sociologic

ANALYSING EVERYDAY LIFE AND CULTURE

sociologic

ANALYSING EVERYDAY LIFE AND CULTURE

SECOND EDITION

Edited by James Arvanitakis

OXFORD
UNIVERSITY PRESS

Oxford University Press is a department of the University of Oxford.
It furthers the University's objective of excellence in research,
scholarship, and education by publishing worldwide. Oxford is a registered
trademark of Oxford University Press in the UK and in certain other countries.

Published in Australia by
Oxford University Press
Level 8, 737 Bourke Street, Docklands, Victoria 3008, Australia.

© James Arvanitakis 2021

The moral rights of the authors have been asserted

First published 2015
Second edition 2021

All rights reserved. No part of this publication may be reproduced, stored in a
retrieval system, or transmitted, in any form or by any means, without the prior
permission in writing of Oxford University Press, or as expressly permitted by
law, by licence, or under terms agreed with the reprographics rights organisation.
Enquiries concerning reproduction outside the scope of the above should be sent to
the Rights Department, Oxford University Press, at the address above.

You must not circulate this work in any other form and you must impose this same
condition on any acquirer.

 A catalogue record for this
book is available from the
National Library of Australia

ISBN 9780190318925

Reproduction and communication for educational purposes
The Australian Copyright Act 1968 (the Act) allows educational institutions that
are covered by remuneration arrangements with Copyright Agency to reproduce
and communicate certain material for educational purposes. For more information,
see copyright.com.au.

Text design by Deborah Johnson
Edited by Laura Rentsch
Typeset by Newgen KnowledgeWorks Pvt. Ltd., Chennai, India
Proofread by Jennifer Butler
Indexed by Mei Yen Chua
Printed in China by Golden Cup Printing

*Links to third party websites are provided by Oxford in good faith and for information only.
Oxford disclaims any responsibility for the materials contained in any third party website
referenced in this work.*

Contents

ACKNOWLEDGMENTS XII
CONTRIBUTORS XIII

PART 1 Introduction and foundations 1

1 **Introduction** 3
   James Arvanitakis
   Introduction 4
   Studying societies … 5
   Let's begin … 11
   Socially constructed 14
   How to use this book 16
   Conclusion 17

2 **Leap into sociology** 20
   Michelle Black and Annelisa Sipos
   What is sociology? 21
   Leap into social analysis 24
   Developing a sociological imagination 26
   What counts as sociological knowledge? 28
   Literacy cultural capital 30
   Succeeding in sociology and beyond 31
   How to research a sociology assignment 34
   Information-finding hacks 38
   To google or not to google 38
   Evaluating information for credibility 39
   Using and citing evidence 39
   Lifelong learning 40
   Conclusion 40

3 **Studying society and culture** 45
   James Arvanitakis
   Introduction 46
   What is society? 49
   What is culture? 51

How societies function	53
Looking for universal rules across societies	58
Postmodernism	59
The interrelated rhombus	60
Conclusion	61

4 Researching the world around us — 65
Maggie Walter and Michael Guerzoni

Introduction	66
Social research and sociological imagination	67
The process of scientific inquiry in social research	68
The research process	70
Researching the social world	73
Social research objectivity and methodology	75
Research methods and real-world sociological research	77
Ethics in sociological research	81
Conclusion	83

5 Modernity and modernisation — 88
Glenda Ballantyne

Introduction	90
What is modernity?	91
Modernisation	92
Modernity: core components	94
Deep dynamics	99
Where are we heading?	100
Conclusion	103

6 Class and class relations — 107
Verity Archer

Introduction	108
So what is class?	109
Adapting Marxism to modern-day working life	112
The market: Max Weber	113

Culture: Pierre Bourdieu — 115
The problem of the underclass — 117
Women and class — 120
Class and place — 121
Is class changing? — 123
How much class mobility is there in Australia? — 124
Conclusion — 125

7 Sex and gender — 131
Denise Buiten

Introduction — 133
Tick the box: sex or gender? — 135
Becoming gendered — 137
Gender and work — 143
The F-word: feminism — 144
Not just gender: intersectionality — 146
Conclusion — 148

8 Power in contemporary society — 152
Lucas Walsh

Three views of power — 153
Spotlight on young people — 166
Conclusion — 168

9 Race and ethnicity — 173
Farida Fozdar

Introduction: race — 174
Changing understandings of race — 177
Race, ethnicity and nation — 177
Racism — 178
The Australian context — 180
The end of the White Australia Policy and the rise of multiculturalism — 182
Conclusion — 190

10 Nation and nationalism in a globalised world — 195
Benjamin T Jones

What is a nation? — 198

When is a nation? — 200

Why is nationalism so powerful? — 203

Are we post-nation? — 206

Conclusion — 208

PART 2 Global issues — 213

11 Globalisation — 215
Duncan McDuie-Ra

Introduction — 216

What is globalisation? — 218

Is globalisation new or old? — 220

Globalisation in practice — 221

Enough with the fish already! — 224

Conclusion — 226

12 Society and the environment — 231
Aisling Bailey

Introduction — 232

Environmental inequality — 236

Climate change — 239

Climate justice — 240

What feeds the economy? — 244

Conclusion — 248

13 Technology and the digital childhood — 254
Joanne Orlando

Introduction — 256

Conclusion — 268

14 Media, social media and generation swipe — 272
Mitchell Hobbs and Clare Davies

Introduction — 274

The media's role and function — 275

	Media content: entertaining or indoctrinating?	278
	Media power and influence	280
	New technologies and old concerns	284
	Conclusion	291

15 Social movements — 301
Karen Soldatic with Nihal Iscel

	Introduction	302
	What is a social movement and how do they work?	304
	Not all movements are progressive	309
	Intersectionality: mapping the margins and working across identities	310
	Human rights and social movements	311
	What might social movements look like in the future?	312
	Conclusion	318

PART 3 Social issues — 323

16 Indigenous Australia — 325
Nikki Moodie

	Introduction	327
	Who are Aboriginal Australians?	327
	Contact	328
	The History Wars: 'It wasn't me'	330
	Aboriginal and Torres Strait Islander activism	333
	The 1967 Referendum	333
	Finding the 'gap'	335
	Blood fetish	336
	Who is Indigenous?	339
	Closing the Gap	340
	The demography of disadvantage	341
	Conclusion	342

17 Youth and young people — 349
Paula Geldens

| | Introduction | 350 |
| | Life stages and social generations | 352 |

	The emergence of 'youth'	356
	Early understandings	357
	Contemporary understandings	360
	Conclusion	364
18	**Deviance and moral panics**	**368**
	Jen Couch and Trudi Cooper	
	Introduction	369
	How social norms are maintained	370
	Sociology and deviance	371
	Why aren't people more deviant?	374
	The making of a deviant: labelling	374
	Totalisation of identity	375
	Dividing practices	377
	Ceremonies of degradation	379
	Mass media and moral panics	379
	Othering	383
	Deviance and resistance	384
	Conclusion: towards inclusion as an alternative to moral panics	385
19	**Work and society**	**390**
	Justine Humphry	
	Introduction	391
	The meaning of work	392
	The rise of global capitalism	394
	The role of digital technology in changing work	396
	Conclusion	402
20	**Society and the world of sports**	**409**
	Mair Underwood with James Arvanitakis	
	Introduction	410
	What is a sociological approach to sport?	412
	Deviance and sport	413
	Gender and sport	417

Sexuality and sport — 421
Conclusion — 425

21 Religion and contemporary society — 431
John A Rees
What is 'religion'? — 432
Where is religion? — 440
When is religion? — 446

22 Conclusion and how to change the world — 454
James Arvanitakis and Mitra Gusheh
Now for the interrelated rhombus — 456
Contrasts and contradictions — 456
The recipe for change — 461
Getting active in other ways — 469
Conclusion — 470

GLOSSARY 472
INDEX 480

Acknowledgments

The author and the publisher wish to thank the following copyright holders for reproduction of their material.

Cover: Stocksy/Jodie Johnson; AFP via Getty Images, Figure 14.4; Alamy, Figure 7.1; Alamy/fStop Images GmbH, p. 2; Anni Dugdale, Box 13.1 & Box 13.2; Getty Images/Jenny Evans, Figure 13.1; Global Footprint Network: www.footprintnetwork.org, Figures 12.1 & 12.2; News Ltd/Newspix; Figure 15.1; Newspix/News Limited, Figures 14.1, 14.2 & 14.3; Shutterstock, p. 1 (arrow on road), Figures 6.1, 18.1 & 20.1; Stocksy/Julia Volk; p. 323; Stocksy/Kevin Russ, p. 213; Stocksy/Lauren Lee, p. 1 (girl on skateboard); Stocksy/Rowena Naylor, p. 214; Stocksy/Sam Burton, p. 324; Youthlaw: http://youthlaw.asn.au/, p. 358.

Thanks to the academics who contributed to the success of the first edition:

- Nikó Antalffy
- Moira Byrne
- Anni Dugdale
- Maria El-Chami
- Anna Halafoff

Every effort has been made to trace the original source of copyright material contained in this book. The publisher will be pleased to hear from copyright holders to rectify any errors or omissions.

Note from James Arvanitakis: Like most authors, such work as this textbook can only be completed because of the support of many colleagues. Though there are too many to mentioned individually, I would specifically like to thank Chrissie Crispin for her research, insights and commitment to the project. Chrissie's work builds on the wonderful efforts of Alexandra Coleman in the first edition of *Sociologic*.

This book is dedicated to the many educators who are devoted to working with students, colleagues and the public to confront the world's grand challenges. There has never been a more important time for us to embrace sociology and the humanities more broadly to understand, analyse and solve the challenges we face.

I would also like to dedicate this book to our colleague Dr Viv Waller who passed away while this second edition was being prepared. Viv was a dedicated educator whose research into environmental practices and knowledge, food waste management, the sociology of information and other areas was well respected.

Finally, as always, a special thank you to my wife Alix Beattie who never says no to an adventure.

Contributors

Verity Archer is a Lecturer in Sociology at Federation University. She writes about the history of social welfare and ideology in Australia. She has a PhD in History from the Australian National University and is a past recipient of the Bob Gollan Award for Labour History and the University of Melbourne's Hugh Williamson Postdoctoral Fellowship for her work on the history of the Australian 'dole bludger'. She is also the Australian representative on the Association of Working Class Academics steering committee.

James Arvanitakis (PhD) is a lecturer in the Humanities and a member of the University's Institute for Cultural and Society. He founded The Academy at Western Sydney University—an Honours College—that received an *Australian Financial Review* Higher Education Excellence Award (2016). James is internationally recognised for his innovative teaching style and was the recipient of the Prime Minister's University Teacher of the Year Award in 2012, an Eminent Researcher Award from the Australia India Education Council in 2015 and Teacher Excellent Award by the Western Sydney Dialogue (2018). In 2019–20, James was the Fulbright Fellow Milward L. Simpson Visiting Professor at University of Wyoming, United States. He continues to research citizenship, hope and the future of universities. A collection of his work can be found at www.jamesarvanitakis.net and on twitter @jarvanitakis.

Aisling Bailey is a Lecturer in Sociology at Swinburne University of Technology and undertook her PhD in Environmental Anthropology at Monash University. As an environmental anthropologist and sociologist, Aisling's research investigates the ways in which the Western dualistic conceptualisation of nature as separated from culture has shaped cultural and economic understandings and behaviour towards the natural environment. In response to a lack of environmental accountability resulting from this disconnection, Aisling's research focuses upon theoretical and practical initiatives that seek to bring people and place together, exploring the ways in which the health and wellbeing of people and place are reciprocally linked. Aisling has worked with organisations including the Centre for Education and Research in Environmental Strategies (CERES) and the community gardening organisation 3000Acres.

Glenda Ballantyne is Senior Lecturer (Sociology) and Deputy Chair, Department of Social Sciences at Swinburne University. In an earlier life she was active in the women's movement and local initiatives to foster intercultural dialogue and active citizenship. Her research interests are focused on migration and cultural diversity, with a focus on 'multiple modernities', nationalism, multiculturalism and interculturalism. She is currently leading an international comparative study on Intercultural Cities and working on a collaboration with the Victorian Multicultural Commission exploring contemporary perspectives on diversity among young Australians explored though their filmmaking practice. Her book *Creativity and Critique: Subjectivity and Agency in Touraine and Ricoeur* (Brill 2007) brought together social theory and philosophy in a hermeneutical interpretation of agency, subjectivity and modernity.

Michelle Black is a Senior Lecturer in Sociology at the Australian Catholic University and a former convener of the Health Sociology thematic group of The Australian Sociological Association (TASA). As a health sociologist Michelle has longstanding research interests in the sociology of trust in complementary and alternative medicine and in substance use and addictions. As an educator, Michelle is committed to helping sociology students develop their confidence in academic research and writing, as well as encouraging a critical awareness of issues in contemporary society. To this end, Michelle has initiated programs on embedding academic literacy into sociology and in researching how engagement in online learning and teaching transforms student learning in sociology.

Denise Buiten is Senior Lecturer in Sociology and Social Justice at the University of Notre Dame

Australia, Sydney. Her research interest is in gender and the media, particularly how understandings of gender-based violence are evolving and changing in media contexts and beyond. She is a Senior Research Associate with the Department of Sociology at the University of Johannesburg, and an International Advisory Board Member for the Association of Applied and Clinical Sociology which aims to promote the practical application of sociological insights to improve social conditions. Denise is passionate about communicating the usefulness of a gender lens for understanding social problems and aims to forward this understanding through both her research and teaching.

Trudi Cooper is an Associate Professor at Edith Cowan University (ECU) in Australia, where she leads the Youth Work degree program. Trudi specialises in the scholarship of teaching and learning and she led a team that received a major grant from the Office for Learning and Teaching to renew the curriculum for Youth Work in Australian universities. In 2006, she received a Carrick Citation for outstanding contribution to learning and teaching. Trudi also leads the Social Program Innovation Research and Evaluation (SPIRE) Group at ECU, which conducts collaborative evaluation and research with government and not-for-profit organisations. In 2010, she was recognised as one of ECU's top 20 researchers. Previously, Trudi lectured in the United Kingdom in youth and community work and, before commencing her academic career, was a youth and community worker. In 2014, she received a special commendation for Leadership in Youth Work in Western Australia.

Jen Couch is a Senior Lecturer in Youth Work and international development at the Australian Catholic University (ACU). Jen has established a national reputation for her work in the area of refugee young people and resettlement and has recently completed the first longitudinal study into refugee youth homelessness. Prior to joining ACU she worked for over 20 years in the community sector in Australia and South Asia. Her work has focused on highly marginalised young people in the areas of refugee settlement, rights and participation, torture and trauma, and capacity building.

Clare Davies is a PhD Candidate and Lecturer in the Department of Media and Communications at the University of Sydney. Her main research interest is exploring the changing nature of the public relations profession in the age of technology. Clare is also a Vice President at one of the world's leading marketing communications agencies. With experience across the private, not-for-profit and government sector, her expertise is in designing and implementing creative communications strategies that bridge the gap between organisations and stakeholder groups. For both local and global clients, Clare develops brand strategies; creative content across earned, owned and paid media; influencer marketing campaigns; social media strategies; brand activations; and media relations programs. Clare's professional experience and research activities give her a unique insight into the ethical behaviours of contemporary public relations practice.

Farida Fozdar is Associate Professor in Anthropology and Sociology at the University of Western Australia. Her research focuses on race relations; migrant and refugee settlement; anti-racism; citizenship; and nationalism. Recent work explores mixed race; diasporas; and postnationalism and cosmopolitanism. She has published widely, as well as authoring reports for government and research consultancies.

Paula Geldens is Executive Dean at UniSA Justice and Society, at the University of South Australia. Prior to this appointment, Paula taught and researched as a sociologist of young people for some 15 years. Paula's research with young people has addressed issues of identity, health and wellbeing, occupational and educational aspiration, and the impacts of place and of community on young people's experiences and life chances.

Michael Guerzoni (PhD, University of Tasmania) serves in the Office of the Pro-Vice Chancellor of Aboriginal Leadership at the University of Tasmania, Australia. Mike's research is focused on the

Indigenising of tertiary curricula and the examination of clerical cultures, attitudes and practice towards child sexual abuse and child protection within Anglicanism and Roman Catholicism.

Mitra Gusheh is a social impact practitioner with 20 years of experience across the higher education and social sectors. As part of her current role as the Executive Manager, Social Impact at the University of Technology Sydney's Centre for Social Justice and Inclusion, she has been responsible for developing the institution's Social Impact Framework. She also leads the Centre's social impact program which seeks to scale and enhance the university's contribution to public good. Previous to this, Mitra worked for a range of not-for-profit organisations where she was responsible for the strategic design, development and implementation of large-scale social change programs. This included establishing Oxfam Australia's national youth program, the design and implementation of an advocacy program on child rights in Sri Lanka, and the design and implementation of an ICT-project in partnership with UNESCO in Nepal.

Mitchell Hobbs is Senior Lecturer in Media and Public Relations at the University of Sydney. He is the Postgraduate Convenor of the graduate coursework programs within the Department of Media and Communications, as well as the Degree Director for the Master of Strategic Public Relations. An award-winning lecturer, Mitchell teaches graduate units in political public relations and strategy selection in corporate communication. His current research focuses on public lobbying strategies; social media and misinformation campaigns; and dating apps. He has previously published on the politics of major media outlets, as well as semiotics, advertising and identity. Mitchell also possesses high-level experience in media relations, including working in political public relations for Prime Minister Julia Gillard.

Justine Humphry is a Lecturer in Digital Cultures in the Department of Media and Communications at the University of Sydney. Her research focuses on mobile mediated work, digital inequalities, communication in public space and smart technology transformation. For her PhD research she examined mobile media and changing discourses and practices of work. She has studied mobile phones and homelessness extensively and conducted collaborative research on mobile antiracism apps in Australia, France and the United Kingdom. Justine has published her research widely, including in the *Routledge Companion to Mobile Media*, the *Routledge Companion to Urban Media and Communication* and the journals of *Media, Culture & Society*, *Information, Communication & Society*, *Communication, Research & Practices*, *M/C Journal* and the *Australian Journal of Telecommunications and the Digital Economy*. Her new project, Smart Publics, researches the social, design and governance implications of smart street furniture with a team from the University of Glasgow.

Nihal Iscel has many years of experience working in the multicultural and disability sectors supporting people from refugee, humanitarian entrant and migrant backgrounds, including people with disability. Nihal aims to contribute to making positive systemic changes and help break barriers for people in minority groups like people with disability, women, children and those from a non-English-speaking background. Nihal's work focuses on supporting people in their successful inclusion and meaningful participation in the wider community: in the economic, social and all aspects of community life; assisting them to build their capacity to independently access the relevant supports and services to meet their individual needs.

Ben Jones is a lecturer in history at Central Queensland University and a Foundation Fellow of the Australian Studies Institute. He has published extensively on Australian politics and history with a focus on national identity and republicanism. His most recent books are *This Time: Australia's Republican Past and Future* (Redback, 2018) and *History in a Post-Truth World: Theory and Praxis* (Routledge, 2020).

Duncan McDuie-Ra is Professor of Urban Sociology at the University of Newcastle. His research focuses on urban frontiers in Asia. His most recent sole-authored project is on skateboarding and urban landscapes in Asia, entitled *Skateboarding and Urban Landscapes in 21st Century Asia: Endless Spots* (Amsterdam University Press). His other recent sole-authored books include *Northeast Migrants in Delhi: Race, Refuge and Retail* (Amsterdam University Press, 2012), *Debating Race in Contemporary India* (Palgrave MacMillan, 2015) and *Borderland City in New India: Frontier to Gateway* (Amsterdam University Press, 2016). He is co-author of *Ceasefire City: Capitalism, Militarism and Urbanism in Dimapur* (Oxford University Press, 2020 with D. Kikon). Recent journal articles have appeared in *Political Geography* (with M. Chettri), *Development & Change* (with M. Chettri), *Space & Culture, Modern Asian Studies, Geographical Journal* (with D. Robinson), and *Area* (with K. Gulson).

Nikki Moodie (Gomeroi) is a Senior Lecturer in Indigenous Studies in the School of Social and Political Sciences at the University of Melbourne. Nikki has a background in political science and sociology, and her research interests include Indigenous policy and governance, Indigenous education, and the surveillance of identity in settler colonial states.

Joanne Orlando studies the intersection of technology, childhood, learning and lifestyle. Her work provides real time insight into how children use technology, and how their uses are impacted by the expectations, knowledge and experiences of key adults in their world including parents, teachers and governments. Joanne works closely with key multinational technology organisations, education, government and the media, to advise on the development of policy and practice that genuinely support children's technology use.

John A Rees is Professor of Politics and International Relations, School of Arts and Sciences, and Research Associate in Religion and Global Ethics, Institute for Ethics and Society, at The University of Notre Dame Australia. John is a published specialist on the theories and practices of religion in international relations. John has been recognised by the Office of Learning and Teaching of the Australian Government for excellence in university teaching. He holds a PhD in International Relations from the University of New South Wales. John is a 2020 Fulbright Senior Scholar.

Annelisa Sipos has been working as a librarian at the Australian Catholic University since 2013 where she supports teaching and learning. She has a strong interest in information and educational design, as well as digital literacy and its contribution to personal fulfilment and effective participation at university and in employment.

Karen Soldatic is an Associate Professor, School of Social Sciences, and Institute Fellow, Institute for Culture and Society, at Western Sydney University. She was awarded a Fogarty Foundation Excellence in Education Fellowship for 2006–09, a British Academy International Fellowship in 2012, a fellowship at The Centre for Human Rights Education at Curtin University (2011–12), where she remains an Adjunct Fellow, and an Australian Research Council DECRA Fellowship (2016–19). Her research on global welfare regimes builds on her 20 years of experience as an international, national and state-based senior policy analyst, researcher and practitioner. She obtained her PhD (Distinction) in 2010 from the University of Western Australia.

Mair Underwood BA (Hons) PhD (Anthropology) is an anthropologist of the body and lecturer in the School of Social Science at the University of Queensland. Mair has a particular interest in body modification and decoration. Recently she has been immersing herself in men's muscle cultures through online ethnographies of bodybuilding communities. She is especially interested in how muscle is connected to gender, and the social lives of those taking performance and image enhancing drugs.

Lucas Walsh is Professor of Education Policy and Practice, Youth Studies in the Faculty of Education at Monash University. His research focuses on the political, economic, cultural, social and technological dimensions of young people's participation—in particular their transitions to post-school life and the implications for educators, service providers and policy makers. He was previously Director of Research and Evaluation at The Foundation for Young Australians. He has worked in corporate, government and not-for-profit sectors, and has held three academic research fellowships. He managed the International Baccalaureate's Online Curriculum Centre in the United Kingdom, and has been invited to advise local, state and federal governments, including the National Curriculum Board and Australian Institute for Teaching and School Leadership.

Maggie Walter is Palawa and a Distinguished Professor of Sociology at the University of Tasmania. She is a long-term member of the steering committee of the Longitudinal Study of Indigenous Children and has published extensively in the fields of race relations, inequality, and research methods and methodologies. Recent publications include *Indigenous Children Growing Up Strong* (edited with Karen L. Martin and Gawaian Bodkin-Andrews, Palgrave McMillan, 2017); *Indigenous Statistics: A Quantitative Methodology* (with Chris Andersen, Left Coast Press, 2013), and *Social Research Methods* (ed.) (4th edn, Oxford University Press, 2019).

PART 1
Introduction and foundations

CHAPTER 1
Introduction

JAMES ARVANITAKIS

CHAPTER OVERVIEW

This book is about studying contemporary society—a fascinating challenge because we are studying something that we are actually part of: that is, we have to look at our everyday experiences and ask, 'Why do we consider this normal?' Like a young child with endless questions about the colour of the sky or what is over the hill at the end of the street, this book encourages a boundless curiosity about the social world around us. This is a challenge because societies are ever changing—sometimes slowly and sometimes very quickly. Even as I sit and write these words today, by the time you read them, some of the topics we discuss may appear to be 'old news'.

What also makes our task challenging is that there is no 'one way' to study society; to understand how societies function, operate and change we need to examine a broad range of theories and theorists. Some of the ideas we encounter you will find interesting and compelling, and others you will not like. The important thing is to keep an open mind and understand that in our studies there is never one person or theory that can provide all the answers. Rather, we need to reflect critically on different perspectives and come up with our own insights and understandings.

This chapter sets out some of the parameters of our investigation into contemporary society and everyday life and outlines the general direction we are going to take in this book. We start by considering pirates in a Sydney supermarket and end by eating a $35 burger!

KEY TERMS

Cultural studies An academic discipline that investigates the symbolic meanings and cultural practices of our everyday experiences.

Culture Encompasses the rules and processes of everyday life and includes the symbolic and learned aspects of human society, such as language, custom and convention.

Epistemology The theory of knowledge and how we learn what we know.

Ontology The way we see the world: how we classify things, people and other entities around us.

Socialisation The process of transmission of culture from one generation to the next; the ongoing social processes by which we learn the norms, customs and values of our society.

Society A social system made up of many smaller parts that share a culture: these smaller parts include both formal institutions (such as schools, hospitals and government) and informal social groups (such as families).

> **Sociology** The study of society. In order to study society, we must look at the interactions within the society of people (both as part of groups and as individuals) and both informal and formal institutions (such as schools, hospitals and government).

Introduction

Welcome to this book!

This book will help you understand and analyse how our contemporary **society** operates. How do we begin such a book? Maybe with something that happened to me a little while ago.

I was having friends over for dinner and I was planning to bake a risotto. I was looking for a specific recipe and could not find it. I knew exactly where it was meant to be—on the back of the Arborio rice packet—but it was not there. So I went back to the supermarket to find the recipe.

The catch was that I already had more rice than I needed and did not want to buy any more. I found the recipe on the back of the packet, and after realising I had left my phone at home, I borrowed a pen and paper, sat cross-legged in the aisle, and began to copy the recipe out.

There I was, a university professor sitting in the middle of a supermarket aisle with a pen and paper and a large packet of rice on my lap writing down the recipe and the steps to follow. I had not really thought about how my actions would be perceived until I noticed some strange glances from my fellow shoppers. I started writing quickly so I could get out of there as soon as possible.

It is at this point that the day really started getting strange. A group of five pirates walked into the supermarket—three men and two women. Granted, they may not have been real pirates, but they were dressed as pirates—eye patches and all. One of the women looked at me and asked what I was doing. After explaining that I was copying a recipe, she asked what I was cooking. The exchange that followed went something like this:

> James: 'I am baking a risotto.'
>
> Female pirate: 'That sounds nice ... how do you do that?'
>
> James: 'It sounds more impressive than it is, but I can explain if you really want me to.'
>
> Female pirate: 'Do you often sit in the middle of a supermarket and write down recipes?'
>
> James: 'Do you often dress like a pirate?'
>
> Female pirate: 'Hey, anyone who is sitting in the middle of a supermarket copying a recipe is in no position to judge what is strange.'
>
> James: 'I never said anything about it being strange ... I was asking a simple question.'

What we need to ask when trying to understand our society is: How 'normal' is such an exchange? Do we consider it strange that someone sits in the middle of a supermarket and writes down a recipe? Do we consider it strange that someone living in contemporary Sydney dresses like a pirate? (And no, it was not Halloween, although it may have been International Talk Like a Pirate Day.)

Also, consider this: How often in everyday life do we talk to strangers in such a random way?

If you do think these events are strange, ask yourself: 'Why?' Did anyone ever tell you that people should not write recipes in the middle of supermarkets or dress like pirates? The answer is probably 'no'. We learn that there are rules in society that we should follow; they are never explained to us or written down, but we learn them. This is the process of **socialisation** (which is discussed in more detail later in this chapter).

These rules are invisible, are all around us, and in many ways are essential to the smooth running of our society. Some are about manners and behaviour; others are about learning what is considered 'normal' and 'natural'; and there are even some about our desires and hopes. Some are explained to us, while we learn others by observing and no one really tells us why we do them. The law enforces some, while others are enforced just as heavily by the opinion of those around us—both friends and strangers.

If you think about it, there are millions of people living in cities all over the world and most of us get along. The question is: How does this happen?

It is deciphering all this—which is a type of 'code'—that is fundamental to understanding our contemporary society. If we can understand these rules, we can understand how our society is organised.

The journey we are about to take in investigating our contemporary society is going to be fun—yes, I said fun—because unlike most books you will read in this area of study, we are not simply looking at theorists and applying their ideas to case studies. Instead, we will be looking at our everyday lives and experiences and seeing which theorists are relevant to us. In this way you will be encouraged to reflect upon your experiences and draw on a wide range of theories to see what is relevant; that is, to unpack the world around you, and not to simply investigate something that is happening 'some place else'. You may find some of these theorists incredibly interesting, many of them relevant and others not so much. Such positions are fine as long as you critically reflect on the issues we discuss and then decide—for as you will see, there are no right or wrong answers.

One more thing before jumping into the main part of this chapter, and that is to answer the question: 'Why study society?'

Studying societies ...

In investigating our contemporary society, we will draw on theorists from two broad schools (or disciplines) of thought: **sociology** and **cultural studies**. The study of society is called 'sociology' and those who study it are referred to as 'sociologists' (see Chapter 2). Sociologists began analysing societies by looking at substantial changes to the social order that occurred through political and industrial revolutions (this is discussed in detail in Chapter 5).

The Industrial Revolution began in the late eighteenth century and changed the way a significant portion of the world operated. For example, this was the first time in history that populations became concentrated around large urban hubs. People headed for the cities, leaving the rural homes that had been in their families for generations—sometimes this was by choice; sometimes it was because they were forced off their land. In the cities they met, interacted and began families with people they may have never encountered before the Industrial Revolution occurred.

> **Critical reflection**
>
> You should note that the movement from rural communities to urban hubs is something that continues today and is creating mega cities (that is, cities with a population of over 10 million). The urban migration process is one of the big challenges confronting policy makers both in Australia and around the world. What are some of the challenges this creates?

During the Industrial Revolution, capitalism became the key organising principle of society, science emerged as the primary source of knowledge (replacing religion and superstition), and the concept of social progress emerged. Political revolutions in France and America changed the relationship between the rulers and the ruled in ways that reverberated across the world.

The changes brought about by such revolutions highlighted how societies can change both slowly and quickly. Furthermore, these revolutions changed the structures of societies, the role of the individual and the relationships that existed within societies. These three dimensions—social structures, the individual and relationships—must each be considered when we attempt to define exactly what society is: this is something we will return to in Chapter 3.

We will also draw on many theorists from cultural studies. This is an academic discipline that investigates the symbolic meanings and cultural practices of our everyday experiences. While sociology looks at social change from a broad perspective across entire societies, cultural studies looks at everyday exchanges between people. Early historians were concerned mainly with the lives of the elite, but cultural studies emerged when theorists became interested in the interactions that ordinary people have. By looking at everyday life, it is possible to gain insights into how our society is arranged, understand why we accept certain things and do not revolt, and realise why we are happy or unhappy.

As noted, one of the challenges of studying contemporary society is that sometimes things change slowly—so slowly and subtly that we often do not even recognise the change. At other times, there is rapid change. As change happens, we can no longer take everyday interactions for granted: what was once accepted as normal may now seem strange.

One example is the decline in letters delivered to our homes. For hundreds of years, this was an accepted—and indeed the most popular—form of communication. Now, the massive impact of the internet has meant that many post offices today rarely deliver letters, as email, social media and mobile technology have become the preferred media of communication. This change started slowly, and people barely noticed it was happening; then it gained momentum, especially as smartphones became more widely available.

At one stage, everyone thought that post offices would disappear, but the internet provided an unexpected advantage: online shopping has made parcel delivery an incredibly popular service! This too started slowly but has now become significant.

Critical reflection

As a sociologist, I am often asked, 'Why should we study society?' The answer I give is usually something like this: 'It is important to understand the world around us. In so doing, we come to recognise why things are the way they are. With such understanding, we can have informed discussions about what traditions of our society are important for us to keep and protect, and what parts we believe we should change.'

An important part of sociology is understanding social change—something we will look at in detail when discussing social movements in Chapter 15. What aspects of our society do you think are important to maintain and what would you like to change?

How do millions of people living together get along?

Over the last few centuries, particularly since the Industrial Revolution, massive urban centres have emerged and for the first time in history more people live in cities than in rural environments. Tokyo, for example, has a population of over 13 million people.

This creates tensions, right?

Every week in the media, we see violent incidents. Sometimes these incidents are between individuals or small groups of people. All too often, we see them in the form of domestic violence directed towards women and children, now one of the leading preventable contributors to deaths and injury to women aged under 45 years in Australia—a heartbreaking statistic indeed (McPhedran 2018). In such situations, we often look at the perpetrator and victim as individuals and wonder what happened.

There are also violent events where society seems to break down. We have seen the Cronulla Riots (2003), the Palm Island Riots (2004) and the tension that emerged in Sydney following the siege of a café when a lone gunman claimed links to terrorist organisations and murdered innocent people (2014). More recently, the spread of COVID-19 in the early part of 2020 created panic buying with reports of fights over toilet paper in suburban Sydney.

When considering these events, the question that most of us ask is: 'Why and how did this happen?' However, many others ask a very different—but just as important—question: 'Why did this not happen before?' Or, as mentioned above: 'In large cities with so many people living in cramped environments, tensions emerge; so why does this not continually happen?'

In our contemporary society we frequently see such violent events. They occur not only in Australia, but also overseas. When we see them in 'foreign' places, we may be shocked, but we often ignore the implications of the violence because we assume there has been some social breakdown that we do not understand. And when such events occur close to home, we are often left searching for simple answers to complicated issues. One of the aims of this book is to decipher many of these issues.

While we do see violent events, Australian society tends to function very well. In fact, while violent events attract the bulk of the media's attention, most days are pretty boring and little happens, even with 25 million of us living in this country!

Moreover, we also see many examples of kindness and empathy, and great efforts to make society function peacefully and justly. For example, in organisations such as Oxfam, Amnesty International, the Edmund Rice Centre, and anti-domestic violence campaigns (including groundbreaking organisations like Reach Out, Our Watch and Australian Women Against Violence Alliance), we see many people—both paid and volunteers—devote their lives to the promotion of a more just society. Such people work for causes including reconciliation, the fight against poverty, misrepresentation, unfair trade relationships, discrimination and exploitation. The bushfires throughout Australia in the 2019–20 summer were battled by both professional firefighters as well as over 150,000 volunteers!

We even see situations where there is violence and hatred side by side with examples of peace and harmony. Sometimes this may even occur around the same issue. For example, while many people support the mandatory detention of refugees, others protest and believe that it is an assault on people's human rights. I have attended protests in support of refugees and seen a wide variety of people, including those from Afghanistan and parts of the Middle East, Anglo-Australians, people of Jewish background, priests, nuns and many others.

So, while some are concerned about many different **cultures** changing Australia and form anti-immigration organisations to stop this from happening, others work for harmony and celebrate difference.

It is by considering such issues that we can find the key to unlocking the 'mysteries' of contemporary society and understanding our experiences in everyday life. No matter where you stand on these complex issues, approach them with a critical mind so you can understand different perspectives (and remember, understanding is different from agreeing).

Here are some other experiences of 'the everyday' that provide insights into our society: Why and how are different roles assigned to males and females? How do nations such as Australia emerge? Why do people protest? Why are you not allowed to vote until you are 18? How can we wear shoes when we know that those very shoes were produced by child labour? Where does racism come from and why does it persist? How can we live in a very wealthy society but still have a homeless population? Why do we give flowers?

To answer these questions, we need to look at society as a whole, as well as the lives of the many individuals within it. This is a challenge, as individuals have their own motivations and desires (see Box 1.1)—answering the questions becomes even more complex when you consider that no two people are the same!

But we do behave rationally … right?

A good friend of mine, who is a medical doctor, always used to argue against me when I explained to her that we rarely act 'rationally' and are often more likely to be irrational. Her position was that medical doctors are trained in such a way that their rational decision-making skills rise above any emotions—irrational or otherwise.

BOX 1.1

Thinking sociologically

SOCIETY IS MADE UP OF COMPLEX INDIVIDUALS

One of the challenges of studying our 'society' and 'culture' is that they are made up of many individuals, and we are unique even though we have much in common.

Many of the dominant ideas that shape the decisions and actions of powerful societal institutions like government, the media and businesses are influenced by classical economic thinking. If this was a first-year economics textbook, one of the first things we would examine is the concept that every one of us is a 'rational' and 'self-interested' being. A central argument I learnt when I studied economics was that each of us is driven to maximise utility (or satisfaction) derived from transactions. We all have unlimited wants, the claim goes, yet the world has limited resources. We therefore make economic decisions based on self-interest in order to maximise our utility, or 'get the most' out of these limited resources. This is a narrow view of how people think and act, intentionally simplified to allow consumer choices to be accounted for in economic models. Contemporary economics includes some more innovative approaches to understanding how people make decisions, including for example alternative behavioural economics and 'happiness economics'. While these emerging fields of research go beyond the classical economists' limited understanding of humans seeking to maximise *economic* utility, they still do not help us understand or explain the full range of relationships and interactions between individuals, groups and institutions in society.

One example is giving someone a bunch of flowers—something that some people do often, and others rarely or maybe never.

If we look at giving flowers 'rationally', we see an act of gifting useless, dying organic matter—for that is all flowers are once they have been cut at their stems.

Giving flowers, however, is rich with cultural and social meanings—from love and sympathy to saying sorry. Rationality does not necessarily play a part, even though choosing which flowers to give, whether to pick them, steal them or buy them, and what size, colour and type of flower all play a part. The flowers that say 'I love you' to mum on Mother's Day are different to the flowers given on Valentine's Day.

So when we think about giving flowers, the last thing we say to ourselves is: 'This is maximising my economic utility.'

Because we are not always rational, because we are all different, and because our priorities are constantly changing, the study of society becomes much more complicated (and more interesting).

This is why we turn to the study of society and culture, which allows us to see individuals as more complex beings. Individuals are not influenced only by economic needs, and do not make only economic decisions. We are also guided by cultural background, socialisation, personal experiences, family, friends, television, music, books and so on. Our choices can also be enhanced by different forms of social privilege and limited by forces of oppression, exploitation or discrimination.

However, I finally got her to agree with me. How? I showed her research on the decision-making skills of doctors. The research showed that doctors can misdiagnose patients not just because of the difficulty of putting a name to symptoms, but also because of 'social factors'.

In a groundbreaking 2007 study, Jerome Groopman found three social factors that influence a doctor's diagnosis. The first factor is the patients the doctor has seen before he or she sees you: if five people come into the surgery before you and they each have the flu, the doctor is likely to conclude that you also have the flu, even if you show only one of the symptoms.

The second is based on the way you look. If you look fit and are young, the doctor is likely to dismiss certain diseases immediately even if you have the symptoms for those diseases. Likewise, it has been found that doctors can dismiss the concerns of patients who are overweight—simply attributing symptoms to their weight with diseases going undetected (Kolota 2016).

The third factor is that doctors make decisions based on how much they like you. The example cited in the Groopman research is of one doctor who liked his patient and did not want to cause him any more discomfort than was necessary. As a result, he decided not to do one extra test that meant he missed a key element in appropriately diagnosing the patient. The patient got sicker and it took another doctor to discover why. The patient eventually recovered, but the fact that he was a friend of the doctor almost led to disaster.

So, even in the most scientific and rational professions, (irrational) social factors play a part. We should never forget this when investigating contemporary society.

We are not born rational or irrational: we are complex social creatures. As such, who we are is not pre-determined; in fact, this idea of being pre-determined, or 'determinism' is a concept that has long been dismissed (see Box 1.2).

BOX 1.2

Thinking sociologically

AVOID DETERMINISM WHEN STUDYING SOCIETY

Another challenge of studying society is that people do not behave in a pre-determined way; that is, we are not like machines pre-programmed to behave in certain ways based on our background.

For example, I have a friend, Charlotte, from Hong Kong who studied in Australia. She told me that because she is Chinese, people often expected her to be good at maths—a subject area she hates and is terrible at!

This supposed innate tendency to be good at maths sounds silly when you think about it, but it is indicative of an issue that we should take seriously.

The idea that someone has inherent traits—be they violent, academic or sporting—has a long history and has been termed 'biological determinism'. Biological determinism suggests that all human nature is inherited, and all human attributes are fixed. Biological determinists disregard or deny the effects of environmental variables or the agency of the individual. Such a viewpoint leads to the idea that criminals cannot be reformed—they are, in effect, 'born that way'. By this reasoning, I am an academic, not because I have studied hard and persisted in obtaining multiple degrees despite setbacks, but because I am somehow genetically programmed for this job like some sort of robot!

Biological determinism, if we take it to its logical conclusion, removes human agency from human responsibility. All blame for failure (or credit for success) is exclusively placed on your genes. According to biological determinism, we have no free will—we only have genetics.

Please note that this does not outright dismiss genetic make-up—studies have shown that genes matter for elite athletes, but so do social factors like having access to the right resources, hard work and persistent training and practice (Epstein 2014).

Let's begin ...

What is society?

I keep on mentioning the word 'society' as though we all know what it means, but what exactly is it?

We will have a detailed discussion of society in Chapter 3, but for now consider this: society is a social system that is made up of many smaller parts, including formal institutions (such as schools, hospitals and government) and informal social groups (such as families). Society encompasses both these parts and the way that they are put together and organised. Hence, society is made up of organisations and the many social relations between people and different groups (Jureidini, Kenny & Poole 2003, p. 16). This is a very brief introduction—as we will see in Chapter 3, understanding and studying society is an incredibly wide area.

What is culture?

We now have a brief overview of the meaning of society, so let's turn to culture. When we hear the word 'culture', we often take it as meaning 'high culture'; that is, we think of priceless paintings or the ballet for example. Or we may think of culture as a formal dimension of belonging to a nationality, such as Australian culture (although what that could be is anyone's guess). We will return to this latter aspect in Chapter 10, where we discuss national identity.

For the purposes of understanding culture in our present context, we should think of it as being broader and encompassing the rules and processes of everyday life. It is with this type of definition in mind that the authors of the *Dictionary of Sociology* (Abercrombie, Hill & Turner 1994, p. 98) describe culture as 'the symbolic and learned, non-biological aspects of human society, including language, custom and convention, by which human behaviour can be distinguished from other primates'; that is, culture determines how our societies are organised, maintained and how they change. (As we will discuss in Chapter 18, there are some sociologists and cultural theorists who challenge the idea of that nature/culture can be so simply divided—but more on that later.)

Consequently, much of the way we act is, as least in part, culturally determined. While there are many things that seem 'natural' in our everyday lives, they are actually shaped by our cultural norms. Think of how babies are given pink or blue clothing depending on their sex. Why does this occur? This is a concept we will return to throughout this book.

One of history's most influential sociologists, Emile Durkheim (1858–1917), argued that every culture makes assumptions about fundamental phenomena. These assumptions set the frame through which we experience the world and are often accepted as the absolute and unquestioned truth. They can include issues about what is 'good' and celebrated in our society, and what is 'bad' and frowned upon.

Another famous and somewhat controversial cultural theorist, Jean Baudrillard (1983), stated that cultures are based on a 'system of signs'. Baudrillard argued that these 'signs' are unconsciously learnt and give meaning to our world. Culture is seen as a world of signs and symbols (or, in Baudrillard's words, 'signifiers'). From this perspective, culture is not only a lived phenomenon, but also a sensory one; that is, we learn to make our cultural experiences part of our senses—explaining why we may 'feel' patriotic at the beginning of a football game when the national anthem is sung!

For Baudrillard, human society is a culturally constructed world of symbols. We humans learn and respond to these symbols in ways that are considered to be culturally appropriate. These are the cultural codes of a society that create a sense of order in a chaotic world.

Socialisation

This brings us to the concept of 'socialisation', which is the transmission of culture from one generation to the next. This is the way that we humans learn the patterns of behaviour, experiences and identities particular to each of our cultures.

For example, think of how we are socialised to greet people and respect personal space. This is something that no one explains to us formally; rather, we learn how to behave over time—we watch, observe and react. When you meet someone, think about how closely you stand to them and the rules that you follow.

Socialisation is an ongoing process: something we learn from birth and continues until death. But while those around influence us, we also do the influencing; that is, we 'socialise' others to behave in a certain way.

Socialisation occurs on many different levels—including the way we speak, the buying of gifts (including the flowers I mentioned above) and how we act (such as not chewing with our mouths open).

Culture and identity

If we combine the concept of culture and how we learn it through the process of socialisation, then we can come to the conclusion that culture in large part determines the type of person we become. According to Van Krieken and colleagues (2005) our identity is the constellation of characteristics that we may regard as part of our 'self', including the way we present ourselves to others.

For example, broader Australian culture places some prestige on being an academic, although this is tempered by the fact that you cannot act as if you are important, or you will be dismissed as arrogant. As such, my identity is balanced between me thinking: 'I am an academic and must act with a certain level of responsibility and according to the rules of academia', combined with my not wanting to be seen as being full of self-importance. Another example would be sportspeople we come to idolise—but who we also expect to be fair, humble and approachable (something we discuss in Chapter 20). When the Australian cricket captain, Steve Smith, was caught working with other players to cheat during a test match in South Africa, there was a massive social backlash that resulted in his suspension and loss of captaincy.

The 'cultural prism' that shapes our identity is not limited to what we do; it is also influenced by our notions of gender, ethnicity, sexuality and so on—all concepts we will return to in coming chapters. There can also be a dark side of having cultural practices that only we understand. This can be seen when we look upon non-members of our culture as being threats, or not as sophisticated as we are.

BOX 1.3

Thinking sociologically

ONTOLOGY

In the study of sociology, there are always terms that mystify many of us—and one such term is '**ontology**'. It is a word that you will come across in sociology and cultural studies, and it refers to the 'science of being'.

The study of ontology is a branch of philosophy that looks at different kinds of objects and their structures and properties, as well as how we relate to these objects in our everyday lives. The simplest way to think of this is to remember that ontology refers to the way we see the world: how we classify things, people and other entities around us.

This means that different fields of research and study have their own ontology that is defined by various factors, such as the key theorists and the history of where the field comes from. For example, as we have seen, sociologists look at individuals very differently from the way that economists do (see Box 1.1). Most mainstream economists believe we are rational decision makers bent on maximising our utility; while sociologists believe we are influenced by many factors (in addition to maximising our utility), such as compassion, fear and concern.

One of the best ways to win an argument is to attempt to understand and recognise the ontologies, or the different ways of looking at the world, that underpin other points of view—like my discussion with my friend the medical doctor. There are various ontological bases for different fields of research such as law, medicine, engineering, economics and music. Where people can come unstuck is by believing that their, often limited, perspective is the only way of seeing or being in the world. Instead, we can adopt a position of ontological pluralism, which acknowledges and values the many different ways of being and seeing. This allows you to examine the differences in (and where appropriate to challenge) the underlying assumptions of different points of view.

Understanding the way that other fields of study see the world is not only about winning arguments, but also about accepting other people's views. For example, my parents grew up in a rural part of Greece and see the world very differently to me. It is not just their opinions that are different; it is also how they actually perceive the world around them. We are very different—but we get along when I try to understand their ontology.

Subjectivity

'Subjectivity' is another of those words we come across in sociology that has a specific meaning in a sociological context and is important to understand when studying contemporary societies. Subjectivity refers to a specific person's (or a subject's) perspective—their knowledge, beliefs, feelings and emotions, desires and principles. It is important that we contrast this meaning with the way the term 'subjective' is used in everyday language, where it refers to someone's opinions that have no apparent justification.

As we will see in Chapter 8, our subjectivity is constituted by—among other things—the power relationships around us. That is, our perspectives and belief systems—including what we consider to be right and wrong—are the result of the relationships around us (both positive and negative). In Chapter 7, we will examine male subjectivity, which refers to the perceptions that someone labelled 'male' has of the world around them. So, males are expected to behave a certain way—which can be contrasted to the way females are expected to behave. As we will see in that chapter, if a male fails to live up to these expectations, he can be bullied and ostracised.

> BOX 1.4
> # Thinking sociologically
>
> ### EPISTEMOLOGY
>
> Another term you may come across in sociology is '**epistemology**', which is the theory of knowledge. Like ontology, it stems from philosophy and is an area of study that deals with how we know what we know, and how we rationalise such knowledge; that is, what logic and values we apply when we are gaining knowledge. There is a long history in the study of knowledge—dating back to Plato (c. 429–347 BCE)—of philosophers and sociologists trying to understand how people learn, make decisions and establish their belief systems.
>
> So, we can ask: In a complex and globalised world, how do we come to know things? What influences this knowledge? How has our process of gaining knowledge changed over time? How does our knowledge structure emerge?
>
> In this book you will sometimes see certain knowledge qualified as 'Eurocentric' or 'Western'. This is to highlight that this knowledge, which is often assumed to be universal, is actually grounded in a particular epistemological tradition. Through colonialism, Eurocentric ways of knowing the world rooted in the European Enlightenment have come to dominate many global knowledge systems (this is discussed further in Chapter 5). Across many fields of academic study, there is a move towards the 'decolonisation' of knowledge. This includes de-centring Western knowledge systems and perspectives; amplifying the voices of Indigenous and other colonised peoples; and valuing their knowledge systems and expertise (Smith 2012). One example that received popular media attention during the 2019–20 Australian bushfire season is the increasing recognition and valuing of the land management, cultural practices and ecological knowledge of Aboriginal and Torres Strait Islander people in reducing the intensity and impact of bushfires (Allam 2020). There is still much work to be done however to challenge and eliminate 'epistemic violence' or harm caused to Indigenous and colonised peoples by the erasure, appropriation and devaluing of their knowledge. You can help by keeping your mind open and appreciating different ways of knowing, being in and seeing the world.
>
> As you read this book, these are some of the questions that you may want to reflect upon, for they may explain why some knowledge is learnt and can be incredibly positive (such as the implementation of human rights language to protect the most vulnerable), and why some knowledge is accepted even when it is incorrect and can have terrible impacts on the world (such as racism).

Socially constructed

A concept that is fundamental in studying society is 'social construction'. When something is socially constructed, it is a phenomenon that is constructed (or invented) by members of a particular culture or society. These constructions exist because people agree to follow certain conventions and to behave in certain ways.

One of the challenges in our investigation of contemporary society is to detect and unmask the social constructions that we, by our very actions, support.

The central idea is that members of a society interacting together form, over time, mental representations of what to expect from each other. Eventually these become embedded in the behaviours we expect and are also reflected in the way that institutions such as schools are organised. In the process, we see the construction shape what we consider to be reality. The structure of society then revolves around this constructed reality that we accept as being both natural and normal.

One example of a social construct is gender roles: that males and females act in different ways. As we will discuss in Chapters 7 and 20, the concept of masculinity is based around how 'real men' are expected to behave: play sports, be tough and not overly emotional. From when we are born, boys are dressed in what we are socialised to think of as being more 'masculine' blue, compared to the 'pretty' pink we give to girls. When I was young, I was repeatedly told that I should 'act like a man'. Though these roles are slowly changing, we are still reminded of the roles men are supposed to play by what is portrayed in the media, the sports boys play (more males play rugby than netball) and the insults dished out to those who do not meet these criteria (such as 'you throw like a girl' or 'put a skirt on').

The reality is, however, that these are constructions: there is no reason why boys should wear blue, and, as a female friend said to me once, 'If you are so tough, try coping with the pain of giving birth'.

BOX 1.5
Thinking sociologically

WHAT IS 'NORMAL'?

If things are socially constructed, then what is natural or normal?

When studying power in Chapter 8, we will learn that the very things we consider 'normal' are themselves socially constructed and vary in different parts of the world. We learn what is normal through formal processes (such as schooling) and informal ones (while observing the people around us), and we behave accordingly. While this is fine in many instances, it can be problematic in others; for example, discrimination based on skin colour used to be considered 'normal' and part of the 'natural' order of things.

Normalisation is a process where both behaviours and ideas are established as normal. This is usually achieved through repetition, ideology, the media, institutions such as schools and hospitals, and even your family (were you ever told that 'young boys (or girls) do not behave like that'?). And, as we will see in Chapter 18, to diverge from this is considered 'deviant'.

A theorist we return to in Chapter 8, Michel Foucault, used the term 'normalisation' to describe the construction of what is acceptable conduct—a norm of behaviour.

If we follow the 'normal' behaviour, then we are rewarded for conforming to this ideal, and if we deviate from it, we are punished.

As noted, many norms that were once established now have been challenged and power structures have broken down. For example, think about how 'sexual norms' have been challenged: homophobia and discrimination against gay and lesbian people are no longer acceptable.

How to use this book

Like most books that aim to introduce a broad range of issues, this book is written in a way that allows you to jump between chapters rather than having to read them in order. There are terms that may be introduced in the earlier chapters that are referred to later in the book. This is why the wonderful publishers have insisted that we include a 'key terms' section at the start of every chapter.

We have also tried to make this book as contemporary as possible—but since I am quite old, my examples and experiences may be different to yours. So, take some of the things I say and apply them to your own experiences. As you do this, check out my blog at <www.jamesarvanitakis.net> (or find me on Facebook and Twitter @jarvanitakis), and feel free to send me your own experiences and examples of how you apply some of the theories I have discussed here.

Most importantly, do not simply accept anything that is said here, even though I have carefully selected the authors of each chapter because they are excellent writers and great teachers. All academics have their own opinions and belief systems; my own epistemology means that I have certain theoretical influences that I favour. In many ways, your job is to challenge these ideas, and, if you still find them relevant, then you should build them into your thinking.

But do me a favour: never believe that one theory or theorist has all the answers. You need to pick and choose what is relevant. Relying on just one theory will lead to blind dogma, not theoretical reflection.

STUDENT VOICE

Alexandra Coleman

❞ My first encounter with social and cultural analysis was through James Arvanitakis' first-year unit Contemporary Society, at Western Sydney University. I had completed Visual Arts, Modern History, Religion and Advanced English at high school, which are all subjects that have undergone a 'cultural turn'—particularly Advanced English—but Contemporary Society was my first formal introduction to the field. I loved it. The lectures and tutorials were the beginning of my foray into social and cultural analysis, and they left me hungry for more.

In one particular lecture, I can distinctly remember learning about social class through a discussion of the humble burger: What does it mean to buy a gourmet burger from a trendy inner-city restaurant for $35, compared to purchasing a cheeseburger from McDonald's for $2? What do these practices signify? How might we theorise these practices as classed and/or classing? (You may not be able to answer these questions now, but you certainly will by the time you have finished reading this book!)

The discussion of the burger, like many other discussions throughout James' unit, encouraged me to critically reflect on my own experiences and practices. This particular discussion prompted me to revisit a memory of eating meat pies: I was in a pie shop with my family and some family friends, the Barratts, and we were all tucking into meat pies using our hands. Sitting at the table nearest was a neatly dressed man eating his pie with a knife and fork (and with a napkin placed delicately on his lap). Geoff Barratt, who was proud of the way he was eating his pie, gestured in the direction of the neatly dressed man, and said 'That bloke wouldn't have a clue how to eat a pie with his hands'.

Though I distinctly remembered this pie-eating episode, I had never considered it in terms of class until completing this unit (with 'hands' signifying a particular type of working-class masculinity and culture).

Mulling over this memory also led me to think more about my own class background, identity and habitus—that is, my ways of being, seeing and acting—as profoundly working class (an identity that has since become ambiguous, and I find myself oscillating between a working-class and middle-class one).

Since that very first incursion into social and cultural analysis, I have gone on to complete an Honours degree, and I am completing my PhD program at the Institute for Culture and Society (Western Sydney University). I continue to be fascinated by class distinctions and I am currently researching the experiences of young people from Cranebrook in Western Sydney who are first-generation university students and graduates of the University of Sydney and the Western Sydney University (two profoundly different institutions with very different student bodies). Cranebrook, like much of Western Sydney, is a social mosaic of economic advantage and disadvantage; it has relatively lower levels of higher education participation but relatively higher levels of trade qualifications compared to the greater Sydney average.

My research, as it stands, will seek to understand the ways the participants talk about their university aspirations and experiences, socio-cultural identity formations, the ways in which place is deeply entangled with identity—particularly how place and class enmesh to constrain access and equity within Australia's higher education system—and the ways young people negotiate social (im)mobility. This project is both near and dear, and draws from my own experiences at both Western Sydney University and the University of Sydney, and my connections to Western Sydney.

I encourage you to theorise your own experiences, practices, histories and identities using the concepts discussed in this book. As you journey through each chapter, you too may begin to see yourself and the world differently—never again will you swallow a story or meaning whole. Munch it slowly.

Social and cultural analysis will give you the tools to understand the complex and kaleidoscopic world in which we live. Most importantly, social and cultural analysis will give you the tools to change the world for the better.

Conclusion

That takes us to the end of Chapter 1, in which I have introduced some broad concepts that set the background for the issues we are going to cover. Hopefully you are already starting to reflect on some of the everyday matters that affect your life in contemporary society.

Summary points

* Society is a social grouping made up of smaller informal and formal institutions.
* While we usually get along—even in cities where millions of people live side by side—there are many examples of things going wrong.
* To study society, we need to draw on theorists from a broad range of disciplines, including cultural studies and sociology.
* Understanding society allows us to discuss and reflect on what dimensions of our culture we want to protect, and what we believe should change.
* No one theory can provide us with all the answers; we should pick and choose elements from different theories.

Sociological reflection

1 List some of your everyday experiences. Why do you think we should study these?
2 What influences your own subjectivity and the way you see the world?

Discussion questions

1 What is contemporary society?
2 Why should we study contemporary society?
3 What are some of the issues and challenges in studying something we are part of?

Further investigation

1 Imagine it is the year 2100 and you are working as an 'alien tour guide', taking newly arrived aliens for a tour. What five things would you show them to portray our society?
2 List five things that you did this morning. Did you follow any cultural rules?
3 Think of some examples of everyday activities. Describe how they reflect wider social relations.

References and further reading

REFERENCES

Abercrombie, N, Hill, S & Turner, BS 1994, *Dictionary of Sociology*, 3rd edn, Penguin, London.

Allam, L 2020, 'Right fire for right future: how cultural burning can protect Australia from catastrophic blazes', *The Guardian*, 19 January 2020: <www.theguardian.com/australia-news/2020/jan/19/right-fire-for-right-future-how-cultural-burning-can-protect-australia-from-catastrophic-blazes>.

Baudrillard, J 1983, *Simulations*, Semiotexte, New York.

Epstein, D 2014, 'The science behind the world's greatest athletes', *Mother Jones*: <www.motherjones.com/environment/2014/07/inquiring-minds-david-epstein-sports-genes/>.

Groopman, J 2007, 'What's the trouble?', *The New Yorker*, 29 January, pp. 36–41.

Jureidini, R, Kenny, S & Poole, M 2003, 'The search for society', in R Jureidini & M Poole (eds), *Sociology: Australian Connections*, Allen & Unwin, Crows Nest.

Kolata, G 2016, 'Why do obese patients get worse care? Many doctors don't see past the fat', *New York Times*, 25 September 2016: <www.nytimes.com/2016/09/26/health/obese-patients-health-care.html>.

Smith, LT 2012, *Decolonizing Methodologies: Research and Indigenous Peoples*, 2nd edn, Zed Books, London.

Van Krieken, R, Habibis, D, Smith, P, Hutchins, B, Haralambos, M & Holborn, M 2005, *Sociology: Themes and Perspectives*, 3rd edn, Pearson Education Australia, Frenchs Forest.

FURTHER READING

Bennett, T & Watson, D 2002, 'Introduction', in T Bennett & D Watson (eds), *Understanding Everyday Life*, Blackwell Publishing, Oxford.

Floridi, L (ed.) 2003, *Blackwell Guide to the Philosophy of Computing and Information*, Blackwell Publishing, Oxford, pp. 155–66.

Giles, J & Middleton, T 1999, *Studying Culture—A Practical Introduction*, Blackwell, Oxford.

Highmore, B 2002, *Everyday Life and Cultural Theory*, Routledge, New York.

Martin, F 2003, 'Introduction', in F Martin (ed.), *Interpreting Everyday Culture*, Edward Arnold Publishers, London.

McPhedran, S 2018, 'FactCheck: is domestic violence the leading preventable cause of death and illness for women aged 18 to 44?', *The Conversation*, 15 April 2018: <https://theconversation.com/factcheck-is-domestic-violence-the-leading-preventable-cause-of-death-and-illness-for-women-aged-18-to-44-94102>.

Miller, T 1998, *Popular Culture and Everyday Life*, SAGE, London.

CHAPTER 2
Leap into sociology

MICHELLE BLACK AND ANNELISA SIPOS

CHAPTER OVERVIEW

Welcome to the study of society!

We, Michelle and Annelisa, the authors of this chapter, are delighted to introduce you to the world of sociological inquiry and to guide your development of skills in academic, information and digital literacy. In this chapter you will be introduced to the study of society and shown how to develop a 'sociological imagination'—a perspective that encourages you to link personal issues with 'macro' social forces. We will explore how sociologists conduct sociological inquiry and the production of sociological knowledge. To become sociologically literate, you need to develop skills in critical thinking and analysis, including the ability to evaluate information, synthesise ideas and incorporate evidence from your reading into your assessments. This chapter is directed at assisting students to accrue sociological skills in *critical thinking* and *academic literacy*. We will build on your existing knowledge of academic and digital literacy and assist you to accrue skills required for success at university.

After reading this chapter, you will be able to:

- Define the term 'sociology'
- Describe the concept of a 'sociological imagination'
- Identify the basic constituents of sociological knowledge
- Understand the concept of 'cultural capital'
- Understand the concept of literacy as a form of cultural capital
- Develop critical thinking skills in sociology
- Develop skills in academic and digital literacy relevant to sociology
- Survive university with confidence!

Key terms

Academic literacy A capacity to write in different styles at university level, to apply academic referencing, to understand academic vocabulary and terminology, to interpret and produce information and academic texts, to research and to evaluate evidence.

Agency The ability (or power) of an individual or group ('agent') to act independently of the external constraints of social structures—making decisions, undertaking actions and confronting authorities.

Cultural capital The social exchange of accumulated cultural knowledge that provides an individual with power and status in society. It is a form of capital based in modes of thinking, dispositions or cultural goods (such as books, art, music, furniture, food and wine).

Expert knowledge Specialised knowledge acquired through professional experience and advanced education. It is also the knowledge that arises from conducting systematic, scholarly research.

Lay knowledge The everyday, common knowledge based on lived experiences.

Scholarly information Encyclopedias, textbooks, journal articles, conference proceedings, or any other information that is written by people with expertise and authority in a subject area.

Social facts A concept identified with the French sociologist, Emile Durkheim (1858–1917), that refers to the way that social forces—external to an individual—influence the feeling, thinking and behaviours of an individual.

Social interaction The interactions within the society of people (both as part of groups and as individuals) and both informal and formal institutions.

Social norms Refers to the shared beliefs, attitudes, values and behaviours of people in a society—that is, a shared understanding of what is normal.

Social research A systematic investigation of society.

Social structures The social systems and institutions that underpin a society and the relationships within it. Social systems include work, education and religion, for example, while social institutions include family, schools, hospitals, government and other institutions that exist within our legal, economic and political systems.

Social theory The frameworks used to explain how society works.

Sociological imagination The capacity to see how social factors influence the life of an individual in society.

Sociology The study of society. In order to study society, we must look at the interactions within the society of people (both as part of groups and as individuals) and both informal and formal institutions (such as schools, hospitals and government).

What is sociology?

To be a good student of **sociology** you must learn to think like a sociologist; that is, acquire the ability to think sociologically. Sociology is, quite simply, a study of society. Of course, sociologists themselves have far more sophisticated definitions of sociology:

> Sociology focuses on the organisation of social life. It looks at how people's lives are influenced by their opportunities and experiences; and the impact that people have on society through taking action and creating change (TASA 2019).

Or:

> the study of the relationship between the individual and society, investigating how human thought, action, and interaction shape and are shaped by society (Germov & Poole 2011, p. 4).

Before we leap into sociology, let us ask you a question: What is a sociologist?

If you cannot answer this question, you are in good company! A 2013 global survey of 16,000 students' parents conducted by social media networking platform LinkedIn found 'sociologist' to be the sixth-most misunderstood occupation: 70 per cent of those surveyed were unable to confidently describe what a sociologist was (Nisen & Goudreau 2013). According to the British Sociological Association (2019) the task of a sociologist is to understand, in a systematic way, the institutionalised patterns of human relationships, to study the reproduction of social institutions at local and global levels, and to provide explanations for shifting patterns of human relationships through the lens of social, cultural, economic or political institutions. In other words, a sociologist applies a systematic study of groups in society and of the **social interaction** of people in society. A social interaction can be an everyday interaction—conversing with a work colleague, posting to social media, or being part of a crowd at a music festival.

Sociology then, is the study of social interactions on an individual's behaviour.

Have you ever been part of a crowd at a sporting event or a music concert? You are not likely to know the majority of people attending the event but are likely to behave in a similar manner to other attendees. What compels individuals to follow conventional rules of behaviour? How are social 'norms' produced and replicated in crowd behaviour? Sociologists recognise that *social change* is produced by collective behaviour of individuals. Sociologists also recognise that an individual has **agency**: that is, an ability to exercise choice and change the behaviour of other people within the constraints of the social structure (more on this later).

As a student of sociology, you will develop skills in critical and social analysis. With these skills you can apply a critical sociological perspective to understand how society influences individuals and how individuals influence society.

That's right: individuals can influence society! While we can focus on high profile individuals like Greta Thunberg—who organised the school strikes for climate change—as changing our society, it is also important to note that less visible individuals like you impact society by taking action and working towards social change. Whenever you sign an online petition or post your opinion to social media, you are effecting change. From a sociological perspective, when an individual acts to exert some level of control over their social relations, then the individual is exercising agency (Sewell 1992).

Sociologists are interested in how individuals exercise agency in relation to structural constraints and opportunities (Lin 2001). The **social structure** is, simplistically, the wider social system that governs the patterned social relationships with which we interact and live, bounded by institutions such as family, health, education, the law, media and politics. To add to this complexity, our social experiences are shaped by *social factors* such as social class, race, ethnicity, gender, age, health status, education, occupation, wealth and income.

Cultural and social norms in society

A society is a group of people who share a culture (Little & McGivern 2019) and interact within a defined space. Closely aligned to 'society' is culture and in Chapter 1, 'culture' is defined as encompassing the 'rules and processes of everyday life'. A cultural group will have shared beliefs, attitudes, values, behaviours and norms—that is, an understanding of what is 'normal'. For example, for a person living in Vanuatu in the Pacific region, it is normal to marry someone chosen for you from an appropriate kinship group, or to participate in 'sister exchange' in which a man owes a wife to a family he has married into. This would be unheard of and very unusual in other places of the world.

Cultural groups can also have many sub-cultural groups. For example, you may identify culturally as 'Australian' but also as 'Chinese-Australian' or 'Indigenous Australian', and if you are an Indigenous Australian, you may also identify culturally with a defined group of people: a 'nation', 'language group', 'clan group' or 'mob'.

A historical constellation of social factors has made Australia a 'unique social environment' (TASA 2019). The vision of Australia in the early twentieth century was as a 'social laboratory' with progressive labour and employment policies (such as the eight-hour work day), female voting, secret ballot for voting at political elections, age pensions and government subsidised health and medical insurance. The vision shifted throughout the course of the twentieth century to incorporate multiculturalism and immigration policy, equal opportunity legislation for workers, public health programs including free immunisation, and a focus on Indigenous and multicultural health and welfare. Society and culture within Australia shift constantly as people and institutions respond to 'macro' or structural changes over time such as political changes, immigration policy, environmental changes, employment practices and gender 'norms'.

While there are many elements of Australian society that we should be rightfully proud of, there are also other elements that should concern us. Throughout this book you will also reflect and research some of the darker sides of our society (both past and present) including racism and exclusion, the treatment of Australia's Aboriginal and Torres Strait Islander population and marginalisation of vulnerable sections of our community.

Critical reflection

Think about your beliefs, values and attitudes towards the following contemporary society topics. Have your beliefs, values and attitudes changed over time?

- Should same-sex couples be able to adopt children?
- What is meant by a 'disabled' person? Should people living with disability be defined as 'disabled'?
- Should women be allowed to participate full-time in the workforce after giving birth?
- Should we celebrate Australia Day on the 26th of January?
- Should the government take more or less action on climate change policy?

Now consider whether your belief is really your own, or whether it is a composite of the beliefs expressed by your family, friends, social media feeds, news media, films, writers, teachers, religious community and political leaders.

Leap into social analysis

Contemporary sociologists seek to understand the connections between people's experiences of daily life, social factors, institutions and other **social structures**, and produce knowledge that explains these connections. To do this, they undertake social research and develop social theory.

Along with anthropology, politics, economics, criminology and human geography, sociology emerged in the mid twentieth century as a popular field for social scientific inquiry. Social scientific inquiry is guided by social theories and concepts. To investigate these theories and concepts, sociologists have developed rules and methods of researching how society influences individual actions and thoughts. **Social theory** explains how society works, and **social research** is a systematic investigation of society. One reason sociologists conduct social research is because as they are 'reflecting on what is going on in modern social life, questions occur to them' (Bryman 2012, p. 5). You will learn more about social research in Chapter 4.

Studying the social world is different to studying physical sciences, such as biology and chemistry. Some scientific research tools, such as clinical experiments, simply do not work in analysing society. Instead, sociologists need specific, unique methods for doing social research. Social research methods including in-depth interviews, online surveys and observations are used by sociologists to explore the social relations in society. For example, a sociologist may be interested in why binge-drinking rates are rising among young people. They may investigate the links between alcohol consumption and young people through interviews or observation studies.

Another important skill set for the sociology student is critical analysis. The Australian Sociological Association (TASA 2019) notes that 'sociology is a perspective on the social world that values critical thinking'. But what is meant, exactly, by 'critical thinking'? When you hear the word 'critical' you may think of disapproving comments or judgments of people and things. In a sociological sense, it is questioning the everyday, commonsense explanations for why the social world is as it is, and considering the influence of power and inequality in everyday life.

Thus, the sociology student must become adept in using social research methods to analyse links between society and the individual. You will need to become sociologically literate, which means learning how to identify how people are influenced by various social phenomena and how we as individuals influence society.

Investigating social life

The sociologist investigates social interactions by doing social research. Box 2.1 showcases a selection of sociological studies published in the *Journal of Sociology* (Issues 1–3, 2019). As you can see from this list, Australian sociologists are involved in a range of exciting, cutting-edge social research. Moreover, social research findings advance **sociological knowledge**.

BOX 2.1
Method to action

TOPICS OF SOCIAL RESEARCH BY AUSTRALIAN SOCIOLOGISTS

- The social networks of immigrants and ethnic inequalities in Australia
- The expansion of global capitalism and the impact on working conditions for call-centre workers in the Philippines
- Young people's experiences and meanings of homelessness
- An exploration of the social determinants of health for Indigenous Australians living in remote communities
- Investigating public trust in social media as a source of information on a global pandemic
- Instruments of control of asylum seekers and volunteers in Australian immigration detention centres
- The relationship between 'social class' and obesity in children
- The cultural norms and beliefs of the Indigenous peoples of Tanna Island, Vanuatu
- Exploring the deviant sub-culture of graffiti 'taggers'
- The changing place of religion in contemporary Australian society
- Perceptions of masculinity among members of an online body building group
- Australian print media representations of intimate partner violence
- Investigating public perceptions of climate change 'risk'.

Individuals are always shaped by the environmental, cultural and social forces around them, as well as individuals shaping that world. You can see from the topics in Box 2.1 that sociologists research the interplay between the individual, society and social institutions. Sociologists typically conduct social research at a *micro* or *macro* level.

Micro—or local—analysis involves studying social interactions, personal experiences and meanings at the individual level. Macro analysis investigates large-scale processes that influence society as a whole (Little & McGivern 2019).

At the micro level, a study into young people and homelessness would explore the meanings associated with homelessness for those young people experiencing it. At the macro level, we would examine the history of homelessness in Australia, the governmental policies affecting rates of homelessness, the social history of benevolence and charity towards homeless people and wider interpretations, globally, of what homelessness is.

Once you start to do social analysis into such topics, you will recognise that society is constantly changing and influenced by past and present factors. The fact that society and culture are *fluid* rather than stable, is what makes sociology so fascinating to study (as well as challenging)—this is something we will explore in more depth in Chapter 3.

> **Critical reflection**
>
> Which of the social research topics in Box 2.1 do you consider to be most important to contemporary Australian society, and why?

Developing a sociological imagination

When we start to see how everything in society is linked and interconnected, we begin to develop what renowned American sociologist, Charles Wright Mills (1916–62), termed a **sociological imagination** (Mills 1959). Mills' concept of the sociological imagination is derived from the conception of a *social fact*. A brief review of the origins of sociology will assist our understanding of a social fact.

Social facts

Contemporary sociology can be traced to the systematic study of European societies that emerged in the early eighteenth century when philosophers such as Voltaire in France and John Locke in England started thinking about the role of society in shaping an individual, and the role of an individual within a society. In 1780 the term 'sociology' was coined by French essayist Emmanuel-Joseph Sieyes (1748–1836) and popularised by the French philosopher Auguste Comte (1798–1857) (Little & McGivern 2019). Comte is remembered as the first scholar to apply a scientific research method to the study of society, or what later became known as the 'science of society' (Van Krieken et al. 2017, p. 15).

French sociologist Emile Durkheim (1857–1917) was influential in establishing sociology as a distinct discipline at the University of Bordeaux in 1895. Durkheim saw the role of sociology as observing **social norms** that bind individuals to a social order and keep a society stable. He theorised that a lack of social norms would result in *anomie*—'a state of normlessness' (Little & McGivern 2019). According to Durkheim, social systems and institutions create the norms and rules by which we live (Durkheim & Solovay 1964). From a sociological perspective, these can be studied as **social facts** that influence how we think, behave and feel on a daily basis. Some examples of social facts include religion, education and learning, money and political practices.

The sociological imagination

Mills (1959) defined a sociological imagination as 'the vivid awareness of the relationship between experience and the wider society', a connection between our personal worlds and public issues. To make this connection, we can investigate the influence on an individual of four interconnected parts:

- *Historical*: How have past experiences influenced a person's present? How has a person's family background influenced the beliefs, values and life choices of the person?
- *Cultural*: How have culture, religion or traditions influenced a person's beliefs, values, attitudes and life choices?

- *Structural*: How have macro systems—such as government, the law, health, globalisation and education—influenced the beliefs, attitudes, values and life choices of a person?
- *Critical*: Why are things as they are? What has influenced a person's values, beliefs and choices to change over time?

These questions can help us to adopt a sociological perspective—an ability to think 'outside the square'; that is, moving beyond our own view of the world and looking at society from a perspective that explores the interactions between macro world systems (such as government, religion, education and law) and the micro worlds of individuals and groups (including beliefs, values, attitudes and life choices).

For example, being unemployed affects us on a personal level. It can cause personal distress and lead to feelings of low self-worth, which can adversely impact our relationships with friends and family. Financially, it can affect our ability to buy everyday goods and services. As a result, unemployed people may become socially isolated. Society values having money and status, so not having a job may disable us from being in the company of people with money and jobs. It may even prevent us from having a romantic relationship. If unemployment is widespread, it impacts society as a whole; it uses up charity resources and leads to increased crime, homelessness and incidence of depression.

The sociological interest is in how the personal experience of being unemployed is linked with a number of social facts including the provision of social welfare, the priorities of the education system and government, the institution of family, and social attitudes towards unemployed people.

If someone is unemployed long term, do they have a social responsibility to be proactive about their situation? Should they find another job? Start a business? Make friends? Be part of the community? Or is society responsible for the wellbeing of a long-term unemployed individual?

We discuss work and society in Chapter 19.

Let's take another example: the simple act of purchasing a pair of trainers. We could argue that trainers do not just have a practical function, they also have symbolic and consumption value. For some consumers, trainers must be a brand and style acceptable to their peer group. The trainers may need a signature 'swoosh' or be a recognisable global brand—these are examples of symbolic consumption. For others, the shoes must not be made from animal products or produced in 'sweat shops' where those working to make the shoes are not paid a fair wage—this is an example of ethical consumption. We can explore the global journey of our shoes—where and how they are made—looking critically at how some people benefit, while others are exploited in the shoe-production supply chain. We can explore the global meanings of a brand of trainers and see how the function of trainers has moved beyond footwear for physical activity to footwear for symbolic consumption. The footwear confers an identity on the wearer as a global consumer.

If you apply a sociological imagination, you will develop an understanding of the macro and micro influences on an individual's everyday-life beliefs, values and behaviours. In short, you will be able to connect an individual's experiences and behaviour within society.

PERSONAL VOICE
Michael Resende

❝ When I was in high school, I was not very academically focused. I was unsure of where I saw myself after completing Year 12. What I did know was I had an intrinsic interest in society and its underpinnings, with a deep curiosity for how it can affect individuals. As a result, I enrolled at Australian Catholic University (ACU) where I studied psychology, which later led me to minor in sociology as I wanted to further explore the more 'social' dimensions of social sciences.

I wasn't sure which pathway to take, but I knew a degree would be the first step to many opportunities in the areas of sociology and psychology. This is evident to me through looking at how I've developed many skills—such as a sociological imagination—over the past three years I've spent studying. In my experience, the sociological imagination helps to understand the different perspectives and approaches to an individual's lived experience, allowing better empathy with others.

As a first-generation immigrant, I had a unique experience of culture growing up which felt noticeably different to my peers. While I appreciated many aspects of my family's culture, I also felt many beliefs and attitudes were outdated and not beneficial to my development into a young adult in the context of living as an Australian. However, through my study of sociology and the development of a sociological imagination, I am better able to understand why and how my experience of culture came to be. A sociological imagination is a great academic tool, and it also contributes positively to your own personal growth. In my experience, taking an empathetic approach to understanding why I was raised with certain cultural values allowed me to better appreciate my culture for what it is. I believe my development of a sociological imagination will continue to provide me with opportunities for further growth in the future.

In addition to the development of a sociological imagination, sociology has also helped me to develop critical thinking skills as well as academic literacy. Before studying sociology, I had little knowledge of how to differentiate between information and evaluate credible sources, and this proved an issue when writing essays. Throughout my studies, I have developed critical thinking skills to evaluate resources and decide if those sources are well researched. This allowed me to better understand the qualities that make a resource credible and as a result, impacted the quality of my academic literacy, as I was able to use resources with more confidence in their legitimacy.

For all these reasons, I continue to have an interest in the area of sociology, with the hopes of pursuing a career relating to social research.

What counts as sociological knowledge?

So, what constitutes 'knowledge' in the study of contemporary society?

To answer this, we need to begin by thinking about what knowledge actually is. Most students come to university assuming that the subjects they learn constitute knowledge because they are produced by academic experts and researchers. These people are seen to hold '**expert knowledge**', by virtue of having experience and qualifications in a field of study.

World-renowned British sociologist Anthony Giddens describes professional workers (such as teachers and doctors) as the 'access points' to expert knowledge systems. The fact that we engage daily with expert knowledge that is not our own—in the fields of transport, engineering, law, health and so on—requires us to have faith or trust in the 'authenticity of the expert knowledge' that experts apply (Giddens 1995, p. 28).

Think about this for a moment: most of us have little to no idea about how a plane works. When we fly, we assume that the engineers who designed the aircraft have expert knowledge in aerospace engineering; likewise, we assume that the pilot has experience and knowledge of flying (and landing!). In other words, we put our trust in a handful of 'experts'—people with specialised knowledge of flight.

> **Critical reflection**
>
> Over the last 24 hours, in what ways have you engaged with expert knowledge? For example, did you attend a medical practitioner? If so, you trusted in the expertise of the doctor, dentist, therapist or other practitioner.

In 1903, sociologist Albion Small defined the sociologist as a person 'studying the facts of society *in a certain way*' (Small 1903, p. 468, emphasis added). What does this mean? Sociologists not only produce expert knowledge in the form of *social theories* and in uncovering *social facts*, they are also interested in the change in *expert knowledge* over time.

Let's take what counted as expert medical knowledge in pre-Modern Europe. Up until the 1600s, *trepanning*—or boring a hole into the skull—was practised to cure seizures, fractures and even mental disorders. The latter were thought to be caused by evil spirits in the brain, which could be released through trepanning. It certainly sounds mighty dangerous! Yet, this approach represented authoritative medical knowledge at that time.

By the eighteenth century, scientific research started to supplant older medical knowledge, and for the first time, doctors were more likely to hold formalised, professional qualifications. Understandings of the human brain were advancing and replacing older medical knowledge, improving outcomes for patients and relegating old techniques to the realms of pseudoscience.

What we see from this example is that expert knowledge can be *contested* and that it can change over time. Indeed, with new research constantly being undertaken and published by scientists and breakthroughs happening regularly, it will continue to change!

Knowledge comes from everywhere

Sociologists recognise that some of the changes in expert knowledge come from the 'bottom up'; that **lay knowledge**—everyday, common knowledge—can influence our beliefs. For example, I may have *knowledge* that a fever is a sign I am ill. I have acquired this knowledge from my family, doctors and media. If I grew up in a different culture, however, I may *know* that a fever is a sign of habitation by evil spirits.

In other words, lay knowledge arises from socialisation. That is, we learn and internalise the everyday norms, knowledge, culture and ideology of our society.

Reflect on your lay knowledge. You probably see it as completely separate to what you read in a textbook, yet, due to individual agency, your everyday beliefs are important and can contribute to lay knowledge. Think about your last comment to social media. How many people may have seen it? Without realising it, you may have imparted knowledge that other people have accepted and shared. In this way, we not only learn through the process of socialisation but also socialise others around us.

This form of everyday, lay knowledge is of interest to sociologists as it contributes to general social knowledge. Have another look at the topics in Box 2.1—you will see that a lot of social research is interested in uncovering people's understandings of social phenomena. What this suggests is that the everyday, lived experiences of 'lay' people is embedded in sociological knowledge.

Literacy cultural capital

As a student, you come to university with existing knowledge—lay knowledge—of **academic literacy**. Some of you have more experience and knowledge than others, but all of you have some exposure to reading, formal writing, research and, in the twenty-first century, digital literacy.

This forms part of what is termed **cultural capital** (we will discuss this concept in more detail in Chapter 6). Cultural capital is the accumulated cultural knowledge of the individual; that is, what is generally acquired as part of a person's upbringing. Cultural capital is seen as important in a person's vocational and educational outcomes.

When we talk about 'literacy cultural capital', we mean language skills (including reading and writing), knowledge of current affairs, research and, in terms of academic literacy, how to write and reference evidence properly, how to research an essay and so forth. But there are other ways to think about literacy cultural capital.

For example, one view is that literacy—in terms of engagement with reading, writing and current affairs—is influenced by our parents. The French sociologist Pierre Bourdieu (1930–2002) (Bourdieu 2007) argued that cultural capital is reproduced through families, and that university-educated, middle-class parents are likely to use the language of the university system in everyday life, making a student feel more familiar with university and with academic literacy. This is (using Bourdieu's theory) more likely to lead to success at university.

So, students come to university with different levels of literacy cultural capital. The authors of this chapter have the view that, whether you have higher or lower literacy cultural capital, you can build on or *accrue* your literacy cultural capital at university. If you are committed to developing academic literacy, then you are giving yourself more chance to succeed at university (Black & Rechter 2013).

The remainder of this chapter is about succeeding in sociology and beyond by developing academic literacies.

PERSONAL VOICE
Merrin Chauncy

❝ After leaving school in Year 10, I attended business college, where I completed secretarial administration studies. I worked in many different administration jobs, including for the Department of Community Services (DoCS); however, I soon got bored. In my time at DoCS I worked in the disability section and discovered that I wanted to work with people and help people.

I realised that I really wanted to go to uni and study social work. I could see that without a degree I would not have the qualifications to obtain a position where I could actually make a difference. I was quite nervous about this because I was a mature-age student.

Sociology fitted really well with social work as it gives one understanding of and insight into social problems. I realised that I brought to uni a lot of valuable knowledge and life experience, however going to a private school, I was not exposed to cultural diversity and unaware of many injustices towards marginalised people. My study of society—for example, racism, the ill-treatment of Australia's Indigenous peoples and the effects of media on society—are all issues I have thought about for years, and have now come to understand from a sociological perspective. In sociology we learnt about how work and leisure are politicised and, having worked for 13 years in disability services, I have brought knowledge of workplace issues—as well as issues around the marginalisation of disabled peoples—to my study of society.

Women especially benefit from the knowledge sociology gives us: although we have come a long way with equality, we haven't come far enough. Knowledge is power and studying sociology has enhanced my cultural capital, my knowledge of the determinants of gender inequality which I have personally experienced.

My studies in sociology have also helped me develop my writing skills. When I first started studying I had little confidence in writing due to my negative experiences throughout school. Now, aged in my thirties I have developed the confidence to write.

I never would have written a piece like this for a book when I first started uni!

Succeeding in sociology and beyond

It is difficult to imagine studying sociology without going online. Where do you turn if you want more information on the sociological imagination? Google, right? Never has it been easier to find information and never has more information been available. However, this wealth of information and its accessibility can be challenging, depending on your level of literacy cultural capital.

This part of the chapter looks at developing academic literacy skills, particularly strategies for increasing your efficiency and effectiveness in finding, evaluating and using information. These skills are essential for succeeding at university and beyond—in your personal and work life.

Information and digital literacy

Information literacy is the ability to find information to meet a need, recognise when you have found enough information, evaluate the information for relevance and credibility, and use that information responsibly.

Information literacy is critical—not just for university, but for fostering personal wellbeing, social connections and employability; it is considered a basic human right (UNESCO 2005).

Digital literacy encompasses a broader set of capabilities that equip a person to fully participate and thrive in a digital society. Digital literacy includes information, media and data literacy, and it also describes behaviours related to communication, collaboration, learning, digital reputation and online identity (Jisc 2014).

At university, you will engage with different technologies and develop specialised capabilities relevant to sociology. For example, using video to interview subjects to interpret and represent culture and society (video ethnography) requires both digital literacy and discipline knowledge. A sociologist might even analyse tweets on a trending topic to identify contemporary social values, which calls for technical skills and a sociological imagination. In fact, researchers in the United States used Twitter and trending tweets to predict the election of Donald Trump in 2016 even though most political commentators argued he had no chance of victory (see Jackson & Sykora 2016).

Information is not created equal

At university, lecturers and tutors expect you to find and refer to **scholarly information** in your assignments. Scholarly information is written by people with expertise in a subject area; authorities on a topic. It is found in encyclopedias, textbooks, journal articles and conference proceedings. Assignments might specify that you use peer-reviewed journal articles. These articles are rigorously reviewed by independent experts before being accepted for publication. Your teachers expect you to use these sources as evidence to support arguments in assessments. As you interpret the ideas of different scholars and theorists, see the connections and differences of their viewpoints, and synthesise the information to analyse or justify a point, you exercise critical thinking skills. By incorporating scholarly sources in your work, you demonstrate your engagement with and understanding of key concepts and theories in sociology.

Scholarly and peer-reviewed information is different to popular sources of information such as magazine articles. Magazines are written for general audiences to entertain or inform. The articles are usually short, easy to read and do not require subject knowledge to understand them. Popular sources are also found on the internet. However, these sources are not generally written by experts or for an academic audience and can be unreliable.

Mainstream media such as newspapers and current affairs programs are important sources for sociology students. They report on social, cultural and political phenomena.

Such sources, along with social media, can also be a yardstick for contemporary values and attitudes. Can media sources be used in university assignments? Aside from considering the reliability of sources—particularly with the advent of 'fake news', 'alternative facts' and 'fast news' (simplified news content)—it depends on the context. An analysis of the media's portrayal of refugees and asylum seekers would be expected to have news and scholarly sources; however, an essay that relied solely on media analyses to support an argument would be penalised.

Popular sources of general information can help us make sense of complex concepts, but it should be used as a starting point only. Lecturers assess the quality of scholarly sources, how well they are used to support a position and whether they have been appropriately acknowledged following a formal referencing style, for example, American Psychological Association Style (APA).

You might be thinking, 'How hard is it to find information? I do it all the time'. And you do. Statistics show that 18 to 24-year-olds mostly access the internet for social networking (95.7 per cent); entertainment (92.9 per cent); and purchasing goods or services (81.2 per cent); with formal educational activities coming in at 56.8 per cent (ABS 2018). However, at university, as mentioned, it is necessary to find scholarly and peer-reviewed information, which can be trickier. So even if you feel confident using the internet, using it for academic study will require different skills.

Critical reflection

Think about your engagement with online information over the last week:

- How many times did you use Google, or another search engine, to find information?
- What type of information were you seeking? For example, health, employment, entertainment?
- Did you go past the first page of results to get the answers you needed?
- Do you know who wrote the information you found?

Now imagine a close friend or family member is looking for information on drug addiction. Why is it important to check that website content is written by people with expert knowledge?

The price of information

Unlike much of the information found on the internet, many journal articles are not freely available. Academic libraries subscribe to journals, which allows their students and staff to access scholarly articles—but not the general public, despite public funding of universities (AOASG 2019). Scholarly content is increasingly being made available through the open-access movement to reduce this inequity and give everybody the right to free information and research. See the end of this chapter for a guide to open-access resources.

As a university student, you are privileged to freely access scholarly content, but this means becoming adept at using your library's online catalogue and databases. Encounters with the university library and databases often start with the first assignment. Before diving into databases, it pays to analyse the task and topic, consider the information required, and search terms.

How to research a sociology assignment

In this section, we outline a step-by-step approach to researching a sociology assignment:
1. Unpacking the assessment task;
2. Analysing the topic;
3. Reading background information;
4. Planning your search—identifying keywords;
5. Planning your search—where to find information; and
6. Smart searching.

We'll apply our research to this example sociology assignment:

> **Analyse how politicians have used their power to shape public thinking on asylum seekers in contemporary Australia. Refer to media coverage and at least six peer-reviewed journal articles in your analysis.**

1 Unpacking the assessment task

What are you being asked to do? It helps to ask yourself questions to make sure you cover essential points. For example:

- Why has this assignment been set? The purpose of the task and learning objectives can help shape your answer.
- What do I need to cover?
- What is the word limit? This is a good guide to the amount of research to do and time needed to complete the task.
- What types of information are required? Scholarly, media, case studies, statistics or government reports? The type of information determines where to look for it.
- When is the assignment due? How long do you have to research, write and revise your assignment?
- Who is going to read the assignment? The audience determines the style and formality of the language to be used. Compare the language used on social media, in magazines, newspaper articles, peer-reviewed journals and textbooks. Which types of writing have power and prestige? Aim to model your writing on the scholarly books and articles you read.

2 Analysing the topic

The next step in the research process is to study the essay question to identify task, content and limiting words.

- Task words tell you how to answer the questions. Look for verbs such as discuss, evaluate, explain, argue, compare and examine. A list of task words and what they mean is available at <www.student.unsw.edu.au/glossary-task-words>.
- Content words contain the main ideas or concepts to be discussed. Content words will become your search terms.

    Essay topics can be wordy, but sometimes a concept is conveyed in a sentence or two. Interpret the meaning and think of a term or phrase that sums up that idea. For example, 'Australians should have the right to decide when they die' is captured by the term 'voluntary euthanasia'.

    Databases work best with keywords and phrases, not sentences. If the question is vague, make it more specific with well-defined concepts for improved search results.
- Limiting words narrow the focus of your response to a time, place, population or type of information.

    Analyse the example topic to determine the task, content and limiting words. Answers are shown below in Box 2.2.

BOX 2.2

Method to action

TOPIC ANALYSIS ANSWERS

- **Task words:** analyse | refer
- **Content words:** politicians | public thinking | asylum seekers
- **Limiting words:** Australia | contemporary (information needs to be current) | media coverage | peer-reviewed journal articles

---

3 Reading background information

With an understanding of the task and topic, the next step is to do background reading. Background reading introduces a topic and helps develop a preliminary understanding of a concept. For our example essay topic, it might include clarifying the difference between asylum seekers, internally displaced people, refugees and economic migrants.

Attending lectures, taking notes and lecture slides are ways of obtaining background information. Subject-specific dictionaries and encyclopedias are also sources of background information.

Background information helps to identify relevant terminology—language used by those with expert knowledge—that can be used as search terms.

If you consult these sources first, you will be better able to evaluate books and journal articles for their relevance to the topic. This can be a good time to meet with your school or faculty librarian for some guidance and tips on the range of sources available to you through the library and its subscription databases.

4 Planning your search—identifying keywords

Planning increases the efficiency and the effectiveness of your searches. Planning involves identifying keywords and related terms, working out where to search, and applying search tips for more effective searching.

Keywords and phrases will be based on the concepts in the essay topic. However, you are not limited to these alone. As we saw above, sometimes you need to interpret a topic to identify keywords or phrases that represent the main ideas. It also helps to brainstorm a topic to identify synonyms and related terms to capture the various ways a topic could be conceived.

Your search query should include the terms you would expect to find in the ideal resource—one that has the answers to all your questions (Russell & MIT 2019). Sadly, this magic paper or book rarely exists! You will need to develop your answer drawing on several resources.

BOX 2.3

Method to action

IDENTIFYING KEYWORDS

The following keywords might be used in a search for information on the example essay topic. Identifying and using alternative terms can help if you are getting too many or too few results.

> Analyse how politicians have used their power to shape public thinking on asylum seekers in contemporary Australia. Refer to media coverage and at least six peer-reviewed journal articles in your analysis.

Politicians	Public thinking	Asylum seekers	Australia
Politics	Attitudes	Political refugees	
Immigration policy	Public opinion	Illegal immigrants	
Government			

---

5 Planning your search—where to find information

Where to search for information depends on the type of information you need. Your assignments might require you to consult both peer-reviewed information and statistics. These are unlikely to be found in the same online source.

You will find some starting points on where to find different kinds of information in Table 2.1.

TABLE 2.1 Where to find different types of information

I need ...	Try here ...
Background information Why: To clarify concepts and identify search terms	Encyclopedias and subject-specific dictionaries such as the Open Education Sociology Dictionary: <www.sociologydictionary.org>. Via a library catalogue. Hint: search for a topic and filter results to reference entries. Choose those relevant to sociology. Your library may also have a sociology subject guide on its website with an overview and links to the most frequently used reference sources. (See for example <https://subjectguides.library.westernsydney.edu.au/sociology>.)
Scholarly and peer-reviewed information Why: To ensure your research is based on expert knowledge in the field	Books and journal articles via a search of your university library or open-access resources.
Statistics and reports Why: To observe and investigate phenomena and problems affecting population groups	Government and organisation websites such as the Australian Bureau of Statistics, Australian Institute for Health and Welfare, The UN Refugee Agency, World Health Organization, and World Bank Open Data Human Development Reports.
Images and videos Why: To research topics, present and illustrate information and witness first-hand accounts of people's experiences	Academic libraries often subscribe to image and video databases. See the open-access guide at the end of this chapter for finding content that can be legally used and shared (Creative Commons).

6 Smart searching

You can improve the effectiveness and efficiency of your searches by understanding a little about how databases and library catalogues work. This will help you to troubleshoot when there are too many or too few results or they are not relevant to your topic.

See Table 2.2 for search basics, along with some tips for refining your searches.

TABLE 2.2 Search tips

Entering this ...	Retrieves this ...
attitudes refugees Australia	Items that include all terms in any order. Use this to combine different concepts. The system automatically combines concepts with AND.
"political refugees" (phrase searching)	Items that mention these words together and in that order.
political refugees	Items that mention both words in any order, when word order is unimportant.
"political refugees" OR "asylum seekers"	Items that contain either or both phrases. Use this when joining similar concepts.
polit* (truncation)	Items that include politics, political, politician(s), politicization and politicisation. Truncation allows you to find word variants and will broaden a search. Many databases use an asterisk for truncation, but check the help function to make sure.

Information-finding hacks

Finding relevant information doesn't have to be hard. Start with what you know. Search the library catalogue and sociology databases such as SOCIndex for a theorist mentioned in lectures, or for a book from a list of recommended readings. Look at the details of an item, including the contents description and subject headings. Subject headings identify the topic(s) of books and articles. Other material that covers similar territory will be assigned the same subject terms (Cargill 2015). Book details and article abstracts (summaries) are a rich source for identifying search terms you might not have considered.

A search for a known item, such as the title of this book, will also retrieve related resources. Other books on the same topic allow you to explore alternative viewpoints. You might also find that concepts are more clearly explained in one book compared to another.

Other relevant sources can be easily found by checking the references listed at the end of book chapters and articles.

A single search rarely yields all the information required. As you search, be alert for terminology and subject headings, which will help to refine successive searches.

BOX 2.4

Method to action

Run a search using the terms: "public thinking" refugees Australia. Note the number of results and the titles of articles and books. Run a second search using the terms: "public opinion" refugees Australia. How do the search results compare?

To google or not to google

Sometimes you need information that is best found on the internet, using Google (believe it or not). For example, statistics and reports from organisations and government departments are readily available. The trick is knowing how to find reliable information online from among commercial websites that aim to sell goods and services, or websites that are biased, misinformed, or present opinions as facts.

Add a specific website's URL before search terms to restrict results to pages from a specific website (Russell & MIT 2019). The same technique can be used to limit a query to a domain, such as educational sites, organisations or government departments, as shown below:

- site:unhcr.org refugees public opinion Australia—this query limits results to information matching these keywords from the United Nations High Commissioner for Refugees website.
- site:org.au gender pay gap—this search limits results on the gender pay gap to Australian organisations, such as the Diversity Council Australia and the Australian Council of Trade Unions (ACTU).

- site:gov.au youth homelessness—this search returns pages on youth homelessness from the websites of the NSW Government, the Australian Human Rights Commission, and the Department of Social Services.

With this technique, you don't need advance knowledge of relevant government departments or organisations: you will discover them in the process.

> **BOX 2.5**
>
> ### Method to action
>
> Run a Google search on a topic of interest. Next add site: followed by a domain or a web address in front of your keywords and rerun the search. Compare the number and quality of the results between the two searches.

Evaluating information for credibility

Once you have found information, the next step is to evaluate it for relevance and reliability. There are different ways to evaluate sources of information. One method, known by the acronym CAARP, evaluates information based on the following criteria:

- *Currency*: Consider when the information was written. Is it still relevant? When was the information or website last updated?
- *Authority*: Who wrote or produced the information? What is their expertise? What are their credentials?
- *Accuracy*: Is the information correct? Is it possible to verify the content?
- *Relevance*: How well does the information meet your needs and relate to what you are researching?
- *Purpose*: Why was the information created?

Using and citing evidence

Whenever you use other people's words, ideas, images, data or content, you must acknowledge your sources by referencing. Referencing or citing serves several functions. Referencing allows you to substantiate your claims and lends credibility to your writing. Referencing allows the reader to locate, verify and evaluate your sources. When you cite the work of others, you demonstrate your engagement with and interpretation of key concepts in sociology. By acknowledging your sources, you respect the creator's intellectual property and protect yourself from claims of plagiarism. Plagiarism occurs when you copy or paraphrase information without crediting sources, which is a form of academic misconduct.

Referencing involves two parts: an in-text citation or footnote, and a complete list of sources with publication details such as author, year and title.

Referencing styles can vary between subjects and schools. The required style is usually indicated in your course unit outline.

Most databases and library catalogues have automatic citation generators, often indicated by a quotation symbol. Use them with caution as the citation may be incomplete. However, once you understand why, when and how to reference and correct a citation, they can be a handy start to documenting and acknowledging your sources.

See the websites listed under 'Referencing styles' at the end of this chapter for guidance on referencing.

Lifelong learning

As you hone these academic skills during your studies, you will be setting yourself up for life after university. Fast-forward and imagine you are working. You have been asked to research and report on the links between poverty and childhood obesity. You know you need primary sources such as health statistics and journal articles reporting new research. You refer to research produced by government departments and organisations. You also consult secondary sources, those that analyse or interpret relevant primary sources, such as journal articles that comment on research. As a digitally and information literate person, you can:

- Find these different types of information;
- Assess it for reliability;
- Analyse the data and research, and interpret it accurately;
- Cite sources so that others can locate and verify your findings;
- Choose appropriate software to write up your findings in different formats (presentation, report, media release, website) and styles according to the intended audience; and
- Share the findings responsibly using relevant communication technologies.

Your report helps to shape policy and make a difference in health outcomes for children in need. This is just one example of how information has value and is influential (Association of College and Research Libraries 2015).

Conclusion

Becoming academically literate takes practice. Like getting ready to run a marathon, you have to work at it over time and you get better the more you practise. The sooner you start applying the skills we have discussed in this chapter to your own learning, the more confident you will feel.

This process becomes incredibly exciting when you apply your skills while developing your sociological imagination and see the way that everything is linked and interconnected. This occurs as you move beyond your own view of the world and look at society from a perspective that explores the influence of both the *macro* world systems on our *micro* world.

This process will allow you to see the world in a different way—and it is one of the most rewarding things that you can experience at university.

Summary points

* Sociology is the study of the individual in society. It focuses on how individual lives are shaped by society, and how individual actions can change society.
* Sociologists contribute to sociological knowledge by developing social theories and providing explanations for how things work, and produce this knowledge using social research methods.
* To refine a sociological imagination, a sociologist considers the conflation of historical, cultural and structural factors on social phenomenon.
* Expert knowledge is held by people with specialised qualifications and experience in a field, and these people are the access points to expert knowledge systems. To navigate our daily life, we develop implicit trust in expert knowledge systems.
* Expert knowledge is not static; it changes over time. Sociologists are interested in how lay knowledge—the everyday, common knowledge of individuals—becomes embedded in expert knowledge systems.
* At university, students accrue skills in academic literacy. The skills form part of their literacy cultural capital—the accumulated cultural knowledge of the individual, and familiarity with forms of academic literacy.
* Academic literacy covers information and digital literacy. Digital literacy is formed by a critical appraisal of online sources of information.
* Scholarly information refers to the thoughts and ideas of subject experts. Students are expected to reference credible, authoritative and relevant evidence in written assessment.
* Library resources, such as discovery tools and databases, contain credible material that students can use to find information about sociology.

Sociological reflection

1. The sociological imagination enables us to see how the social world influences the individual. To develop a sociological imagination, we need to think 'outside the square'. Apply your sociological imagination to the following simple, everyday behaviours:
   - A decision to buy ethically harvested food products;
   - A decision to go on a diet to shed 10 per cent of body weight;
   - A decision to devote one's life to the service of others.
2. Dieticians with expertise in health and nutrition will commonly advise that a daily diet should consist of fresh fruit and vegetables, protein, unsaturated fat, whole grains and a litre of water; and to combine a healthy diet with moderate exercise. Have a look at the diet advice in a magazine or on social media. How does the 'expert' advice of a dietician compare and contrast to the 'non-expert' advice of social media commentators or magazine writers?
3. Surviving and succeeding at university means acquiring and using academic literacy skills in formal written assessment. Suppose you are given an essay to write on the following topic:

'In Australia some people believe there is no social class, and with hard work you can achieve whatever you set your mind on. Argue for or against this proposition.'

What are the steps involved in writing the essay? First, consider what the topic requires you to do—to argue. Which keywords or terms would you use to find academic evidence, and where would you locate this evidence? How would you plan the essay?

Discussion questions

1. Develop a sociological imagination by writing a social biography. Interview another student about their family, education, culture, religion, work experience and what they want to do after university. Write a brief social biography of the social influences that have shaped the beliefs, values and life choices of that student.
2. List some of the common, everyday beliefs about what causes climate change. You may want to ask some of your classmates what they believe about the causes of climate change. Compare the lay beliefs of students and peers on climate change causation with those of scientific experts, politicians and other public commentators.
3. What do you consider to be the three most important issues in contemporary Australian society? How could you investigate public opinions on these issues using social analysis?
4. How could you research and critically analyse the topic of 'racism' in society?

References and further reading

REFERENCES

Association of College and Research Libraries 2015, *Framework for Information Literacy for Higher Education*: <www.ala.org/acrl/standards/ilframework#value>.

Australasian Open Access Strategy Group (AOASG) 2019, *What is Open Access?*: <https://aoasg.org.au/what-is-open-access/>.

Australian Bureau of Statistics (ABS) 2018, 'Household use of information technology, Australia', *2016–17*, Cat. No. 8146.0, ABS, Canberra: <www.abs.gov.au/ausstats/abs@.nsf/mf/8146.0>.

Black, M & Rechter, S 2013, 'A critical reflection on the use of an embedded academic literacy program for teaching sociology', *Journal of Sociology*, 49(4), 456–70.

Bourdieu, P 2007, 'The forms of capital', in AR Sadovnik (ed.), *Sociology of Education: A Critical Reader*, Routledge, New York, pp. 83–96.

British Sociological Association 2019, *What is Sociology?*: <www.britsoc.co.uk/what-is-sociology/origins-of-sociology/>.

Bryman, A 2012, *Social Research Methods*, 4th edn, Oxford University Press, Oxford.

Cargill, J 2015, 'Finding the evidence for practice in social work', in M Pack & J Cargill (eds), *Evidence Discovery and Assessment in Social Work Practice*, pp. 36–64 (DOI: 10.4018/978-1-4666-6563-7.ch002).

Durkheim, E & Solovay, S 1964, *The Rules of Sociological Method*, 8th edn, trans. SA Solovay & JM Mueller, GEG Catlin (ed.), Free Press, New York.

Germov, J & Poole, M 2011, 'The sociological gaze: linking private lives to public issues', in J Germov & M Poole (eds), *Public Sociology*, Allen & Unwin, Crows Nest, pp. 2–18.

Giddens, A 1995, *The Consequences of Modernity*, Polity Press, Cambridge.

Jackson, T & Sykora, M 2016, *How Our Tool Analysing Emotions on Twitter Predicted Donald Trump Win*: <https://theconversation.com/how-our-tool-analysing-emotions-on-twitter-predicted-donald-trump-win-68522>.

Jisc 2014, *Developing Digital Literacies*, London: <www.jisc.ac.uk/full-guide/developing-digital-literacies>.

Lin, N 2001, *Social Capital: A Theory of Social Structure and Action*, Cambridge University Press, New York.

Little, W & McGivern, R 2019, *Introduction to Sociology*, 1st Canadian edn, BC Campus OpenEd: <https://opentextbc.ca/introductiontosociology/>.

Mills, C 1959, *The Sociological Imagination*, Oxford University Press, London.

Nisen, M & Goudreau, J 2013, '10 jobs that are impossible to explain to your parents', *Business Insider Australia*, 13 September.

Russell, D & Massachusetts Institute of Technology 2019, *The Joy of Search: A Google Insider's Guide to Going Beyond the Basics*, MIT Press, Cambridge, MA.

Sewell Jr, WH 1992, 'A theory of structure: duality, agency, and transformation', *American Journal of Sociology*, 98(1), 1–29.

Small, AW 1903, 'What is a sociologist?', *American Journal of Sociology*, 8(4), 468–77.

The Australian Sociological Association (TASA) 2019: <www.tasa.org.au>.

United Nations Educational, Scientific and Cultural Organization (UNESCO) 2005, *Information Literacy*: <www.unesco.org/new/en/communication-and-information/access-to-knowledge/information-literacy/>.

Van Krieken, R, Habibis, D, Smith, P, Hutchins, B, Martin, G & Maton, K 2017, *Sociology*, 6th edn, Pearson Australia, Melbourne.

FURTHER READING

Bernstein, B 2003, *Class, Codes and Control: Towards a Theory of Educational Transmission*, Routledge, New York.

DiMaggio, P 1982, 'Cultural capital and school success: the impact of status culture participation on the grades of US high school students', *American Sociological Review*, 47(2), 189–201.

Durkheim, E 1964, *The Rules of Sociological Method*, trans. SA Solovay & JM Mueller, Free Press, New York.

Edwards, M 2015, *Writing in Sociology*, SAGE, Thousand Oaks, CA.

Jaeger, MM 2011, 'Does cultural capital really affect academic achievement? New evidence from combined sibling and panel data', *Sociology of Education*, 84(4), 281–98.

Johnson, WA, Rettig, RP, Scott, GM & Garrison, SM 2010, *The Sociology Student Writer's Manual*, Prentice Hall, Upper Saddle River, NJ.

Lanning, S 2012, *Concise Guide to Information Literacy*, ABC-CLIO, Santa Barbara, CA.

JOURNALS

Journal of Sociology, SAGE journals: <https://journals.sagepub.com/loi/JOS>.

WEBSITES

Australian Bureau of Statistics (ABS)—Australian Social Trends: <www.abs.gov.au/socialtrends> (see snapshots of Australia for other insights into contemporary Australian society)

Australian Bureau of Statistics (ABS)—Census: <www.abs.gov.au/census> (for a profile of the Australian community, including your own community)

Australian Catholic University Library—Find open access resources guide: <https://libguides.acu.edu.au/open-access-resources/key-resources> (for websites to discover open-access resources including textbooks and journals)

Australian Catholic University Library—Help Yourself: <https://library.acu.edu.au/help/guides/help-yourself> (for help on researching assignments, finding and using databases, search tips, searching the internet and evaluating information using CAARP criteria)

British Sociological Association (BSA): <https://www.britsoc.co.uk> (for information on the origins of sociology, what sociologists do, sociology careers and how sociology research is conducted)

Purdue Online Writing Lab (Purdue OWL): <https://owl.purdue.edu/owl/purdue_owl.html> (for help with academic writing, conducting and using research, and citing resources)

The Australian Institute of Health and Welfare (AIHW): <www.aihw.gov.au> (for data and reports that can be used to inform decisions related to the health of Australians)

The Australian Sociological Association (TASA): <www.tasa.org.au> (for information on sociology, careers in sociology, and numerous links to sociology resources)

REFERENCING STYLES

American Psychological Association Style: <www.apastyle.org>

Modern Language Association Style: <www.mla.org/style>

The Chicago Manual of Style Online: <www.chicagomanualofstyle.org>

CHAPTER 3

Studying society and culture

JAMES ARVANITAKIS

CHAPTER OVERVIEW

You are reading this book because you are interested in the study of society. So far, we have explored why studying society and culture is both important and interesting (Chapter 1) and also how we can use the sociological imagination and skills in academic and digital literacy to do this (Chapter 2). This chapter will dig deeper into what we mean by society and culture and discover how these everyday words are layered with complexity when we study them academically. We will also consider how society and culture change across time and place.

So, what exactly do we mean when we use the word 'society'?

Although commonly used in our everyday language, 'society' describes a series of complex phenomena. To understand this complexity, we need to examine and understand the various structures that make up a society, and also consider how these different parts work together.

Since the formal study of society began, sociologists have sought to understand how societies form, operate and change by asking a series of questions. For example, do societies materialise and progress 'naturally', or are they the result of specific processes?

Related to this, we must also consider the many different types of 'culture' that can be found in societies. This word, too, carries great complexity. In everyday language, the word 'culture' might refer to the 'artefacts' of a specific society: language, the arts and music. In this book, however, we look beyond beautiful objects, music and theatre and dance, to delve into the 'culture of the everyday'.

For those who are part of a society, culture can often seem invisible, but it is what makes our society function. Here, we are talking about our everyday practices and expectations: from the way we greet each other, or how close we stand to one another when talking, the different expectations men and women carry, or how we define what it means to be 'successful'. It can also be about the expectations of 'young people', our attitudes to sexuality and so on.

In this chapter, our journey begins by reflecting on how a society and its everyday culture change across time and place—throughout history and in every corner of the planet. How do we understand the way people organise shared spaces, whether it is cyberspace or a neighbourhood or a global city? The variations across time and place, in different parts of the world and also different generations, are enormous. Can you imagine a society without mobile phones or the internet? How much more complicated would it be to organise seeing a movie with your friends? How did your parents or grandparents manage it?

After reading this chapter, you should be able to:
- Define the words 'society' and 'culture'
- Understand the different parts of a society
- Explain that societies and cultures change across time and place
- Understand how societies change
- Intelligently discuss this quote from Shakespeare: 'All the world's a stage, / And all the men and women merely players' (*As You Like It*, Act 2, scene 7, line 140).

KEY TERMS

Agency The ability (or power) of an individual or group ('agent') to act independently of the external constraints of social structures—making decisions, undertaking actions and confronting authorities.

Conflict theory A social theory linked with Marxism that argues different individuals and groups have different levels of resources and power. These groups come into 'conflict' as the more powerful aim to exploit the less powerful, who in turn resist and fight back.

Grand narrative A theory that attempts to explain social history through a single 'master' idea, such as 'class conflict' or 'conflict theory'.

Postmodernism A movement of thought in the late twentieth century that was sceptical of any grand narrative.

Social contract Society's tacit acceptance of how we will be governed and the laws we will follow.

Social structures The social systems and institutions that underpin a society and the relationships within it. Social systems include work, education and religion, for example, while social institutions include family, schools, hospitals, government and other institutions that exist within our legal, economic and political systems.

Socially constructed The concept that society is built by individuals and groups through various social processes. In turn, the processes established shape expectations for those individuals and groups.

Society A social system made up of many smaller parts that share a culture: these smaller parts include both formal institutions (such as schools, hospitals and government) and informal social groups (such as families).

Introduction

'Apple!'

This may seem a strange way to start an investigation into contemporary **society**, but it is as good a place as any. Why? The reason is that when we begin looking at society, we should start by asking ourselves: 'What does it mean to me?'

When you reflect on the word 'apple', do you picture a piece of fruit? It may be green or red, large and shiny and perfectly shaped, or smaller, crunchier or fresher. Regardless of the details, most of us can conjure up an image of an apple. Or did your mind turn first to a computer or some communication device?

The chances are that the split is between a piece of fruit or a branded computer or device.

Now, when you say the word 'society', what image springs to mind? There is a good chance that each one of you reading this book will have a very different image: what you see in your head is likely be different to the person sitting next to you.

For example, my image of society includes people in suits, towering skyscrapers, endless traffic jams, cafés, restaurants and even streets dotted with homeless people. This society is busy, urban, rushed—sometimes to the point of rudeness—filled by strangers going about their daily lives without acknowledging each other.

On a packed train in this society, we sit side by side in silence. Unless something happens to encourage a different behaviour, I can sit squashed between two strangers with no personal space and not say a word. That is kind of strange if you think about it in those terms, don't you think?

There is diversity in this image: there are people from different backgrounds, indicated by visual and verbal signs, such as skin colour and other physical features, or language spoken. Cars are everywhere, alongside buses, motorcycles, scooters, pushbikes, ferries, train tracks, and maybe trams.

Is this the only vision of society? The answer is obviously 'no'.

Those who grew up on acreage or on a farm, and rarely travelled to the city, would have an image of 'society' that is very different. You may even be uncomfortable with this vision of a bustling and impersonal city as a society. If you live in a remote part of Australia or on another continent, you will hold different images of society in your mind.

When I worked in the Solomon Islands, I noticed that the tallest building in the national capital, Honiara, was only three storeys high. The population is 40,000 people: this is about 1 per cent of the more than 4 million people living in Sydney. Most roads there are unsealed, and there are relatively few cars. Although there is significant poverty in the Islands, I did not see homeless people, like I do in Sydney.

More recently I spent almost a year working in the state of Wyoming, United States. This is a rural state often referred to as 'cowboy country' full of ranches, massive four-wheel drives and wide-open spaces. When I moved there, one of the hardest things I had to adjust to was how quiet it was: in fact, I initially found it hard to sleep because it was too quiet!

Now, take a moment and think of a farm that is part of your society. Visualise it. What do you see?

Do you see lots of people bent over their work on the side of a steep hill? This is what you would see if you visited rice farmers who dominate the rural landscape in places such as Thailand or Vietnam. If you are from Australia, the chances are that this is nothing like the vision of a farm that you imagined, and in the United States, most people would say, 'We don't have farms; we have ranches.'

Imagine you were born 50 years ago …

Now try another thought experiment: imagine you were born 50 years ago. This was in the midst of the Cold War—when the Soviet Union and the United States were threatening each other with nuclear warfare. In the 1970s, no matter where in the world you were born, your understanding of society would be very different—even if you lived in the same street as you do now.

Returning to Sydney for our 1970s vision, there would have been a far less diverse population. There were comparatively few cars and no skyscrapers, and no one would have been talking on their mobile phone (or on WhatsApp or playing *Mario Kart*). The word 'globalisation' did not exist and no one had thought up Facebook or Instagram.

Fifty years ago, there was only one type of 'apple'—the fruit!

Now jump 50 years ahead ...

There is more: Can you imagine what society will be like in 50 years from now? Think of a movie such as *Terminator: Dark Fate* (2019) that imagines robots taking over the world, or *Bumblebee* (2018), where robots fight one another. Or *Star Wars: The Last Jedi* (2017), where space travel is like driving a car.

This may seem far-fetched, but we really have no idea what our society will look like in 10, let alone 50 years. And things can change very quickly.

In the 10 years between 2010 and 2020 the following things appeared in our society: Instagram (2010), Spotify (2011), Uber (2012), Apple Watch (2014), AirPods (2016) and TikTok (2019). The decade before that we had the emergence of smartphones, GPS devices, tablets, 'the cloud' for data storage and millions of different apps. In one generation, mobile phones have shrunk from weighing 10 kilograms and talk time has grown from 10 minutes. As you know, smartphones can now connect you to friends and family all over the world, hold your diary and email, deliver newspapers and magazines, and store a bunch of games (all of which can distract you from study!).

If I asked, 'Would you rather lose your phone or your wallet?', what would you answer? If I asked that of your parents when they were your age, they would likely say, 'How can you lose your phone? It's sitting on the table in the hallway connected to the socket in the wall!'

Societal changes also mean that our 'culture' changes; that is, the way we live our everyday lives and our relationships to each other. These changes mean that we live very different lives from our parents and grandparents. Think of the way you start the day: waking up. Twenty years ago, households had alarm clocks that would ring or buzz or turn on the radio. Today people rely on their phones. Many people wake up, check emails and their social networks, and scroll through newsfeeds and notifications all before they even get out of bed.

This has changed the way we think, relate to each other and see the world. In other words, our society has changed along with technological developments that impact on our behaviour, our thoughts and our relationships, which are all parts of everyday culture.

And because our society today is the stuff that science fiction movies could not imagine 30 years ago, we can say with confidence that it is almost impossible to predict what the world will look like in 10 or 20 or 50 years.

What does this tell us?

The initial insight that this provides is that *the concept of society is complex and changing*. There are multiple factors that contribute to this, as indicated by the examples above. And remember that technological advances are not just about smartphones and internet access, but also about such things as international travel, medicines that prolong life, automation and dating.

Consequently, the first point to highlight is that the meaning and vision of 'society' depends on who you are, and when and where you live (both within and across national borders, and also within the same city, town or village). It also depends on your values and beliefs, health and education, and many other social factors.

The second point is that there is no pre-determined path that a society will take. That is, the way we choose to live and structure society does not occur by magic, but slowly develops—and this process takes place differently in different places. For example, in some parts of Europe and South America, the siesta is an enduring practice. Can you imagine doing that in Australia? (Maybe, as an experiment, ask your lecturer to break in the middle of the class so everyone can have a 20-minute nap?)

This brings us to the third point, which is related to the above two points: the way that societies are structured and operate arise from the decisions and actions of human beings. *People* have decided that university lecture rooms should be designed with your lecturer standing up the front. *People* have decided that you should not vote or drink alcohol until you are 18 years old (or in other parts of the world until you are 21 years old). *People* have introduced laws that prevent us from driving after a few drinks and give the police power to randomly breathalyse us—something that a few decades ago was totally acceptable.

As such, our contemporary society can be referred to as being '**socially constructed**': something that is built through various social processes, not something that has emerged naturally, or by magic.

Finally, if *people* have designed society in a certain way, then *we have the capacity to change society*. While the society around us may seem natural, it is constructed by humans and can therefore be changed by humans. This means that each individual can confront the **social structures** around them and effect change. Of course, this varies according to who you are, your access to education, your family connections and the resources available to you. Nevertheless, each of us has at least some ability to influence the shape and direction society takes. This is usually described as having '**agency**'—something we will return to in later chapters (including Chapters 5 and 22).

Critical reflection

Describe some of the ways in which your experience in society may be different from that of your parents by considering the role social media plays in your everyday life. How did good and bad news travel around social circles before social media?

What is society?

So, now we know that societies change across time and place, we can explore more deeply the question: 'What is society?'

To answer this, we first need to ask some more questions:

- Is society more than just a group of individuals living in close proximity? That is, when a group of individuals come together for a reason, is something specific created? Something we call 'society'?

- Are there invisible bonds that bind us and ensure we generally get along?
- If we accept there are such bonds, is violence an example of these bonds breaking down?
- What are the factors that drive societies to change?
- What is the link between society and culture?

The study of society is called 'sociology' and those who study it are referred to as 'sociologists' (something we discussed in Chapter 2). Those who study culture are referred to as 'cultural theorists' undertaking 'cultural studies'. You may think it strange that there is a split between the two pursuits, as each must understand its relationship to the other. In most of this book, we group social and cultural concepts together—it is when you get deeper into the study of society and culture that the gaps become more important.

BOX 3.1

Thinking sociologically

DEFINING 'SOCIETY'

A society is a social system made up of many smaller parts or institutions that can be formal (such as churches, prisons, schools and government bodies) or informal (including family and social groups).

These social systems have established structures and rules, and involve people living and working together in the pursuit of both self-interest and social harmony (Andersen, Logio & Taylor 2012).

Society, then, is made up of both its parts and the way that these parts are put together and organised. Therefore, it is comprised of organisations *and* social relations.

Society is, however, more than just structures and relations, as it includes individual 'agents'—people, with agency, who make up the society and attend its institutions. Many of these people have shared identities that are expressed in common cultural forms such as language, dress, religion and eating habits. These individuals are an active part of the way the structures and relations of the society are organised.

As we learnt in Chapter 1, the birth of sociology came about as scholars and other thinkers in Western Europe began analysing substantial changes to the social order that occurred during political and industrial revolutions. As we will see in Chapter 5, these changes significantly altered the way the world worked, particularly with regard to urbanisation and work patterns. This was a period of huge upheaval, and altered structures, relationships and perceptions—particularly perceptions of 'the individual'.

One huge change that occurred during this time, for example, is that time went from being perceived as *seasonal* (a time to plant seeds, a time to harvest crops, a time to preserve those crops for the winter months) to being perceived as *linear* and moving forward (running out of time today, this must be finished tomorrow!). Think of the term 'progress': it means 'moving forward', and today it usually describes technological change—in medicine, communication and so on. This meaning did not really exist before the massive changes associated with the Industrial Revolution and the way time was reconceived, and as you will see in Chapter 5 the idea of (and belief in) 'progress' became one of the defining features of modern society.

At this point it might be helpful to note—and reflect on the fact—that many sociological theories and accounts of society are based in societal changes that originated from one small part of the world (Western Europe) during one particular period of history (the Industrial Revolution). Many of these changes, including capitalism, were aggressively imposed on the rest of the world through the expansionist policies of European powers, such as England and France; a process known collectively as 'imperialism' (Petras & Veltmeyer 2013). We also need to remember, however, that the imposition of these processes has been resisted and altered in a variety of ways across different parts of the world. This means that although the legacy of imperialism remains the foundation for many of the global rules, systems and institutions that exist today there is no singular or universal experience of modern society (an area that is discussed in greater detail in Chapter 5). It is important that we constantly question and consider the implications of this in our work as sociologists.

What is culture?

Now that we have established what we mean by society, let's turn to discuss what is meant by 'culture'. As mentioned above, the study of culture at universities is, unsurprisingly, referred to as 'cultural studies'. Cultural studies emerged as a field of interest from a series of different academic fields. (In fact, different countries around the world have different traditions of cultural studies—making this theoretical environment both challenging and interesting.)

The focus here is on everyday experiences; that is, how culture creates and transforms individual experiences, everyday life and relationships with those around us (McLennan 2005). Importantly, culture is never seen as fixed or stable, but like society, constantly changing.

Cultural studies researchers and theorists are interested in understanding how our everyday cultural and social practices relate to the systems of power around us. As we study culture, we should be constantly raising questions about the form that our culture takes and who benefits: which notions of culture appear to dominate, and which are ignored? 'Power' is a huge topic of its own with many different meanings, and this is discussed in more detail in Chapter 8.

In contrast to sociology that focuses on societal-wide structures and trends, cultural studies tend to focus more on the *everyday* experiences of individuals: how we shape our identity and how our identity is shaped by the many forces around us. In fact, as you will see below when reading about Erving Goffman, the exact shape of our identities comes into question.

One example that can highlight the difference between sociology and cultural studies is the way we would approach studying the changing media landscape. Only a generation ago our ability to access the news was limited to traditional media—television, radio and newspapers. There were a few media outlets and we consumed (or watched) media, rather than produced media content (as we do on TikTok or Instagram).

From a sociological perspective, we may be interested in understanding how the diffusion of media changes our social relationships. For example, in the United States, those who vote Republican tend to watch news outlets like Fox News and those that vote Democrat watch CNN.

This helps explain why people are becoming more divided around controversial issues like gun control or immigration as these two news sources present radically different interpretations of events.

These large-scale trends capture the imagination of sociologists. In contrast, cultural theorists look for ways that this new environment is reflected in our everyday interactions: how we behave on Facebook or the personality we portray on Instagram. Culture includes the way we communicate, the symbols that give meaning to the world around us, and how everyday habits change over time. A cultural theorist might be interested in how our identities are shaped by this changing media landscape and through the different ways we act in this context: for example, do we say things or like posts on Facebook that we may not be willing to support in the real world?

The famous sociologist, Anthony Giddens (2001, p. 2) reminded us that: 'Sociology is the study of human social life, groups and societies … It teaches us that what we regard as natural, inevitable, good or true may not be such, and that the "givens" of our life are strongly influenced by historical and social forces.' Cultural studies extend this concept by further unpacking how all these factors shape and are shaped by our identities and the other ways we give meaning to our experiences.

> **BOX 3.2**
>
> # Thinking sociologically
>
> ### PERSPECTIVES ON IDENTITY AND CULTURE: ERVING GOFFMAN AND JUDITH BUTLER
>
> Erving Goffman (1922–82) was a very influential American sociologist who was interested in the rituals of our everyday social interactions. Goffman's key theoretical development was that our identities are not stable and independent but rather are constantly remade as we interact with others: something that became known as dramaturgical theory.
>
> Think of it this way: the way you behave and the type of identity you have with your family may be quite different to that which you have with your football team, or your friends, or at work.
>
> For theorists like Goffman and Judith Butler (see below), identity is something that is developed, acted out and even achieved rather than innate. Furthermore, our identities are not always about individual choice but subject to the social world and expectations around us. The social expectations associated with who we are shapes and limits our behaviours.
>
> When we know someone well and then we see them in a different environment, we may be surprised by how differently they behave. The behaviour may be so different that we feel like they are not being their 'real' or 'authentic' selves.
>
> We hear this about reality television stars when their friends say, 'No, they are not mean or nasty, deep down they are really nice people.'
>
> Goffman, however, argued that this idea of an 'authentic' or 'true self' does not exist—we are always performing our various selves. This is not to say that we are fakes or fraudulent, rather it indicates the importance of being accepted by the social group we interact with.
>
> In other words, Goffman felt that 'the self' was the result of the social situation we find ourselves in at any given time. We are constantly changing because there is no dimension of who we are—our identity—that is not shaped by the social world.
>
> Further, this social world we are interacting with is shaped by the culture and social norms around us.

Judith Butler is another influential theorist who looks at identity, but focuses on its gendered dimensions. Butler explores the idea of why we create gendered identities. Butler's writings can be hard to unpack but in essence her position is that there is no physical identity that precedes our social work. This is because everything about who we are—including our bodies—are shaped by the social world around us (see Chapter 7 for more detail on Judith Butler and her theories).

How societies function

Now that we have defined society and culture and determined that each varies significantly across time and place, we turn to the question of how societies function. In undertaking this task, we could look at hundreds of theorists, philosophers and other thinkers—and some textbooks do exactly that. This textbook, instead, is designed to lay the foundations of understanding, so that you can later delve both more broadly and more deeply into theories of society and culture from different world views. We will shortly highlight just three broad approaches to learning about how societies function.

Before discussing these, it is important to keep in mind that societies do not emerge fully formed. Societies slowly evolve—though sometimes things can change quickly. When I was writing this chapter, we were in the middle of the COVID-19 pandemic. All of a sudden, a majority of Australians started working or attending school from home—something unthinkable four weeks before hand. This has changed the way Australians interact and socialise and may well have longer-term implications.

Regardless, societies are seen to evolve. This concept of 'social evolution' is a relatively recent idea and was first identified by French philosopher Auguste Comte (1798–1857). By examining historical events, Comte concluded that societies progress or evolve over different time periods (Pickering 1993).

Though this idea of evolution is relatively recent, it is something we are quite comfortable with today. Evolutionary progress first appeared in the nineteenth century with the seminal work of Charles Darwin (1809–82) and his groundbreaking book *On the Origin of Species* (2009, original work published 1859). The northern Australian city of Darwin was named in his honour because Darwin's observations of Australian animals were an important contribution to his development of evolutionary theory.

You may be familiar with Darwin from studying biology or you might have seen the (average) movie *Creation* (2009) about his life and struggles with religion. Darwin's theory of evolution challenged the previous dominance of biblical understandings of creation in Europe. Evolutionary theory has never been disproved, and is therefore widely accepted, yet initially Darwin was mocked and ostracised for disproving the 'hand of God' version of how different species came to be.

Herbert Spencer (1820–1903) transferred Darwinian evolutionary theory to the study of society, arguing that social evolution is a natural process (Mingardi 2011). His conclusion was that governments and other institutions should never interfere with evolutionary social process. It was actually Spencer who first used the phrase 'survival of the fittest' (Darwin spoke of 'natural selection'). Spencer asserted that some societies are simply destined to die out and disappear.

It is hard to know what Spencer was thinking, but the application of his theory had devastating effects: it was used to justify colonial attitudes and violence towards indigenous societies. Having caused the death of huge numbers of Indigenous peoples through direct conflict, displacement or slavery through the pursuit and theft of land and resources, colonial powers invoked the 'survival of the fittest' in attempts to rationalise their actions. For those Indigenous people who did survive, it was then assumed that they would 'naturally' die out—resulting in 'protectionist' and 'assimilationist' government policies (these are covered in Chapter 16).

Do societies evolve? Should governments promote certain types of social progress? Why do we get along most of the time? What binds institutions and individuals together?

We now introduce three approaches to exploring these questions: the **social contract**, the organic analogy, and **conflict theory**.

The social contract

In Chapter 1, I referred to some examples of the types of things that can happen when the bonds that link us begin to break down. Though we can list a number of examples of societies breaking down, we can cite many more examples of things working; for example, if you are sitting at uni and reading this to prepare for your next class, the chances are that your day has been relatively uneventful compared to a day of riots.

The first approach we will consider for understanding how societies function, takes us back to a time and place where riots were commonplace—the period of political revolution across Western Europe in which in the philosophies of the European Enlightenment arose (see Chapter 5). Thomas Hobbes (1588–1679) was one of the early philosophers to raise questions about social order at this time. Hobbes' somewhat bleak view was that if there are no 'restraints' on people such as laws and regulations backed by police, violent conflicts are inevitable (Haworth 2012). He famously described the human experience without social restraints as 'solitary, poor, nasty, brutish and short' (Hobbes 1998 (original work published 1651), p. 84). You would not want to get stuck sitting next to him on a long plane flight!

But what sort of restraints can you place on people in free societies?

For Hobbes the answer was to understand ourselves as being in some sort of *contract* with the society to which we belong. This 'social contract' summarises how we will be governed and the laws we will follow, and what rights and freedoms we are willing to give up in order to be protected.

To briefly expand: the social contract assumes that you 'tacitly' accept the contract from the moment you enter a society (via birth or as an 'outsider' being accepted). By 'tacitly', we mean that your presence as a member of the society is evidence that you have accepted the terms of the contract. You did not actually shake hands on it, or sign along the dotted line!

Rather, this is a silent contract, and its catchcry, as you will find in the Australian Constitution, is for 'peace, order and good government'. Thus, individuals accept the laws of the land and in return we live in a peaceful, orderly society. In return for our acceptance, the lawmakers and government will ensure 'good government', which is defined as both external and internal. External good government is protection of the territory (national security). Internally, the government organises essential social services, again focused on peace and order (police, health, education). As in any contract, there must be *mutual agreement.*

The social contract is enforced in formal and informal ways simultaneously. Police officers cruise our roads and are called to crime scenes. Judges punish convicted offenders. At the same time, individuals and groups monitor everyday practices, from saying 'please' and 'thank you' to being suspended from a sporting club for rough play or fined by a library for not returning that book in time.

But there is much we do not agree with. For example, while we support the police in many ways, most of us do not think they should target specific groups simply because of their cultural background—something that is discussed in Chapter 9. I am sure that, as you read this, there are some things you agree with, and others you do not agree with!

It is important to understand that the social contract changes as society and its expectations change. For instance, not so long ago, university students fulfilled their part of the social contract by completing their studies. The Australian Government fulfilled its part by funding institutions and students—there was little, if any, debt associated with obtaining a degree and income support such as Austudy was relatively readily available. Now the burden of the students' part of the contract has increased: not only are students expected to study, but also many of you need to work as income support has become increasingly difficult to access. Also, if students are claiming Youth Allowance, they must be careful not to breach the rules or they will be penalised.

Some breaches of the social contract are not just social but also criminal, and some who criminally breach terms of the contract end up in jail. To be penalised for breaking the law, a whole set of institutions and arrangements must swing into action: police statements, court proceedings, verdicts and punishments and even rehabilitation can all be understood through the lens of the social contract.

Just as important are the informal rules that we follow. Think of something like the way we adjust our presence around personal space. Do you stand right next to someone when you speak to them? Do you eat with your mouth open? Such informal rules are important dimensions of the social contract that we follow. While we are not punished by law if we breach these rules, it will be harder to make friends if you are rude or inconsiderate—a social punishment of sorts.

Hobbes argued that without the social contract, society would break down, and held that a strong social contract creates a society, binds it together, and keeps it functioning in a peaceful and orderly way.

Now, you do not have to accept this Hobbesian view of society. For some it is controversial because acceptance of the social contract is tacit, and nobody asked us if we wanted to be born into such a society. On this view, a binding contract requires autonomy: we must have opted *into* the contract of our own free will.

Consider this in these simple terms: we work and pay taxes. The payment of taxes is part of the social contract. My taxes are used to fund things I agree are important, such as schools and hospitals. My taxes also fund things that I see as unimportant or morally wrong, such as subsidies to big mining companies, or detention centres where asylum seekers, looking for a better life, are indefinitely trapped. When the Australian Government breaches all sorts of human rights conventions that it has previously signed—spending billions of dollars in the process—I consider it to have violated its part of the social contract. The same thing might be said when the government lies or breaks election promises, because people relied on those promises to make up their mind about their vote. In a democratic system such as ours, a government that lies to the electorate, or makes promises it cannot or will not keep, has broken its side of the contract.

There is a further problem here: the uneven power relationship between the parties to the social contract. For example, while the Australian Government can fine me or throw me in jail for breaching my end of the contract, I have limited ability to hold it to account when I feel let down by it. I can vote for or against a government every few years, but it is still a very unbalanced relationship based on the different levels of power. Put simply, the government has a lot more power than individuals (something we will return to in Chapter 8).

You have now been introduced to social contract theory (so you need no longer find the word 'theory' intimidating, as many students do!). If we are more than just a group of individuals living in a shared space, and something is formed when we come together, we can understand that 'something' as a 'society'. The important thing to gain from Hobbes is that he *theorised* this invisible bond that holds societies together and operates in the shared interests of its citizens in 'peace, order and good government'.

This idea of the 'social contract' has remained influential today. In fact, many contemporary government policies focused on unemployment benefits or payments to single parents are based on the idea of 'mutual obligation', which draws on the social contract (Holdsworth 2016).

The organic analogy

The second approach regarding the invisible bonds that bind us comes from two of the theorists I mentioned above, Auguste Comte and Herbert Spencer. These men (and it is indeed all white men to whom the 'birth' of sociology is attributed) saw society as being like other 'organic' beings. In this sense, society is like the human body: it is an organism made up of systems and interrelated parts. This perspective has become known as the 'organic analogy' or 'consensus' (Giddens et al. 2013).

The organic analogy has been an influential perspective. Its proponents argue that to understand society we must first examine the component parts and then further understand how the different parts are interrelated and interdependent. The argument is that like any 'natural' organism, all parts are reliant on each other, and there is an equilibrium at which the whole operates most effectively. If part of the organism malfunctions, the organism might break down, or it might repair itself, depending on its health, strength, resilience, maintenance and so on.

There are two main ways this plays out: through competition and cooperation. Let us start with cooperation. Talcott Parsons (1902–79) saw society functioning and progressing in a cooperative manner. According to Parsons, this cooperation could be seen in processes of negotiated ideologies. Members of societies collectively establish patterns of life that reflect the ideologies held by different individuals and groups. The size of the society (or organism) does not change the basic framework: no matter how big or small, all the different parts cooperate to make up the whole. This view of how societies work is broadly referred to as 'structural functionalism', meaning that *all* the structures in society have a function (Turner 2013).

Let us look at an example. One way that we can 'divide' society into component parts is by categorising employers and employees. Managers (or bosses) and staff—or those who own the business and workers—may appear at odds with each other, with different aims, pay scales and responsibilities. You may at first think that these two broad groups have opposing interests as the workers want maximum wages, but the managers want to limit these to maximise their income. The organic analogy, however, argues that the different groups are interdependent, relying on each other and working cooperatively in the long run. (We will return to the relationship between workers and bosses in Chapter 6.)

Why do owners and workers need each other? The workers rely on the financing of the bosses to ensure that they are paid for their labour. The bosses rely on the workers to do the work, or there would be no product to sell. It is the workers who produce what is sold, whether in farming, manufacturing or computer coding. While there are competing interests regarding pay scales and privileges, society functions because such groups must cooperate like any organic system to survive. The alternative to cooperation is competition, which we will consider in the next section.

Conflict theory

A school of thought that falls under the broad category of competing interests is known as 'conflict theory' (Bartos & Wehr 2010). This is the 'competition' side of the 'cooperation and competition' framework and is almost a direct response to the organic analogy and other theories of cooperation.

Conflict theory claims that different sections of society have different forms of power and access to wealth, as well as competing interests. As a result, the component parts of a society *compete* rather than cooperate. Society, overall, is in constant conflict over resources and power arrangements, and much of the perceived cooperation is in fact coercion.

A society in conflict is bound by the control that the powerful groups exercise over those who are less powerful.

If we return to the example of bosses and workers, we can understand how conflict between these groups is seen to be inevitable. The workers have less power to ensure they receive a living wage, while bosses have far greater power and a different goal: to keep wages as low as possible and maximise profits. In this scenario, the more powerful bosses are also highly likely to have influence with political leaders. When those political leaders form government and pass laws, they can ensure that employment and industrial laws (associated with setting wages and work conditions) suit the bosses. If the workers decide to protest against low wages or dangerous conditions by striking, the political leadership may move to put further legal structures in place to support the influential bosses. Some examples include making strikes illegal, so that police then arrest strikers and strike leaders. In this example, the bosses and political leaders work together in competition with the workers—who are also working together to protect their own interests. These types of conflicts are usually understood as 'class' conflict. We will discuss class struggle and influential theorist Karl Marx in Chapter 6.

It is important to note that conflict theory continues to be popular today. One theorist is Slovenian philosopher Slovaj Zizek, whose work crosses everything from conflict theory, popular culture and psychoanalysis. Zizek (2012) draws on conflict theory when discussing his concepts of 'ideology' and how we are influenced by contemporary belief systems (or ideologies) even if we do not think we are.

As we have seen, these are three very different ways of looking at the way societies function. You may be left wondering: 'Which one is the best?'

Ultimately the decision is up to you: you may prefer one or see important dimensions of all three approaches when attempting to understand society. Each of the three theories is important to our efforts to analyse contemporary society. At this point, we are learning that there are different ways of seeing the same thing, and that each may be relevant. Remember, societies and cultures change, so the degree of relevance—or influence—of different theories can change over time.

> **Critical reflection**
>
> Think of a person or group of people whose actions have dramatically altered the trajectory of a particular society. How might you frame their actions using one of the social theories considered in this chapter?

Looking for universal rules across societies

As previously mentioned, the philosopher Auguste Comte thought that societies followed a linear evolutionary path—gradually moving from simple to more complex. Since the time of Comte, the classification of different societies, and allocating particular societies a place on this path, has itself evolved (Fevre & Bancroft 2010).

Karl Marx (1818–83) is one theorist who also argued that societies followed a linear evolutionary path with 'universal rules'. Marx defined societies on the basis of their 'mode of production'—or how people organise themselves to produce goods and services. This allows us to classify different societies, both today and throughout history, along different phases of production, such as slave-based, feudal, industrial and post-industrial societies. Each one of these marks a period of massive change as society moves along a clear path (Fevre & Bancroft 2010).

If we combine these various concepts—that is, the different things that bind societies together, along with the notion of an evolutionary path—we find something worth noting: many who have studied society have looked for *universality* in human interaction. That is, the search is for ingredients that will unlock the secrets as to what makes societies function across the human experience. In human societies, as with a community of bees or ants, there is a role for each part and we need to identify what that role is in order to understand how it works and changes, be it in cooperation or conflict.

This search for both the 'natural' ingredients that make societies function and the 'natural' evolutionary path that societies are said to follow has dominated a great deal of sociological thought over the past 300 years. This type of theorising is described as a **grand narrative** that looks for broad, large rules that can be applied across time and space to almost all human journeys and arrangements.

Postmodernism

A relatively recent break in this type of thinking is **postmodernism**. Emerging in the late twentieth century, this philosophical movement is characterised by scepticism, relativism and a challenge to the above centuries-old perspectives that search for natural rules or evolutionary processes. Postmodernism, among other things, argues that each society follows its own path and this path is not natural but subject to human negotiation and actions, or the *agency* we mentioned earlier.

One example is the way that postmodern thinkers challenged the concept of 'progress'. Rather than seeing society as progressing, for example, postmodernists claimed that societies move in positive and negative directions simultaneously. As we will discuss in Chapter 5, rather than society travelling through processes of modernity, we concurrently experience 'multiple modernities'.

There are many dimensions to postmodern thought but here I will outline only three to highlight the differences with more traditional sociological theories.

The first is the dismissal of an objective natural reality. *Postmodernists dismiss this idea and see multiple truths.* For example, a major debate in Australia known as the 'History Wars' re-examines earlier claims about the British colonisation of Australia (see Chapter 16). This debate has revealed that, far from being 'settled' (a version of history that was taught in schools up until the 1980s), Australia was invaded and occupied by an imperial power, causing the deaths of countless Indigenous Australians. However, others defend the traditional standpoint, saying that the British carried out a process of peaceful settlement—acknowledging that while deaths did occur, these were a by-product of the settlement process.

My view is that the continent and its islands were invaded, not peacefully settled. So how do we deal with the memory of the early colonists? Do we look at them as murderers, complicit in the act of invasion, or as explorers and pioneers? Maybe you think that it all depends on the individual settlers and their own experience? Or maybe we can think of them as being both these things? When it comes to 'truth', you are encouraged to weigh up the different arguments and reach a conclusion—or several conclusions—and these conclusions may be modified over time.

As such, there is no single or simple truth here, but something much more complicated. *You* are learning the skills to interpret specific pieces of knowledge, information, facts and arguments—something we covered in detail in Chapter 2.

The second dimension is based on the point I raised above: *postmodernists do not accept the concept of progress*. This very concept is based on the idea that through reason and logic, we can change ourselves and society for the better as we become more humane and enlightened. Postmodernists do not accept that science and technology are mechanisms of human progress: think of the destruction caused by the scientific advances in weapons that have seen millions of people die in conflicts around the world.

The third dimension that contrasts postmodern thought to more traditional thinkers is the *refusal to accept the 'grand narratives'* of the many theories. For postmodernists, these theories are problematic not only because they are false, but also because they force complex histories across the world into one simple story privileging one viewpoint and dismissing the complexity and diversity of our experiences.

The interrelated rhombus

Before concluding this chapter, I want to introduce a concept called the 'interrelated rhombus'. It is not a theoretical tool. Rather, it is designed to assist your understanding of the different ways to study society.

As I have discussed in this chapter, there are many ways to look at any phenomenon, and each has its advantages and limitations. Different viewpoints, through a process of academic research and reflection, build different ways of seeing the world and gaining insights. Consequently, for every aspect of society we study, we can examine it from a variety of perspectives and academic disciplines.

If these ideas are new for you then your head is probably spinning right now! Hopefully this final concept can serve as an anchor—something you can return to as you begin to make sense of how to navigate the complex and changing ideas of society and culture I have introduced here.

FIGURE 3.1 The interrelated rhombus.

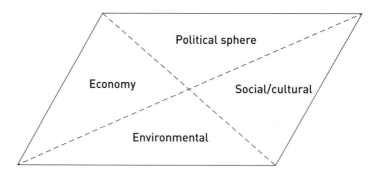

Let us look at the bushfires of 2019–20. While we may initially think of this as an 'environmental issue', there are other ways to look at it. For example, most scientists argue that the extent of the bushfires was a result of human induced climate change, the government's failure to design a climate policy that effectively reduces carbon emissions, and Australia's inability and unwillingness to work with the rest of the world to find a solution to the climate crisis. Others argue that the bushfires had nothing to do with climate change but blamed political positions that opposed backburning and hazard reduction.

As such, we can look at the incidents of these fires being as much about a failure in politics and policy, as an environment issue. Further, one of the arguments against stricter action on climate change is that it will negatively impact jobs and the economy—so now we can understand that this is also an economic issue!

If we are serious about responding to climate change, we need to significantly change our behaviours to reduce energy consumption and waste. This would require us to travel less, buy fewer goods, reduce use of air conditioners and other such behavioural changes—all things that are social. This will also challenge our consumption patterns—patterns that drive our capitalist economy and culture.

Right in the middle of the rhombus is our identity and social self. That is, how we see the world and how we are shaped by it. Likewise, our actions and behaviours also shape the various dimensions of the world around us. Our different experiences shape who we are and then the way we behave re-shapes our political, social, cultural, economic and environmental worlds.

In other words, while we may focus on the social and cultural in this book, we need to be aware that there are many ways of looking at the same problem. The aim of the rhombus is to highlight the interrelated nature of all such phenomena. A political event is never simply a political event. Likewise, environmental issues can impact across political, social, cultural and economic spheres. As a result, we must know that all these areas are interrelated. As we progress through this book, always remember that we may be presenting only one or two ways to look at any phenomenon—but I am sure you will be able to think of others.

Conclusion

How to conclude such a chapter that begins with an apple, looks at social evolution and ends with the 2019–20 bushfires?

Hopefully from this chapter you can see that the concept of society is complex, and that it embraces social relations between individuals and groups, social structures, identity, norms and social roles. With the concept being so open to interpretation, there are arguments that the term could be dropped all together, but just because it is a complex concept, it does not mean we should ignore it. In fact, we must continue to cast a critical eye over it.

Finally, it is important that we do not see our relationship with society as being a one-way street. Society influences individuals, for sure. But individuals not only influence society, they also build and run the institutions and arrangements that define a society. If we change our behaviours, we can also change the people and society around us. This is why studying society is such a fascinating thing to do!

Summary points

* Meanings and visions of society vary, depending on who you are, where you live (both within and across national borders, and also within the same city), the time period in which you live and your value systems.
* There is nothing 'natural' about the way that our society is organised; that is, the way we choose to live and structure our society does not occur magically along a pre-determined path, but develops according to a variety of factors. In this way, we can think of our contemporary society as being *socially constructed*.
* A society is a social system made up of many interrelated smaller parts or institutions that share a culture, and these can be formal or informal.
* The reasons that societies function the way they do are complicated. Although many people throughout history have presented different understandings, there is no simple or single answer.
* As the 'interrelated rhombus' highlights, we should attempt to look at many dimensions of contemporary society from a variety of perspectives.

Sociological reflection

Do you think the social contract, the organic analogy and conflict theory continue to offer relevant ways of understanding different societies?

Discussion questions

1. What does a society consist of?
2. What binds a society together?
3. How does a society transform over time?
4. What are some of the issues that can drive change in a society?
5. Why does a society remain stable over time?
6. What are some of the social structures that may limit our ability to change a society?
7. Why are there so many different types of society?
8. Is society the same as culture? How are they different? How are they similar?
9. What is the difference between sociology and cultural studies?

Further investigation

1. Download a podcast from triple j's *Hack* radio program that explores a contemporary issue you feel passionate about. *Hack* is a national radio show that delivers daily commentary on a range of current affairs from the viewpoints of young Australians. Use the 'interrelated rhombus' to consider the different ways this contemporary issue can be understood.

2. What social theory do you think best represents the interactions between Aboriginal and Torres Strait Islander peoples and the British colonialists in Australia in the nineteenth century? Does this social theory continue to represent more contemporary social relations between Aboriginal and Torres Strait Islander peoples and Anglo-Australians? Why or why not?

References and further reading

REFERENCES

Andersen, M, Logio, K & Taylor, H 2012, *Understanding Society: An Introductory Reader*, 4th edn, Cengage, Cincinnati, OH.

Bartos, O & Wehr, P 2010, *Using Conflict Theory*, 2nd edn, Cambridge University Press, Cambridge.

Darwin, C 2009, *On the Origin of Species*, Oxford University Press, Oxford (original work published 1859).

Fevre, R & Bancroft, A 2010, *Dead White Men and Other Important People*, Palgrave MacMillan, Basingstoke.

Giddens, A 2001, *Sociology*, 4th edn, Polity Press, Cambridge.

Giddens, A, Duneier, M, Appelbaum, R & Carr, D 2013, *Introduction to Sociology*, 9th edn, WW Norton & Co, New York.

Haworth, A 2012, *Understanding the Political Philosophers*, 2nd edn, Routledge, London.

Hobbes, T, 1998 *Leviathan*, Oxford University Press, Oxford (original work published 1651).

Holdsworth, L 2016, 'The impact of mutual obligation for sole parents', *Journal of Sociology*, 53(3), 607–21.

McLennan, G 2005, 'Power', in T Bennett, L Grossberg & M Morris (eds), *New Keywords: A Revised Vocabulary of Culture and Society*, Blackwell Publishing, Oxford, pp. 274–78.

Mingardi, A 2011, *Herbert Spencer*, Continuum, New York.

Patrick, A 2013, *Downfall: How the Labor Party Ripped Itself Apart*, ABC Books, Sydney.

Petras, J & Veltmeyer, H 2013, 'Introduction', in *Imperialism and Capitalism in the Twenty-first Century: A System in Crisis*, Ashgate, London, pp. 1–17.

Pickering, M 1993, *Auguste Comte: An Intellectual Biography*, vol. 1, Cambridge University Press, Cambridge.

Turner, J 2013, *Contemporary Sociological Theory*, SAGE, Los Angeles, CA.

Zizek, S 2012, *Less Than Nothing: Hegel and the Shadow of Dialectical Materialism*, Verso Books, London.

FURTHER READING

Anderson, N & Schlunke, K 2008, *Cultural Theory in Everyday Practice*, Oxford University Press, Melbourne.

Barker, C 2012, *Cultural Studies: Theory and Practice*, 4th edn, SAGE, London.

Barker, C 2004, *The SAGE Dictionary of Cultural Studies*, SAGE, London.

Beilharz, O & Hogan, T (eds.) 2012, *Sociology: Antipodean Perspectives*, 2nd edn, Oxford University Press, Melbourne.

Bennett, T, Grossberg, L & Morris, M (eds), 2005, *New Keywords: A Revised Vocabulary of Culture and Society*, Blackwell Publishing, Oxford.

Giddens, A & Sutton, P 2013, *Sociology*, 7th edn, Polity Press, Oxford.

Holmes, D, Hughes, K & Julian, R 2011, *Australian Sociology: A Changing Society*, 3rd edn, Pearson Education, Frenchs Forest.

Jureidini, R & Poole, M (eds) 2003, *Sociology: Australian Connections*, 3rd edn, Allen & Unwin, Crows Nest.

Macionis, J & Plummer, K 2012, *Sociology: A Global Introduction*, 5th edn, Pearson Education, Harlow.

Marr, D & Wilkinson, M 2003, *Dark Victory*, Allen & Unwin, Crows Nest.

Ritzer, G (ed.) 2012, *The Wiley-Blackwell Companion to Sociology*, John Wiley, Malden.

Scott, J & Marshall, G 2009, *A Dictionary of Sociology*, Oxford University Press, Oxford.

Turner, B, Abercrombie, N & Hill, S 2006, *The Penguin Dictionary of Sociology*, Penguin, London.

Walsh, K 2014, *The Stalking of Julia Gillard*, Allen & Unwin, Sydney.

Williams, R 1983, *Keywords: A Vocabulary of Culture and Society*, revised edition, Oxford University Press, New York.

Wray, M (ed.) 2013, *Cultural Sociology: An Introductory Reader*, WW Norton & Co, New York.

MOVIES

Amiel, J (dir.) 2009, *Creation*, Recorded Picture Company & BBC Films, London.

Johnson, R (dir.) 2017, *Star Wars: The Last Jedi*, Lucasfilm Ltd., Los Angeles, CA.

Knight, T (dir.) 2018, *Bumblebee*, Paramount Pictures, Los Angeles, CA.

Miller, T (dir.) 2019, *Terminator: Dark Fate*, Paramount Pictures, Los Angeles, CA.

CHAPTER 4

Researching the world around us

MAGGIE WALTER AND MIKE GUERZONI

CHAPTER OVERVIEW

Is inequality in Australia growing or diminishing? What is the effect of rising housing prices on the level of homelessness and crime rates in Australian towns and cities? Why is closing the Indigenous/non-Indigenous socio-economic gap proving so difficult?

As you saw in Chapter 2, sociologists by definition seek answers to these and many other important social questions. As also discussed in Chapter 2, research is the way that sociologists find answers that contribute to our understanding of the social world, as well as to forming solutions to some of the social issues of our day and age.

Research therefore is the driving force of sociology in its overarching aim of making theoretical and empirical sense of the world around us. Through research, sociologists collect, interpret and analyse data to produce high-quality evidence. How we conduct that research, however, varies widely. There are not only myriad pressing social questions that need to be answered, but there also is a broad suite of methods available to undertake such investigations.

Understanding the practices, methods, methodologies and conventions of sociological research is central to understanding sociology as a discipline and society more broadly. The purpose of this chapter is to provide you with a broad understanding of the nature and uses of social research. We first explore the key facets of producing quality social research, along with an overview of its key methods, methodologies and practices. We then use a set of practical examples to demonstrate how social research can, and is, being conducted and disseminated within Australia.

After reading this chapter, you should be able to:
- Explain how sociological research is conducted using processes of scientific inquiry
- List the 10 steps of the social research process
- Describe at least four common social research methods used by sociological researchers and how they are applied to contemporary social issues
- Explain why ethical principles need to be rigorously observed in planning and conducting sociological research
- Understand the link between theory and empirical data in research.

> **KEY TERMS**
>
> **Data** Information collected and/or analysed to answer research questions. Data comes in all manner of forms—surveys, content analysis, secondary data and so on.
>
> **Empirical** Data that is collectable and related to observable social phenomena.
>
> **Ethics** A set of values that guide how we interact with others and data in the practice of research.
>
> **Method** The technique used to collect and analyse research data.
>
> **Methodology** How to approach the research that is to be undertaken. It is more than just the method used—it also represents how the researcher sees the world around them.
>
> **Mixed methods** A research process that combines both qualitative and quantitative research.
>
> **Qualitative research** Research that focuses on the investigation and understanding of opinions, motivations, experiences and feelings.
>
> **Quantitative research** Research that aims to explain phenomena by collecting numerical data that are analysed by using mathematically based methods, including statistics.
>
> **Sociological research** Research that seeks to advance our understanding of social phenomena and the social world.
>
> **Theory** An explanation for patterns of meaning or trends and the relationship between the key concepts that we find in our data.

Introduction

Sociology is a discipline of inquiry and our focus is the world around us: it is an investigation into understanding how societies, as well as the institutions and persons within them, operate. Sociology's central task is to engage with the important social questions of our time and place, and contribute to the formulation of possible measures to address and improve or overcome overarching social issues and challenges.

In the current era, our fields of research have widened as countries around the world experience a period of unprecedented social, political and cultural change—something that we will unpack in greater detail in the following chapter. The pace and impact of these changes varies markedly across locations, communities, and social and cultural groups. Sociological research, therefore, is at the forefront of building the knowledge base to understand and explain the nature, dimensions and implications of these changes. Our challenge is to engage critically with these complex social and cultural phenomena and policy environments, as well as measure and describe them. This provides the foundation for governments and institutions, as well as individuals, to appropriately interact and respond to social phenomena rather than seeing and approaching issues as facing only some 'individuals' (such as obesity) or placing them in the 'too hard' basket.

These ongoing societal transformations are often global in origin, but manifested at the national and local level. For example, Australia, in common with other Western nations, has a rapidly ageing population. Indeed, one out of every seven Australians ('older Australians') in 2017 were at or above the age of 65 (AIHW 2018). We are also witnessing an increase in the number of older Australians remaining in positions of employment. As of January 2018,

13 per cent of older Australians (10 per cent of older women and 17 per cent of older men) were still working, an increase from the 2006 rate of 8 per cent (4 per cent of older women and 12 per cent of older men, see AIHW 2018). An ageing population will likely place a strain on our health services (especially given the rise of age-related diseases such as Alzheimer's), see an increase in poverty levels among the aged, require increased federal budget for the Age Pension, and increase demand for care workers and services. The retirement aspirations of older Australians and the social impacts of longer work lives are therefore pressing social questions being addressed by sociologists.

Research from the Australian Bureau of Statistics (2017) found that 50 per cent of employed Australians surveyed wished to retire at around the age of 65–69, 20 per cent at 70 years of age or older, and 23 per cent wished to retire in their early 60s (ABS 2017). The leading considerations for determining retirement plans amongst participants included financial security (34 per cent of women and 41 per cent of men) as well as one's health and ability to continue working (21 per cent for both sexes, ABS 2017). Such factors must be considered in light of broader socio-economic trends, such as increases in the cost of living and changes to superannuation entitlements, rather than individual decision making alone.

The consequences of this population shift will significantly shape Australia. Later retirement, Wolcott (1998) found, could adversely affect intergenerational support, as well as financial and asset transfers among family members. The value of the unpaid caring and support work undertaken by many retirees for grandchildren and aged parents, therefore, is a factor in assessing the value of and necessity for longer working lives. Any delay in retirement is also likely to have an effect on housing affordability—something on the minds of many young Australians who are priced out of the housing market (Della Bosca 2018).

Social research and sociological imagination

Sociological research is not just any research about social issues; it has distinguishing features. A key factor is its framing by the concept of sociological imagination (Mills 1959)—something discussed previously in Chapter 2.

The sociological imagination is that frame of mind that allows us, as sociologists, to move outside our personal perspectives and experiences to recognise that social outcomes are more than just the result of what people do at an individual level. Rather, from a sociological imagination perspective, social outcomes are shaped by the broader social context, the period in history and the overarching cultural understandings. In this way, by developing a sociological imagination, we learn to see the intersection of (social) structure and (personal) agency in how we understand the world, and that which occurs within it, around us. It is one of the unique gifts that sociology as a discipline has to offer, and will change the way you live in the world and interact with others.

As discussed in Chapter 2, this intersection reinforces the sociological understanding that our actions (agency) do not occur in a social vacuum. Instead, what people do and the choices they make are shaped and influenced by structural factors, such as social and political institutions, social and cultural norms, and the key social forces of race, gender and class.

For example, while marriage and relationship breakdown is experienced at the personal level (see Vaughan 1990), data from the Australian Bureau of Statistics (ABS 2007) indicates that up to one third of Australian marriages end in divorce. The data indicates that Australian divorce rates represent a social pattern, not just a personal problem. The research literature finds that social factors such as the change in societal attitudes towards gender roles and commitment within relationships, and changes to women's life options, opportunities and aspirations, as well as changes to the laws governing divorce (that is, 'no-fault divorce'), are also involved in any explanation for divorce rate changes (see Hewitt 2008). We see that divorce rates in Australia peaked with the introduction of no-fault divorce in 1976, and though have steadily decreased since then, remain at a higher rate than before the changes to divorce law came into effect (see AIFS 2019). In other words, the personal issue of marital breakdown is also a public issue and is situated in a broader socio-legal and socio-cultural context.

The process of scientific inquiry in social research

Sociological research must abide by specific criteria. As mentioned earlier, there are different approaches to undertaking social research, and the one you choose will depend on what you are attempting to investigate. In this section, we will look at how inquiry from the traditional sciences is applied to social research—and, as we will see, not everyone agrees with this approach (that is to be expected and is okay!).

Social research that uses the process of scientific inquiry as its basic guide for practice is frequently summed up as involving three steps, which we will discuss in greater detail below:

1. Observation;
2. Analysis; and
3. Interpretation.

Researchers collect **data** (through *observation*) on a social phenomenon using an appropriate research **method**: these may include surveys, interviews and participant observation. The researchers then *analyse* these data and explain (or *interpret*) the results theoretically. The discussion that follows demonstrates how this process operates, using the social phenomenon outlined in Box 4.1.

BOX 4.1

Everyday sociology

HOMELESSNESS

Homelessness is a significant social problem in Australia. Homelessness is typically thought of as people sleeping rough; however, staying temporarily with friends or relatives, accessing emergency accommodation or living in boarding houses, while less visible, are also forms of homelessness. Using this definition, the Australian Bureau of Statistics (2018) estimated that there were 116,427 homeless people in Australia on the night of the 2016 Census of Population and Housing.

But how do people become homeless? More critically, how can people move out of homelessness? And are there social or cultural factors related to the moving out of, or staying longer term in, homelessness?

Observation

To answer the questions raised in Box 4.1, social researchers Chamberlain and Johnson (2011) collected data from two organisations working with people who were homeless or deemed at risk of becoming homeless. They studied data on more than 4000 adult clients (aged 21 years and over).

It is important to note that as part of the ethical procedures of undertaking research, only those who gave written consent for their files to be part of the study were included. Also, the way in which the data was recorded meant that no client could be identified.

Of this group 70 per cent were male, around half were aged between 21 years and 34 years, and nearly all were unemployed or not in the labour force. More than 80 per cent were single and 10 per cent were in a family with a child aged under 18 years.

The researchers supplemented the case study data obtained from the client files by conducting 65 in-depth interviews with people who were or had been homeless.

Analysis

After the data was collected, analysis was used to identify five typical pathways into homelessness:

- The first was housing crisis, where a financial crisis such as job loss meant the person could no longer maintain a home: 19 per cent of client files.
- The second was family breakdown—either fleeing from domestic violence or losing the family home at the end of a relationship: 11 per cent of client files.
- The third was substance abuse, which affected the person's capacity to maintain stable housing and used up finances: 17 per cent of client files.
- The fourth was mental illness and the consequent breakdown or loss of supportive family relationships: 16 per cent of client files.
- The fifth, and most common, pathway was the continuation of homelessness from youth into adulthood: 35 per cent of client files. Disturbingly, 42 per cent of this group had previously been in state care. The length of homelessness was also associated with this pathway.

Those whose homelessness related to a housing crisis or family breakdown were the least likely to experience long-term homelessness (more than 12 months). Only about a third of each group were still homeless after a year.

Those whose homelessness related to substance abuse, mental health issues or youth-to-adult homelessness progression were more than twice as likely to experience long-term homelessness.

Of the youth-to-adult transitions, 85 per cent were experiencing long-term homelessness.

Interpretation

Chamberlain and Johnson concluded that homelessness pathways point to the structural and cultural factors that constrain the choices people can make.

Those more likely to be long-term homeless tended to establish different social practices that allowed them to adapt to their situation, including building networks of support. However, structural factors—such as the availability of support services and the quality and resources of those services, as well as local labour and housing markets—also directly impacted on the likelihood of those at risk becoming, or staying, homeless.

The researchers' interpretation was that while those who are homeless retain some agency in how they live their lives, their choices are constrained by social and cultural factors, and by structural factors. Personal agency was utilised, but within the constraints of the level of social support available, and this was especially true for those who were likely to be homeless long term.

Always be systematic and public

The above example outlines how research is undertaken, but how do you know what is 'good research', that is, research that has integrity and can be trusted? To begin with, no matter what research you are doing, you must always be systematic and public:

- *Systematic* means that research should proceed through a structured, coherent and sequential process.
- *Public* (or open) means that the research needs to be publicly shared—something that can be done through publications and conferences.

There are also criteria for reliable and valid research findings:

- *Reliability* refers to the consistency of the research. Research is reliable if we are confident that, using the same **methodology** and same techniques, we are likely to produce similar results in another study.
- *Validity* refers to the extent to which the research being undertaken actually reflects or measures what the researcher intends it to reflect or measure. For example, if we are investigating poverty we need to be clear about how we define 'poverty'. Does it mean, in quantitative research, household income that falls below 50 per cent of the median household income? Or, in qualitative research, does the term 'poverty' reflect the respondents' own understanding of themselves as being poor?

The degrees of reliability and validity act as quality control indicators for research. We need to be thorough and precise, as these criteria will not only ensure quality but also effect how our research is received.

The research process

The research process can be broken down into two phases. The first phase establishes the research foundation and includes six steps that need to occur before the first piece of data can be collected. Each step is necessary in its own right—skipping or skimping on any of them will raise the risk that the quality or integrity of the research may be compromised. For example, if we skip the 'identifying the research topic' step, we are likely to end up with a whole lot of data about a topic, but not a specific focus. This lack of focus will hinder the carrying-out of our research and undermine our ability to analyse or interpret the data in a coherent way.

In this section, we will present the steps in a logical and linear order. Please note that research is never this simple and you may need to move back and forward as you discover new things! For example, after a detailed review of the literature in Step 2, you may go back to re-identify your research topic in Step 1 (maybe even multiple times).

Phase 1

The six steps of Phase 1 of the research process are as follows.

STEP 1: IDENTIFYING THE RESEARCH TOPIC

While our topic choice is unlimited, in order to be valid the topic must have sociological relevance and be able to be investigated within a research project. 'Motherhood', for example, is too broad a topic for a research project. A specific aspect of motherhood, however, such as 'breastfeeding experiences', has the potential to be investigated from a number of dimensions.

STEP 2: REVIEWING THE SOCIOLOGICAL, THEORETICAL AND EMPIRICAL LITERATURE

All research needs to be informed by research already undertaken on the topic. Reviewing the existing literature ensures that our research question has not already been answered. It also ensures that our research design is informed by a critical examination of earlier findings. For example, research indicating that women from lower socio-economic backgrounds are more likely to cease breastfeeding earlier than mothers from middle-class backgrounds might influence us to delve more deeply into this topic.

STEP 3: SPECIFYING THE METHODOLOGY AND THE THEORY THAT WILL INFORM THE RESEARCH

Our methodology is how we approach the research. It is more than whether we use a quantitative or qualitative approach; it is based around the researcher's standpoint (see below for more detail on methodology).

Our methodology also informs which theories make most sense to us. A female researcher, for example, may be more likely to use a feminist conflict perspective than a male researcher.

STEP 4: DEVELOPING THE RESEARCH QUESTION

A research topic is not enough. We need to address a specific research question. For the topic of breastfeeding experiences, we might develop our research question as:

> How do new mothers from low socio-economic areas negotiate their interactions with services that promote/support breastfeeding?

The research question should contain all key concepts under investigation. In our example research question, we have to decide how we classify an area as 'low socio economic', and to determine what 'new mother' means. We might decide that suburbs in areas that have a low score on the Australian Bureau of Statistics Social Economic Indicators for Areas (SEIFA) are 'low socio-economic', and that mothers who have given birth within the past year are 'new'. Such decisions can be informed by the literature review in Step 2.

STEP 5: DECIDING ON THE RESEARCH METHOD

The research question also informs the choice of research method. The research question about breastfeeding, for example, may lend itself to qualitative rather than quantitative methods. We might therefore decide to conduct a series of in-depth interviews with new mothers, and we might also decide to conduct some participant observation at service organisations.

STEP 6: ADDRESSING THE ETHICAL DIMENSIONS OF THE RESEARCH

All sociological research has ethical dimensions and research projects will generally require approval from a Human Research Ethics Committee (HREC)—we discuss this towards the end of this chapter.

In the breastfeeding research, we would need ethics clearance before any women could be recruited for interviews. This is because any research involving people as research participants or subjects must demonstrate that the benefits outweigh any risks of causing harm to the people we are researching. Our ethics application would also need to address how our research design addresses any ethical issues that may arise throughout the research process. For example, it would need to address whether being questioned about breastfeeding might make some young mothers feel anxious and guilty if they are not breastfeeding. We must explain how we intend to manage this risk, and how to respond if participants do experience unease or distress.

Phase 2

The second phase of the research process is the collection, analysis and interpretation of data, and can be broken down into four steps. If we have undertaken Steps 1–6 in a rigorous way, then the undertaking of Steps 7–10 should be relatively straightforward.

The four steps of Phase 2 of the research process are as follows.

STEP 7: SELECTING THE RESEARCH SAMPLE

Before we collect data, we need a research sample. A sample does not have to be people; if we are undertaking discourse analysis, for example, our sample is likely to be communications such as newspaper articles or political speeches (commonly referred to as 'texts').

In the breastfeeding example, our sample could be a group of new mothers. To recruit our sample, we might place posters advertising the research in child health clinics in our selected area. All potential respondents need to be fully informed about the study before they can consent to participation.

STEP 8: COLLECTING THE DATA

Eventually, at Step 8, we collect our data. In our example, the data are collected via in-depth interviewing with new mothers: the interviews are recorded and transcribed. We would also have detailed information from the participant observations at the service organisations, contained within a field notes journal (within which researchers log their observations and experiences as they go about their research).

STEP 9: ANALYSING THE DATA

How we analyse the data depends on our research method. In our example we would probably use thematic analysis (commonly used when analysing interviewing data). This involves identifying themes in the transcribed interviews and coding and categorising these as they arise. Alternatively, if we were examining the way that drug use (for instance, 'ice') is portrayed in the media, we could do a content analysis of an over-time sample of newspaper articles. These processes help us make meaning of our data that can be used to glean shifts in societal attitudes and, in some instances, moral panics (which we will discuss in Chapter 18). If we are using a quantitative method such as surveys, we would analyse our data using statistical techniques; for example, we would run statistics on how many new mothers decide to find alternatives to breastfeeding.

STEP 10: INTERPRETING THE RESULTS

The final step is to interpret our results through our theoretical framework determined at Step 3 and ask: 'What do our results mean, sociologically?'

For example, we may have found that many of the new mothers interviewed found the professionals advising them on breastfeeding to be judgmental and felt that they were being patronised. They may have also reported that they responded to this by limiting their contact and honesty with health centre staff. From a feminist perspective—something we will discuss in Chapter 7—we could interpret these results as indicating that the middle-class and gender frameworks of the health professionals are operating to alienate some new mothers from their services.

To meet the criteria of public and open research noted above, most sociological research is peer reviewed—that is, it is reviewed by other scholars in that field—before it is published as a report, book or journal article. Peer review examines the process of the research as well as the results and findings as a way of safeguarding the quality and accuracy of published research.

For sociology students, as well as other researchers, this means that when you read a research article or book, all 10 steps of the research process should be apparent. You should be able to see what the researcher did, what guided and facilitated that process, and how they came to the conclusions presented.

> **Critical reflection**
>
> 1   Why is it important that social research follows the process of scientific inquiry?
> 2   Is it possible to do good social research without this process?
> 3   What are the risks if sociological research is done outside the framework of scientific inquiry?

Researching the social world

Sociological research is similar to other types of research in that it combines **theory** and **empirical** data in how it seeks to understand the social world.

By the term 'empirical' we mean 'of the real world': empirical data, whatever the type and source of these data, are both observable and can be analysed. For example, we might be interested in how supermarket shopping is influenced for the adult shopper by the presence of a child. To test whether there is any influence, we need to collect empirical data, perhaps by spending time in a supermarket observing and recording the purchasing behaviour of people shopping with small children.

To turn our observations into empirical data, we have to determine a way of measuring the phenomena. It's not enough to say we saw shoppers buy something after their toddler threw a tantrum; that is anecdotal. To be empirical, data collection—and specifically the *recording* of data—needs to be more rigorous. So, we could observe the selections of shoppers in a set aisle—such as in the chocolates aisle—for a series of set time periods. Using this technique we might observe that over a period of two hours (1–3pm) we observed 14 instances of purchases made at the insistence of a small child and nine instances where an item was requested by the child but not purchased. We would record other details such as the child's age and gender, the gender of the adult, the item(s) purchased, the forms the child's insistence took and how the shopper dealt with the child's insistence. Now we have a set of data we can analyse.

The analysis of the data from such a study might indicate that the adult is more likely to purchase the item if the child continues their insistence for more than two minutes. We might even find a linear relationship between the amount of time that the child is insistent and the likelihood that the item will be purchased.

Our empirical data, therefore, are telling us quite a lot about the 'what, how and where' of the social experience of shopping with a small child. But they give us only hints on 'why'.

We also need theory

For the 'why', we need theory. Theory can be defined as a set of ideas that provide an explanation for the relationships between concepts or occurrences in a particular sociological phenomenon. You may know that in the hard sciences theories are used to explain why certain things in the universe occur or are the way they are (for instance Darwin's Theory of Evolution to explain variations in living creatures). In sociology the purpose of a theory is to explain, in sociological terms, what the analysis of our observations reveals about something occurring within our society. It is important to stress that sociological theories *explain* social patterns and social meanings: they do not predict!

In our hypothetical example we might explain the adult shoppers' behaviour from a *structural functionalism* perspective (see Chapter 3). Structural functionalism's theoretical base is that to be functional, a society must have a set of social norms that are shared and adhered to by its members. Adherence to these norms in a society is reinforced by the expectations and responses of others. Non-adherence is likely to be viewed as deviant and socially sanctioned (rebuking, snide remarks, vehement glances). A supermarket is a public place where social roles, such as shopper and parent, are performed. In mainstream Australian society, parents can be judged by others by both the appearance (clean, well-dressed) and behaviour (manners, obedience, charm) of their child. A child crying or screaming, or rolling on the floor crying and screaming, is likely to bring negative attention and thus a judgment on the overall parenting ability of the caregiver. Giving the child what it wants, despite the adult not wanting to purchase that particular item, is therefore a swift way of avoiding negative social experiences. No one wants to be *that parent* at their IGA.

Theorising is not just about the classical sociological theories. Any time we interpret our results we are theorising! It is also worth remembering that a theory is just an explanation of an observed social phenomenon; it is not a truth, even if popular or vogue.

Theories can and do change as a result of more research, and there can be multiple and often competing theoretical explanations for the same social phenomena. For example, is unemployment best explained as deviance and laziness by those who are unemployed in their unwillingness to conform to social norms in taking a job (functionalism), or is it better explained as being a structural outcome of a labour market designed to limit the power of workers compared to that of employers (conflict theory)? Our understanding of the 'why' of unemployment depends not just on our data, but also on our understanding of the way the world is—a topic covered in the next section.

Social research objectivity and methodology

Social research is focused on people and social relationships—even when we are not researching people directly but using secondary sources such as speeches or newspaper articles. Social research is, therefore, human research in two ways. Not only is our research largely concerned with people and specific groups of people, but we researchers are people ourselves. This means that the experience, understanding and approach we bring to our research are important ingredients of that research and can impact on research involved in both social and physical sciences (Walter 2019; Jewkes 2012).

This is why we need to engage with the ideas of objectivity and rationality.

These concepts are associated with the beginning of sociology and Auguste Comte's (1975) claim that the objective and rational principles of natural science research can be applied in the study of society. But the rules of the natural sciences cannot be directly and seamlessly transferred to sociological research. A social group or institution is not the same as the set of elements on the periodic table or a flock of seagulls. As such, we cannot study that group in the same way as we would study the chemical properties of zinc, for example. Sociology is not a lab coat science. Not only are there ethical issues involved in how we treat a group of people, we also cannot rely on either ourselves as researchers, or the social group under investigation, to be completely objective and rational within the research; because we are all human.

It is easier to understand this fairly complex idea with a practical example.

Think about a social topic that interests you. Now think about *why* that topic interests you. Usually it is because it is a social phenomenon that you yourself have experienced or are familiar with or connected to (e.g. general anxiety disorder amongst adolescent boys). But our personal understanding means we already have some ideas—we are already approaching the topic from a particular angle (e.g. understanding what causes or triggers such anxiety). This does not mean that we will go into our research with set ideas on what the outcomes will be, or—more damagingly—should be; the process of social inquiry helps ensure that we approach the research with an open mind and are diligent about the transparency and even-handedness of our research practice. But this does mean that we cannot ever claim to be completely objective or even rational (you might remember the discussion about rationality in Box 1.1).

The twin concepts of objectivity and rationality also link to understanding research *methodology*.

Methodology has been defined as the theoretical lens through which the research is designed and conducted (Walter 2019). This lens refers to more than our theoretical framework. It also incorporates our world views and perspectives, inclusive of our experiences and how we see ourselves positioned in relation to our social world.

For example, if you are a middle-class, Euro-Australian male, no matter how non-sexist, non-racist you are, and how much you believe in social equality, these social attributes, alongside how they position you within your society, will influence *how* you understand, perceive and respond to social phenomena relating to class, gender and race (see Bourdieu 1984).

This *social position* in turn is linked to who we are. Some dimensions of our own positioning to be considered include:

- Our *epistemological* position—how we define, value and prioritise knowledge and knowledge sources;
- Our *ontological* position—how we see the world and understand reality; and
- Our *axiological* position—the values that inform how we see the world.

These positions will influence the way we perceive and approach the social phenomena we are researching. They also influence the *theoretical frameworks* that make most sense to us.

The final element of a research methodology is the *research method* (the technique or practice we use to gather data).

Figure 4.1 outlines the elements of a methodology and how they intersect to influence our research approach.

FIGURE 4.1 Elements of a research methodology.

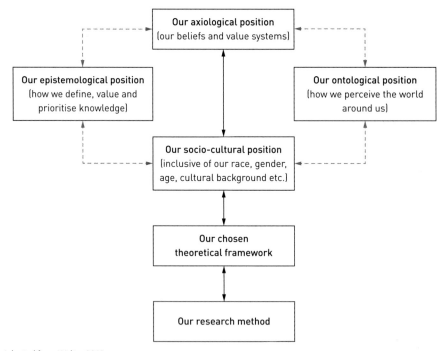

Source: Adapted from Walter 2019

> **Critical reflection**
>
> Look at the following list of social research topics. Rank them 1 to 5 based on how interested you would be to conduct research on that topic, with 1 being the topic you would find most interesting:
>
> - Voting patterns among older (aged 65+ years) Australians
> - Reasons people give for choosing a cat as their pet
> - Changes in health practices amongst Australians to minimise risk of heart disease
> - Attitudes of religious Australians towards same-sex marriage
> - Media streaming practices of young Australians (legal paid-services versus illegal)
>
> Now reflect on why you have ranked each of these issues as you did. What was the issue you gave your number 1 ranking to? Why? What is it about this issue that makes it more interesting to you than the others?
>
> For most people, these reasons will be linked to a personal aspect of the topic. Perhaps you love cats or have a family member affected by heart disease. Think about these reasons and how they might impact on the way you would approach research on the topic.

Research methods and real-world sociological research

The methods used to collect sociological data are many but fall into two main categories: quantitative and qualitative.

Quantitative research is any research that collects or uses data that can be coded into numbers and statistically tested. Methods include surveys, secondary data analysis of data collected by others (such as Census data) and structured interviews. Quantitative methods often collect or use data from a large number of subjects, such as national surveys that use 'probability sampling', so the findings can be used to present conclusions related to the whole population.

Qualitative research tends to focus on smaller groups of people, or smaller sections of society. The focus of qualitative research is not on generalisable data, but a nuanced understanding of social situations and the meanings that individuals and groups attach to those situations. Qualitative research emphasises the subjective experiences of social phenomena. Methods include the various forms of observation, focus groups, in-depth interviews and narrative work.

It is important to note that one method of research is not better than the other: the one you employ will be dependent on your research goals. Increasingly, many researchers are employing a combination of both qualitative and quantitative methods—something described as **mixed methods**—to improve the scope and rigour of their inquiry through a process known as triangulation (see Graham 2016).

The following section details some of the most common methods used by Australian sociological and cultural researchers, with examples of recent research using that method.

Surveys and statistical analysis

As noted, quantitative analysis most commonly relates to research using data collected through surveys or through the secondary analysis of data collected by another researcher. The key purpose of surveys is determining social patterns and trends through the comparative analysis of responses from (usually) a large number of respondents. They have a number of unique qualities.

The need for *comparability* means that the respondents must give their responses in circumstances that are as similar as possible. This in turn means that the questions included in the survey need to be pre-set and must be the same for each respondent. The methods of collection also need to be as similar as possible.

The responses must also be able to be coded numerically, but this does not mean that answers to the questions in the survey have to be numbers. For example, with categorical data such as a person's gender, the responses are often coded 1 for male and 2 for female.

BOX 4.2

Method to action

SURVEYS

While mobile telephones and smartphones have brought a number of benefits to social connectivity, the device's facilitation of 'sexting' (the sending of images, rather than suggestive text) amongst young people has been identified as a social problem. This is particularly concerning given that some forms of sexting breach Australian child pornography laws; laws that young people may not be aware of, nor intentionally seek to break.

To investigate the sexting behaviours and perceptions of Australian youth, Murray Lee and colleagues (2015) conducted an online survey with 2243 youth and young adults aged 13–25+ (52 per cent female, 47 per cent male, <1 per cent identified as other), with 42 per cent of the sample 16–18 years of age.

The scholars found that 50 per cent of participants aged 16–18 had sent a sexual video or picture via SMS and 70 per cent had received such content. The majority of participants in this age category had sent sexual content to one person before (44 per cent male, 52 per cent female). It was found to have been more common for males to receive content from multiple people, with 43 per cent of 16–18-year-old males having been sent material from 2–5 persons. Conversely, females of this cohort reported to have received sexual content from mainly one person (44 per cent). Patterns of behaviour were explained by participants as stemming from a desire to be 'fun and flirty' and tended to be undertaken within the context of a dating relationship.

The authors concluded that a harm minimisation approach may be an effective and realistic measure to regulate 'consensual' sexting amongst young Australians and cautioned against a heavy-handed legislative approach.

BOX 4.3
Method to action

SECONDARY DATA ANALYSIS

The use of early-childhood education in Australia is the norm for many families, offering many benefits to the development, nurturing and care of children. But have you ever wondered what young children think about attending these services, in contrast to the expectations of the parents?

In 2017 a study by Karen Martin was published examining how Indigenous children experience early-childhood education, and the expectations and motivations their parents had in enrolling their children in these programs. Martin used secondary data analysis of quantitative and qualitative data from The Longitudinal Study of Indigenous Children (also known as LSIC, specifically Waves 2–4), which has been collecting data annually from two cohorts of Indigenous youth from 11 sites on mainland Australia since 2008. Parent data was drawn mainly from Wave 2 (a sample of 1671) and children from Wave 3–4 (a sample of 1394 and 1269 respectively).

Using this data, Martin found that:

- 63 per cent of the youth were happy about attending pre-school; 33 per cent shared that they found pre-school a fun place to be;
- 78 per cent responded that their teacher was nice to them; and
- 62 per cent found that other children were nice to them.

Children shared that they particularly enjoyed drawing, painting, play time and playing with their friends. Parental expectations of the early-childhood education included the development of their child(ren)'s academic skills, interpersonal skills, independence, physical skills, Indigenous and cultural identity, and to further school attendance and enjoyment:

- 37.4 per cent of parents saw a good education involving leading their child to finish year 12;
- 26.4 per cent as leading to their child to study at university; and
- 16.34 per cent as enabling their child to obtain employment after schooling.

Martin concluded that parents send children to pre-school as they see the service as integral for their hopes for their child's future. Children, whilst not yet appreciating this, enjoy pre-school for the care, intellectual stimulation and socialising they receive.

Discourse analysis

Discourse analysis is a research method that uses forms of recorded communication (texts, films, political speeches, opinion pieces, newspaper articles and so on). The aim is to provide a critical understanding of how language is used and deployed, and for what purpose.

This method makes explicit the social and political context in which the communication(s) are situated. In discourse analysis the use of language is seen as a *performative* activity; that is, language not only describes what is happening, but also helps shape peoples' understanding of it (Jacobs 2019). Critical discourse analysis is one variant of the method used by social scientists (Jacobs 2019).

An example of how language can shape our understanding of reality is a government inquiry in which the conduct of an organisation's employees is described as an 'error of judgment' or 'mistake'. This creates the image of workers committing a once-off or unintentional failure, perhaps due to fatigue, or at worst, incompetence. However, if the conduct is described using legal language such as 'fraud' or 'embezzlement', a very different image emerges in our minds.

As such, the term 'discourse' in discourse analysis relates to the construction of language (written or spoken) that can influence readers' thinking on a topic. It examines discursive strategies deployed within recorded texts to persuade the reader of the veracity of an ideological argument. Discourse analysis is therefore related to sociology's role of revealing structures of power within society, because dominant discourses shape the way a society operates. For example, attention to nuanced or obfuscatory language is necessary to expose attempts to evade responsibility, manipulate or coerce others and shift blame.

BOX 4.4

Method to action

CRITICAL DISCOURSE ANALYSIS

Clerical abuse within religious institutions has been one of the leading criminal concerns of the twenty-first century in Australia and across the world. Notwithstanding the launching of a number of inquiries in Australia, the United States and most recently the United Kingdom, some experts believe we are only scratching the surface about what we know about this horrible crime. Churches have been criticised for their attempts to evade responsibility for clerical abuse and the historical silencing of victims.

Researchers Guerzoni and Graham (2015) used critical discourse analysis to investigate the role of the confessional and the Melbourne Response compensation scheme in the institutional secrecy and inaction of the Roman Catholic Church in Victoria, Australia regarding child sexual abuse. In this study, 28 documents (1394 pages) from a governmental inquiry were sorted via 'structural coding' (see Saldaña 2012) and thereafter analysed for the discursive practice (see Jacobs 2019) employed by clergy and church officials. Attention was particularly given to how the 'techniques of neutralisation' (see Sykes and Matza 1957; Cohen 1993) were used to justify their acts and omissions towards the concealment of abuse knowledge and not reporting crimes to police.

Their results demonstrate that the Church and its senior clerical leaders possess a Janus-faced approach in this area: on one hand it would be conveyed that there was a commitment to survivors, justice and compliance with legal requirements; however, when pressed about the confessional and the Melbourne Response, it was shown there were appeals to higher (mostly religious) loyalties as a means of justifying non-compliance with the legal requirements to report matters to and collaborate with law enforcement. Discursive practice is used to emphasise the importance of compliance with canon or religious law rather than statutory and civil law.

Qualitative interviewing

Interviewing is one of the most commonly used qualitative research methods and can take a number of different formats. In Box 4.5 you will see that the researchers use a more standard (semi-structured) framework when interviewing bisexual young women from rural Tasmania.

The key purpose of an interview is to explore the meaning of social phenomena. This includes specifically the meaning that people make of social situations, contexts and lived realities. In-depth interviewing is often also referred to as 'semi-structured interviewing'. This means that, unlike the highly structured format of a survey, the interview is guided by the interviewer, but the interview can follow its own unique path. Each interview does not have to include exactly the same questions or exactly the same format.

In-depth interviewing seeks to answer social questions through understanding the meanings people bring to their experiences. The way it is undertaken reflects this purpose (Travers 2019). Thus, it is not usually necessary to interview a large sample of people. Rather, the aim is to reach 'saturation point' (Willis 2019); that is, the point where any additional interviews are no longer revealing significant new insights on the topic.

BOX 4.5
Everyday sociology

SEXUALITY AND HEALTH CARE

While there has been an increase in understanding of the sexual health of lesbian and gay Australians, a knowledge gap remains in relation to the health of bisexual women; particularly those living in rural areas. This raises the questions of: 'What are the experiences of young bisexual women in respect to sexual health care?' and 'What are the rural health needs of these women?'

An article by Ruby Grant and Meredith Nash (2019) records the findings of semi-structured interviewing (undertaken between 2015 and 2016) with 15 Tasmanian bisexual women from rural areas aged between 19 and 26 years old (n=20). Participants expressed that it was not easy for them to access inclusive health services in rural areas, and that when accessing such services they looked out for symbols that indicated its gender inclusivity (e.g. rainbow sticker) to measure their safety. It was shared by some participants that negative experiences in some instances, through judgmental questions from GPs concerning sexual health, and positive experiences in others, by the use of gender-neutral language (e.g. partner), shaped whether they ceased or continued attending that clinic respectively.

The authors concluded that it is pressing for medical practitioners to be conscious of and exercise inclusive practice for LBGTIQ persons, especially in rural areas where access to medical services is limited.

Ethics in sociological research

The final important aspect of sociological research for this chapter is ethical research.

Ethics is a set of values that guide our behaviour and how we interact with others. To be ethical in research means that we must abide by ethical principles in the conduct of our research (Banks 2019).

While most researchers are well-intentioned and driven by a commitment towards the common good, the power differences between the researcher and those who are the subject of research means that it cannot be left up to individual researchers to decide what is ethical research and what is not.

In Australia, research practice is governed by the principles laid out in the *National Statement on Ethical Conduct in Research Involving Humans* developed by the National

Health and Medical Research Council in 2007, and recently updated (NHMRC 2018). Central principles in this statement include:

1 Respect—recognising the inherent dignity and autonomy of research participants;
2 Beneficence—the duty of researchers to maximise the benefits of the research, especially to its participants, and to minimise any risk of harm and discomfort;
3 Justice—ensuring that certain groups do not bear an unequal burden of research and that the benefits of research are also fairly distributed to all groups in society;
4 Research merit and integrity—that the research is safe for participants and researchers and that its results will be of value;
5 Informed consent—that all respondents are fully informed about the research and what it will involve before they consent to be a participant; and
6 Anonymity and/or confidentiality—that respondents are guaranteed that their participation and data will not be identifiable.

Within institutions that conduct research, such as universities and research centres, HRECs are charged with ensuring that researchers abide by ethical principles. This means that before researchers can begin collecting data, they must submit to the appropriate HREC an application outlining what their research is about and how it will be conducted. The HREC will only give ethical clearance for the research to proceed once its members are satisfied that the research and the researchers are ethical.

The *National Statement on Ethical Conduct in Research Involving Humans* (2018a) covers many situations and circumstances, but it also has limitations. For example, it does not necessarily address the values and principles of non-Western peoples in Australia. This gap has been recognised formally in the case of Aboriginal and Torres Strait Islander peoples, through the development of the *Ethical Conduct in Research with Aboriginal and Torres Strait Islander Peoples and Communities: Guidelines for Researchers and Stakeholders* (2018b) and *Keeping Research on Track II* (2018c). These guidelines, developed by Aboriginal and Torres Strait Islander people, refer to values and ethical principles specific to Indigenous-based research. These include:

- Spirit and integrity—this overarching value refers to recognition of the continuity of Aboriginal and Torres Strait Islander peoples over time and the need for research to maintain the coherence of Aboriginal and Torres Strait Islander values and cultures, shown through the agreement to submit to each of the following research values;
- Cultural continuity—recognising and respecting Indigenous interpersonal relationships and connection with Country as an integral component of their continuing culture. It prompts acknowledgement and discontinuation of research practices that disregard, disrespect and disrupt communities and their observance of culture;
- Equity—that there is a mutual obligation between the researchers and those who are the subjects of the research;
- Respect—that the research is built around the dignity and autonomy of participants combined with respect for Aboriginal and Torres Strait Islander culture, values and mores;

- Equality—that Aboriginal and Torres Strait Islander peoples are equal participants in the research, and that they have the right to have different culture, values and mores; and
- Survival and protection—that the research does not pose risks to, or marginalise, Aboriginal and Torres Strait Islander culture or collective identity.

These guidelines are especially important given that Aboriginal and Torres Strait Islander people have been over-burdened as the subjects of research. Sociology, as well as disciplines such as anthropology, history and the health sciences, have over the past two centuries conducted extensive research among Indigenous people. Not all of that research has respected Indigenous cultures and values. The marginalised and heavily disadvantaged position of Aboriginal and Torres Strait Islander people, which is discussed in Chapter 16, has meant that frequently they were not given any option about participation and were unable to influence how the research was interpreted.

Critical reflection

Imagine that you are part of a research team that is investigating the reasons why parents do, or do not, get their children fully immunised. You find, as part of your analysis of the immunisation data in your region, that children who are identified as Aboriginal or Torres Strait Islander are underrepresented among those who are fully immunised.

You decide that you need to interview a sample of Aboriginal and Torres Strait Islander parents to try and find out the reasons for the lower immunisation rates. Think about the following ethical issues that will arise as part of your research practice. How would you:

- Establish a respectful relationship and trust with the parents?
- Find out what cultural values and mores you will need to take into account and respect? (Remember, there is no one Indigenous culture or value set—these vary across Australia.)
- Recognise and minimise the effect of your own cultural values and mores within the research?
- Provide for equality and reciprocity in the relationship and the research?
- Ensure that the research does not marginalise or devalue Aboriginal or Torres Strait Islander culture and collective identity?

Conclusion

Social research is a key part of what it is to 'do' sociology. It provides the means for sociologists to answer or seek further knowledge about key social issues.

As sociologists, we research the phenomena that shape and form our social world. In doing so we gain a greater sociological understanding, which influences social policy and social discourse, and contributes to social justice. But to be of value sociological research needs to be ethical, conducted using social inquiry methods and conducted with rigour throughout the research process.

Summary points

* Research is the primary means of achieving sociology's aim of making theoretical and empirical sense of the world around us. Sociological research has distinguishing features. It is informed by a sociological imagination and uses scientific inquiry as its basic guide for practice.
* Sociological research is also systematic in that it uses an established research process to ensure research findings are valid and reliable. Sociological research requires a combination of observable and analysable data and sociological theory in how it seeks to understand the social world.
* Our research methodology is the lens through which we approach our research. Our methodology is shaped by our social position and our epistemological, axiological and ontological position, and our research can never be completely objective.
* There are a wide variety of social research methods available to sociologists, usually categorised as either qualitative or quantitative.
* Ethics is a set of values that guides how we relate to others, and ethical research is research that abides by ethical principles in its conduct.

Sociological reflection

1 Explain why researching social questions is more than measurement or description. Why is it so important that we are critically engaged with the complex social and cultural dimensions, discourses and policy environments of these questions?
2 Think of a social issue that is really important to you. How would you go about researching it? What theoretical framework would make most sense to you? What would the difficulties be in conducting this research?
3 Reflect on ethics within social research. What are some of the ways that the power differentials between researchers and those participating in the research might facilitate unethical research practices? What consequences would this have on the research data?

Discussion questions

1 What is the sociological imagination?
2 How does a sociological imagination shape how sociologists research?
3 Explain the criteria for scientific inquiry—observation, analysis and interpretation—in your own words.
4 What are the first six steps of the research process?
5 Why is it important for researchers to follow all steps in the research process?
6 What are the different roles of empirical data and theory in research?
7 What's the difference between a method and a methodology?
8 Pure objectivity is desirable but unobtainable in social research. Why?
9 What is the difference between qualitative and quantitative research methods?
10 Explain the basic tenets of in-depth interviewing.

Further investigation

1 Go to the NHMRC website and work your way through the page on human research ethics at <www.nhmrc.gov.au/about-us/publications/national-statement-ethical-conduct-human-research-2007-updated-2018>.

2 Using your library's database find at least two sociology research articles relating to a topic that intrigues you. Compare the two. How do they differ in their approach, research question, theoretical framework, findings and interpretations?

References and further reading

REFERENCES

Australian Bureau of Statistics (ABS) 2007, 'Lifetime marriage and divorce trends', *Australian Social Trends Cat. No. 4102.0*, ABS, Canberra.

Australian Bureau of Statistics (ABS) 2017, 'Retirement and retirement intentions, Australia, July 2016 to June 2017', *Cat. No. 6238.0*, ABS, Canberra.

Australian Bureau of Statistics (ABS) 2018, 'Census of population and housing: estimating homelessness, 2016', *Cat. No. 2049.0*, ABS, Canberra.

Australian Institute of Family Studies (AIFS) 2019, 'Divorce rates in Australia': <https://aifs.gov.au/facts-and-figures/divorce-rates-australia>.

Australian Institute of Health and Welfare (AIHW) 2018, 'Older Australia at a glance, *Cat. No AGE 87*, AIHW, Canberra.

Banks, S 2019, 'Ethics and social research', in M Walter (ed.), *Social Research Methods*, 4th edn, Oxford University Press, Melbourne, pp. 83–115.

Bourdieu, P 1984, *Distinction: A Social Critique of the Judgement of Taste*, trans. R. Nice, Routledge and Kegan and Paul Ltd, London.

Chamberlain, C & Johnson, G 2011, 'Pathways into adult homelessness', *Journal of Sociology*, 49(1), 60–77.

Cohen, S 1993, 'Human rights and crimes of the state: the culture of denial', *Australian and New Zealand Journal of Criminology*, 26(2), 97–115.

Comte, A 1975, *Positivism: The Essential Writing*, Harper Textbooks, New York.

Della Bosca, L 2018, 'Older Australians holding the property market steady', *Your Live Choices,* 13 August: <www.yourlifechoices.com.au/finance/property/seniors-steadying-property-market>.

Graham, H 2016, *Rehabilitation Work: Supporting Desistance and Recovery*, Routledge, New York.

Grant, R & Nash, M 2019, 'Young bisexual women's sexual health care experiences in Australian rural general practice', *Australian Journal of Rural Health*, 27, 224–28.

Guerzoni, MA & Graham, H 2015, 'Catholic Church responses to clergy-child sexual abuse and mandatory reporting exemptions in Victoria, Australia: a discursive critique', *International Journal for Crime, Justice and Social Democracy*, 4(4), 58–75.

Hewitt, B 2008, *Marriage Breakdown in Australia: Social Correlates, Gender and Initiator Status*, Social Research Policy Paper No. 35, Department of Families, Housing, Community Services, and Indigenous Affairs, Canberra.

Jacobs, K 2019, 'Discourse analysis', in M Walter (ed.), *Social Research Methods*, 4th edn, Oxford University Press, Melbourne, pp. 316–40.

Jewkes, Y 2012, 'Autoethnography and emotion as intellectual resources: doing prison research differently', *Qualitative Inquiry*, 18(1), 63–75.

Lee, M, Crofts, T, McGovern, A & Milivojevic, S 2015, 'Sexting among young people: perceptions and practices', *Trends & Issues in Crime and Criminal Justice*, 508, 1–9.

Martin, K 2017, 'It's special and it's specific: understanding the early childhood education experiences and expectations of young Indigenous Australian children and their parents', *The Australian Educational Researcher*, 44(1), 89–105.

Mills, CW 1959, *The Sociological Imagination*, Oxford University Press, New York.

National Health and Medical Research Council (NHMRC) 2018a, *National Statement on Ethical Conduct in Research Involving Humans (2018)*, NHMRC, Commonwealth of Australia, Canberra: <www.nhmrc.gov.au/guidelines-publications/e72>.

National Health and Medical Research Council (NHMRC) 2018b, *Ethical Conduct in Research with Aboriginal and Torres Strait Islander Peoples and Communities: Guidelines for Researchers and Stakeholders*, NHMRC, Commonwealth of Australia, Canberra.

National Health and Medical Research Council (NHMRC) 2018c, *Keeping Research on Track II: A Companion Document to Ethical Conduct in Research with Aboriginal and Torres Strait Islander Peoples and Communities: Guidelines for Researchers and Stakeholders (2018)*, NHMRC, Commonwealth of Australia, Canberra.

Saldaña, J 2012, *The Coding Manual for Qualitative Researchers*, SAGE, London.

Sykes, G & Matza, D 1957, 'Techniques of neutralization: a theory of delinquency', *American Sociological Review*, 22(6), 664–70.

Travers, M 2019, 'Qualitative interviewing methods', in M Walter (ed.), *Social Research Methods*, 4th edn, Oxford University Press, Melbourne, pp. 265–95.

Vaughan, D 1990, *Uncoupling: The Turning Points in Intimate Relationships*, Oxford University Press, New York.

Walter, M 2019, 'The nature of social science research', in M Walter (ed.), *Social Research Methods*, 4th edn, Oxford University Press, Melbourne, pp. 3–28.

Willis, K 2019, 'Analysing qualitative data', in M Walter (ed.), *Social Research Methods*, 4th edn, Oxford University Press, Melbourne, pp. 341–64.

Wolcott, I 1998, *Families in Later Life: Dimensions of Retirement*, Working Paper No. 14, Australian Institute of Family Studies, Melbourne.

FURTHER READINGS

Alston, M & Kent, J 2008, 'The big dry: the link between rural masculinities and poor health outcomes for farming men', *Journal of Sociology*, 44(2), 133–48.

Amir, LH & Donath, SM 2008, 'Socioeconomic status and rates of breastfeeding in Australia: evidence from three recent national health surveys', *Medical Journal of Australia*, 189(5), 254–356.

Bentley, M, Kerr, R, Scott, F, Hansen, E, Margin, P & Bonney, A 2019, 'Exploring opportunities for general practice registrars to manage older patients with chronic disease: a qualitative study', *Australian Journal of General Practice,* 48.7, 451–6.

Bryman, A 2015, *Social Research Methods*, 5th edn, Oxford University Press, Oxford.

Fairclough, N 1992, *Discourse and Social Change*, Polity Press, Cambridge.

Flood, M 2007, 'Exposure to pornography among youth in Australia', *Journal of Sociology*, 43(1), 45–60.

Harrigan, N & Goldfinch, S 2007, 'A trans-Tasman business elite?', *Journal of Sociology*, 43(4), 367–84.

Newton, J 2008, 'Emotional attachment to home and security for permanent residents in caravan parks in Melbourne', *Journal of Sociology*, 44(3), 219–32.

Walter, M (ed.) 2019, *Social Research Methods*, 4th edn, Oxford University Press, Melbourne.

Zivkovic, T, Warin, M, Davies, M & Moore, V 2010, 'In the name of the child: the gendered politics of childhood obesity', *Journal of Sociology*, 46(4), 353–74.

CHAPTER 5

Modernity and modernisation

GLENDA BALLANTYNE

CHAPTER OVERVIEW

A key concept for understanding contemporary societies is 'modernity'. Sociologists use this term to refer to the intellectual, cultural, economic, political and technological developments that began transforming social life in the seventeenth century, ushering in a historic shift away from traditional ways of life. The changes involved were so unprecedented, thinkers at the time had to find brand new ways to make sense of the world—and one of these new ways of thinking was the development of sociology itself! Since then, 'big picture' sociology has been devoted to understanding these changes, how they impact on us today, and how society is evolving.

These developments emerged first in Western Europe, but by the twentieth century they had transformed societies around the world. Their impact has been momentous. They overturned forms of social organisation that human beings had lived with for thousands of years, and ultimately transformed what it means to be human. The advent of modernity has opened up previously undreamed-of possibilities for human beings, but it has also created new forms of destruction, conflict and constraint.

Understanding this complicated picture and the dynamics pulling in different directions is crucial if we are to find our way into comprehending our contemporary society, and work towards a viable, equitable future. In this chapter, we look at the institutional 'infrastructure' of modern societies and explore what is so distinctive about modern ways of thinking, before examining the sometimes contradictory trends shaping contemporary social life and its evolution.

After reading this chapter, you should be able to:
- Define the term 'modernity'
- Identify the main differences between traditional and modern societies
- Identify the key components of modernity
- Describe the underlying dynamics shaping modernity and its transformations
- Explain in what ways modernity is ambiguous.

KEY TERMS

Agency The ability (or power) of an individual or group ('agent') to act independently of the external constraints of social structures—making decisions, undertaking actions and confronting authorities.

Bureaucracy A type of organisation based on rational principles, hierarchy of authority and written rules, and staffed by full-time officials.

Capitalism An economic system based on the private ownership of wealth, which is invested to produce profit. Its driving principle is the accumulation of profit, which demands ever-increasing levels of consumption.

Colonialism The political rule, and often cultural domination, of one nation over another.

Democracy In a general sense, the 'rule of the people'. There are different interpretations of democracy, encompassing the principles of the participation of citizens in political decision making, the presence of civil liberties and equality.

Democratic revolution The idea, sparked by the American Revolution (1775–83) and the French Revolution (1789–99), that people should have a say in how they are governed.

Individualisation The expansion of the scope of individual preference and choice in defining our identities, our life paths and our relationships.

Industrial revolution The economic and related social transformations produced by industrialisation.

Industrialisation The harnessing of advanced forms of energy to power mechanised production. It involves the application of science and technology to industrial processes.

McDonaldisation George Ritzer's term for the intensification of rationalisation in contemporary societies. It refers to the extension of the principles of fast-food restaurants—such as efficiency, calculation and predictability—to more and more spheres of social life.

Modernisation The social processes that brought about the transition from traditional to modern societies. These include industrialisation, urbanisation, rationalisation, and a shift in consciousness that fostered the idea that human beings have agency.

Modernity The social structures and ways of thinking that have been shaped by the industrial, scientific and democratic revolutions.

Multiple modernities The many different forms that modernity takes around the globe. Patterns vary across nations, regions and civilisations.

Nation state A political community in a recognised territorial space in which a centralised government exercises authority to rule on behalf of a national community or communities; among its citizens, there is a strong sense of belonging to a shared community. Note that Chapter 10 of this book discusses nation states.

Nationalism A set of symbols and beliefs that provide the sense of being part of a single political community; also refers to loyalty to and promotion of the nation.

Neoliberalism The political ideology and economic policies that promote a 'pure' form of capitalism, as free as possible from government regulation.

Rationalisation The spread of precise calculation and efficiency as the primary principles for social organisation.

Scientific revolution The origins of modern Western science in the sixteenth century, based on detached observation, evidence and reason.

Traditional societies The range of pre-modern societies. These varied widely, but all were non-industrial, primarily rural, and characterised by meaning-based rather than reason-based world views.

▷

Introduction

Have you ever thought about what your life would have been like if you had been born 300 years ago? You might think first about the absence of material comforts we take for granted: your television, the internet, your smartphone. Technology was rudimentary by our standards, with production, transport and communication relying on people and animal 'muscle power'. Unless you were very wealthy or powerful, you would have had very basic shelter, worked the land, walked on your rare trips to neighbouring villages or townships, and heard 'news' through word of mouth, or possibly from someone who could read a newspaper. And then there would have been the food. 'Gruel' is a meal that comes to mind—cereal or rice boiled in milk or water.

But 'standard of living' in this sense is not the only part of social life that has been revolutionised over the past several centuries. In the pre-modern world, the majority of people had little say in how they were governed. In fact, they lived strongly predetermined personal lives, governed by social expectations, religious doctrine or tradition. Social hierarchies were rigid, and questioning them was virtually unthinkable because they were considered to be divinely ordained.

Our world—of hi-tech production, mass consumption, global communication networks and individualistic orientation—is in many respects a major advance on life in **traditional societies**. It offers us unheard-of levels of wealth, and unprecedented opportunities for personal fulfilment and creativity. At the same time, however, we often have the feeling we are caught up in a relentless, even inhuman system, and sometimes we have the nagging doubt that we have lost something important.

On closer inspection, many of our 'choices' seem rather shallow. We have gained individual freedom, but seem to have lost community feeling. What is more, the technological developments that have vastly expanded wealth and created quite extraordinary opportunities for communication around the globe, have also intensified the destructive impact of warfare, subjected us to new forms of surveillance, and unleashed environmental destruction.

The emergence of **modernity**, it seems, has been a double-edged sword; our modern world is both exciting and disturbing, offering us great opportunities and throwing up new dangers. The future shape of our societies, and perhaps even our planet, depends on how we collectively manage the promises and threats thrown up by modernity. Disagreement over the best way forward is inevitable. One thing is sure, though: we will be in a much better position to choose wisely between the options before us if we understand the forces that created modernity, and the dynamics that are shaping its evolution.

In this chapter, we will try to get a handle on this thing called 'modernity'. First of all, we will look at the way modernising processes unfolded around the world, identifying the core components of modernity. Then we will look at the deep dynamics that have shaped modernity and its continuing evolution. To conclude, we will reflect on where we are heading.

Let us start, though, by getting an initial idea about what we are talking about!

What is modernity?

We will be trying to answer this question throughout the chapter, but let us begin with a definition. As Van Krieken and colleagues (2010, p. 7) point out, sociologists generally use the term 'modernity' to describe:

> the complex range of phenomena associated with the historical process, commencing in the 17th century, which saw Western societies change from a feudal to a capitalist economic framework, with most of their populations migrating from rural, village settings to towns and cities, as well as moving beyond Western Europe in the process of colonising much of the rest of the world.

This gives a very useful starting point—the tricky bit will be pinning down that 'complex range of phenomena'! We will look at the core components in a moment, but first some background might help.

There are three landmarks in European history that helped bring about the transition from traditional to modern societies. The scale of their impact is evident in that they are all referred to as 'revolutions' (Furze et al., 2015, p. 10):

- The first was the '**scientific revolution**'. With its origins in the mid-sixteenth century in Europe, this revolution overturned traditional ways of thinking, based on belief and speculation, by insisting that knowledge about the world must be based on detached observation, evidence and reason.
- The second was the '**democratic revolution**'. Sparked by the American Revolution (1775–83) and the French Revolution (1789–99), this revolution overturned traditional forms of political power and authority by fostering the idea that people should have a say in how they are governed.
- The third was the '**industrial revolution**'. Unfolding in the eighteenth century, this revolution triggered dramatic economic changes by applying science and technology to production processes.

These revolutions helped create the political and economic institutions that are at the centre of modernity, such as the industrial capitalist economy and the nation state. Just as importantly, however, they created distinctively modern forms of consciousness (or ways of thinking). In their own ways, each of these revolutions helped create a very revolutionary idea: things can be different to how they are. For us, this seems obvious. But to bring about this new outlook, the pre-modern ideas that the social order is divinely ordained and that the proper way to do things was how they had always been done, had to be overturned.

Tied up with these revolutionary ideas was another—the idea that human beings could be in control of their lives. Sociologists refer to this development as a growing sense of human **agency** (which we discussed in Chapter 3). In traditional societies, people had little control over their lives, and mostly believed their destiny was determined by God, or by fate. Together, the scientific, democratic and industrial revolutions gave human beings the possibility of greater control over their destiny, and with it a new conception of themselves as agents.

Before we launch into our exploration of the economic, political and cultural components of modernity, it will be helpful to think about *how* this form of social organisation has come to dominate the world.

Modernisation

The term '**modernisation**' refers to the processes of social change involved in the transition from traditional to modern societies. **Industrialisation** is one of the most important, but so too are the emergence of nation states and the spread of capitalism. Along with these go other processes including urbanisation and the setting up of mass education systems. We can see straight away that modernising processes such as these unfolded gradually, over long periods of time. They were consolidated in Europe over the nineteenth and early twentieth centuries. In other parts of the world, they began later and in many cases are still occurring (and given the upheaval they cause, are being resisted by some).

If we take a global perspective on modernisation, two points stand out. The first is that the emergence of modernity was tied up with the rise of Western global power, which saw European powers **colonise** vast swathes of territories and countries around the globe (see Box 5.1). This was a factor in the way modernisation occurred in Europe—European countries had access to the natural resources of their colonies. The cotton mills of England, for example, relied on cotton extracted under British rule in India. Western global power was also a crucial factor in the way modernisation has unfolded around the world. As noted in Chapter 3, many European powers aggressively imposed modernisation in the colonies they ruled. So for many people in the world, modernity arrived via a gunboat.

BOX 5.1

Sociology in history

COLONIALISM

From the sixteenth to the twentieth century, European powers imposed, often brutally, political control over vast swathes of territories and countries around the globe in a process called colonialisation (this is also discussed in Chapter 9). One way to map this process is to think of the national languages of contemporary societies around the world. Why is English widely spoken in India? Why is Spanish spoken so extensively in South America, and Portuguese used in Brazil? And think about Africa, where English is spoken in Nigeria and Ghana, French in Algeria, and German in Namibia.

The second point to note is that modernising processes have unfolded in markedly different ways around the world. Non-Western countries have been greatly influenced by Western patterns of modernisation, often not by choice, but their diverse social and cultural contexts have seen modernity unfold in distinctive ways. A quick glance at India, China or Turkey (or Yemen, which we will examine in Chapter 11) shows this diversity. China does not have a democratic political system. India's vibrant democracy has a more 'communal' element than the Western version, where there is a focus on individual rights. Arranged marriages are still common in India, but often in a modern form, where the partners willingly participate and can accept or reject the match. In Turkey, some highly educated women choose to wear the veil while being politically active in Islamist political movements.

Recognising this diversity has led to a significant shift in the way sociologists understand modernity. For a long time, many thought the European pattern was *the* model of modernity. It was often taken as the benchmark for all modernising societies, and any divergence from it was taken to be a sign of incomplete or imperfect modernisation. More recently, a new perspective has challenged this Eurocentric view. The **'multiple modernities'** approach argues that while the same core components are present in all modernities, social and cultural legacies always shape the forms they take (see Box 5.2). There are, according to this approach, multiple ways of being modern, and the Western way is only one among many.

Sociologists are now studying the many different forms of modernity in earnest. These studies are fascinating, and key to understanding the full experience of modernity. For this introduction to the concept, though, we will focus on the pattern of modernity that emerged in Western Europe, in particular the core components of:

- Industrialisation;
- Capitalism;
- The nation state;
- Culture; and
- Identity and agency.

BOX 5.2

Thinking sociologically

DIFFERENT EXPERIENCES OF MODERNITY

As noted above, there are many sociologists who discuss the concept of 'multiple modernities' and criticise the idea of a single narrative of modernity. Their position is to raise concerns about some of the fundamental underlying (and often unspoken) assumptions connected to the dominant Eurocentric account of modernity. Some points raised include the assumption of linear progress inherited from the philosophy of the European Enlightenment, the centring and universalising of a vision of the world that is rooted in European imperialism, and a racialised hierarchy that has traditionally placed European society as superior. These are complex but important ideas to unpack if we are to more fully understand our modern world (Hall & Gieben 2011).

Many of the core components of modernity explored in this chapter are philosophically grounded in the ideas of European philosophers that culminated in the mid-eighteenth century in a period of European intellectual history that came to be known as the Enlightenment (Hamilton 2011). In his (1874) essay, *An answer to the question: what is Enlightenment?* Immanuel Kant identified five principles central to Enlightenment thought: liberty, progress, equality, reason and dignity. These principles continue to underpin the core institutions and laws of contemporary nation states and international frameworks like the United Nations Declaration of Human Rights. While there are many positive aspects of such thinking, it is important that we also look below the surface and critique some of its assumptions.

One set of problems we can identify is that though they may have been conceived as 'universal' ideals they were only ever intended to apply to a narrow subset of humanity—basically to respectable European (white) men. In order to resolve this apparent contradiction, a clear boundary was needed between those entitled to 'universal' rights and those who were excluded. It is within this context that philosophers from the eighteenth and nineteenth century evolved the concept of what it means to be 'fully human'—with different kinds of people being defined as more or less human (Balibar 1994).

Many of the prejudices that continue to be experienced by different groups of people in our society today can be traced back to this idea. For example, ideas such as women being regarded as less rational than men, disabled people being considered less capable than able-bodied people and the racial discrimination that arises from the idea of a racial hierarchy that positioned 'civilised' European (white) people as morally superior and as legitimate rulers. As we will see in later chapters, such ideas justified imperial projects including colonisation and the dispossession and exploitation of other 'inferior' people that this entailed.

Many of the challenges to the dominant and singular view of modernity come from those positioned at the margins of this world order based on European (white) supremacy, including Black, Indigenous, feminist and queer scholars. They question both the universal assumption that modernity equals progress and also the terms on which this is judged. These different perspectives are explored in later chapters, but what is important to hold in mind whilst wrapping your head around this force called modernity is that (like everything we study as sociologists) it arose in a particular social and historical context and was driven by specific social and political factors. Furthermore, and perhaps even more importantly, the resulting injustices are not confined to history but are ever-present in different peoples' lived experiences of modernity.

This is why we use the term 'multiple modernities': for the experiences of the many processes of modernity have been beneficial for many, while disastrous for others. As sociologists, we need to recognise these complexities.

Modernity: core components

Industrialisation

One of the core components of modernity is an economic structure based on industrial production. Industrialisation led to a massive increase in productivity: it was 10 times more productive than agricultural production reliant on human and animal 'muscle power', and 100 times more powerful than that of hunters and gatherers. At the same time, it accelerated technological change, setting in motion a process of ongoing innovation (Nolan & Lenski 2010).

Industrialisation has produced much greater levels of wealth than any previous form of society, but this is not the only change it has wrought on our lives. It prompted a massive population migration into towns and cities. Living in large cities created more diverse communities and fostered greater cultural creativity but at the same time weakened the strong kinship ties, sense of community and collective sentiments that had characterised pre-industrial societies. Furthermore, in industrialised and urbanised societies more individualistic attitudes flourished, replacing sentiments such as virtue and honour that had guided life in pre-modern societies.

Capitalism

A second key feature of modern economic systems is **capitalism**. In Europe, the spread of capitalism was closely intertwined with industrialisation, and the industrial capitalist economy that swept away the agrarian-based feudal system. Peasants and serfs became urban factory workers, and the 'bourgeoisie'—who invested their accumulated capital in the new factories—replaced feudal landowners as the main owners of wealth.

Capitalism changed more than just the economy. It transformed the way people relate to each other in a very profound way. In the feudal system, peasants had been little more than the property of feudal lords, and exchanged their labour for shelter and a tiny proportion of what they produced. Industrial workers in the new capitalist economy were 'freed' from their ties to particular lords, and exchanged their labour for a wage.

A radical change in sentiment followed from this development. While power and economic differences between feudal nobles and serfs had been extreme, the nobles and the serfs had also been bound together by longstanding traditions and a host of mutual obligations. In the new economic system, those ties dissolved, and traditional values such as pride and honour were replaced with those of naked self-interest and the unconstrained pursuit of profit (Macionis & Plummer 2012). As Karl Marx famously said, this left the new industrial workers 'free' to starve—something we discuss in Chapter 6.

Capitalism has been a dynamic economic system, but it has also been prone to crises, such as the Great Depression that preceded the Second World War and the Global Financial Crisis of 2007–08. It has also been an adaptable system. Workers fought for and achieved some reforms that improved their working conditions, and after the Great Depression, in some parts of the world these reforms were coupled with a 'welfare state'—a concept that refers to countries providing a 'safety net' for the most vulnerable members of society. In other parts of the world, capitalism has been coupled with a stronger guiding hand of government. In its 'pure' form, however, it is based on a 'free' market—free from government regulation and concern for other social values, such as equity or fairness.

The nation state

Another core component of modernity is the **nation state**, something we discuss in Chapter 10. This distinctly modern type of state (or political apparatus) differs significantly from political administrations of the pre-modern era, such as empires and kingdoms. In contrast to modern nation states, the boundaries of these pre-modern states were fluid, and rulers often had limited control over their subjects and territory. In empires, rule was frequently from a distance and depended on local political structures. In kingdoms, monarchs technically ruled, but actual control of territory was mostly in the hands of regional feudal lords. Few people had strong emotional connections with such states, identifying primarily with their village or region, local lord or tribe.

The rise of the nation state was a crucial factor in the emergence of modernity, because it provided a stable political and institutional framework for the development of industry and capitalism. It also brought about some significant shifts in the way people are governed, and changed relationships between those who belonged to nations and those who were considered 'outsiders'.

NATIONALISM

The first change in the way people are governed has to do with the emergence of a new nationalist form of collective identity. In contrast to the citizens of pre-modern states, citizens of nation states have a strong sense of belonging to a shared community—the shared community of a *nation*. Historically, the idea of a nation was built on the idea of a common ethnicity, but more recently some conceptions of the nation have tried to be more 'cosmopolitan', defining the nation simply in terms of shared values and adherence to the laws and political system of the land. Both conceptions are modern developments, fostered by political elites to generate loyalty to the new nation states.

Nations are symbolic entities, based on the belief that members share a common history, along with language and culture. Benedict Anderson (1983) points out that nations are 'imagined'—a nation is not a community where people know each personally, but a set of shared symbols and practices that generate a sense of loyalty to fellow members. In Australia, national symbols include the ANZAC legend, ideas of egalitarianism, thongs and 'barbies'.

Being imagined, however, does not make the nation an insubstantial thing. On the contrary, identification with the nation is frequently profound. We feel its strength when we care passionately about Australian athletes at the Olympics, or when some us feel compelled to make sacrifices—even to the point of laying down our lives—to defend 'our' nation. In some cases, this sentiment takes the form of militaristic ideologies that argue for the superiority of one's own country and traditions. Nationalism in this form has been at the centre of many conflicts, and is still used to justify war or 'ethnic cleansing'.

BUREAUCRATIC ADMINISTRATION

The second shift in the way people are governed is connected to the development of bureaucratic administration. Administration in pre-modern societies was patchy and partial. Status, privilege and social position were more important in the appointment of officials than competence, and the work of administration was often a part-time sideline undertaken by a person of high social standing. As one of the founding figures of sociology, Max Weber (1864–1920) pointed out that modern nation states needed a different kind of administration. Capitalism in particular required that 'the official business of public administration be discharged precisely, unambiguously, continuously, and with as much speed as possible' (Weber 1978, p. 974). The development of extensive **bureaucracies** in modern nation states has served this purpose.

Bureaucratic organisation of government administration clearly has much going for it and is crucial to the running of complex modern societies. But sociologists have long identified a troubling side effect: bureaucratic administration has allowed government control over citizens to become more centralised, more intensive and more far-reaching. Bureaucratic state agencies—such as prisons, the police force, the tax office and departments of human services—reach into more and more parts of our lives, and can encroach on individual rights and freedoms. Weber feared that growing bureaucratisation had the potential to crush human creativity and reduce people to being 'only a small cog in a ceaselessly moving mechanism' (1978, p. 988).

DEMOCRACY

The third shift in the way people are governed is associated with a move towards **democracy**. Not all modern nation states are democratic. The case of China demonstrates that it is possible to have a modern, industrialised and capitalist economy without democracy. However, the modern world has seen a significant trend away from the despotic rule of monarchs, emperors and sultans, and many countries have political systems in which citizens elect political representatives, and there are civil liberties such as freedom of association and speech.

We should note, however, that this is not a pre-determined pathway. Many researchers have recently raised concerns about the emergence of 'new despotisms': that is, nations that once seemed on a pathway to democracy and have changed course (Levitsky & Ziblatt 2019).

The democratic ideal also operates in modern societies in broader ways. The aspiration to extend democracy throughout social life has been a central feature of modernity, particularly through the mobilisation of *social movements*. Social movements differ from political parties in that they mobilise outside the formal political system and are characterised by a much looser, informal and fluid form of organisation (see the discussion in Chapter 15). Their ambitions are often very different to those of political parties—they are often seeking to change values of their societies rather than to gain political power. While rarely achieving political control, social movements have greatly influenced modern societies. The workers' movement won many reforms that alleviated the harshness of industrial capitalism. Similarly, the 'new' social movements since the 1960s have achieved reforms in the areas of civil, women's, and gay and lesbian rights, and brought about significant cultural shifts in these areas. The ecology and Occupy Wall Street movements have challenged the logic of industrial capitalism and the kind of thinking and behaviour it encourages (Ballantyne 2006a; Ballantyne 2006b).

Culture (and counterculture)

Just as central to modernity as the new economic system and the new forms of politics are new forms of culture and consciousness. Three cultural innovations in particular are core elements of modernity.

The first is the *dominance of the scientific outlook*. Modern science has had many major, direct impacts on the emergence of modernity. Most obviously, it underlies the technological developments that fuelled industrialisation, and have continued to provide us with new medicines, new gadgets and new communication networks. But the rise of science has also changed how we *see* the world. In traditional societies, people saw the world as profoundly imbued with meaning, and thought it to be governed by magic or mystical forces. The 'world' in this sense encompasses both nature and society. Some believed that spirits inhabited nature; others that a person's fate was at the mercy of a multitude of warring gods; and others that God created the universe for a purpose. In modernity, in contrast, the world is mainly viewed through the prism of scientific thinking. From a scientific point of view, the world is an objective reality, without inherent meaning, and we turn to scientific observation and reasoning to gain knowledge of it. Many people hold religious beliefs, but for the most part they see them as compatible with science. In the words of Max Weber, the world has become 'disenchanted'.

The second cultural innovation is the *shift from tradition to instrumental rationality as the principal mode of human thought*. 'Instrumental rationality' is not concerned with reasoning about what we should be aiming for, as a society or as individuals, but with calculating the most efficient means to an end. In traditional societies, sentiments and beliefs passed from generation to generation governed behaviour, and notions of 'God's will' or preserving the past would often determine a person's path of action (Macionis & Plummer 2012). In modernity, for most of us, the principle of efficiency carries much more weight. Think about your decision to undertake a university degree. You probably spent more time calculating whether the cost of your course and time involved undertaking it will be outweighed by future income, than you did considering its value in preparing you to be a good citizen. This is not a personal criticism! It is a reflection of our contemporary culture and circumstances.

The third cultural innovation is the *belief in progress*. The idea that human beings and their societies could be improved, or even perfected, used to be entirely foreign to traditional ways of thinking, but it became a driving force in the early period of modernity. Scientific knowledge and rational thinking were seen as key to progress, fostering the belief that science can provide the answers to all the questions and problems that confront human beings, including those of society.

The influence of the ideals of science, rationality and progress was greatly fostered by the Enlightenment. But the rise of scientific, rational thinking was also contested. Playing a key role in a 'counterculture' was another philosophical movement that sought to discover new forms of meaning and creativity. Philosophers—and writers, poets and novelists—associated with the Romantic movement favoured emotion over reason and creativity over formal rules, and valued ideas of human connection with nature and artistic originality. They encouraged the idea that our truest selves are to be found within our 'inner depths', and were interested in the distinctive identities of folk cultures, and ethnic and national groups.

Identity and agency

These cultural shifts have had a profound impact on the way we see ourselves. The Canadian social philosopher Charles Taylor (2008) has explored the 'modern identity'. In traditional societies, he points out, people were defined by their position in the social order. Such social orders were very hierarchical, and they were also fixed. They were thought of as 'divinely ordained', and it was unthinkable to challenge them: people 'knew their place'. In modernity, we are no longer defined in these terms; we are, rather, '*self-defining*'.

As we noted at the beginning of this chapter (as well as in Chapter 3), underlying this shift is a new sense of human 'agency'. In modernity, people have a much greater sense of themselves as agents: able, up to a point, to take action independently of social structures.

However, when we look at this more closely, things get more complicated—and rather more interesting! Taylor (2008) points out there are two quite different modern ideas of agency. The first is the widespread view that our agency stems from our capacity to use reason to control our emotions. The second is the idea that we are agents because we have the capacity to express ourselves creatively (Taylor 2008).

Deep dynamics

We have an idea of the core components of modernity now. But what are the underlying dynamics that shaped its unfolding? If we stand back and look at the components we have just examined, we can see that there is no single dynamic that defines modernity; rather, there are two distinct, and rather contradictory, trends that are evident.

The pursuit of wealth and power

The first dynamic is an intensification of the pursuit of wealth and power. Of course, people have sought wealth and power throughout human history. But in pre-modern societies, the pursuit of wealth and power was tempered by other values, such as honour, tradition or notions of 'doing God's will'. In modernity, this pursuit has become a core value.

Maximising wealth and power are not only the main goals for many individuals, they are the principle on which the modern institutions of the industrial capitalist economy and the bureaucratic nation state are based—and for many people, it is even how we measure success. Industrial technology is deployed to promote efficiency at the cost of humanness, as for example in the production lines on which people have little room for human skill or creativity. Capitalism, as we have seen, is based on the principle of maximising profit—and it often maximises profit with little consideration for creativity and desire to express ourselves as individuals. Similarly, the bureaucratic state is geared to maximising control over its territory and citizens.

Underlying this dynamic is a whole new way of thinking, which was summed up by the Greek–French social theorist Cornelius Castoriadis as a 'vision of rational mastery'. Its essence is an aspiration to control nature and society through the application of reason (Smith 2014).

Autonomy and creativity

The second dynamic pulls in the opposite direction. As well as the pursuit of power and wealth, we see in modernity a heightened aspiration to freedom and creativity. Castoriadis uses the term '*autonomy*' to describe this aspiration (Adams 2014)—referring to freedom from the rule of others or, to put it another way, the capacity to be in charge of or 'govern' oneself. It applies to both individuals and collectives. Democracy is one of the most significant sites of autonomy in modernity, but the ideal of autonomy also motivates many social movements. Some important examples have been the struggle of nations for independence from colonial rule, and the struggle of women as a group against the dependence created by patriarchal systems, for instance when women are denied work or relegated to poor-paying jobs, or are seen as 'objects' rather than as 'subjects' engaged in their own life projects.

This dynamic also encompasses the growing aspiration to and opportunity for human *creativity*. Creativity too can be individual or collective. It is expressed in works of art, but also in our daily lives, in how we dress, listen to or make music and create social networks.

Modernity, it seems, is a very ambiguous social form, characterised by tensions and contradictions. It is for these reasons we need to acknowledge both the countless benefits of modernity as well as the many problems and challenges that have emerged.

Where are we heading?

So what lies in store for us? Has society not radically changed again in recent years? Some have argued that we are now moving beyond modernity, into a new epoch of 'postmodernity'. The concept of postmodernity suggests that the modern era is giving way to a new period in which belief in science, rationality, progress and enlightenment no longer hold sway, and the patterns of social life established in modernity are being transformed.

However, many sociologists argue that the emerging social patterns constitute a new phase within modernity. I am with them. If we look closely at some of the main developments, we can see many continuities, and the ongoing presence of the deep dynamics of modernity. Here are three examples of what I mean.

Individualisation

The first example is what sociologists have termed **individualisation**. German sociologists Ulrick Beck and Elisabeth Beck-Gernsheim (2002) have explored a recent trend in our life paths and our personal relationships, particularly evident in the Western world. They argue that since the late twentieth century, both have become significantly less constrained by social expectations stemming from the family, religion and tradition. At the same time, social developments associated with the unfolding of modernity have increasingly expanded our options. Key factors are rising levels of education and living standards, and the opening up of opportunities for work for women. The result, they suggest, is not simply that we are now freer to create our own life path, but that we are *forced* to do so. Now, 'more people than ever before are being forced to piece together their own biographies and fit in the components as best they can … the normal life history is giving way to the do-it-yourself life history' (Beck & Beck-Gernsheim 2002, p. 88).

Individualisation has also had a big impact on personal relationships, including families and marriages. Even love and sexuality are being transformed. As Beck and Beck-Gernsheim put it, it is 'no longer possible to pronounce in some binding way what family, marriage, parenthood, sexuality or love mean, what they should or could be; rather these vary in substance, norms and morality from individual to individual and from relationship to relationship' (2002, p. 5). And on top of this, 'Love is becoming a blank that lovers must fill in themselves' (2002, p. 5).

These changes are very significant. But as Beck and Beck-Gernsheim point out, these changes have their roots in long-term developments that began in the early stages of modernity. Individualisation increased as social and geographical mobility created by the new economic relationships of industrial capitalism and urbanisation began breaking up people's dependency on the pre-industrial family. What is more, the intensification of this trend in the late twentieth century is related to developments unfolding within the capitalist economy.

While this trend altered traditional family relationships, individualisation has also created new possibilities for individual autonomy. As a result, many people have embraced it for the self-determination it offers.

BOX 5.3

Everyday sociology

INDIVIDUALISATION AT THE MOVIES

We can trace the long unfolding of 'individualisation' in the sphere of personal life through two relatively recent movies. In the 2005 film of Jane Austen's *Pride and Prejudice*, we see how the early modern shift towards individual choice and freedom affected women's place in society. In the early 1800s, when the story was set, family and class structures determined women's life course. Marriage was virtually the only choice open to women and was therefore a major source of their identity. We also see the importance of a woman's 'reputation'. The constraints of social rank and hierarchy are at the heart of the narrative, with the class differences between Elizabeth and Mr Darcy a major obstacle to their marriage. What the story chronicles, though, is the beginning of the breakdown of these structures and expectations; we see the emergence of the idea that romantic love should be a basis for marriage, and that social conventions and rank can be challenged.

The intensification of individualisation in the last half of the twentieth century is nicely shown in the film *Pride* (2014). Set in 1984, the title refers to the emergence of the Gay Pride movement, and the film tells us a lot about growing diversity and choice in sexual identity and relationships. But the title also refers to the pride the Welsh miners had in their working-class identity and traditions, and this gives us a glimpse of the sources of identity that predominated over the course of the twentieth century. Particularly in Western societies, class identities associated with workers and the 'middle class' were strong, and many people proudly identified with their working-class origins. The decline in this sentiment over recent decades is tied up with increasing individualisation.

Consumer society

Another major change in modernity in the second half of the twentieth century was the dramatic expansion of the significance of consumption in our lives. In the first phases of modernity, consumption still met relatively basic needs for the bulk of the population. In the 1960s and 70s, however, we entered a new era. We now buy clothes that last for only a season and update our phones and devices at an ever-accelerating rate. More and more parts of life have been turned into commodities that we purchase; for example, we buy experiences (entertainment, travel), health (we go to gyms in our fancy sports gear), and love and caring (in the United States, people pay others to sit with their dying parents). At the same time, goods have become more than functional; now they are markers of our lifestyle and identities, and we increasingly define 'who we are' in terms of the things we consume (Langer 1996).

There is lively debate among sociologists about the meaning of this change in our societies, but most connect our new consumption patterns to the deep dynamics of modernity. Some connect it to the pursuit of profit and expanding **rationalisation**. Beryl Langer (2006), for example, points out that the rise of consumer society was prompted not by the 'needs' of consumers/workers, but by the needs of capitalism: demand had to be increased to match the greater output of the new techniques of mass production. George Ritzer (2000) points out that the principle of instrumental rationality saturates our new patterns of production and consumption. He coined the term **McDonaldisation** to sum up the four basic elements of rationalisation: efficiency, calculability, uniformity and predictability, and control through automation. If you want to see what he means, think for a minute about the McDonald's chain, with its thousands of outlets churning out near identical burgers around the globe. The company uses precise calculations to generate maximum output and maximum uniformity, all with maximum efficiency.

Other sociologists take a different view of the new role of consumption in our lives. They argue that new levels of consumption have provided us with new resources for expressing our creativity and defining our identities. They point to niche markets, local variations in the products of global chains such as McDonald's, and the ways people 'personalise' the commodities they buy, using them in individual and creative ways (Woodward 2011). Another focus in this area is the rising trend for sustainable and collaborative consumption. That is, consumers focus on buying 'fair trade' coffee and boycotting products that have a problematic environmental history. Collaborative consumption is the move to share goods and services.

Still, this interpretation connects with the deep dynamics of modernity; from this point of view, the new trends in consumption are more connected to the dynamic of growing self-expression and self-determination.

Neoliberalism

One last sign of a new phase of modernity is the rise to global dominance of **neoliberalism**. In this context, 'liberalism' refers to a political philosophy of maximum individual and economic freedom from government control. Liberalism was the political framework in which capitalism emerged, and it was only over many years that regulations to improve working conditions (think 12-hour days, child labour and unsafe machinery in what were known as 'the Satanic mills' of England) and protect the vulnerable were instituted.

*Neo*liberalism refers to the recent political movement to return to policies that promote a 'pure' form of capitalism, as free as possible from government regulation. Two of its main planks are the privatisation of government-owned utilities and the deregulation of as much of the economy as possible. Neoliberalism has gathered momentum in the period of globalisation since the 1980s, and many sociologists see it as the most significant trend reshaping contemporary societies around the world (Walby 2009).

Neoliberalism is transforming our lives in very significant ways. Two examples that might be relevant to you are that work is becoming more precarious, and education more expensive! The global spread of neoliberalism has also been identified as a key factor in increasing inequalities that have fuelled the rise of populist movements such as those supporting Donald Trump and Brexit (Sandel 2018). As the very term suggests, however, this trend has direct connection to earlier phases of modernity that privilege the pursuit of wealth.

Conclusion

This has been a long journey—we have travelled from the 1550s to the 2020s all in one chapter! Hopefully the trip has shown how radical the changes brought about by modernity have been. Along the way, we have also seen that modernity is a very distinctive and very dynamic type of society. No social entity is ever static, but modernity—more than any social type that preceded it—has been characterised by ongoing, rapid change. It is also highly contradictory, with core developments pulling in different directions. We cannot predict exactly what our societies will look like in the future, but we can expect that our path ahead will be shaped by the deep dynamics of modernity.

Summary points

- The transition from traditional to modern societies brought about a spiral of change unprecedented in human history.
- Modernity emerged first in Western Europe, but has developed in distinctive ways around the globe, creating 'multiple modernities'.
- Modernity is a social form that is full of tensions and conflicts.
- The key tension is between a vision of infinitely expanding rational mastery of nature and society, and the individual and collective aspiration to autonomy and creativity.
- Modernity has created new opportunities for expressing human agency and autonomy, and new forms of constraint.
- These dynamics continue to shape the unfolding of modernity, even as it undergoes major transformations.

Sociological reflection

1. Reflect on what life would have been like 300 years ago. What would a regular day look like? What would be different about your 'world view'?
2. Compare your life to that of your grandparents. How is your experience of relationships, love and sex different from theirs?
3. Reflect on where you see Australia, and the world more generally, heading. Are things getting better or worse? Or both?

Discussion questions

1. How do modern societies differ from traditional ones?
2. What are some of the key institutions of modernity?
3. What distinguishes modern ways of thinking from traditional ones?
4. What are the deep dynamics that underlie modern institutions and consciousness?
5. In what ways is modernity ambiguous?
6. Is society becoming 'McDonaldised'?
7. Is there a downside to the growing individualisation of our life paths?
8. Has consumer society made us more creative, or more manipulated? Does it make us happy?
9. In what ways, if any, should governments regulate the capitalist economy?

References and further reading

REFERENCES

Adams, S 2014, 'Autonomy', in *Cornelius Castoriadis: Key Concepts*, Bloomsbury Publishing, London.

Anderson, B 1983, *Imagined Communities: Reflections on the Origin and Spread of Nationalism*, Verso, London.

Balibar, É 1994, 'Racism as universalism', in *Masses, Classes, Ideas: Studies on Politics and Philosophy Before and after Marx*, Routledge, London.

Ballantyne, G 2006a, 'Gender', in P Beilharz & T Hogan (eds), *Sociology: Time, Place and Division*, Oxford University Press, South Melbourne, pp. 383–7.

Ballantyne, G 2006b, 'Social movements', in P Beilharz & T Hogan (eds), *Sociology: Time, Place and Division*, Oxford University Press, South Melbourne, pp. 420–5.

Beck, U & Beck-Gernsheim, E 2002, *Individualization: Institutionalized Individualism and its Social and Political Consequence*, SAGE Publications, London.

Furze, B, Savy, P, Webb, R, James, S, Petray, T, Brym, RJ, & Lie, J 2015, *Sociology in Today's World*, 3rd edn, Cengage Learning, South Melbourne.

Hall, S & Gieben, B (eds) 2011, *Formations of Modernity: Understanding Modern Societies an Introduction Book 1* (reprinted). Polity Press, Cambridge.

Hamilton, P 2011, 'The enlightenment and the birth of social science', in S Hall & B Gieben (eds), *Formations of Modernity* (reprinted), Polity Press, Cambridge.

Langer, B 1996, 'The consuming self', in A Kellehear (ed.), *Social Self, Global Culture*, Oxford University Press, South Melbourne, pp. 57–8.

Langer, B 2006, 'Consumption', in P Beilharz & T Hogan (eds), *Sociology: Place, Time and Division*, Oxford University Press, South Melbourne, pp. 250–4.

Levitsky, S & Ziblatt, D 2019, *How Democracies Die: What History Reveals about Our Future*, Penguin Books, London.

Macionis, J & Plummer, K 2012, *Sociology: A Global Introduction*, 5th edn, Pearson Prentice Hall, Harlow.

Nolan P & Lenski, J 2010, *Human Societies: An Introduction to Macrosociology*, 11th edn, McGraw-Hill, New York.

Ritzer, G 2000, *The McDonaldisation of Society*, Pine Forge Press, Thousand Oaks.

Smith, K 2014, 'Modernity', in S Adams (ed.), *Cornelius Castoriadis: Key Concepts*, Bloomsbury Publishing, London.

Sandel, M 2018 'Populism, Trump and the future of democracy', *Open Democracy*: <www.opendemocracy.net/en/populism-trump-and-future-of-democracy/>.

Taylor, C 2008, 'The making of modern identity', in S Seidman & J Alexander (eds), *The New Social Theory Reader*, 2nd edn, Routledge, Abingdon.

Van Krieken, R, Habibis, D, Smith, P, Hutchins, B, Haralambos, M & Holborn, M (eds) 2010, *Sociology*, 4th edn, Pearson, Frenchs Forest.

Walby, S 2009, *Globalization and Inequalities*, SAGE Publications, Los Angeles, CA.

Weber, M 1978, 'Conceptual explosion', in G Roth & C Wittich (eds), *Economy and Society*, University of California Press, Berkeley, CA.

Woodward, I 2011, 'Consumption and lifestyles', in J Germov & M Poole, *Public Sociology: An Introduction to Australian Society*, Allen & Unwin, Crows Nest, pp. 151–68.

FURTHER READING

Gare, A 2015, 'Social movements', in *Wiley-Blackwell Encyclopedia of Social Theory*, John Wiley and Sons Ltd, Chichester.

Germov, J 2007, 'The new work ethic', in J Germov & M Poole, *Public Sociology: An Introduction to Australian Society*, Allen & Unwin, Crows Nest, pp. 363–86.

Giddens, A 1991, *Modernity and Self-identity: Self and Society in the Late Modern Age*, Stanford University Press, California.

Gray, I 2011, 'Urbanisation, community and rurality', in J German & M Poole, *Public Sociology: An Introduction to Australian Society*, Allen & Unwin, Crows Nest, pp. 461–77.

Ritzer, G 2001, *Explorations in the Sociology of Consumption: Fast Food, Credit Cards and Casinos*, SAGE, London.

Taylor, C & Lee, B (n.d.), 'Modernity and difference', in *Multiple Modernities Project*, Centre for Transcultural Studies, Philadelphia, PA: <www.sas.upenn.edu/transcult/promad.html>.

Smith, C 2006, 'On multiple modernities: shifting the modernity paradigm', unpublished paper, University of Notre Dame, Notre Dame, IN.

MOVIES

Warchus, M (dir.) 2014, *Pride*, BBC Films, London.

Wright, J (dir.) 2005, *Pride and Prejudice*, Working Title Films, London.

CHAPTER 6

Class and class relations

VERITY ARCHER

CHAPTER OVERVIEW

James Arvanitakis, who put this book together, tells the following story in his lecture on class:

It is a cool winter's morning and I'm sitting in a café at a beach in Sydney with a good friend. We have just had a swim in the sea and we're talking about the merits of what makes a good coffee when she turns to me and states: 'You swim like a public schoolboy.'

I am a little stunned. 'Sorry,' I replied, 'What did you say?'

She smiles and repeats: 'You swim like a public schoolboy. Where I grew up in Tasmania, I went to a private school. We had access to pools and swimming lessons and my friends and I are all good swimmers. When we used to go swimming at the Launceston Gorge, we used to make fun of the boys from public schools who couldn't swim very well. You swim like one of them.'

She is right—I did go to a public school, and the only access we had to swimming pools was at the annual swimming carnival. I begin to protest, but after thinking of the way she left me behind in the water, I withdraw my protests and sink behind my three-quarter flat white.

This concept of *dividing* people by their access to different levels of income and resources is known as 'class analysis'. The issue of class has been debated by sociologists and cultural theorists since their respective disciplines came into existence. One reason for this is that, although class essentially refers to social groups defined by their access to economic resources, the exact meaning of 'class' varies. While some argue that we should define class in terms of wealth, others believe that status is more important.

In modern societies such as Australia, many believe that class is now irrelevant. The aim of this chapter is to lay out some of arguments around this topic—you can then assess the evidence.

After reading this chapter, you should be able to:

- Describe the different ways in which Karl Marx, Max Weber and Pierre Bourdieu define and/or approach 'class'
- Explain the complex relationship between class and gender
- Explain the concept of the 'underclass' and reflect on its usefulness in social analysis
- Examine any situation of economic disparity (including any within your own life) using the lenses of the different types of class analysis.

KEY TERMS

Alienation A process present in pre-socialist economies, whereby a person is separated from their true nature and highest purpose in life via the labour process, and in particular, by selling their labour power. A worker could be alienated from themselves, from other workers, from their working life and from the product of their labour.

Class A process of ordering people in society by a set of divisions based on both real and perceived differences in social and economic status.

Cultural capital The social exchange of accumulated cultural knowledge that provides an individual with power and status in society. It is a form of capital based in modes of thinking, dispositions or cultural goods (such as books, art, music, furniture, food and wine).

Economic capital For Bourdieu, this is simply cash, or capital that an individual can convert to cash, such as property, businesses and shares.

Exploitation For Marx, this is the nexus of class relations. Capitalists, who own the means of production, exploit workers by paying them less than the full value of their labour. The gap between the full value of the worker's labour and their wage determines the extent to which the worker is exploited.

Habitus Acquired modes of thought and unthinking dispositions learnt in early childhood. People who move between habitus (for example, when a working-class person enters an elite university) may suffer cleft-habitus, an uncomfortable form of social dislocation.

Life chances A Weberian term used to describe opportunities in life; the likelihood of gaining the things we desire. While we may think that opportunities are the result of talent and effort, they are enabled and/or constrained by the class and status of our families, and by other structures that constitute our social location, such as gender, ethnicity and social capital.

Social capital For Bourdieu, the resources and benefits that derive from our social networks.

Social stratification The ranking of individuals or groups based on factors such as income, wealth, occupational status and education.

Socio-economic status A system of ranking based on a combination of Weber's 'class' and 'status' categories of power.

Status A Weberian term to describe the degree of power possessed by an individual on the basis of honour or prestige.

Surplus value The portion of the value of a product or service that exceeds the cost of producing it; that is, the labour of producing it.

Symbolic capital When cultural capital is legitimated or not legitimated by others, it becomes symbolic capital. What is deemed valuable or not valuable by others is always objectively determined by the dominant middle classes.

▷

Introduction

There is a myth in Australia that we are a fair-go and evenly democratic society. The word '**class**' rarely, if ever, appears in public debates. We like to think of ourselves as an egalitarian bunch, where mobility is fluid and where effort and talent are the most important factors in determining social position—in other words, people 'get what they deserve'. We like to think we are all, pretty much, somewhere in the middle, class-wise. This belief that we are an equal society is a core part of our national identity.

In fact, you might say that 'class' is almost a dirty word in Australia. Mention 'the c-word', as Australian author Tim Winton did in an interview, and you will probably get a very funny look. Winton wrote about this in an article for *The Monthly* magazine:

> During a recent interview, a journalist pulled me up for using the c-word.
> '*Class*?' she asked with lifted eyebrow. 'What do you mean?'
> I found myself chewing the air a moment. Had I said something foul, something embarrassing to both of us? (Winton 2013–14)

Even some sociologists have disputed the existence of class, as Jan Pakulski and Malcolm Waters did in their 1996 book *The Death of Class*. Others, such as feminist author bell hooks, have noted that the concept simply fell out of fashion:

> Nowadays it is fashionable to talk about race or gender … the uncool subject is class. It's the subject that makes us all tense, nervous, uncertain about where we stand (hooks 2000: vii).

So what is class?

One of the 'fathers' of sociology, Karl Marx (1818–83), predicted many things that did not happen, such as the increasing impoverishment of the masses, a world revolution led by workers against the capitalist exploiters, and a socialist utopia—which he termed 'communism'—where capitalism and selfishness gave way to cooperation and self-fulfilment. We have seen communism in action—and while there are some wonderful ideals, more often than not the implementation has been disastrous. The communist dictator Joseph Stalin, for example, was responsible for the enslavement and execution of millions of people.

Yet social scientists come back to Marx time and time again, either to develop and adapt his ideas, or to reject and argue against his analyses. Whether you agree with Marx's ideas or not, they remain important—even in a country such as Australia—and should not be dismissed out of hand. For example, for many people, Marx's theories of 'exploitation' and 'alienation' (discussed below) reflect our own feelings about work and wages and their impact on our physical and emotional life. In fact, the last time you and your friends sat at the pub or a café and complained about work—your frustrations, your pay, your hours—you may well have sounded like a pack of raging Marxists!

Marx was not even 30 when he wrote his first major work *The Communist Manifesto* in 1848. In it, he and his long-time friend and collaborator Friedrich Engels reflected on the condition of the workers (or working class) in Europe in the early stages of the Industrial Revolution (see Chapter 5). Engels was the son of a factory owner and he had seen firsthand the appalling conditions under which men, women and children laboured, for low wages and for long hours. To paraphrase Thomas Hobbes, life was seen as being lonely, nasty, brutal and short, and Marx and Engels thought the economic system was to blame.

If Marx and Engels were writing today, they might take their inspiration from the working conditions in retail and hospitality, or in call centres, or from the relationship between multinational companies and their employees in places such as McDonald's, Walmart in the United States, or sweatshops in Bangladesh. But whatever the size of the company, however

FIGURE 6.1 Exploitation: in just 30 minutes, a worker in this sweatshop might create goods that are equivalent to the value of her wage for an entire week.

physical or mental the work, if the worker works more hours than he or she needs to, in order to generate a wage, then the extra toil generates *profit* for the owner.

For example, it may take a machinist in a developing country 30 minutes to generate goods equivalent to the value of their wages for a week. The gap between the full value produced by the worker's labour and the wage paid to the worker is called **surplus value**. Marx referred to this appropriation (or stealing) of the worker's labour power as '**exploitation**'. For Marx, 'exploitation' is the key to understanding the structure of classes.

Understanding exploitation

The term 'exploitation' is loaded with negative meaning and invites moral condemnation, but in Marxist theory—although this moral aspect is present—exploitation really refers to the process whereby profit is extracted from resources (for example, Rio Tinto *exploits* natural resources in the Pilbara by mining for iron ore). In Marxist theory, workers, or more specifically their *labour power*, is the resource from which capitalists extract profits. In other words, the *bourgeoisie* (capitalist class) extracts profit from the labour effort of the *proletariat* (working class).

There is one other class that occupies neither the position of the exploiter nor the exploited: that of the *petit bourgeoisie*. The petit bourgeoisie own businesses and tend to work for themselves. As such, they tend not to employ other workers and 'exploit' their labour power for profit (although in the contemporary context, we can argue that this has changed). So, we can see that it is this relationship to the process of exploitation that gives us our three-class structure in classical Marxism.

This describes a Marxist class structure, but does not explain how it works. How is it that the capitalist class is able to exploit the working class?

The core of the answer to this question lies in the ownership of the means of production. Look at it this way: what would you like to do when you finish your degree? Your answer may be something like: become an accountant, a social worker or a teacher.

Did it occur to you to 'do' something that does not generate a wage? Probably not. If you do not own something that generates profit, such as a company, or investment properties (more on this later), then you will probably never have the luxury of thinking outside the parameters of spending your days in wage-generating work.

I would like to spend my days reading books, walking on the beach, chatting with friends and family, and writing my memoirs, but because I do not own something that generates profit, I sell my labour power to a university in exchange for a wage. Because I am forced to sell my labour to survive, I am a part of the proletariat. The proletariat may own property—such as a car and maybe even a house—but they own nothing *productive* except their own labour power, and they must sell this in exchange for wages. I use my labour power to generate a product (education), which the university sells to students in exchange for fees.

Marx did not talk about workers in the public service or organisations such as universities that, in Australia, are a somewhat strange mix of profit-generating business and government institution. But if Marx were alive today, he would be forced to consider the many different economic entities that have emerged, including universities, government corporations and not-for-profit organisations.

Some people who work for capitalist organisations earn a huge amount of money. Think about bank managers, lawyers … and professional footballers! In 2017 AFL player Dustin Martin signed a contract with the Richmond Tigers that saw him earn an estimated $1.2 to $1.3 million per season in 2018 and 2019. Surely he is not 'working class'? Yet according to Marx, yes he is! The AFL generates far greater profit from the labour power of its players than it pays them in the form of a wage. The AFL generated a $50.4 million profit in 2018. Martin is an exceptional case. Today, the starting salary for rookies is $71,500 after a 20 per cent pay rise was granted in 2017 (at the time of the AFL players' dispute in 2011 it was $35,000)—see Schmook and Gaskin 2017. But then Marx was not really interested in the amount a worker is paid. He only really cared about the *gap* between a worker's earnings and the value of the worker's labour power.

Understanding alienation

For Marx, exploitation has another sinister element that affects class relations. It leads to **alienation**, whereby a person is separated from their true nature and highest purpose in life via the labour process, and in particular, by selling their labour power.

Let me explain! Marx believed work to be central to human fulfilment. But he thought that working for a capitalist—rather than for oneself or the community—would always lead to the worker becoming alienated, both from the product of the labour and from one's own true self. Perhaps Dusty Martin had always dreamed of being an elite footballer. The same probably cannot be said of the cashier at Bunnings or the telemarketer in a call centre in India (next time you get a call, be nice).

But let us return to the process of exploitation. We have seen that Marx saw the ownership of the means of production as the core of the exploitation process. However, he also identified other aspects that helped create exploitation, including religion, ideology and politics. While these things are not the *reason* for exploitation and class structure, they can all support the capitalist in the quest for profit; they combine with the owners of the means of production to form what Marx called a *superstructure*, which further drove exploitation.

Adapting Marxism to modern-day working life

Erik Olin Wright (born 1947) is a contemporary Marxist whose work adapts classical Marxism to modern-day economies. His work represents what we call 'analytical Marxism', which is an attempt to scientifically define and clarify concepts such as class and empirically test them.

Wright does not accept everything Marx said. One departure from Marx, for example, is Wright's argument that class is not the primary explanation for everything. Instead, Wright says that the focus should be on how class affects various other aspects of social life. So while class may not be the key explanation, its impacts are never absent.

Another focal shift is Wright's concern with the micro level of the individual and their decision making. Classical Marxism looks at the macro level; that is, at large-scale processes. Wright, however, sees class as a set of locations occupied by individuals who make decisions; people can occupy class locations, but they can't *be* classes. For Wright, 'to be in a class location is to be subjected to a set of mechanisms that impinge directly on the lives of individuals as they make choices and act in the world' (Wright 1989, p. 189).

Wright attempts to address four aspects missing from Marx's concept of class structure:
1 The 'middle class';
2 People not in the paid labour force, including children, the unemployed and full-time homemakers;
3 Capitalist assets owned by employees (employee share schemes); and
4 The way that class locations can change over time.

To address some of these deficiencies, Wright's class model includes not just the three classes we discussed above, but 12 classes! Wright arranged these 12 classes according to Marx's original idea of exploitation—or the relative relation that each class has to the 'means of production'—and also according to:
- Relation to authority;
- Relation to scarce skills; and
- Number of employees.

Within his schema, Wright recognises that some categories of employee—such as high-level managers and workers with rare skills and expertise—are able to command wages that actually *exceed* the product of their labour.

Holding multiple class positions

Wright then went further to show that people can hold multiple class positions. For example, the billionaire media proprietor Rupert Murdoch began his working life as a part-time journalist at the Melbourne *Herald*, but his family owned it. His father was preparing him to take over the family business: News Ltd. Wright would say that Murdoch's class location at that point in time is twofold, but that his capitalist class location (as part of a capitalist family) probably overshadowed his 'stint' as a worker.

Wright also applied this multiple class positioning to children and full-time homemakers to explore the role that the class structure plays in the lives of people not in the labour market. He said that children and full-time homemakers occupy an indirect class position; they are tied to the class structure through their personal relations within the family and can therefore identify with the class interests of the family as a whole.

Homemakers also have a 'shadow' class position. This is the position they would occupy should they become separated from the class position of the family (for example, through divorce).

Wright did a lot of work attempting to reconcile feminist analysis with Marxist class analysis. Later in this chapter, I will examine some of the intersections between class and other social categories, such as gender and race. (Note that gender is discussed further in Chapter 7 and race in Chapter 9.)

The market: Max Weber

Max Weber (1864–1920) was a German sociologist who wrote mainly at the beginning of the twentieth century. Although he wrote a good half-century after Marx, it sometimes feels as if he is having a conversation with Marx, as he engages with the same themes but reaches very different conclusions.

First, Marx believed that economic structures were at the heart of our social relations, while Weber sought to explain social phenomena as the consequence of individual actions. We call Weber's approach '*methodological individualism*', while describing Marx's method as '*structuralism*'.

Second, in keeping with a structuralist approach, Marx viewed classes as independently existing phenomena. He spoke of classes *doing* things, and he thought that a class could gain 'consciousness' and act in its own self-interest. In contrast, Weber's methodological individualism led him to conclude that, unlike individuals, classes did not and could not actually exist. He did not reject 'class' as a concept, but he thought it could never go beyond just that—a concept. Weber saw the term 'class' as being useful for describing a collection of individuals in comparable economic situations.

Third, Weber rejected class as the primary organising principle for social relations. Instead, he thought that power and domination were more important in the great social struggle of 'who gets what'. And as you will see in Chapter 8, power is complicated. (Stop for a moment and think of the different people in your life who have 'power' over you. Your boss? Your peers? Politicians? Your football coach?)

In order to account for the multitude of rankings in society, Weber came up with three types of power:

1. Class (unequal access to scarce and valued resources within the market);
2. **Status** (social standing); and
3. Party (the ability to exercise power over others via institutions such as the legal system, political parties and clubs).

Although Weber saw these as distinct categories, applicable within different time scales, contemporary theorists who follow this line of thinking (known as 'neo-Weberians', such as John Goldthorpe (1996)) have attempted to bring them together to inform Weberian class categories. In fact, the term **socio-economic status** is based on a combination of Weber's 'class' and 'status' categories.

Weber's discussion of 'life chances'

Weber (1978, p. 69) said: 'a class situation is one in which there is a shared typical probability of procuring goods, gaining a position in life, and finding inner satisfaction'. In other words, Weber was saying that a class situation is one that shows us how likely it is that an individual person will lead the type of life that involves attaining scarce and valued resources, including a good education, a high-paying job, a house in a good neighbourhood, health, safety and freedom from violence. Right now, in Australia, there are children being born to different families in different class positions. Those babies have done nothing, but already we can use empirical evidence to assess their different chances in life. A baby born to an Indigenous family in a precarious housing situation in Redfern is statistically less likely to attain scarce and valued resources than a white baby born to two doctors living in an owner-occupied house in Sydney's Rose Bay.

Weberians commonly use the language of '**life chances**' instead of class, because it is generally considered that members of a 'class' share common life chances. So how are life chances determined? Weber thought that the market distributed life chances on the basis of what the individual brings to the market. This might then lead us to an income-based definition of class. For example, a radiologist in Australia can earn over $700,000 per year, but she may not own her own practice. Her credentials give her power within the market, and it is a safe bet that she and her children will be able to attain almost any valued and scarce resources they choose!

Weberians are fond of what we call **social stratification** analysis. Marx saw classes as dependent entities (one cannot exist without the other), but theorists who use stratification—or 'merit-based'—analysis tend not to worry about this. Sociologists have adopted the term 'stratification' from geology, where it describes the distinct layers within a rock. This means the theorist can apply layer upon layer of social positions within an economic structure, and because the layers are not interdependent, they can shift and change at any time. In theory, it is possible to have as many economic classes as there are people.

But surely, if it is possible for every person to belong to a different class, then there would be no such thing as class; there would only be individuals? Weber explained that while an endless number of *economic classes* are possible, it is an 'empirical fact' that there are only really four *social classes*. To delineate these, Weber first looked to the ownership and non-ownership of

property to create two great classes (this may sound familiar). But then he further split each of these social classes in two, based on 'the kind of property and the kind of services that can be offered in the market' (Weber 1978). The resulting four classes are:
- The 'dominant entrepreneurial and propertied groups';
- The petit bourgeoisie;
- Workers with formal credentials (the middle class); and
- Workers without formal credentials (the working class).

Weber felt that movement *within* these social classes was fluent, but that movement *between* them was not.

Culture: Pierre Bourdieu

If the French sociologist Pierre Bourdieu (1930–2002) were alive and working in Australia today, he would probably be engaged in a detailed analysis of 'bogans', 'cashed-up bogans' and 'hipsters'. This is because Bourdieu saw culture—and specifically *taste*—as determining our position within social space. He did not so much define classes but rather provided the grounding for a new theory of class that focused on *class culture*.

So, is 'class' the same as 'culture'? Although Bourdieu regarded culture as the most important element of class distinction, he did not dismiss the importance of economics. He thought that class represented the degree to which a person held or did not hold three types of capital:
- **Economic capital**: command over economic resources (like Marx);
- **Social capital**: access to networks of prestige and influence (a little like Weber); and
- **Cultural capital**: associated with taste, lifestyle and the arena of consumption; for Bourdieu, cultural capital directly influences the accumulation of economic and social capital over time.

Bourdieu also spoke of **symbolic capital**, which is the conversion of the three forms of capital into something like honour or prestige.

So how does one 'get' capital? Largely, through **habitus**—acquired modes of thought and dispositions—or habits. As an example of how habitus may affect the composition of capital, Bourdieu spoke of the ways in which food can play an important part in marking the boundaries of class. Parents teach children to consume food appropriate for their social rank and to reject food outside their class boundaries. Thus the working classes distinguish themselves via the consumption of common, hearty and filling foods (which can also be quite fatty). Anxieties over a potential lack of food can often lead to a desire to never be without, so filling the stomach is the most important aspect of eating.

The upper classes, on the other hand, distance themselves from the working classes via a display of 'elite' taste, which often involves eating for nutrients, as well as eating rare and exotic foods. A highly refined knowledge of food and, in particular, wine, allows the upper classes to distance themselves from the working classes.

But if the working classes begin to adopt the tastes of the upper classes, those tastes shift— in effect, redrawing the boundaries. Take for example, wine. New Zealand Sauvignon Blanc (or

Sauv Blanc) was, a little over a decade ago, the height of sophistication. Its popularity among the upper classes resulted in it flooding the Australian market. Today, Coles BWS has half of its white wine fridge devoted to it, with prices ranging from $8 to $30. As a result, those with elite taste have stopped drinking it and it is rare to see a New Zealand Sauv Blanc on the wine list at a fancy restaurant.

Likewise, in the original version of this chapter written in 2015, I wrote that the upper classes might select organic quinoa as an indicator of elite taste. By 2018 students were pointing out that organic quinoa salads were now available in your local shopping centre food court and therefore very likely to be consumed by your 'everyday bogan'. In just three years, quinoa had become generic and unfashionable to the upper classes!

Was Bourdieu a snob?

In case you think Bourdieu was a snob, it is important to understand his deeper analysis. He explained that symbolic capital is a form of violence against the working classes. It is the powerful and hegemonic middle classes that determine what is 'good taste' and what is not. In deeming working-class habits and aesthetic choices to be bad taste and not worthwhile, they devalue the working-class person culturally: this is a sort of 'double whammy' when combined with economic disadvantage (Bourdieu 2000).

In Australia, when a person from the working class is labelled a 'bogan', it might have this effect. Labelling someone a 'cashed-up bogan', or CUB, is slightly different. Sociologists Barbara Pini and Josephine Previte (2013) have pointed out that, as a result of the resources boom, previously low-waged, blue-collar workers have obtained wages that sometimes surpass the 'taste makers' in the middle class. The term 'cashed-up bogan' can serve to put them back in their 'rightful' place, at least culturally.

STUDENT VOICE

Anonymous

❝ I hail from Merbein, a locally infamous suburb 10 minutes away from the 'rural city' of Mildura. Merbein is very much working class. I live on a street where drug raids, deafening music and domestic disputes are the norm. There is a palpable divide between the haves and the have-nots, and this can be witnessed in almost every component of daily life.

One of the most common indicators of class is where you eat. For instance, you have Langtree Avenue with its juxtaposition of the bogans' Original Souvlaki Inn and Subway on one side, and the opulent Grand Hotel on the other. The working classes and upper classes inhabit the same street, but they don't intermingle. They are adjacent but separate. I have a distinct memory of attending a birthday party at the Pizza Café, which is part of the Grand Hotel, and feeling utterly out of place. This was where my friends, mostly from families of wealthy vineyard owners, dined all the time. Their ingrained social rituals and inside jokes formed an elaborate script, both spoken and unspoken, which I felt incapable of comprehending. For them, it was just another day, but for me it was an exhilarating intrusion into an unfamiliar world.

The children of the wealthy vineyard owners mostly go to

the private school, St Joseph's College. St Joseph's students are charmingly referred to by the public-school students as 'St Hoes', a clear manifestation of the class envy harboured by angst-ridden adolescents. Their extravagantly priced school uniform, featuring ties, offers a stark contrast to my old school's dress code, which has casual clothes. But in a small town like Mildura, it would be unfeasible to entirely segregate the classes by school. Indeed, some girls at my school, Mildura Senior College, would take every opportunity to flaunt their wealth with the latest brand names, leaving the rest of us feeling like sacks of potatoes.

There is a widely documented gap between rich and poor growing wider, and Mildura is no exception to this phenomenon. There's a dramatic split between the cramped, ugly rentals and the palm-tree lined mansions. Socio-economic issues are becoming increasingly dire, as evident in the soaring drug and crime rates. To those who truly know Mildura, the highly visible upper-class minority serves as an amusing distraction from the issues plaguing the town.

Admittedly, it is Mildura, so few people lead truly extravagant lifestyles relative to the city. In Mildura, the ultimate display of cultural capital is taking your jet ski down to the river, and perhaps enjoying an overpriced glass of wine at Trentham Estate. In a small town, social capital (who you know) is of utmost importance, with judgments fired rapidly on the basis of who you choose to associate with. In Mildura it's common to hold the narrow-minded attitude that 'people get what they deserve'. Indeed, there seems to be little acknowledgement of the relationship between private troubles and public issues, and that our life chances are determined not only by our character and efforts, but inevitably by the class and status we are born into.

Critical reflection

Stop for a moment and visualise two scenarios:

- A mother and child sit in a park where they eat a large meal from a well-known fast-food outlet known to be unhealthy.
- A mother and child sit in a park where they eat carrot sticks and homemade hummus. Does your mind automatically 'class' the two families?

The problem of the underclass

Around the mid-1970s, in most Western countries unemployment began to rise rapidly. At about the same time, family structures changed. The introduction of no-fault divorce in Australia meant a rise in single-parent, female-headed families. These families were often asset-poor and cash-poor, and came to be concentrated in state-run housing, which shifted to the outer-suburban regions where access to jobs and services was further limited. New suburbs sprang up where cheap house-and-land packages offered hope for achieving the Australian dream, but this dream was rarely fulfilled, as a lack of economic, cultural and social resources led to greater poverty.

Employment shifted too. The process of deindustrialisation in the 1980s removed opportunities for high school leavers without university qualifications and led to a geographical shift of jobs away from the suburbs and regional areas to the inner cities, where the knowledge economy was located. Rural and regional areas suffered terribly—with the major industries gone, getting by meant getting out. Everyone wanted to move to the inner cities where the jobs were located, but demand for housing and rising prices locked out all but the top earners. A spatially located 'underclass' was born.

Despite all the theoretical rigour that has been applied to understanding the working class, scant attention has been paid to theorising *the* underclass (that is, the 'working poor' and the unemployed). It is often taken for granted that this class just 'is'; but we can use our critical sociologist's eye to unpack this characterisation.

First, it is important to note that the notion of an 'underclass' has a moral element. It is a package deal that brings with it a range of unhelpful stereotypes that can have a negative effect—emotionally and within the public sphere. The term 'underclass' originated, in part, from the work of the American political scientist Charles Murray (born 1943). Murray advocated rolling back welfare payments, arguing that the underclass had been seduced into a welfare-dependent culture, which he saw as including crime, a lack of family values, 'anti-social behaviour' and disrespect for taxpayers.

Second, the underclass thesis also intersects with racial welfare imagery in the United States (something we touch on in Chapter 9). As Ann Tickamyer and Debra Henderson note:

> In the United States poverty is commonly given a black and disreputable face and then alternately ignored and demonised, part of a legacy of institutionalised racism that obscures the complexity of its demographics, causes and consequences (2009, p. 50).

By labelling poverty as a Black problem, powerful (mostly white) people can detach from it, fail to empathise, and sometimes attribute class position to racial/cultural characteristics. Tickamyer and Henderson point to a long tradition of characterising Black Americans and Native Americans as lazy, unable to take personal responsibility for themselves and their families, unable to delay gratification, and ultimately dependent on public welfare.

Applying this to the Australian context

Does this sort of thing happen in Australia?

Well, yes. Non-Indigenous Australians often apply these stereotypes to Indigenous Australians. A 2014 SBS documentary series called *First Contact* took six non-Indigenous Australians into Aboriginal Australia for an extended period and documented their reactions. In one episode, a white woman speaks to an Aboriginal woman about poverty and welfare in her community. 'Put yourself in their shoes', the Indigenous woman says. 'There are no jobs out here. They've got no education.' The white woman responds with a fairly common view: 'I wouldn't be in their shoes', she says, 'because I strive.'

> ### Critical reflection
>
> Reflect on what these two women are saying and what it tells us about their individual backgrounds and circumstances.
>
> Perhaps we, as sociologists, should begin to ask some questions about how the 'underclass' can be reincorporated into traditional (or even new) class theories.

STUDENT VOICE

James Arvanitakis

❞ I had never thought about how my background affected my time at university until years later when I had a chance to reflect on class structures and class relations.

This story now seems quite funny but at the time it made me feel like I didn't belong and that I was, to put it mildly, dumb.

After finishing high school I just scraped into university. This was a big deal as I was going to be the first person in my family to attend university. As a working-class child of Greek immigrants—my dad was a labourer and mum ironed for a living—we celebrated when I received my offer letter. My parents hoped that attending university would result in financial stability—something they could only dream of growing up in war-ravaged Greece.

The day before university started, I went to my father and asked him what I should take with me. My father was working in the backyard. He stopped what he was doing, looked up and said: 'Ask your mother'. As someone who left school at seven years old, I should not have been surprised by this answer, but why he thought my mother would know more I am not sure.

My mother was in the kitchen preparing the evening meal: roast lamb stuffed with garlic and coated with oregano and olive oil—yes, a Greek classic. I asked my mum what I should take to university, and she stopped, looked into the distance and said:

> Take your passport so everyone knows who you are ... And also, I will pack you some lamb. That way you can make friends.

The next day I went off to university with my passport, some paper and a pen, and a large plastic container full of lamb.

I arrived early and made my way to the front row, directly in front of the lecturer, waiting to hear the first words of what I expected to be a mathematics lecture. I remember being overwhelmed and intimidated by the other students: they seemed so comfortable, when I felt like an imposter. But I was also excited. The lecturer walked in, looking larger than life, and welcomed us all to his 'Advanced Asian Cinema' class. I laughed, thinking it was a joke: I mean, film was something you watched, not studied.

It was not a joke. I had to make a decision: get up and make my way out of the class in front of everyone, or save myself the embarrassment but miss my first ever (scheduled) university lecture. Too scared to move, I sat through the class, petrified that I would be asked a question.

I felt so stupid that I went home early. Being at uni was never a comfortable experience: I often failed, was too scared to ask anyone for help, didn't know that there were opportunities to travel overseas to study, and had no one at home to ask about terms such as 'ontology'. I almost dropped out 100 times and it took me five years to finish my first degree.

All this is hard to imagine now that I am a professor and

have been given a number of awards, but my class background meant that I nearly missed out on the one thing I love doing more than anything else: being an educator. I was lucky to break class barriers, but many of my friends from school never did.

> **Critical reflection**
>
> How would welfare recipients fit into the structures or theories developed by Marx, Weber and Bourdieu? Can you think of a new class structure that might incorporate welfare recipients? Remember that not all welfare recipients are out of the workforce, and that many are engaged in work within the home, caring for children or the elderly; while others are engaged in volunteer work, training or 'Work for the Dole' programs.

Women and class

One of the biggest problems with classes is that they are made up of people: people who come from broad backgrounds with different ethnicities and cultures; people who are young and old; women and men; and people of different religions. As such, class is not just class. It can take a different shape and can be experienced differently depending on your own lived experience.

Traditional class analysis has struggled with the question of women and class. We can often have a very 'male-centric' understanding of class without even realising it. And it is not just theorists who are guilty of male centrism when it comes to class. Until very recently, women were often asked, 'What does your husband do?' as one of the first questions when meeting a stranger. The family's class position was viewed as a direct correlate to the man's occupation and gave people a sense of whether the woman in question was 'worth knowing' or not.

Further, most class theories revolve around waged labour, and women sometimes do not fit as neatly as men into traditional class positions. The reality is that most women in families work fewer hours in the paid labour force than men, and for lower wages; and some work only in their own home and for no wages at all. In that case, perhaps a woman's class position *should* reflect that of the main earner. (The different experiences between men and women are discussed in Chapter 7.)

When we think about women and class we can sometimes come up with more questions than answers: Can a woman within a family unit have a class position independent of the family unit? If not, exactly what relationship should a husband's class position have to his wife's class position? How is money negotiated within a family, and can this alter a woman's class position, or even set up a class position *within* the family? Can unpaid domestic labour or caring work be a measure of class position? If so, does a woman working both outside and within the home hold multiple class positions? If class is not actually a structure, but rather something cultural, how is this process 'gendered'? What counts as cultural capital for a man? What counts as cultural capital for a woman? How do men experience class? How do women experience class? What does this say about 'class' as a category? I told you there were a lot of questions!

While some feminists in the 1970s started dismissing class analysis for ignoring women, bell hooks asked: 'Why hasn't feminism done much for working-class women?' (hooks 2000). The answer was multifaceted. hooks argued that while middle-class white feminists were writing about the dissatisfaction women felt with being confined to the home, the majority of women were in fact in the workforce, working long hours for low wages. These working-class women were also responsible for the care of children and household labour. While women with high levels of education and decent household incomes saw the workforce as 'freedom', freedom for working-class women meant something quite different. It meant the ability to *choose* between working and not working. If feminism argued only for equal access to higher-status positions, it ignored the economic plight of millions of working-class women for whom higher wages in working-class industries, for their spouse and for themselves, would mean the ability to choose to *work less*, and perhaps even indulge in some rest and leisure!

This example tells us that class experience is 'gendered', and gender experience is 'classed'.

Class and place

I grew up in a factory town on the north-west coast of Tasmania. There was one big factory, the APPM pulp mill, that employed around 4000 people. The smaller factory, Tioxide, produced paint pigment and employed around 450 people. By the time I finished high school, APPM had sold the pulp mill to a different company and most of its operations had moved offshore. A few years later, Tioxide also closed and our town suffered one of the highest unemployment rates in Australia.

There were additional flow-on effects. No one had money, so shops closed down; and with such a huge number of job hunters, anyone with a job was in constant fear of losing it. This made workers easy prey for unscrupulous employers. The town has never recovered and, in policy-speak, we could say that the residents are 'socially excluded', with high levels of second-generation joblessness, physical and mental health issues, and drug dependency.

I tell this story not because it is remarkable, but because it is common. Around Australia, as in the United States and Western Europe, there are hundreds of stories like it.

Researchers are now beginning to pay close attention to how location might affect class. Location has always been central to class.

Suburbs take on a class character and this appears to be because of—or reinforced by—property prices. In turn, growing up in a particular location can have a strong influence on a person's position in life. 'Slums' and 'ghettos' are spatially concentrated poverty, while old money tends to reside in the scenic and charming older suburbs. In Melbourne and Sydney, the wealth tends to be in the east, while to the west of major cities lie the old working-class suburbs, now gentrified to a certain extent by the recent relocation of work and the subsequent push to the inner cities.

Zora Simic (2008) has written about class and the west in Sydney, where the idea of a 'westie' is not just a description of where you live, but a description of your class character, based on where you live. In a sense, the suburb can inhabit you as much as you inhabit it.

Understanding ghettos

One person who has examined class and spatial location extensively is the United States-based sociologist Loïc Wacquant (2008). We can look at his work on the American ghetto to see if it has anything to offer us in Australia. Wacquant started writing about ghettos when he moved to Chicago from France, where he had been a student of Pierre Bourdieu. He was shocked to discover firsthand what he described as 'urban desolation, racial segregation, social deprivation and street violence concentrated in this *terra non grata* that was universally feared, shunned and denigrated by outsiders' (Wacquant 2008, p. 116).

In his studies of the American ghetto, Wacquant not only talked about the spatial concentration of class, but about the way in which a *place* can *class* a person. Within every advanced economy, he said, there are certain abandoned areas. The people within these spaces bear the stigma of living somewhere that no one else wants to live. The residents become symbols of poverty and internalise the ghetto, losing pride and fracturing community ties. They may also be targets for law enforcement and suffer prejudice from employers.

Wacquant refers to these places as 'hyperghettos' to distinguish them from the old working-class communities of the 1950s.

> **Critical reflection**
>
> Wacquant's ethnographic studies concentrate on the hyperghettos of Chicago. Do you think any of what he says applies to us, here in Australia? Why or why not?

In Australia, while each major city has its disadvantaged suburbs, the disadvantage gap is greatest when we examine the urban/rural-regional divide. People such as Peter Saunders and Melissa Wong (2014, p. 144) have ranked locations in terms of their economic prosperity, finding that:

> city residents have the highest incomes by a considerable margin, are more likely to own considerable assets, have the lowest poverty rates and are the least reliant on government benefits for income.

High levels of income support reliance in regional areas reflects both the lack of jobs in those areas and that people with low incomes are likely to move to regional areas to access cheaper housing. This divide has escalated in recent years with urban—particularly inner-city—housing values growing at a much greater rate than rural-regional properties.

The upshot of all this is that the people who need jobs cannot afford to live where the jobs are located.

Finally, it is worth noting that it can be harder to escape class in places where everyone knows your business. So, living in a rural or regional area and being from a particular class of origin can have a huge effect on your reputation—with teachers and peers, with potential employers, and with welfare and law enforcement. Thus the effects of class can vary depending on spatial location.

Is class changing?

When in 2014 French economist Thomas Piketty published his English translation of *Capital in the Twenty-First Century,* he managed to do something few academic economists before him had done; he sold a lot of books. At the point of writing this chapter in 2019, *Capital in the Twenty-First Century* had sold over 2.5 million copies worldwide. In June 2019 a documentary feature based on the book premiered at the Sydney Film Festival. Many regarded it as 'the right book at the right time'. It spoke to people who believed the gap between rich and poor had been growing and that it was now harder to jump from one side of the gap to the other.

For those who wondered why, Piketty had answers: he said it was because r > g.

The concept of r > g is Piketty's shorthand way of saying wealth, in today's society, grows faster than economic output. In other words, the wealthy are getting wealthier via the increasing returns on capital investments (such as property, dividends and capital growth), while those with little to no wealth, people who rely on income from wages (or from welfare), are merely staying afloat, or in some cases going backwards, in spite of their hard work. When we consider how skewed wealth distribution is in most countries (in Australia the top 20 per cent own 62 per cent of the wealth while the bottom 20 per cent own just 1 per cent) we can begin to fathom the importance of Piketty's findings.

CEOs and other super-earners' salaries have forged ahead in recent years (Apple CEO Tim Cook received $190.5 million in 2018), but for most other workers, wages have stalled or gone backwards in real terms relative to the cost of living. This means the divide between those who earn money from wages and those who earn money from investments grows wider.

The r > g phenomenon is easy to relate to when we look at our own housing crisis. Renters who are using only their own wages to save for a house deposit are chasing something that's moving faster than they are; quite like using an escalator to chase a hot air balloon!

Piketty and his team of researchers spent 10 years looking at long-range historical data related to the distribution of wealth and income across the globe dating back to the seventeenth century. The team included Australia among the eight rich countries it analysed. They found that the r > g model dominated across all the nations studied throughout most of history. Wealth lost its power and gave way to wage incomes only briefly, between the 1930s and 70s. This was mainly due to the economic shocks caused by the World Wars and the Depression of the early twentieth century that wiped out a great deal of hereditary wealth and ushered in grand redistributive policies, including a suite of welfare advancements. These shocks settled from the 1980s onward, and changing political circumstances resulted in neoliberal reforms that favoured wealth and to a large extent rolled back redistribution. Wealth inequality once again began to escalate beyond wage inequality. Looking back at the work of Weber and Marx, who were writing in the nineteenth century, we can see that their analysis largely reflected this class arrangement.

So if wages no longer have the same impact on economic position, what does this mean for Australia and for our understanding of 'class'? Focusing on property investments, Ilan Wiesel, a senior lecturer in urban geography at the University of Melbourne, says it's now more accurate to talk about Australia being divided into three asset-based classes: the renting class, the home-owning class, and the property elite. The property elite are a group who derive income primarily from returns on property investments. The home-owning class gain wealth for retirement via capital gains on their own home. The renting class spend, on average, around a third of their income on rent and, without appreciable assets, find it difficult to save for the future. Their retirement, Wiesel notes, will be vastly different to that of the other two classes.

In a climate of $r > g$, the economic situation of one's family of origin becomes more important as children leverage off the wealth of their parents to make investments of their own. We often talk about the wealth divide being an intergenerational issue, with young people locked out of the housing market and baby-boomers who bought cheap and paid off early, reaping the rewards. It's safe to say that the older generation's wealth will be passed on to their children, so in a climate of $r > g$, your parents' economic situation will probably determine yours.

Piketty believes it is likely that we will see a return to a world similar to nineteenth century Europe. We may even begin to notice a growing 'leisure class' of people who, far from gaining prestige from their job title, actually need not work at all! Apart from a short blip in the twentieth century, this class arrangement has been the norm. Piketty is keen to point out, however, that normal is not the same as 'natural'. He believes this trajectory can (and should) be altered via state intervention and redistributive polices such as a wealth tax.

Piketty warns us that if current trends continue, democratic systems may be in grave danger and 'the consequences for long-term dynamics of the wealth distribution are potentially terrifying'.

How much class mobility is there in Australia?

We are raised to believe that if we work hard, we can achieve anything we want. But how frequently do we actually see 'class mobility', or people moving up the class ladder? Because of the many different theoretical positions on class, it is hard to measure 'class' mobility but we can, and do, measure income and wealth mobility.

We measure intergenerational mobility using the relationship between an individual male's earnings and his father's earnings on a scale of 0 to 1. Given the complicated nature of female employment over the life cycle, we concentrate on comparing father–son earnings. If the number is 1, then we can predict the son's earnings with 100 per cent accuracy based on what his father earns. This implies no social mobility. If the number is '0', then the son's earnings have no relationship to his father's, implying high mobility. The Australian Productivity Commission 2018 report 'Rising Inequality', noted that countries with high inequality tend to have low intergenerational mobility while countries with low inequality tend to have high intergenerational mobility.

Without looking at the answer below, do you think Australia has a high or low level of social mobility?

Professor Dan Andrews (Harvard University) and Andrew Leigh (a former economics professor at the Australian National University (who in 2010 became a federal Labor Party politician) found in 2009 that Australia had an intergenerational elasticity of earnings in the range of 0.2 to 0.3. Building on this work and using a longer range of Household Income and

Labour Dynamics Australia (HILDA) data, Murray and colleagues found in 2017 that Australia's rate of elasticity was 0.41 (a stronger correlation between father–son earnings). In other words, Australia has a moderate (but perhaps decreasing) level of social mobility: more socially mobile than the United States, not as socially mobile as Sweden, and about equal with the United Kingdom.

Asset ownership is steadier between generations, with family of origin being the biggest predictor of the rate and value of home ownership. For most people in Australia, their major asset is the family home. Recently, due to a range of factors including tax breaks, we have seen a widening of the wealth gap, as those who own their own house (or a significant portion of it) are able to buy more houses to use as investment properties. Demand for properties, particularly those close to the centre of major metropolitan cities such as Melbourne and Sydney, has driven house prices up. People who do not yet own houses are finding it more and more difficult to purchase a first home. But, as we have already seen, a middle-to-high wealth/income within your family of origin is likely to result in parental assistance when it comes to buying a house.

The Australian Housing and Urban Research Institute (AHURI) found that people receiving large bequests from family are also more likely to accumulate wealth in housing because they are often able to purchase houses that have higher rates of capital growth, for example high-value houses in central metropolitan areas. People from working-class backgrounds often experience delayed asset accumulation due to a lack of parental assistance. They are also likely to be shut out of high-value housing with high rates of capital growth and be paying off a mortgage into later life. We see that those who started out with parental assistance and bought early will have been mortgage-free for many years.

The gap becomes even wider when a young person reaches middle age and inheritance comes into play. People from wealthy backgrounds are likely to inherit a house worth perhaps three times as much as someone from a poor background might inherit. This is further exacerbated when we look at the divide between rural and regional house values, and metropolitan house values. All of this, of course, assumes that your parents own a home.

With a relatively fixed transfer of intergenerational wealth and a mediocre rate of intergenerational earnings elasticity, we have to wonder whether Australia can live up to its own egalitarian mythology.

Conclusion

This chapter has highlighted that class remains an important tool of analysis, particularly if we combine it with other categories of analysis. Throughout this book, we will return to the issue of class—despite many arguing that it is less important in a contemporary society than gender, ethnicity, religion and other factors.

What is important—and what I have hopefully highlighted—is that class *does* count. It is the mechanism by which power, privilege and inequality are often distributed and institutionalised in contemporary societies. Beyond the rhetoric of equal opportunity, class exists and influences peoples' life chances.

Class shapes attitudes and life choices. We can think about certain parts of any major city where the elite live: in Sydney it is Vaucluse; in Adelaide, it is the Adelaide Hills. It explains why we may or may not feel comfortable in these suburbs, or why some of these areas have access to a greater number of services and facilities (such as parklands) compared to poorer areas of the city. Class can be used to explain why so many of our politicians went to private schools and why James swims like a public schoolboy.

Summary points

- Although Karl Marx regarded class as an objective phenomenon, it is very difficult for us as sociologists to reach this conclusion.
- Class is differently constructed and applied depending upon your theoretical perspective.
- Class is not an independent phenomenon. It intersects and interacts with other advantages and disadvantages derived from gender, race and geography, so that different people experience class differently.
- While economic factors form the base of most class analysis, culture can also play an important part in 'classing' the individual. The legitimation (or non-legitimation) of someone's culture can affect their class experience.
- Despite popular mythology, evidence shows that Australia is only moderately socially mobile between generations and relatively stagnant when it comes to intergenerational wealth.
- The wealth divide has grown faster and more dramatically than the wages divide, meaning our understanding of how society is 'classed', and what this means, may be changing. Family of origin is becoming more important. We may soon see the return of a 'leisure class' made up of people who need not work at all!

Sociological reflections

1. What are the links between politics, media and the 'underclass' thesis? Can you think of anything that you have seen on television or read in the newspaper that might have depicted an underclass?
2. Describe how Bourdieu's cultural capital may be ethnically or historically specific.
3. Describe how someone's geographical location can influence their class position and their experience of class.

Discussion questions

1. What is 'class'?
2. To what extent is class present in Australian society?
3. How relevant are the theories of Marx, Weber and Bourdieu to Australian society? Is one more relevant than another?
4. If Piketty's analysis is right and the gap between those who hold wealth and those who don't continues to grow, how might our society change? Should we do something about it? If so, what?
5. In what ways can you see class and gender interacting within society? What about class and race? Or class and geography?
6. Is class inevitable or should class division be contested?

7 In mid-2019, SBS aired the third season of its three-part documentary series titled *Struggle Street*, which explores hardship and resilience among communities often described as 'impoverished'. *Struggle Street* has attracted much attention, and debate has been polarised between those who argue that the show is 'poverty porn' and those who argue that the show offers a 'sensitive' and 'exposing' portrayal of the suffering and loss endured by those Australians who have been 'left behind'.

  a Watch an episode of *Struggle Street* and consider the ways in which the participants are represented. Is the portrayal sensitive or derisive?

  b Read Steven Threadgold's article '*Struggle Street* is poverty porn with an extra dose of class racism' and Nathan Rees' article '*Struggle Street*: Western Sydney has many more stories of hardship like this'. Summarise and critically evaluate both sides of the debate.

  c Read Tim Winton's article 'Some thoughts about class in Australia: the C word' <www.themonthly.com.au/issue/2013/december/1385816400/tim-winton/c-word>, and consider the ways in which *Struggle Street* plays into the anxieties of a nation that has become increasingly segregated by social class.

References and further reading

REFERENCES

Andrews, D & Leigh, S 2009, 'More inequality, less social mobility', *Applied Economic Letters*, 16(15), 1489–92.

Australian Housing and Urban Research Institute (AHURI) 2018, *How are Intergenerational Wealth Transfers Impacting First Home Purchases?*, AHURI Brief: <www.ahuri.edu.au/policy/ahuri-briefs/how-are-intergenerational-wealth-transfer-impacting-first-home-purchases-in-australia>.

Bourdieu, P 2000, *Distinction: A Social Critique of the Judgment of Taste*, trans. Richard Nice, Routledge, London.

Goldthorpe J 1996, 'Class analysis and the reorientation of class theory: the case of persisting differentials in educational attainment', *British Journal of Sociology*, 45, 481–506.

hooks, b 2000, *Where We Stand: Class Matters*, Routledge, New York.

Marx, K & Engels, F 1967, *The Communist Manifesto*, Penguin Books, London (original work published 1848).

Murray, C, Clark, R, Mendolia, S & Siminski, P 2017, *Direct Measures of Intergenerational Income Mobility for Australia*, September 2017, IZA Institute of Labour Economics, Bonn, Germany.

Pakulski, J & Waters, M 1996, *The Death of Class*, SAGE, London.

Piketty, T 2014, *Capital in the Twenty-First Century*, Harvard University Press, Cambridge, MA.

Pini, B & Previte, P 2013, 'Bourdieu, the boom and cashed-up bogans', *Journal of Sociology*, 49(2–3), 256–71.

Productivity Commission, 2018, *Rising Inequality? A Stocktake of the Evidence*, Commission Research Paper, Canberra.

Rees, N 2015, '*Struggle Street*: Western Sydney has many more stories of hardship like this', *The Drum*, 7 May: <www.abc.net.au/news/2015-05-07/rees-western-sydney-has-many-more-stories-of-hardship-like-this/6452224>.

Saunders, P & Wong, M 2014, 'Locational differences in material deprivation and social exclusion in Australia', *Australasian Journal of Regional Studies*, 20(1), 113–58.

Schmook, N & Gaskin, L 2017, 'Players get 20 per cent pay rise in new CBA', *AFL News,* 20 June: <www.afl.com.au/news/44107/players-get-20-per-cent-pay-rise-in-new-cba>.

Simic, Z 2008, 'What are ya?: negotiating identities in the western suburbs of Sydney in the 1980s', *Journal of Australian Studies*, 32(2), 223–36.

Threadgold, S 2015, '*Struggle Street* is poverty porn with an extra dose of class racism', *The Conversation*, 6 May: <http://theconversation.com/struggle-street-is-poverty-porn-with-an-extra-dose-of-class-racism-41346>.

Tickamyer, A & Henderson, D 2009, 'The intersection of poverty discourses: race, class, culture and gender', in B Dill & R Sambrana (eds), *Emerging Intersections*, Rutgers University Press, New Jersey.

Wacquant, L 2008, Ghettos and anti-ghettos: an anatomy of the new urban poverty, *Thesis Eleven*, 94, 113–18.

Weber, M 1978, *Economy and Society: An Outline of Interpretive Sociology*, University of California Press, Los Angeles, CA (original work published 1922).

Wiesel, I 2016, 'How the housing boom is remaking Australia's class structure', *The Conversation,* 17 October 2016: <https://theconversation.com/how-the-housing-boom-is-remaking-australias-social-class-structure-66976>.

Winton, T (2013–14), 'Some thoughts about class in Australia: the C word', *The Monthly*, December 2013: <www.themonthly.com.au/issue/2013/december/1385816400/tim-winton/c-word>.

Wright, EO 1989, *The Debate on Classes*, Verso, London.

Wright, EO 1997, *Class Counts: Comparative Studies in Class Analysis*, Cambridge University Press, Cambridge.

FURTHER READING

Connell, R 1977, *Ruling Class, Ruling Culture*, Cambridge University Press, Cambridge.

Connell, R & Irving TH 1980, *Class Structure in Australian History*, Longman Cheshire, Melbourne.

Delphy, C & Leonard, D 1992, *Familiar Exploitation: A New Analysis of Marriage in Contemporary Western Societies*, Polity Press, Cambridge.

Goldthorpe, J 1987, *Social Mobility and Class Structure in Modern Britain*, 2nd edn, Clarendon Press (original work published 1980).

Hollier, N 2004, *Ruling Australia: The Power, Prestige and Politics of the New Ruling Class*, Australian Scholarly Publishing, Melbourne.

Peel, M 2003, *The Lowest Rung: Voices of Australian Poverty*, Cambridge University Press, Cambridge.

Pini, B & Leach, B 2011, *Reshaping Gender and Class in Rural Spaces*, Ashgate, Farnham, UK.

Pusey, M 2003, *The Experience of Middle Australia: The Dark Side of Economic Reform*, Cambridge University Press, Cambridge.

Sawer, M & Hindess, B 2004, *Us and Them: Anti-Elitism in Australia*, API Network, Perth.

Skeggs, B 1997, *Formations of Class and Gender: Becoming Respectable*, SAGE, Thousand Oaks, CA.

Western, M et al. 2007, 'Neoliberalism, inequality and politics: the changing face of Australia', *Australian Journal of Social Issues*, 42(3), 401–18.

TELEVISION

First Contact (SBS, 2014): documentary series.

Struggle Street (SBS, 2019): three-part documentary.

CHAPTER 7

Sex and gender

DENISE BUITEN

CHAPTER OVERVIEW

Picture these scenarios.
- In a hospital, a baby is born. The first thing that is said when the baby is delivered is: 'It's a girl/boy!' Once this happens, the parents can name the child, and eager friends and family rush out to buy pink or blue blankets, little dresses or little pants, dolls or toy trucks.
- On the street, someone does a double take as they walk past a person who doesn't seem to conform to gender norms. They crane their neck as they try to identify and categorise this person's sex and gender identity. This is curious because they are strangers.
- While a girl looks into the mirror with disappointment at the shape of her body, wishing to be thinner, a boy looks into the mirror with disappointment at the shape of *his* body because he wishes he was more built. The diet industry responds; billion-dollar industries focused on weight-loss still primarily target women and products aimed at bulking up still mostly target men.
- On a weekday, scores of women can be seen in malls and parks walking their young babies and meeting with their mothers' groups to discuss the joys and perils of parenthood. There are a handful of new dads among them, walking and playing with their young babies, and some stay-at-home dads even join the mothers' groups. In numbers, however, dads who visit the park during the week stand out as the relative exception compared to women.
- Girls and boys file into school each day. Many of them are separated by gender. Some schools offer different subjects to girls and boys. There are also separate toilets and changerooms for girls and boys. A debate has broken out at a local school about whether a trans-boy should be 'allowed' into the boys' toilet.

We live in a highly 'gendered' world; that is, a world in which gender categories play a significant role in our everyday lives. Gender is so ubiquitous, so all-present, that very often we don't even notice it. But social researchers have shown that gender impacts on the interests we pursue, the way people interact with us, the kinds of work and play we engage in, and our access to various material and social resources. Young babies and toddlers are dressed, spoken to and played with in subtly different ways according to their gender, based on expectations set at (or even before!) birth. Often, this is unconscious; while parents and teachers believe their interactions with children are devoid of stereotypes, sociological research shows us that subtle but important differences creep in nonetheless, and that these build to have an impact on the kinds of things girls and boys end up doing more or doing better (Fine 2010).

Adults' worlds are highly gendered too. For example, women and men experience a different distribution of their labour at work and at home and dominate in some careers more than others.

As sociologists, one of the things we learn to develop is a *gender lens*: that is, the ability to 'see' or to notice gender in our everyday lives. As a budding sociologist, you may be surprised once you develop this lens how much you start to notice the world being shaped by gender in myriad ways.

How gender appears in daily life has of course changed over the years, slowly transforming many of the scenarios above. Women and men today expect different things from life than women and men from the 1950s. Most schools are now co-ed, usually offering the same subjects to all students. Ideal body shapes for men and women have changed over the years. More fathers are taking extended paternity leave and playing a more active role in the lives of their young children. Some parents encourage their children to play with toys associated with both boys and girls. Gay, bisexual, transgender and various other gender non-conforming people occupy greater spaces in public life and culture than they did even a decade ago.

Still, while gender has evolved over the years, it has not disappeared. We know from sociological research that gender is always *there*, influencing our upbringing, work, pay, parenting, body image and much more. Furthermore, gender roles and relations are not the same everywhere; gender plays out in different ways according to place and time. Sociologists aim to study the ways in which gender manifests in different spaces, at different times and among different people around the world, and to investigate how and why this is evolving and changing.

You may have noticed that in talking about gender here we have not restricted ourselves to the experiences of women and girls. In fact, while it is often assumed that gender is a female issue, or that feminism is all about women and their rights, gender analysis and indeed much feminist scholarship is interested in the experiences of men and women, boys and girls and indeed people who do not identify with these gender categories. The study of masculinities is one of the most prolific in modern gender and feminist social research, and 'queer studies', which critically examines diverse sexual and gender identities and power relations, is an established and expanding area of research. As such, gender is about everyone, and as we move through this chapter you may start to consider how gender impacts on your own life.

This chapter explores the fundamentals of gender analysis, including an introduction to what we mean by gender, how it relates to biology, and how gender roles and identities are developed in our lives.

After reading this chapter, you should be able to:
- Define gender and distinguish between 'sex' and 'gender'
- Discuss the relationship between sex and gender; namely, whether gender is the natural result of sex, or whether it is socially determined
- Describe some of the ways in which humans become gendered and identify ways in which this has happened in your own life
- Consider the role of other aspects of our identity (such as race, class or sexuality) and their influence on how we experience gender

- Define feminism in its most basic terms and demonstrate an awareness of the ways in which approaches to feminism differ
- Start to develop a 'gender lens' through which you 'see' gender in everyday life.

KEY TERMS

Biological determinism The belief that human traits and behaviours are created by genes and biology, rather than social factors.

Feminism A diverse set of theories and actions that have the following elements as their starting point: that gender is a significant element of social organisation, that gender relations are patriarchal, and that this inequality needs to be transformed.

Gender Social and cultural traits associated with males and females that shape roles, behaviours and expectations around what it means to be a man (masculine) or a woman (feminine).

Gender performativity The ways in which gender is constructed by the repetitive performing or acting out of gender conventions.

Intersectionality The interconnected nature of social categories such as gender, race, class, (dis)ability and sexuality that create overlapping systems of inequality.

Patriarchy A social system in which men and masculinity are privileged, and women and femininity made subordinate.

Sex The biological categories: male and female.

Social construction A social phenomenon or category created by society, such as gender.

Socialisation The process of transmission of culture from one generation to the next; the ongoing social processes by which we learn the norms, customs and values of our society.

Introduction

In our everyday lives, we seldom question or even notice **gender**. We take gender largely for granted, entering the gender-appropriate toilet, shopping in the gender-appropriate section of the department store and often making or hearing universalising declarations about gender such as 'women love flowers' or 'men hate shopping'. But where do these ideas and behaviours come from, and what exactly *is* gender?

To answer this question, let us conduct a thought experiment: How would we explain gender to an alien? Imagine we were being visited by an alien race from a planet with no gender. On this planet, there is no masculine or feminine—there is no gender distinction. They have come to Earth to study and understand our way of life, and have noticed that we have this thing called 'gender' that distinguishes between 'boys' and 'girls', 'men' and 'women', who live and work in somewhat different ways. They want to know more about it.

What would you say? How would you explain the scenarios we have sketched at the beginning of this chapter? For example, if the aliens ask why we have separate toilets, or schools, or why 'women' humans tend to look after the baby humans for greater periods of time. Why, for example, in some cultures do 'girl' humans want to be slender, while 'boy' humans want to be muscular? And where do humans 'get' gender from—how do we know which roles to play, and why do we play them?

Take a moment to consider how you would explain this to someone who has never experienced gender.

Your answer says a lot about which theories of gender have most influenced you. Did you talk about nature and natural differences, such as hormones or other biological differences? Did you explain gender as a social phenomenon, pointing out how gender is taught to us by parents, educators and the media? Or did your answer include a combination of the above? For example, some of you might have talked about social pressures and the media in relation to body image differences, and also included biological differences such as the ability to breastfeed or nurturing instincts in relation to childcare. At the heart of the question 'What is gender?' is the debate and associated theories regarding whether gender is a natural consequence of our physical sex, or the result of social engineering. Consider the discussion of the sociological definition of gender below. You might notice how this definition relates to the debate above.

No one definition of 'gender'

Gender is a term that has been defined in a variety of ways. Since the 1970s, when 'gender' became common parlance within the social sciences, it has largely been used to distinguish from biological **sex**; that is, male or female (Pilcher & Whelehan 2004). As distinct from sex, gender denotes the *social and cultural* traits associated with males and females, namely masculinity and femininity. That is, gender shapes roles, behaviours and expectations around what it means to be a man (masculine) or a woman (feminine) (Pilcher & Whelehan 2004). These constructs of gender impact on the social organisation of society in a number of ways (Scott 1986), as we have seen in the scenarios outlined at the beginning of this chapter, including patterns of behaviour and the distribution of labour and resources.

Within sociology, therefore, gender is largely understood as a *social* phenomenon, as something that is taught to us in various ways and that reflects the norms of our culture. As such, gender is also something that differs across time and space—because it is taught, it can vary depending on our cultural background and the period of time we find ourselves in. We *learn* to become boys and girls, men and women or, as French existentialist and founding feminist scholar Simone de Beauvoir (1973) famously wrote: 'one is not born, but becomes, a woman'. While sex refers to a relatively fixed set of characteristics attached to being male or female at birth, gender is changeable. Sociologists have for a number of decades aimed to understand the ways in which gender works as a social phenomenon, and how it manifests diversely in different cultural and temporal spaces.

The question does remain within sociology, however, as to how sex and gender may be linked. Does our biological sex influence our social gender (and maybe even vice versa)? As we shall see, there are diverse theories about this, and the relationship between social gender and biological sex is not a simple or uncomplicated one to determine.

Tick the box: sex or gender?

We have all had to tick the box at some time—the many forms of paperwork today that ask us to indicate our gender by ticking either the 'male' or 'female' box. Consider this in light of the discussion above. What strikes you?

You may have noticed that, for sociologists, the terms 'male' and 'female' refer more to sex than to gender. In theory, too, if gender is social and changeable, then while most males identify as men and most females identify as women, someone male could identify in terms of gender as a 'woman' and a female could identify as a man. Transgender people, for example, identify with a gender that does not correspond with that which is commonly assumed to go with their assigned sex. Within some cultures, certain members of a community may be raised as a gender that does not correspond with their sex. The fa'afafine of Samoa hold a recognised identity within their communities as a third gender, born male in terms of sex but possessing and raised to express both masculine and feminine qualities. Translated, 'fa'afafine' means 'in the manner of a woman', and this is not regarded as deviant or problematic, but rather as a legitimate identity and role within the community: we will return to this topic of 'deviance' in Chapter 18.

Such variations of gender identity have led feminist and gender scholars to argue that gender, as a social category, is changeable across time and space. This view represents a **social constructionist** perspective of gender: this means that gender differences between men and women are viewed as being developed not through biology, or even individual choice, but through the collective influence of society. The social world is viewed as constructing and attaching meaning to gender, and therefore also shaping human behaviour.

Most sociological theories of gender tend towards the social constructionist end of the spectrum of sex/gender theories.

At the other end of the spectrum are theories that are classified under **biological determinism**. These theories consider gender to be a natural consequence of biology—for example Darwinian theories holding that differences between men and women make evolutionary sense. From a biological determinist perspective, we come to be masculine or feminine due to the influence of different hormones, brain structures and other physical characteristics of sex; biology is considered destiny.

Sociologists tend to analyse gender in terms of its social dimensions. However, this is not to suggest that all sociologists deny the existence of certain physical differences between men and women. Rather, for sociologists the social forces that shape our gender identity are highly significant, as evidenced in the differences across place and time in how societies have interpreted what it means to be a man or a woman. This also means that, even where physical differences may exist, these differences are given meaning and elaborated upon through social forces. The physical ability of being able to breastfeed, for example, leads us to attach the idea of 'nurturing' to females, even where some females may not be able to or choose not to breastfeed or have children. We come to view femininity itself as nurturing, layering social meaning onto the physical function of breastfeeding.

The sex/gender distinction

The sex/gender distinction within sociology enables us to acknowledge physical differences while investigating the significant role of social dimensions shaping our gender. Nonetheless, while this distinction has been widely embraced within sociological circles, some social theorists also question the immutable, fixed biological basis for sex. Anne Fausto-Sterling's (2008; 2000) analysis of the social construction of sex is an example of this. She argues that even sex categories such as male or female are impacted upon by social forces, not just biological ones. In the first instance, the assumption that there are only two sexes, which are fully distinct from one another, is a social assumption, she argues, rather than a biological fact.

This dualism (male/female) ignores variations along the spectrum of male and female physical traits, including the existence of intersex persons who are born with both male and female physical elements. Recent events in the world of sports demonstrate this. Athletes, such as South African runner Caster Semenya, present with bodies that do not fit neatly into a single sex category, raising controversial debates about whether or not they can participate in 'women's' sport. The more we find out about the human body, the more we find that 'maleness' and 'femaleness' are quite complex and varied; for example, both 'male' and 'female' athletes present with different hormone levels that may impact on performance—at what point do 'unusual' hormone levels exclude them from participation in competitive sport? Bodies, it seems, might better reflect a continuum of sexed experiences.

The assumption of sex dualism for Fausto-Sterling (2000; 2008) is born out of the social desire for fixed categories that provide a rationale for our society's gender order. The physical differences themselves, she argues, are layered with social meaning, so that we come to view any detected differences in the brain or hormones through the lens of our assumptions about gender, using biological evidence selectively to support our own cultural ideas about gender.

The distinction between sex and gender, while useful, can also mask the strong relationship between them. Rather than sex being fixed and unchangeable, it responds to social ideas about gender. For example, societies that value physical strength in women might see more physical strength developed and manifested among females in their society. Men and women evolve physically to fit in with the social expectations of their culture. Recent scientific research has also shown how both brains and genes can in fact change and respond to environmental circumstances, raising questions about the notion of biological 'hard-wiring' or the neat distinction between nature and culture (Fine 2018; Keller 2016). Instead, it appears that rather than the biological shaping the social, the social world can also shape physical realities.

As we can see, the relationship between sex and gender is not as simple as one might assume, and theorising in this area continues to evolve. For sociologists, however, it is important to note that gender refers to *more* than biology; it refers to the social characteristics of masculinity and femininity usually associated with males and females, and the myriad theories relating to how these social distinctions come about and impact on our lives.

Becoming gendered

So how do we 'become gendered'? That is, what is the process by which we learn to identify as masculine or feminine and become a man or a woman? It is, first of all, important to note that the process of becoming gendered is ongoing; it not only takes place during childhood, but happens continually throughout our lives through various social interactions with other individuals, groups and even organisations that we come into contact with. *How* gendering happens is a question that continues to occupy social thinkers. Some of the best-known foundational theories that attempt to explain these processes are outlined below.

> **Critical reflection**
>
> If a class of nine-year-olds was asked to talk about their least favourite things about being their gender, what might they say? Where do these ideas about gender come from?

Gender socialisation

The first and most basic is the theory of gender **socialisation**. Gender as a social construct is taught through the various spaces we live in day to day and as we have already noted, the various people we come into contact with. These spaces can include our homes and schools, as well as media and community spaces, with social inputs from people such as parents, teachers, peers, journalists and celebrities.

Ideas about gender are reinforced by rewarding or negatively sanctioning our behaviour. For example, a little boy may be rewarded for activities and abilities associated with his gender ('look how strong you are!') or negatively sanctioned for activities and behaviours that are not ('big boys don't cry!'). According to socialisation theory, when all these experiences are added up over time, the messages that are conveyed teach him what is expected of him in terms of his gender. While there may be alternative messages that challenge traditional ideas about gender included in his experiences, the overall pattern of his social interactions reinforces particular ideas about gender to the point where he internalises those messages. In turn, he comes to identify as 'masculine' according to his cultural context and is likely to model those gendered expectations in a similar way to others around him, becoming a socialising agent himself. Socialisation is something that occurs intensively during childhood, but can continue to occur in adulthood as he engages with peers, the workplace, and the mass media, for example, all of which will express ideas about masculinity.

Sociologists apply socialisation theory in a variety of ways to understand gender. Talcott Parsons (Parsons & Bales 1956), for example, wrote on gender roles in the 1950s, focusing on the learning of these roles from our parents within a nuclear family setting. He argued that learning to identify with and play separate gender roles has a practical *function* within society. According to Parsons, while women play a more expressive role (meeting emotional needs), men play a more instrumental role (meeting practical needs and demonstrating leadership), roles he considered *complementary* to one another.

This well-known sociological theory of gender has been widely criticised within sociological circles for proposing that unequal gender roles are 'functional' and therefore somewhat natural, justified and not reasonably subject to change. For many sociologists, the 'expressive role' of women has led to lower status in a society that regards leadership and monetary income—the traditional 'instrumental role' of men—as having a higher value. This instrumental role is also associated with greater levels of social and economic power. As such, Parsons' notion of complementary gender roles acquired through socialisation masks the inequality of these roles—assuming they are largely natural and perpetuating a system in which women are subordinated. It has also been argued that just as women are capable of and should be able to play leadership roles, men should not be assumed to be less nurturing; this is a cultural, rather than natural, tendency that can be changed. As such, when it comes to socialisation theory, variations exist.

Socialisation theory has also been applied in a more critical sense, looking at socialisation not as a neutral, functional process but as one that shapes and perpetuates unequal power relationships.

While socialisation theory offers a good starting point for exploring gender as a social construct, the concept of socialisation more broadly has been criticised for assuming that the process of becoming gendered is a relatively passive, one-directional one. Gender is seen as learnt or picked up from others, implying that human beings absorb gender messages largely without challenge, resistance or action on their own part. In response to this criticism, various theorists have attempted to identify some of the more active ways in which people participate in the process of becoming gendered.

Symbolic interactionism

The work of a well-known sociologist, Erving Goffman (1959), has been referenced and adapted to understand processes of gender socialisation in more active terms. Goffman (who you read about in Chapter 3) was a *symbolic interactionist*: that is, studying and theorising in relation to the face-to-face interactions of human beings in daily life. His 'dramaturgical' analysis posited that people interact in ways similar to the actors in a stage play; that is, human beings learn to identify and play various social roles that are dependent on the place and time they find themselves in, including their real or imagined 'audience'. People pay attention to, and adapt their behaviour in accordance with, the real or anticipated reactions of those around them. In regards to gender, this could include adapting our stage play of life by restricting or enhancing behaviours based on what is regarded as appropriate for one's gender, and thereby 'performing' gender.

A woman may, for example, dress, sit or talk in a way that is intended to elicit a positive response from (and avoid negative responses from) the people in her daily life. This performance is dependent on context; her cultural background and the time period she is in will determine what is considered appropriate feminine conduct, and she will therefore adapt her daily interactions based on her cultural audience. In so doing, she is actively and continually 'performing' her gender on the stage play of life.

Gender performativity

The notion of **gender performativity**—or the manner in which we continually act out and demonstrate to others expected gender roles and behaviours—is a useful concept to advance our analysis of how gender is acquired. The idea of performativity suggests that gender is not just passively absorbed through a one-way flow of socialisation influences, but rather that we actively participate in our gendering in both reinforcing gender norms and resisting them. While performativity acknowledges that all gendered behaviour is shaped by our cultural audience, and therefore has social origins, it also acknowledges that we consciously as well as unconsciously adapt the ways in which we present our gender.

Doing gender

'Doing gender' is a concept related to performativity, developed by West and Zimmerman (1987), that has been used, revisited and adapted by scholars in various ways over the last few decades (including prominent feminist theorist Judith Butler). Principally, this refers to the series of tiny actions that, all together, create gender in our everyday lives, including the way we groom and dress, speak (tone and language), sit, stand, walk and gesture. Through the use and repetition of various actions encoded by our culture as masculine or feminine, we act out—or *do*—our gender each day. For example, you may notice that women and men in many Western social contexts sit in somewhat different ways—women are more likely to cross their legs (regarded as feminine), while men are more likely to sit with their legs wider apart (regarded as masculine). This is an example of 'doing gender' in everyday life.

Being gendered from this perspective is an active rather than passive state. However, this does raise the question of choice and how it stacks up against the forces of socialisation. By saying that we 'do gender', sociologists are not implying that this is a pure individual choice. Sociologists are interested in how society shapes the individual, and as such, doing gender is regarded as being constrained by the cultural options made available to us. To refer back to our example above, while some women may sit with their legs wider apart, most would not—they would have witnessed women sitting with their legs crossed thousands of times, far more than the alternative; they would feel the social pressure to sit gender-appropriately and possibly even face negative social sanctions or responses if they were to break this gender code. In crossing their legs, they actively participate in their gendering, demonstrating it to the world around them, but in a way that is limited according to the contours of their culture.

People who 'do gender' in ways that transgress or resist gender norms may also face consequences, such as discrimination, as a result of these actions. In this way, while there is a recognition of choice and agency, this is constrained and shaped by the ways in which society holds people accountable to current gender norms. With the rise of social movements advocating for the rights of gender non-conforming people, and the increasing visibility of people who 'do gender' in non-conforming ways, 'doing gender' in transgressive ways becomes more possible and likely. In this way, 'doing gender' is more than individual choice, but is shaped by the wider, collective context.

> **BOX 7.1**
> ## Sociology in history

DOING GENDER IN EVERYDAY LIFE—EXPLORING BODY LANGUAGE

Erving Goffman, who we discussed in Chapter 3, undertook a study of gender in advertising in 1979 that showed the active performing of gender. He argued that models for advertisements are encouraged to pose in ways that code them as masculine or feminine.

For example, male hands in advertising are shown as holding objects firmly and with intent, while feminine hands lightly hold—almost caress—objects delicately, or just finely trace the edges of objects. Women are often depicted touching themselves with their hands, whether it be with their hands to their face, hugging themselves protectively or gently touching their necks; while men's hands are usually seen touching objects and other women rather than themselves. Women are often shown lying down or draping themselves on a sofa, appearing inactive and sexually available, or when standing are shown posing off-kilter, bashfully bending a knee or posing with bent torsos. This is contrasted with masculine subjects who are more often shown confidently facing head-on, with their bodies square.

These poses convey messages about gender, particularly around women as vulnerable (lying down defenceless, touching their necks or mouths), sexually available (touching themselves seductively and lying down in sexually available positions) and delicate (hands caressing and tracing objects). In comparison, masculinity is depicted as stronger and more assertive. The images in Figure 7.1 are similar to those from Goffman's 1979 study—do you agree that these poses show the 'performance' of gender? What messages about gender can you see communicated in these poses?

Goffman's study was done some time ago. But let us now consider some more recent advertisements. Select a magazine or set of magazines to analyse, or snap some photographs of advertisements on billboards or in shop windows at your local shopping centre; have a look at some of the advertisements of the brands you follow on Instagram, or look up some brands of the clothing you like online and see what their website advertising looks like.

Have a close look at the images you have gathered. What messages about gender are communicated through these modern advertisements? Do you see gender 'performed' in similar and/or different ways to the 1950s images in Figure 7.1?

We often walk past advertisements without really noticing them. What you have done—looking closely at advertisements in the world around you and considering them in relation to social theory—is the work of a sociologist. In paying close attention to gender, you are engaging in gender analysis and developing a 'gender lens', whereby you notice gender in the world around you, seeing it afresh and thinking it through critically.

Sometimes, it is easier to 'see' gender in the world around us when we consider the alternative to what we know. What would happen, for example, if we saw female models for advertisements posing in ways that we associate with male models, or saw male models posing the way female models normally do? What would this look like, and what would our reaction be?

FIGURE 7.1 What messages about gender can you see communicated in these poses?

While advertising is a very distilled form of gender performance, and we are unlikely to see people posing in these same ways in everyday life, one can observe subtler forms of gender performance occurring in other settings. Go to a place where you can see men and women gathering—your university, local shopping centre or a nightclub, for example—and note down your observations about the ways in which women and men in these settings dress, stand, sit, walk, talk and gesture. Can you see masculinity and femininity being 'performed'? What kinds of actions are part of this performance, and what do they communicate about gender, or about what it means to be a man or a woman?

PERSONAL VOICE

Anonymous—Growing up a 'real man'

❝ James Arvanitakis has asked me to write about my first recollection of encountering ideas about the masculine gender. While the memory of the incident I'm going to relate to you remains vivid, the significance, underlying ramifications and reasons behind it have only just become clear to me.

The incident in question took place on a Saturday morning in the winter of 1981. I was six years old and my twin brother and I had just started playing Rugby League. My mother would stay at home and look after our sister so this was just for the 'boys'. It was often the only time we spent with our father, which made football even more important to us. My dad had played for an established League team and this was a big deal in our house—there were photos everywhere and dad talked about the game with reverence.

It was the fourth game of the season. It started like all the rest, and soon enough had become a blur of running and tackling, with me occasionally looking over at my father to try and guess his opinion of my performance. It was after one such peek that I attempted a tackle and heard a snap.

It was loud and clear, and straightaway my arm tingled and my hand refused to work properly. As a six-year-old, this was an odd sensation and I didn't know what to make of it. I assumed that as I had heard the snap so clearly, everyone else had too. As I waited for the coach to come running my arm began to throb. When no one came to help me, I rejoined the defensive line—with my limp arm hanging at my side—and tried in vain to tackle the opposition. The more I tried the worse my hand felt.

At this point the coach came on to the field and asked what was wrong. I explained about the snap, tingling, numbness and pain. The coach noticed the swelling and escorted me off the field.

I can remember that as I walked off the field my father yelled that I should stop being a 'sissy' and keep playing. He yelled 'it's not netball' and that I should 'toughen up'. Once I was on the bench, my father quickly confronted the coach and forcefully asked why I had been replaced. My coach responded swiftly and clearly: 'His arm is broken … I don't think he should play anymore today, do you?' My father turned promptly and glared at me. He said nothing, yet I knew exactly what he was thinking.

The pain started to get worse and as I waited for my brother to finish so I could go to the doctor, all I could do was wonder why my father was so upset with me. I started to feel this pang in the pit of my stomach, overriding the pain in my arm. (Later I would discover this feeling was guilt.) After a few minutes my father stopped pacing up and down the sideline and he once again confronted my coach. My father insisted that I be returned to the field, while my coach's response was short and to the point: my arm was broken and since I didn't want to play anymore that was the end of the matter. With that my father turned on his heel and made a beeline for me on the bench.

As he stood over me, I became aware that I was letting him down and disappointing him, and I was embarrassed. Dad started to try to shame me into playing by saying: 'I didn't realise that you were such a little sissy. Next week we can dress you in a skirt and mum can take you to the netball so you can play with the other girls.'

With that all the other boys next to me started to laugh. I got cranky and replied: 'I never asked to come off, the coach made me. Honest dad, I'll play if he'll let me', all the while hoping that the coach wouldn't let me play.

My father again confronted the coach, who tried to explain that with my arm broken, it would not do the team or me any good to rejoin the game. Dad interrupted and said the words that solidified my personality for life: 'This is a man's game and pain is a part of life. Better he learn to deal with it rather than run away from it like a girl! He wants to play. If you don't let him, next week *we* will go and play for another team. The decision is yours.'

Looking back, I'm sure that the 'we' my father referred to was more about him than me, as he was playing for the A-grade squad at the same club, but at the time it made me feel important.

The coach asked me if I really wanted to play, and said he understood it was my decision. I looked over his shoulder at my father who nodded his head silently. I said 'yes' and was returned to the field.

For the remainder of the game—roughly 15 minutes—I fought back tears from the agony in my right arm and played as hard as I could, ignoring the pain as best I could.

As I recall the event today, the key thing I remember is looking over at my father as he beamed from ear to ear, a smile seldom seen before or after that day as I continued up and down that field ignoring every sensible urge I had to sit down and cry—proving my masculinity and confirming his at the same time. The game finished and we went straight to the emergency room from the field. As we arrived at the hospital, my father—for the first time without it being a reply—said: 'I love you boy and I couldn't be more proud of you.'

It may sound strange, but it is one of my best memories of growing up.

Gender and work

Gender has very real implications for the material aspects of our lives. One of the clear ways we can see this is through gender differences in earning power and financial circumstances. In Australia, for example, more women than men attend university, and graduates enter paid employment at very similar rates and at similar pay levels. Return in 15 years, however, and things have shifted. Overall, men are earning more than women and engaging in higher rates of full-time employment. Fast-forward to retirement and women in Australia are retiring with significantly less superannuation than men and are more likely to live in poverty. What is going on here?

The Gender Pay Gap (GPG) has been the topic of significant debate in Australia and around the world. As reported by the government in 2019, the gender pay gap sits at 14 per cent (Workplace Gender Equality Agency 2019).

What does this mean? Does it mean that women are earning 14 per cent less for the same job than men? No. The answer is not so simple.

Perhaps women and men earn differently due to different patterns in part- and full-time employment? We know that women, particularly women who become parents, are more likely to work part-time than men due to gendered roles and expectations around parenthood. Therefore, we might expect that women earn less than men, if working part-time, and this affects their overall income and superannuation. Of course, a sociologist would not assume that these patterns of work are a pure 'choice'; differing cultural norms around 'fatherhood' and 'motherhood' would significantly shape the decision of which partner in a heterosexual partnership would spend more time at home.

However, the GPG is not the result of women working part-time at greater rates than men: this is not what it measures. The GPG is based on average weekly full-time equivalent earnings. In other words, for someone who works part-time, the GPG would measure what they would earn if they were working full-time, based on their current rate of earnings. What factors contribute to this gap?

Feminist sociologists have argued that while we often think of the economy as based around paid employment or 'productive work', the economy actually relies on a range of different forms of 'work' or 'labour', some of which is not paid. For example, having someone to care for children and the household is necessary in order for a parent to participate in the paid workforce. Sometimes this unpaid work, called 'reproductive work' is outsourced, for example to cleaning or childcare services (these are often lowly-paid jobs). However, much of it is done without pay, more often by women than men.

Hochschild (1989) called the work completed outside of the paid work day the 'second shift', with women engaging in more household and childcare work regardless of paid employment. The gap between women's and men's contribution to reproductive work identified by Hochschild has reduced in Australia in recent years, but remains nonetheless. This second shift supports paid employment, yet is unpaid and undervalued, and stems from ideologies of gender that link women to nurturing roles.

The extent to which someone is responsible for this unpaid labour can have a bearing on their ability to work long hours or take on roles that require higher levels of travel or responsibility. Further, more senior roles tend not to be available at part-time, whereas lower-paid roles might be. If social norms position women as primary caregivers and nurturers, we can therefore see how it might impact on their 'choice' to work part-time, the kinds of paid work they can and do undertake, and therefore their likely level of pay. Taking time off work or reducing to part-time work will also shape long-term earning potential; those who remain in full-time employment across the life cycle are likely to be earning far more later in life than those who do not.

Gendered patterns in reproductive labour are not the only source of the GPG, however. Gender socialisation impacts on what kinds of careers women and men gravitate towards. Research studies show that subtle, and often unconscious, socialisation factors shape the kinds of careers men and women end up pursuing (Fine 2010). These include the tendency to encourage boys into maths and sciences and assume a greater capacity in girls as nurturers or verbal communicators. The impact of seeing—or not seeing—role models of the same gender in particular professions or classrooms also plays a role. Professions associated with 'femininity' such as teaching, childcare or the 'soft sciences' have tended to be paid less than professions associated with 'masculinity' such as science and technology. Gender socialisation, therefore, can shape people's career preferences in a way that has a bearing on their income. Gender socialisation can also contribute to subtle, unconscious bias in hiring or workplace performance evaluations; sociological research has shown that while overt discrimination is waning, unconscious bias along lines of race, class and gender is very prevalent.

As we can see, direct gender discrimination in rates of pay is not the main source of the GPG; instead, it is far more complex than that and reflects the collective influence of gendered patterns in reproductive labour, gender socialisation and more. While the GPG is reducing in many parts of the world, its resilience reminds us that gender shapes how we work and earn in important ways.

The F-word: feminism

What comes to mind when you hear the word '**feminism**'? In 1913, Rebecca West was famously quoted as saying:

> I myself have never been able to find out precisely what feminism is: I only know that people call me a feminist whenever I express sentiments that differentiate me from a door mat or a prostitute.

While all of us have probably heard about feminism and have a sense of what it is about, many of us don't actually know very much about the feminist movement or feminist theory. This section will give a brief overview of the key concerns of feminist theory and activism.

One of the most important things to know about feminism, at the outset, is how diverse it is. Activists and scholars identifying as 'feminist' look at a range of issues in relation to gender, and often disagree with one another on what gender inequality is and how to address it. There are also various strands of feminism, each with a different theoretical underpinning and approach to gender issues. It may therefore be more accurate to say *feminisms*.

The other important thing to note about feminist theory is that it is both a discipline in and of itself (a distinct and recognised field of study) like sociology or economics or politics, and a theoretical approach that is located within other disciplines. This means that feminist theory is not only applied in feminist and gender studies, but also in sociology, economics, politics, history, art, theatre and many more. In fact, feminist theory has been instrumental in transforming the ways in which many disciplines approach their subject matter, by making gender dynamics visible within these different areas and challenging gendered assumptions made within various disciplines.

One example centres around traditional economics that tended to focus on 'productive' or income-generating activities. Feminist scholars were among those who advocated for unpaid work, such as child care and household work, to be considered as labour within economic analyses. The argument was that, without looking at these forms of unpaid work mostly performed by women, our view of the economy will be incomplete. What would happen, for example, if women suddenly stopped providing free child care and household work? Would men engaged in income-generating activities be able to work in the manner in which they do? Would they need to hire someone to do that work for them, thereby radically changing household expenses? As we can see, looking at those areas of the economy related to women makes a difference in how we understand the economy as a whole. These are the kinds of ideas that feminist theory has been involved in developing.

What exactly is feminism?

But let us take a step back for a minute. What *is* feminism? If feminist work is so diverse, what do feminisms have in common? There are three common key elements to all feminist theory and scholarship.

The first is that *gender is regarded as a key organising social force*—that is, as central to the way in which society is structured and to our experiences of life—and therefore gender is an important concept to employ in social analysis. As we have seen, while much feminist work has focused on women, this can also include analyses of men's experiences and the importance of masculinities.

The second common element all feminisms hold is that *gender relations are characterised by inequality*. Literally meaning 'rule of the father', **patriarchy** broadly describes the nature of this inequality, which sees women—and indeed the feminine—largely subordinated within the gender order socially and economically. Scholars theorising patriarchy, such as Sylvia Walby (1990), argue that the concept is a contested one, meaning that there are different interpretations regarding what it is, how it operates, and how men and women are affected by it. As we will see later in this chapter there are some scholars who have attempted to theorise how patriarchy may also adversely affect some men. However, the key idea within feminist scholarship relates to inequality in gender relations, especially—but not limited—to women.

The third common element is that *feminisms see this inequality as unjust and in need of change*. In other words, feminist theorists and scholars are not content to declare that inequality exists, and are unlikely to argue that it is natural, unavoidable or desirable. For feminist thinkers, gender inequality is worthy of action to achieve a more egalitarian gender order. Again, feminist scholars differ greatly in terms of how they think this should best be achieved, or even on what a gender utopia may look like. However, they do agree that action to change the gender order is important, and within feminist scholarship the goal of research is to understand gender relations better in order to hopefully effect change down the line. This does not mean that feminist theorists are always directly involved in activism themselves. Nor does it mean that feminist research is skewed; indeed, most feminist work relates to how to pursue research in a way that is rigorous and thorough. It does, however, mean that the analyses undertaken by feminist theorists demonstrate a critical perspective on gender inequality and may be used to effect change.

Not just gender: intersectionality

Gender is not just about gender. This may seem like a strange statement, but trends in social research and theory are moving towards this position.

What do we mean by this?

Simply that gender as a social construct does not exist on its own. Instead, it is accompanied and influenced by a variety of other social forces, including race, class, (dis)ability, sexuality and more. One cannot understand gender without understanding how these various factors impact on the meaning and experience of being a man or woman, a boy or a girl. This is called **intersectionality**, or the ways in which different social forces intersect (which we will also discuss in Chapter 9).

Many feminist activists from the 1960s emerging out of the United Kingdom and United States were keen to assert that women's experiences of gender were universal, and that as such women needed to stick together. However, a wave of criticism against this argument also emerged from activists who argued that not all women's experiences were the same. In fact, for women who did not possess membership to privileged social groups (of, for example, white, middle-class, heterosexual, able-bodied women), gender oppression was cross-cut with other forms of oppression (for example, Crenshaw 1991; 1989; hooks 1989; 1984; Rich 1980). Black women in contexts of racial inequality experienced oppression at the hands of white women. Gay women found themselves marginalised within many corners of the feminist movement.

When Betty Friedan wrote her famous feminist book *The Feminine Mystique* in 1963, she spoke of the oppressive limitations placed on suburban women. Arguing that women were imprisoned by social expectations to be the perfect housewife—well-presented with well-kept homes and children—and that what women needed to liberate them was to enter the paid workforce, her book became a key reference point for the feminist movement. However, many activists began to criticise her for assuming the white, middle-class, heterosexual, able-bodied, married experience of suburbia to be the experience of 'women' in general under patriarchy. As bell hooks (1984, p. 2) observed:

> She did not discuss who would be called in to take care of the children and maintain the home if more women like herself were freed from their house labour and given equal access with white men to the professions. She did not speak of the needs of women without men, without children, without homes. She ignored the existence of all non-white women and poor women. She did not tell readers whether it was more fulfilling to be a maid, a babysitter, a factory worker, a clerk or a prostitute than to be a leisure class housewife. She made her plight and the plight of white women like herself synonymous with a condition affecting all American women.

Criticisms such as this highlight that gender is influenced by a variety of factors. The roles, expectations, privileges, limitations and daily experiences of being a man or a woman, boy or girl, are impacted upon by one's membership to other social groups. As such, feminist activists and scholars have increasingly advocated for gender analysis to incorporate intersectionality—an analysis of other aspects of our identity, and the ways in which they cross-cut with gender.

Michael Kimmel, a male feminist writer and speaker, has often told the story below to demonstrate the idea of intersectionality, or that we cannot understand the meaning and experience of gender without understanding the impact of other social categories. His story illustrates how privileged groups within society, whether due to gender, race or class, often find it more difficult to 'see' their own privilege and the way in which it impacts on other aspects of their identity. His story illustrates the critique of gender universality that emerged in the feminist movement, that the experience of gender and gender inequality is different for diverse men and women.

PERSONAL VOICE
Michael Kimmel

❝ I often tell a story about a conversation I observed in a feminist theory seminar that I participated in about a decade ago. A white woman was explaining to a black woman how their common experience of oppression under patriarchy bound them together as sisters. All women, she explained, had the same experience as women. The black woman demurred from quick agreement. 'When you wake up in the morning and look in the mirror,' she asked the white woman, 'what do you see?' 'I see a woman,' responded the white woman hopefully. 'That's the

> problem,' responded the black woman. 'I see a black woman. To me race is visible, because it is how I am not privileged in society. Because you are privileged by race, race is invisible to you. It is a luxury, a privilege not to have to think about race every second of your life.' I groaned, embarrassed. And, as the only man in the room, all eyes turned to me. 'When I wake up and look in the mirror,' I confessed, 'I see a human being. The generic person. As a middle class white man, I have no class, no race and no gender. I'm universally generalizable. I am Everyman.'
>
> Source: Kimmel 2005

Intersectionality and men

Intersectionality impacts not only on women's experiences of gender, but also on men's. Australian feminist scholar R. W. Connell (2007; 1987) developed a theory that aims to explain the different position of men under patriarchy, and how this is shaped by intersectional social forces. Arguing that not all men experience gender in the same way, or accrue the same privileges under patriarchy, Connell introduced the idea of *hegemonic* (or dominant) masculinity. This is the form of masculinity that is ascribed the most social and economic power in society—the ideal form of masculinity to which the greatest privilege accrues. In Western societies this would tend to be a white, middle-to-upper-class, heterosexual, able-bodied masculinity. Men who do not fit within the confines of this construct will have less power—a lower allocation of the 'patriarchal dividend'—than men who do, creating a *hierarchy of masculinities*.

For example, black men have historically experienced discrimination at the hands of more privileged white men, and even white women. Gay men have also in some contexts been regarded as 'not real men' and faced discrimination for not meeting the ideals of a hegemonic masculinity. This demonstrates the variability of the experiences of men (as with women) in accordance with other social forces in their lives. A man who does not meet the criteria of a hegemonic masculinity will still, according to Connell, experience certain privileges under patriarchy as a man, but the extent and type of privileges will vary.

Conclusion

Sociologists seek to understand the ways in which gender manifests in different contexts and to comprehend changes to gender relations across time. Whoever we are, we are all gendered in some way, with an impact on our identity, access to resources and life experiences of various kinds. This is why an analysis of gender is so central to understanding society—if gender shapes us all, it is relevant to all areas of life.

The strong presence of gender and feminist analyses in such a variety of disciplines within the social sciences is testament to this, and as our 'gender lens' or ability to 'see' gender around us is sharpened, so it becomes more and more difficult to look around us and not notice the impact of gender on our lives.

Summary points

- Gender and feminist theory is about more than women; it relates to men and women, boys and girls, as well as to those who identify beyond these binary categories.
- Within the social sciences, 'gender' is widely distinguished from 'sex'. Gender denotes the *social and cultural traits* constructed around masculinity and femininity (the roles, expectations and meanings attached to being a man or a woman). Sex refers to the *biological distinction* between male and female.
- While sex is relatively fixed, gender is socially malleable, changing across time and space, so that what it means to be a man or woman, boy or girl, is shaped by a variety of social influences.
- There are a number of theories that attempt to explain how we become gendered, or how we learn to be masculine or feminine, men or women. For example, *socialisation* theory argues that we learn gender through the reinforcement of certain behaviours by people and other influences (such as media) around us. The notion of *doing gender* refers to the ways in which we actively participate in and play out our gender roles.
- Feminist theory is diverse, represented by a range of approaches to understanding and addressing gender relations. However, feminist theory has as its common premise that gender is a central concept for social analysis, that gender relations are unequal or patriarchal; and that more egalitarian gender relations should be pursued.
- Gender cannot be understood in isolation from other social categories such as race, class, (dis)ability and sexuality. Gender and feminist theory, therefore, is increasingly intersectional, studying the ways in which gender interacts with other social forces.

Sociological reflection

1. *Doing gender photo essay*: In groups of two or three, create two photographs that demonstrate the ways in which you/your peer group 'do gender' in a particular context; for example, body language, speech, adornment or dress. Your photographs should aim to evoke discussion about gender and its performance in everyday life. You should then present your photos and a brief description of the ideas they raise to the class. Be creative! (And remember, for ethical reasons if you are photographing people outside your group you will need to seek their permission to take and use these images.)

2. *Gender and baby clothes research expedition*: Visit a baby clothing store or the baby clothes section of your local department store. Make notes about the different colours, images and words used on the designs for boys and for girls (as well as unisex baby clothes, if these exist). What do these tell us about what is expected of girl and boy children? What role do clothes play in gender socialisation? Write a mini report on your findings.

Discussion questions

1. How have you become gendered? Consider your childhood, youth and adulthood. Where have you learnt—and where do you continue to learn—about what it means to be a man or a woman? Write a reflective piece on your own processes of becoming gendered.

2. What do you love and hate most about being the gender you are (a man or a woman, or any other gender you identify with)? Write down five things you love and five things you hate about being this gender. What do these things reveal to you about masculinity and/or femininity in your cultural context? Use your list as a basis to reflect on the assumptions made about your gender, and the privileges and limitations of different gender roles.

3. What does feminism mean to you? Do you believe in gender equality? If so, would you identify as a feminist or not? Reflect on your relationship to the notion of gender equality and the idea of feminism.

References and further reading

REFERENCES

Connell, RW 1987, *Gender and Power: Society, The Person and Sexual Politics*, Stanford University Press, Bloomington, CA.

Connell, RW 2007, *Masculinities*, 2nd edn, University of California Press, Berkeley and Los Angeles, CA.

Crenshaw, K 1989, 'Demarginalizing the intersection of race and sex: a black feminist critique of antidiscrimination doctrine', *University of Chicago Legal Forum*, 1989, 139–68.

Crenshaw, K 1991, 'Mapping the margins: intersectionality, identity, and violence against women of color', *Stanford Law Review*, 43(6), 1241–300.

De Beauvoir, S 1973, *The Second Sex*, Vintage Books, New York.

Fausto-Sterling, A 2000, *Sexing the Body: Gender Politics and the Construction of Sexuality*, Basic Books, New York.

Fausto-Sterling, A 2008, *Myths of Gender: Biological Theories about Men and Women*, Basic Books, New York.

Fine, C 2010, *Delusions of Gender: The Real Science Behind Sex Differences*, Icon Books Ltd, London.

Fine, C 2018, *Testosterone Rex: Unmaking the Myths of Our Gendered Minds*, Icon Books Ltd, London.

Friedan, B 1963, *The Feminine Mystique*, WW Norton & Company, New York.

Goffman, E 1959, *The Presentation of Self in Everyday Life*, Anchor, New York.

Goffman, E 1979, *Gender Advertisements*, Harper and Row Publishers Inc, New York.

Hochschild, A 1989, *The Second Shift: Working Parents and the Revolution at Home*, Viking Penguin, New York.

Holmes, M 2009, 'Learning and doing gender in everyday life', in *Gender in Everyday Life*, Routledge, Abingdon, pp. 34–57.

hooks, b 1984, *Feminist Theory: From Margin to Centre*, South End Press, Cambridge.

hooks, b 1989, *Talking Back: Thinking Feminist, Thinking Black*, South End Press, Boston.

Keller, EF 2016, 'Thinking about biology and culture: can the natural and human sciences be integrated?', *The Sociological Review Monographs*, 64(1), 26–41.

Kimmel, M 2005, 'Why men should support gender equity', in *The Role of Women in World Peace and the Role of Men and Boys in Gender Equity: Women's Studies Review, Fall 2005 Special Edition (Symposium Proceedings)*, Lehman College, New York, pp. 102–14.

Parsons, T & Bales, RF 1956, *Family Socialization and Interaction Process*, Psychology Press, London.

Pilcher, J & Whelehan, I 2004, *50 Key Concepts in Gender Studies*, SAGE, London.

Rich, I 1980, 'Compulsory heterosexuality and lesbian existence', *Signs*, 5(4), 631–60.

Scott, JW 1986, 'Gender: a useful category of historical analysis', *The American Historical Review*, 91(5), 1053–75.

Walby, S 1990, *Theorizing Patriarchy*, Basil Blackwell, Oxford: <https://libcom.org/files/Theorizing%20Patriarchy%20-%20Sylvia%20Walby.pdf>.

West, C & Zimmerman, DH 1987, 'Doing gender', *Gender and Society*, 1(2), 125–51.

West, R 1913, 'Mr Chesterton in hysterics. A study in prejudice', *The Clarion*, 14 November.

Workplace Gender Equality Agency 2019, *Australia's Gender Pay Gap Statistics*: <www.wgea.gov.au/data/fact-sheets/australias-gender-pay-gap-statistics>.

FURTHER READING

Butler, J 1990, *Gender Trouble: Feminism and the Subversion of Identity*, Routledge, London and New York.

Butler, J 2004, *Undoing Gender*, Routledge, London.

Kimmel, MA, Hearn, J & Connell, RW 2004, *Handbook of Studies on Men and Masculinities*, SAGE, Thousand Oaks, CA.

Millet, K 1969, *Sexual Politics*, Doubleday and Co, New York.

Oakley, A 2005, *The Ann Oakley Reader: Gender, Women and Social Science*, Polity Press, University of Bristol.

O'Reilly, J, Smith, M, Deakin, S & Burchell, B 2015, 'Equal pay as a moving target: international perspectives on the forty years of addressing the gender pay gap', *Cambridge Journal of Economics*, 39(2), 299–317.

CHAPTER 8

Power in contemporary society

LUCAS WALSH

CHAPTER OVERVIEW

In 2019, youth climate protests took place around the world. Galvanised by 15-year-old activist Greta Thunberg, students began to strike during school days. Jonas Kampus, aged 17 from Switzerland, said that: 'For people under 18 in most countries, the only democratic right we have is to demonstrate. We don't have representation … To study for a future that will not exist, that does not make sense' (Carrington 2019).

This might resonate with people of all ages, but as we shall see, not everyone feels this way—notably some senior Australian politicians. Such activism is in contrast to a longer-term concern that many young people—amongst whom you, dear reader, may be one—are disengaged from politics, indifferent, naïve, immature or members of 'gangs'. The reality is more complex.

In this chapter, we speak about power. Some people appear to have it and others don't. Even for those who seem to possess it, power can be fleeting. Just look at the removal of Australia's Prime Ministers from power within their own parties over the last decade: Kevin Rudd, Julia Gillard and Tony Abbott went from leading the country to being 'backbenchers' overnight, and Malcolm Turnbull left politics altogether. Relations of power are unstable.

Of course, power does not only reside in conventional political institutions such as government. It permeates everyday life. Knowledge is equated with power; money, too. Sometimes power is equated with both: as one news outlet points out, Google's revenue in 2017 'would be 59th in the world by GDP if it were a country' (Belinchón & Moynihan 2018).

Power is tragically visible in the violence of wars throughout the world. We speak of the power of music and education, and even the power of love. It swirls virally across social networks, in which 'influencers', for example, have power to alter the moods, aspirations and political actions of their followers. From the image of a lone Chinese protestor confronting tanks in Tiananmen Square in 1989 to Femen activists exposing their breasts in 2013, power can emanate from images, speech and sound. At the same time, it can be elusive and illusory.

There are useful ways of thinking about power and its operation across these diverse settings. This chapter will explore some of these by explaining power in relation to young people, with examples ranging from education to citizenship, health, technology and working in the gig economy.

The purpose of this focus on young people is to provide some real-world contexts in which we can explore different understandings of power.

After reading this chapter, you should be able to:
- Explain how different forms of power 'operate' in contemporary society
- Describe how power can be seen and understood through different 'lenses'
- Apply these lenses to understand power in your own life.

KEY TERMS

Covert power Power that is exerted when an issue or issues are excluded from discussion in decision making. In this way, issues not on the agenda are neither discussed nor decided. It is evident when, for example, 'a person or group—consciously or unconsciously—creates or reinforces barriers to the public airing of policy conflicts' (Bachrach & Baratz 1970, p. 8).

Disciplinary power Power that reflects a move away from overt power through physical punishment to the expansion of a kind of disciplinary net over the moral character of individuals (Foucault 1977). Rather than being purely restrictive of behaviour, disciplinary power is productive, influencing and controlling the ways that people think about and see the world.

Hegemony The dominance of one state, social group or ideology over others.

Instrumentarian power Power that shapes human behaviour toward the ends of others (namely corporations) through automated networked devices, things and spaces (Zuboff 2019).

Lukes' third face of power Power that is characterised by the capacity to change, shape or regulate the wants of someone without their knowledge.

Overt power Power that exists in a direct gain of preference in a visible conflict. It takes place when actor A has the power over actor B to the extent that A can get B to do something that B would not otherwise do (Lukes 1974, p. 12).

Three views of power

In 1974, Steven Lukes released a short but influential book titled *Power: A Radical View*. This book provides insight into visible power, covert power and also Lukes' third face of power. In this chapter, we will not only explore these faces of power, but also delve deeper into the analyses of power by French philosopher, Michel Foucault, and American scholar, Shoshana Zuboff. We shall use these as lenses to view examples of power in action. While some are gruesome and provocative, it proves useful to view one's own life through each of these lenses because they all have relevance to our everyday experiences.

As a starting point, picture a lecture theatre in which rows of students face the teacher who is located at the front. The teacher collects detailed information about students, such as assessment and possibly attendance. There is also the online learning component, which enables a vast amount of information about student participation to be collected and analysed. Run according to strict timetables, classes are typically structured and both students and teachers are expected to behave in certain ways. Inappropriate behaviour might result in the exclusion of a student.

The lecturer sets the agenda for classes, deciding what will be taught and in what sequence, and what will be left out of the curriculum. The seating layout immediately suggests how people are *ordered* within the space. Power not only flows through people and knowledge, but also through the very architecture of the room.

Power can be seen flowing throughout this environment, from the visible authority of the teacher to the ways in which students 'behave' in the classroom. Power is also 'relational': that is, the power that any individual has within the classroom may change in different contexts and even within the classroom. A student, for example, may have power outside of that setting; perhaps they manage others at work.

As a lecturer myself, I may be knowledgeable and appear authoritative in the lecture theatre, but at home I am just a forgetful husband who is forever looking for his car keys.

Many different kinds of power are evident in any specific space and at any single time, some of which we will now examine.

1   Overt power

Between 1957 and 1959, political scientist Robert Dahl conducted a study in the city of New Haven, Connecticut. He was interested in how power structures operate in American democracy—particularly how government and other actors exert power and influence. Dahl (1970) argued that 'virtually no one is completely beyond the reach of some kind of political system' (p. 1) and that we are all subject to a 'pattern of political relationships' (p. 4).

But how do we understand power? According to Dahl, the simplest way to think of power is as enabling the possibility of imposing one's will upon the behaviour of another.

From here, we draw our first view of power: *A* has power over *B* to the extent that *A* can get *B* to do something that *B* wouldn't otherwise do (Lukes 1987, p. 12). From now on we shall call these actors *Alex* and *Ben*.

Power here is concerned with 'ruling over' and domination, rather than through influence: it exists in a direct gain of preference in an overt or obvious conflict. This view of **overt power** echoes a classic definition provided by the sociologist Max Weber, who defined power as 'the possibility of imposing one's will upon the behaviour of other persons' (Weber, cited in Rheinstein 1954, p. 323). He viewed power to be evident in probably all social relationships.

Weber's definition features a focus on the individual, as does the work of Bachrach and Baratz (1970). Like Dahl, these views also share a focus on human behaviour and are therefore described as 'behaviourist' approaches.

How is overt power evident in everyday life? We see it most visibly in law enforcement. Breaking a law comes with a threat of imprisonment, fine or other deprivation. It is also evident in exclusion from a classroom as described above.

Critical reflection

How is overt power visible in the workings of government and society more broadly? Do you exercise overt power in your life, such as at home, playing sport or at work? Who else has power in these settings?

2 Covert power

While overt power is something that we all recognise, we need to dig deeper by looking at 'covert' power. Bachrach and Baratz did this by focusing their analysis of power away from specific interactions over specific issues. They formulated their view of power while studying poverty, race and politics in the American city of Baltimore. In particular, they focused on 'various decisions by the mayor and various business leaders to deflect the developing demands of Baltimore's blacks from becoming politically threatening issues' (Lukes 1974, p. 37). Their analysis provides our second lens through which to view power: **covert power**.

The best way for us to think of covert power is that it exists when a group or individual decides the agenda or priorities. By doing this, those who set the agenda decide what can be discussed and what is excluded.

In this situation, individuals gain or lose through 'a mobilisation of bias'. This emerges, in the words of Bachrach and Baratz, from:

> ... a set of predominant values, beliefs, rituals, and institutional procedures (rules of the game) [that] operate systematically and consistently to the benefit of certain persons and groups at the expense of others (1970, p. 43).

In this situation, issues that may threaten decision makers and those in power are bypassed by excluding them from a given agenda of decision making. Items not on the agenda are never decided and 'non-decisions' occur (Bachrach & Baratz 1970, p. 44).

When issues are excluded from discussion in decision making, covert power is taking place. As Bachrach and Baratz argue, this occurs 'consciously or unconsciously' and 'creates or reinforces barriers to the public airing of policy conflicts' (1970, p. 8).

BOX 8.1

Everyday sociology

POWER AT A PARTY

Imagine that you are holding a party in which the aim is for everybody to have a good time. In drawing up the guest list, certain people are deliberately excluded because they may not get along.

To understand how covert power has worked here, we would look at who eventually made the invitation list, and what the implications are for those excluded—perhaps they find themselves home alone on Saturday night, see images from the party on social media and are not happy to be missing the fun. Here, the hosts of the party are exerting covert power.

An example of covert power occurred during the process of developing a new model of funding schools in Australia. The so-called 'Gonski Review' sought to formulate a more equitable model of school funding (Gonski et al. 2011). School funding in Australia is unusual because a significant level of Commonwealth Government funding is allocated to support non-government ('independent') schools. It could be argued that this is unfair because non-government schools can charge fees and thus generate revenue to fund their operations, whereas government schools rely on funding derived from public revenue with relatively little funding sourced by the parents of the students or elsewhere.

Placing aside the debate about the merits of public versus private schooling, in setting the agenda for the Gonski Review, the former Gillard Government decided that no school should be worse off as a result of any possible funding reform (Gillard 2010). Consequently, this decision significantly shaped the approach and findings of the review, in that the option of reducing funding to both government and non-government schools was effectively excluded. It could be argued that this supported the interests of elite private schools (from which many politicians are alumni). Regardless, it meant that some areas of possible reform were excluded from the Gonski agenda.

Debate was reignited in 2017 when the funding formula was again changed. Known as 'Gonski 2.0', one consequence of this was an anticipated reduction of Australian government funding to Catholic schools (in the order of billions of dollars over a decade). This led to influential displays of both overt and covert power through media, election and direct campaigning about the number of students who could be affected at Catholic schools. In particular, a Catholic advocacy group targeted two federal byelections in Longman (Queensland) and Batman (Victoria) warning parents of possible fee rises and the closure of schools (Goss 2018). Catholic Education even used automated phone calling in Batman to campaign for the major Labor opposition party. Eventually, the government capitulated and walked away from the proposed changes (Maiden 2018).

> **Critical reflection**
>
> How might covert power shape your own life? Who sets the agendas that shape your world and can you influence them? If so, how? How important is what is left off the agenda?

3 Lukes' third face of power

In his work, Lukes (1974) proposed a third type of power that allows for a kind of latent or hidden conflict between the interests of decision makers and excluded parties. This view seeks to move beyond the 'behaviourist' dimensions discussed above which focus on actual decisions, outcomes and observable conflicts. Bachrach and Baratz argued that: 'If there is no conflict, overt or covert, the presumption must be that there is consensus on the prevailing allocation of values' (1970, p. 49). Lukes (2005, pp. 27–8) disagreed and suggested something very different:

> The most effective and insidious use of power is to prevent conflict in the first place ... to assume that the absence of grievances equals genuine consensus is simply to rule out the possibility of false or manipulated consensus ...

In this way, **Lukes' third face of power** seeks to move beyond a focus on observable and actual conflict to an interpretation of power according to which *Alex* may exercise power over *Ben* by not only getting *Ben* to do what *Alex* wants, but also by 'influencing, shaping or determining' *Ben*'s 'very wants' (Lukes 1974, p. 23). The very things that *Ben* wants and desires are shaped by *Alex*. This exercise of power may impact upon people unconsciously.

Consequently, Lukes develops a view of power by asking a very *powerful* question: 'to what extent and in what ways are social actors, whether individuals or collectives, constrained to think and act in the ways they do?' (1977, p. 3).

BOX 8.2
Thinking sociologically

CITIZENSHIP, CONTROL AND THE MODERN STATE

British sociologist Anthony Giddens argues that modern citizenship developed within a 'dialectic' of control (1982, p. 29). Giddens contends that from the late sixteenth century, citizenship formed in a two-way expansion of state sovereignty. This firstly involved a build-up of administrative power that included the development of technologies to survey and regulate citizens through institutions (such as prisons and schools). The second part of this expansion involved convincing the population that it was in their interests for this expansion to happen and consequently that they co-operate to enable it to happen peacefully. The growth of this form of modern democracy meant that the state could gradually rely less on force alone to regulate its populace by fostering a population who *wanted* to be regulated (Held 1989). According to Giddens, the expansion of state sovereignty in turn helped to foster the identity of subjects as citizens.

We shall return to this historical development later on.

Lukes' three-dimensional view of power not only takes into consideration decision making and non-decision making, but also the way that power moves to suppress latent (or hidden) conflicts within any society (Lukes 1974). It offers 'the prospect of a ... sociological and not merely personalised explanation of how political systems prevent demands from becoming political issues or even from being made' (Lukes 1974, p. 38).

According to Lukes' three-dimensional view, any understanding of power must take into consideration that which may limit what someone can even conceive or imagine. It may take the form of an ideological limitation such as the way someone's values and beliefs shape their view of the world. A challenge is identifying whether and how people's minds have been manipulated. Adu-Gyamfi sums up this difficulty:

> It seems that the third dimension operates invisibly and can only be seen in retrospect. Until people realise that what they have been used to for years is actually not in their interest it becomes difficult for the researcher to identify power's third dimension (2013, p. 1768).

To examine this form of power therefore, we need to look beyond observable behaviour and towards the 'social forces and institutional practises that shape people's interests and prevent people from knowing their real interests' (Adu-Gyamfi 2013, p. 1768).

This links with the work of Antonio Gramsci—who wrote some of his most well-known work while in jail as a political prisoner during the Second World War—which proposed a theory of cultural power (or **hegemony**). Manifest through ideology, this form of power is used more indirectly than overt power by making people believe in and consent to the ruling authority (this could be the state and or the ruling capitalist class). Norms and values that maintain the real power of elites are so pervasively promoted that they come to seem like the 'common sense' values of all (Gramsci 1971). This can happen through various means, including education.

> **Critical reflection**
>
> If you think back to the first few chapters of this book, consider how many 'normal' and 'common sense' things we have asked you to challenge. By doing so, you are delving into understanding Lukes' third face of power.

Other ways that this form of power works includes an absence of necessary resources, skills or knowledge—which is why many of us argue that education is an important way to confront power. That means we can see education as potentially a place that both makes us succumb to power, as well as having the potential to confront it. We can see this in debates about human-induced climate change: many of our economic classes make us accept the fact that we must continue to expand the economy for us to maintain and improve living standards. We accept it as 'normal' and 'desirable' even if it means that this perpetuates the damage to our environment. But it is also at school that we learn about the causes of climate change, how we can assert our democratic rights (such as taking part in a school strike) as well as what alternatives are available!

BOX 8.3

Everyday sociology

CAN BUSINESS FILL THE VOID CREATED BY GOVERNMENT INACTION ON CLIMATE CHANGE?

Continuing our conversation about climate change, despite the overwhelming scientific consensus about human-made climate change, the Australian government has been criticised for being too slow to respond in a substantial way. Exploring the role of business in acting on climate change, it has been asked: 'To what extent should we trust that business—which in the past has typically worked against climate goals—has changed its spots, and will be a leader in the climate movement?' (Purtill & Afshariyan 2019). There is a salient question of the covert power exerted by vested corporate interests over setting government agendas.

Reflecting Lukes' third face of power at a deeper level is the role of education.

In response to the student strikes for action on climate change in 2018, then Resources Minister, Matt Canavan, said that students should 'be at school to learn about how you build a mine, how you do geology, how you drill for oil and gas, which is one of the most remarkable scientific exploits of anywhere in the world that we do ... These are the type of things that excite young children' (AAP 2018).

Was Minister Canavan's vision one of learning or manipulation or both?

Critical reflection

This third face of power is based on the idea that as we are consciously and unconsciously shaped by values, ideologies and systems, so too is the manifestation and operation of power. One feminist view, for example, is that patriarchy—the domination and oppression of women by men—shapes all power relations (Millett 1970; see also Chapter 7). Despite the recognition of a need for gender equality in contemporary society, men continue to earn more money, dominate the boards of corporations and hold more positions of public office, all of which amount to significant economic and political power.

When Ukrainian 'radical feminist' Femen protesters exposed their breasts as an act of wilful protest and defiant expression of autonomy, it could be argued that this subversive act was undermined by seeking to attract the male gaze and appeal to the male objectification of women. This attempt at subversion ironically might reinforce a view that women are only paid attention to when they expose their physical selves.

On the other hand, it could also be argued that they are deliberately manipulating a system (namely, the media) to raise public awareness of their causes. What do you think?

Controversy over Femen's 'sextremism' highlights another dimension of power, which underpins our fourth and final lens.

4 Relational and disciplinary power

Our final view of power seeks to move beyond the binary of ruler and the ruled. Here power is conceptualised within a relational field: that is, it exists in the relation between people. It has no centre and cannot be rationalised into specific portions or actors.

This takes us into the world of French philosopher, Michel Foucault. His influential book, *Discipline and Punish* (1977), begins with a gruesome recount of the execution of servant Robert-François Damiens in 1757 for attempting to murder King Louis XV. Drawing from coverage of the event by the *Amsterdam Gazette* and other historical documents, Foucault describes Damiens' punishment through rituals of public torture and dismemberment that took place before the main door of the Church of Paris. Damiens' final moments were recorded in horrific detail—even though I enjoy the occasional horror film, the account is still unpleasant reading.

Pleading to God for pity, Damiens' brutal punishment was a visible display of the power of the French Monarchy during a time when the use of dark dungeons, removal of limbs and other nasty displays of authority were routine. By publically torturing and executing Damiens, the King displayed his authority and power over his subjects.

Foucault then contrasts this with the rules drawn up 80 years later for 'The House of Young Prisoners in Paris', which reflect a new form of individual and social regulation. Examples of these rules included:

> 17. The prisoners' day will begin at six in the morning in winter and at five in summer. They will work for nine hours a day throughout the year. Two hours a day will be devoted to instruction. Work and the day will end at nine o'clock in winter and at eight in summer ...
>
> 19. The prayers are conducted by the chaplain and followed by a moral or religious reading. This exercise must not last more than half an hour ...
>
> 21. Meal. At ten o'clock the prisoners leave their work and go to the refectory; they wash their hands in their courtyards and assemble in divisions. After the dinner, there is recreation until twenty minutes to eleven ...
>
> 22. School. At twenty minutes to eleven, at the drum-roll, the prisoners form into ranks, and proceed in divisions to the school. The class lasts two hours and consists alternately of reading, writing, drawing and arithmetic (Foucault 1977, p. 6).

The birth of the modern prison and use of these rules reflected new regimes of power. Foucault uses Jeremy Bentham's 'Panopticon' to illustrate this new form of social regulation. The Panopticon is the building that you may see in the middle of a prison yard. It was designed in the late eighteenth century to enable large numbers of prisoners to be viewed from a single tower looking onto all of the cells. The Panopticon allows a guard to view all the prisoners, but the prisoners cannot tell when they are being watched, encouraging them to behave well at all times.

Many prisons that used this model also featured glass ceilings to enable natural light so that prisoners could be constantly viewed throughout the day. They reflect an approach based on surveillance and 'rehabilitation'. This became common practice and even Australia's early convict prisons like Port Arthur were modelled on this!

The types of daily regimes described above were attempts to develop 'a new mode of obtaining power of mind over mind' (Bentham, in Bozovic 1995, p. 31).

This shift from torture to a new penal style coincides with the Age of Enlightenment in Western Europe—part of the processes of modernity discussed in Chapter 5. Imprisonment utilised the regulation of behaviour and instruction as a means of reordering individuals by shining a light on 'problem' behaviour and to cultivate moral self-regulation. The shift is significant because it reflected a wider change in the methods of ordering people in general.

From the Enlightenment, there was a move from physical punishment to the expansion of a kind of disciplinary net over the moral character of the individual (Foucault 1977). So where the very public and brutal execution of Damiens reflected a deliberately violent display of overt power by Church and Monarchy, the regulation of individuals shifted towards the use of institutions of the state such as prisons and schools to correct 'immoral' behaviour of the individual and develop 'good citizens'. This approach informed the development of hospitals (including 'mental asylums'), as well as the classrooms and lecture theatres that we commonly sit in today.

DISCIPLINARY POWER

In this section, we are going to unpack Foucault's ideas a bit more. One part of Foucault's work was his discussion around 'governmentality' or the art of government (Foucault 1991). Governmentality as part of modernity became focused on the logics of regulation, influence and control directed at how people think, behave and see the world.

As part of this, Foucault argued that '**disciplinary power**' emerged. Disciplinary power is *productive* rather than being restrictive of our behaviour. That is to say, power here works by having us behave a certain way rather than restricting our behaviour. In Australia, for example, we are expected to be employed, save for a house and contribute to the economic wellbeing of our nation. The power yielded by the state is not just focused on stopping us doing certain things, but through education and financial incentives, also works to make us behave in a certain way and strive for certain things.

This key feature of Foucault's approach looks at power at a micro level: that is, on the personal and everyday level. By drawing attention to shifting micro (or everyday) practices within broader historical changes, Foucault provides a critical model through which to understand modern power, rule and authority:

> To say that power took possession of life in the nineteenth century, or to say that it has, thanks to the play of technologies of discipline on the one hand and technologies of regulation on the other, succeeded in covering the whole surface that lies … between body and population (Foucault 2004, p. 253).

According to this approach, it is perhaps more appropriate to think of the way 'power influences through *Ben*' rather than '*Alex* influences *Ben*'. Power can be seen as acting *through* relationships in dynamic and multiple ways.

As such, power is relational. For Foucault (2004), no one is external to power as there is no 'power over' us as we see in a binary between rulers and ruled. Rather than looking at power residing with one person or group, we should study power based on relationships, as it is these relations that determine the elements in which power operates.

Today, for most of us to feel that we are integrated into society, we use the 'technologies' of 'self-discipline' to meet some of the expectations I mentioned above. The responsibility to meet these expectations is placed upon you as the individual—and you are seen at fault if you fail to live up to these expectations. The term 'technology'—which we discuss in more detail below—is used here in the sense that it is a systematic application of a body of knowledge. So rather than relying on the first type of power through direct rule and punishment, governments have become quite skilful at making citizens enact policy objectives on themselves.

> **BOX 8.4**
> ## Everyday sociology
>
> **PERSONAL HEALTH IN CONTEMPORARY SOCIETY**
>
> Where institutions of public health grew tremendously within the expansion of the welfare state during the twentieth century, the recent decline of welfare states throughout the world has often been accompanied by a shift onto models of prevention, seeking to develop individual citizens who take 'better' care of themselves. In doing so, they seek to prevent the development of negative health issues that may draw resources from the public purse.
>
> Public campaigns to increase the use of sunscreen and to promote weight-loss and cessation of smoking are all techniques seeking to shape individual citizens to ease financial burdens off the state. Self-regulation and a perception of individual choice are all ways by which the state can enforce order via a kind of 'remote-control'. This type of disciplinary power is significant in that governments regulate people by fostering moralities and behaviours in individuals to regulate themselves to meet the policy objectives of the state.

The other thing for us to think about is that power is 'dynamic'. According to this relational perspective, 'the successful enforcement of power depends as much on a coercer's force as on others' acquiescence to it. At all times, both parties—privileged and disadvantaged— are simultaneously undergoing and exercising power' (Severs, Celis & Erzeel 2016, p. 350).

We often forget how the English Westminster system of political representation (that heavily influenced the formation of Australian democracy) used to exclude women from voting. Prior to legislation granting women the vote in 1918, such exclusion was then taken by many men and women as given. Even during debates in English parliament immediately leading up to 1918, 'powerful men in Parliament were trying to stop votes for women' (Gillett 2018). One male MP said that:

> Women are likely to be affected by gusts and waves of sentiment ... Their emotional temperament makes them so liable to it. But those are not the people best fitted in this practical world either to sit in this House ... or to be entrusted with the immense power which this bill gives them.

Another argued that:

> There are obvious disadvantages about having women in Parliament. I do not know what is going to be done about their hats. How is a poor little man to get on with a couple of women wearing enormous hats in front of him? (Gillett 2018)

As the power of those adult white males crumbled, so too did a longstanding binary perception that women are powerless.

For intersectionality theorists, the observation that 'one is never just privileged or oppressed ... dissolves rigid distinctions between the so-called powerful and the powerless ...'

In so doing 'it draws attention to the productive aspects of power, namely, the ways in which the exertion of power invariably also produces possibilities for resistance' (Severs, Celis & Erzeel 2016, pp. 350–1).

Notably, when the vote was given to women, it applied only to those over the age of 30! Contemporary debates about lowering the current voting age continue to be laden with assumptions over the 'maturity' of younger people to vote. Former Australian MP Lindsay Tanner has argued against lowering the voting age to 16 because at this age Australian citizens have 'less connection with the world of adult responsibility than any previous generation of that age, as people enter full-time employment, purchase homes and establish families a good deal later than in earlier times' (Tanner 2011, p. 38). As such markers of 'adulthood' are somewhat fluid if not arbitrary. Tanner's patronising tone is inescapable: it serves to infantilise young people who prior to voting can work and pay taxes but not be eligible to vote for political representatives who will determine how their taxes are spent (Walsh 2012). And yet many young people resist this this exertion of power. In the case of our protestors at the start of this chapter, the dismissive tone of the response by some 'adults' appears to galvanize them to further action.

Technologies of self-discipline

Disciplinary power is used by states instead of brute force to instigate new forms of **social training**. Social training is concerned with processes of normalisation that seek to order citizens, not just at a collective level, but at the very granular or micro level of the individual. The use of routines, from school timetables to medically prescribed personal fitness regimes, are examples of social training. Power is understood as a multiplicity of relations immanent in the sphere in which they operate, and which constitute their own organisation.

A contemporary of Foucault's approach, Nikolas Rose (1996), suggests that techniques of normalisation entrench patterns of domination. These patterns are embedded through governmental strategies that 'autonomize' and 'responsibilize' the citizen as subject: that is, they make us autonomous individuals responsible for our own success or failure. These strategies involve fostering a 'subjectivity'—or way of seeing the world—in which the individual becomes 'an entrepreneur of itself, seeking to maximize its own powers, its own happiness, its own quality of life, through enhancing its autonomy and then instrumentalizing its autonomous choices in the service of its own lifestyle' (Rose 1992, pp. 150–1). Responsibility for the self is shifted from the state to the individual. Personal responsibility becomes the main lever through which social ends can be achieved. Notions of individual freedom, competition and entrepreneurialism are valorised and so pervasive in liberal democracies as to appear 'normal' and desirable.

Consequently, modern government is, by Foucault's definition, about the calculated and systemic ways in which the behaviour of citizens is shaped. Accordingly, *governmentality* is about the development of expert systems by the state designed to regulate and alter the public and private conduct of citizens. For Rose, *expert systems* of human conduct produced by various authorities, such as school teachers, play an important role.

Ian Hunter's (1994) analysis of the rise of state education in the United Kingdom takes a Foucauldian approach to understand how schools are charged with 'moral training' of students by instilling a self-governing principle in them to further the needs of the state.

To illustrate how strategies of governance are redirected to the regulation of the self, let's briefly return to the lecture theatre and classroom. Foucault uses Bentham's model of the Panopticon to emphasise the ways by which behavioural norms are internalised via technologies of regulation. The modern school employs these disciplinary technologies. In the classroom, students are overtly compelled to behave in certain ways under the gaze of the teacher, whose visible authority defines the parameters of acceptable, normal conduct. Students gradually incorporate these codes of conduct into their own moral framework so that the normalised self maintains self-surveillance in order to avoid punishment for 'inappropriate' behaviour. Ideally, students learn to regulate themselves.

BOX 8.5
Everyday sociology

WORKING IN THE GIG ECONOMY

Young people today face changing worlds of work—something you will learn in more detail in Chapter 19. This is evident in the rise of the 'gig' economy. As traditional careers are replaced by a 'portfolio' of jobs across one's lifetime, in some sectors employers require employees to use Australian Business Numbers (ABNs) to work as contractors. In this way, they change from being employees to businesses working with other businesses. Where work traditionally involved a transaction of the employee's time and effort for money, workers define themselves and are defined by employers as a business with a brand (Gershon 2017).

The gig economy is promoted as enabling individual ('entrepreneurial') workers to have more flexibility in how, when and where they work. But as individual businesses they might forgo the provision of employee entitlements, such as increased pay during public holidays and other benefits. In 2019, food delivery company Deliveroo was sued by former delivery rider, Jeremy Rhind, for allegedly failing to pay the minimum wage, penalty rates and superannuation. Where the hourly minimum wage in Australia is $19.49, Rhind reportedly said that he was paid $9 per delivery and struggled to earn the minimum wage (Chau 2019).

Different faces of power are evident here: the role of employer and employee is changing alongside the relationship between the two. Deliveroo has a certain power over delivery riders by enabling them to work. Rhind has the power to not choose to undertake the labour of delivery. He is also possibly at risk of exploitation by Deliveroo.

At a deeper level, the meanings of work and career are changing in ways that promote choice and flexibility of employees, but which also arguably reinforce and boost corporate profitability and power.

SURVEILLANCE CAPITALISM

The business model of Deliveroo is enabled through social media and an unprecedented concentration of power. In 2018, the average Australian male aged 14–24 spent just under nine hours (528 minutes) per week on social media. The average woman in the same age group spent more than double this time (Croft 2019). Amongst other uses, social media has become a powerful tool for campaigns such as the #MeToo movement against sexual harassment and assault. As social media has become pervasive, power flows through life in ways that are not always visible.

Alongside these 'democratised' uses of technology is a concentration of enormous power. When using ostensibly 'free' online services such as Facebook, the saying goes that 'If you're not paying for it, you become the product'. But Shoshana Zuboff (2019) suggests that more is going on: the rise of 'surveillance capitalism'. This emergent form of capitalism:

> describes a market driven process where the commodity for sale is your personal data, and the capture and production of this data relies on mass surveillance of the internet. This activity is often carried out by companies that provide us with free online services, such as search engines (Google) and social media platforms (Facebook) (Holloway 2019).

Under surveillance capitalism, internet users like you and me 'are … the objects of a technologically advanced and increasingly inescapable raw-material-extraction operation. Surveillance capitalism's actual customers are the enterprises that trade in its markets for future behaviour' (Zuboff 2019, p. 10).

The surveillance economy is a 'new economic order that claims human experience as free raw material for hidden commercial practices of extraction, prediction and sales …' (Zuboff 2019, p. viii). Companies such as Google, Facebook and Microsoft exploit and manipulate human behaviour through pervasive advertising.

Zuboff proposes '**instrumentarian power**' as a form of power to emerge from surveillance capitalism. This power shapes human behaviour (such as Google) through automated networks of devices, spaces and things. Following Zuboff's thesis, it becomes possible to envisage a concentration of corporations mediating, colonising and profiting from all human life (and possibly all life). This new corporate power infiltrates all human knowledge and interests, monetising our every human experience. Governments and organisations such as the European Union are struggling to keep pace with this technological development (Scott, Cerulus & Overly 2019).

Zuboff argues that surveillance capitalism is 'marked by concentrations of wealth, knowledge and power unprecedented in human history', posing a grave threat to individual freedom and democracy through 'a coup from above: an overthrow of the people's sovereignty' (Zuboff 2019, p. viii).

Critical reflection

What are the implications of Foucault's understanding of power in relation to Luke's three faces of power discussed above?

Can you see examples of disciplinary or instrumentarian power in your own life?

Is it possible to resist domination?

Spotlight on young people

Like all theories you will come across in this book, these different views of power do not neatly fit together, but provide useful ways of understanding power in contemporary life. With this in mind, the final part of this chapter will explore these views in relation to the experiences of a group of young change-makers in Australia who participated in a case study about how they view their capacity to make social and political change. Some were volunteers at their local council, while others were social entrepreneurs participating in a leadership program that provides opportunities for mentoring, peer learning and skills development to enable them to improve their social impact (Walsh, Black & Prosser 2018).

Before we explore these young people's perspectives of power in detail, the wider context of young people's participation provides insight into broader experiences of young people and power.

Like in many other liberal democracies throughout the world, research has consistently shown that many young people in Australia feel remote from decision-making processes and political institutions (Harris & Wyn 2009). Political parties and politicians are not seen to reflect young people's values and interests. Many do not feel that they can exercise overt power through the democratic process. In fact, a survey in 2019 found that just over half (55 per cent) of Australians aged 18–29 years expressed a preference for democracy, compared with 68 per cent of Australians over 30 years old. Nearly a third (30 per cent) of those aged 18–29 said that 'in some circumstances, a non-democratic government can be preferable' (Kassam 2019). Despite the powerful role played by democratic citizens in the twentieth century, such as through the civil and women's rights movements, political representatives and institutions seem very distant and, for some, less desirable today.

Young people often feel the overt power of the state. In the Australian state of Victoria, for example, police can 'move on' people, including those involved in peaceful protests. Protestors are also subject to overt power because they can be prevented from entering a particular public space and even imprisoned (Williams 2016). Throughout the world, governments have overtly discouraged protests against inaction in response to climate change (for another example, see BBC 2014).

It could also be argued that the act of discouraging protesters from having their message heard is a form of covert power. As discussed above, school protestors were criticised by the Australian government for missing school to attend climate change protests in 2018. Minister Canavan said at the time that 'Walking off school and protesting, you don't learn anything from that …' and 'The best thing you learn about going to a protest is how to join the dole queue [to collect government benefits]', adding 'That's what your future life will look like, up in a line asking for a handout, not actually taking charge of your life and getting a real job' (AAP 2018). But 14-year-old Harriet O'Shea Carre said: 'We have to sacrifice our education, which is something we really value, so we're showing them that … this is even more important than our education'.

The discouragement and exclusion of young people from the agenda of governments is linked to a form of ageism: that is, stereotyping and discrimination against people on the basis of their age. This occurs as governments contradictorily expect young people to pay taxes when working and obey laws (that for most school students are determined by representatives for whom they are not entitled to vote), but are suspicious of young people because they are young and decry them when they take action on issues such as climate change.

These perspectives only explain part of the picture. Young people are seeking to make an impact and influence political and social change through other means. Driven by issue-based or 'choice' politics, the evidence suggests that young people are engaging in activities that aren't necessarily visible in the conventional ways that we understand political participation (Walsh & Black 2018). One way is through social enterprise, through which young people reject the idea that corporations and governments are best able to determine the most effective allocation of resources to social ends. Drawing from the resources and techniques of government, business and not-for-profit sectors, social enterprises often work between and across conventional channels of participation, power and influence.

BOX 8.6

Everyday sociology

CASE STUDY OF YOUNG PEOPLE'S EXPERIENCES OF POWER

In the final profile of this discussion, we shall look at the experiences of young people and their perceptions of power in action. As part of my research, we conducted focus groups with young people, such as social entrepreneurs, seeking to make change and the extent to which they believe that they have the power to influence society (Walsh & Black 2018). Their testimonies were analysed and categorised using Lukes' conceptual approaches to power (Walsh, Black & Prosser 2018).

The results were really interesting and illustrate how dimensions of power intersect and overlap.

Firstly, many felt the overt controlling influence of adults.

Moving into the second dimension of power, 'adults' denied young people entry into decision-making on issues of direct concern to them. One female suggested that young people may be discouraged by the lack of 'avenues' to engage powerful entities. Another participant felt constrained because young people 'haven't had the same amount of time to build up social and financial power to overcome some of those barriers'.

Some felt empowered at the local level because they had the opportunity to be considered 'experts' and could thus influence agenda-setting (and thus covert power).

But Lukes' third face of power presented challenges. One had difficulty finding 'what's true and accurate information ... You get a lot of information but you have to wade through the crap [and] to get to the truth is pretty hard for a lot of people'. This young person found that some Indigenous communities, for example, 'aren't told anything ... they just don't receive that information so they can't even actually make an informed choice because they don't even have the information to start with and that's one of their biggest barriers.'

It was suggested that young people 'might feel disempowered because they don't know that they have such powers ... young people don't know that if they lobby a certain person, like organisations, they can actually make a change or force those people to make a change—to do something.'

At a deeper level, echoing Gramsci there was awareness of predominant values that operates systematically against young people because they are young. A mobilisation of bias against young people is reflected in the view that 'society doesn't put young people in the top job and we see that in the Government, we see that with big organisations ... taking responsibility off young people.'

Discussions highlighted how young people are negatively portrayed by those in positions of power and 'how as a society we problematise young people so young people are a problem to solve ... " Young people are viewed suspiciously because of a perception that 'if you didn't give them something to do they'd be doing something wrong.'

Illustrating the relational nature of power, one young person observed that what constitutes 'youth' itself has shifted across time:

> So a hundred years ago, women were having babies at fifteen and that was normal. Now they're not having babies till thirty because you know you're not responsible at fifteen, you're not responsible at sixteen, why would you have children? And then you go way back to the 1400s and Joan of Arc led an entire country to victory at the age of sixteen. We now treat our sixteen-year-olds like they can't wipe their own arse and they need to be, like, managed or they need to be sorted out. So I think we're slowly taking responsibility off young people and the less responsibility you have, the less influence you have on society ...

Critical reflection

The final comment above highlights a tension in the responsibilisation of young people. On the one hand, they view it as their individual responsibility to make change but at the same time encounter forces that strip responsibility from them because they are young. Do any of the characterisations of young people described above resonate with you? Do young people have power? What types of power (or possible lack thereof) are evident in their testimonies? In the twenty-first century, does government have more, less or the same power? What about social media influencers or corporate mediators of information, such as Google?

Does anyone really have power?

Conclusion

This chapter has highlighted that power can be understood in many ways. No single definition fully explains the complex ways in which power 'works' in society. They are interrelated and power needs to be understood in historical context.

Lukes proposes that these views 'can be seen as alternative interpretations and applications of one and the same concept of power, according to which *A* exercises power over *B* when *A* affects *B* in a manner contrary to *B*'s interests' (1974, p. 27). The perspectives discussed in this chapter also suggest that power can be relational and flow beyond any given actor.

Evident in all social relations, power seems to be inescapable.

Summary points

- Sociologists investigate the ways in which power operates in society and how they enable and disrupt forms of social integration.
- We should think about multiple forms of power rather than any single notion of power.
- Power needs to be understood in the context of social and political development from pre-modern to modern society. Just prior to the Age of the Enlightenment is a useful place to begin.
- There is an important link between the characteristics of modernity identified in Chapter 5 and how power now operates in our society: power no longer exclusively resides in the hands of a queen or king. Rather, it is everywhere in, for example, the way our choices are limited or subtly controlled and the different ways that we seek to influence each other.

Sociological reflection

1. Describe how the nature and use of power has changed in the transition to modernity.
2. How does it differ across historical and spatial contexts?
3. What are the links between the issues raised by Michel Foucault in his discussion of power and some of the characteristics of modernity described elsewhere in this book.
4. List some ways that the different kinds of power are evident in your life.

Discussion questions

1. What is power and in what different ways does it operate?
2. Do young people have power?
3. Does anyone have power?

References and further reading

REFERENCES

Adu-Gyamfi, J 2013, 'Can children and young people be empowered in participatory initiatives? Perspectives from young people's participation in policy formulation and implementation in Ghana', *Children and Youth Services Review* 35, 1766–72.

AAP 2018, 'Climate change protest will lead to dole queue, minister tells students', *Sydney Morning Herald*, 30 November 2018: <www.smh.com.au/politics/federal/climate-change-protest-will-lead-to-dole-queue-minister-tells-students-20181130-p50jbt.html>.

Bachrach, P & Baratz, MS 1970, *Power and Poverty*, Oxford University Press, New York.

Bendix, R 1977, *Max Weber*, University of California Press, Los Angeles.

Belinchón, F & Moynihan, R 2018, '25 giant companies that are bigger than entire countries', *Business Insider*, 25 July: <www.businessinsider.com/25-giant-companies-that-earn-more-than-entire-countries-2018-7?r=AU&IR=T>.

Bentham, J 1995, *The Panopticon Writings*, M Bozovic (ed.), Verso, London.

British Broadcasting Corporation (BBC) 2014, 'Occupy Parliament Square protest camp prevented', *BBC News*, 24 November: <www.bbc.com/news/uk-30155308>.

Carrington, D 2019, 'Youth climate strikers: "We are going to change the fate of humanity"', *The Guardian*, 1 March: <www.theguardian.com/environment/2019/mar/01/youth-climate-strikers-we-are-going-to-change-the-fate-of-humanity>.

Chau, D 2019, 'Deliveroo sued by former worker who alleges exploitation and underpayment', *ABC News*, 28 August: <www.abc.net.au/news/2019-08-28/deliveroo-case-ex-worker-alleges-exploitation/11454870>.

Croft, P 2019, 'Communicating more effectively with students? There's an app for that', *Campus Review*, 21 January: <www.campusreview.com.au/2019/01/communicating-more-effectively-with-students-theres-an-app-for-that/>.

Dahl, RA 1970, *Modern Political Analysis*, 2nd edn, Prentice-Hall Inc., New Jersey.

Foucault, M 1977, *Discipline and Punish*, Penguin Books, England.

Foucault, M 1991, 'Governmentality', trans. R Braidotti, rev'd C Gordon, in G Burchell, C Gordon & P Miller (eds), *The Foucault Effect: Studies in Governmentality*, University of Chicago Press, Chicago, pp. 87–104.

Foucault, M 2004, *Society Must be Defended*, Penguin, London.

Gershon, I 2017, *Down and Out in the New Economy: How People Find (Or Don't Find) Work Today*, University of Chicago Press, Chicago.

Giddens, A 1982, 'Power, the dialectic of control and class structuration', in A Giddens & G MacKenzie (eds), *Social Class and the Division of Labour: Essays in Honour of Ilya Neustadt*, Cambridge University Press, New York, pp. 29–45.

Gillard, J 2010, *Speech delivered in Brisbane, Queensland*, 16 August: <http://electionspeeches.moadoph.gov.au/speeches/2010-julia-gillard>.

Gillett, F 2018, 'Women's suffrage: 10 reasons why men opposed votes for women', *BBC News*, 29 April: <www.bbc.com/news/uk-43740033>.

Gonski D, Boston, K, Greiner, K, Lawrence, C, Scales, B & Tannock, P 2011, *Review of Funding for Schooling. Final Report*, Department of Education, Employment and Workplace Relations, Canberra.

Goss, P 2018, 'Explaining Australia's school funding debate: what's at stake', *The Conversation*, 18 July: <https://theconversation.com/explaining-australias-school-funding-debate-whats-at-stake-100023>.

Gramsci, A 1971, *Antonio Gramsci Prison Notebooks*, Lawrence and Wishart, London

Harris, A & Wyn, J 2009, 'Young people's politics and the micro-territories of the local', *Australian Journal of Political Science*, 44(2), 327–44.

Held, D 1989, *Political Theory and the Modern State*, Polity Press, Cambridge.

Holloway, D 2019, 'Explainer: what is surveillance capitalism and how does it shape our economy?' *The Conversation*, 25 June: <https://theconversation.com/explainer-what-is-surveillance-capitalism-and-how-does-it-shape-our-economy-119158>.

Hunter, I 1994, *Rethinking the School: Subjectivity, Bureaucracy, Criticism*, Allen & Unwin, Sydney.

Kassam, N 2019, *Lowy Institute Poll 2019: Australia and the World*: <www.lowyinstitute.org/publications/lowy-institute-poll-2019>.

Lukes, S 1974, *Power: A Radical View*, Macmillan Press, London.

Lukes, S (ed.) 1977, *Essays in Social Theory*, Macmillan Press, London.

Lukes, S (ed.) 1987, *Power*, New York University Press, New York.

Lukes, S 2005, *Power: A Radical View*, 2nd edn, Macmillan, London.

Maiden, S 2018, 'How the Catholic schools sector outplayed the Coalition', *The Guardian*, 5 November: <www.theguardian.com/australia-news/2018/nov/06/how-the-catholic-schools-sector-outplayed-the-coalition>.

Millett, K 1970, *Sexual Politics*, Abacus, London.

Purtill, J & Afshariyan, N 2019, 'Can business fill the void created by government inaction on climate change?' *Triple J Hack*, ABC, 4 September: <www.abc.net.au/triplej/programs/hack/can-business-fill-the-void-of-inaction-on-climate-change/11479282>.

Rheinstein, M (ed.) 1954, *Max Weber on Law in Economy and Society*, Harvard University Press, Cambridge, MA.

Rose, N 1992, 'Governing the enterprising self', in P Heelas & P Morris (eds), *The Values of the Enterprise Culture: The Moral Debate*, Routledge, London, pp. 141–64.

Rose, N 1996, Governing Advanced Liberal Democracies, in A Barry, T Osborne & N Rose (eds), *Foucault and Political Reason: Liberalism, Neo-Liberalism and Rationalities of Government*, University College Press, London.

Scott, M, Cerulus, L & Overly, S 2019, 'How Silicon Valley gamed Europe's privacy rules', *Politco*, 22 May: <www.politico.eu/article/europe-data-protection-gdpr-general-data-protection-regulation-facebook-google/>.

Severs, E, Celis, K & Erzeel, S 2016, 'Power, privilege and disadvantage: intersectionality theory and political representation', *Politics*, 36(4), 346–54 (DOI: https://doi-org.ezproxy.lib.monash.edu.au/10.1177/0263395716630987).

Tanner, L 2011, 'Window dressing: the mirage of political reform', *The Monthly*, 73, November, 36–9.

Walsh, L 2012, 'More mixed messages about youth participation', *Youth Studies Australia*, 31(2), 3–4

Walsh, L & Black, R 2018, *Rethinking Youth Citizenship After the Age of Entitlement*, Bloomsbury Academic Publishing, London.

Walsh, L, Black, R & Prosser, H 2018, 'Young people's perceptions of power and influence as a basis for understanding contemporary citizenship', *Journal of Youth Studies*, 21(2), 218–34.

Williams, G 2016, 'The legal assault on Australian democracy', *QUT Law Review*, 16(2), 19–41 (DOI: 10.5204/qutlr.v16i2.651).

Zuboff, S 2019, *The Age of Surveillance Capitalism: The Fight for a Human Future at the New Frontier of Power*, Profile Books, London.

FURTHER READING

Australian Broadcasting Corporation (ABC) 2018, 'Students strike for climate change protests, defying calls to stay in school', 30 November: <www.abc.net.au/news/2018-11-30/australian-students-climate-change-protest-scott-morrison/10571168>.

Hoar, Q & Nowell Smith, G (eds) 1999, *Selections from the Prison Notebooks of Antonio Gramsci*, ElecBook, London.

Jones, P 2008, *Introducing Social Theory*, Polity Press, Cambridge, UK.

Lukes, S 2005, *Power: A Radical View*, 2nd edn, Macmillan, London.

Rose, N 1999, *Powers of Freedom: Reframing Political Thought*, Cambridge University Press, Cambridge, UK.

Zuboff, S 2019, *The Age of Surveillance Capitalism: The Fight for a Human Future at the New Frontier of Power*, Profile Books, London.

CHAPTER 9

Race and ethnicity

FARIDA FOZDAR

CHAPTER OVERVIEW

In 2011 I undertook a survey to find out how common it was for people to fly flags on their cars for Australia Day, and what sort of message they were trying to send in doing so.

The results were simple enough—while for many people car flag flying is simply a celebration, people who fly car flags do tend to be less positive about minorities (Muslims, asylum seekers, Asians); more fearful that their culture and values are under threat; more proud of Australia's history; and more likely to think Australia is the most important country in the Asia–Pacific Region.

When I reported the results in a press release, I interpreted this as a form of racism. You will understand why after reading this chapter.

The general public did not, and the research became a topic of heated debate around Australia Day 2012. It generated lots of media coverage and blog discussion. One of my favourites is from Fat Aussie Barstard (sic) who had over 280,000 hits for his rant against the research, and against me, who he assumes to be a male Muslim (I'm a female atheist), before it was taken down from YouTube.

Over the years, there have been many debates about how certain national symbols represent racism. One example was when the Australian hip-hop artist, 360, ignited a similar controversy by suggesting on ABC's *Q&A* that the Australian flag had come to represent racism. More recently, Aboriginal players refused to sing the national anthem at a State of Origin rugby league game because they argued the flag does not represent them—but rather represents a history of racism. We cover the complexity of symbols such as flags and anthems when we discuss the nation and state in Chapter 10.

In this chapter we extend many of these issues and consider why race and racism are such difficult subjects to talk about while never being far away from the public's attention. We will also try to understand why Australians are often sensitive about them.

After reading this chapter, you will be able to:
- Identify the difference between race and ethnicity
- Define key concepts such as race, racism and multiculturalism
- Explain how and why race and ethnicity are implicated in Australian identity
- Describe various approaches to anti-racism
- Recognise how race affects the way you see the world and your opportunities.

> **KEY TERMS**
>
> **Assimilation** The process of becoming similar to something; the absorption of minorities into the mainstream culture.
>
> **Integration** The process of mixing, blending into a unified whole, with adaptation from both sides.
>
> **Ethnicity** The categorisation of groups of people on the basis of cultural characteristics and shared heritage; belonging to a group bonded by the common historical linkages of language, tradition, religion and/or cultural practice.
>
> **Intersectionality** The interconnected nature of social categories such as gender, race, class, (dis)ability and sexuality that create overlapping systems of inequality.
>
> **Multiculturalism** Policies that support the maintenance of different cultural groups within one society. The term is also used to mean cultural diversity, whether that is supported by policy or not.
>
> **Race** The hierarchical categorisation of groups of people on the basis of physical characteristics such as skin colour or eye shape.
>
> **Racism** Ideology and practices that discriminate against people based on assumptions about their biological or cultural inferiority.
>
> **White Australia Policy** A legislated practice that started at Federation and continued for almost 70 years, which essentially ensured that 'people of colour' could not migrate to Australia and made it difficult for those already living in Australia to remain.

Introduction: race

The term '**race**' is usually used in relation to differences between groups of people based on biological characteristics including physical (sometimes called 'phenotypical') features such as skin colour, hair type, the shape of people's faces, and the shape and colour of the eyes (Brace 2005). Most of us think we can distinguish between an 'Asian' and a 'Pacific Islander'. But what do we mean by 'Asian'—a Korean, a Malay, an Indian (Parsi or Malayali?), or one of the range of peoples from China? What about Hazara Afghans, or some Russians, who look quite 'Asian'? This is before we even begin to consider the range of 'Pacific Islander' people. The more you think about it, the more difficult it becomes to take the concept of 'race' for granted. And yet we do.

In fact, as we will also discuss in Chapter 16, there is no genetic basis to 'race'. Race is, as we will outline, a 'social construction' rather than a biological reality (Delgado & Stefancic 2001). Over the centuries, humans have always had ways of categorising themselves (such as religion, income earned, or language spoken). While racial categories are something we take for granted now, they are a relatively recent invention, emerging only in the eighteenth century, as a result of combining Darwin's ideas on evolution with the imperial and religious ideologies used to justify colonial expansion.

As you will see in reading this chapter, there are three main problems with race as a system of categorisation:

1. Firstly, racial categorisations are often ascribed social characteristics; that is, a person's personality is presumed to be related to their physical characteristics, accompanied by

presumptions of a hierarchy that sees groups of people as more and less civilised based on this categorisation—this is the basis of **racism**.

2 A second problem is that the physical distinctions related to racial categories are taken as 'essential'; that is, something fundamental that cannot be changed.

3 A third problem is that this division of people into racial categories is seen as a natural, universal phenomenon—a law of nature (Goldberg 1993).

Social scientists have pointed out that there is nothing absolute about race. In fact, as we noted, it is a *social construction* (as discussed in Chapter 3). Michael Banton, in his book *Racial Theories* (1998), showed how theories about race are influenced by the social and political circumstances of the time in which they developed, demonstrating this process of construction. Some of these processes are outlined below.

The Human Genome Project demonstrated that there is no genetic basis for the category of 'race', and that noticeable physical variations between human beings—such as height or skin colour—are largely the result of environmental factors over long periods of time. Genetic analysis can be used to establish relatedness, but no genetic marker can be identified as belonging to one 'racial group'. In fact, what we now know is that at the DNA level there is more genetic difference between any two individuals within a 'race' than there are group differences between two 'races' (de Plevitz & Croft 2003, p. 11). However, despite the absence of a scientific basis for race, it has become a powerful idea.

Science, colonialism and the Bible

The concept of 'race' is a relatively recent phenomenon (Brace 2005). The actual term comes from biological definitions of differences between categories of living things. You might have done this in biology, where living things are classified into taxonomies. Race is the last or most precise classification in the biological division of living things into kingdom, class, order, genus, species and race. It is a way of bringing a sense of order to an apparently chaotic world through categorisation. When such a system is applied to groups of people, however, it implies essential, permanent differences, based on biological factors, but with a whole range of other implications. The term 'race' became popular as a result of biblical, biological and colonialist thinking. While biology offered the terminology—and colonialism the desire—to classify humans into different groups, the Bible provided the explanation for why there were physical differences between groups. From this perspective, since we all descended from Adam and Eve, we should look the same. But according to the Old Testament, physical differences resulted from God's punishments, such as the mark of Cain and the curse of Ham: both passages from the Bible that were interpreted as an explanation for black skin. Thus, the Bible was understood as saying that being Black was a punishment and slavery was deserved.

The medieval Christian concept of the 'Great Chain of Being' also supported the notion of racial distinctions. This was the idea that all living things form a divinely inspired hierarchy, from amoebae to humans. Humans are at the top of the chain, connecting it to God (Banton 1998; Brace 2005). Lower forms of life were seen to exist in order to serve those higher on the chain. The corollary of such thinking is that the 'lower races' should serve the 'higher races', as part of God's plan. With European colonial expansion, the 'discovery' of different peoples could be explained using this notion of the chain—linking colonised peoples in the service of their colonisers. However, with the Age of Enlightenment, more 'scientific', though still problematic, explanations became popular (see also Chapter 5).

Carl Linnaeus (1707–78), a Swedish naturalist known as the 'father of modern taxonomy', identified four 'human' types: European, African, Asiatic and American. The classification was based on place of origin, skin colour and supposed character traits. Thus American 'Indians' were classified as coming from the Americas, being reddish in colour, and being stubborn and easy to anger; Africans were assumed to be black, relaxed and negligent; Asians constructed as yellow, avaricious and easily distracted. Of course, the European 'race' was categorised as white, gentle and inventive.

A clear hierarchy is established in this early classification. Linnaeus summed it up in his famous remark: 'Europeans are governed by laws, Asians by opinions and Africans by caprice' (von Linne 1997, p. 13). In the Australian context, the similarity between African and Austro-Melanesian physical features was extrapolated to assumptions about aggression and laziness among the Indigenous peoples (Hollinsworth 2006, p. 32).

In his 1871 book *The Descent of Man*, Charles Darwin suggested that the extinction of the 'savage races' with their 'smaller brains' was inevitable, as they would be unable to adapt to competition from Europeans. This 'Social Darwinism' was used to justify social inequality. If natural selection (not just biological, but social) occurred to ensure that only the fittest survived, then, as noted above, the dominance of some 'races' by others was evidence that they were entitled to their privileged position.

Hollinsworth (2006) outlines the ways in which such thinking was reflected in nineteenth-century arguments about Australian Aboriginal and Torres Strait Islander peoples being closer—in their capacity for logical thinking, creativity, justice and benevolence—to animals than to Europeans. The fiction of *terra nullius*—the idea that the land was simply vacant of people—justified the appropriation of land. Physical and cultural genocide was seen as simply speeding along a natural process. Many argue that these fictions and practices continue to influence some of Australia's policy making today (Moreton-Robinson 2015, Matthews & Arvanitakis 2019).

The racial hierarchy was so effective as a technology of colonial power that it was often internalised by colonised peoples. Franz Fanon (1970) argued in *Black Skin, White Masks*, that colonised peoples often internalise the negative stereotypes of their colonial oppressors, taking on the norms, values and opinions of the dominant group, accepting their inferior position, and ultimately supporting their own domination. The result, for many, has been a perpetuation of oppression over generations.

> **Critical reflection**
>
> What is your immediate reaction when you see someone that looks different from you? Are you 'colour blind'? Do you try to avoid stereotyping people based on their physical appearance? Think about steps you could take to improve your acceptance of people's differences.

Changing understandings of race

In the early part of the twentieth century, social scientists and others started to challenge these ideas. Australian historian Jane Lydon (2012) has shown how the use of photographs of colonised peoples, particularly those who were enslaved, began to change people's perceptions of the differences between them and others, demonstrating their common humanity.

Among social scientists, anthropologist Franz Boas led the charge, arguing that there was no correlation between physical and other attributes such as intelligence, creativity or aggression (1983, original work published 1911). There were also important critiques by Black sociologists beginning with WEB Du Bois (1940), challenging and changing conceptions of race.

Eventually the United Nations released the following statement:

> there is no proof that the groups of mankind differ in their innate mental characteristics, whether in respect to intelligence or temperament ... for all practical social purposes, 'race' is not so much a biological phenomenon as a social myth (UNESCO 1950, pp. 138–9).

Despite this, the concept persisted. Through the 1970s and 80s anthropologists were divided on the 'reality' of 'race', and debate among social and biological scientists continues (see Lieberman et al. 2001, p. 75). In a series of papers and books published in the 1980s and 90s, for instance, the psychologist Philippe Rushton argued that different climates produced a hierarchy of difference among the 'races' (Saini 2019). Thus 'Mongoloids' were seen as superior, with 'Caucasoids' a close second. 'Negroids', on the other hand, were seen as significantly inferior with 'the smallest brains, the largest genitalia, the lowest intelligence, the largest number of offspring, and the least parental care' (Lieberman et al. 2001, 74).

You can see how the thinking of hundreds of years ago is reflected in these ideas.

Race, ethnicity and nation

The many problems with the idea of race linking phenotype to civilisation, culture and mental capacity meant a new concept was needed. '**Ethnicity**' became the term of choice and was popularised in the social sciences from the 1970s onwards. While 'race' tends to be used to categorise other groups, 'ethnicity' more commonly refers to self-identified groupings formed on the basis of shared culture and a feeling of connection. (Though it should be noted that theorists such as Stuart Hall argue that race and ethnicity are intertwined (Davis 2004).)

The word 'ethnic' comes from the Greek word *ethnos*, meaning 'nation'. However, rather than meaning a political grouping, which is generally how we use the word 'nation' now, nation originally meant people united by common descent. In contemporary usage, 'ethnic' continues to denote a form of unity and commonality among a people, and to draw a boundary between an 'us' and a 'them'. One of the founding fathers of sociology, Max Weber (1864–1920), developed the following definition of 'ethnic group' after visiting the United States and observing the ways in which Greeks, Irish, Germans, African Americans and Native Americans were grouped together and treated differently. For Weber, an ethnic group refers to:

> human groups (other than kinship groups) which cherish a belief in their common origins of such a kind that it provides a basis for the creation of a community. This belief

may be based on similarities of external custom or practice or both, or on memories of colonisation or migration. The question of whether they are to be called an 'ethnic' group is independent of the question whether they are objectively of common stock ... (Runciman 1978, pp. 364–5)

A more detailed definition was developed by J Milton Yinger:

> An ethnic group perceives itself and is perceived by others to be different in some combination of the following traits: language, religion, race and ancestral homeland, with its related culture. A group that is different only by race is not an ethnic group (1981, p. 250).

Ethnicity, like race, remains a contested concept. Anthropologist Frederik Barth (1969) emphasised that the study of ethnicity must focus on the ongoing boundary negotiations between groups. In reality, groups are never culturally discontinuous, but they are constructed as such in people's practices of exclusion and inclusion, ascription and self-ascription.

It is easy to see how ideas about ethnicity, race and nationality get conflated. There are two ways in which we can conceive of 'belonging' in the nation state, one of which relies on similarity of ethnicity, and often race, and the other of which uses the more political concept of the state. Members of 'ethno nations'—nations with shared 'ethnicity'—see themselves as 'belonging' together on the basis of a shared language, culture, traditions and history (Gellner 1996), and solidarity is based on presumed intrinsic and emotional connections between members. This often has a more or less explicit racial basis—thus ethnicity, race and nation become conflated. Civic nationalism, on the other hand, is premised on commitment to a common destiny and government through shared civic institutions (see the discussion in Chapter 10 as well as Smith 2005).

Racism

Bulmer and Solomos (1999, p. 4), in their introduction to *Racism*, suggest that racism is an ideology of racial domination based on:

1 Belief that a designated racial group is either biologically or culturally inferior; and

2 The use of such beliefs to rationalise or prescribe the racial group's treatment.

The terms 'cultural racism', 'new racism' and 'neo-racism' (Barker 1981; Blaut 1992; Balibar 1991) recognise that modern racism is less about assumptions of biological superiority and inferiority based on phenotype. Instead, it reflects a tendency to see the world in terms of cultural hierarchies that maintain practices that exclude certain minority groups, whether these groups are 'racially' different or not. It is based on the idea that various cultures are incompatible and should not co-exist in the same society. While the old racism justified processes of colonisation, the new racism is associated with predominantly white nations seeking to restrict or control migrants (Balibar 1991), and is linked to nationalism. It is also associated with racialisation—a process by which some members of a society (Muslims, for example) come to be seen in racial terms as distinct, culturally alien, groups.

It is also important to note that the terms 'prejudice' and 'racist attitudes' tend to be used synonymously (Pedersen & Barlow 2008).

STUDENT VOICE
Gabrielle

❝ I remember the first time I realised my background may have made me different. I was around five years old and the teacher pulled me out of the classroom at the start of the day and asked my mum if 'it was true that my father was really *Māori*'—I guess I had been to visit my nan that weekend and had shared a story in class, possibly about eating lambs' tails or some story that made me love my visits to the coast. I didn't mind because I loved *Te Reo*, or *Māori* class, I loved learning about our history and *Māorianga* (practices of being *Māori*).

In primary school, being part of both worlds was not too problematic. Apart from that first memory, I remember being proud of my heritage and I didn't really fit in anywhere anyway, so the fluidity of my ethnicity wasn't too bothersome. There were also some *Pākehā* (white New Zealander) students whose parents encouraged them to learn *Te Reo* and be a part of *Kapa Haka* (*Māori* performing arts).

At high school, when students from various schools came together, the question of my ethnicity became a little more of a conundrum. First, I was challenged often about 'how *Māori* I was'; second, I was in the top academic stream of the high school and in the 'A' netball team, whereas the majority of my *Māori* peers were in the lower streams. And while in primary school both *Māori* and *Pākehā* girls had played netball—and really well—over the summer between intermediate and high school, many of my *Māori* friends started drinking and didn't enrol much in sports at high school.

During this time, I remember feeling very much on a fence. I heard teachers making comments about how 'bad' the *Māori* kids were, or my *Pākehā* friends talk about my *Māori* friends being lazy, their style or attitude (many of them were pretty fierce). I noted that if I chose *Māori* as my language elective, I automatically got placed in the lowest level biology class (I ended up being one of only two students who passed the course). I chose to keep attending *Māori* class, but would rarely say anything if either group was mouthing off at the other. Somewhere through my high school journey, I accepted and internalised being *Māori*. I am not sure if it is related, but I too started skipping classes. Sometimes I would tell teachers I was held up in the *Māori* room and they wouldn't question where I was.

Skip to the current day and, having worked in England, Ecuador and now in Australia, my observations of race have still been as that individual sitting on the fence and observing the privileges of whiteness, and the frustrations of the non-white to negotiate their mixed identities. Some moments where whiteness come to mind are the paradox of being on a beach in Ecuador and lying in a bikini to get a tan while my Ecuadorian peers sat on the beach covered head to toe in clothing and with an umbrella so they would maintain their 'whiter skin'. Or visiting Mitchell Plains, a coloured neighbourhood in South Africa with my then-boyfriend, and having his family tell me they had never had a white person in their house, and apologising. I told them my grandparents' and uncle's houses in New Zealand were similar in size and they didn't believe me.

> Undertaking a 'whiteness' course at university was extremely confronting to me, because even though my skin colour is white, *Māori* was my predominant identity choice. In making this choice, I had made invisible a large part of my heritage, while enjoying the privileges of this. Therefore, making whiteness visible for me has been both about coming to terms with my white privilege and also making whiteness relevant within my *whakapapa* (family tree) and acknowledging both sides of my heritage, instead of only my *Māori* family.
>
> *Ko Gabrielle tāku ingoa, Ko Ngāti Kahungunu mātou ko Ngāti Pākehā tāku iwi*—My name is Gabrielle, my tribe is *Ngāti Kahungunu* and *Pākehā*.

The Australian context

Having looked at the origins of 'race' thinking, its relationship to ethnicity and some of the theories about how it is perpetuated, it is time to turn to the Australian context and see how this sort of thinking has influenced the way we see ourselves and treat each other.

Most Australians are migrants (or their descendants), and for much of Australia's history migration has been limited to people who were racially white. The first people on the Australian continent, Aboriginal and Torres Strait Islander peoples, have lived here for at least 50,000 years. Before 1788, there were approximately 260 different language groups, and 500 dialects spoken across Australia (see Chapter 16).

Colonial Australia was also multicultural from the arrival of the First Fleet in 1788, with a number of people of Jewish and black African backgrounds among its mainly English and Irish passengers (Pybus 2001). Subsequently, people of other races migrated. South Sea Islander people (referred to as 'Kanakas', a derogatory term used by traders which meant 'boy'), were brought—often against their will or through deception—as indentured labour to work on plantations in Queensland. By the late 1830s thousands of people of African ancestry had settled in Australia. The first ship of 120 Chinese people (referred to by the derogatory term 'coolies') arrived in 1848 and many more came later, like others, to mine for gold. In Western Australia, people from India and the West Indies were among the first free settlers. In the 1850s, with the discovery of gold, over 600,000 people flooded to Australia from the United Kingdom, continental Europe (especially Germany), China, the United States, New Zealand and the Pacific (Jupp 2001).

The English settlers brought with them prejudices that were amplified by their insecurity at living on the 'edge' of the British Empire. Thus, White Australians from the time before Federation were strongly fearful of outsiders (xenophobic) and pro-white. This resulted in an environment of fear and desire to impose a British society and regimes of control onto the Indigenous community—something that Patrick Wolfe (2016) argues is reflective of other colonial experiences such as Blacks and Native Americans in the United States, and of Ashkenazi Jews in Western Europe.

In this climate, the new Australian Federal Parliament passed the *Immigration Restriction Act 1901*, one of its very first pieces of legislation. This Act formed the basis of the **White**

Australia Policy, which sought to exclude non-Europeans from Australia. While the Act did not directly discriminate against particular racial groups, it allowed discrimination at an informal level, thus keeping voters happy. It did this through the notorious *Dictation Test*, which was applied by immigration officers and which prohibited from entering Australia:

> [a]ny person who when asked to do so by an officer fails to write out at dictation and sign in the presence of the officer a passage of fifty words in length in an European language directed by the officer.

In practice, the Act enabled immigration officers to deny entry to any person deemed 'undesirable'. If an officer detected coloured skin, they could exclude someone simply by requiring them to complete the Dictation Test in a language they could not possibly know, such as Welsh. The documentary *Admission Impossible* (Morgan (dir.) 1992) provides firsthand accounts from immigration officers who had to apply the policy on a daily basis, using their own discretion, based on the skin colour, eye shape and hair of the would-be immigrants.

Additionally, shipping companies were fined if they were found to have brought a prohibited immigrant to the country, and so they would err on the side of caution by accepting 'white only' passengers. As Jupp (2007, p. 10) succinctly states: 'A message was sent out to the world that "coloured" people could not settle in Australia. They did not.'

The effectiveness of the Act (as well as other legislation that made it difficult for non-whites already in Australia to remain) is clear in the pattern of immigration that existed between 1901 and the Act's repeal in 1958. During the gold rush, in the second half of the nineteenth century, some 50,000 Chinese lived in Australia. By 1901 this figure was about 30,000, and by 1947 it was down to less than 10,000 (Choi 1975, p. 42). A similar pattern occurred with other non-European immigrants already in Australia, such as Japanese and Pacific Islanders (Jupp 1991, p. 50).

Back to diversity

It was not until the post-Second World War era that diversity again became a feature of the Australian population. It took a while for attitudes to change, however. The Minister for Immigration at the time, Arthur Calwell, commented that 'two Wongs don't make a White' (Jayasuriya & Pookong 1999, p. x), demonstrating the tone of flippant racism that remained. And *The Bulletin*, one of Australia's most popular magazines, retained its masthead 'Australia for the White Man' until 1961.

The slogan of the times was also insightful: 'populate or perish', which meant that the nation had to be populated by the British in order to retain it as a home for white British descendants. Even the Irish were suspect—while they shared physical similarities with the English, Welsh and Scots, they were Catholic and seen as inferior. This inferiority was represented in images of Irish people drawn as 'black' and monkey-like in appearance (Roediger 1991).

During the decades that followed the Second World War, the perceived inferiority of the Irish became secondary to the desire to create a united 'White Australia'. Immigration programs were launched to attract new migrants from the United Kingdom, including the provision of assisted passages for families and skilled workers that enabled people to travel for a small fee in return for fulfilling certain conditions of settlement. Over 300,000 people arrived from the United Kingdom between 1945 and 1958 in response (Appleyard 2001). However, the numbers were not enough to allay insecurities and fears of invasion, and so the 'immigration net was, reluctantly, cast wider and wider' (Collins 1988, p. 10), first incorporating people from Scandinavian countries and then gradually other European nations.

This resulted in a shift in Australian social policies, from 'White Australia' to **'assimilation'** as post-war migrants faced the challenge of adapting to 'one of the "whitest" countries in the world' (Jupp 2007, p. 10). The overriding goal was to ensure 'Anglo-conformity' (Jayasuriya 1997, p. 60) even as people of non-Anglo backgrounds were imported to meet the economic needs of the nation. There was a clear expectation that the new migrants would speak English, accept the employment that was offered—or, in the case of displaced persons (refugees of the Second World War), imposed on them—and become 'Australian' as quickly as possible in their attitudes and behaviours. It was assumed that this would be easier for those immigrants who 'looked' British, thereby justifying the continued implicit operation of the White Australia Policy.

So, the vast majority of the population, even in 1971, remained of British and European descent, with some from Italy, Greece, Yugoslavia, Germany, the Netherlands and Poland. People from northern European countries did, in fact, appear to assimilate very quickly. Large populations of Germans and Dutch, for example, became the ideal 'invisible migrants', disappearing into the existing population—often at great personal cost as they purposely left behind their identity, language and other national traditions.

The end of the White Australia Policy and the rise of multiculturalism

The White Australia Policy, while waning, did not officially end until 1973, when the Whitlam Government declared that race, ethnicity, religion and cultural background would no longer be grounds for admission or exclusion from immigration to Australia, and British migrants would no longer receive preferential access to citizenship. Instead, entry was based on a 'points system', where applicants were allocated points for factors such as their existing connection to Australia through family links, educational qualifications, occupation, work experience, English language skills and age (Collins 1988). At the same time, policies began to change to support immigrants retaining aspects of their culture 'with rights to power and participation' in the Australian public sphere (Martin 1975, p. 78). It was this newly emerging discourse that gave rise to the government adopting policies that supported **multiculturalism**.

The policy of multiculturalism emerged out of a growing sense that racial discrimination—at least in its overt forms—was unacceptable. As Markus (1994, p. 174) points out, 'the notion that all should conform to a unitary "Australian way of life" was abandoned, and the various ethnic groups were encouraged to define their own lifestyle'. This included promoting ethnic organisations.

However, the extent of this 'encouragement' is debatable. The language of Australia has remained English and, in spite of the provision of translation services, those who do not speak

English are widely disadvantaged. In terms of race, people who may have lived in Australia for generations are frequently asked 'Where are you from?' if they do not look Caucasian—something documented by Hatoss (2012) in his article about Australians from a Sudanese background. Furthermore, the 'Australian way of life' re-emerged during the Howard Government (1996–2007) as a central tenet of Australian Government policy, re-envisioned through the construction of the new citizenship test, with its emphasis on British historical contributions to the establishment of Australia, and its focus on Enlightenment values and Christian heritage (Fozdar & Spittles 2009).

Christina Ho (2013) has argued that Australian multicultural policy, while always being about acknowledging and respecting Australia's culturally diverse society, has been through three phases with differing degrees of positive engagement with cultural difference. The social justice phase (1970s to 80s) focused on recognition and support. This was followed by a focus on the economic contributions of migrants, which she characterises as productive diversity (1980s to 90s). Most recently we have seen a shift to the linking of statements and policy about multiculturalism with social cohesion (2000s to the present). This version of multicultural **integration** looks more like assimilation, and the targets of fears about social cohesion are inevitably those not just culturally, but 'racially' different from the mainstream.

It is useful to distinguish between the theory of multiculturalism, the fact of multiculturalism (diversity of population) and policies of multiculturalism, which support that diversity in various ways. A number of countries, Australia and Canada among them, have explicitly adopted policies of multiculturalism that recognise minorities rather than subsuming them into a homogenous mass (Taylor 1994) and seek to ensure equitable redistribution of resources (Kymlicka 1995). Thus, the goal of such policies is to ensure ethnic minorities co-existing within a nation state have the right to retain aspects of their culture and are treated in an equitable way. In Australia and Canada multiculturalism has become a marker of political and social identity (Moran 2016; Kymlicka 1995).

Race, ethnicity and Australian nationalism

Going back to the connections between race, ethnicity and nationalism, it is important to consider how Australians conceive of 'Australianness'—and there is much contradictory evidence.

In the Australia Day flags study referred to at the start of this chapter, several questions explored how Australian nationalism is related to traditional views about white Australia (see Fozdar, Spittles & Hartley 2014). For example, one question asked whether respondents believed the White Australia Policy had 'saved Australia from many problems experienced by other countries'. Around 41 per cent of those with car flags ('flaggers') agreed—significantly higher than the 23.9 per cent for those without flags ('non-flaggers'). Here are some other interesting statistics:

- 39.5 per cent of flaggers believed that being born in Australia was important to being truly Australian (compared to non-flaggers, at 18.3 per cent);
- 36.9 per cent agreed that having Anglo-Australian ancestry was important to being truly Australian (compared to 14.4 per cent); and

- 23.2 per cent felt that being Christian was important to being truly Australian (compared to 16.9 per cent).

It is also interesting that flaggers were more negative towards minorities than non-flaggers. Positivity towards Muslims and asylum seekers, both racially constructed groups, was very low among both groups, but significantly lower among flaggers. Only 19.6 per cent of flaggers felt positive towards Muslim Australians compared with 26.8 per cent of non-flaggers; and only 9.9 per cent of flaggers were positive towards asylum seekers (versus 24.7 per cent).

Interestingly, 38.8 per cent of flaggers felt positive towards Asian Australians compared with 48.6 per cent of non-flaggers. There was little difference between flaggers and non-flaggers in terms of positive attitudes towards Indigenous Australians, with less than half the respondents feeling positive towards this group (43.2 per cent versus 45.6 per cent).

These results, like those of other scholars, suggest that quite a strong vein of support for a homogenous (White) Australia remains in the twenty-first century, and that this is associated with nationalism.

STUDENT VOICE
Kwasi Tettey

❝❞ I have lived in Australia for quite some time now. I moved from New South Wales to Western Australia to do my PhD. Besides Australia, I have visited, lived and worked in other parts of the world—more than 10 countries, including Peru, Canada, the United States, the United Kingdom and many parts of Europe. It is only in Australia and most especially Western Australia that I came to realise that the colour of my skin matters to some people that I do not even know.

In Sydney, I remember that after finishing work one day, I walked with a colleague to the bus stop. Other people were also waiting for the bus. My colleague asked me if I saw one of the girls 'perving' at me, and I said 'no'. He then said, 'Do you know, I hate you guys because you come to Australia and take our girls?' 'Which guys?' I asked, to which he replied, 'You blacks.' I thought it was funny, but it obviously was not to him because he refused to speak to me for the next few weeks.

This was not my only encounter with racism in Sydney. One evening, I was waiting for the bus at Randwick. Someone driving past stopped, beeped his horn to draw my attention, gave me a middle finger and sped off. I was the only black person there, and had not done anything to provoke such a response, so it is difficult to say that his motivation was not skin-colour related.

The racism became a bit more 'serious' when I moved to Western Australia. Growing up in Ghana, culturally I was brought up to ask people if they were okay if I thought they needed help. In the United States, for example, if I went shopping and saw elderly people labouring to push their grocery-packed trolleys, most often I would go and ask if they needed assistance. Some would answer in the affirmative, others would say no. There was no time that I felt awkward doing this. However, this was not the case when I moved to Western Australia.

One day, I was in the city and it was peak hour and the train platform was packed. Through the throng, I saw a young woman with a baby in a stroller on the platform. She also had many grocery bags and other pieces of luggage beside her. When I saw the train arriving, I looked around to see if she was with anyone and, most importantly, if anyone was going to help her. When no one did, I asked if she needed help to carry her things onto the train. She looked me up and down scornfully and then screamed: 'You're black anyway. I don't want your fucking hands on my stuff.' To say that I was surprised is an understatement. She managed to get the stroller and her things onto the train in four trips—no one helped her. We sat across from each other in the train. Someone came up to me, shook my hand and said within her hearing: 'Good on you man, I hope this isn't gonna stop you from helping someone again.' But in all candidness, since then, I have found it difficult approaching white people I do not know to ask if they need help.

I was narrating this experience to a Ghanaian academic friend here, and he told me about a similar experience. He was shopping with his three-year-old son and saw that a trolley in which a toddler was sitting had tipped over. As he bent down to help the boy up, his mother came and pushed him aside, asking him not to touch her child.

These experiences have been culturally confronting. I am teaching my two children about Ghanaian culture, but I have been wondering whether to encourage them to ask someone if they need help if they are in Ghana but not if they are in Australia, most especially if the person is white. However, if I said that, would it not be racist?

I thought my colour was not an issue any more in Perth until a couple of years after this incident, when I was ambling with my white wife in Fremantle, pushing a stroller. Four white boys who were driving past started yelling, 'Hey black man, you black man.' A middle-aged (white) man sitting at a nearby bus stop got up in anger and went and kicked the side of the car as it stopped at the traffic lights, telling them: 'You shouldn't be bastards.' The boys got out of the car, one wielding a bottle. I was considering whether to snatch the bottle from him, but my wife stopped me. A fight erupted between the boys and the man, who was seriously injured by the bottle, ending up in hospital. I felt very sorry for the man who, in my defence and by reason of my skin colour, was attacked and beaten.

It concerns me that such racist behaviours and actions occur in the presence of my children. Quite recently, I went bushwalking with my wife and the kids at Heirison Island, East Perth. As I was playing with my four-year-old son, we saw five people cruising past on the Swan River and my son waved at them. Unexpectedly, one of them started laughing hysterically and kept calling out: 'Fucking black, go home.' I had explained to my son in the past that it is discourteous to use such words. With that in mind, he was able to draw inferences from what he had heard and asked: 'Daddy, why is that man not being nice to blacks?' 'Probably, because I am different,' I said. His next comment was: 'But I'm different too. Look at my hair! Does that mean people won't be nice to me?' A difficult question to answer. My wife and I have thought several times about moving to a more cosmopolitan country, or to Melbourne or back to Sydney, but we are not sure that will solve the problem given that racism is prevalent in these cities as well.

As part of my PhD research into the effects of race and ethnicity on job satisfaction, I was shocked to hear several nurses I interviewed saying that they had seen Aboriginal patients in hospitals being given fewer pain relief drugs because of a perception that they feel pain less than other races. This and some of the other examples I have given, illustrate that traditional racism still exists in Australia.

I came to sociology from a background in agriculture, believing that nature and biology are everything. I landed in sociology by accident, but I am so glad I did because it has given me a framework for understanding that race is not 'natural', as we are led to believe, but a social construction. In Ghana, members of certain tribes who historically fought and conquered other tribes consider themselves superior 'humans' to the members of the vanquished tribes. We call this 'tribalism' in Ghana, but I call it 'racism', because sociology has led me to realise that whether discrimination occurs between races, ethnicities or tribes, it is still racism.

WHITENESS

Historically, studies of 'race' have tended to objectify those who are different, while those in power (who in the context of European colonisation are 'white people') remain invisible and evade scrutiny. More recently, social scientists and Black activists have argued that white privilege (or whiteness) must also be examined in order to understand the bases of structural inequality.

Inequality is, after all, a relationship between the subordinate and the privileged. Whiteness studies asks: What is the meaning of 'whiteness' and how does it inform assumptions about and opportunities for those who 'lack' whiteness? How is white privilege maintained? Such questions are as much political as they are theoretical (Doane 2003, p. 6).

> ### Critical reflection
> Think about your circle of friends and family. To what extent does your network represent racial and cultural diversity? Why do you suppose this is? (Consider issues of race, class, ethnicity, gender, etc.)

Whiteness Studies begins from the assumption that race is a social construction—as we discussed above. Yet it recognises that race-based power structures privilege some and disadvantage others. A study of the 1970s American economic recession showed how the white majority used the recession to claw back many of the political and economic gains achieved by minorities in the 1960s (Omi & Winant 1994). White working-class men felt they had been disadvantaged, even discriminated against. Affirmative action programs, and other measures aimed at reducing inequalities based on race, were seen as forms of racial discrimination in reverse. The Australian Critical Race and Whiteness Studies Association, which is a vibrant group of scholars exploring issues of whiteness in Australia, argues that it is therefore important to 'notice race' in order to move towards a more just and egalitarian society.

However, 'noticing race' is not necessarily easy. One of the main arguments of Whiteness Studies is that whites are often rendered invisible, while they contribute to the 'noticing' of other races, or, rather, the races of 'others'.

In the Australian context, the first significant contribution to Whiteness Studies was by anthropologist Ghassan Hage (1998). Hage asked why so many Australians 'worry' about the nation, and in particular about 'multiculturalism'. He argued that whiteness and Australianness are closely interconnected, allowing some people to be identified as more rightfully competent and legitimate in their statements about the nation's past, present and future. So, it is on the basis of her 'whiteness', and thus her 'Australianness', that Pauline Hanson (1996) believes she is able to treat Indigenous Australians, Asian Australians and Muslim Australians as outsiders with inferior rights over Australia.

Whiteness continues to confer privilege in Australia. A study of contemporary British immigrants in Australia found that they see themselves as 'the norm'—as 'fitting in' in unproblematic ways (Schech & Haggis 2004). At the same time, studies of newly arrived black Africans, as well as longer-established Vietnamese communities, find that they face difficulties in fitting in and feeling like they 'belong' in Australia.

One problem 'whiteness' scholars have met is that since 'race' has become a taboo subject, this silences discussion about racial privilege. As Cowlishaw (2004, p. 60) argues: 'Speaking of race was feared to reproduce racial inequality, but not speaking about race did nothing to destroy it.' In order to avoid being accused of reproducing racist discourses, many people assert a form of 'colour-blindness', whereby race is simply not mentioned. Rather than stopping racism, however, this creates a situation where it is possible for white people to avoid acknowledging the racial basis of their privilege.

> **Critical reflection**
>
> Has your race been an advantage or a disadvantage in your life, and the opportunities you have had? How?

INTERSECTIONALITY

Like gender and class, race overlaps with other issues. We have already noted how race is connected to class and gender, but also generation, age, disability and sexuality, to produce complex patterns of inequality.

Intersectionality focuses on the overlapping categories of discrimination that people face (see Chapter 7; see also Anthias & Yuval-Davis 1993). The concept of intersectionality arose out of critiques by Black feminists of white women's assumption that experiences of oppression were the same for all women. Instead, they argued, Black women experience a double jeopardy, disadvantaged by both race and gender.

> **Critical reflection**
>
> Could ALP Senator Penny Wong ever become Prime Minister of Australia? What barriers would she face?

Anti-racism

As people have become more aware of the social construction of race, and the effects of racism, anti-racism movements have gained momentum. Advocates argue there are two main reasons to oppose racism:

1. It is morally and philosophically wrong, from a human rights perspective; and
2. It damages people by distorting social relations and undermining opportunities. This manifests in material, social and psychological ways.

Hollinsworth (2006, p. 275) suggests there are four main approaches to anti-racism.

1. 'Cultural awareness training' teaches people about different cultures to raise knowledge, understanding and empathy, but it tends to homogenise and essentialise culture, and may confirm stereotypes. An example would be the provision of lists of cultural characteristics of different ethnic groups, such as those provided by government departments and others to make people aware of 'difference'.
2. 'Racism awareness' focuses on making white people aware of the privilege they enjoy as a result of their race. This approach can be alienating, as it tends to lay blame solely at the feet of whites, simplifying a complex process.
3. 'Anti-racism strategies' tend to be more broad-based, recognising that complex power relations are the cause of racial domination. Such strategies focus on material and cultural factors that reproduce racism, targeting interventions at the political level.
4. Finally, the 'social justice' approach sees racism as one aspect of a complex of intersecting factors including class, gender, sexuality, disability and age, which produce advantage and disadvantage. Social justice interventions are political, but also aim to reduce inequities at the material level, by ensuring equitable access to resources.

It can be seen that the first two approaches focus on the individual, offering training designed for professional or personal development. The second two are broader and are directed at the political and ideological levels.

Interventions can also take the form of everyday activities such as 'bystander anti-racism' (see Nelson, Paradies & Dunn 2011): challenging people's 'false beliefs' and stereotypes, and encouraging empathy and dialogue. Encouraging interactions between people from different backgrounds—a process known as 'the contact hypothesis'—has also been shown to decrease prejudice and stereotyping (Pettigrew & Tropp 2006). There are also ideological and language-based ways in which racism can be challenged—think of the ways in which the words 'Muslim' and 'terrorism' so often occur together in the media and in politicians' speeches, and what a difference encouraging people to stop conflating the two would make.

But there are also more material interventions. To address the structural disadvantage that perpetuates racial inequality, affirmative action strategies have been used, for example, by allocating a certain quota of university places or jobs for minorities.

Legislation against racism is also effective. Laws set the moral limits of societies. They are designed to regulate our behaviour. Australia has a number of laws designed to reduce discrimination on the basis of race and ethnicity. There has been ongoing discussion about changing one such law, section 18C of the *Racial Discrimination Act 1975*, to make it lawful to offend, insult and humiliate people on the basis of their race or ethnicity. This has been criticised as sending the wrong signal about the type of society we want to promote.

BOX 9.1
Everyday sociology

The media is often criticised for perpetuating racist stereotypes but the media can also be used to take up the cause of anti-racism. Three examples in recent years show the power of mainstream and social media in raising awareness about racism.

ADAM GOODES

One of the best contemporary Australian footballers, Australian of the Year, and anti-racism advocate, Adam Goodes, left the game prematurely in 2015 due to an ongoing campaign of racial abuse. Two documentary movies, 'The Final Quarter' and 'The Australian Dream' tell the story of Adam Goodes' life and decision to leave the game he loved due to a sustained campaign of on-field booing and other abuse, including being called an 'ape'.

In 2019, as the documentary 'The Final Quarter' was released, the AFL and its 18 clubs issued an unreserved apology for the sustained racism that had driven Goodes out of the game. They said:

> Adam, who represents so much that is good and unique about our game, was subject to treatment that drove him from football. The game did not do enough to stand with him, and call it out. Failure to call out racism and not standing up for one of our own let down all Aboriginal and Torres Strait Islander players, past and present. Our game is about belonging. We want all Australians to feel they belong and that they have a stake in the game. We will not achieve this while racism and discrimination exists in our game … We will stand strongly with all in the football community who experience racism or discrimination. We are unified on this,

and never want to see the mistakes of the past repeated (ABC News 2019).

BLACK LIVES MATTER

Black Lives Matter began as a hashtag on Twitter (#BlackLivesMatter) in the United States and became an ongoing activist movement against systemic racism and violence faced by Black Americans. The initial impetus was the acquittal of a white man of murder, after he shot dead unarmed African-American teenager, Trayvon Martin, in Florida in July 2013. The movement's profile was raised through other Black deaths, often at the hands of police. Over a number of years demonstrations in support of 'black lives' have been held across the United States and elsewhere. The movement is not only against the murder of black people, but against high incarceration rates, racial profiling, inequality and marginalisation. It has extended to recognising intersectionality (queer, trans, disabled, women). The movement spread through tweets (over 30 million in 2015 according to Wortham, 2016) and memes. The use of social media has also been important in improving the ability to record and share incidents of police violence, raising awareness about the issue.

THE ONLINE HATE PREVENTION INSTITUTE

This independent Australian site seeks to reduce the risk of harm generated by online hate content. Their targets are racism, violent extremism, anti-Semitism, anti-Muslim hate, racism against Indigenous Australians, as well as a range of non-race/ethnicity-based online content. Their site provides advice on how to report on-line hate, as well as a range of resources.

> **Critical reflection**
>
> 1 You are a cultural diversity expert, and have been asked by the Health Department of the United States to provide a list of characteristics of Australians so that American health workers can treat Australians in a culturally appropriate way. What would your list look like? What are some of the difficulties of this sort of approach to developing 'cultural sensitivity'?
> 2 Watch a movie, a series and some news on SBS. Reflect on the ways in which ethnic difference is presented on this channel, compared to commercial stations. Consider how SBS makes a contribution to anti-racism.

Conclusion

This chapter has attempted to demonstrate the ways in which the idea of race developed, and some of the consequences of the ubiquity of this concept. It has argued that Australia has always had a complex relationship with racial and cultural diversity and that this is related to its sense of nationhood and identity. It concluded with a discussion of approaches to challenging racism.

Summary points

* Race is a social construction that has real effects.
* Race is a relatively recent idea, but has been sustained by religious, colonial and class-based thinking.
* Analysis of the effects of racial thinking must include recognising the privileges of whiteness.
* Ethnicity is considered by some to be a more acceptable way of thinking about difference, being based on cultural rather than biological difference, but it also has its limits.
* Australia's history has been plagued with racial discrimination, particularly its long history of allowing only white immigrants to settle, and its treatment of its Indigenous peoples.
* Policies of multiculturalism have made Australians much more accepting of racial and cultural difference, although some barriers remain.

Sociological reflection

1 To what extent does race remain a useful concept?
2 Consider how race, ethnicity, religion, class and gender are linked.
3 Should sociologists engage in programs to reduce racism?

Discussion questions

1 Is the Australian flag a racist symbol?
2 Should immigrants conform to Australian values?
3 Do you think someone's race/ethnicity can affect his or her life chances and expectations?

References and further reading

REFERENCES

ABC News 2019, 'AFL apologises unreservedly for failures over racism faced by Adam Goodes', Australian Broadcasting Corporation, 7 April 2019.

Anthias, F & Yuval-Davis, N 1993, *Racialized Boundaries: Race, Nation, Gender, Colour and Class and the Anti-Racist Struggle*, Routledge, London.

Appleyard, R 2001, 'International migration policies: 1950–2000', *International Migration*, 39(6), 7–20.

Balibar, E 1991, *Race, Nation, Class: Ambiguous Identities*, Verso Books, London.

Banton, M 1998, *Racial Theories*, Cambridge University Press, Cambridge.

Barker, M 1981, *The New Racism: Conservatives and the Ideology of the Tribe*, Junction Books, London.

Barth, F (ed.) 1969, *Ethnic Groups and Boundaries: The Social Organization of Culture Difference*, Universitetsforlaget, Oslo.

Blaut, J 1992, 'The theory of cultural racism', *Antipode*, 24(4), 289–99.

Boas, F 1983, *The Mind of Primitive Man*, Greenwood Press, Westport, CT (original work published 1911).

Brace, C 2005, *Race is a Four Letter Word: The Genesis of the Concept*, Oxford University Press, New York.

Bulmer, M & Solomos, J (eds) 1999, *Racism*, Oxford University Press, Oxford.

Choi, C 1975, *Chinese Migration and Settlement in Australia*, Sydney University Press, Sydney.

Collins, J 1988, *Migrant Hands in a Distant Land: Australia's Post-War Immigration*, Pluto Press, Sydney.

Cowlishaw, G 2004, 'Racial positioning, privilege and public debate', in A Moreton-Robinson (ed.), *Whitening Race: Essays in Social and Cultural Criticism*, Aboriginal Studies Press, Canberra, pp. 59–74.

Darwin, C 1883, *The Descent of Man and Selection in Relation to Sex*, Appleton and Co., New York (original work published 1871).

Davis, H 2004, *Understanding Stuart Hall*, SAGE Publications Ltd, London.

Delgado, R & Stefancic, J 2001, *Critical Race Theory: An Introduction*, New York University Press, New York.

de Plevitz, L & Croft, L 2003, 'Aboriginality under the microscope: the biological descent test in Australian law', *Law and Justice Journal*, 3(1), 105–21.

Doane, A 2003, 'Rethinking whiteness studies', in A Doane & E Bonilla-Silva (eds), *White Out: The Continuing Significance of Racism*, Routledge, London, pp. 3–18.

Du Bois, WEB 1940, *Dusk of Dawn: An Essay Toward an Autobiography of a Race Concept*, Oxford University Press, Oxford.

Dyer, R 1997, *White*, Routledge, London.

Fanon, F 1970, *Black Skin, White Masks*, Paladin, London.

Fozdar, F & Spittles, B 2009, 'The Australian citizenship test: process and rhetoric', *Australian Journal of Politics & History*, 55(4), 496–512.

Fozdar, F, Spittles, B & Hartley, L 2014, 'Australia Day, flags on cars and Australian nationalism', *Journal of Sociology* (DOI: 1440783314524846).

Gellner, E 1996, *Mapping the Nation*, New Left Books, New York.

Goldberg, T 1993, *Racist Culture*, Blackwell, Cambridge, MA.

Hage, G 1998, *White Nation: Fantasies of White Supremacy in a Multicultural Society*, Pluto Press, Annandale.

Hanson, P 1996, 'Maiden speech', *Parlinfo Web*, Parliament of Australia: <http://parlinfoweb.aph.gov.au/piweb/view_document.aspx?ID=41338&TABLE=HANSARDR>.

Hatoss, A 2012, 'Where are you from? Identity construction and experiences of "othering" in the narratives of Sudanese refugee-background Australians', *Discourse & Society*, 23(1), 47–68.

Ho, C 2013, 'From social justice to social cohesion: a history of Australian multicultural policy', in A Jakubowicz & C Ho (eds) *'For Those Who've Come Across the Seas': Australian Multicultural Theory, Policy and Practice*, Australian Scholarly Publishing, North Melbourne, pp. 31–41.

Hollinsworth, D 2006, *Race and Racism in Australia*, Thomson/Social Science Press, South Melbourne.

Jayasuriya, L 1997, *Immigration and Multiculturalism in Australia*, School of Social Work and Social Administration, University of Western Australia, Perth.

Jayasuriya, L & Pookong, K 1999, *The Asianisation of Australia? Some Facts about the Myths*, Melbourne University Press, Melbourne.

Jupp, J 1991, *Immigration*, Sydney University Press, Sydney.

Jupp, J 2001, *The Australian People: An Encyclopedia of the Nation, its People and their Origins*, Cambridge University Press, Cambridge.

Jupp, J 2007, *From White Australia to Woomera: The Story of Australian Immigration*, Cambridge University Press, Melbourne.

Kymlicka, W 1995, *Multicultural Citizenship: A Liberal Theory of Minority Rights*, Clarendon Press, Oxford.

Lieberman, L, Loring Brace, C, Harpending, H, Jackson, F, Marks, J, Rushton, P, Relethford, J, Smedley, A, Stolcke, V & Weizmann, F 2001, 'How "Caucasoids" got such big crania and why they shrank: from Morton to Rushton/Comments/Reply', *Current Anthropology*, 42(1), 69–95.

Lydon, J 2012, *The Flash of Recognition: Photography and the Emergence of Indigenous Rights*, NewSouth Books, Sydney.

Matthews, I & Arvanitakis, J 2019, 'Whose island home? Art and Australian refugee law', *UNSW Law Society Court of Conscience*, 4, 19–26.

Markus, A 1994, *Australian Race Relations, 1788–1993*, Allen & Unwin, Sydney.

Martin, J 1975, *The Economic Condition of Migrants*, Commission of Inquiry into Poverty, Australian Government Publishing Service, Canberra.

Moran, A 2016, *The Public Life of Australian Multiculturalism: Building a Diverse Nation*, Springer, London.

Morgan, A (dir.) 1992, *Admission Impossible*, Film Australia National Interest Program.

Moreton-Robinson A 2015, *The White Possessive: Property, Power, and Indigenous Sovereignty*, University of Minnesota Press, Minneapolis.

Nelson, J, Paradies, Y & Dunn, K 2011, 'Bystander anti-racism: a review of the literature', *Analyses of Social Issues and Public Policy*, 11(1), 263–84.

Omi, M & Winant, H 1994, *Racial Formation in the United States: From the 1960s to the 1990s*, Routledge, New York.

Pedersen, A & Barlow, F 2008, 'Theory to social action: a university-based strategy targeting prejudice against Aboriginal Australians', *Australian Psychologist*, 43, 148–59.

Pettigrew, T & Tropp, L 2006, 'A meta-analytic test of intergroup contact theory', *Journal of Personality and Social Psychology*, 90, 751–83.

Pybus C 2001, 'A touch of the tar: African settlers in colonial Australia and the implications for issues of aboriginality', *London Papers in Australian Studies*, Menzies Centre for Australian Studies, London, 3.

Roediger, D 1991, *The Wages of Whiteness: The Making of the American Working Class*, Verso, London.

Runciman, W (ed.) 1978, *Weber: Selections in Translation*, trans. E Mathews, Cambridge University Press, Cambridge.

Saini, A 2019, *Superior: The Return of Race Science*, Beacon Press.

Schech, S & Haggis, J 2004, 'Terrains of migrancy and whiteness: how British migrants locate themselves in Australia', in A Moreton-Robinson (ed.), *Whitening Race: Essays in Social and Cultural Criticism*, Aboriginal Studies Press, Canberra, pp. 176–91.

Smith, A 2005, 'Civic and ethnic nationalism', in P Spencer & H Wollman (eds.), *Nations and Nationalism: A Reader*, Rutgers University Press, NJ, pp. 177–83.

Taylor, C 1994, *Multiculturalism: Examining the Politics of Recognition*, Princeton University Press, Princeton, NJ.

United Nations Educational, Scientific, and Cultural Organization (UNESCO) 1950, 'On race', *Man*, 50, 138–9.

von Linne, C 1997, 'The God-given order of nature', in E Eze (ed.), *Race and the Enlightenment*, Blackwell Publishers, Cambridge, pp. 10–14.

Wolfe, P 2016, *Traces of History: Elementary Structures of Race*, Verso Books, London.

Wortham, J 2016, 'Black tweets matter', *Smithsonian Magazine*, September: <www.smithsonianmag.com/arts-culture/black-tweets-matter-180960117>.

Yinger, J 1981, 'Towards a theory of assimilation and dissimilation', *Ethnic and Racial Studies*, 4(3), 249–64.

FURTHER READING

Fozdar F, Wilding R & Hawkins M 2009, *Race and Ethnic Relations*, Oxford University Press, Melbourne.

Reynolds, H 1987, *Frontier: Aborigines, Settlers and Land*, Allen & Unwin, Sydney.

WEBSITES

Australian Critical Race and Whiteness Studies Association: <www.acrawsa.org.au> (a vibrant group of scholars exploring issues of whiteness in Australia)

The Online Hate Prevention Institute: <https://ohpi.org.au/>.

University of Western Sydney, The Challenging Racism Project: <www.uws.edu.au/ssap/ssap/research/challenging_racism> (for practical ways in which racism can be challenged)

TELEVISION

Darling, I (dir.) 2019, *The Final Quarter*, Shark Island Productions, Woollahra, NSW.

Gordon, D (dir.) 2019, *The Australian Dream*, Madman Entertainment, East Melbourne, Victoria.

Morgan, A (dir.) 1992, *Admission Impossible*, ABC and Film Australia, Lindfield, NSW.

CHAPTER 10

Nation and nationalism in a globalised world

BENJAMIN T JONES

INTRODUCTION

Imagine you are overseas at a crowded backpacker hostel in a big city. You can hear many different accents and languages being spoken as you make your way to reception to check in. You learn that you are sharing a large room with seven other travellers. How would you introduce yourself to your new roommates? You would probably start by saying hello and telling them your name. Chances are, one of the very first questions they would ask you, and one of the first questions you would ask them is, 'Where are you from?'

Like gender, ethnicity and religion (or lack thereof), nationality is a significant building block in the construction of most people's identity. We imagine—and it is important to remember that it is an imagining—that certain nations have particular traits, and these are often applied to the citizens of those nations. For example, if one of your new roommates is German you might assume that they are efficient, organised and interested in watching a Bundesliga football match with you later in the day. These are just stereotypes, of course, and they may not be accurate at all. In fact, rarely does an individual tick all the stereotype boxes assigned to their nation(s). Nevertheless, we are interested in people's nationality because we think it gives us some insight into them.

What happens when a person does not fit the image we might have of certain nations? For some, it is so disconcerting that they demand an explanation.

Australia is a multicultural country and home to a multiplicity of ethnicities. Despite this, a national stereotype persists that a 'real Aussie' is an athletic, easy-going, white person who enjoys drinking beer and spending time surfing at the beach. If someone says they are Australian but does not fit this description, particularly if they are not white, they frequently face an intrusive follow-up question: 'Where are you *really* from?'

This question is so persistent that in 2018, comedian Michael Hing released a documentary series with the same title. He speaks to many non-white Australians whose families have lived in the country for multiple generations. Despite being born in Australia they are still asked where they 'really' come from. Part of the reason for this is the merging of **ethnicity** and nationality in the popular imagination. Even though modern Australia is built on unceded Aboriginal land, it is unlikely that a white Australian would be asked where they really come from.

You may have noticed the word 'imagination' popping up frequently. This is due to the influence of Benedict Anderson who published a book in 1983 describing nations as *Imagined Communities*. In a famous line, he claims that, 'all communities larger than primordial villages of face-to-face contact (and perhaps even these) are imagined' (Anderson 2006, p. 6).

What he meant is that, even in small nations, a person will never actually meet the vast majority of their fellow citizens. Despite this, they feel as though they share a special bond with these millions of strangers through a shared imagination; a sense of belonging to the nation.

Teaching in Rockhampton on the east coast of Australia, I often give my students the following thought experiment: if a person from Perth, Western Australia and Auckland, New Zealand, were competing in a major sporting event, who would they cheer for? Reflexively, they usually respond, 'The Australian, of course!' But why is this an obvious answer? From Rockhampton and other cities on the east coast, Auckland is geographically closer than Perth. New Zealand shares many political and cultural features with Australia. The two countries have fought in wars together and enjoy friendly relations. In the late nineteenth century, delegates from New Zealand even attended the federation conferences with the view to join the new Australian state. The fact that they ultimately decided to remain separate can be considered an accident of history. Yet most Australians are likely to feel a stronger connection to someone from Perth while someone from Auckland is seen as foreign. And what would happen if Western Australia decided to declare themselves an independent nation? For Anderson, our imaginations would adjust, and my students would come to think of Perth as equally foreign.

Anderson's view belongs to a broader theory of nation and nationalism called **modernism**. Modernism suggests that nations are relatively recent constructions, inherently novel, and artificial (we covered this in detail in Chapter 5). They arose in the wake of the Industrial Revolution in response to a need to foster a sense of common identity by those in power over large areas. One of the most important modernists, Ernest Gellner, compared the nation to a modern army (1983). In the same way an army trains recruits to behave in certain ways and even to think in certain ways, so too does the nation. The strong sense of patriotism one might feel for their country, Gellner argues, is not an organic outpouring of feeling but the end result of national training. Through schooling, national rituals (like ANZAC Day and Australia Day), public monuments, the media, national songs and celebrations, the idea of the nation is created.

This theory is not accepted by everyone. Those who challenge modernists insist that nations are not artificial creations but have at their core something real or natural. This theory is loosely called **primordialism**, a term popularised by Edward Shils. He claims that nations, like families, demand great loyalty because they are rooted in 'the tie of blood' (1957, p. 142). Another influential primordialist, Clifford Geertz, argues that nations are not mere constructs but are authentic if they include a sense of 'givens' (1993, p. 259). If it is simply a 'given' that your community will practice a certain religion, speak a particular language and follow certain cultural practices, this creates a genuine and powerful sense of national identity that cannot be easily disregarded.

One final theory discussed in this chapter is **ethno-symbolism**. Articulated by Anthony Smith, this view rejects the modernist position but does not accept that all nations have ancient or natural pasts. He outlines certain elements that must be in place for a nation to develop. In a way, this position sits between Anderson's imagined community and primordialism.

What this shows us is that nations and nationalism are contested topics and far from simple. Particularly if you lean towards the modernist view, it should also be clear how malleable the concept of nation is. Rogers Brubaker goes as far to say that nation is a 'category of practice' (2010, p. 10). In other words, the way nationhood is practiced through popular culture forms our perception of the nation. There is nothing intrinsically white about the nation we call Australia, but a great deal of effort was put into creating this perception. For three quarters of a century after it was established in 1901, an overtly racist immigration system was in place, known popularly as the White Australia Policy. Since the 1970s Australian governments have pursued a policy of multiculturalism and have actively 'practiced' a new understanding of the nation. This can be seen as a shift from ethnic nationalism (where race and culture are prioritised) to civic nationalism (where **citizenship** and shared values are prioritised).

Although a strong majority of Australians support multiculturalism, the concept of nation is still contested. Pauline Hanson's One Nation party, for instance argues against multiculturalism and immigration. Some far-Right groups such as Reclaim Australia seek a return to ethnic nationalism and what they imagine the nation used to be. What this shows us is that citizenship is not necessarily the same as nationality. In many parts of the world, a legal citizen may not be fully accepted as a legitimate member if they do not fit into the hegemonic narrative of that nation. Equally, an individual may have multiple heritages and not wish to be wedded to a single nationality.

This chapter will discuss the difference between nation and state, and also explore the way nationalism impacts society. We discuss not only what a nation is but when a nation comes into being. You will be asked to consider why nationalism is such a powerful force and if that power is waning or gathering strength. Finally, we will consider the idea of 'post-nations' and if the phenomenon of globalisation and the existential threat of climate change will make nations redundant.

After reading this chapter, you should be able to:
- Define the terms 'nation' and 'state' and explain how they are distinct yet connected
- Explain the difference between modernism and primordialism
- Understand why nationalism is so powerful even in a globalised world
- Give a considered opinion as to whether the concept of nations is losing relevance.

KEY TERMS

Citizenship Legal membership of a political community, normally a state (that is, a 'country') that provides individuals with both rights (or protections and provisions) and obligations (or loyalty and duties).

Ethnicity The categorisation of groups of people on the basis of cultural characteristics and shared heritage; belonging to a group bonded by the common historical linkages of language, tradition, religion or cultural practice.

Ethno-symbolism A theory that nations originate in both the historical development of ethnicity and the creation of a modern political community.

> **First Nations** A term used initially to describe the Indigenous peoples of Canada. It is now widely used in the United States, Australia and other places. Unless otherwise specified, it refers to Indigenous peoples globally.
>
> **Imagined community** A theory that in the modern world, members of nations are bound together by a constructed image of how fellow members live the same way and share the same values.
>
> **Modernism** A theory that nations were created in the Industrial Revolution by the need to develop a large-scale sense of community, identity and order.
>
> **Nation** A group of people with a common identity and a public culture rooted in ethnicity or created by industrial society.
>
> **Nation state** A political community in a recognised territorial space in which a centralised government exercises authority to rule on behalf of a national community or communities; among its citizens, there is a strong sense of belonging to a shared community.
>
> **Nationalism** A set of symbols and beliefs that provide the sense of being part of a single political community; also refers to loyalty to and promotion of the nation.
>
> **Primordialism** A theory that nations are timeless because they are rooted in the language and culture of pre-modern societies.
>
> **Sovereignty** The autonomous power to exercise supreme legal and political authority over a given domain, commonly measured in territorial terms.
>
> **State** A form of modern political organisation where a government exercises sovereign power over a population of citizens. Often synonymous with 'country'.
>
> **Transnational actor** A community or political movement that defines its identity or activity beyond the sovereign boundary of the state.

What is a nation?

The 1994 Commonwealth Games in Victoria, Canada, was won by Australia with 87 gold medals. Two of those gold medals were won by Indigenous sprinter Cathy Freeman. After winning the 400 metre event, she took a victory lap carrying both the Australian and Aboriginal flags.

This sparked a great deal of controversy as some felt she should only carry the flag of the state she officially represented. The head of the Australian team, Arthur Tunstall, was apoplectic. He immediately sent a directive to all Australian athletes threatening that they would be sent home if they waved any flag other than the Australian flag. Freeman defied this order. After winning another gold, this time in the 200 metre event, she again completed a victory lap with both flags. The incident sparked a debate about national identity in Australia. Like Tunstall, some expressed the view that a citizen can only express loyalty to one nation and that any other display of allegiance is a form of national betrayal. Freeman's decision to celebrate both her Australian and Aboriginal identities was controversial in 1994 but widely celebrated by the end of the decade. When Sydney hosted the 2000 Olympic Summer Games, she was given the honour of lighting the cauldron. Her victory in the 400 metre final and celebration, again proudly carrying both flags, is remembered as one of Australia's greatest sporting moments.

The response to Freeman's success reveals a great deal about national identity and the debates in Australia at the time. Although she was reprimanded by Tunstall and sections of the media, she was defended by the prime minister, Paul Keating. In 1992, Keating delivered the historic Redfern Address, which highlighted the violence and dispossession Indigenous people had endured in Australia and called for reconciliation. At a global level, 1993 was declared by the United Nations the International Year of the World's Indigenous People. By the time Freeman won her gold medals in 1994, Australia was thinking deeply about national identity. The concept of nation was changing from a homogenous group to a diverse one. Some years later, Tunstall even appeared alongside Freeman in a television advertisement for Bushells Tea. In a friendly repartee, he asks, 'Like any of the new flags Cathy?' She replies, 'Yeah, nothing I'm wrapped in though'. This light-hearted reference to her victory laps suggests that even Tunstall had moderated his view over the years.

Reflecting on her decision to display both flags, Freeman said that the reason she runs is 'for my people and my country' (White 2010, p. 193). It is significant that these are not, for her, the same thing and we can see the nation and state being disentangled. Freeman was proud to represent the Australian state but was also motivated to celebrate her people and culture. She reflects in her memoir that, 'This was my race and no one was going to stop me telling the world how proud I was to be Aboriginal' (White 2010, p. 193). Through an act of bravery and defiance, Freeman was able to show a televised audience of millions, that many nations exist within the one Australian state.

Imagine again that you are in the backpacker hostel, meeting new people and introducing yourself. Many of the people you speak to might simply state they are Egyptian, or Chinese, or Iranian, meaning that they are both from that state and identify (at least to some extent) with the dominant national culture. In these cases, there is no (or little) distinction between 'my people' and 'my country'.

It is likely, however, that some travellers may give a more nuanced answer: 'I am Korean-American', 'I am Nigerian, but I live in England', 'My family is Indian, but I am Dutch'. In an increasingly globalised world, it is unsurprising that many people feel a close bond to two or more nations even if they only hold citizenship in one state.

It should be clear at this point that nation and state are different things even if they often go together. A **state** is a political organisation with a government that represents citizens (in a democracy the citizens will have a say over who represents them, in other systems they will not), has a largely accepted territory (even if there are border disputes or contested zones), and is a recognised member of the international order of states. Often the word 'country' is used interchangeably with state. Although the international body that meets in New York is called the United Nations, it is a forum for dialogue between states, not nations. The state is a relatively new concept and for most of world history there was no international order of states. In Europe, the modern concept of states is often traced to the Treaty of Westphalia in 1648 (McGrew 2011). **Nation** is a much older idea and refers to a people with a common identity and culture, often rooted in claims to shared ethnicity that include but are not limited to language, religion and history.

When you bring them together, you have the **nation state**.

The nation state

The nation state is a ubiquitous term and it is sometimes assumed that both elements always go together. This is not the case. You can have a nation without a state. The Kurdish people, for instance, can collectively be seen as a **transnational actor**. They are a group with a shared identity, history and culture. They have a flag and a geographical region known as Kurdistan, but they lack statehood. Along with an international diaspora, the Kurdish people are spread out across parts of other states, namely Turkey, Syria, Iraq and Iran.

There are many other examples of nations that do not have a state. Since the 1980s, the Indigenous peoples of North America, and more recently Australia, have increasingly used the term 'First Nations' to refer to their various people groups and cultures. For instance, my university is on the land of the Darumbal nation in central Queensland. Although these nations are not states they have ancient histories and have survived colonisation and dispossession.

It is much less common to have a state without a nation. States like Switzerland and Belgium are possible examples where there is one state but no single nation. The former Czechoslovakia is another example where the state was built to accommodate at least two distinct nations. In 1993, however, it split to form two nation states: the Czech Republic and Slovakia. Known as the 'velvet divorce', this peaceful dissolution can be seen as evidence that many people prefer to live in a nation that is also a state.

For our purposes here, this illustrates that nation and state are different things and even if we often bundle them together, one can exist without the other.

When is a nation?

Even though we use the term 'nation' often in everyday life, it is far from a simple concept. Scholars debate exactly *what* defines a nation, but it is also contested *when* a nation comes into existence. On 24 October 1995, a famous debate took place between two of the leading thinkers on nationalism at Warwick University: Anthony Smith and one of his academic mentors Ernest Gellner. Although they agreed on many aspects of nation and nationalism, a key point of contention was when a nation emerges. Particularly in the wake of the Second World War and observing the process of mass decolonisation in the 1950s and 60s, many scholars were interested in nationalism as a cultural phenomenon and field of study. As we have seen, the theory of modernism understands the creation of nations to be the result of modern society from the eighteenth century. Especially if nations are imagined, as Anderson argues, there was no way to communicate and reinforce that imagination on a large scale before the invention of the printing press and the development of mass media.

Consider the example of Italy. The process of unification (*Risorgimento*) and the creation of the Italian state only took place in the nineteenth century. A popular saying from the time, often attributed to Massimo d'Azeglio is, 'We have created Italy, now we must create Italians'.

The comment reveals a self-awareness. The nation is something that can be constructed and **nationalism** is the ideological glue that gives it power and legitimacy. Through a set of symbols that appeal to human emotions—a national flag, national anthem and other songs, national schooling, and the construction of a national mythology—a sense of national community is fostered and reinforced over time. For modernists like Gellner, even though unification leaders may have evoked the Roman Empire to give the nation a sense of permanency and history, it was still a modern construction. Like New Zealand's decision not to join the Australian federation, Italian unification can be considered an accident of history. For modernists, had some areas not joined, our imaginations would have adapted and the map of Italy we recognise today could have looked very different.

Another prominent modernist, Eric Hobsbawm, used the term 'invention of tradition' to describe the 'comparatively recent historical innovation, the "nation", with its associated phenomena: nationalism' (2012, p. 13). Smith agrees that nationalism is modern but rejects the inference that nations are, therefore, necessarily modern. Although his ethno-symbolism approach can be considered a form of primordialism, Smith does not believe that nations are natural or eternal. Nor does he accept that every ancient society or empire can be conceived of as a nation. Rather he suggests that various nations have different 'pedigrees' and can be traced to different starting points (2002). Smith points out that medieval historians can discern a sense of nationhood well before the Enlightenment. When the English and French fought in the Hundred Years' War in the fourteenth and fifteenth centuries, for instance, was there a concept of nation and political community? Both modernists and primordialists have to consider if those who fought and died in this conflict did so out of loyalty to the nation. When nations come into being depends a great deal on how a nation is defined. What qualities do you look for?

In the ethno-symbolism approach, the emphasis is on 'symbolic and social elements that compose collective cultural identities' (Smith 2002, 14). Smith draws the following distinction between an *ethnie* and a nation:

- An *ethnie* is a named community with shared origin myths, memories and one or more element(s) of common culture, including an association with a specific territory.
- A nation is a named community possessing a historic territory, shared myths and memories, a common public culture and common laws and customs (adapted from Smith 2002, p. 15).

The distinction is an important one for Smith. Not every group with shared memories and culture is a nation. There also need to be the elements of shared territory, language, economic life, public culture and common law. Smith's approach encourages us to consider the more subjective elements of nationhood. What constitutes a public or official culture? What is a shared memory? Who are the national heroes and for what reasons are they celebrated? Can these memories be contested? Let's return to Australia as a case study.

To ask when the Australian state emerged is relatively straightforward. This took place on 1 January 1901. But to ask when the Australian nation emerged is far more complex. Surely this did not happen overnight. It is implausible that there were no shared memories and no collective identity on 31 December 1900 and these all emerged the following day. There must have been some sense of nation that preceded the state. So perhaps the Australian nation came into being at some point in the nineteenth century? But it gets more complicated than this. For most white Australians, the collective identity was not solely Australian but Australian British. Australian school children would learn the names of British kings and queens, they would sing *Rule Britannia* and other British patriotic songs and more broadly would share in the collective imagination of being British. So, for many of the elements that Smith identifies like shared memories and public culture, Australia might be considered a British nation in 1901.

Again, it can be useful to consider the Olympic Games. Australia has hosted twice: Melbourne in 1956 and Sydney in 2000. Even though the games took place in the same host country in the same century, the public display of nationhood to the world was very different. In 1956, Australia presented itself to the world as a white, British nation. The games were opened by the Duke of Edinburgh on behalf of Queen Elizabeth II. When an Australian won a gold medal, *God Save the Queen* was played. All the forms and rituals combined to send a clear message that this was a British nation made up predominantly of British people (even if they had been transplanted from their homeland).

The message at the Sydney 2000 games was very different. They were opened by the Australian Governor-General and the unique Australian anthem was played for every gold medal. An elaborate opening ceremony showed a progression from Indigenous land to British colonies, to independent nation. So perhaps the Australian nation emerged in the twentieth century, not the nineteenth? But if so, why did Australia reject becoming a republic in a national referendum just a year earlier in 1999? Why does the British flag still sit at the top left of the national flag?

It gets even more complicated. Cathy Freeman insisted on waving both the Aboriginal and Australian flags to demonstrate that there are other nations in the Australian state. The **First Nations** of Australia occupied their lands for several millennia before white contact and have survived violent dispossession. For many years, First Nations have fought for the rights that most nations take for granted: the right to self-determination and **sovereignty**. For settler-colonial societies like Australia, this can be a complex and difficult process. This difficulty is exacerbated by the origin stories of the nation, often used to justify, if not glorify the dispossession. Chris Budden notes that the dichotomous language of resourceful settlers and 'primitive' Indigenes 'were not factual descriptors but the narrative used to defend and explain dispossession and violence' (2011, p. 64). Robert Clarke argues that this narrative has been repeated and institutionalised over 200 years (2016). A further issue, as Aileen Moreton-Robinson reminds us, is that there is an 'incommensurable difference' between the sense of belonging understood by Indigenous and non-Indigenous peoples (2015). Taiaiake Alfred also highlights this incommensurability and is particularly wary of modern treaties as a tool of redress. He warns that the treaty process can be 'an advanced form of control, manipulation, and assimilation' (1999). In Australia, First Nations largely rejected a government-led campaign to recognise them in the constitution and set out their own terms for having their voice heard and their sovereignty respected.

In 2017 the First Nations National Constitutional Convention met and endorsed the Uluru Statement from the Heart. The powerful first line on the Statement declares that: 'Our Aboriginal and Torres Strait Islander tribes were the first sovereign Nations of the Australian continent and its adjacent islands, and possessed it under our own laws and customs'. Among the recommendations of the Statement is a constitutionally enshrined Indigenous body that must be consulted on matters concerning them by the federal parliament. This would allow for a form of co-sovereignty where First Nations are recognised as legitimate nations, deserving the same self-determination other nations enjoy. If embraced, the enactment of the Uluru Statement would be a historic moment. As Megan Davis explains, 'the descendants of the ancient polities can unlock what is sorely lacking in this country, a fuller expression of Australian nationhood' (2018, p. 13).

So when did the Australian nation begin? The First Nations of what we now call Australia occupied their lands over 60,000 years ago. A British Australian nation was formed in the nineteenth century and a multicultural Australian nation emerged in the late twentieth century. As for a fully independent Australia, perhaps that is coming in the twenty-first century. It is a complicated answer to a deceptively simple question, and that is just one example. When did the Russian nation begin? Or Turkey, or South Africa, or Japan? Nations are messy and the theories of nation often come unstuck or at least need major qualifiers when we apply them to specific case studies. This should give us pause to reflect on whether any grand narrative of nations—modernist or primordialist—is going to be accurate or even compelling in all cases and all periods.

> **Critical reflection**
>
> You should now have a basic understanding of modernism, primordialism and ethnosymbolism. Which theory do you find the most convincing? Depending on the examples you choose, sometimes nations can seem very new or very old. Canada, for instance, only federated in 1867 and might be considered a 'new' nation even though its First Nations people were there for a long time before European contact. The People's Republic of China was established in 1949 and only recognised by many other nations in the 1970s. Despite this, it would feel strange to call China a 'new' nation. It depends greatly on your definitions of the nation and the state.
>
> Consider the nation(s) you are a citizen of. When did it begin? Does it have an independence date? Does it have an ancient history? Is your nation also a state? If so, when did it achieve statehood? Is this the same time, in your opinion, that it became a nation? Is there more than one nation within your nation state?

Why is nationalism so powerful?

The iconic 1942 film *Casablanca* is set in Morocco during the Second World War. In the movie, and in real life, Nazi Germany had occupied France and established the puppet state known as Vichy France. With national emotions running high, the movie focuses on an American nightclub owner named Rick. In a famous scene, a group of Nazi officers loudly sing German patriotic songs, which greatly upsets many of the nightclub's French regulars. With a nod of approval from Rick, the band plays the French national anthem, *La Marseillaise*. As soon as the music starts, the regulars jump to their feet and give a stirring rendition of the song, drowning out the Germans. As they sing, tears can be seen in their eyes. It is an emotional scene and finishes with defiant cries of 'Vive La France!'

How is it that these songs stir such deep emotions? Why did hearing the German songs provoke such disgust? Why did singing *La Marseillaise* feel so triumphant? Part of the reason this scene is so powerful is because it showed genuine national feeling. Several of the extras in the scene were refugees who had fled their countries before the Nazi occupation. Patriotic songs (especially the national anthem) become important symbols of the nation. In this context, the German songs were a reminder of the occupation, loss of sovereignty and losing one's home. Singing *La Marseillaise*, with its themes of freedom and love for France, was a way of showing defiance and resisting occupation. Released during the Second World War, the scene was a source of inspiration, not only to the French diaspora but to all who supported France. Even in American cinemas, some viewers were inspired to stand and sing along. As Zoë Jensiene Godfrey notes, 'on first glance, it is just a song. Yet to have such widespread societal impact, it is obviously more' (2019).

Even three quarters of a century later, the scene from *Casablanca* continues to stir deep emotions. In the wake of several terrorist attacks in France in 2015, it was shared widely online as a show of solidarity and defiance. This is the power of nationalism.

While the leading theorists disagree on the origins of nation, there is a general consensus on the purpose of nationalism: at its heart is a desire to legitimise the nation and justify its claims to sovereignty.

Smith describes it as 'an ideological movement for attaining and maintaining autonomy, unity and identity …' (2010). John Breuilly argues that its main purpose is to assert that the nation has the 'right to existence and recognition, and that to secure this right the nation must possess autonomy, often understood as [being] a sovereign nation state' (2013, pp. 1–2). Gellner agrees and notes that 'nationalism is primarily a political principle' (1983, p. 1). In other words, the purpose of nationalism is to justify and defend the nation state. Even though Smith would argue the nation itself is much older while Gellner would consider it a modern construct, they would both see nationalism as serving this political function.

Linking the nation with who we are?

Part of the reason why nationalism is so powerful is because national identity can become fused with our personal identity. When this occurs, we can perceive attacks on the nation or even the symbols of the nation to be an attack on our self.

Many nations have laws prohibiting the burning of the nation's flag for instance. Why is this so? It's just a piece of cloth with no feelings or emotions; yet burning the flag can be seen as a grave insult against the nation. Consider the national anthem also: some people stand, remove their hat, and place their hand on their heart when the anthem plays and become furious when others do not do the same.

In 2016, American football star Colin Kaepernick decided not to stand for the anthem in protest of the treatment of Black Americans. This small, silent protest grew into a significant activist movement for Black rights (Haerens 2019). It seems strange that one person deciding to kneel or stand, sing or remain silent, would spark such outrage and emotion but again, this is the power of nationalism. Those who opposed Kaepernick saw it as a great insult. Those who supported him saw it as an important protest. Both sides recognised that the anthem was a powerful symbol of the nation.

Nationalism is also powerful because it can be used to create a strong sense of us and them—friends and enemies. By creating a clear sense of what the nation is, it also establishes what the nation is not. This is its essential ideological function. It appeals to a human desire for a sense of belonging and community, but also a tendency to view different groups as 'Other'.

Consequently, nationalism can create a sense that certain behaviours, ideas, and even people do not belong—these are labelled 'un' (unAmerican, unJapanese, or unBrazilian). For this reason, nationalism is often viewed as a dangerous and potentially harmful ideology that should be resisted. For scholars in the twentieth century, there appeared to be a strong correlation between nationalism and xenophobia, racism, expansionism and violence. The Holocaust and other genocides were at least partly the result of a race-based nationalism. As Grace Cheng notes, especially for those who study human rights, nationalism can be seen as the ideological justification for 'the exclusion—and sometimes extermination—of Others' (2012, p. 3).

The potential for nationalism to be used in a harmful way is undeniable, but this does not necessarily mean that nationalism itself is a bad thing. In a provocative book, Yael Tamir argues that nationalism is not an inherently evil idea that feeds on our worst impulses (2019). She suggests that it can be, and historically has been, a force for good.

Civic nationalism is built around patriotism, shared citizenship and common values. Ethnic nationalism, by contrast, focuses on shared ethnicity. This could be based on language and culture but can also include ideas of race. As such, civic nationalism is seen as more inclusive and compatible with liberal values (Hoffman & Graham 2015, p. 268). Most forms of nationalism combine the two but may place a greater emphasis on one or the other. Hans Kohn, who coined the terms, argued that civic nationalism is associated with Western Europe while Central and Eastern Europe has been influenced more by ethnic nationalism (1962). When Tamir defends nationalism, she is referring specifically to civic nationalism.

Working within a liberal-democratic framework, Tamir argues that civic nationalism can be used to foster a sense of community and promote the common good. She identifies with the political Left but argues that the 'malaise of our age' is loneliness and this is exacerbated by the emphasis liberalism places on individual rights (2019, p. 53). A nationalism that is rooted in democracy and respect for human rights can help fight loneliness by providing a sense of community and belonging (even if it is imagined).

This is a controversial position and one might ask if the places that embrace a strong nationalism really are any less lonely. The violence of the twentieth century also serves as a caution against embracing nationalism too readily.

> **Critical reflection**
>
> Flags are one of the most visible symbols of the nation. They are displayed when world leaders meet, at international sporting events, and on national holidays and celebrations. Some flags indicate which religion is associated with the nation (the Swedish flag contains a Christian cross while the Malaysian flag has an Islamic crescent), others suggest a political ideology (the flag of China is red, the colour of communist revolution), and some are relatively neutral (the Canadian flag features a maple leaf).
>
> What are the elements in your national flag and what do they symbolise? Do you support the current flag or think it should change? Should it reflect things like religion and political ideology?
>
> How would it make you feel to see your national flag burned or defaced in some way? Would you react differently to seeing it burned by your fellow citizens in a protest, as opposed to seeing it burned by foreign nationals?

Are we post-nation?

This might seem like a strange question. The world that we know is mostly made up of nation states and it is difficult to imagine an alternative. It is unlikely that humanity will return to a system of empires or local tribes. Through globalisation, however, it is conceivable that the nation is gradually having less significance and international bodies are becoming more important. With breakthroughs in technology we may come to see ourselves united as members of the same species and global citizens rather than divided by our various nationalities.

One particular driver of this sentiment is the existential challenge we all face through human-caused climate change. Climate change is a direct challenge to national sovereignty because its cause and reach go beyond any one nation. It is not the case that nations who dramatically cut their carbon emissions will experience less climate change. Nor is it true that the nations who burn the most coal and cause the most pollution will suffer the worst results. As a planet, we will face the consequences of human-caused climate change together. This is why groups like the Intergovernmental Panel on Climate Change have been formed and why some world leaders use international forums to call for collective action.

Climate change is one clear example where we might think of ourselves as post-nations but there are others. Most national economies rely heavily on importing and exporting goods with other nations. As commerce and contact between nations has increased, we have seen the creation of multinational economic zones. Perhaps the most significant of these is the European Union (EU). By creating a single market and currency for its member states, proponents of the EU argue that they have created a superpower that can rival the United States or China. This is why it was seen as such a shock when the United Kingdom voted to leave the EU in 2016. As the twentieth century came to a close, especially with the fall of the Soviet Union and the end of the Cold War, it seemed logical, even inevitable, that the world would increasingly globalise and share a reasonably uniform liberal democratic ideology. One scholar, Francis Fukuyama, even called this period the 'End of History' (1992). Instead, we are seeing a revival of nationalism in many parts of the world. So we need to ask ourselves: Why are we as a species so attached to the idea of nations?

Tamir identifies two types of nationalism: separatism and anti-globalisation (2019, pp. 8–9). The first is a kind we have seen many times in history—a distinct nation wanting independence and sovereignty. In the twentieth century, this included many parts of Asia and Africa that won independence from their European colonisers after the Second World War. In the twenty-first century, those in Scotland who seek to leave the United Kingdom or those who want Catalonia to be independent of Spain have formed separation movements spurred by nationalism.

The other type—anti-globalisation—can be understood as a rejection of globalisation and a feeling that leaders have forsaken the nation. There is a great appeal to place the focus back on the nation, especially from working class people who worry (with or without cause) that their jobs have been moved overseas or taken by foreign migrants.

Donald Trump's election campaign to become President of the United States in 2016 used the slogan 'Make America Great Again'. A big part of his message was anti-globalisation. He argued that 'elites' use globalism to become wealthy and undermine national sovereignty. Two of his signature promises were explicitly nationalist and anti-globalisation. The first was to build a large physical wall on the Mexican border. The second was to ban people from certain Muslim-majority nations travelling to the United States. The nature of these promises and his election victory itself is evidence of a global resurgence of nationalism. Other populist leaders like Viktor Orban in Hungary, Matteo Salvini in Italy, Marine Le Pen in France and Pauline Hanson in Australia have enjoyed a surge in popularity built around promises to put their nation first and oppose 'global elites'.

At the end of the last century, it was usually the political Left who campaigned against globalisation. Progressive activists in the 1990s campaigned against large international corporations like McDonald's and Coca-Cola, arguing that they were undermining national sovereignty through exploitation of workers around the world and making huge profits. More recently, the proposed Trans-Pacific Partnership (TPP) trade agreement was of great concern to the Left who saw it as an opportunity for corporate greed. The Left opposed it because it supposedly undermined workers' wages and conditions; they demanded 'fair not free trade'. As part of his election campaign, Trump also opposed the TPP, arguing it was an 'attack on America's businesses'.

It is a strange development that the political Right have taken over the anti-globalisation mantle. The emphasis, however, is different. Supporters of Brexit, like supporters of Trump and other populist leaders, tend to be very concerned about immigration and their nation losing its imagined identity.

As an extremely wealthy individual Trump is, by definition, part of an elite. Having made huge sums of money through global trade, there is no small irony that he is the one leading this new nationalist movement against global elites. Anti-Trump advertisements in 2016 pointed out the irony that his branded ties were made in Mexico and other Trump products were also made overseas (Lee 2016). The fact that he still won on a nationalist platform speaks to the power of nationalism—though not the only contributing factor to his victory, it was certainly an important one.

For the time being, it appears that neither the political Left nor the political Right want to move to a post-nation world. Even though humanity will have to face global problems collectively, it appears this will be handled within national frameworks. Whether we consider the nation to be something real, natural, constructed, or artificial, it is a force that will remain for the foreseeable future.

Conclusion

Nations and nationalism are complex. Because there are so many variations of nationhood that have been shaped by their own time and context, we should approach with caution any grand narrative or overarching theory that claims to give a full and universal definition. What has been demonstrated, is that nation and state are different things even if they do often go together. Each reader will have to make up their own mind whether the nation is entirely constructed and modern or if it is based on natural primordial elements. It is also for the reader to discern if nationalism is inherently destructive or if elements of it can be tamed to provide a greater sense of belonging and community. Finally, as we face transnational problems like climate change, refugee crises, human trafficking and others, will we inevitably move to a post-nations era? And is that desirable? Or is the power of nation and nationalism too strong and will we always be bound to them? Is this desirable? This chapter has offered more questions than answers but they are important ones to contemplate if we are committed to making the twenty-first century less bloody than the one before.

Summary points

- The definition of a 'nation' is contested. Some understand nations to be rooted in culture and ethnicity, while others believe them to be linked to citizenship and political community. This reflects different beliefs about the origins of nations as either grounded in pre-modern social practices, or as a way of creating identity in modern industrial societies.
- The 'nation state' combines the identity politics of the 'nation' with the power politics of the 'state' to create powerful social practices, symbols and understandings that are used to define who is 'inside' and who is 'outside' a political community; who are 'friends and allies' of a country; and who are 'enemies and threats' to the state.
- The nation state is legitimised by the ideology of nationalism, which contends the nation state is unique and worthy of sovereignty. Nationalism has been combined with racism to justify terrible acts of violence. Some claim that it can also be a force for good and that it appeals to a human need for belonging and identity.

Sociological reflection

1. Contrast the flags and national emblems of three nations from different continents. What do the differences in symbolism convey about the different ways each country understands itself? How are these representations similar?
2. Place the following five identity sources in a hierarchy of importance to you:
   a. Your gender;
   b. Your citizenship;
   c. Your ethnic heritage;
   d. Your religious background;
   e. Your socio-economic background.

   Why have you chosen this hierarchy? Compare your answers with a friend. Is their hierarchy of importance the same as yours?
3. Thinking about your own nation(s), do you consider yourself more of a 'modernist', or more of a 'primordialist'?
4. List some of the people held up as national heroes for a particular nation state. What did they achieve? Why do you think they were chosen to be celebrated? Are other kinds of citizens left out? Who do you think should be celebrated as a national hero?

Discussion questions

1. Define the concept of 'nation' in 100 words or less. Compare your description with that of a classmate.
2. Define the 'state' in 100 words or less; include three characteristics of 'states' in this definition.

3   Which has more merit: 'modern' or 'primordial' understandings of the origins of nations? Discuss your views with others.

4   Why do nation states seem to represent themselves via similar modes such as flags, wartime remembrance, national monuments and claims to uniqueness? Does this make states all the same (and therefore not unique), or does it allow plenty of space for diversity?

5   Should nation states or international organisations such as the United Nations have more power in international society?

6   Consider some of the independence movements around the world (Scotland, Catalonia, West Papua, Kurdistan, Palestine). Do you support them? Should any nation that wants to become an independent state be allowed to do so or are there certain criteria?

7   Why is the study of nationalism important for understanding global contemporary society?

8   Is it inevitable that humanity will move to a post-nation world? Is this desirable?

9   Are you a 'nationalist'? Explain your answer using the concepts of this chapter.

References and further reading

REFERENCES

Alfred, T 1999, *Peace, Power, Righteousness: An Indigenous Manifesto*, Oxford University Press, Oxford.

Anderson, B 2006, *Imagined Communities*, revised edition, Verso, New York.

Breuilly, J 2013, *The Oxford Handbook of the History of Nationalism*, Oxford University Press, Oxford.

Brubaker, R 2010, 'Migration and membership', *Journal of Interdisciplinary History*, 41, 61–78.

Budden C 2011, 'The necessity of a second peoples' theology in Australia', in SB Bevans & K Tahaafe-Williams (eds.), *Contextual Theology for the Twenty-First Century*, James Clarke & Co, Cambridge.

Cheng, G 2012, *Nationalism and Human Rights: In Theory and Practice in the Middle East, Central Europe, and the Asia-Pacific*, Palgrave Macmillan, New York.

Clarke, R 2016, *Travel Writing from Black Australia: Utopia, Melancholia, and Aboriginality*, Routledge, New York.

Davis, M 2018, 'The long road to Uluru: walking together: truth before justice', *Griffith Review*, 60, 13–45.

Fukuyama, F 1992, *The End of History and the Last Man*, New York Free Press, New York.

Geertz, C 1993, *The Interpretation of Cultures: Selected Essays*, Fontana Press, California.

Gellner, E 1983, *Nations and Nationalism*, Blackwell/Cornell University Press, New York.

Godfrey, ZJ 2019, 'Praise the Lord and pass the ammunition: propaganda music as a governmental marketing tool during the WWII era', in L Abrams & K Knoblauch (eds.), *Historians Without Borders: New Studies in Multidisciplinary History*, Routledge, Oxford.

Haerens, M 2019, *The NFL National Anthem Protests*, ABC-CLIO, Santa Barbara.

Hobsbawm, E & Ranger, T (eds) 2012, *The Invention of Tradition*, Cambridge University Press, Cambridge.

Hoffman, J & Graham, P 2015, *Introduction to Political Theory*, 3rd edn, Routledge, Oxford.

Kohn, H 1962, *The Age of Nationalism: The First Era of Global History*, Greenwood Press, Westport.

Lee, MYH 2016, 'How many Trump products were made overseas? Here's the complete list', *Washington Post*, 26 August.

McGrew, A 2011, 'Globalization and global politics', in J Baylis, S Smith & P Owens (eds), *The Globalization of World Politics*, 5th edn, Oxford University Press, Oxford, pp. 14–33.

Moreton-Robinson, A 2015, *The White Possessive: Property, Power, and Indigenous Sovereignty*, Minneapolis, University of Minnesota Press.

Shils, E 1957, 'Primordial, personal, sacred, and civil ties', *British Journal of Sociology*, 8, 130–45.

Smith, AD 2002, 'When is a nation', *Geopolitics*, 7(2), 5–32.

Smith, AD 2010, *Nationalism: Key Concepts*, Polity Press, Cambridge.

Tamir, Y 2019, *Why Nationalism*, Princeton University Press, Princeton.

White, L 2010, 'Gender, race, and nation at the Sydney 2000 Olympic Games: mediated images of Ian Thorpe and Cathy Freeman', in L Fuller (ed.), *Sexual Sports Rhetoric: Global and Universal Contexts*, Peter Lang, New York, pp. 185–200.

MOVIES AND TELEVISION

Curtiz, M (dir.) 1942, *Casablanca*, Warner Bros. – First National Pictures, Los Angeles, CA.

Hing, M 2018, *Where Are You Really From?*, SBS Australia: <www.sbs.com.au/ondemand/program/where-are-you-really-from>.

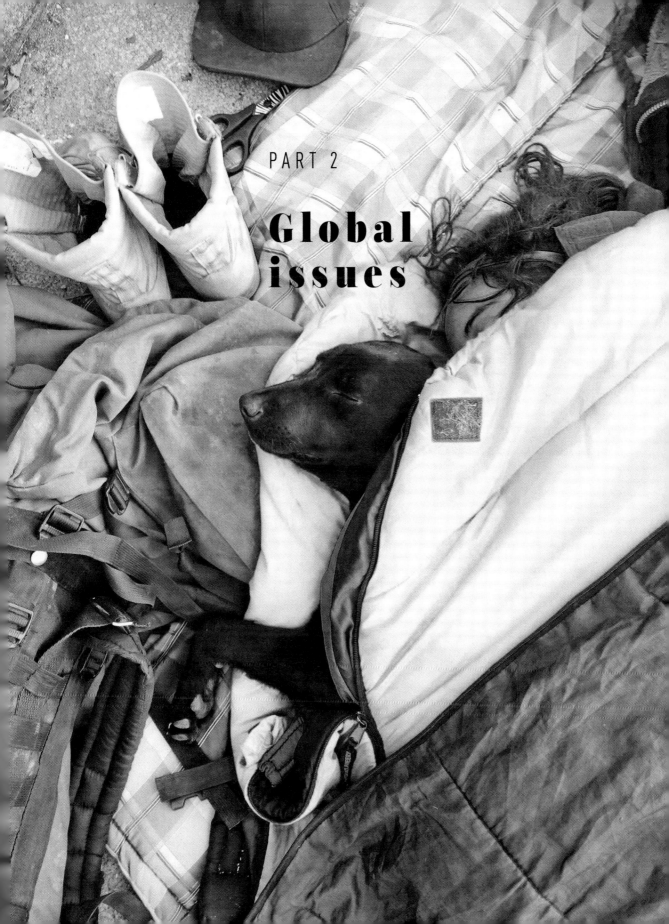

PART 2

Global issues

CHAPTER 11
Globalisation

DUNCAN MCDUIE-RA

OVERVIEW

Globalisation is a term used by so many people to describe so many things that it often seems impossible to pin down. In this chapter we will explore the social implications of globalisation through three brief cases from the one city, Al-Hudaydah, in Yemen. Yemen is an unusual place to start a chapter on globalisation, especially as in recent years the country has fragmented due to conflict and the people have experienced great suffering. Usually an introduction to the idea will begin in the United States—the biggest consumers of things made around the globe; or in China—the biggest manufacturers of things that are sold around the globe. Others begin by talking about the number of corporations that are in control of more money than many countries, in an attempt to juxtapose the economic might of some with the economic dependency of others. Some begin by looking at a single object or commodity, such as a brand of cola or a type of mobile phone, and analyse where it is made and where it is sold. Other approaches focus on the volume of things that move around the world: networks, transactions and connections at a global level.

All of these are useful ways to approach globalisation—but they have all been done before! Yemen has been chosen for this chapter for two reasons. First, Yemen is a small country with a small population that is often depicted as being opposed to the kinds of influences brought on by globalisation. So if we can find evidence of globalisation in Yemen then we stand a good chance of being able to find it almost anywhere.

Second, it is always helpful to think of globalisation as a situated phenomenon. The idea and the examples frequently used to illustrate globalisation can be very abstract and always seem to be happening 'out there', driven by invisible forces. To avoid this it is beneficial to think of globalisation being experienced in particular locations: in particular societies. Globalisation connects societies and it can change them, but the people experiencing its impacts live somewhere. They live in a society with its own formal and informal institutions, individuals and communities as we have learned about in the earlier chapters of this book. This chapter encourages you to think about how globalisation shapes life in society, how people in society react and their agency, or, the actions they take.

Before continuing, it is important to note that Yemen has been in the news a lot in the last five years as a civil war grips the country. The war is an acceleration of divisions that have been building for decades (Lackner 2019; Stookey 1982; Wedeen 2009) and some of these issues are referred to in this chapter. Having spent time in Yemen and having made good friends there, it is especially heartbreaking to watch. The events in this chapter describe everyday life in a complex society and I hope that they assist you in understanding globalisation and working towards a more just and peaceful world.

After reading this chapter, you should be able to:
- Define globalisation
- Give examples of globalisation in different contexts
- Discuss the aspects of society that globalisation impacts
- Discuss the aspects of society upon which globalisation has a minimal impact.

> **KEY TERMS**
>
> **Backroads** The geographies of globalisation that are often unseen but are vibrant.
>
> **Globalisation** A contested term—often described as the processes that bring the world closer together, for others it is something to be opposed.
>
> **Left–Right political spectrum** A system of classifying political ideologies, positions and parties.
>
> **Occupy Movement** International progressive socio-political movement that, using many global technologies, opposed social and economic inequality brought on by the global financial crisis.
>
> **Supraterritorial** The ability of a state to engage with its citizens or corporations beyond its borders.

Introduction

The city of Al-Hudaydah is located on the Red Sea Coast in Yemen, a republic sharing part of the Arabian Peninsula. Al-Hudaydah has a diverse population drawn from different parts of the mostly mountainous country of Yemen and from other countries sharing the Red Sea like Eritrea, Sudan and Somalia. Along the waterfront, fishing boats bring their catch to the shore and offload it at the fish market. Here customers come from all over to buy fresh yellowfin tuna, kawa kawa, Indian mackerel and king fish. Some fish will be bought by seafood companies and sold as frozen fish or processed products to nearby countries like Saudi Arabia, Qatar and Egypt. It may also be sold to places much further away like Nigeria and South Africa, Spain and France, or even Malaysia and Thailand.

The strange thing is that many of these places have their own fisher peoples going out in boats, communities that live from fishing, ministries in their governments that promote trade of their own fish, and their own companies freezing fish and shipping them to other parts of the world. In global terms Yemen has a small fishing industry, yet there are fish being caught there and eaten thousands of kilometres away, often by people living by the sea! At the same time, in the area behind the fish market there are many hungry residents of Al-Hudaydah asking for leftover fish or any scraps that they can take home and cook.

According to the World Food Programme, Yemen has one of the highest malnutrition rates in the world and almost 12 million people depend on direct food aid just to survive (WFP 2019). Even before the civil war there were an estimated 5 million people dependent on direct food aid (WFP 2014), indicating a severe food crisis even in times of 'peace' (always a relative term in the recent history of Yemen). The Food and Agriculture Organization of the United Nations has labelled Yemen one of the most food-insecure countries in the world, meaning that it does not produce enough food to feed its population and depends on food imported from abroad (FAO 2014). The province of Al-Hudaydah is one of the worst affected areas, yet there are thousands of fish caught here every day that are sent to other countries.

Meanwhile, along the coastline one kilometre from the fish market is a large construction site where a hotel is being built. There are two towers going up side by side. Each tower faces the Red Sea and is about 10 floors high—low for some cities but high in Al-Hudaydah. At the bottom of each tower a construction team is hard at work building swimming pools. The developers of the hotel are a South Korean company and they hope to attract tourists from Bahrain, Kuwait and the United Arab Emirates to the hotel complex upon completion. As construction winds up for the day the labourers put down their tools and climb into the back of pickup trucks to be driven back to their accommodation. They are from North Korea, brought to Yemen to work on the project and living in a dormitory where they cook their own food and sleep. They rarely go out into the city. The area where the hotel is being built used to be a long public walkway along the edge of the sea. Parts of the walkway are still intact and there are a few small kiosks, a children's playground and some benches along the wide cement footpath. There is a wall between the walkway and the sea. Along this wall there are small shelters built by the homeless residents of the city, many who have fled fighting in neighbouring countries or difficult conditions in Yemen itself. Yemen has very high rates of poverty and unemployment, especially among its youth. This makes the presence of construction workers from a faraway country—which itself has serious economic problems—in a city where there are thousands of unemployed local people looking for work even more peculiar.

Finally, a short walk from the construction site is a large restaurant. In the evening the restaurant is well lit, a contrast to the dark streets where no electricity is wasted. Fish is the speciality, with accompanying freshly made bread, yogurt and salads. The restaurant has two floors, one for solo diners on the ground floor and one for families upstairs. In the upstairs dining area there is a television mounted on one wall. The television receives a broadcast of the Middle East Broadcasting Center, or MBC as it is more commonly known. MBC is the first private satellite broadcaster in the region, run from Beirut in Lebanon. The channel MBC2 is showing an American film starring Kevin Costner and Robin Wright called *Message in a Bottle*—a slow-paced romantic film—and a group of diners and staff have crowded around the television to watch it. As more people finish their meals they also move closer to watch it, especially children and teenagers, impatient in waiting for their parents to finish eating. Downstairs the male solo-dining crowd is watching a broadcast of the Bundesliga, the top division of the German soccer league. The game is being played in heavy rain in Dortmund, a contrast to the very hot, dry air outside that is somewhat eased by a sea breeze.

These three sites raise multiple questions about contemporary society. Let's start with the fish. Is it really better economically to send fish to Spain than to sell it to locals? Is it really cheaper to buy fish from Yemen than the fish caught in Spain itself? With such high levels of hunger, malnutrition and food insecurity why doesn't the government of Yemen stop companies sending fish outside the country so that the local population can eat them? These are all very logical questions.

Let's ask similar questions of the hotel being built further along the coast. How can it be more efficient to bring workers to Yemen from North Korea with so many local people needing work? Why is a South Korean company building a hotel on the Red Sea in the first place? Who is likely to go and stay there? Where will they come from? How will they get there? Will the tourists boost the local economy? Will they eat the local fish or will they stay behind the walls of the resort, enjoying the swimming pools and eating food flown in from somewhere else?

And finally, what are Yemenis doing watching an American love story and a German soccer match beamed in from Lebanon? Is this what we would expect in a society usually depicted as anti-Western?

Imagine yourself in Al-Hudaydah confronted with these contradictions and confusions. How would you explain them? What would you identify as the processes, the dynamics, the 'things' that are happening? Are they just a few isolated coincidences specific to a city on the coast of Yemen? Or do they reflect bigger things taking place in the world? If instead of Al-Hudaydah you were standing in Sydney, Australia or Toronto, Canada or Mumbai, India, or Córdoba, Argentina—what would be the same and what would be different? In all these places you are likely to find things that are very specific to the place; things that are hard to find anywhere else. These could be specific objects you can buy, foods you can eat, the way people talk and act, the way they dress or the landscape they do these things in. In all these places you are also likely to find things that are easy to find in other places: brand-name sneakers, soft drinks, a European soccer match on television, blue jeans, a skyscraper, a slum. Think about how you might explain these to a friend or someone in your family. Many people trying to understand these things would use the term globalisation to explain them to someone else and even to themselves.

What is globalisation?

Globalisation is hard to define because it relates to so many different things happening in so many different places. In fact many people are far more comfortable identifying globalisation than defining it. As Ulrich Beck argued almost 20 years ago, 'globalisation makes possible things which, though perhaps always there, remained hidden during the stage of the welfare-democratic taming of capitalism' (2000, p. 2). In some ways we 'know it when we see it', but it can be hard to go into depth about exactly what it is we are witnessing. This is made even harder given that many of the things that cross the globe are very difficult to see: data, electronic transactions, messages through social media apps (Kitchin 2014). Globalisation has many definitions, and during the 1990s and early 2000s there was a great deal of writing on the topic as scholars in sociology, cultural studies and political science (among other fields) tried to make sense of the changing world around them.

> **BOX 11.1**
> # Thinking sociologically
>
> ### DEFINING GLOBALISATION
>
> Jan Aarte Scholte, one of the preeminent critical thinkers on globalisation, defines it as 'a reconfiguration of social geography marked by the growth of transplanetary and supra-territorial connections between people' (2005, p. 8). There are some important things to point out about this definition.
>
> First, 'reconfiguration' suggests that globalisation builds on connections and networks that previously existed. In this way reconfigured implies that something older has been rearranged into a new form, a new configuration. Second, social geography is the thing being reconfigured. How then to understand this term? One answer is to think of the relationship between society and space. Social geography is therefore concerned with the 'geographical aspects of social provision, social reproduction, social identities and inequalities' (Pain 2004, p. 650).
>
> So what is the new form of social geography? For Scholte the new form is characterised by growth of connections between people and between the societies they live in. Scholte believes this is taking place on a trans-planetary scale: that is, people in any location on the planet can be connected to other people in any other location. These connections are also supra-territorial, in that they are not limited by territory: by borders, by natural barriers, by distance.
>
> If we now put all of this together we can think of globalisation as the rearrangement of connections between people living in different parts of the world that affects:
>
> 1. The things they have access to such as work, services, health care, education, food and other commodities (provision);
> 2. The transfer of inequalities between generations of people in a society (social reproduction);
> 3. The way people see themselves and others (social identities); and
> 4. Inequalities within and between societies.

It is important not to *over-determine* globalisation. In other words we must be careful that we don't hold globalisation responsible for everything that changes in a society (Kiely 2005a). Scholte also cautions against this. He writes that globalisation has 'not erased primary pre-existent social structures such as territorialist geography, capitalist production, state governance, national identity …' (2005, p. 8). However he does argue that globalisation has changed the way territory, state, capital, nation and modernity are *understood* and the ways they *operate*. Not everywhere and not all the time, but certainly enough to make us take the concept seriously as a major factor shaping our world.

Christine Knowles has challenged us to think of globalisation at different scales. In her 2014 book *The Flip-Flop Trail: A Journey Through Globalisation's Backroads* Knowles follows the production of one of the most ubiquitous commodities in the world: low-cost footwear. Knowles maps the trail of flip-flops from Kuwait where they begin as a petroleum biproduct, to the Korean Peninsula, China, Djibouti and Ethiopia via lots and lots of shipping containers, entangling and ensnaring lives and livelihoods along the way. For Knowles the concept of the '**backroads**' is crucial. The backroads are 'counter-geographies of globalisation' that meander 'the quiet backroads of globalisation, roads that [are] unseen, [but] are alive with traffic' (2014, p. 12). Knowles argues that the backroads offer a view of the 'connective tissue' of globalisation that is 'less neat, finished, predictable, settled and routed than the familiar theorists (of globalisation) suggest' (2014, p. 14). She adds that journeys along these backroads, these trails, 'expose the missing [urban] geographies of globalisation' (2014, p. 193), insisting globalisation is 'an unstable, shifting, contingent mass of ad hoc-ery, with pockets of opportunity within overwhelming landscapes of precarity' (2014, p. 193). This is a major challenge to the idea that there is some coherent plan or set of ideas driving globalisation. When viewed from the backroads, it is a much more random set of trails. It is just that there are millions of these trails connecting places, people and things at any one time.

Is globalisation new or old?

If this chapter were being written a decade ago, it would have been written very differently. The term globalisation was everywhere and was used all the time to explain just about anything.

There were also lots of books making cases either for globalisation as a force for economic growth and prosperity (Bhagwati 2004; Freidman 1999), against it as a force that increases inequalities, poverty and perpetuates injustice (Klein 1999; Stiglitz 2003), and those seeking to bridge the 'great divide' (Held & McGrew 2007). Others sought to critically analyse globalisation and examine its potential for achieving, and denying, a more just world (Kitching 2001; Kiely 2005b; Sassen 1998). In recent years globalisation has become a more taken-for-granted phenomenon and the diametrically opposed pro and anti positions have given way to more situated studies of globalisation's impacts and of the areas of life where its impact is minimal. Some authors have even explored the return of the state following the global financial crisis and the return of heavy controls over migration in much of the world (Barrow 2005; Jessop 2010): in fact, this changing shape of the nation state is discussed in Chapter 10 by Benjamin Jones.

The rise of the **Occupy Movement** and the accompanying advances in social media have also drawn attention away from what was the older 'anti-globalisation' movement, made popular by landmark protests such as at the World Trade Organization meeting in Seattle in 1999 (Smith 2001). The Occupy Movement takes a firm stand against exploitative global capitalism, social injustice and inequality, while using the tools of global connectivity to organise and protest. As Jacquelien van Stekelenburg argues, the Occupy Movement shows 'how people are becoming increasingly connected as individuals rather than as members of a community or group' (2012, p. 55)—a shift that has the potential to reimagine democracy itself (Razsa & Kurnik 2012). At the same time globalisation has faced pressure from politicians buoyed by populist agendas in the United States, Europe and Latin America. The idea that opposing globalisation will bring jobs 'back' to stagnating economies is powerful, if challenging in practice, and anti-globalisation is now a common feature in mainstream politics at various points on the **Left–Right political spectrum** (Hu & Spence 2017). It seems globalisation is being opposed from 'above' and from 'below'.

During the same period, debates about whether globalisation is good or bad were also accompanied by debates about whether it is old or new. There are many scholars who argue that globalisation is not new; rather it is a new name for older processes such as the spread of European power and violence through colonisation and mercantilism from the fourteenth to the twentieth centuries, the internationalisation of trade and commerce, and the creation of international institutions to govern a more connected world (Arrighi 2005; Paul & Thompson 1996). Others argue that the current scale of connectivity and the emerging consensus between influential governments and institutions is unprecedented and the ways in which technology has changed the ways we understand time and space, especially national borders, is unlike any other time in history (for a discussion see Harvey 2003; 2007).

Globalisation in practice

We can return to the export of fish from Al-Hudaydah to illustrate this point. Al-Hudaydah is certainly on globalisation's backroads, if we stick to Knowles' terminology. There are many things that are largely unaffected by globalisation. Small crews on wooden fishing boats are using nets to catch yellowfin tuna in the Red Sea in much the same way as they have for centuries. Fisherfolk earn money from selling their catch or by being paid for working on someone else's boat. This money then goes to supporting their family, paying for somewhere to live, sending their children to school, supporting parents or siblings, buying food and saving to buy land or a boat—an asset to make the future a little easier. Fishing is risky and there are a lot of things that can affect the livelihood of a fisher. Like most people, they may fall sick and not be able to go out to sea. They may have a family member who is sick and have to take care of them or spend money to send them to hospital. There are other issues like weather patterns, seasonality and the behaviour of the fishing fleets of other nations.

There are also security and safety concerns. Pirates are always a risk and they may seize the fisher's catch. The fisher may be arrested by the Eritrean authorities and put in prison if they cross the maritime border. They may have an accident on a boat or ashore that means they can't earn. There may be no fish to catch—a legitimate concern with overfishing, large commercial trawlers and climate change altering the behaviour of the catch. Life is as precarious as ever.

Other things have changed dramatically. A large number of the fish are sold to exporters and factories. These exporters take advantage of the difference in the price they can buy fish for and the price people will pay for the same fish in other parts of the world. They have costs too. They must buy the fish, store it, package it and transport it. Even with these costs they can fetch more for the fish by selling it outside Yemen than they can just selling it to locals.

The Government of Yemen wants to encourage the export of fish to grow the economy and so it tries to make it easier for exporters to send fish all over the world by reducing taxes and other costs. Aid donors also encourage the government to boost its exports. The government, in other words, wants to gain from globalisation; it has changed the way the government operates in this sector of the economy. At the same time, other countries can limit the costs of Yemeni fish entering into their country and being sold to their population. For example, the European Union has a zero per cent tariff on fish from Yemen. Usually the tariff would be 8 per cent as a way to protect local European farming communities, but the European Union knows that Yemen is a poor country and that fish exports are important for the economy. Many other countries do the same. Thus it is more profitable to sell fish overseas than locally.

At the same time Yemen imports almost 85 per cent of its food. The Government of Yemen tries to tax food coming into the country to give local farmers and fishers some advantage over imported food. But as the country doesn't produce enough food to feed the population, taxing imports too high would make the cost of food very high for locals. With millions of people depending on food aid in Yemen this creates a very complicated scenario for the government. This has been made even worse by the recent civil war in the country. Furthermore, since joining the World Trade Organization (WTO) in 2014, Yemen must agree to several trade rules, and that means they have to limit the amount they tax imported food.

What has changed and what remains the same?

The biggest change is that Yemeni fish are being eaten all over the world. They are flying on planes and transported on ships to be sold in markets as far away as South Africa and Singapore. There are new opportunities for Yemeni food companies to sell to more buyers and they stand to make more money selling the fish globally than locally. A fish caught off Al-Hudaydah on Monday could be eaten in Europe on Thursday or Friday. Thousands more tonnes are canned in local factories and consumed all over the world months later. These are the **supraterritorial** connections that Scholte is talking about.

So how are these connections recalibrating social geography? Sticking with fish in Yemen, demand means that some Yemenis are able to set up companies to trade fish. Other companies that transport, store, can, freeze and pack the fish will also benefit. These companies will employ people—crucial anywhere but especially in a country with such high unemployment—who can provide better for their families and their employment may be the difference between their children going to school or having to work at a young age. Lawyers will help draw up contracts. The relevant ministries will approve export licences. Labourers at the port or the airport will load the goods and the same process will be repeated in Lagos, Nigeria, or in Kiev in the Ukraine.

So far so good! However, what happens when the buyers of Yemeni fish stop buying or start paying less? There might be cheaper fish coming from somewhere else. Consumers might be wary of fish from Yemen following health scares over metal contamination. Or what if the fish can't get to the customers as happened in 2014 when Houthi rebels seized the capital of Yemen, Sana'a? Or under conditions of armed conflict where control of Al-Hudaydah has changed hands several times in recent years? If supraterritorial connections are essential to people's lives, incomes and futures, what happens when the connections are shut down, even for a short time?

Back in Al-Hudaydah there are other issues to consider. The price of fish is subject to fluctuations in the global marketplace. The price fishers will get will depend on the buyers from the export company. The buyers will set prices based on what the fish can fetch on global markets that day, or even that hour—prices are updated continually and communicated through the internet, satellite, or even by phone; another form of connectivity. All kinds of changes can affect the price the fish are fetching, such as a new tariff on imported food in Malaysia reducing demand; a worker's strike at a port in Croatia meaning the fish are not being offloaded so the buyer has found another supplier; or a sudden rise in demand in Spain as the weather gets warmer. Connectivity creates new opportunities but also new vulnerabilities.

For the fisherfolk out on the boats, the price they get for the fish—or their bosses get—goes up and down based on factors outside their control. Other factors could also be at play not caused by connectivity directly but exacerbating its impacts, such as pollution and overfishing making it harder to catch as many fish, which in turn may mean less pay. At the same time the costs of other things in fishers' lives—rent, food, medical bills, children's school fees—rarely get any lower.

Inequalities

Here we can see the potential for greater inequalities within the society. Exporting fish has made some people more comfortable and others more vulnerable. However, their fates are tied to each other and to events outside their control. It also might have an impact on the next generation. If fishing goes well the next generation might have a chance to do other kinds of work. If fishing doesn't go well, let's say the children of fishers are not able to continue at school, or that the boys stay but the girls leave earlier, and the inequalities within the society and between boys and girls in the society may be reproduced for the next generation. This may alter their own perceptions of who they are, what they do and where they fit in society; in other words, their identity. Globalisation does not cause all these inequalities, but as we have discussed above, it can have a major impact on them.

Back to defining globalisation

Let's return to our definition for a moment. Globalisation does not just bring inequalities within societies into focus, but inequalities between societies too. In relative terms, someone in Spain will pay more for a fish than someone in Yemen, which is why there is a market for sending fish there in the first place. When compared to Yemen, an individual in Spain earns more money. This may not necessarily mean that this individual in Spain is wealthy in their own society, they may just be getting by, but considering their income they may be prepared to pay 10 euros per kilogram of fish. This is much more than someone in Yemen will be willing—or able—to pay, so there are profits to be made by selling the fish to Spain. At first glance one society benefits (Spain gets the fish it can afford) at the cost of another (Yemen sends all its fish away and in return fishers make meagre wages). In some accounts of globalisation this example might be used to say the West profits from globalisation while the rest of the world gets a bad deal. Yet it is not that simple.

Importing fish from Yemen has an impact on the fishing industry in Spain. Cheaper imported fish means that it is harder for Spanish fishers to make a living. There may be less work for fishers as the profits can only be made on a larger scale on big fishing boats. So with less work for local fishers some may have stopped working in that industry all together. Some may work in fish farms, some may be unemployed, some may have migrated to cities to work in other jobs, some may have gone into further education. This will also influence their own perceptions of their place in society: their identity. This can also be why people start to support politicians who adopt an anti-globalisation position, promising to bring jobs back to a particular society or rekindle some lost past glorious greatness. There are many possibilities. The point to be made is that the societies are connected in new ways—their social geography has been recalibrated.

Now imagine that this small scenario with the fish is played out a million times each day in locations all over the world. Spain doesn't just import fish from Yemen; it is the fourth largest fish importer in the world after the United States, China and Japan (FAO 2014, p. 50). Spain gets fish from places close by like Morocco, France and Portugal, but also from far away like Argentina, China, Ecuador and Chile. Yet Spain is also a major fish exporter too! The ninth largest in the world.

Furthermore, Yemeni fish exporters don't just sell to Spain. So while trade with Spain may be going, er, swimmingly, there might be problems in other markets that affect local life back in Al-Hudaydah. And this is just fish—there are millions of commodities moving around the world to different markets, all trying to take advantage of increased connectivity and small differences in costs, trading rules, taxes and profits that are constantly shifting. It all seems out of control (Sassen 1996).

Enough with the fish already!

There are other things going on in our case that we must revisit. Let's go back to the hotel. The hotel is being built for tourists coming from other places to Al-Hudaydah. Some locals may go and stay there but the main guests will be from other countries. Here we can see another aspect of globalisation: mobility. People have always moved. Yet in the present era it is easier, cheaper and faster to move between different locations throughout the world. Mobility studies have evolved rapidly with the onset of new methodological and conceptual challenges brought about through globalisation (Urry 2007).

Research into mobilities is concerned with flows of people and goods in an increasingly connected world. In other words, it centres analysis on the people, objects and ideas that are mobile and the contexts that shape and are shaped by their mobility. A focus on mobility accounts for the ways advances in technology, transport and infrastructure alter where people move to, the length of time they stay and the degree of movement back and forth to 'home'. Technology also enables more frequent contact with home and with migrants living and working far away, bolstering familial and cultural networks and reducing the need and desire for local assimilation. Complex patterns of mobility 'are closely entwined with institutional regimes enabling and constraining movement, reconfiguring sociality and labour toward new forms of collaboration and exploitation' (D'Andrea, Ciolfi & Gray 2011, p. 150). In other words, mobility in a globalised world is not random. People follow opportunities for work; capital follows opportunities to profit, and in many cases to exploit cheaper labour; and institutional regimes—the laws, policies, agreements and agencies of individual countries and of groups of countries—allow people and goods to move or stop them from doing so.

The construction workers

This brings us to our North Korean construction workers building the hotel. What are these men (and they are all men in this case) doing so far from home? Why aren't there local people working on the hotel?

Well there are a few possible answers. The first is that the cost of paying the North Korean labourers is lower than paying local workers even when factoring in the cost of flying them to Yemen, keeping them in accommodation and feeding them. In some other parts of the world this would seem to be the most likely answer: Bangladeshi construction workers in Malaysia or Nepali construction workers in Qatar are both examples where the costs of the migrant labour are so much lower than local labour that they are preferred. Also, in both Malaysia and Qatar the government allows work visas for this type of work to make sure construction keeps on moving, and also because this type of work is not attractive to locals so there is a shortage of people to do it. Globalisation has increased the mobility of workers in relatively low-paid industries like construction but also in relatively high-paying industries like finance and tertiary education. At the same time, mobility for other kinds of workers, migrants and refugees is getting more difficult.

In the case of Yemen it is hard to imagine that North Koreans would be paid a lot less than locals given Yemen is a poor country and there are a lot of people looking for work. There are probably some other factors involved. The developers of the hotel are from South Korea, a dynamic and globally connected economy, and its professionals work all over the world. In this case the South Korean developers needed workers that speak their own language—something they would not find among the local population. Bringing workers from South Korea is out of the question, as they would demand higher wages. So the developers arranged to bring workers from North Korea who will work for a low amount but also understand the language of the developers.

Global inequalities also play a part here. As a very poor and very isolated country, North Korea has a surplus of workers in desperate need of employment and income to support their families. There are many workers willing to live in a faraway country for a few months—even in a very hot climate with strange food, a different language and very different religious and cultural customs. As very few North Koreans get the chance to travel outside their country, the construction workers will return with some much-needed income and also stories, experiences and knowledge of the wider world. This too is a form of connectivity along the backroads.

Many studies explore the experience of migrants in a globalised world, though many of these are focused on the experience of migrants in the West, or in cosmopolitan cities like Hong Kong or Dubai. Far less attention is given to the almost invisible mobilities of construction workers, maids and farm hands between developing countries.

Western films, music and other cultural products

With fish moving in one direction, workers in another, we can also see the consumption of fairly ubiquitous Western culture: a Hollywood film and a German soccer match in the same city. Many analysts of globalisation are obsessed with cultural consumption and the idea that it is universalising societies around the world, erasing local differences, and making everyone in the world similar. Usually this is discussed as 'Westernisation'. It can cause a range of reactions in different societies, most notably the desire to protect local culture or to ban or demonise culture from outside in the hopes of stopping its influence.

There are a few issues to discuss here. The notion that local cultures are so weak that they could disappear in the face of movies and pop songs from another part of the world seems like an overreaction. It is true that various cultural outputs—films, pop music, celebrities, sporting stars—have a global reach; indeed you can find posters of the footballer Lionel Messi everywhere from Bamako in Mali to Bangkok in Thailand. However, local cultures can be very resilient. They are also fluid. They are not frozen in time and are in the process of constant change, but it is doubtful that they would be changed by something like watching the Bundesliga. Contemporary societies tend to have hybrid cultures—cultures mixed from all kinds of influences. Though it should be noted that for some small communities including many of the world's indigenous peoples there is a very real threat of languages disappearing, the loss of traditional knowledge between generations, and in some cases, the forced integration into dominant cultures.

It is also true that non-Western culture is also consumed globally: Bollywood films in Afghanistan and Kenya, Korean pop music and television in Myanmar and Mongolia, and Arab pop music made in Cairo is blasted from Tanzania to Australia.

Watching *Message in a Bottle*—the insipid 1999 film starring Kevin Costner—in Al-Hudaydah is unlikely to dramatically alter local practices, belief systems, or social relationships. It may provoke some curiosity about another part of the world. Someone may even be tempted to style their hair after the starring actor. It may shape people's aspirations for a different future in another country; a world seemingly perfect and free from daily struggles. Though it should not be assumed that people are naïve about life elsewhere. What makes this case interesting is the keen audience for an American film in a country perceived to be very anti-Western. The film is likely just being enjoyed as entertainment, not as a geopolitical statement; just another trans-planetary connection.

Conclusion

We started this chapter by taking events occurring within a square kilometre of one another in a small city on the coast of the Red Sea. From these we have been able to think about globalisation through a commodity (fish), labour (construction workers), consumers (tourists coming to the hotels), and culture (soccer and Kevin Costner). From a tiny patch of the planet we can witness all of these global processes coming from different directions.

Imagine what it would be like to enlarge that patch to five square kilometres. Imagine still if instead of a relatively isolated place like Al-Hudaydah the patch was in Cairo, Hong Kong, London, Moscow, Shenzhen, Singapore or Melbourne, Sydney or any other Australian city. Imagine the global processes originating and arriving in a small patch of land in one of these metropolises in just one 24-hour period. It is almost unfathomable: the financial transactions, the text messages, the emails, the freight, the aeroplanes, the trains, the ships, the cargo. While this boggles the mind there are other things to consider. Consider what does not make it into these cities: the people denied entry, the customs regulations that stop some things arriving, the laws that deny certain people visas.

All of these things are the result of policies and laws made by governments, laws that can also be changed. In the present era there are many measures being undertaken by some governments to make changes, to assert control over globalisation. Consider also the places where these things—these flows of goods and transactions—originate, where they pass through, and where they may ultimately end up after their time in one of these urban hubs. At each stop there is a society, shaped in part by what it produces, what flows through it, and what gets dumped there.

Summary points

★ Globalisation involves multiple processes in multiple locations. It is not a single thing, driven by one group of people, one country, or one way of organising society. Globalisation refers to unprecedented connectedness between societies that changes the way we think about distance, territory and borders.

★ While many older ways of connecting people and societies resemble globalisation, the intensity of connections in the contemporary era and the reduced importance of physical barriers make it different to the past.

★ Connectivity, much of it made possible through advances in technology, increases the mobility of goods and people across the globe. However, mobility is also constrained by laws, by borders and by politics.

★ Globalisation can be best analysed through focusing on a particular context, or place, and on particular things being globalised—in this case a commodity (fish), labour (construction workers) and culture (film/soccer).

★ Globalisation connects societies and can have a major impact on the lives of people in these societies, their livelihoods, their wellbeing, their knowledge, and their sense of their own place in their society and the world. These impacts affect people living now and in future generations.

★ It is important not to over-determine globalisation as the main explanation for everything that takes place in a particular context. It may have a powerful influence, and it may have a very small one or none at all. Therefore it is important to analyse globalisation through cases and contexts.

Sociological reflection

1 Would you describe your life as globalised? Why? How might this compare to your parents' or grandparents' era?
2 How mobile are you? Are you able to enter and leave other countries easily? Are there others who face much more difficulty? Why is this?
3 What actions do you undertake in your everyday life that might impact someone else through an interplanetary connection?

Discussion questions

1 What is globalisation?
2 Why do some people oppose globalisation?
3 Should people be allowed to work wherever they want in the world?
4 Has globalisation's time passed?

Essay topics

1. Should globalisation be regulated? If so by whom?
2. Should governments try to control mobility across their borders? Or should there be no borders at all?
3. What are the pros and cons of this for different societies, say Yemen and Singapore?
4. Does globalisation threaten local cultures and societies?
5. Given recent political events in the United States, Europe and Latin America, is globalisation under threat?

Further investigation

1. The next time you go to the supermarket, have a look at where the goods you are buying are produced. You will notice a large range of places of origin. If you have the chance to go to a large wholesale food market in the city where you live, and if the vendors will tell you the truth, find out where the fish, the garlic or the apples come from. You will be surprised (or maybe not) to find that a lot of the unprocessed food—or 'fresh' food—comes from overseas and that a lot of these same food products are also produced in Australia. Think of how your choice is linked to the lives of others far away and how this affects society closer to home. Imagine geo-tagging the origins of all these goods and mapping them. What might it look like?
2. When you next encounter the term globalisation in the media, record the segment or broadcast, or copy the story. What is the view of globalisation being given in this case? Is it pro or anti? What is being globalised in the story? Are the different impacts in the different societies considered? How might you tell the story differently? What would you focus on?

References and further reading

REFERENCES

Arrighi, G 2005, 'Globalization in world-systems perspective', in R Appelbaum & W Robinson (eds), *Critical Globalization Studies*, Routledge, New York, pp. 33–44.

Barrow, CW 2005, 'The return of the state: globalization, state theory, and the new imperialism', *New Political Science*, 27(2), 123–45.

Beck, U 2000, *What is Globalization?*, Polity, Cambridge.

Bhagwati, J 2007, *In Defense of Globalization: With a New Afterword*, Oxford University Press, Oxford.

D'Andrea, A, Ciolfi, L & Gray, B 2011, 'Methodological challenges and innovations in mobilities research', *Mobilities*, 6(2), 149–60.

Food and Agriculture Organization of the United Nations (FAO) 2014, *The State of the World's Fisheries and Aquaculture 2014*, FAO, Rome.

Friedman, T 1999, *The Lexus and the Olive Tree*, Farrar, Straus & Giroux, New York.

Harvey, D 2003, *The New Imperialism*, Oxford University Press, Oxford.

Harvey, D 2007, 'In what ways is the "new imperialism" really new?', *Historical Materialism*, 15(3), 57–70.

Held, D & McGrew, AG 2007, *Globalization Theory: Approaches and Controversies*, Cambridge University Press, Cambridge.

Hu, F & Spence, M 2017, 'Why globalization stalled: and how to restart it', *Foreign Affairs*, 96, 54–63.

Jessop, B 2010, 'The "return" of the national state in the current crisis of the world market', *Capital & Class*, 34(1), 38–43.

Kiely, R 2005a, *The Clash of Globalisations: Neo-Liberalism, the Third Way, and Anti-Globalisation*, Brill, Leiden.

Kiely, R 2005b, 'Globalization and poverty, and the poverty of globalization theory', *Current Sociology*, 53(6), 895–914.

Kitchin, R 2014, 'Big data, new epistemologies and paradigm shifts', *Big Data & Society*, 1(1) (DOI: 2053951714528481).

Kitching, G 2001, *Seeking Social Justice through Globalization: Escaping a Nationalist Perspective*, Penn State Press, University Park, PA.

Klein, N 1999, *No Logo: Taking on the Brand Bullies*, Picador, New York.

Knowles, C 2014, *Flip-flop: A Journey through Globalisation's Backroads*, Pluto, London.

Lackner, H 2019, *Yemen in Crisis: Road to War*, Verso, London/New York.

Pain, R 2004, 'Social geography: participatory research', *Progress in Human Geography*, 28, 652–63.

Paul, H & Thompson, G 1996, *Globalization in Question*, Polity, Cambridge.

Razsa, M & Kurnik, A 2012, 'The Occupy Movement in Žižek's hometown: direct democracy and a politics of becoming', *American Ethnologist*, 39(2), 238–58.

Sassen, S 1996, *Losing Control?: Sovereignty in an Age of Globalization*, Columbia University Press, New York.

Sassen, S 1998, *Globalization and its Discontents: Essays on the New Mobility of People and Money*, New Press, New York.

Scholte, JA 2005, *Globalization: A Critical Introduction*, Palgrave Macmillan, London.

Smith, J 2001, 'Globalizing resistance: the battle of Seattle and the future of social movements', *Mobilization: An International Quarterly*, 6(1), 1–19.

Stiglitz, JE 2003, *Globalization and its Discontents*, WW Norton & Company, New York.

Stookey, R 1982, *South Yemen: A Marxist Republic in Arabia*, Westview Press, Boulder.

Urry, J 2007, *Mobilities*, Polity, Cambridge.

Van Stekelenburg, J 2012, 'The Occupy Movement: product of this time', *Development*, 55(2), 224–31.

Wedeen, L 2009, *Peripheral Visions: Publics, Power, and Performance in Yemen*, University of Chicago Press, Chicago.

World Food Program (WFP) 2014, 'Yemen': <www.wfp.org/countries/yemen>.

World Food Program (WFP) 2019, 'Yemen-Emergency': <www.wfp.org/emergencies/yemen-emergency>.

FURTHER READING

Brennan, T 2003, *Globalization and its Terrors: Daily Life in the West,* Psychology Press, Abingdon.

Mathews, G 2011, *Ghetto at the Center of the World: Chungking Mansions, Hong Kong*, University of Chicago Press, Chicago.

Mathews, G, Ribeiro, GL & Vega, CA 2012, *Globalization from Below: The World's Other Economy,* Routledge, New York.

Tsing, AL 2005, *Friction: An Ethnography of Global Connection,* Princeton University Press, Princeton.

MOVIE

Mandoki (dir.) 1999, *Message in Bottle*, Bel Air Entertainment.

CHAPTER 12

Society and the environment

AISLING BAILEY

CHAPTER OVERVIEW

As a child, I grew up in a small, rural Irish village and had great freedom to enjoy the nearby fields, rivers and trees. When my family and I migrated to Australia, we moved to suburban Melbourne, and the close connection I had experienced with the natural environment was lost. Ever since, I have been exploring the importance of connecting with the natural environment and trying to forge a new connection within an urban setting.

If you live in a city and have spent time bushwalking or hiking, you may know the feeling I am describing.

Rural village life is very different to urban city life. This difference reflects the significant transition many societies around the world have experienced as a consequence of urbanisation. The majority of the world's population now live in urban settings—the result of a trend that began centuries ago and likely to continue and even increase.

Though the natural environment is featuring less in our daily lives, it is becoming increasingly important that we consider the natural environment in our daily choices. In this chapter, you will be introduced to the field of environmental sociology, and some of the important areas of work within this field. These include patterns of environmental inequality, the societal implications of climate change and societies' role in addressing it, patterns of consumption highlighting significant differences between developed and less developed nations, the ways in which the societal institution of the economy operates with detrimental environmental consequences, and how we can affect the change that is needed to help address the environmental issues of our time.

After reading this chapter, you should be able to:
- Understand the role of dualistic thinking in shaping our behaviour in society
- Have an awareness of environmental inequality within societies and across the globe
- Appreciate that society has an important role to play in addressing climate change
- Recognise the relationship between consumption practices and the natural environment
- Recognise the current economic model's lack of environmental accountability
- Appreciate the role of connection in addressing environmental problems.

KEY TERMS

Carbon pricing The application of a price on carbon, internalising the environmental cost of carbon emissions, within the context of climate change.

Circular economy In recognition of the limit in availability of resources, they are instead recovered and reused in this economic system, rather than being disposed of.

Climate justice Justice that aims to ensure that those more likely to experience environmental risk and harm as a consequence of climate change are heard, can participate in decision making affecting them, and are supported so that they can be resilient.

Ecological economics An economic model that internalises environmental costs and operates at a sustainable level in response to the knowledge that resources are finite.

Ecological footprint An ecological measure of the impact of a person's lifestyle.

Environmental inequality The unequal distributions of environmental risk and harm, and unequal access to environmental amenities.

Environmental justice Justice that aims to bring about accountability and seeks to prevent environmental inequality for both current *and* future generations.

Environmental racism The unequal distribution of environmental risk and harm, and unequal access to environmental amenities on the basis of 'race'.

Holism A conceptualisation recognising the reciprocal links between nature and culture.

Human Exemptionalist Paradigm A way of viewing humans as superior to and exempt from the natural world.

Nature/culture dualism A conceptualisation of nature and culture as two opposing and disconnected elements.

New Ecological Paradigm A way of viewing humans as interdependent with the natural world.

Overshoot The point after which the share of resources available to ensure sustainability are expended.

▷

Introduction

As we have been discussing throughout this book, our world is a complex whole and understanding the many variations and interconnections of phenomena within it is challenging. Some cultures' languages frame understandings of the world's phenomena through the use of binary oppositions. For example, in the English language, the night/day binary opposition has been applied to understand the trajectory of the sun's light around the world over the course of 24 hours. The terms night and day focus our attention on two contrasting extremes and distract our attention away from the variations of light in between these extremes. Another example can be found in the framing of gender—something discussed in detail in Chapter 7—creating a view that people are either men or women, when research shows that gender exists on a spectrum.

Thinking in terms of binary oppositions may hold initial appeal for their simplicity and apparent ease of understanding, but they can have detrimental consequences—as in the case of gender—as they overshadow the variations that exist between the two points. This is also true of the binary opposition between nature and culture that underpins more traditional sociological thought (see Chapter 1 and Box 12.1 below). Thinking of nature as the opposite of culture creates a sense of difference and disconnection between the two, when in fact they are reciprocally linked in important ways. Most fundamentally, without clean air, water, food and shelter provided by the environment, human societies cannot survive.

How people frame their understanding of their relationship with the environment plays an important role in informing environmental behaviour. If people do not recognise the ways in which their life is shaped by and shapes the natural environment, their actions are less likely to take the environment into account.

When the dualistic framing is challenged through applying a **holistic** (or inclusive) framing, an opportunity emerges for people to recognise their interdependence with the natural environment (Bateson 1979). Yet a disconnected conceptualisation has informed the ways in which many of us understand our relationship with the natural environment, and this in turn shapes the way we behave towards nature.

Like other phenomena explored in this book, it is important to note that cultural and societal engagement with the environment varies across time and place. However, industrial and post-industrial societies have engaged with the environment in ways that have proven to be detrimental to the environment, evident in pollution, unmanageable waste, species loss, habitat loss, the exploitation of finite resources and climate change. The results have been devastating for both the environment and societies: think of the impacts of the bushfires in Australia over the 2019–20 summer!

The behaviour of industrial and post-industrial societies has not been *environmentally accountable*: that is, our society has historically used and even depleted environmental resources without thinking of the consequences. This is a direct result of our society's way of thinking that we are disconnected from the environment. How people understand something shapes the way in which people behave towards it. In the pursuit of societal progress, industrial and post-industrial societies have developed in a way that now appears to challenge, if not threaten, our way of life, and that of future generations.

Concerningly, the many problems resultant from the environmentally unaccountable behaviour of industrial and post-industrial societies are adversely impacting societies that have largely not contributed to these problems. This is evident for example, in the case of sea-level rise experienced by low-lying Pacific Island nations.

BOX 12.1
Thinking sociologically

THE NATURE/CULTURE DUALISM

A number of factors have contributed to the development of the **nature/culture dualism** within Western cultures. One of the earlier influences comes from Cartesian Philosophy, a method of philosophical inquiry that emerged in the seventeenth century from the work of René Descartes (1596–1650). Cartesian philosophy put forward the idea that a person's mind or soul was the vehicle through which they could understand and make sense of the world.

It is argued that this way of rational thinking involved *disembodiment*: that is, the separation of people's minds from their bodies and from being emplaced within the world. This resulted in the centring of the rational (and cultured) human, with lesser significance placed on the environment (Casey 1996).

Dualistic thought also exists within cultures not influenced by Cartesian philosophy (Maybury-Lewis 1989). The twentieth century anthropologist Claude Lévi-Strauss put forward the idea that there was an innate tendency towards dualistic thinking right around the world (Lévi-Strauss 1976) and that this tendency reflected a desire for symmetry in an asymmetrical and dynamic world (Almagor 1989). This assertion is challenged by others who argue that while dualist thought is evident in many different parts of the world, it is not evident in every single culture and therefore is not innate (Maybury-Lewis 1989). This offers hope for the possibility of connected or holistic ways of thinking about and understanding our relationship with the natural environment gaining greater currency.

There are a number of intellectual fields that recognise the importance of interconnections between nature and culture. Some examples identified by Gregory Bateson include 'systems theory, cybernetics, holistic medicine, ecology and gestalt psychology' (1979, p. 218). Phenomenology, too, is an intellectual field that seeks to bring our attention to interconnections, through the vehicle of sense-experience (Merleau Ponty 2006). Each of these fields represents ways of thinking that encourage us to recognise that anything and everything we try to understand, is part of a dynamic and complex whole. In this way, these fields challenge disconnected ways of thinking and promote connected ways of thinking.

Environmental sociology

This focus on the social to the exclusion of the environment is evident within early sociology. This is hardly surprising as the very focus of sociology's intellectual contribution is the social. However, in the early 1970s, sociologists such as Michelson (1970) and Burch (1971) were challenging this social focus through the creation of 'human ecology' as a specific area of study. The target here was the interrelationship between human society and the biophysical environment. Through the 1970s this area developed into what became known as 'environmental sociology', defined as: 'the study of interaction between the environment and society' (Catton & Dunlap 1978, p. 44).

Early sociology was influenced by the 'Dominant Western Worldview', encapsulated by the ideas that unlike other species, humans have a cultural heritage; that human experience is largely determined by social and cultural influences; that the biophysical environment is unimportant in shaping human experience; and that the cumulative nature of culture means we can forever experience social and technological progress, capable of solving all social problems (Catton & Dunlap 1980, pp. 24–5). Catton and Dunlap critiqued this early sociological stance, challenging the idea that humans were capable of escaping 'environmental influences and constraints' (Catton & Dunlap 1980, p. 25). Identifying this way of thinking as one that excluded people from having to face environmental limits, Catton and Dunlap named this the '**Human Exemptionalist Paradigm**' (Catton & Dunlap 1978).

Within the Human Exemptionalist Paradigm, we can recognise the influence of dualistic thinking described above. Environmental sociology raised concerns with dualistic thinking evident in the Human Exemptionalist Paradigm in shaping many societies' environmental behaviour across the world. In critiquing the way we humans were harming the environment with little recognition of the damage, these sociologists created a new paradigm that would recognise our interdependence with the environment: the '**New Ecological Paradigm**'. Developed by Catton and Dunlap, this paradigm recognises that humans are one of many interdependent species; that human life is influenced by the environment; that human life is dependent upon particular environmental conditions; and finally that there are environmental limits to the growth of human societies (1980). In this way, the New Ecological Paradigm recognises that humans are shaped by their interdependence with the natural world, reflecting a holistic conceptualisation.

If disconnected understandings of nature as separated from culture have played a role in shaping societies' environmentally unaccountable behaviour, it follows that connected understandings have the capacity to encourage us to behave more environmentally accountably. With connected understandings of the human relationship with the environment, the possibility exists to inform societies that we must be responsible to confront the many environmental challenges we currently face.

> **BOX 12.2**
> # Thinking sociologically
>
> ### CONNECTED UNDERSTANDINGS
>
> Holistic thinking, expressed in the example of the New Ecological Paradigm, has great potential for encouraging us to recognise our interconnection with the natural environment. How we think about our relationship with the natural environment shapes our behaviour right through from an individual level to a societal level. It is hoped that a turn to holistic thinking will facilitate a shift towards societal practices that take the natural environment into account.
>
> Holistic thinking can be difficult to achieve within a societal context that distances us from the natural environment, however. Looking to the work of Indigenous scholars and others who bring a holistic understanding of relationships with the natural environment to their work can therefore help us to learn about holistic paradigms. For example, Indigenous scholars have made a significant intellectual contribution to the development of research methodologies and theoretical frameworks for incorporating holistic thinking into academic practice (see for example, Tuck & McKenzie 2015). However, an important note of caution should be heeded, articulated thoughtfully by Deborah Bird Rose:
>
> > There is always the possibility that people who perceive a lack in their own culture will be drawn to a romantic and nostalgic glorification of other cultures and seek to transplant another culture's ethical system into their own. The attempt is misguided. Every culture is the product of particular beings living particular lives within the particular options and constraints of their own received traditions, their modes of production and so on, none of which can be readily transplanted (Rose 1988, p. 378).

Care should therefore be taken not to appropriate Indigenous peoples' knowledge or to perpetuate stereotyped or essentialised representations of Indigenous peoples. Instead we can strive to learn in a thoughtful and respectful way, for example through centring and amplifying the voices and perspectives of Indigenous peoples and acknowledging their contribution to our understanding of the interconnectedness of people and the environment (or nature and culture)—knowledge that has historically been 'rendered invisible' due to an 'assumption of superiority of Western knowledge over Indigenous knowledge systems' (Langton 1998, p. 9).

Deborah Bird Rose sought to learn about non-human-centred ways of thinking, or what we might describe as holistic ways of thinking, from the Nganinman and Ngaliwurru people in the Yarralin and Lingara communities of the Northern Territory. As part of this journey, Rose was educated on the central concept of Country.

An example presented by Rose in her journey to understanding Country is that of the River Fig Tree. This tree offers wood and fruit to humans, and fruit to birds, ants, fish and turtles. One of Rose's teachers from the community, Riley Young Winipilin, explained that:

> When you go fishing and the figs are ripe, you can eat some for yourself, and then throw some into the water to attract the attention of turtles ... the time when the figs are fruiting is also the time when turtles (are) ... good to eat (Rose 2005, p. 296).

Further, Indigenous people from the community shared that the time in the year that people can hear the cicadas sing, announces that the figs are ripe, and that the turtles are ready to eat (Rose 2005, p. 297). These interconnected relationships helped Rose understand how 'the life of most living things is for others as well as for itself' (Rose 2005, p. 296).

The insights into human relationships with the natural environment offered by what Rose identifies as Indigenous philosophical ecology (2005), challenge anthropocentric thinking and the idea that human needs and desires should be prioritised over other life processes. Instead, ideas of kinship with nature, such as in the form of totemic groups, bring the non-human world into moral considerations; and help us to understand that the natural environment is not run by people, but invites people to connect and engage with it.

Environmental inequality

Environmental problems, whether air and water pollution, bushfires, or flooding, are faced right around the world by all kinds of people, and of course by many other species. Every environmental problem is of concern no matter where it occurs, and it is hoped that these problems are appropriately addressed. However, research shows that particular vulnerable groups within societies—including for example those with lower socio-economic status and ethnic minorities—are more likely to experience environmental risk and harm than others. These groups are also thought to have less access to environmental amenities such as parks and beaches.

Such disproportionate exposure to environmental problems as well as exclusion from environmental amenities is a concept know as '**environmental inequality**'. Patterns of environmental inequality occur within nations but can also be seen on an international scale. These patterns are common enough for us to conclude that such inequalities do not happen by chance.

Knowing this can be disheartening, but this also means that there is scope to challenge environmental inequality. We, as sociologists, are well positioned to identify areas of environmental inequality locally and internationally, to better understand the cause and impact of these inequalities, and to assist in creating positive change informed by evidence.

When seeking to understand why particular groups within a society may be more likely to experience environmental risk or harm than others, the level of power different groups hold in society may provide some answers. (We discussed the concept of power in sociology in detail in Chapter 8.) As noted above, one group within society more likely to experience environmental risk or harm are those with lower socio-economic status. An example that illustrates this relates to past associations of wealth and privilege with the 'West End' of London in England, and associations of the working class with the 'East End' of London. It appears that this east/west class-based separation, interestingly evident in other cities throughout England, relates to the direction and dispersal of pollution blown from factory chimneys into the east of cities at the time of Industrialisation (Heblich, Trew & Yanos 2016). In Australia, similar patterns can be found regarding the location of industrial zones closer to historically lower socio-economic status neighbourhoods. This was highlighted recently when chemical factory fires to the north and west of Melbourne took place, leading to health concerns for local populations and pollution of local waterways (EPA 2019a, 2019b).

Critical reflection

Why do you think powerful groups within society are less likely to face environmental risk and harm? Which aspects of our society facilitate this inequity? How could these aspects of society be changed to achieve environmental equity?

Other members of societies who appear more likely to experience environmental risk and harm are people who experience racism. This has given rise to the concept of '**environmental racism**' which is described by Robert Bullard as:

> ... environmental policies, practices, or directives that differentially affect or disadvantage (whether intentionally or unintentionally) individuals, groups, or communities based on race or colour (2002, p 35)

Environmental racism then is similar to environmental inequality and could be described as the unequal distribution of environmental risk and harm, and unequal access to environmental amenities on the basis of 'race'.

There are a number of cases around the world in which Indigenous peoples, for example, have suffered as a result of uranium mining, testing and waste storage. Within South Australia the British undertook nuclear testing through the 1950s and 60s. In Maralinga two major tests and numerous minor tests were carried out:

> the Maralinga Tjarutja people lived a mostly peaceful existence on this land for tens of thousands of years ... Radioactive exposure from the fallout affected both military

personnel and members of the Anangu community, who also suffered from a loss of culture and identity after being displaced from their traditional lands. Some communities witnessed the death of many of their elders, consequently leaving the younger generations to figure out their cultural responsibilities on their own. Many cultural connections have also been lost due to the death of many young people caused by intergenerational radioactive poisoning (Borg 2017, pp. 23–4).

Sadly, a more recent example can be found within a research discussion paper submitted by the Australian Institute of Aboriginal and Torres Strait Islander Studies (AIATSIS) to the Uranium Mining, Processing and Nuclear Energy Review Taskforce. The submission provides preliminary data showing that Indigenous people living adjacent to uranium mining and milling processes within the Kakadu region suffered a 90 per cent higher incidence rate of cancer than the general Indigenous population of the Northern Territory (Tatz, Cass, Condon & Tippett 2006). In response to such inequality, there are calls for recognition of the 'disproportionate impact of nuclear-weapon activities on indigenous peoples' around the world' (UNODA 2017).

Environmental justice

Over decades, there have been many calls for the recognition and change of unequal distributions of environmental risk and harm. Those calling for reforms are part of a broader effort termed **'environmental justice'**. Environmental justice is defined as:

> [a] mechanism of accountability for the protection of rights and the prevention and punishment of wrongs related to the disproportionate impacts of growth on the poor and vulnerable in society from rising pollution and degradation of ecosystem services, and from inequitable access to and benefits from the use of natural assets and extractive resources ... This applies both to vulnerable parts of society today, and how unsustainable use of resources and ecosystem services can create risks for securing equity and justice for future generations (Keuleers & Sekhran pp. 5–6).

Environmental justice aims to bring about accountability and seeks to prevent environmental inequality for both current *and* future generations. This recognition for justice both within and across generations is an important dimension of the environmental justice movement. Environmental justice is a direct response to international patterns of environmental inequality.

Another example is the way Australia has been dealing with waste. Until recently, Australia was exporting a significant proportion of our recyclable and other waste materials to China and less developed nations, rather than processing our waste material locally. This practice shifts the burden of dealing with waste, much of which poses health risks to populations and the environment, from wealthy nations with significant resources, to developing and less developed nations. However, China, and other nations have been implementing restrictions to this practice, causing significant logistical difficulties locally with regard to the export of plastics in particular (Pickin & Trinh 2019).

Electronic and electrical waste, otherwise known as e-waste, is another example. E-waste currently flows from developed nations to less developed nations, causing significant health concerns for populations and environments exposed to it. The scale of e-waste is increasing as greater numbers of people around the world are using electronic devices and replacing them more frequently (Baldé, Forti, Keuhr & Stegmann 2017). The global amount of e-waste in 2016 was 44.7 million metric tonnes: to put this into perspective, it is the equivalent of 4,500 Eiffel towers! In 2021 global e-waste is predicted to increase to a total 52.2 million metric tonnes (Baldé, Forti, Keuhr & Stegmann 2017). The proportion of e-waste collected and recycled around the world is just 20 per cent. What exactly happens to the remaining 80 per cent is of concern as e-waste contains hazardous components that can pollute air, water and soil, and can significantly endanger people's health (Baldé, Forti, Keuhr & Stegmann 2017).

Manufacturing undertaken by transnational corporations is another area in which environmental inequality can be seen taking place on an international level. Most transnational corporations originate in wealthy nations but establish their manufacturing and processing hubs in less developed countries. Undertaking business manufacturing and processing in less developed nations often presents lower labour costs as well as fewer and less stringent environmental regulations around manufacturing and processing practices. As highlighted by Wallerstein (2004), most production involves environmental damage in the form of chemical waste, exhausting resources, or long-term changes to the local environment. This leaves other populations and future generations to deal with the consequences. The power dynamics between developed and less developed nations evident in relation to environmental inequality reflect the legacy of colonisation in a contemporary globalised form (Wallerstein 1974).

One of the many environmental consequences of locating manufacturing and processing practices in less developed nations is poor air quality. Citizens of wealthy nations face fewer years of life lost as a result of poor air quality, compared with citizens of China and India for example, with some people in India losing up to 12 years of life as a result (AQLI 2020).

One way that this dynamic between developed and less developed nations is explored is through the 'sociology of ecologically unequal exchange'—with research in this area finding increasing levels of environmental inequality (Jorgenson 2016). Additionally, sociological research has found that increasing levels of foreign investment within less developed nations, which has the potential to lead to cleaner processes, has instead led to extraction and production practices that are dirtier, with resultant costs to environments and human wellbeing (Jorgenson 2016). Nations currently seeking to develop are following the path of industrialisation set by Europe and its settler colonies of the past. Reliance upon fossil fuels within this process may appear to be economically cost-effective, however the true cost, the environmental implications and limits of this development, are increasingly becoming evident.

Climate change

According to the United Nations Intergovernmental Panel on Climate Change, human activities now account for an increase in temperature of 1° Celsius above pre-industrial levels (IPCC 2018). To put this in perspective, NASA estimates that during the Ice Age, average temperatures across the earth were on average 4 degrees cooler.

The effects of this temperature increase are already being felt around the world—including in Australia—through extreme weather events that are challenging the way we live. The United Nations' Paris Agreement was formulated to encourage nations around the world to commit to reducing their emissions so that average temperature increases are well below 2° Celsius above pre-industrial levels, and preferably do not increase by more than 1.5° Celsius above pre-industrial levels. Expert climate scientists have suggested that limiting a temperature increase to 1.5° Celsius could save several hundred million people from climate related risks and associated poverty, that it could save 10 million people from the dangers of sea level rise, and that it could reduce the number of people left without sufficient water by 50 per cent (IPCC 2018).

Scientifically, it is known that net zero emissions need to be achieved globally by 2050 in order to limit a temperature increase to 1.5° Celsius above pre-industrial levels. Technologically, many of the innovations needed to reduce emissions are already in existence. Recent analysis from the Australian National University Energy Change Institute, for example, show that it is possible for Australia to rely upon 100 per cent renewable energy by the 2030s if current installation rates of windfarms and solar photovoltaic systems continue (Baldwin, Blakers & Stocks 2018). What the authors in this report identify is the need for the Australian Government to provide policy certainty for the renewable energy industry to invest and continue to expand: something missing in Australia over the last two decades.

In order for scientific knowledge and technological innovation to be applied, societies have a significant role to play in facilitating these changes. As the Report of the Secretary General on the 2019 Climate Action Summit and the Way Forward in 2020 states in relation to a global level: 'while this goal is within reach, to achieve it would require urgent and unprecedented social and economic transformation' (2019, p. 3).

Critical reflection

Through the use of science and technology we have the knowledge and tools required to make the transformations needed to achieve net zero emissions by 2050 in Australia. What has prevented this from being put into action? What role could society play in helping to achieve net zero emissions by 2050?

Climate justice

Underpinning the kind of social and economic transformation that is needed to address climate change, is the concept of '**climate justice**'. The aim of the climate justice movement is to respond to climate inequality: that is, the uneven distribution of both environmental amenities and climate change risk. This brings a human rights lens to the climate crisis (United Nations Sustainable Development Goals 2020).

As we have discussed above, there is a close link between existing inequalities, and vulnerability to the hazards of climate change. It is important to embrace the notion of climate justice because it addresses the effects of climate change on the most vulnerable (World Economic and Social Survey 2016). Specific issues that must be addressed include growing food insecurity, health problems, heat stress, displacements and involuntary migration (World Economic and Social Survey 2016). Data shows that of the 6457 weather-related disasters taking place between 1995 and 2015 globally, low-income nations experienced the most significant losses to life and other adverse effects (World Economic and Social Survey 2016). Further, as we saw in the Australian bushfires over the 2019–20 summer, it is the poorest communities that are the most vulnerable (Grounds 2020).

Extreme weather events can challenge and undermine the capacity of less developed nations. As such, it is important to address inequality more generally to give these nations the best chance of coping (World Economic and Social Survey 2016). The ethos of climate justice would be to ensure that the concerns of vulnerable groups are heard, that they can participate in decision-making processes affecting them, and that they are in a position to exercise resilience. Environmental problems including climate change are closely interconnected with social issues such as inequality. Understanding the complexity of relationships between societies and the environment is an important first step in achieving climate justice and environmental justice more broadly.

Consumption of the Earth's resources

Another important environmental issue we face that is closely linked with our society is consumption. Though much consumption relates to what we need to live our lives, a great deal of what we consume is unnecessary and can lead to environmental problems such as excess waste and resource exploitation. Consumption sits on a spectrum, with some people in the world unable to consume a sufficient amount for survival, right through to those consuming much more than they need. As such, consumption also intersects with issues of inequality and power between people within societies, and between nations around the world.

Consumption is also linked to economic considerations, as higher levels of consumption are seen to drive economic growth. Following the end of the Second World War, many nations were seeking to reinvigorate their economies through growing consumption. Within the United States, this sentiment is captured within the writings of economist Victor Lebow:

> Our enormously productive economy demands that we make consumption our way of life, that we convert the buying and use of goods into rituals, that we seek our spiritual satisfactions, our ego satisfactions, in consumption. We need things consumed, burned up, worn out, replaced, and discarded at an ever-increasing rate (1955).

The post-war years in places like the United States did indeed witness an increase in consumption. In some societies, a rise in consumption levels made life easier and certainly contributed to economic growth. However, concerns exist around the cost of excess consumption to the natural environment evident in the challenges outlined above. Also, as has become increasingly evident in wealthy nations, consumption alone is unable to provide personal fulfillment.

The impacts of excess consumption are the focus of the World Wide Fund for Nature's (WWF) annual 'Earth **Overshoot** Day' report. The WWF report looks at 'sustainable living' The report outlines that in order to live sustainably into the future, only a certain level of the Earth's resources can be used over the course of a period of time. Each year, WWF advises by which time the limit of available resources to live sustainably over the course of one year have been used up in their entirety. Unfortunately, Earth Overshoot Day is taking place earlier each year. In 2019 for example, Earth Overshoot Day fell on 29 July (WWF 2019): this means that the share of resources available to ensure sustainability were expended just over halfway through the year, and from this date onwards, resources were being taken away from levels needed for future generations. To put this into perspective, the last time that the level of resources consumed were at a sustainable level was in 1970 (WWF 2019). Since 1970 then, consumption levels have been too high and are not sustainable.

Consumption of the Earth's resources also poses important questions and concerns around equity. WWF provide additional calculations to see when Earth Overshoot Day would be if the whole world lived as particular nations do. To illustrate the variation of resource consumption, if the whole world lived as Australians do, Earth Overshoot Day would have fallen on 31 March 2019. In comparison, if the whole world lived as Indonesians do, Earth Overshoot Day would have fallen on 18 December. The broader pattern apparent in Figure 12.1 is that developed nations' resource use is much greater than in poorer nations, and that few nations are consuming at sustainable levels.

FIGURE 12.1 Country Overshoot Days 2019.

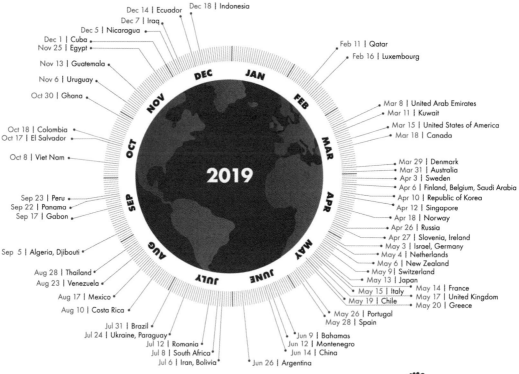

Another way in which the environmental consequences of consumption are conveyed is through an **ecological footprint**. Ecological Footprint Calculators invite you to enter information regarding your lifestyle and generate data to show how many Earths would be required if everyone in the world lived as you do: see Figure 12.2. If everyone lived as Australians do, more than four Earths would be needed (WWF 2019).

> **Critical reflection**
>
> It can be quite confronting to hear that over four Earths would be needed if everyone in the world were to live like we do in Australia. Why might it be important for people to focus on what they can do in response to an issue like this? Why might it be important to look at Australia as a whole rather than focusing on individual behaviour when trying to understand this issue?

If we are honest with ourselves, we need to answer some difficult questions regarding consumption levels, and also uncomfortably, about population levels.

FIGURE 12.2 We would need 4.1 Earths if the whole world lived as we do in Australia.

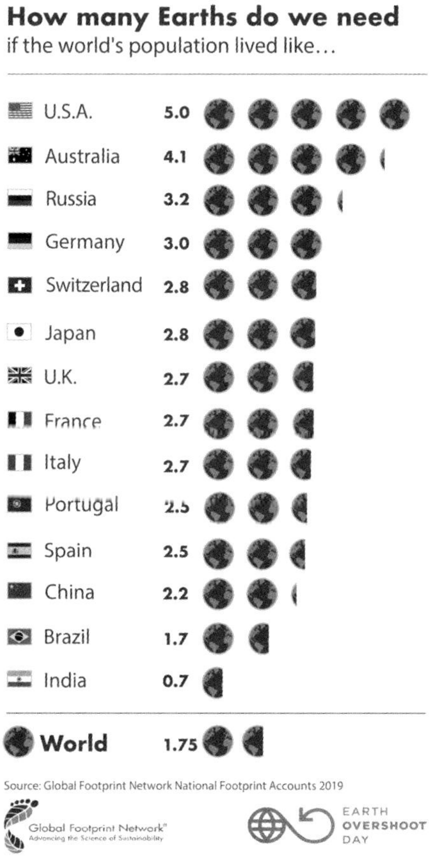

How many Earths do we need
if the world's population lived like…

Country	Earths
U.S.A.	5.0
Australia	4.1
Russia	3.2
Germany	3.0
Switzerland	2.8
Japan	2.8
U.K.	2.7
France	2.7
Italy	2.7
Portugal	2.5
Spain	2.5
China	2.2
Brazil	1.7
India	0.7
World	**1.75**

Source: Global Footprint Network National Footprint Accounts 2019

Some people hope that through the use of renewable energy and other technological innovations, the capacity for Earth to carry more people will be increased. Others are concerned that as we are already overshooting the Earth's capacity to sustainably support current population levels, changes need to take place. Questions about population are further complicated given that much of the world's population is currently living in poverty.

There are no easy answers in addressing these many issues. Research does confirm that some of the reasons behind high birth rates relate to poverty and a lack of education opportunities for women. If issues like poverty and education access were addressed, the burden of an increasing population may ease.

What feeds the economy?

Consumption levels reflect what people need to live only up to a certain extent. It can be argued that consumption levels amongst particular groups of people, and in particular nations, are much higher than they need to be.

Let me ask you a question: how many pairs of shoes do you think we each need? Some of you may say 10, others 20, and some of you may be crazy about sneakers and have 50 pairs! Think of this: I remember feeling amazed and puzzled as to why anyone would need more than 3000 pairs of shoes, as Filipino politician Imelda Marcos owned. This is an extreme example, though it helps to illustrate a culture of excess that exists, and one that many in society aspire to achieve.

Cultures of excess are incredibly beneficial for the economy, and specifically for the internationally recognised measure of market value, Gross Domestic Product (GDP). GDP refers to the total amount of money spent on goods and services within a nation, usually reported on a quarterly and annual basis. Each nations' GDP levels are frequently compared as though in competition. This measure of market value can be associated for example, with the level of opportunity within a nation. Increasing GDP is therefore appealing to many, as it shows that a nation's economy, and opportunity, is growing.

Economic growth has been seen as something capable of addressing many social problems. For example, if a nation's education sector is in need of investment, economic growth is considered one way in which additional financial resources can become available to government, in order to invest in education.

Economic growth, however, does not always equate to more money in the hands of government nor are the benefits shared equally across the population. In fact, the opposite can be true: economic growth takes place when concerning things happen. For example, when a war takes place, money changes hands to produce and deploy weaponry. Likewise, when an environmental disaster takes place, like the Australian bushfires, money changes hands to clean up the mess. All of this contributes to a rise in GDP but does not necessarily make our lives better.

With only a limited amount of resources available on Earth, many of us puzzle over how the economy can be expected to grow indefinitely. Resources provide the goods within an economy, and sustain the population providing services. As resources are limited, this appears to pose a challenge to the aspiration of continuous economic growth. In fact, if you have studied any economics, one of the first challenges that would have been raised was: how do we deal with unlimited wants and limited resources!

Additionally, as has been discussed, current global resource use is not at a sustainable level. This leads some environmentalists and economists to be critical of pursuing economic growth, as it is already having detrimental environmental consequences. In this way, the current economic model can be seen to operate in a way that is disconnected from considerations of the natural environment. This is evident in the calculation of the price paid for goods and services, which doesn't capture or reflect the environmental cost, referred to as a 'negative externality'.

There have been a number of different responses to these challenges. Some argue that technological innovation alone will facilitate continuous economic growth by drawing on renewable resources. Others embrace change, including a call for a **circular economy**; a call for a new ecological economic model and initiatives internalising environmental costs, such as placing a price on carbon. Each of these different responses seek to change the way in which the economy operates by taking environmental considerations into account.

The concept of a circular economy presents a different economic model by recognising that resources relied upon by the economy are finite. Seeking to address this limitation, the circular economy changes the way resources are managed. Within the current economic model, resources flow through the economy in a linear way. For example, resources follow the linear trajectory of being extracted, developed and finally disposed. The circular economy offers an alternative trajectory that is not linear, but rather circular, where resources are recovered and reused (Gregson, Crang, Fuller & Holmes 2015). It is therefore possible to recognise within a circular economic model, an acknowledgement of the way in which the environment plays a vitally interconnected role.

Drawing on such concepts, **ecological economics** acknowledges and responds to environmental limits. Ecological economics seeks to address the modern environmental crisis as it acknowledges that environmental destruction is intertwined with how the current economic model operates (Spash 2011). It challenges the desire for increasing consumption levels, which are considered responsible for 'the persistence of distributional inequity, global poverty and the imposition of pollution and environmental degradation on the poor, (Spash 2011, p. 359). This challenges the dominant economic model by highlighting that the Earth's resources are finite. As a field, social ecological economics is committed to recognising:

> environmental problems requiring behavioural and systemic change, continued economic growth through material and energy consumption being unsustainable and politically divisive, poverty and distribution as major economic concerns, a need for balancing power at different spatial scales, a central role for ethical debate, envisioning markets as social constructs with numerous flaws, political economy, design of alternative institutions, public participation, empowerment and engagement as necessary to address the science-policy interface, recognising the importance of 'others' (both human and non-human) (Spash 2011, pp. 366–7).

Ecological economics draws on broader ideas also evident in environmental sociology, as it acknowledges the interconnections between society and the environment. While not seeking to change the current economic model as a whole, **carbon pricing** is one initiative that seeks to internalise the environmental cost of carbon emissions within the context of climate change. Placing a price on carbon sends the message that the environmental harm from carbon emissions has a cost that should be recognised. In 2012, Australia adopted a carbon price, which was in place until 2014. Over this two-year period, carbon emissions significantly dropped in the electricity, transport, industrial processes and agriculture sectors (Department of the Environment 2014). Australia's carbon price was removed from 1 July 2014, and as a consequence Australia's carbon emissions as a whole have increased.

Currently, the European Union utilises an Emissions Trading System (ETS) that includes a cap on the amount of emissions permissible each year and that cap is set to gradually decrease. This system has shown success in reducing emissions (European Commission 2020). It is clear that economic efforts to recognise the interconnections with the environment are beneficial for the environment. Societal institutions such as the economy therefore have the capacity to operate in more sustainable ways when their reliance on the environment is recognised.

Who in society shows environmental concern and why?

In order to address environmental issues, efforts must be made throughout societies: not just us as individuals, but also our institutions. As has been discussed, there are important efforts underway in relation to the societal institution of the economy; for example, to address environmental issues. No doubt further efforts are required across business and government to ensure that their operations and policies sufficiently take the environment into account.

Within society, it is important and helpful to be aware of those groups who are more likely, and those who are less likely, to be concerned about environmental issues. Australian Bureau of Statistics data from 2012 reveals some interesting patterns worthy of consideration. Where people live seems to play a significant role in the level of concern held. For example, the urban/rural divide appears relevant, showing that those living in capital cities, compared with those living outside capital city areas, are more likely to be concerned about environmental issues in Australia (ABS 2012). Additionally, across the country, people in particular states and territories appear to have higher levels of concern about climate change than others: specifically, highest levels of concern were expressed by people living in the Australian Capital Territory, Tasmania and Western Australia (ABS 2012). What people earn also appears to play a significant role in shaping the level of environmental concern held. Australians with earnings in the highest quintile represented the largest proportion of those concerned about environmental issues (ABS 2012). Interestingly, it was also found that women were more concerned than men about climate change, water shortages and waste (ABS 2012).

As sociologists, we need to be aware of these issues. People on lower incomes may rely on extractive industries such as coal, and any push to change our economies to slow down our reliance on such industries need to take these anxieties into account. Understanding why some people have higher levels of concern than others could help to highlight underlying inequalities or differences throughout society that may benefit from being addressed, as well as leading to opportunities to further generate an environmentally engaged society. Despite some of the concerns, I think that there is good reason to be optimistic. The majority of Australians, when surveyed in 2019, agreed with the following statement: 'Global warming is a serious and pressing problem. We should begin taking steps now even if it involves significant costs' (Lowy Institute 2019). As we will discuss in the final chapter, we can all play a part!

Generating environmental action through connection

An important way to generate environmental engagement requires little more than creating opportunities for connection. Connections with each other and with place can lead to people transforming their environmental concern into action. Research has shown that creating a sense of collective identity can be effective in generating action: that is, when people feel connected to others in seeking to achieve something, they are more likely to take action (Breinlinger & Kelly 1996). And remember—understanding these connections is what sociology is all about!

Being connected to and having the support of others is beneficial. In Australia, people have come together to protect priceless rivers from being dammed when alternatives existed; protected farm land and underwater aquifers from chemical laden hydraulic fracturing fluid; protected vulnerable species; and protected the environment from waste more generally. These initiatives have simply looked for sustainable alternatives!

These achievements relied upon people connecting with one another and an element of hope: that is, the willingness to put into action our beliefs that a better world is possible (Arvanitakis 2016). People are more likely to become involved and take action when they feel that their participation will lead to their goals being achieved (van Zomeren, Postmes & Spears 2008). This is one good reason to remain hopeful about achieving environmental change.

Alternatively, if people feel that their action won't lead to the kind of environmental change they would like to see, they will be less likely to participate. With few people participating, change will therefore be less likely.

Connecting with the natural environment is another simple step that holds the capacity to generate environmental action. When people feel connected to a particular place, they hold a greater desire to take care of those places (Proshansky, Fabian & Kaminoff 1983). If you have dived at the Great Barrier Reef, bushwalked the Blue Mountains or spent time at Kakadu, you feel a connection to the beauty and uniqueness of these places and likely want to see them protected for yourself, your family and future generations. Connecting with a particular place, even a local park or river, can generate wellbeing, which in turn can serve as a motivator for people to care for the environment more generally (Hartig, Kaiser & Bowler 2001). Facilitating opportunities for people to connect with natural settings—particularly in the context of increasing urbanisation—is beneficial for both our society and natural environment.

Childhood appears to be a particularly significant time for generating a sense of connection with the natural environment. When children have the opportunity to connect and engage with the natural environment, they are more likely to act with respect towards the natural environment as adults (Kaltenborn 1998). With an increasing number of young families residing in cities, and in apartments without gardens, ensuring the inclusion of public green space holds great environmental value.

Conclusion

Many of the environmental problems faced today result from a lack of connection. In our thoughts, nature has been framed as something separate and different to us—something that was briefly discussed when we unpacked the concept of modernity. In our consumer behaviour in this globalised world, the interconnections we have with the people who make the products we consume, and the places that supply the resources for those products, are hidden from our view and are therefore far from our thoughts. We think of the economy as a neutral system that simply measures the 'value' of what people buy and sell, when in fact it was designed in a particular way reflective of dualistic thinking, leaving the true value of the natural environment out of all calculations.

As sociologists, we need to explore the influence of the nature/culture dualistic conceptualisation, and to offer a more comprehensive understanding of the social world that takes the natural environment into account. What is needed now is connection. Individually, it is possible to provide ourselves with the opportunity to connect with the natural environment, so that through our experiences we can help to recognise that we are part of the natural environment. We can make the effort to find out what impact a particular product we wish to purchase has had on people and places far away from us, and if we can't find that information, we can call on businesses to disclose this information. We can call on economists and others to ensure that the economic system we use reflects the true value of the environment. Faced with environmental problems and the huge challenge that is climate change, people can come together to generate the critical mass that is needed for societal and environmental change.

Summary points

* The nature/culture dualism has discouraged societies from recognising their interdependence with the natural environment.
* A holistic conceptualisation recognising the reciprocal links between environments and societies has the capacity to inform environmentally accountable behaviour.
* Within the field of environmental sociology, the Human Exemptionalist Paradigm describes a societal view that humans are exempt from the natural environment, and the New Ecological Paradigm seeks to encourage recognition of human interreliance with the natural environment.
* Environmental sociology has developed in response to the awareness that societal experiences are informed by the natural environment, and that societal behaviour has a significant impact upon the natural environment.
* It is clear that there are patterns of environmental inequality in existence, with particular groups more likely to suffer from environmental risk and harm, and to have less access to environmental amenities than others.
* Environmental justice and climate justice seek social and environmental accountability, and to ensure that populations experiencing environmental risk and harm are heard, can participate and are supported.
* It is important to recognise that consumer behaviour is interconnected with the natural environment. There is a need for sustainable consumer behaviour.
* Current economic practices have taken more from the natural environment than it can sustainably withstand. There is a need for an alternative, environmentally accountable economic model.
* It is important to understand why some people in society show environmental concern and others do not. If inequalities underly these patterns of concern, sufficiently addressing them could result in environmental benefits.
* Connecting with each other and connecting with place can help to address environmental problems.

Sociological reflection

1 If you think about the area in which you live, can you identify whether lower socio-economic status neighbourhoods are closer in proximity to industrial zones, or to the location of a waste facility, compared with higher socio-economic status neighbourhoods? On what basis might someone argue that this is something that should be accepted? What kinds of arguments could be put forward to challenge an unequal distribution of environmental risk and harm?

2 What might help people shift away from pursuing a culture of excess and move towards adopting a culture of sustainability? In thinking about this, it might be helpful to explore why people do pursue a culture of excess: What does this offer? What are some of the current associations of sustainable lifestyles?

3 What do you believe needs to take place in order to prevent the worst effects of climate change? What do you think has been preventing effective action taking place? How can this be challenged?

Discussion questions

1. Some people in society benefit financially as a result of environmental risk and harm. How is this currently accepted and how can this be challenged?
2. If consumers knew how many carbon emissions were produced in the creation of a product, would they change their shopping habits and behaviour?
3. What kind of initiatives could help to facilitate and encourage greater engagement with the natural environment?
4. Do you think compensation should be offered to those who suffer as a consequence of climate change if those suffering were not responsible for climate change?
5. How does social stratification relate to environmental risk and harm?

References and further reading

REFERENCES

Air Quality Life Index (AQLI) 2020, *Years of Life Lost Relative to WHO Guidelines*: <https://aqli.epic.uchicago.edu/pollution-facts/>.

Almagor, U 1989, 'Dual organisation reconsidered', in D Maybury-Lewis & U Almagor (eds.), *The Attraction of Opposites: Thought and Society in the Dualistic Mode*, University of Michigan Press, Michigan, pp. 19–32.

Arvanitakis, J 2016, *From Despair to Hope*, Penguin, Sydney.

Australian Bureau of Statistics (ABS) 2012, 'Environmental views and behaviour, 2011–12': <www.abs.gov.au/ausstats/abs@.nsf/Lookup/4626.0.55.001main+features32011-12>.

Baldé, CP, Forti, V, Keuhr, R & Stegmann, P 2017, *The Global E-waste Monitor*, United Nations University (UNU), International Telecommunication Union (ITU) & International Solid Waste Association (ISWA), Bonn/Geneva/Vienna.

Baldwin, K, Blakers, A & Stocks, M 2018 'Australia's renewable energy industry is delivering rapid and deep emissions cuts', *The Energy Change Institute*, Australian National University, Canberra.

Bateson, G 1979, *Mind and Nature: A Necessary Unity*, EP Dutton, New York.

Borg, M 2017, 'Little known South Australian history: uncovering the truth behind the nuclear weapons project at Maralinga', *Oral History Australia Journal*, 39, 23–31.

Breinlinger, S & Kelly, C 1996, *The Social Psychology of Collective Action*, Routledge, New York.

Bullard, RD 2002, 'Confronting environmental racism in the twenty-first century', *Global Dialogue*, 4(1), 34–48.

Burch, WR Jr 1971, *Daydreams and Nightmares: A Sociological Essay on the American Environment*, Harper & Row, New York.

Casey, E 1996, 'How to get from space to place in a fairly short stretch of time: phenomenological prolegomena', in S Feld & KH Basso (eds.), *Senses of Place,* School of American Research Press, Santa Fe, New Mexico, pp. 13–52.

Catton, WR Jr & Dunlap, RE 1978, 'Environmental sociology: a new paradigm', *American Sociologist*, 13, 41–9.

Catton, WR Jr & Dunlap, R E 1980, 'A new ecological paradigm for post-exuberant sociology', *American Behavioural Scientist*, 24(1), 15–47.

Climate Action Summit 2019, *Report of the Secretary General on the 2019 Climate Action Summit and the Way Forward in 2020*, United Nations, New York.

Department of the Environment 2014, *Quarterly Update of Australia's National Greenhouse Gas Inventory*, June 2014, Commonwealth of Australia, Canberra: <www.environment.gov.au/climate-change/climate-science-data/greenhouse-gas- measurement/publications/quarterly-update-australias-national-greenhouse-gas-inventory- june-2014>.

Dunlap, RE 2008, 'Promoting a paradigm change: reflections on early contributions to environmental sociology', *Organisation & Environment*, 21(4), 478–87.

European Commission 2020, *EU Emissions Trading System (EU ETS)*, European Union: <https://ec.europa.eu/clima/policies/ets_en>.

Environment Protection Authority (EPA) 2019a, *Campbellfield Fire EPA Statement*, Environment Protection Authority, Victoria: <www.epa.vic.gov.au/about-epa/news-media-and-updates/news-and-updates/campbellfield-fire-epa-statement>.

Environment Protection Authority (EPA) 2019b, *EPA Continues to Support Recovery Efforts in West Footscray*, Environment Protection Authority, Victoria: <www.epa.vic.gov.au/about-epa/news-media-and-updates/news-and-updates/epa-continues-to-support-recovery-efforts-in-west-footscray>.

Gregson, N, Crang, M, Fuller, S & Holmes, H 2015, 'Interrogating the circular economy: the moral economy of resource recover in the EU', *Economy and Society*, 44(2), 218–43.

Grounds, M 2020, 'Australia's bushfires demonstrate that the poorest suffer most from the climate crisis', *Geographical*, 20 February: <https://geographical.co.uk/opinion/item/3600-australia-s-bush-fires-demonstrate-that-the-poorest-suffer-most-from-the-climate-crisis>.

Hartig, T, Kaiser, FG & Bowler, PA 2001, 'Psychological restoration in nature as a positive motivation for ecological behaviour', *Environment and Behaviour*, 33, 590–607.

Heblich, S, Trew, A & Yanos, Z 2016, *East Side Story: Historical Pollution and Persistent Neighborhood Sorting*, CESifo Working Paper Series No. 6166, Bristol.

Intergovernmental Panel on Climate Change (IPCC) 2018, *Sixth Assessment Report*, United Nations, New York.

Jorgenson, AK 2016, 'The sociology of ecologically unequal exchange, foreign investment dependence and environmental load displacement: summary of the literature and implications for sustainability', *Journal of Political Ecology*, 32, 334–49.

Kaltenborn, BP 1998, 'Effects of sense of place on responses to environmental impacts: a study among residents in Svalbard in the Norwegian High Arctic', *Applied Geography*, 18(2), 169–89.

Keuleers, P & Sekhran, N 2014, *Environmental Justice: Comparative Experiences in Legal Empowerment*, United Nations Development Programme.

Langton, M 1996, 'What do we mean by wilderness? Wilderness and terra nullius in Australian art', *The Sydney Papers* 8(1), 11–31.

Langton, M 1998, *Burning Questions: Emerging Environmental Issues for Indigenous Peoples in Northern Australia*, Centre for Indigenous Natural and Cultural Resource Management, Northern Territory University, Darwin.

Lebow, V 1955, 'Price competition in 1955', *Journal of Retailing*, XXXI(I).

Lévi-Strauss, C 1976, *The Savage Mind*, Weidenfeld and Nicolson, London.

Lowy Institute 2019, *Lowy Institute Poll 2019*, Lowy Institute, Melbourne.

Maybury-Lewis, D 1989, 'The quest for harmony', in D Maybury-Lewis & U Almagor (eds.), *The Attraction of Opposites: Thought and Society in the Dualistic Mode*, University of Michigan Press, Michigan, pp. 1–17.

Merleau Ponty, M 2006, *Phenomenology of Perception*, Routledge, London.

Michelson, WH 1970, *Man and His Urban Environment*, Addison-Wesley, Reading, MA.

Pickin, J & Trinh, J 2019, *Data on Exports of Australian Wastes 2018–19*, Australian Government, Department of Agriculture, Water and the Environment.

Proshansky, HM, Fabian AK & Kaminoff, R 1983, 'Place-identity: physical world socialisation of the self', *Journal of Environmental Psychology*, 3, 57–83.

Rose, DB 1988, 'Exploring an Aboriginal land ethic', *Meanjin*, 47(3), 378–87.

Rose, DB 2005, 'An Indigenous philosophical ecology: situating the human', *The Australian Journal of Anthropology*, 16(3), 294–305.

Spash, CL 2011, 'Social ecological economics: understanding the past to see the future', *American Journal of Economics and Sociology*, 70(2), 340–75.

Tatz, C, Cass, A, Condon, J & Tippett, G 2006, 'Aborigines and uranium: monitoring the health hazards', AIATSIS Research Discussion Paper 20, Australian Institute of Aboriginal and Torres Strait Islander Studies, Research Section.

Tuck, E & McKenzie, M 2015, *Place in Research: Theory, Methodology, and Methods*. Routledge Advances in Research Methods, Routledge, New York.

United Nations 2020, *Climate Justice*, Sustainable Development Goals: <www.un.org/sustainabledevelopment/blog/2019/05/climate-justice/>.

United Nations Office for Disarmament Affairs (UNODA) 2017, *Treaty on the Prohibition of Nuclear Weapons*, United Nations, New York.

van Zomeren, M, Postmes, T & Spears, R 2008, 'On conviction's collective consequences: integrating moral conviction with the social identity model of collective action', *British Journal of Social Psychology*, 51, 52–71.

Wallerstein, I 1974, *The Rise and Future Demise of the World Capitalist System: Concepts for Comparative Analysis*, Cambridge University Press, Cambridge.

Wallerstein, I 2004, *World-Systems Analysis: An Introduction*, Duke University Press, Durham.

World Economic and Social Survey 2016, *Climate Change Resilience: An Opportunity for Reducing Inequalities*, Economic and Social Affairs, United Nations: <www.un.org/development/desa/dpad/publication/world-economic-and-social- survey-2016-climate-change-resilience-an-opportunity-for-reducing-inequalities/>.

World Wide Fund for Nature (WWF) 2019, *July 29: Earth Overshoot Day 2019 is the Earliest Ever*: <https://wwf.panda.org/wwf_news/?350491/Earth-Overshoot-Day-2019>.

FURTHER READING

Bateson, G 1979, *Mind and Nature: A Necessary Unity*, EP Dutton, New York.

Bullard, RD 2005, *The Quest for Environmental Justice: Human Rights and the Politics of Pollution*, Sierra Club Books, San Francisco.

Carson, R 1962, *Silent Spring*, Houghton Mifflin Company, Boston.

Catton, WR Jr 1982, *Overshoot: The Ecological Basis of Revolutionary Change*, University of Illinois Press, Champaign.

Eyles J & Williams, A 2008, *Sense of Place, Health and Quality of Life*, Ashgate, Hampshire.

Plumwood, V 2001, *Environmental Culture: The Ecological Crisis of Reason*, Routledge, New York.

MOVIES

Davies, S (dir.) 2019, *Climate Change: The Facts with David Attenborough*, BBC Studios, London.

Fox, L (dir.) 2007, *The Story of Stuff*, Free Range Studios, San Francisco, CA.

Gorelick, S, Norberg-Hodge, H & Page, J (dirs.) 2011, *The Economics of Happiness*, Local Futures.

WEBSITES

Global Footprint Network: <www.footprintcalculator.org/> (Global Footprint Network is an international non-profit organisation founded in 2003 that envisions a future where all can thrive within the means of our one planet. The Network has offices in the United States and Switzerland).

United Nations—Sustainable Development Goals: <www.un.org/sustainabledevelopment/sustainable-development-goals/> (the Sustainable Development Goals are overseen by the Division for Sustainable Development Goals (DSDG) in the United Nations Department of Economic and Social Affairs (UNDESA) and aim to achieve sustainability and equity for communities and people).

CHAPTER 13

Technology and the digital childhood

JOANNE ORLANDO

CHAPTER OVERVIEW

Children today are growing up in an era immersed in and defined by digital technology. Internet-enabled smartphones, tablets and laptops influence all aspects of our modern life including how we work, play, think, learn, create, relate and even fall in love. For hundreds of millions of children, from the moment they enter the world, they are steeped in a steady stream of digital communication and connection—from the way their medical care is managed and delivered to the online pictures of their first precious moments.

Not only are children surrounded by digitally charged social settings, they themselves have become prolific and skilled users of technology. Children often begin using technology around the age of two and by the time they reach adolescence, technology is fully embedded in their life; in fact, many teenagers would be unable to separate their online social life from their offline social life (Pew Research Center 2018).

It is of no surprise that technology is having an enormous impact on **childhood**. Social media, videogames and messaging platforms such as WhatsApp and Snapchat have become important social sites for children and young people. Their extensive engagement on these platforms strongly influences how they connect with others, who they connect with, how they engage with their world, and how they position and reposition themselves within it.

There is, however, ongoing anxiety by adults regarding children's technology use. It has become commonplace to refer to young people as addicted to or obsessed with technology (Sahlberg 2019). Media headlines consistently highlight the dangers of technology for today's youth with messages such as, 'Video Games and Online Chats Are "Hunting Grounds" for Sexual Predators' (*New York Times* 2019), 'Social Media Savvy Teens More Susceptible To Eating Disorders' (*The Asian Age* 2019), and 'Two Thirds of Parents and Grandparents Say Childhoods Getting Worse' (Young 2019). There may be some truth to these sentiments, however it is important to look past these often superficial and one-sided observations to understand why children and young people are engaging in these activities and why adults are pushing back.

The social unease that surrounds children's technology use is explored in this chapter, providing an important case study of how sociology can help us better understand the relationships between technology and society. The 'techno' and 'social' components of modern childhood are probed in some depth, along with the history and components of constructions of childhood. A key question asked within the chapter is how our concerns regarding children's technology use relate to our **social construction** of how we expect children to act, and what we understand 'childhood' to be. A possibility posed is that the dominant construction of childhood may no longer fit with today's digital era.

Many of you will become involved in industries that relate to children, young people and/or technology usage. Perhaps you will create new technologies that will mediate and transform our social relations, or perhaps you will be responsible for guiding children's wellbeing. Some of you will be parents. Others will work as policymakers who work to assist educators, parents and children and young people themselves to navigate the technical complexities that now shape our contemporary society. To achieve this, you need to understand how technology is changing experiences of childhood (and parenthood) and transforming the world we live in. By understanding the dynamics between children, technology and the social complexities that underpin their relationship, we will be able to make informed and meaningful decisions about how best to manage technologies and social relations.

After reading this chapter, you should be able to:

- Compare children's technology use in various social settings from the perspective of adults and from that of children
- Present key case studies that show critical thinking on the impact of technology on children's social worlds
- Critically analyse factors that inform social policies that relate to children's technology use
- Apply key concepts to critically evaluate socio-techno systems in our everyday lives.

KEY TERMS

Actor–Network Theory (ANT) An approach to social theory that treats technologies as networks of human and non-human actors. ANT calls for symmetry, with human and non-human actors being treated and discussed in the same terms.

Child development domains Five domains in which children mature and grow: language development, cognition, learning, physical development and social development.

Childhood The age span ranging from birth to adolescence.

Digital technology Computerised devices such as a laptop, tablet and/or a mobile phone and related systems, methods and processes.

New Sociology of Childhood Social construction of childhood in which childhood identities are interpreted as multidimensional and children are active constructors of their own identities.

Snapchat A social media platform that young people use to post statuses, updates, photos, and videos to friends to comment on. Posts automatically disappear after 24 hours.

Social construction The view that attitudes and behaviour in relation to the idea of 'childhood' are the unique products of particular time periods, societies and cultures.

Social media Websites and apps that enable users to create and share content or to participate in social networking.

Social settings The range of environments that children engage in socially including home, school and other institutions.

Techno-social life Seamless integration of technology into our social lives.

Introduction

I interviewed a six-year-old boy as part of my ethnographic research in Australian family homes. I was examining how children's technology use influences children's engagement in home life, including parent–child relationships. In my talk with the boy he was explaining to me how he uses Siri, the voice assistant on his iPad. In that explanation, he told me that Siri is his best friend.

Here's a brief section of our talk:

Boy: ... *I talk to Siri all the time*

Me: *What do you say?*

Boy: *All kinds of things ... she helps me with my homework, answers questions about what I want to know. She sings to me and tells me jokes ... She is really smart!*

Boy: *Siri is my best friend*

> **Critical reflection**
>
> What are your first thoughts when you consider the boy in this scenario? Is it that the boy is lonely? Do you think that he should be playing with friends at the park instead of sitting in his room talking to a bot? Think of yourself at the age of six—what were the social activities that you engaged with and why? Think laterally, for example, what social factors enabled you to take part in those activities. And what social factors inhibited you in taking part in other social activities? How did adult conceptualisations of children and childhood influence your participation in these social activities?

The boy's emotional connection with Siri was not due to a negative or neglectful family environment. As I mentioned, this was a real situation taken from my research with the boy and his family. I had spent many hours observing and talking with the family and I could see that the boy had a loving and supportive home life. His access to his voice assistant Siri, whenever he needed it, made him feel emotionally secure. From his perspective, it was like having another adult around to look after him, and this was comforting to him.

Let me explain.

Younger children feel more secure when they know an adult is there to protect them (Berk 2012). Siri has an adult voice, and from the boy's perspective, she was a substitute grown-up, always there for him whenever he needed answers. Children of that age ask a lot of questions, and no parent can be attentive 24/7, therefore the additional 'adult-like' attention he gained via Siri gave him emotional safety.

The idea of a young boy seeking solace in a bot is something we might see in a sci-fi movie. It would often be portrayed as a twisted shift in the social world; an 'end of the world' scenario when all hope is lost. Yet here we have what seems to be a well-balanced boy, living in a well-adjusted contemporary family, who feels a friendship and emotional connection with his bot—Siri.

Is this the new 'normal' for children growing up in the digital age? Should we be worried? Is this what we should come to expect to be a part of childhood now? If you were his parent, would you feel at ease with this connection? Should we as sociologists be concerned?

Technology has become more important to us than expected

Over time, technology has become much more than something we simply own. Technologies, as Mackenzie and Wajcman (1999) point out, bundle together devices and the human skills to work them, maintain them and bring them into our daily lives. New technologies involve new ways of doing things—know-how as well as actual devices; they involve integrated systems of activities, materials and distributed processes that have revolutionised our social world.

To understand how sociologists understand technology today it is important to look back at some of the key developments in how we think about the relationship between science, technology and society. A useful starting point is the work of Thomas Kuhn and his 1970 book *The Structure of Scientific Revolutions*.

BOX 13.1

Thinking sociologically

THOMAS KUHN AND SCIENTIFIC REVOLUTIONS

By Anni Dugdale

Historian Thomas Kuhn (1922–96) inspired a change in the way that sociologists see science and scientists. Prior to Kuhn, science was seen as the place where scientific facts were tested objectively, beyond the reach of culture and social elements. The new sociology of science, however, set out to seek explanations for the content of science, showing how scientific statements of fact were outcomes of social processes: scientists themselves were influenced by biases, relationships and all the things that make people human!

Kuhn gave sociological explanations for major scientific paradigm changes within disciplines. Paradigms combine:

- Ways of thinking (accepted theory and beliefs);
- The types of questions acceptable to a scientific community; and
- The kinds of instruments and devices used to extend the boundaries of knowledge.

An example of a scientific revolution and paradigm change given by Kuhn is the shift in astronomy in the sixteenth century from the Ptolemaic paradigm—where the Sun and planets rotate around the Earth—to the Copernican paradigm, where the Sun replaces the Earth at the centre. The usual story told about this scientific revolution is that it was much delayed in its social acceptance due to the opposition of the Catholic Church, which banned Copernicus' book and had Galileo (who publicised the Copernican system) tried by the Inquisition for heresy. The Church opposed the displacement of man from the centre of God's creation. The Bible was interpreted literally, and the Bible stated that the Earth was at the centre of the universe, so Copernicus—who delayed publishing his book until just before his death—and Galileo were labelled heretics.

Kuhn showed that science was not practised outside of society and that scientific revolutions—far from being driven by objective facts—were, indeed, social processes. The patterns he identified in the production of scientific knowledge laid the foundations for a transformation in the way sociologists think about the relationship between science, technology and society.

Just as the sociology of science catalysed by Thomas Kuhn set out to show how social factors shape scientific knowledge, sociologists of technology argue that social, cultural and political processes shape technologies. In doing so they argue against the idea of *technological determinism*, in which technological developments, scientific discoveries and their applications are considered pretty much inevitable, operating independently of context and human intervention. The consequences of this way of thinking are twofold. On the one hand, technological determinists claim that society should leave the decisions about science and technology to scientists and engineers since the development of science and technology proceeds by its own internal logic and momentum. On the other hand, we are disempowered as we feel we have no choice but to take on new technology. In this view of the world, the best people can do is to try and adapt.

The sociology of technology, instead, seeks to understand and explain how technology both helps to shape and is shaped by social and cultural factors. One of the more influential figures to theorise this kind of relationship between technology and society is Bruno Latour.

BOX 13.2
Thinking sociologically

BRUNO LATOUR AND ACTOR–NETWORK THEORY

By Anni Dugdale

The **Actor–Network Theory (ANT)** approach developed by Bruno Latour (1987) sees socio-technical systems as networks of people and things, networks of material elements, semiotic elements (meanings, symbols and ways of understanding and talking about the world around us), and human behaviours. ANT pays particular attention to how agency (understood as a capacity to act) is distributed across this network (among both human and non-human entities) and considers it a relational rather than fixed pre-determined property.

> ANT is known as the 'sociology of translation'. 'Translation' here is a play on different meanings, as it can refer to translating from one language to another; translation in the geometrical sense (the movement of an object on a page); or the transformation of an object. ANT traces the processes and negotiations that move human and non-human actors into new networks, thereby transforming them. Just as it is not possible to exactly translate meaning from one language to another—because the meaning of a word depends on its relations with all the other words in a language system—so too ANT argues that the meaning of any element in an actor network is relational and depends on its position in the network.
>
> For example, in your car, what is the process of deciding to wear a seatbelt? While you can start the car without doing up the seatbelt, cars today produce a loud and annoying sound until you 'buckle up'. Doing the right thing in this situation is not an entirely human moral decision, but is partially distributed to a non-human actor: the car!
>
> In some parts of the world, the seatbelt in some cars automatically snakes around you and does itself up, and you cannot engage the gears until this action is complete. Here the action—doing up the seatbelt—is fully distributed to things (Latour 1997).

The term **techno-social lives** (Chayko 2018) is often used to describe the seamless integration of engagement with technology across different **social settings** and the activities within them. This integration happens for both adults and for children.

For those who live in societies rich in digital communication such as Australia and the United States, these technologies offer on-tap opportunities to share information, identify interpersonal commonalities, and to interact and form social connections with a range of people for a range of purposes. These connections are created at almost every social juncture imaginable. We use technology for simple correspondences such as using our smartphone to message friends or to find out about new community events, to interactions that have significant impact on our lives, such as using an online dating site to meet a new partner (Fullwood & Atrill-Smith 2018) or shaping our online **social media** identity to influence how others interpret us and our actions.

We are communicating with others readily, easily and frequently, forming genuine relationships and becoming part of meaningful social groupings at an unprecedented rate, pace and scope (Chayko 2018). An important impact is that rather than socialising within a relatively few tightly knitted groups, people now tend to become part of numerous, far-reaching, diverse social networks that they expect will meet many of their social, emotional, and even economic needs. Today, technology enables communities, networks, societies and even individual selves to be created, established and maintained. In the box below, you can see how technology has reshaped the community of street artists and their practices.

PERSONAL VOICE
How technology has transformed street art

❝ My name is Alix Beattie and I am a PhD candidate at Western Sydney University. My research area focuses on street artists and how this media transforms and activates urban environments. Part of my research focuses on the way technology and social media has created online communities for street artists as well as audiences who love (and sometimes hate) street art. These communities have created conversations that have not been previously possible.

Street art uses the urban environment as a canvas and is used as a way of discussing and projecting ideas of the artist into the public realm. Artists communicate messages and ideas through imagery.

Prior to social media, street art was limited to the physical world. It is described as an ephemeral or 'temporary' artform because it is painted over, constantly changing and sometimes vandalised. With the introduction of the internet and specifically social media this once ephemeral artwork is now permanently documented and preserved in the digital world (Brown 2015). By creating this digital existence, conversations with audiences are now taking place online and continuing long after the artwork has gone. Through 'likes', sharing and comments, the artworks are now embedded into the digital world.

Artists creating these works now have the ability to speak to the audience and contextualise their message through online communities. Prior to such online communities, the artist could rarely speak to audiences.

An example of this is Sydney-based street artist E.L.K who was authorised to create a mural at Bondi Beach (see Figure 13.1). The work acknowledged the number of asylum seekers that have committed suicide over the past 10 years while being held as part of Australia's mandatory detention regime. The mural received Australia wide media attention and conversations, shares and likes reverberated through the internet and social media: many praising the work and others criticising E.L.K's message. While the mural was destroyed some days later by members of the public, it is now embedded in the virtual world and the conversations created about Australia's treatment of refugees continue.

FIGURE 13.1 'Not Welcome to Bondi' by Luke Cornish.

By using social media to document and provide context to the audience, artists are able to connect with other artists (MacDowall & De Souza 2018). These networks created an opportunity for collaboration as well a sense of community for artists. This has changed the once solitary art practice into a collective space for artists to network and collaborate.

This can be seen through the use of the hashtag #bushfirebrandalism—an artist collective who are using their artworks to discuss the issues around climate change in Australia. The Australian bushfires of 2019–20 summer were news around the world. Likewise, the work of the artists have created conversations about climate change and the need to continue all forms of activism to force global leaders to respond.

> **Critical reflection**
>
> How has technology influenced your friendship/social circle? Do you agree with the following statements? Answer yes or no. The more yes answers, the more influence technology has had.
>
> - I need technology to connect with friends.
> - I meet new friends via technology.
> - Likes on my social media posts are important to me.
> - I use social media to invite friends to events.
> - I like to spend time in digital spaces simply hanging out with friends.
> - I met my romantic partner online.
> - I have more social contact with my existing friends because of social media.
> - I understand my friends better because of my engagement with them online.

Techno-social world of children

It should come as no surprise that the impact of technology on children has been huge. Not only are they immersed in a world driven by technology, they have also emerged as prolific users of digital technologies; particularly in their use of smart touchscreen devices such as smartphones and iPads.

One third of internet users globally are children and adolescents under 18 years old (UNICEF 2017). Children often begin using smart devices when they are toddlers—around the age of two (Orlando 2019). The use of technology and the presence of it in their lives grows exponentially into their teen years. Research has found that 98 per cent of teens in digitally rich countries such as Australia and the United States own a mobile device and use it on average for nine plus hours per day (Pew Research Center 2018).

To understand how technology is impacting children's social worlds it is important to understand how they use it, how they interpret their use, and its value for them. Mobile devices such as smartphones and tablets have been the game changer for children in terms of ease of use, and regularity of use. As I will explain in the next section, that is part of the reason for the massive influence technology is having on them.

Why children are so good at using technology

Children are well-known for having great technology skills—something that has skyrocketed since the introduction of mobile devices. The term 'Digital Natives' (Prensky 2001) is often used to refer to their almost innate ability to use technology. What makes children—even very young children—so tech-savvy? How is it possible that some three-year-olds seem to understand technical concepts their grandparents and parents can't even fathom?

Considering this phenomenon from a child development perspective makes it clearer. Child development is often grouped into five **child development domains**: language development, cognition, learning, physical development and social development (Berk 2012). As explained below, the design features of touchscreen devices perfectly match children's development from an early age. Understanding this alignment is key to understanding their prolific use of technology and how it impacts them.

Design requires exploring and discovering

Using a touchscreen necessitates an exploratory approach. Have you ever noticed this? It requires clicking, finding and discovering, then more clicking, finding and discovering. This fundamental design element perfectly matches how children play. The exploratory design of mobile devices favours children over adults because of children's natural affinity for exploratory learning and problem-solving (Lucas et al. 2014).

Physically easy to manipulate

Touchscreen devices are physically easy to use. Features such as 'tapping' and 'swiping' (Orphanides & Nam 2017) make it easy for children as young as two years old to use technology. Mobile devices are also easily picked up and carried by children (just like a toy). It is for these design reasons that children will repeatedly choose to use technology and will often stay using it for a greater length of time (Arnott, Grogan & Duncan 2016). This may be interpreted as obsessive technology use, however for children it's about engaging in an activity they experience to be physically easy.

Visually rich design that is easy to manipulate

Unlike laptop use, which tends to require more developed literacy skills, mobile devices do not require high levels of reading and writing. This makes engaging with the content easy for children as they can navigate apps and search lists using visual cues such as images or symbols with varying levels of literacy skills (Orlando 2019).

Flipped positions: adults learn from tech-savvy children

The alignment of touchscreen design features with children's development means that children become very skilled users of technology early in life. By the time they are teens they are often highly prolific technology users. Such high skill levels and insights are enhanced because of children's enthusiasm for such technologies and their willingness to experiment. While skill levels vary across children and adults, the reality is that many children are or will become more skilled at using technology than their parents or teachers.

Below are some common scenarios in families. Have you experienced any of them?

- Dad purchases a new smartphone. He asks his 11-year-old daughter to set it up for him.
- A pre-schooler picks up her aunt's phone and takes a selfie.
- Instead of asking their parent, a 10-year-old asks 'Google Home' or 'Alexa' to answer their homework questions.
- Mum cannot work out how to use the new application on her laptop she needs for work. She asks her 15-year-old son to explain it to her.
- Dad is struggling to upload a video to social media. His 13-year-old helps him.

Historically, adults are the wise, experienced possessors of knowledge, and children learn from adults. This is still the situation today across most facets of life. Children go to school to learn from adults, and children learn from their parents at home. Adult advice and guidance are an ongoing, day to day reality of growing up.

Learning to use **digital technology** is often the exception. Technology has contributed to shifts in the culture of adult and child relationships (Correa et al. 2015). In families, it has become the norm for children to be the technology brokers guiding their parents in how to use digital technology (Nelissen & Van den Bulck 2017). Correa and colleagues (2015) call this process 'bottom-up technology transmission', by which they mean that children influence their parents' connection, use, and understanding of both traditional and new technologies. This is an important shift given that technology is one of the most valued commodities of our era.

This new reality is also important to schools. While teachers may be the holder of knowledge of the curriculum, technology is often used to learn the curriculum. School teachers are often confronted with the new (and at times harsh) reality that their students know more about the technology used in the classroom than they do (Orlando 2014). This can lead to teachers feeling a loss of status and professionally disempowered.

Children having more knowledge than adults alters the established parent–child, teacher–student roles and the traditional practices of adults and children within those roles (Nelissen & Van den Bulck 2017). Knowing more than their parents and teachers about technology means that in comparison to other aspects of their life, children often use technology and engage online more independently, with less expert adult guidance. This shift in knowledge brokerage also contributes to and confirms the idea that technology is part of youth culture and that adults are less technologically able (Orlando & Attard 2016). This change can be confronting for many adults who realise that children are likely to know more about technology than they ever will. It challenges their conceptualisation of adult–child hierarchy and can be interpreted as loss of social status for adults in their technological engagement with children across various social settings, including home and school (Orlando 2014).

As sociologists then, we must reflect on the changing nature of relationships between children, young people and adults: How does this re-shape families, communities and societies? Does this new-found independence mean that the power relations between young people and adults that you have seen discussed in other chapters change in other aspects of life?

Significant changes to childhood

Children's skilled technology use has facilitated a wide range of changes for them ranging from how they learn, communicate, grow and interpret their place in this world. As Abbasi, Ting and Hlavacs (2017) note, the fundamental shift in how children choose to spend their time has resulted in a culture unlike that experienced by previous generations. Although most children who are online view it as a positive experience, many parents, educators and policy makers worry that immersion in screens and the internet is making children depressed, creating internet dependency and contributing to health issues such obesity (UNICEF 2017).

In some ways, the fears of predators tracking children, or young people being lost in social media, is reflective of the moral panics discussed in Chapter 18. As stated, it is important that we look beyond the media headlines to understand the complex social changes that are taking place and how we can respond.

In this section, then, we will focus on the changes to the social world of children and young people that stem from the use of technology. While digital technology use does not have uniform effect on children (or adults), the changes highlighted below are emerging as significant.

1 Childhood social experiences no longer only local

Prior to digital technology, children predominantly talked and played with friends from the local school, or who lived in their neighbourhood, or whom they knew through their family. Technology has extended their social connections and environments beyond the local.

A typical 'pre-technology' social scenario would be meeting with a friend who lived in their street, rummaging through the toy box and playing a game based on the toys at hand. Teens might ring friends from school on the phone and talk about the day's events. Children would go to the local park or meet at the local shopping centre to hang out. The adults in their life were also part of their local network. What they did and who they did it with was largely very visible and familiar to the adults who cared for them.

For the first time in history, children's social worlds are no longer confined to the local; and technology has been a significant influencing factor. Technology has extended children's social world to now inhabit both face-to-face, local social groups (Holt & Holloway 2006), and non-face-to-face and non-local connections. This therefore extends the people they connect with, and the ideas, information, values and perspectives they engage with. Today's children engage in their world with breadth and complexity in a way that no other generation of children has ever been able to.

For example, a typical social scenario for a 15-year-old now may be to take a photo of themselves on **Snapchat**, add a rainbow-puking Augmented Reality lens to it and send it to their Snapchat friends, who may be a combination of personal and online-only friends. After posting they might then view stories of Snapchat users from around the globe to see what's happening elsewhere, maybe something like a music concert in Los Angeles.

We can see this play out in many ways. Greta Thunberg, the successful environmental activist, is an example of how connections beyond the local not only impact an individual child/adolescent, but also have more broad ranging impacts on the social worlds they are engaging with. While Greta's work is a highly visible example, young people's engagement with their broader social worlds impacts both parties to varying degrees and with varying consequences.

2 Play more personal, more private and profitable

Mobile devices are contributing to children's recreational activities becoming more personal, more private and less supervised (UNICEF 2017). Children are moving away from shared home entertainment, such as the whole family watching the same TV show, towards more individualised, solitary content-viewing via streaming services such as Netflix and YouTube. For example, half of 5 to 15-year-olds now watch services such as Netflix and Amazon, often on their own devices and independently (Ofcom 2019). As a result, parents have fewer opportunities to directly monitor what their children are watching, and children have more control and choice over content.

These new media formats are also providing the opportunity for children to 'produce and create' their own tech-savvy content such as YouTube videos, videogames, apps and online commercial businesses. This has given rise to a wave of 'young' technology creatives in the form of 'influencers' (online celebrities), videogaming stars, reality stars, wellbeing experts and lifestyle vloggers. More broadly as Watkins (2019) states, this youth-produced content has contributed to a new version of the innovation economy in which young entrepreneurs cultivate their technology skills with social media networks to bring their new ideas and products to the world.

3 Continuously 'plugged into' their social world

Children and young people primarily interface with the internet via social media networks and digital content platforms such as Snapchat, Instagram, TikTok and YouTube. These interactive tools allow us to generate and share content, create personalised profiles and develop online social networks (Obar & Wildman 2015). They have the potential to increase both the scope and intensity of social interactions.

Such social media networks facilitate the ongoing opportunity for children and young people to be in touch socially almost continuously (Chayko 2018), constantly receiving posts in their feed, and regularly posting their own updates. Always 'open' and always 'on', online social networks and communities can help deepen friendships and provide young people with a deep-seated sense of connectedness, of feeling 'plugged in' to a unit larger than oneself, and of being super-connected (Chayko 2018).

Can you relate to this? Do you use these networks as real-time portals for connecting, building support networks from friends and online groups, as well as for seeking advice?

Social networks can also be used as a canvas for identity expression (McDool et al. 2020). Young people can use their online identity to choose how to represent themselves and to express how they want others to see and interpret them. This can allow them to break free from established identities and social relations they may have at school, within their family or other social space, that they no longer want to be confined by.

This positivity however is far from unanimous. Young people can feel pressure to always be online, and to portray their life in a positive and likeable way. Their friendships also play out differently online. A study by Pew Research Center (2018) investigating the digital lives of 700 teens found that approximately half the teens interviewed (43 per cent) unfollowed others on social media because they acted differently online than in person, and/or posted political or social views they disagreed with.

Social media use can be linked to more frequent social comparisons, which are more likely to be negative. One of the most significant points of comparison is physically appearance (McDool et al. 2020). The material young people choose to present online also represent selectively idealised (rather than real) versions of their true lives (Pisano et al. 2017).

From a sociological perspective, the ways children and young people use technology raises questions regarding what this means for the social relations between young people. How does this shape whom children and young people befriend and relate to, how they communicate with them, how they express themselves in their social worlds, and how they negotiate online and offline social relationships? How do the public and global interactions that are now everyday practices online impact children and young people, and their interactions with their parents and other adults in their life?

> **Critical reflection**
> - With these changes to childhood, what do you think that children have gained and lost?
> - What are the consequences of having near-constant availability to one another? Has face-to-face interaction and community been displaced by these new technology-enabled practices?
> - Do you think that reliance on social media as a form of social connection leads to disconnection and social isolation, and making us lonely? If this is the reality for adults, what are the consequences for children who have known no other social world?
> - Do you think it's normal for children to act this way? Could we say that it is the new normal?

Adult interpretations of digital childhood

There is no doubt that technology is having a major influence on childhood today, and it should therefore be of no surprise that these changes are being hotly debated by adults. Many adults feel loss of control, uncertainty and/or fear that children's lives are being negatively affected by technology. As we have discussed, the way young people use technology is also changing the relationships they have with adults. The term *moral panic* is often used to describe the huge push back from adults in relation to children's technology use.

Other adults, however, are in awe of children's capabilities with technology and identify positive gain in them leveraging technology for learning, career and overall success in life. With so many social commentators discussing the likelihood that technologies will continue to disrupt many industries, such digital skills are also seen as necessary for achieving success.

At no other time have children's agency, skill and independence been so highly profiled. Our constructions of childhood are therefore powerful determinants of how accepting we are of the changes to childhood that have emerged, and how we support children in their use of technologies. The idea that childhood is a social construct means that there is no universal understanding of what childhood means. Rather, the ways we perceive children are products of culture and time, and as with social constructions we have discussed throughout this book, will vary across time and place (Ariés 1962).

There are currently two dominant constructions that underpin debates about childhood. The core difference between them relates to the way adults interpret how children should and shouldn't engage within their world (James, Jenks & Prout 1998). Both constructions are outlined below. While you read the next section, a key question to consider is whether the conflict between these two constructions is negatively impacting children growing up today and the support they do or do not gain from adults, institutions and governments who care for them.

Social construct: Children are Vulnerable

The view of childhood as a time of helplessness and vulnerability is the dominant way of viewing children today. The common saying 'Children are so innocent', derives from this construction. Core to this interpretation of childhood is that children are weak, less able and dependent, and we must protect them from bad influences (Qvortrup 2009).

A priority in this construction of childhood is to protect the innocence of children for as long as possible and to mourn lost innocence when we see our children growing up, when we hear them swear for the first time, and when we see them being devious and sneaky.

Knowing that this is the dominant construction of childhood helps in understanding the unrest regarding unfamiliar changes to childhood activity such as children using technology (Robinson 2013).

Social construct: The Agentic Child

This construction is drawn from the **New Sociology of Childhood** that is based on the understanding that childhood identities are multidimensional, and that children are active constructors of their own identities (Mayall 2002). Framing children as active participants in their social world means they are constructed as skilled social operators who actively use (observe, listen, question, argue, agree, negotiate, manipulate) other people to learn from, rather than being constructed as innocent victims.

Constructing children as agentic—having agency—is counter to the moral panic that has surrounded children's use of technology, which has defined children as naïve, innocent, vulnerable and in need of protection (Norozi & Noen 2016). This framework allows a more hopeful account of how technologies can be used to contribute to more socially and educationally just outcomes for children because it positions them in the field of transformation. Conceptually this framework has a focus on agency and negotiation.

Critical reflection

- Which social construction of childhood do you most align with? How has this affected your own analyses of children and the decisions you have made in relation to them?
- Do you think that multiple constructions of childhood negatively or positively affect children?
- Do you think that there is a place for both constructions of childhood?

Constructions influence adult interpretations of child technology use

Each construction of childhood prioritises different types of support, policies and legislation regarding children in their technology use. The 'Children are Vulnerable' construction positions technology as corrupting children, and children as in need of protecting. In this scenario, cyber-safety and closely monitoring children's activities become key concerns. Policies, strategies and tools to support and protect children are justified from this perspective.

Surveillance apps that allow parents to secretly view their child's internet browsing history are an example of this.

The 'Agentic Child' construction focuses on helping children be skilled and active technology users who can leverage the best of technology for their needs. Coding classes that help children develop computer science skills are an example of this. This construction still accepts the need to protect children from online danger, however this is not the singular focus.

Adults do not necessarily align with one construction of childhood or another. Instead the construction they draw on, and the intensity in which they do so, depends on the age of the child, gender, ethnicity, class and other social factors (Norozi & Noen 2016). For example, entry into the world of social media suddenly gives children of any age a relatively independent space in which to test out 'risky behaviours' that they may not be mature enough to cope with. For this reason, many adults see the need to protect children and younger teens from social media. Similarly, many adults identify the value in children learning technology skills that may support future career success, which is why coding classes for children of all ages are often fully enrolled.

Conclusion

In this chapter, we have used the changing nature of children's use of technology to provide insights into the relationship between technology and society. In so doing, we have unpacked the 'digital childhood' from multiple layers: children's technology skills, children's 'digitally' mediated engagement with their social worlds, and adults' interpretations of digital childhood. What is clear are the significant changes that have occurred in what children do, who they connect with, and their interpretations of their world and their place in it.

Drawing on the insights in the sociology theories presented in this chapter, we must avoid simple interpretations of the relationship children and young people have with technology. Rather than seeing children and young people as merely vulnerable with no sense of agency, we need to understand that some of the moral panic that has set in is driven by the fact that adults feel overwhelmed by both the knowledge that young people have of digital technologies, as well as by the technology itself. These insights allow us to contemplate a more nuanced position than simply banning smartphones or the use of all technology.

Ensuring that children are supported in a meaningful, balanced and healthy way in their technology use in schools, in homes and in social and health policy requires a deep understanding of children's techno-social worlds. It also requires acknowledging our own reflexivity in how we act on and interpret the actions of children as well as in our own understanding of technologies used.

As sociologists, this gives us insights into the way technology shapes our society, as well as how social priorities, 'moral panics', hopes and the changing expectations of young people shape technology. This is one topic that is likely to become increasingly complex as new technologies such as autonomous vehicles driven by artificial intelligence and complex algorithms will continue to re-shape our lives.

Summary points

* Technology has become a ubiquitous part of our lives and continues to create a generational gap.
* Young people's knowledge of this technology has created a threat to adults who, for the first time, feel they know less about a topic than young people.
* The use of contemporary communication technologies by young people creates a moral panic.
* We should think critically about the impact of technology on children's social worlds. In so doing, we need to recognise both the benefits and risk of technology and ensure that such analysis informs social policies.

Sociological reflection

1. Technological innovation is often claimed to be driving economic development and social progress. It is seen, for instance, as leading the way to greater freedom of choice. But are these innovations making us happier?
2. It is often claimed that the internet enhances social equality by empowering young people. What do you believe?
3. Young people are often seen as vulnerable to internet technologies. What is your experience and what do you believe?

Discussion questions

1. What is technological determinism and why do most sociologists disagree with this theory?
2. To what extent do you as a consumer and user of technology have agency?
3. With your classmates, outline a technology policy for your local school.
4. Critically analyse the child development domains. Do you agree with this approach? Justify your position.

References and further reading

REFERENCES

Abbasi, A, Ting, D & Hlavacs, H 2017, 'Engagement in games: developing an instrument to measure consumer videogame engagement and its validation', *International Journal of Computer Games Technology*, 1(10).

Ariés, P 1962, *Centuries of Childhood*, Penguin Books, Middlesex, UK.

Arnott, L, Grogan, D & Duncan, P 2016, 'Lessons from using iPads to understand young children's creativity', *Contemporary Issues in Early Childhood*, 17(2), 157–73.

Berk, L 2012, *Child Development*, Pearson Education, USA.

Brown, BA 2015, 'Digitized street art', *Media Art and the Urban Environment*, 5, 267–84.

Chayko, M 2018, *Superconnected: The Internet, Digital Media, and Techno-Social Life*, SAGE, Thousand Oaks, CA.

Correa, T, Straubhaar, J, Spence, J & Chen, W 2015, 'Brokering new technologies: the role of children in their parents' usage of the internet', *New Media & Society*, 17, 483–500.

Fullwood, C & Attrill-Smith, A 2018, 'Up-dating: ratings of perceived dating success are better online than offline', *Cyberpsychology, Behavior, and Social Networking*, 21(1), 11–15.

Holt, L & Holloway S, 2006, 'Editorial: theorising other childhoods in a globalised world', *Children's Geographies* 4(2), 135–42.

James, A, Jenks, C & Prout, A 1998, 'Childhood in social space', in A James, J Chris & A Prout (eds), *Theorizing Childhood*, Polity Press, pp. 37–58.

Kuhn, TS 1970, *The Structure of Scientific Revolutions*, 2nd edn, University of Chicago Press, Chicago, IL.

Latour, B 1987, *Science in Action: How to Follow Scientists and Engineers Through Society*, Harvard University Press, Cambridge, MA.

Latour, B 1997, 'Where are the missing masses? The sociology of a few mundane artifacts', in WE Bijker & J Law, *Shaping Technology/Building Society: Studies in Sociotechnical Change*, MIT Press, Cambridge MA.

Lucas, C, Bridgers, S, Griffiths, T & Gopnik, A 2014, 'When children are better (or at least more open-minded) learners than adults: developmental differences in learning the forms of causal relationships', *Cognition*, 131, 284–99.

MacDowall, L & De Souza, P 2018, '"I'd Double Tap That!!": street art, graffiti, and Instagram research', *Media, Culture & Society*, 40(1), 3–22.

MacKenzie, D & Wajcman, J 1999, *The Social Shaping of Technology*, 2nd edn, Open University Press, Buckingham.

Mayall, B 2002, 'Studying childhood', in B Mayall (ed.), *Towards a Sociology for Childhood*, Open University Press, Buckingham, pp. 9–26.

McDool, E, Powell, P, Roberts, J & Taylor, K 2020, 'The internet and children's psychological wellbeing', *Journal of Health Economics*, 69 (https://doi.org/10.1016/j.jhealeco.2019.102274).

Nelissen, S & Van den Bulck, J 2017, 'When digital natives instruct digital immigrants: active guidance of parental media use by children and conflict in the family', *Information, Communication & Society*, 21(3), 375–87.

New York Times 2019, 'Video games and online chats are "hunting grounds" for sexual predators', 8 December: <www.nytimes.com/interactive/2019/12/07/us/video-games-child-sex-abuse.html>.

Norozi, S & Noen, T 2016, 'Childhood as a social construction', *Journal of Educational and Social Research*, 6(2), 75–80.

Obar, J & Wildman, S 2015, 'Social media definition and the governance challenge: an introduction to the special issue', *Telecommunications Policy*, 39(9), 745–50.

Ofcom 2019, 'Life on the small screen: what children are watching and why': <www.ofcom.org.uk/__data/assets/pdf_file/0021/134832/Ofcom-childrens-content-review-Publish.pdf>.

Orlando, J 2014, 'Veteran teachers and technology: change fatigue and knowledge insecurity influence practice', *Teachers and Teaching*, 20(4), 427–39.

Orlando, J 2019, 'Young children's home technology use: responsive qualitative methods for a sensitive topic', in N Kucirkova, J Rowsell and G Falloon (eds), *The Routledge International Handbook of Learning with Technology in Early Childhood*, Routledge, pp. 435–59.

Orlando, J & Attard, C 2016, 'Digital natives come of age: pressure, device conflict, novice pedagogical knowledge, and the reality of today's early career teachers' using technological devices to teach mathematics', *Mathematics Education Research Journal*, 28(1), 107–21.

Orphanides, A & Nam, C 2017, 'Touchscreen interfaces in context: a systematic review of research into touchscreens across settings, populations, and implementations', *Applied Ergonomics*, 61, 116–43.

Pew Research Center 2018, 'Teens' social media habits and experiences', November: <www.pewresearch.org/internet/2018/11/28/teens-social-media-habits-and-experiences/>.

Pisano, L, Mastropasqua, I, Cerniglia, L, Cimino, S & Erriu, M 2017, 'Adolescents' online and offline identity: a study on self-representation', *Journal of Health Economics*, 5(3).

Prensky, M 2001, 'Digital natives, digital immigrants. Part 1', *On the Horizon*, 9, 1–6.

Qvortrup, J 2009, 'Childhood as structural form', in J Qvortrup, W Corsaro & MS Honig (eds), *Palgrave Handbook of Childhood Studies*, Palgrave, pp. 21–33.

Robinson, K 2013, *Innocence, Knowledge and the Construction of Childhood. The Contradictory Nature of Sexuality and Censorship in Children's Contemporary Lives*, Routledge, London.

Sahlberg, P 2019, 'Sleepless, distracted and glued to devices: no wonder students' results are in decline', *Sydney Morning Herald*, 6 December: <www.smh.com.au/education/sleepless-distracted-and-glued-to-devices-no-wonder-students-results-are-in-decline-20191204-p53gvs.html>.

The Asian Age 2019, 'Social media savvy teens more susceptible to eating disorders', 5 December: <www.asianage.com/life/health/051219/social-media-savvy-teens-more-susceptible-to-eating-disorders.html>.

United Nations International Children's Emergency Fund (UNICEF) 2017, *The State of the World's Children 2017. Children in a Digital World*, UNICEF, New York: <www.unicef.org/publications/files/SOWC_2017_ENG_WEB.pdf>.

Watkins, C 2019, *Don't Knock the Hustle: Young Creatives, Tech Ingenuity, and the Making of a New Innovation Economy*, Beacon Press, USA.

Young, S 2019, 'Two thirds of parents and grandparents think childhoods are getting worse', *The Independent*, 10 July: <www.independent.co.uk/life-style/health-and-families/childhood-uk-parents-action-children-survey-government-cuts-a8995551.html>.

CHAPTER 14
Media, social media and generation swipe

MITCHELL HOBBS AND CLARE DAVIES

CHAPTER OVERVIEW

Today's society is saturated by media images and networked by communication technologies. Video games, television, radio, newspapers, magazines and social media all provide us with countless hours of entertainment as we immerse our consciousness within different media 'texts'. As the media are ubiquitous, and their pleasures self-evident, many of us do not consider the impact that media and communication technologies have on our daily lives. In many ways, the media are so commonplace that using them seems as natural as breathing, with our mobile phones, game controllers, television remotes and other devices being an extension of our bodies and capacity to interact with the world.

The concept of 'affordance' is useful here as it refers to the relationship between the capabilities of an object, such as an 'app' on your mobile, and its perceived uses (Gibson 1979). For example, interactions between people via social media apps are shaped by perception and emotional experiences, including social understandings of the technology and its associated meanings, risks, possibilities and limitations (Bucher & Helmond 2018). We knowingly use and reach out through communication technologies to connect and share, using the affordances provided by the technology to enrich our lives in many ways—sometimes small, other times significant—but often meaningful (Humphreys 2005).

Yet our familiarity with media texts and communication technologies can serve to mask their many social and cultural impacts. Some of these impacts are positive—such as the educational outcomes obtained from watching a documentary or apps tailored to how and where you want to consume your news. Other impacts are more negative, such as the common phenomenon of 'trolling', where someone seeks to cause offence by publishing hateful and provocative comments on social media (Munro 2014).

Other media effects have both positive and negative dimensions. Examples here include the phenomenon of 'sexting', which can be seen as a pleasurable form of sexual play between consenting individuals. It can also be a source of anxiety and harassment should private images be inappropriately distributed beyond the intended recipient (see Albury & Crawford 2012; Hasinoff 2013). Similarly, photo sharing applications like Instagram have provided new ways of connecting and have given rise to new forms of entrepreneurial activity (Abidin 2018). And yet, some researchers have suggested an association between social media and a decrease in psychological wellbeing, with some users of Instagram experiencing 'status anxiety' as a result of social comparisons (see Mackson, Brochu & Schneider 2019).

In order to understand how the media influences our lives we must engage our 'sociological imaginations'. This involves thinking critically about the operations of the mass media and social media, including the ways in which our values are influenced by media content.

After reading this chapter, you should be able to:
- Define important sociological concepts such as 'public sphere', 'fourth estate', 'cyberspace', 'liquid surveillance' and 'networked intimacy' and expand your understanding of 'moral panics' as outlined in Chapter 18
- Explain how the media influences how we see, experience and engage with the world
- Understand the power of social media and some of the dangers associated with sharing too much online.

KEY TERMS

Cyberspace Electronically mediated and simulated space in which individuals play, debate, create and form relationships. Cyberspace is used to refer to the virtual spaces created by the digital computing technologies of the internet.

Fourth estate The conceptualisation of the news media as guardians of democracy and the public interest. Fourth estate journalism is that which scrutinises the activities of social elites (including politicians) to expose abuses of power and ensure accountability.

Framing The process of selecting and highlighting some aspects of a story or situation in order to influence how the audience interprets an event or issues.

Liquid surveillance A sociological concept that emphasises the diffused, mobile and flexible methods of surveillance, from CCTV cameras on the streets to software that tracks our digital footprints. Liquid surveillance can come from government agencies, corporations, social networks, partners and parents, and even employers.

Mass communication The transmission of information to large audiences. Mass communication is made possible in advanced industrial societies because of mass media technologies.

Mass media Diversified communication technologies that reach a large audience and include print (books, newspapers, magazines, etc.), recordings (CDs, DVDs, digital data files, etc.), cinema, radio, television and the internet.

Media power The concentration of power in the media. This has three primary aspects: discursive power (the ability to influence how we think and act regarding particular phenomena); access power (the ability to control which voices and perspectives are present within the public sphere); and resource power (the ability to use media assets to leverage certain policy outcomes).

Moral panic An overreaction to events (that are often relatively isolated or seemingly inconsequential), the understanding of which is informed by the media, where particular people or actions are labelled as a threat to society and to the wellbeing of the majority of the population. This leads to widespread anxiety and fear, and calls for urgent policy action.

> **Public sphere** A concept used to discuss the networked areas of public life in which ideas, information and knowledge are exchanged and debated. The media help to constitute society's public sphere by providing news and information, which is the raw material people use to discuss matters of public concern.

Introduction

Let us begin with you reading this book. Do you have your phone or computer near you with music playing? Are you checking social media sites for updates? Or are you monitoring the news or some sporting event? Maybe you are listening to a podcast or messaging someone as you read.

You are constantly connected—something that only a few years ago was available to very few people. Now, most of us are interacting in the virtual world and we see no real gap between the material (or real) world and the things we do online.

The changes that occur in society fascinate sociologists. As such, we aim to explore the various impacts of media and communication technologies in order to understand the forces shaping our daily experiences. As will become clear in this chapter, the media are powerful institutions that can influence how we feel about each other and ourselves.

For example, fashion and lifestyle magazines can influence how we dress, as well as reinforce body or beauty ideals that might be difficult for most of us to attain. Such textual representations can reinforce social inequalities, where success is perceived to be gained by those who acquire possessions and a standard of living (Bulmer 1975). Likewise, the media can also shape our politics and drive social change, with the topics of 'media bias' and 'political propaganda' being of central concern.

The media are also accused of having the power to 'corrupt and deprave' (McCullagh 2002), especially in regard to representations of sex and violence to susceptible members of the community. As such, concerns have led to different forms of censorship and content classification schemes. The media are worthy of study for many different reasons and it is the goal of this chapter to introduce some of the important issues and debates associated with 'the sociology of the media'.

This discussion takes place at an exciting time in our history. The old media of the twentieth century (specifically newspapers, television and radio) are being displaced by the digital media of the internet. This is not only occurring in terms of popularity, but in the way the internet is soaking up audiences, advertising revenue and journalism (Burns 2013). Moreover, the distinction between old and new media is becoming increasingly blurred, as digital computers and the internet make formerly distinct media industries—such as music, print and television—undergo a process of *convergence*.

The mobile phone epitomises this trend towards convergence, with the device now performing the function of a radio, music player, television, gaming computer, web browser, mail box and so on. In the digital age of convergent technology, newspapers are as likely to be read online as they are on paper; television programs are increasingly streamed 'on demand' rather than seen when a network decides to broadcast them; and blogs, mobile phones and webcams allow everybody to become 'digital content producers' and, at times, 'citizen journalists' (Charles & Allan 2019).

John Keane (2018) has argued that this growth of computerised media networks has given birth to the era of 'monitory democracy', where no topic is immune from public scrutiny; and communicative abundance multiplies this storytelling to audiences. Everyday citizens can now use their phones to expose abuses of power and hold authorities—such as the police and other institutional elites—accountable.

In order to understand the various ways in which the media and social media influence our daily experiences, we must examine media cultures and technologies from different sociological perspectives. As noted earlier in this book (including in Chapter 3), sociology has several broad schools of thought that offer different approaches to understanding social phenomena (Giddens 2009):

- *Functionalist theories* seek to explain the social roles of the media and their effectiveness with regards to binding societies together through the mass distribution of a shared culture.
- *Conflict theories* focus on the ways different media can reinforce social inequality by excluding certain groups and their perspectives from media programs and news stories. Conflict theorists are also concerned with issues such as the ownership and control of media systems, as well as the representation of different political and social issues.
- *Interactionist theories* focus on the micro level of society, such as on individuals and their use of media technologies, and the sociological significance of 'mediated' interaction.
- *Postmodern theories* are broadly concerned with the tenuous connection between media representations, or 'texts', and their ability to reflect or communicate 'reality'.

While all of these schools of thought have areas of similarity and mutual agreement, their different perspectives also offer distinct insights.

Rather than providing a lengthy discussion of different schools of thought, this chapter seeks instead to focus on key concepts and recent issues in order to offer a concise introduction to the central debates. This discussion begins by considering the media's role in potentially creating an 'enlightened' society.

The media's role and function

Perhaps one of the most important sociological concepts related to the media's role in society is that of the **public sphere**. According to the German sociologist Jürgen Habermas (1992), the media constitute part of a broader 'public sphere', which is the area of public life in which ideas, information and knowledge are exchanged and debated. The media help to constitute society's public sphere by providing information and news. Habermas is not, however, a functionalist. He is more critical, in that he believes the public sphere has undergone a process of decline, corrupted by commercial forces and self-interested communication.

Habermas (1992) argues that the public sphere first emerged in eighteenth-century Europe as a forum for citizens to engage in rational dialogue and learn about public affairs. At the time, newspapers and books served to spread information and knowledge. While the early European public sphere was not inclusive—as it excluded ethnic minorities, women, and working-class men—nevertheless it did create more knowledgeable and egalitarian societies as citizens became better informed and began to expect more from their leaders. Indeed, as the public sphere continued to spread throughout the nineteenth and twentieth centuries, it saw reason, science, the rule of law and democratic values challenge authoritarianism, superstition, corruption and ignorance. (At this point, it is important that you notice the link with 'modernity', discussed in Chapter 5.)

The public sphere conceptualised by Habermas (1992) effectively saw the development of political rights and democratic values, promoting ideas such as free speech, freedom of the press, freedom of assembly and the right to privacy (Tucker 1998).

A key concept within Habermas' broader theory of the public sphere is that of '*ideal speech situations*'. This concept argues that the media and **mass communication** technologies have the potential for bringing about better societies, provided individuals participate freely and truthfully in exchanging information and logical reasoning. This means that when we exchange information, we must be able to support our claims and be prepared to genuinely listen and reflect on the arguments of others. Through facilitating the exchange of factual discourse, the news media and other sources of factual information (including the academic press) can create 'communicative reason'; that is, rational and broadly consensual understandings of the world (Habermas 2003).

Habermas' work shows how the media—including the commercial media—can play an important role in representative democracies such as Australia. For instance, within the public sphere, we are connected to our elected representatives and the policy-making processes of our governments. Communication networks, such as the news media and social media, allow us to learn about policies and politicians, and they provide a way for public support and concerns to be communicated to our elected representatives (Hobbs 2016). This can be done through opinion polls, direct communication to politicians and critical media publicity (Davis 2010).

The growing ubiquity of communication networks makes digital technologies a revolutionary force in the public sphere (McNair et al. 2017). The public can now participate in political debates on platforms such as Twitter, Facebook or YouTube and are not limited by geography (McNair et al. 2017). Indeed, social media constitute a global networked public sphere, much larger in scope than the regional and national public spheres constituted by mass media in the form of newspapers and broadcasting (McNair et al. 2017). This networked public sphere is allowing for new social and political movements, as people debate issues and mobilise to take action (see Castells 2012).

While this media can add to public debates, there are also increasing concerns to the rise around social media including phenomena like 'echo chambers' and 'filter bubbles' (where we only access the information we agree with), and fake news (Hern 2017). As such, while the public sphere is networked and theoretically open, in practice people may only experience a subsection of it based on their own preferences, reinforcing their existing beliefs.

The communicative link

This communicative link between the structures of government, elected representatives and the public is important because Australian citizens are expected to participate meaningfully in the democratic process by voting in elections. Indeed, since 1924, Australia has had a system of compulsory voting for most of our population (Young 2007). This somewhat radical democratic obligation—as we are one of the few democracies that enforce this civic responsibility—sees 92 per cent of eligible Australian citizens voting in federal and state elections (Tiffen 2012). Without a factual and ideologically diverse news media, the notion of an 'informed citizenry' is not possible (Jones & Pusey 2010).

The fourth estate

Another key function of the news media that is relevant at this point concerns their role as the '**fourth estate**' of democracy (see Schultz 1998). This old idea comes from the development of the press in the United Kingdom in the eighteenth century. As society's 'fourth estate', the press saw it as their role to be 'watchdogs' or 'guardians' of the public interest, who would work to expose abuses of power or maladministration by social and political elites. This popular conception of a 'watchdog press' spread to many nations, becoming a core part of the cultures of journalism in the world's oldest democracies, including Australia.

Indeed, journalism in Australia today continues to be guided by this 'fourth estate' ethic. Journalists and other serious producers of the news see it as their democratic duty to closely scrutinise all aspects of political life in order to ensure that the community's elected representatives and business elites are held accountable and that the 'public interest' is protected (Schultz 1998). Journalists can thus be a positive democratic force when exposing abuses of power. They also act as vehicles for knowledge within the public sphere and help to facilitate rational discussions and decision making.

Media also entertains

The media performs other integral functions, perhaps the most obvious of which is entertainment. Indeed, rather than consuming large quantities of 'quality' news to learn about issues and events, often we are merely seeking to be entertained or distracted from our busy lives (Blumler & Katz 1974).

This dimension of media consumption is also an important area of interest for sociologists, as the most common and profitable forms of **mass media** are the entertainment media: television, music, magazines, films and televised sporting events. The entertainment media are part of society's broader 'popular culture' and are often seen as being less valuable than the 'high culture' of the serious arts such as theatre and opera—something that is obviously debatable (see Rowe, Turner & Waterton 2018).

So the role of the media depends on your views

From a functionalist perspective, the entertainment media act to reduce social tension in society. They do this by allowing people to briefly forget about the rigours of employment or their personal circumstances. They also provide relaxing talking points for us when we speak to friends, family and colleagues.

In mass communicating programs, the media also help to reinforce a common national culture, which reflects societal norms and values. For instance, televised sporting events become part of a collective cultural experience and reinforce social expectations (see also Chapter 20).

This is part of the process of 'socialisation' that helps to impart certain values, ideas and beliefs into children and adults, and thus reproduces the social and cultural patterns of our society. Moreover, the international distribution of media products enhances the 'glocalization' of culture (Robertson 1995), with local cultural products influenced by global cultural imports coming from Hollywood, Bollywood, and other centres of media production. In the twenty-first century, global brands and celebrities are key ingredients in our daily dose of media culture.

Media content: entertaining or indoctrinating?

While the media have the ability to entertain, inform and foster social cohesion, many sociologists are also concerned by the media's power to do the opposite; that is, the media can 'dumb down' political events or issues. The media can also play a role in effectively masking exploitation, inequality and other issues.

Habermas (1992; 2006) argued that the public sphere has undergone a process of devolution as market forces see commercial self-interest replace genuine and informed debate with the presentations of 'ideologies and viewpoints'. The French sociologist Pierre Bourdieu (1998, p. 71) agrees, arguing that 'the field of journalism' is 'permanently subject to trial by market, whether directly, through advertisers, or indirectly, through audience ratings'.

Others, such as Neil Postman (2005) and Robert Putnam (2000), have argued that the media undermine civic participation. This is because individuals spend more time being passively entertained than meaningfully participating in their communities. Likewise, Zygmunt Bauman (2002, p. 169) argues that the 'substance of democratic politics' is undermined by news media content that is increasingly the symbolic equivalent of junk food: 'aimed at immediate consumption and similarly speedy excretion'.

Arguments about the negative social influences of the media often have their roots in Marxist theories of power and social inequality (see Chapter 6). Karl Marx (1979, p. 59) famously wrote that the 'ruling ideas' of every age have been 'the ideas of its ruling class'. Conflict theorists expanded on Marx's observation, arguing that media institutions help to promote the ideas of the ruling classes in order to justify the social hierarchy of society.

For instance, in the mid-twentieth century, the Frankfurt School scholars—such as Max Horkheimer and Theodor Adorno (2002) and Herbert Marcuse (2013)—argued that the media are part of a 'culture industry' that produces a standardised and shallow 'mass culture'. Horkheimer and Adorno (2002) argued that, while the media's content is seductive and pleasurable, it effectively *creates a prison for the mind*, undermining our capacity for critical thinking and creative activity. Habermas (2006) suggests that market forces have commercialised political discourse as a form of entertainment where events are dramatised, and complex issues are simplified to 'promote civic privatism and a mood of antipolitics' (p. 422). Marcuse (2013) asserted that the media engender 'false needs' for consumer lifestyles. These 'false needs' are shaped by commercial media and social forces and create a materialistic culture (Marcuse 1964). In short, according to the Frankfurt School, the media renders us passive 'cultural dopes' and 'mindless consumers'.

Likewise, the French Marxist sociologist Louis Althusser (1977) argued that the media constitute part of an 'ideological state apparatus' (ISA) that helps to reconcile citizens to the social inequalities created by capitalism. This occurs as the media disseminate a type of 'dominant ideology' that supports big business and capitalism by presenting social and economic inequalities as natural and inevitable features of society.

But wait ...

While it is clear that some parts of the media are indeed ideological and can be mind-numbing, these critiques are outdated and do not adequately account for the current diversity of media forms and effects. We can also readily identify programs that amuse and *inform*, and which make a positive contribution to our daily lived experiences.

Indeed, the commercial media can provide quality news and current affairs, as well as complex dramas and informative lifestyle programs (something that Marxist accounts of the media tend to ignore or trivialise). Accordingly, while it is important to be critical of media content, we need to avoid totalising (or generalising) accounts and have a more empirically grounded, and thus evidence-based, understanding of media influences.

It is also important that we continue to monitor patterns of media production and consumption, especially at a time when YouTube and social media are challenging traditional sources of news and current affairs for viewers, especially young adults (Park et al. 2018). Indeed, while media diversity has brought new cultural forms and allowed for a generation of DIY content creators and curators outside of the established media elite (Bruns 2018), we must also make sure we are not becoming captured by ideological echo-chambers (Jamieson & Cappella 2008) or algorithmic filter bubbles (Pariser 2011) that merely reinforce our existing worldviews in a myopic way.

The Pew Research Centre has been tracking this in the United States and the results are concerning. For example, increasingly people only access news and information sources that confirm their own beliefs (Mitchell et al. 2016). This has been a leading source of the political divide that now characterises the United States (Arvanitakis 2019).

BOX 14.1

Thinking sociologically

NEWS, CURRENT AFFAIRS AND ENTERTAINMENT

Can you identify an example of a news and current affairs topic that was altered through digital and social media technologies? How have these technologies influenced the news agenda? There are two examples below.

1. Vaccines can protect against serious infectious diseases. Yet lack of vaccination has become a public health problem with the World Health Organization (WHO) listing 'vaccine hesitancy' in the top 10 threats to global health (WHO 2019). The increase in vaccine hesitancy can be due to the way in which digital and social media technologies aid the facilitation of conspiracy theories. This prompted Facebook to take action in providing 'more ways to connect people with authoritative information about vaccines on Facebook and Instagram' (Facebook 2019).

> **2** In 2017, the *Australian Marriage Act 1961* was updated to allow for same-sex marriage. The growing number of countries who have legalised same-sex marriage can be attributed to digital and social media platforms that connect, motivate and amplify political expression, leading to the popularity of the Marriage Equality Movement (Gibson 2018).

Media power and influence

In contrast to the totalising accounts discussed earlier, 'political economic' approaches to studying **media power** offer a more focused assessment. Part of the conflict theory school of thought, political economy seeks to understand how economics (such as market forces) and politics (such as Left/Right political ideologies) can influence media content. Often, political economy focuses on media ownership and the workplace cultures that operate in newsrooms—all issues that can influence the tone and stance of the news media on particular issues. The British academic John Street (2001) is a leading exponent of this approach and argues that we need to identify three main forms of media power: 'discursive power', 'access power' and 'resource power' (Street 2001, p. 232).

While we will discuss these in more detail below, you will notice some overlap with the discussions on power in Chapter 8.

Discursive power

Discursive power refers to the media's control of information and is perhaps best expressed in the adage that 'knowledge is power'. Discursive power is the media's ability to shape how people think about a particular event, person or issue, using certain words that '**frame**' our understanding of the topic. In its most crude form, discursive power is most clearly seen in the media of authoritarian societies such as North Korea. Here, the state seeks to control information to prevent their citizens from seeking greater democratic freedoms. This is done by creating slanted news (or blatant and deliberate bias) and through critical omissions of important content (such as not mentioning stories that might present the government in a negative light).

In contrast, in liberal democracies such as Australia, discursive power tends to take a more complicated and subtle form: persuading the audience to view a particular event or issue according to a 'preferred perspective' (Hall 1980).

For instance, in regard to the Australian news media's coverage of asylum seekers, emotive words such as 'illegal immigrants', 'illegals' and 'boat people' communicate different meanings to 'asylum seeker' or 'refugee'. The more emotive terms construct a more conservative 'frame' that influences the audience's perception of this issue (see *Media Watch* 2009). Likewise, Rupert Murdoch's Fox News in the United States uses words such as 'illegal immigrants', 'illegals', 'adult illegals' and 'illegal aliens' that echo and support President Donald Trump's rhetoric on immigrant 'invasion' (see Mackay 2019).

Access power

In contrast, *access power* refers to the pathways and opportunities available to the public for the expression of their ideas and concerns in the media. As such, access power is about opportunities to participate in the media, and thus in the public sphere.

On one level, access power refers to issues pertaining to media ownership, with monopolies and conglomerations seen as forces undermining the diversity of public expression. Habermas (2006) argues that this use of media power is a perceived crisis that distorts the public sphere. For instance, in Australia, Rupert Murdoch's News Corp accounts for 65 per cent of capital city and national daily newspapers sales, which makes it a powerful political instrument when it decides to take a united position on a particular politician or political party (Hobbs & McKnight 2014).

On another level, access power is concerned with the potential for certain cultural and political 'tastes' of certain audiences to be excluded. This can happen because of 'market failure'—where the commercial media sector chases the largest and most financially lucrative audience demographic and therefore excludes other groups (Street 2001).

Resource power

Finally, *resource power* refers to the influence that major media companies wield over the workings of governments. While in terms of setting and implementing a public agenda the media are a weaker force than government, they are nonetheless capable of influencing the processes of government through 'agenda setting'. This occurs when the media:

- Campaign for a particular policy initiative;
- Cover certain issues in depth while ignoring other issues; and
- Expose information that might be detrimental to the government.

Furthermore, as major social institutions, the media have the lobbying power of any other big business. Indeed, this lobbying power can lead to a form of *market capture*, where governments might be reluctant to regulate against the commercial interests of major media conglomerates as this might provoke hostile coverage of their policies. Accordingly, 'resource power' highlights the intertwined and mutually dependent relationship between governments and the media.

BOX 14.2

Everyday sociology

MEDIA POWER AND RUPERT MURDOCH

Rupert Murdoch (born 1931) is perhaps the world's most famous media proprietor. In 1952, he inherited a small newspaper, the *Adelaide News*. From these relatively humble beginnings, Murdoch went on to build one of the world's largest and most globalised media companies, and became a person courted by presidents and prime ministers around the world.

Between the 1950s and 70s, Murdoch proceeded to take over several major newspapers in Australia and founded the national daily newspaper, *The Australian*. These assets made Murdoch a major player in Australian politics, as different prime ministers sought the support of his news media (Hobbs & McKnight 2014).

For example, at the 1972 election Murdoch instructed his newspapers to support Labor leader Gough Whitlam. Three years later, his newspapers famously turned on the government and vocally campaigned for its defeat (Hobbs & McKnight 2014).

Not satisfied with being merely a powerful media mogul in Australia, Murdoch expanded News Corp into the United Kingdom and then the United States. He also diversified his media holdings by expanding into film and television. His most powerful acquisition in the United Kingdom, *The Sun* newspaper, heavily supported Murdoch's preferred prime ministerial candidates at British elections, including Margaret Thatcher and later Tony Blair (McKnight 2012). In the United States, Murdoch's major news media supported the Republican Party's presidential candidates, commencing with Ronald Reagan in the 1980s.

In Australia in 1987, Murdoch took over the Herald & Weekly Times media group, making News Corp the country's dominant newspaper publisher and a powerful political instrument (Tiffen 2014). This expanded corporation would be largely neutral regarding the Hawke and Keating Governments, but would later throw its support behind John Howard and his conservative government (Tiffen 2014).

From the mid 1990s it was Murdoch's American Pay TV channel *Fox News* that best expressed his media power. This channel supported George W Bush at the elections of 2000 and 2004 (McKnight 2012). *Fox News* also campaigned against Barack Obama at the 2008 and 2012 elections. One example of the channel's recent political bias was a *Fox News* journalist being 'shutdown' and demoted after attempting to report on Donald Trump's relationship with Stormy Daniels, a pornographic film producer/director/actor, in the lead up to the 2016 presidential campaign (see Mayer 2019). A survey found Americans who voted for Donald Trump heavily relied on *Fox News* as their main source of political news, whereas Hillary Clinton voters did not rely on any one source (Sutton 2017).

In recent years, Murdoch has continued to show his interest in Australian politics. He was hostile to the Gillard Government and instructed his newspapers to campaign against Kevin Rudd at the 2013 federal election: see Figure 14.1. Often cited as the key contributor to the downfall of Malcolm Turnbull in 2018, Murdoch reportedly told Seven West proprietor Kerry Stokes 'Malcolm has to go' and pushed for a leadership change (see McIlroy 2018). When Stokes pointed out that a leadership challenge would guarantee a Labor government within a year, Murdoch brushed aside concerns, saying he would put up with three years of a bad Labor government to make this happen.

Murdoch arrived in Australia 10 days ahead of the August 2018 leadership spill that coincided with the launch of News Corp's hostility towards Turnbull: see Figure 14.2. Channel Nine political editor Chris Ullham accused News Corp of destabilising the government (see *Nine News* 2018). Murdoch-owned TV program *Sky News* was dominated by guests who attacked Turnbull over his leadership and decision-making including his energy policy. Likewise, News Corp newspapers attacked the ALP's policies and praised the Coalition. By week's end, Murdoch's work was done. Scott Morrison replaced Turnbull as Prime Minister after defeating Peter Dutton in a Liberal party ballot. News Corp spent the week afterwards praising the Morrison government: see Figure 14.3.

Accounts by former News Corp editors and journalists have described Murdoch as a 'frustrated politician' who cannot leave politics alone (Hobbs & McKnight 2014).

Critical reflection

When does the news media's role as a 'watchdog' become replaced by ideological or commercial self-interested reporting? Further, what should be done about it?

FIGURE 14.1 An example of Murdoch's political influence on the Rudd Government.

FIGURE 14.2 An example of Murdoch's political influence on the Turnbull Government.

FIGURE 14.3 An example of Murdoch's political influence on the Morrison Government.

New technologies and old concerns

Since the 1990s, new technologies have been transforming the media landscape and offering 'new media' platforms, content and pathways for networking and connecting. Driving this change is the development and widespread uptake of digital computing, the internet (the global network of interconnected computers) and the World Wide Web (the system of interlinked hypertext documents and websites). Digital media are no longer 'new'—they have transformed the way media is produced and consumed.

Whereas in the twentieth century the mass media produced content for the public in a unidirectional flow of content, digital media allow audiences to become more active in both media consumption and production, with audiences able to create and share media online (Bruns 2013). Indeed, so profound are the changes brought about by digital computing technologies that many believe they have transformed political participation (Castells 2014).

Manuel Castells (2001) has argued that the internet enables new combinations of work and self-employment, individual expression, collaboration and sociability. In recent years, Castells (2012) has also shown how political activists can utilise the internet to spread their messages around the world, and thus drive social and political change.

One example in Australia is the organisation GetUp!, which is a progressive campaigning community with an online membership of over 1 million people (see <www.getup.org.au>); we will discuss more examples in Chapter 15 when looking at social movements. While several academic disciplines are interested in the study of the internet, sociologists are primarily concerned with the impacts the technology is having on social life. The sociological approach seeks to understand the ways in which the web gives rise to '**cyberspace**', the term used to describe the online virtual space in which computer-mediated communication occurs between individuals.

Interactions in cyberspace are of course quite different to face-to-face interactions. For instance, it is easier to manufacture a virtual identity that highlights our positive attributes and conceals other aspects of our lives, in what is an extension of the 'presentation of self' identified by Erving Goffman (1959): see Chapters 3 and 7. Likewise, the ability to be anonymous in cyberspace makes it easier to engage in a wide range of antisocial behaviours such as cyberbullying, trolling, sexual harassment, racism and revenge porn (the latter of which refers to the distribution or publication of sexually explicit images or video of an individual without their permission). For others, anonymity means being able to protect themselves—for example through the use of online support services for gay young people in areas where exposing their sexuality may put their safety at risk.

Additionally, many people find the creative freedom of being able to create an online identity, or persona, an empowering aspect of the digital age (Marwick 2015). Indeed, the internet and social media have allowed us to create profiles and avatars that enable us to connect in ways that can overcome time and distance, such as making international friendships in online games or finding an old friend on a social media site.

> BOX 14.3
> ## Thinking sociologically
>
> **CYBERSPACE: SOCIAL OR ANTISOCIAL?**
>
> How do digital and social media platforms create opportunities to share positive information and connect with 'like-minded' people anonymously? On the other hand, how do the affordances of these technologies influence antisocial behaviours?

Divided opinions

Sociologists are divided in their assessments of the internet's impacts, with some seeing it as merely a benign technological extension of older forms of community and communication, and others seeing it as having new and worrying social consequences. For example, in *The Virtual Community*, Howard Rheingold argues that the internet has both positive and negative repercussions for society. His view is that cyberspace is occupied by 'virtual communities', which he defines as:

> social aggregations that emerge from the Net when enough people carry on ... public discussions long enough, with sufficient human feeling, to form webs of personal relationships (2000, p. 5).

Rheingold believes that being part of a virtual community is much the same as being part of regular community, albeit one in which we participate with a disembodied form (Giddens 2009). For instance, in cyberspace we interact, argue, solve problems, tell jokes, gossip, feud, fall in love and fall out again, much like we do in real-world communities. Rheingold's work shows that the good and bad aspects of the internet—from the creation of lifelong friends to being vilified and attacked—are merely manifestations of the desires and capacities of human nature.

And here comes social media

The virtual communities explored in Rheingold's (2000) research are an increasingly obvious aspect of the web, particularly since the advent of social media. Social media is essentially internet-based applications that allow the creation and exchange of user-generated content, such as the sharing of text, photos, news stories and blogs. Popular social media applications include Facebook, Twitter, LinkedIn, Instagram, WhatsApp, Messenger and so on. The largest single social media platform is Facebook, which had 2.41 billion active users in 2019 (Facebook 2019). Globally, 2.1 billion people use Facebook, Instagram, WhatsApp or Messenger every day (Facebook 2019).

The rapid rise of social media has raised some old concerns about technology and its impacts on society (something we discussed in Chapter 13). Some scholars, such as Christine Rosen (2007), have criticised social media for contributing to a 'culture of narcissism', where we post status updates and images with the intent of manufacturing a positive public persona in order to satisfy our egos. The 'selfie' is just one dimension of this form of self-promotion. Other scholars have been critical of the ways in which social media changes relationships with our friends, so that we spend less time engaged in 'quality' interactions.

Sherry Turkle in *Alone Together* argues that 'these days, insecure in our relationship and anxious about intimacy, we look to technology for ways to be in relationships and to protect us from them at the same time' (2011, p. xii). Turkle (2011) believes that, as a result of mediated connectivity, people are developing problems in regard to truly relating to each other, as they are increasing shying away from more complex face-to-face conversations in favour of superficial interactions on social media.

Similarly, Taina Bucher's (2012) research shows how Facebook operates according to a series of algorithms that determine which of your friends are visible in your newsfeed, and thus with whom you communicate on a routine basis. Facebook also provides a very structured form of interaction (such as the 'like' buttons and birthday reminders), which shape how we do 'friendship maintenance' within that space: a phenomenon that Bucher (2012) argues is artificial when compared to interactions in face-to-face settings.

The emergence of emojis as a way to manage digital relationships through digital pictograms was investigated by Stark and Crawford (2015). They found that emojis are new representations of digital feeling that lure users to social media platforms where businesses extract emotional data and harness consumerist worldviews. Facebook (2016) continued to capitalise on this form of social expression through the launch of *Reaction*s, an extension of the 'like' button where emojis representing 'love', 'haha', 'wow', 'sad' and 'angry' can be instantaneously expressed on posts in user News Feeds. When COVID-19 emerged and much of the world went into lockdown, Facebook also introduced a 'care' emoji.

Ellis and Goggin's (2013) work highlights some of the social benefits brought by social media, especially for people living with disabilities. The ability to broadcast themselves, share information and comment has allowed a greater representation of disability than was present in earlier public spheres. Platforms such as YouTube provide people with the ability to produce, upload and share their own content about their everyday lives, making visible common problems as well as potential solutions (Ellis & Goggin 2013).

The interactive and participatory nature of social media is, then, reshaping the news and entertainment media and allowing for new forms of community and connection. Social media also enables a 'visual self-presentation strategy' (Marwick 2015, p. 139), that is closely aligned with celebrity culture and conspicuous consumption (Redmond 2018; Marwick 2015). The interactive and participatory nature of social media creates variations of the 'self', no longer bound by time and place. This shift from traditional media to social media platforms and online self-representation has allowed for new types of human intimacy as well as new paths to fame and celebrity.

BOX 14.4

Everyday sociology

LIQUID LOVE AND DIGITAL INTIMACY

Perhaps one of the most important impacts of social media on relationships have been those connected to the rapid uptake of dating and hook-up apps. Dobson, Robards and Carah (2018) assert that such apps monitor, modulate and control digital intimacies. They argue that algorithms dictate who receives attention and to what kinds of performances.

The potential impacts of dating and hook-ups apps for social structures like monogamy is explored through the theory of 'liquid love' (see Hobbs, Owen & Gerber 2017). Zygmunt Bauman (2003) believed that computer dating is symptomatic of 'liquid love', arguing that rampant individualisation, consumerism and technological change are liquefying formerly solid social structures, including the notion of a life-long romantic partner. Bauman theorised that mediated communication is leading individuals to pursue transient connections, with dating being transformed into a recreational activity (Bauman 2003, p. 65).

However, while these theories can help us consider the social meanings and uses of dating apps, research has shown that concerns about a 'death of relationships' and a commodified hook-up culture are overblown, with 'many users feeling empowered by the technology and using it to find both short-term lovers and long-term life partners' (Hobbs, Owen & Gerber 2017). For Hobbs, Owen, and Gerber (2017), dating apps give rise to networked intimacy, bringing new freedoms, opportunities and pleasures, as well as old and new anxieties about risk, self-image and love.

Another interesting development has been the way such dating apps are helping people stay connected during COVID-19. Researcher Lisa Portolan (2020) has outlined how such apps are helping negotiate the social distancing environment but still ensuring people can socialise—even if mediated through online technologies.

Social media influencers

Social media platforms have generated new opportunities for ordinary people to transform into 'social media influencers' or 'internet celebrities' (Djafarova & Trofimenko 2018; Khamis, Ang & Welling 2016; Turner 2014). A type of 'opinion leader' for the digital age, influencers shape audience attitudes by employing rich multimodal narrations of their everyday life, allowing audiences to believe they are accessible, believable, authentic and intimate (Dhanesh & Duthler 2019; Stoldt et al. 2019; Abidin 2016; Khamis, Ang & Welling 2016; Senft 2013). Such exposers create a 'parasocial relationship' (Horton & Wohl 1956) between the influencer and their followers, in that there is no real-world connection between them, but instead an asymmetrical relationship between a micro-celebrity and their audience. The parasocial relationship that develops makes influencers valuable cultural intermediaries, who can use their cultural capital to set trends and manipulate the actions of their followers. Indeed, platform features such as comments, likes and shares now function as a form of social currency (Marwick 2015) assigned to those who have 'attracted, and continue to attract, the most eyeballs' (Abidin 2014; Abidin & Brown 2018).

The power to reach and influence networked audiences has made the social media influencer a valuable commodity for businesses and communication agencies. Influencers allow organisations and brands to package commercial messages within content that is likely to be actively sought by a specific market. Influencers can then leverage this dynamic for commercial outcomes, with many pursuing sustainable careers by using their 'personal brand' to sell a product or service (Archer 2019; Stoldt et al. 2019; Abidin 2018; Duffy 2018). Whether the advantages brought by this economic independence, DIY-celebrity status and entrepreneurial activity are outweighed by more critical concerns regarding the commodification of youth cultures and the spread of covert marketing is an ongoing debate (see Figure 14.4).

One critical concern here for sociologists is the extent to which commercial relationships have been disclosed, so that audiences can identify authentic opinions and posts from sponsored content. In the interest of promoting ethical practice, various regulatory and self-regulatory bodies for marketing and public relations professions have been encouraged to update their guidelines to account for the use of social media influencers. Consequently, the United States Federal Trade Commission (FTC) has revised their Endorsement Guides to stipulate that influencers must disclose paid relationships as 'knowing about the connection is important information for anyone evaluating the endorsement' (FTC 2017). Similarly, in March 2017, the Australian Association of National Advertisers (AANA) amended the Advertiser Code of Ethics, requiring that paid social media posts must clearly state '#ad or similar wording' (AANA 2017). However, questions remain regarding the effectiveness of these guidelines, with many organisations and influencers wanting to avoid disclosing a commercial partnership that might undermine the authenticity of a carefully crafted post.

FIGURE 14.4 An example social media influencer's post.

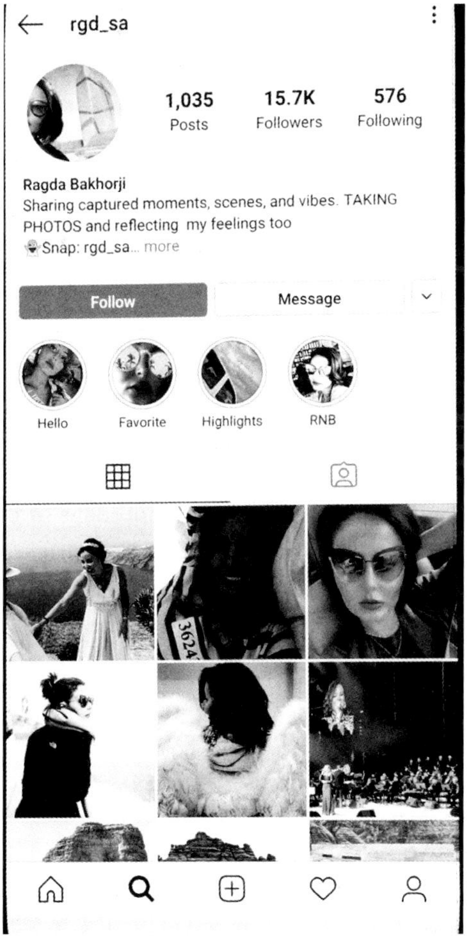

Finally, there is also surveillance

Social media also raises an old concern regarding power and surveillance in society. Indeed, corporations and governments can now track our interactions and activities online. Corporations are able to monitor our web browsing activity so that they can target advertisements to our key word searches.

Likewise, social media sites such as Facebook team with agencies and corporations to target advertisements to specific users based on their interactions with company pages and the demographic details on their profile. For instance, somebody who recently indicates that their relationship status is single on Facebook might soon find dating advertisements appearing in their newsfeed. Moreover, 'liking' a band on social media sites might result in advertisements for similar music concerts in your city. Such advertisements blur the line between what was once considered an intrusive marketing message and potentially useful information.

Online surveillance by government is perhaps slightly more concerning than that conducted by corporations. Governments, of course, have an obligation to protect citizens from crime and danger, and thus their intelligence agencies seek to identify potentially criminal activity by tracking the digital footprints of suspect individuals. Such policing is necessary in order to combat the new networking capabilities of terrorists, paedophiles and other criminals who can use the internet to further their illicit activities.

However, in recent years, several news stories have emerged that have raised serious concerns regarding a potential abuse of government power in regard to spying on citizens. For instance, in 2013 Edward Snowden, a private contractor working at the National Security Agency (NSA)—a key counter-intelligence and surveillance agency in the United States—leaked an estimated 1.7 million intelligence files to the news media. These files were gathered by the intelligence agencies of Australia, Canada, New Zealand, the United Kingdom and the United States, which share data as part of a global system of counter-intelligence and espionage. Snowden's leaked files show that the NSA was collecting millions of emails and contact lists, searching email content, tracking and mapping the location of mobile phones, and tapping into Google and Yahoo data to collect information from millions of account holders worldwide (Gellman & Soltani 2013a, 2013b, 2013c; Savage 2013). More recently, NSA documents revealed that the United Kingdom's electronic surveillance agency, the Government Communications Headquarters (GCHQ), ran an operation called 'Optic Nerve', which secretly intercepted and recorded millions of images of Yahoo webcam chats, 'regardless of whether individual users were an intelligence target or not' (Taylor 2014). These images included 'substantial quantities of sexually explicit material, from more than 1.8 million Yahoo user accounts globally' (Taylor 2014).

In Australia, government intelligence agencies have extended their powers of surveillance, making it easier to obtain digital information about the internet activity of Australian citizens. The Abbott Government moved to make further extensions to security laws (Grubb & Massola 2014; Grubb 2014), making it a requirement for internet and phone providers to store 'metadata' (such as information about which websites you visit) for two years. These data retention laws allow intelligence agencies to access your digital footprint (Home Affairs 2019).

More recently, the Facebook-Cambridge Analytica scandal garnered public attention worldwide. Cambridge Analytica, a political consulting firm, harvested personal data from millions of Facebook profiles to influence voting behaviours in the 2016 presidential election of Donald Trump in the United States and Brexit in the United Kingdom (ABC News 2018a). Similarly, American intelligence officials claim the Russian government interfered with the presidential election by spreading false information as a tactic to elevate Donald Trump to the presidency (ABC News 2018b). Over the course of the election, politically damaging information was released on the internet and circulated by fake social media accounts on pro-Trump topics such as immigration and gun control. Advertisements criticising Hillary Clinton were also placed on social media using hashtags such as '#Hillary4Prison', '#TrumpTrain' and '#MAGA'.

Donald Trump would later capitalise on concerns regarding fake news, appropriating the term to dismiss stories that framed him in a negative light, even when written by established journalists with verified facts. His call to boycott fourth estate media outlets such as CNN (see

Grynbaum & Lee 2019) comes at a time when audiences can select from an array of media outlets that align with their worldviews—returning us to the 'echo-chambers' mentioned above.

The expanding powers of surveillance in democracies such as Australia, the United Kingdom and the United States has raised old questions about 'who watches the watchers' to make sure surveillance agencies behave responsibly and only target criminals, and not others who might be legitimately critical of the government. Such activities also raise concerns about a '*surveillance society*', where 'Big Brother'—a term that originated with George Orwell's famous novel *1984*—is always watching you.

Two concepts are particularly useful here:

- The first comes from the work of Michael Foucault (1977) and refers to the Panopticon (see Chapter 8), an eighteenth-century design for a prison surveillance tower where guards could continuously monitor prisoners. As the prisoners could not see when they were being watched, they behaved as if they were under constant surveillance. This concept applies to modern societies in that we feel increasingly visible, due in part to digital surveillance and an image-conscious culture, and so govern our behaviours as if we are being watched.
- The second comes from Zygmunt Bauman and David Lyon (2013), who argue we are living in an age of '**liquid surveillance**'. Whereas terms such as 'Panopticon' and 'Big Brother' imply a top-down hierarchy of surveillance and social control, the concept of 'liquid surveillance' emphasises the diffused, mobile and flexible methods of scrutiny that come from government agencies, corporations, social networks, partners, parents and even employers (such as when an employer covertly checks your Facebook profile to assess your 'true' character). In the age of liquid surveillance, we must all think twice before posting something that might damage our future selves.

Conclusion

In this chapter, we have highlighted how the media have both positive and negative implications for our daily experiences. On the one hand, media technologies can educate, entertain and connect us in new and wonderful ways. On the other hand, media technologies can also exploit members of the community, warp how we see events and issues, and even provide space for criminality and hate. Indeed, the media and social media reflect both the best and worst aspects of human nature and are thus a reflection of the angels and demons inside all of us.

As sociologists, it is our job to analyse and understand the media's different functions and impacts. In so doing, we can work to minimise harm to vulnerable community members, while also ensuring that values of openness and inclusion remain central to the public sphere.

Finally, it is important to continue to ask questions about the role of the media. Are we amusing ourselves to the point that we no longer care about serious issues overseas or within our communities? Do the media have the power to corrupt moral values or cause violence? How do the media portray certain sections of our society? What are the impacts of hyper-sexualised portrayals of women in video games or violent pornography on the web? How is power being structured and contested online? How much power should government agencies and corporations have in regard to tracking our digital footprints?

In answering these questions it is important to avoid feeding a '**moral panic**' (see Chapter 18). We should not dismiss the concerns of intelligence agencies, but we also need to ask questions regarding new forms of surveillance and social control. As sociologists, we should engage in cool-headed and impartial research and reflection about the forces that influence our daily experiences, and all of human society.

This is what makes sociology both an empowering and important social science.

Summary points

* The media are part of society's public sphere and can help to create informed citizens and democratic societies.
* The news media are the 'fourth estate' of democracy, which vigorously protects the public interest by exposing corruption, government failings and abuses of power.
* Media texts are representations of the world. As such, texts are infused with different worldviews that help to frame the meaning of an event or issue.
* There are three main forms of media power: discursive power, access power and resource power.
* Cyberspace and social media allow for the creation of 'virtual communities' that are similar to traditional forms of community.
* Digital technologies have changed the way people interact in their intimate relationships and with family and friends.
* Social media allows ordinary people to become content producers, and at times, micro-celebrities.
* The popularity of digital and social media platforms has increased the prevalence of fake news and the misuse of personal data.
* Increasingly, governments and corporations are using digital media to conduct surveillance on their citizens.
* The media have both good and bad aspects, which reflect the nature of the human spirit.

Sociological reflection

1. Describe some of the ways in which your understanding of the world is influenced by the media.
2. What are the positive and negative impacts of social media on your everyday life? Do you feel social media enhances your life?
3. Think of your favourite television programs, video games, magazines and digital media. How many hours each week do you spend immersed in media content? Does this undermine quality time with family and friends?

Discussion questions

1. Are we amusing ourselves with media to the point that we no longer care about serious issues or community participation?
2. Do the media have the power to 'corrupt and deprave' by exposing us to hyper-sexualised portrayals of women in video games or online pornography?
3. Are different forms of censorship an appropriate response in regard to regulating offensive content, or is this an attack on freedom and free speech?
4. How is power structured and contested online? How much power should government agencies and corporations have in regard to tracking our digital footprints?

5 How have digital media changed the media landscape? What are the implications of declining revenue for newspapers and television networks?

6 What are the positive and negative social influences of social media? Is social media merely about ego and posturing, or are there other social benefits and pleasures?

Further investigation

Download the *Good Game* feature on 'Racial representation in games': <www.abc.net.au/tv/goodgame/stories/s3703899.htm> (*Good Game* 2013). *Good Game* is an ABC television program that discusses the culture and products of the video game industry. In addition to its weekly reviews of new video games, it regularly broadcasts segments that explore the history, culture, economics and social issues associated with this media sector.

After watching the feature, discuss and answer the following questions.

1 Why is there a distinct lack of diversity when it comes to racial representation in games?
2 How do social stereotypes become textual features? Are they damaging for society?
3 Are women also misrepresented in video games? If so, why?
4 What other social issues are associated with video games?

References and further reading

REFERENCES

ABC News 2018a, 'Cambridge Analytica harvested data from more than 87 million Facebook users, whistleblower says', 18 April: <www.abc.net.au/news/2018-04-18/cambridge-analytica-employee-testifies-before-uk-committee/9670192>.

ABC News 2018b, 'Facebook boss Mark Zuckerberg tells Congress the company is in an "arms race" with Russia', 11 April: <www.abc.net.au/news/2018-04-11/facebook-boss-mark-zuckerberg-fronts-united-states-congress/9639764>.

Abidin, C 2014, '#In$tagLam: Instagram as a repository of taste, a brimming marketplace, a war of eyeballs', in M Berry & M Schleser (eds.), *Mobile Media Making in the Age of Smartphones*, Palgrave Pivot, New York, pp. 119–28.

Abidin, C 2016, 'Visibility labour: engaging with influencers' fashion brands and #OOTD advertorial campaigns on Instagram', *Media International Australia*, 161(1), 86–100 (DOI: 10.1177/1329878X16665177).

Abidin, C 2018, *Internet Celebrity: Understanding Fame Online*, Emerald Publishing Limited, Bingley, UK.

Abidin, C & Brown, ML 2018, *Microcelebrity Around the Globe: Approaches to Cultures of Internet Fame*, Emerald Publishing, Bingley, UK.

Albury, K & Crawford, K 2012, 'Sexting, consent and young people's ethics: beyond Megan's story', *Continuum*, 26(3), 463–73 (DOI: 10.1080/10304312.2012.665840).

Althusser, L 1977, 'Ideology and ideological state apparatuses', in L Althusser, *Lenin and Philosophy*, New Left Books, London, pp. 121–76.

Archer, C 2019, 'How influencer "mumpreneur" bloggers and "everyday" mums frame presenting their children online', *Media International Australia*, 170(1), 47–56 (DOI: 10.1177/1329878X19828365).

Arvanitakis, J 2019, 'The fracturing of our media and our community', *Open Forum Australia*, 23 November: <www.openforum.com.au/the-fracturing-of-our-media-and-our-community/>.

Australian Association of National Advertisers (AANA) 2017, 'Clearly distinguishable advertising': <http://aana.com.au/content/uploads/2017/01/AANA_Distinguishable-Advertising-Best-Practice-Guideline__Final.pdf>.

Bauman, Z 2002, *Society Under Siege*, Polity Press, Cambridge.

Bauman, Z 2003, *Liquid Love: On the Frailty of Human Bonds*, Polity Press, Cambridge.

Bauman, Z & Lyon, D 2013, *Liquid Surveillance: A Conversation*, Polity Press, Cambridge.

Blumler, JG & Katz, E 1974, *The Uses of Mass Communication*, SAGE Publications Ltd, Newbury Park, CA.

Bourdieu, P 1998, *On Television*, The New Press, New York.

Bruns, A 2013, 'From prosumption to produsage', in R Towse & C Handke (eds) *Handbook on the Digital Creative Economy*, Edward Elgar Publishing, Cheltenham, UK, pp. 67–78.

Bruns, A 2018, *Gatewatching and News Curation: Journalism, Social Media, and the Public Sphere*, Peter Lang, New York.

Burns, L 2013, *Understanding Journalism*, SAGE Publications Ltd., London.

Bucher, T 2012, 'The friendship assemblage investigating programmed sociality on Facebook', *Television & New Media*, 14(6), 479–93 (DOI: 10.1177/1527476412452800).

Bucher, T & Helmond, A 2018, 'The affordances of social media platforms', in J Burgess, A Marwick & T Poell (eds), *The SAGE Handbook of Social Media*, SAGE Publications Ltd., London, pp. 233–53 (DOI: 10.4135/9781473984066.n14).

Bulmer, M (ed.) 1975, *Working-Class Images of Society (Routledge Revivals)*, Routledge, London (DOI: 10.4324/9781315637112).

Castells, M 2001, *The Information Age: Economy, Society and Culture, Vol. I: The Rise of the Network Society*, Blackwell, Oxford.

Castells, M 2012, *Networks of Outrage and Hope: Social Movements in the Internet Age*, Polity Press, Cambridge.

Castells, M 2014, 'The impact of the internet on society: a global perspective', in F González, (eds), *Ch@nge: 19 Key Essays on How Internet is Changing our Lives*, BBVA, Bilboa, pp. 132–33.

Charles, M & Allan, S 2019, 'Citizen journalism', in TP Vos & F Hanusch (eds), *The International Encyclopedia of Journalism Studies*, John Wiley & Sons, Inc., pp. 1–8.

Davis, A 2010, *Political Communication and Social Theory*, Routledge, New York.

Dhanesh, GS & Duthler, G 2019, 'Relationship management through social media influencers: effects of followers' awareness of paid endorsement', *Public Relations Review* (DOI: 10.1016/j.pubrev.2019.03.002).

Djafarova, E & Trofimenko, O 2018, 'Instafamous'—credibility and self-presentation of micro-celebrities on social media', *Information, Communication & Society* (DOI: 10.1080/1369118X.2018.1438491).

Dobson, A, Robards, B & Carah, N 2018, *Digital Intimate Publics and Social Media* (DOI: 10.1007/978-3-319-97607-5).

Duffy, BE 2018, '#Dreamjob: the possibilities and perils of a social media career', in M Deuze & M Prenger (eds), *Making Media: Production, Practices and Professions*, University of Amsterdam Press, Amsterdam.

Ellis, K & Goggin, G 2013, 'Disability and social media', in J Hunsinger & TM Senft (eds), *The Social Media Handbook*, Routledge, New York, pp. 126–43.

Facebook 2016, 'Reactions now available globally': <https://newsroom.fb.com/news/2016/02/reactions-now-available-globally>.

Facebook 2019, 'Company information: our mission': <http://newsroom.fb.com/company-info>.

Federal Trade Commission (FTC) 2017, 'The FTC's endorsement guides: what people are asking': <www.ftc.gov/tips-advice/business-center/guidance/ftcs-endorsement-guides-what-people-are-asking>.

Foucault, M 1977, *Discipline and Punish*, Penguin Books, England.

Gellman, B & Soltani, A 2013a, 'NSA collects millions of e-mail address books globally', *The Washington Post*, 14 October.

Gellman, B & Soltani, A 2013b, 'NSA infiltrates links to Yahoo, Google data centers worldwide, Snowden documents say', *The Washington Post*, 30 October.

Gellman, B & Soltani, A 2013c, 'NSA tracking cellphone locations worldwide, Snowden documents show', *The Washington Post*, 4 December.

Giddens, A 2009, *Sociology*, 6th edn, Polity Press, Cambridge.

Gibson, R 2018, *Same-Sex Marriage and Social Media*, Routledge, London (DOI: 10.4324/9781315179773).

Gibson, JJ 1979, 'The theory of affordances', in R Shaw & J Bransford (eds), *Perceiving, Acting and Knowing*, Lawrence Erlbaum, Hillsdale, USA.

Goffman, E 1959, *The Presentation of Self in Everyday Life*, Pelican Book, London.

Grubb, B 2014, 'New laws could give ASIO a warrant for the entire internet, jail journalists and whistle blowers', *Sydney Morning Herald*, 23 September.

Grubb, B & Massola, J 2014, 'What is "metadata" and should you worry if yours is stored by law?', *Sydney Morning Herald*, 6 August.

Grynbaum, MM & Lee, E 2019, 'Boycott AT&T to punish CNN, Trump suggests: business/financial desk', *New York Times*, June 4: <www.nytimes.com/2019/06/03/business/media/trump-att-boycott-cnn.html>

Habermas, J 1992, *The Structural Transformation of the Public Sphere: An Inquiry into a Category of Bourgeois Society*, Polity Press, Cambridge.

Habermas, J 2003, *Truth and Justification*, MIT Press, Cambridge, MA.

Habermas, J 2006, 'Political communication in media society—does democracy still enjoy an epistemic dimension? The impact of normative theory on empirical research', *Communication Theory*, 16, 411–26. Based on a paper presented at the 56th ICA Annual Convention, Dresden, Germany.

Hall, S 1980, 'Encoding/decoding', in S Hall, D Hobson, A Lowe & P Willis (eds), *Culture, Media, Language*, Hutchinson, London, pp. 128–39.

Hasinoff, AA 2013, 'Sexting as media production: rethinking social media and sexuality', *New Media & Society*, 15(4), 449–65.

Hern, A 2017, 'How social media filter bubbles and algorithms influence the election', *The Guardian*, 22 May: <www.theguardian.com/technology/2017/may/22/social-media-election-facebook-filter-bubbles>.

Hobbs, M & McKnight, D 2014, '"Kick this mob out": the Murdoch media and the Australian Labor Government (2007 to 2013)', *Global Media Journal: Australian Edition*, 8(2), 1–13: <www.hca.uws.edu.au/gmjau/?p=1075>.

Hobbs, M 2016, 'The sociology of spin: an investigation into the uses, practices and consequences of political communication', *Journal of Sociology*, 52(2), 371–86 (DOI: 10.1177/1440783314562414).

Hobbs, M, Owen, S, & Gerber, L 2017, 'Liquid love? Dating apps, sex, relationships and the digital transformation of intimacy', *Journal of Sociology*, 53(2), 271–84 (DOI: 10.1177/1440783316662718).

Home Affairs 2019, *Data Retention Obligations*: <www.homeaffairs.gov.au/about-us/our-portfolios/national-security/lawful-access-telecommunications/data-retention-obligations>.

Horkheimer, M & Adorno, TW 2002, *Dialectic of Enlightenment: Philosophical Fragments*, Stanford University Press, Stanford, CA.

Horton, D & Wohl, RR 1956, 'Mass communication and para-social interaction', *Psychiatry*, 19, 215–29.

Humphreys, L 2005, 'Cellphones in public: social interactions in a wireless era', *New Media & Society*, 7(6), 810–33.

Jamieson, K & Cappella, J 2008, *Echo Chamber: Rush Limbaugh and the Conservative Media Establishment*, Oxford University Press, Oxford.

Jones, PK & Pusey, M 2010, 'Political communication and media system: the Australian canary', *Media, Culture & Society*, 32(3), 451–71.

Keane, J 2018, *Power and Humility: The Future of Monitory Democracy*, Cambridge University Press, Cambridge (DOI:10.1017/9781108348997).

Khamis, S, Ang, L & Welling, R 2016, 'Self-branding, "micro-celebrity" and the rise of social media influences', *Celebrity Studies*, 8(2), 191–208 (DOI: 10.1080/19392397.2016.1218292).

Mackay, R 2019, 'Donald Trump and Fox News warned of a migrant "invasion" before El Paso gunman struck', *The Intercept*, 6 August: <https://theintercept.com/2019/08/05/el-paso-gunmans-fear-migrant-invasion-echoed-donald-trump-fox-news/?comments=1>.

Mackson, SB, Brochu, PM & Schneider, BA 2019, 'Instagram: friend or foe? The application's association with psychological well-being', *New Media & Society*, 21(10), 2160–82 (DOI: 10.1177/1461444819840021).

Marcuse, H 1964, *One-Dimensional Man: Studies in the Ideology of Advanced Industrial Society*, Beacon, Boston.

Marcuse, H 2013, *One-Dimensional Man: Studies in the Ideology of Advanced Industrial Society*, Routledge, New York.

Marwick, AE 2015, 'Instafame: luxury selfies in the attention economy, *Public Culture*, 27(175), 137–60 (DOI: 10.1215/08992363-2798379).

Marx, K 1979, *Collected Works*, Lawrence & Wishart, London.

Mayer, J 2019, 'The making of the Fox News White House', *The New Yorker*: <www.newyorker.com/magazine/2019/03/11/the-making-of-the-fox-news-white-house>.

McCullagh, C 2002, *Media Power: A Sociological Introduction*, Palgrave, London.

McIlroy, T 2018, 'Rupert Murdoch, Kerry Stokes and the downfall of Malcolm Turnbull', *Australian Financial Review*: <www.afr.com/politics/rupert-murdoch-kerry-stokes-and-the-downfall-of-malcolm-turnbull-20180921-h15ox2>.

McKnight, D 2012, *Rupert Murdoch: An Investigation of Political Power*, Allen & Unwin, Sydney.

McNair, B, Flew, T, Harrington, S & Swift, A 2017, *Politics, Media and Democracy in Australia*, Routledge, New York (DOI:10.4324/9781315771311).

Media Watch 2009, 'The problem with "illegals"', ABC, 27 April: <www.abc.net.au/mediawatch/transcripts/s2553917.htm>.

Mitchell, A, Gottfried, J, Kiley, J & Eva Matsa, K, 2016 *Political Polarization & Media Habits,* Pew Research Centre, Washington.

Munro, P 2014, 'Everyday sadists: inside the mind of an online troll', *Sydney Morning Herald*, 7 December.

Nine News 2018, 'They're waging a war on the PM: Uhlmann takes aim at News Corp': <www.9news.com.au/national/they-are-waging-a-war-on-the-prime-minister-uhlmann-takes-aim-at-news-corporation/7fd3125c-101b-4b51-86b0-da28651afb62>.

Orwell, G 2000, *Nineteen Eighty-Four*, Penguin Books, London.

Pariser, E 2011, *The Filter Bubble: What the Internet is Hiding from You*, Penguin, London.

Park, S, Fisher, C, Fuller, G & Lee, JY 2018, *Digital News Report: Australia 2018*, News and Media Research Centre, University of Canberra.

Portolan, L 2020, 'The safest sex you'll never have: how coronavirus is changing online dating', *The Conversation*, 31 March: <https://theconversation.com/the-safest-sex-youll-never-have-how-coronavirus-is-changing-online-dating-134382>.

Postman, N 2005, *Amusing Ourselves to Death: Public Discourse in the Age of Show Business*, Penguin, New York.

Putman, R 2000, *Bowling Alone: The Collapse and Revival of American Community*, Simon Schuster, New York.

Redmond, S 2018, *Celebrity*, Routledge, Boca Raton, FL.

Rheingold, H 2000, *The Virtual Community: Homesteading on the Electronic Frontier*, MIT Press, Cambridge, MA.

Robertson, R 1995, 'Glocalization: Time-space and Homogeneity- heterogeneity', in M Featherstone et al. (eds), *Global Modernities*, SAGE, London, pp. 25–44.

Rosen, C 2007, 'Virtual friendship and the new narcissism', *The New Atlantis: A Journal of Technology and Society*, Summer: <www.thenewatlantis.com/publications/virtual-friendship-and-the-new-narcissism>.

Rowe, D, Turner, G & Waterton, E (eds) 2018, *Making Culture*, Routledge, London.

Savage, C 2013, 'NSA said to search content of messages to and from US', *The New York Times*, 8 August.

Schultz, J 1998, *Reviving the Fourth Estate: Democracy, Accountability and the Media*, Cambridge University Press, Cambridge.

Senft, TM 2013, 'Microcelebrity and the branded self, in *A Companion to New Media Dynamics*, Wiley-Blackwell, Oxford, pp. 346–54 (DOI: 10.1002/9781118321607.ch22).

Stark, L & Crawford, K 2015 'The conservatism of emoji: work, affect, and communication', *Social Media + Society* (DOI: 10.1177/2056305115604853).

Stoldt, R, Wellman, M, Ekdale, B & Tully, M 2019, 'Professionalizing and profiting: the rise of intermediaries in the social media influencer industry', *Social Media + Society* (DOI: 10.1177/2056305119832587).

Street, J 2001, *Mass Media, Politics and Democracy*, Palgrave, New York.

Sutton, K 2017, 'Pew study: Fox News was no. 1 news source—for Trump voters', *Politico*, 18 January: <www.politico.com/blogs/on-media/2017/01/study-fox-news-is-no-1-news-source-for-trump-voters-233773>.

Taylor, M 2014, 'GCHQ's interception and storage of Yahoo webcam images condemned', *The Guardian*, 28 February: <www.theguardian.com/world/2014/feb/27/gchq-interception-storage-webcam-images-condemned>.

Tiffen, R 2012, 'Spin doctors, news values and the public interest: the Bermuda Triangle of policy debate', in M Ricketson (ed.), *Australian Journalism Today*, Palgrave Macmillan, Sydney, pp. 16–27.

Tiffen, R 2014, *Rupert Murdoch: A Reassessment*, NewSouth Publishing, Sydney.

Tucker, KH 1998, *Anthony Giddens and Modern Social Theory*, SAGE Publications, London.

Turkle, S 2011, *Alone Together: Why We Expect More From Technology and Less From Each Other*, Basic Books, New York.

Turner, G 2014, *Understanding Celebrity*, 2nd edn, SAGE Publications Ltd, Los Angeles, California.

World Health Organization (WHO) 2019, 'WHO in emergencies': <www.who.int/emergencies/en/>.

Young, S 2007, 'Following the money trail: government advertising, the missing millions and the unknown effects', *Public Policy*, 2, 104–18.

FURTHER READING

Andersen, B 2012, 'Job hunters stalked on social media', ABC, 21 March: <www.abc.net.au/news/2012-03-21/job-hunters-stalked-on-social-media/3904004>.

Arsenault, A & Castells, M 2008, 'Switching power: Rupert Murdoch and the global business of media politics: a sociological analysis', *International Sociology*, 23(4), 488–513 (DOI: 10.1177/0268580908090725).

Elliott, J & Mazzetti, M 2013, 'World of spycraft: NSA and CIA spied in online games', *ProPublica: Journalism in the Public Interest*: <www.propublica.org/article/world-of-spycraft-intelligence-agencies-spied-in-online-games>.

Franklin, B 1994, *Packaging Politics: Political Communications in Britain's Media Democracy*, Edward Arnold, London.

Good Game 2013, 'Racial representation in games', ABC, 5 March: <www.abc.net.au/tv/goodgame/stories/s3703899.htm>.

Greenwald, G, Grim, R & Gallagher, R 2013, 'Top-secret document reveals NSA spied on porn habits as part of plan to discredit "radicalizers"', *The Huffington Post*, 26 November.

Habermas, J 1984, *The Theory of Communicative Action, Vol. I: Reason and the Rationalisation of Society*, Polity Press, Cambridge.

Habermas, J 1990, *Moral Consciousness and Communicative Action*, MIT Press, Cambridge, MA.

Habermas, J 1996, *Between Facts and Norms*, Polity Press, Cambridge.

Lumby, C 1999, *Gotcha: Life in a Tabloid World*, Allen & Unwin, Sydney.

McCullagh, C 2002, *Media Power: A Sociological Introduction*, Palgrave, London.

Merton, RK 1957, *Social Theory and Social Structure*, rev. edn, Free Press, Glencoe.

Stevenson, N 2002, *Understanding Media Cultures: Social Theory and Mass Communication*, SAGE Publications Ltd., London.

MOVIES

Condon, B (dir.) 2013, *The Fifth Estate*, DVD, Touchstone Pictures, Los Angeles, CA.

Levinson, B (dir.) 1997, *Wag the Dog*, DVD, New Line Cinema, Los Angeles, CA.

CHAPTER 15
Social movements

KAREN SOLDATIC WITH NIHAL ISCEL

CHAPTER OVERVIEW

Social movements are a central feature of how change is made in the world: they bring people together who have strong concerns about an area of life that they wish to see change or remain the same. While we often associate social movements with street protests, most often social movements bring together people in less visible ways to confront power collectively.

Social movements can start with a small group of people who are focused on a local issue, such as the building of new roads that would affect their homes and community. They can swiftly become very large if people are forced to come together to stop something from happening imminently, such as the 2003 global protests against the invasion of Iraq, the 2019 Youth Climate Strike or the Black Lives Matter protests in 2020. Most often, social movements are working quietly on issues, drawing upon advocacy strategies such as meetings with local councils and parliamentary members, trying to influence policy makers in government departments, or working through community-based organisations.

The reasons why people come together vary significantly as individuals are spurred on by a range of motivations. People are often ignited to join a social movement because they feel working in collaboration with others collectively is likely to have a greater impact on the issue. People also participate in social movements in very different ways: some protest, others lobby and many sign petitions and donate funds. Participation is often associated with the time people have to commit, the types of skills and resources they can contribute, or their level of personal comfortability to become fully involved.

After reading this chapter, you should be able to:
- Define the term 'social movement'
- Gain an understanding of the different types of actions, tactics and strategies social movements use to achieve their goals
- Describe why and when social movements form
- Understand the importance of identity for those participating in social movements
- Identify the different ways people engage with social movements including activism, advocacy, or being an 'ally'.

> **KEY TERMS**
>
> **Aboriginal and Torres Strait Islander peoples** A collective name for the First Peoples of Australia and their descendants. While this phrase can't include the diversity of languages, cultural practices and spiritual beliefs of Australia's First Peoples, it is preferred over 'Indigenous'. In this chapter you will note that 'Aboriginal and Torres Strait Islander' and 'Indigenous' are used interchangeably.
>
> **Campaign** A sustained, organised public effort making collective claims on specific authorities and institutions such as governments, corporations and the global governance institutions.
>
> **Collective action** A variety of actions (such as campaigns) taken by a group of people with a specific set of objectives and goals to achieve a shared purpose.
>
> **First Peoples** A broad, collective term describing the indigenous peoples of an area. Depending on the country, phrases such as 'First Peoples' and 'First Nations' can have specific meanings (for example, in Canada).
>
> **Human rights activism** Campaigns that utilise the language, processes and institutions of human rights to position their collective action and organising.
>
> **Indigenous** Any ethnic group originating and surviving in an area subject to colonisation. A lower-case 'i' is used when writing about general issues, such as 'the global indigenous rights movement'.
>
> **Intersectionality** The interconnected nature of social categories such as gender, race, class, (dis)ability and sexuality that create overlapping systems of inequality.
>
> **Social movement** A large grouping of people and organisations that focus on specific social, political or cultural issues with the aim of achieving, resisting or reversing social change.

Introduction

Social movements are all around us. Every day millions of people across the globe are involved in social movements. Some of the most recent examples to come across our media networks include large-scale street protests in Hong Kong for greater democratisation (2019–20); the Brexit movement in the United Kingdom to leave the European Union and the counter movement 'Remain Campaign' (beginning in 2016); or the First Nations Peoples of Australia's long-term struggle for recognition, self-determination and Treaty with the constitutional reform campaign culminating with the 'The Uluru Statement from the Heart' campaign in 2019. These are just some of the social movements that have occurred in our world recently that have been reported within the mainstream news and on social media platforms such as Twitter and Facebook.

You too could be, or have been, involved in a social movement, directly or as an ally of a social movement. You may or may not be fully aware that you have participated in a **campaign** or action that has been generated by activists, advocates or ally members of social movements around a particular cause. Have you signed a petition to end the use of palm oil to save the forests for the orangutans in Indonesia? Maybe you were part of the global climate strikes as a student over the past couple of years? Or, maybe you have just 'liked' an organisation on

Facebook, such as Oxfam, because their campaign on child slavery and labour made you aware of how the coffee you drink or chocolate you eat was produced.

There have been multiple theories, speculations and comments about social movements, particularly in regard to how we can best define them. There has been significant research into understanding social movements including considering the ways in which **collective action** comes about. That is, research into the underlying causes that have thrust people to work together to achieve change (or stop change from happening). Often, this means thinking through carefully the different types of actions, tactics and strategies social movements utilise to achieve their objectives and goals.

As we will discuss in this chapter, social movements have changed over time, and they will change in the future with the advances of technologies such as social media platforms. We can therefore expect that both the underlying factors and conditions that bring people together and also the ways in which groups of people come together to mobilise and create social movements, will change.

It is important to note first, that different people think about and understand social movements from different perspectives. Political scientists examine how social movements impact local and national politics and the electoral system, particularly within democratic states (Byrne 2016). Often psychologists examine the group dynamics of social movements, how people make group decisions to mobilise for a particular campaign, how they collectively decide upon the actions the group will take, and how the group builds consensus among new members to maintain momentum of the campaign (Byrne 2016). Philosophers think through the moral and ethical dimensions of social movements; that is, why people see the issue as important enough to actively support and get behind. Questions such as, 'When do people decide to act collectively to create a world that they see as good, fair and just?' are central to philosophical deliberations on social movements (Byrne 2016).

In this book, we are exploring social movements from a sociological perspective. This means that we are interested in a different, but similar, set of questions to the disciplines of political science, psychology and philosophy. As sociologists, we are seeking to understand how social movements are formed, how they influence social change, and how they position their actions, strategies and tactics collectively to achieve the change they wish to see. For example, we might seek to understand why some social movements undertake radical street protests, while others focus on highly targeted media campaigns, or in other cases why advocacy and deliberation may be the most strategic orientation. This chapter will draw upon some of the most recent examples of social movement campaigns and activism in Australia and internationally to explore and examine these sociological questions.

We will also illustrate the critical importance of these sociological questions in informing our understanding of social movements and the people involved in social movements through drawing upon the life narrative of one of the authors—Nihal Iscel. Through Nihal's reflective contribution about her experiences of working in different roles and capacities in social movements, we will begin to see how being involved in social movements often changes over time. This change may be driven by external demands of a changing socio-political landscape; a shift in the objectives and goals of the social movement; or by tensions that arise because of one's ethical and moral commitment to the campaigns objectives and goals the deeper one becomes involved in a social movement. All of these are 'normal' dilemmas for people involved in social movements and are continuously grappled with over time as a social movement participant.

Significantly, Nihal's exploration of her own journey as an advocate, activist and ally reveals how social movement actors often need to make decisions about when to engage in radical street protest—taking a more confrontational approach—or when to advocate through dialogue and policy deliberations with those in power. As Nihal illustrates for you, certain decisions are not only tactical and strategic, but also often the only possibility as all other avenues to drive change have been exhausted. Interestingly, what you will learn from Nihal's journey is that often being involved in a social movement means that you will occupy all three positions simultaneously: working as an advocate, protesting on the street as an activist and working as an ally in support of others. Through Nihal's descriptions of her own experience, you will be able to identify and understand the dimensions of social movements in the real world and what it means to be involved in social movements as a process and identity.

What is a social movement and how do they work?

Even though different theorists and disciplines try to understand social movements from a range of perspectives, generally, it is well accepted that social movements result from people coming together to collectively organise for social change or, to try to stop something from changing as they want it to remain the same (Byrne 2016). The issue the group are focused on may be either short or long term. It often contains a number of moral or ethical dimensions for those involved, such as ending violence against women, stopping Aboriginal deaths in custody, or ending child labour.

One example of a long-term social movement is First Nations Australians' (**Aboriginal and Torres Strait Islander peoples**) struggles for sovereignty, rights and Treaty. It is well documented that First Nations peoples have resisted European invasion and settler-colonialism since the first moments of invasion (Walters 2010).

An example of a short-term social movement campaign is the Twitter media campaign that garnered national support in December 2019 to demand the Australian Prime Minister, Scott Morrison, to return from his holiday in Hawaii during the worst bushfires in Australia's history. While the movement of First Nations peoples has been a sustained campaign lead by **Indigenous** Australians and their allies over more than 250 years, the latter was a short, loosely connected network of Australian citizens coming together to make a single demand.

These two very different campaigns illustrate the different ways social movements organise to bring people together with a clear set of objectives and goals. Significantly, as contrasting campaigns, they also demonstrate how different tactics and strategies are adopted to ensure that the core message of the campaigns are heard by a broader public. The more people involved the more pressure there will be on governments, institutions, businesses and organisations to respond to the social movement campaign in some way.

Most importantly, both campaigns illustrate the spatial and temporal dimensions of social movements. That is, for Australia's First Nations peoples, the campaign is longstanding and seeks to address past injustices with colonial invasion and settler-colonial dispossession, violence and enduring systems of governance. Additionally, it is oriented towards a future vision of Australia as First Nations peoples seek to transform their relationship with the Australian state and non-Indigenous citizens. It is thus a long-term campaign to put an end to enduring forms of racism and Indigenous inequality. It has involved diverse forms of activism and advocacy at the local and national levels around issues of recognition within the Australian constitution, laws, policy and programming. It has also involved building global alliances with other First Nations peoples in settler-colonial states such as Canada, New Zealand and the United States, who have collectively worked to gain support from global governance institutions such as the United Nations to realise an International Declaration on the Rights of Indigenous Peoples. Although some progress has been made on these issues in recent years, given the size and scale of transformation of Australian society required, the struggle for the recognition of First People's sovereignty, rights and Treaty, continues.

The Twitter and social media campaign to put pressure on Australia's Prime Minister to return from an international holiday during the catastrophic bushfire crises over the summer of 2019–20 was a short-term online campaign. It was highly targeted and drew upon highly emotive tactics of public shame through suggesting that the Prime Minister was recoiling from his responsibilities as the leader of the nation in its time of crisis and while citizens were deeply suffering. This campaign brought together diverse and many unaligned people through the use of technological platforms including Twitter, Instagram and Facebook—there was no street protest. The use of technologies and social media made the absence of Prime Minister Morrison from Australia highly present in people's everyday lives. The ongoing representation of the Prime Minister's absence immediately increased political pressure on the Australian Government. The movement's target, Prime Minister Morrison, and its objective, for the Prime Minister to return from holiday and demonstrate leadership, were clear, coherent and direct. It demonstrates how a simple campaign can very quickly achieve its goal. The demand for change was small with few, if any, structural reforms required to meet the movement's core demand. Yet it was only through sustained social media and mainstream media engagement that this result was achieved.

These two social movements and their campaigns illustrate the central role of collective action and some of the ways in which collective action can draw on diverse skills, knowledge and strategic alliances across a range of publics to build networks with potential campaign allies and to maintain momentum to build a mass social movement. Further, they show how building broad traction and take-up of the social movement's objectives and goals involves illustrating the moral and ethical dimensions behind the objectives and goals; that is, clearly identifying and expressing the 'right thing to do given the circumstances'. Skilled engagement through cartoons, catchy hashtags and visual imagery can help to build broad base appeal, and to maintain traction through widespread coverage.

Whether these skilled strategies and tactics are part of a long-standing campaign such as the struggle for Indigenous rights, sovereignty and Treaty, or a short term campaign with a tight focus, social movement capacities to attract, build and sustain broad public support is a critical component of their work. Further, if we reflect globally on the Brexit movement or the mass protests for democratisation in Hong Kong, we can see these strategies, tactics and practices employed across each of these social movements.

Why and when do social movements form?

This leads us to core questions around why and when social movements form. That is, at what point do people identify an issue that they see as important?

As Moira Byrne (2016) argued, social movements are likely to have always existed in some form as long as collective groups of people have lived together and developed shared rules, regulations and institutions. Byrne (2016) has identified that many social movements within Western societies such as the United Kingdom, Europe, Canada and the United States, have emerged out of the process of colonial conquest and power such as the fight to end slavery. Importantly, it is not just those directly affected who are mobilised to participate in, or lead, social movements. Often, movements involve allies, advocates and activists who socially, morally and ethically disagree with a situation that oppresses other people, even if they are a beneficiary of such a situation.

BOX 15.1

Sociology in history

WAVE HILL WALK-OFF

One of Australia's most influential protests occurred on 23 August 1966 by the Gurindji people in the Northern Territory. It started a social movement that changed Australia's culture, the relationship between the state and Indigenous people and continued the momentum of recognising the complex and rich history of Australia's First Nations people.

On that day, Vincent Lingiari of the Gurindji people and 200 fellow Indigenous stockmen, domestic workers and their families, walked off the Wave Hill Cattle Station. The strike, initially, was about fair wages and conditions: the Gurindji people were enclosed within the property and forced to work for only basic rations (Meakins 2016). The strike escalated, however, to be a fight for land rights and justice.

Historically, the Gurindji people have faced many injustices as a result of colonisation. Some 80 years beforehand, they had been dispossessed of their lands to make way for pastoralists across Central Australia. There is also evidence of a series of abuses including massacres, stolen children and forced labour (Meakins 2016).

To appease the strikers, the pastoralists offered better wages and working conditions. Lingiari and the Gurindji people, however, demanded nothing less than the full return and ownership of their lands.

After walking away from Wave Hill Station, Lingiari led the strikers on 30 kilometres to Wattie Creek, where they stayed and protested for nine years.

At the time, the idea of returning land to Aboriginal people as the original owners was unheard of by most Australians. As such, Vincent Lingiari understood that he needed to raise awareness and build a broad coalition of support. To do this, he toured the country, sought support from other First Nations peoples across Australia, spoke to Trade Unions and the broader Labour Movement, met with social justice groups and parliamentarians, and gave countless interviews to the media.

This built support across the nation that raised awareness both about the treatment of the Gurindji people and of Australia's Indigenous peoples more generally.

In 1975, Lingiari and the Gurindji people finally achieved what they set out to do. Gough Whitlam became the first Australian Prime Minister to return land to First Nations people—the moment is symbolically captured in Figure 15.1.

FIGURE 15.1 Gough Whitlam symbolically hands back land to Vincent Lingiari and the Gurindji people.

This small strike built momentum that brought about changes to Australian culture and society that continues to this day. Unbeknown at the time, the Gurindji people's fight for land rights was a significant step in changing and reforming Indigenous–settler colonial relations in Australia.

The dispossession and plight of our nation's Aboriginal people was recognised across the nation and there began a discussion of responding to past injustices. These discussions led to a profound change in attitudes and in 1967 over 90 per cent of Australians voted to support the count of Indigenous Australians in the national Census. This had significant impacts on Aboriginal policy-setting in this country (Soldatic 2018).

The campaign for change continued with the Aboriginal Tent Embassy established outside Parliament House, Canberra, in 1972 (Foley, Schaap & Howell 2013).

The Wave Hill Walk-Off has grown into a social movement that continues to agitate for social change. Some 50 years later, the actions of the Gurindji people continue to shape the landscape of Australian society (Hodgson 2011). Most importantly, the Gurindji's protests and actions along with other Indigenous protests—such as that lead by Charlie Perkins and the Freedom Rides (1966)—show the power of collective actions in changing history for the long term (Curthoys 2002).

This and many other stories are outlined in the Australians Together website and resources: <https://australianstogether.org.au>.

The collective organising and mobilising of the labour movement that emerged during the Industrial Revolution in the late seventeenth century provided the basis of contemporary Trade Unions. This provides us with an example of how social movements can evolve over time (Biyanwila 2009). Workers, agricultural labourers, landless peasants and crafts persons— exposed to highly exploitative and dangerous workplaces and conditions frequently resulting in death and/or injury—often combined with everyday citizens to create mass social movements with the aim of changing both the industrial workplace and bringing about broader social reforms.

Collectively, these different groups mobilised through an array of diverse actions. Throughout this period there was extensive protest actions and civil unrest. For example, the term 'Luddite' originates from the organised social movement of skilled weavers and textile workers who lost their jobs and incomes through industrial mechanisation (1811). The Swing Riots (1830) was the combined social movement of agriculture workers, labourers and landless peasants in mass civil unrest (see Biyanwila 2009).

While economic reforms largely referred to the wages and conditions of male workers at the time, the labour movement formalised as the Trade Union movement in many Western countries and placed pressure on governments for other social reforms such as public health care, free public education, and better public sanitation to diminish disease, disability and unnecessary death (Biyanwila 2009). As leading social movement scholar Alain Touraine (2002) has argued, these social movements have been critically important also for a strong democratic society that is fair, just and egalitarian in its commitments to all of their citizens, not just a few with economic and political power.

During the 1960s and 1970s, social movements changed markedly as people began to collectively organise around civil rights and identity. Examples include the African-American civil rights movement lead by Martin Luther King Jr. and Malcolm X; the Australian Indigenous Rights movement in relation to civil rights and the constitutional referendum of 1967; and the feminist movement and the emergence of the environment movement (see Chapters 7, 9, 12 and 16).

More recently, we have witnessed new social movement mobilisation and campaigns to further civil rights around core areas of identity. For example, in Australia we have seen the mass mobilisation of diverse citizens through social movement advocacy, activism and campaigns for equal marriage rights for members of the LGBTIQA+ community. This social movement campaign highlighted the ways in which non-heterosexual couples were discriminated against in a multitude of ways and faced unique injustices and inequalities as they were unable to legally marry or be legally recognised in a de-facto relationship. The implicit heteronormative framing of law and policy impacted and diminished their everyday lives—both private and public. (By heteronormative, I am referring to the position that believes the norm or default sexual partnership is between a male and a female.)

For example, longstanding LGBTIQA+ partnerships were often denied 'next of kin' status in relation to emergency health care and medical procedures such as when a partner was dying or required emergency medical intervention. Therefore, long-term partners were often denied access to their loved ones in the last moments of their lives, even, for example, after being together for more than 20 years (Power 2015). Thus, the focus of the marriage equality social movement was a struggle for recognition so that the LGBTIQA+ community no longer experienced these forms of daily injustices in all areas of life.

The social movement for marriage equality is also a good example of changes in the focus of social movements—from a politics of redistribution (social and economic inequality) of the early Trade Union movement (worker's rights) and the Abolitionists (anti-slavery) with the rise of the industrial revolution and industrial capitalism, to that of the politics of recognition (unjust differences experienced when identifying as belonging to a particular group). What we have seen is that social movements have come to focus more on issues of personal identity and how public laws, policies and attitudes impact upon our personal lives and choices. This was a trend identified by Fraser (1997), who argues that social movements based in wealthy nations, have become more focused on concerns with the recognition of one's social identity since the 1990s. This has seen collective action for the specific issues people experience because they identify with and belong to a specific identity group, such as the LGBTIQA+ community and the movement for marriage equality.

Not all movements are progressive

We should also remember that not all social movements are progressive—they can also be 'conservative, reactionary or regressive' (Martin 2015, p. 25). Therefore, we should not assume that social movements are always associated with struggles for justice, rights and equality. At a global scale, we have witnessed the emergence of reactionary social movements in the United States that supported the election of TV billionaire personality Donald Trump. In the United Kingdom, the Brexit campaign to leave the European Union was a nationalist movement. And of course, in India, Hindu Nationalism and the Modi Government emerged out of the Hindutva movement of 'ethnic absolutism' and in turn, millions of Muslim Indian citizens are now stateless (Sur 2019). These are clear examples of social movements that focus on identity of difference with little regard for injustices experienced by others (see Soldatic & Johnson 2020). Therefore, we cannot assume that all social movement campaigns will lead to rights, dignity and respect for citizens; in fact, the impact of their demands may be detrimental to the wellbeing and security of others (Martin 2015).

In Australia too, an increasing rise of conservative and reactionary social movements has been observed (Stanley 2015). The clearest example is the 2019–20 campaigns for new legislation by reactionary groups against the reforms won by the marriage equality social movement. With the new marriage equality laws in place, the reactionary social movements argue that they now need protection for their beliefs and practices, and the right to discriminate against those who do not necessarily practice a similar set of beliefs.

At the time of writing, the negative impact of such reactionary social movements in Australia, and their demands of religious discriminatory protections, has been highlighted by a combined public statement opposed to this reactionary social movement:

> We call on the Australian Parliament to introduce laws that appropriately strengthen that shield of protection for people facing discrimination because of their religious beliefs or because they don't hold religious beliefs. Equally, we caution the Australian Parliament against laws that would give some people within society a 'sword' to use their beliefs to harm others by cutting through existing anti-discrimination protections. We will oppose any new laws which would give religious groups a license to discriminate against others in a way that would sanction mistreatment or wind back the clock on equality (Twenty10 2019, p. 1).

This collective effort from a range of social movement organisations and their representatives illustrates the importance of understanding the objectives and goals of social movements, what they seek to achieve by their campaigns, and who will be dis/advantaged if they are able to achieve their campaign objectives and goals.

Critical reflection

What do you think are some of the weaknesses of a social movement approach to thinking about society?

Most significantly, this example illustrates the importance of analysing social movement campaigns and the organisations, groups and peoples involved, to fully comprehend the demands and who may or may not directly benefit, and who is or will be disadvantaged in the long term. Importantly, these examples also illustrate why, when and how social movements form, activate and mobilise; that is, those motivating forces that give rise to, mobilise and sustain social movements over time. At times, it is to drive change to address what they understand as particular injustices and ensure equality for their specific concern; at other times, it is in reaction to the growing power of a group that has been less privileged historically and is now challenging another group's historical position of power; and sometimes, it is to ensure that things remain the same as they do not agree, or see just, the changes that are proposed.

These tensions always exist when people are required to live together, as different groups have significantly different commitments to what they understand as 'what is good', 'what is right' and 'what ought to be'. It is this very struggle that will ensure that social movements will remain a central component of our societies into the future.

Intersectionality: mapping the margins and working across identities

Across the globe, we have also seen the rise of 'new social movements.' These have emerged with the rise of identity politics and argue that social movement mobilisation, activation and campaigns often do not account for the complexity of people's everyday lives. Women of colour have been leading thinkers in identifying the ways in which issues of race and gender intersect to give rise to the unique injustices that they face (Brown et al. 2017). This is what African-American legal scholar Kimberle Crenshaw (1991) coined as **intersectionality**, where one's lived experience of multiple marginal identities results in overlapping systems of oppression—intersectionality is discussed in Chapter 7.

Due to this complexity, social movements across time have grappled with the broad base of their membership to ensure fair, just and equal representation. For example, women of colour and women from the Global South have extensively argued that the global women's movement has largely focused on gains for White women who already often experience a high level of privilege because of both their whiteness and middle-class status (Moreton-Robinson 2000). Chandra Talpade Mohanty (2003) has argued that the transnational women's movement has to prioritise the injustices of women within the Global South to be truly representative of women on a global scale.

An example Mohanty (2003) draws upon is in the area of work, access to the labour market and professionalisation of White middle-class women's labour. It is now well documented that White middle-class women's access to high-paid, skilled work has become dependent upon on the poorly paid, highly exploitative labour of migrant women to care for their children while they are at work (Parranas 2015). Thus, women's movement campaigns for wage justice and economic parity need to ensure that this provides opportunities for all women, and not just a small minority who are already experiencing a level of privilege and power. It should be noted that while Parranas's work focused on the United States, migrant workers—both men and women—are also vulnerable to exploitation in Australia (Doherty 2016).

A more recent example to illustrate the importance of intersectionality in thinking about social movements is the #MeToo campaign, which aims to increase the awareness of sexual assault and violence (me too, 2020). Even though this social movement was ignited by working-class women of colour, one of the core criticisms of the outcomes of this movement is that the primary beneficiaries have been white middle-class women (Harris 2018). Penny Griffin (2019, p. 556) argues that understanding the 'intricate web of practices that enable certain types of gendered identity and socioeconomic privilege to intersect, in powerful and potent ways' is critical for social movements to achieve the social change they set out to accomplish. In so doing, they should not be co-opted for the benefit of others or marginalise further those who sit on the fringe of the movement.

A number of activists, advocates and allies have argued that to counter these issues of intersectional power within social movements, it is critical for those who care for these issues to ensure they are also a priority for all social movements (Gurung 2020). For example, Trans Queer Disabled activist Zahari Richter (2020) explains that he has to raise issues of trans and queerness within the disability movement, and issues of disability within the trans queer movement. Richter suggests that the only way to overcome these tensions within social movements is to offer a deep intersectional analysis of the impact of social movement campaigns and in turn, propose practical strategies and actions that align with the broader movement's objectives and goals. What is required, Richter argues, is to expand the boundaries of social movements. This is demonstrated through Nihal Iscel's personal journey—outlined below—through social movements as a migrant disabled woman of colour. As you will be able to identify, Nihal continually acts in ways that transform and expand social movement agendas and campaigns to ensure that those who live on the margins and experience multiple axes of power in their lives are also included in, and benefit from, any social change achieved.

> **Critical reflection**
>
> How would a strong, collective single identity within a social movement be exclusionary to individuals that identify across a range of identities (e.g. a young queer person who is also from a poor migrant family)?

Human rights and social movements

Another interesting change in social movements globally is the increasing focus around issues of human rights and the rise of **human rights activism**. According to De Sousa Santos (2007), human rights have become the dominant language of social movements across the globe. This is due to the integration of national economies into the global economy and institutions, and its impact on people's everyday lives in addition to the broad scale acceptance of human rights in international law. Primarily, the international human rights system enables social movements to confront power through formal systems, institutions and processes, and give credibility to their local level concerns, struggles and claims for rights, justice and equality. Social movements, therefore, utilise the unified language, institutions and structures of human rights to build traction around their concerns, actions and campaigns.

One of the key reasons that 'human rights discourse' is attractive for social movements is that it is a recognised global language that has been ratified into international and national laws, policies and programs (Ife 2016). Further, via the United Nations Treaty system, citizens can take their grievances against governments to the United Nations and have them independently reviewed (Ife 2016). For example, in the case of *Toonen v Australia* (1994), Nicholas Toonen drew upon Article 17 of the International Covenant on Civil and Political Rights to illustrate that Tasmania's criminalisation of homosexuality violated his right to privacy that was protected with Australia's ratification of this Treaty. In response to this, 'the Commonwealth Government passed a law overriding Tasmania's criminalisation of homosexual sex' (HREOC 2020, p. 1). This single case was supported by the broader LGBTIQA+ community across Australia, and illustrates the ways in which social movements strategically position human rights to make broader structural change at the local level (Dondoli 2015).

The use of human rights as a core organising principle is what Keck and Sikkink (1998) have argued is 'boomerang' social movement activism and advocacy. This gives social movements the capacity to strategically select individual cases that will lead to broad structural change at the local level. The idea of the 'boomerang' is that you mount the campaign at an international level that will drive pressure on national governments to drive local laws, policies and social practices and attitudes (Soldatic 2016).

Further, through the international system of human rights, social movements have access to various powerful processes. For example, by working with formal civil society organisations, informal social movements can submit 'shadow reports' to the United Nations. These reports can be used to challenge claims of national governments—offering an alternative understanding of what may be experienced on the local level. Nihal explains the importance of these global systems, institutions and the language of human rights for disability groups in Australia and their central role in bringing about real change for disabled people. The discourse of human rights has been extremely generative for social movements and is something that is likely to continue.

What might social movements look like in the future?

It is difficult to say exactly what social movements will look like in the future. The world is changing—and changing rapidly. Interestingly, while the 1990s and 2000s have been dominated by issues around identity, such as the LGBTIQA+ movement and the refugee movement, older issues around the politics of redistribution such as income inequality, poverty and the right to decent, secure work and social protection are now re-emerging. The impact of COVID-19 on many people's livelihoods saw new demands for income redistribution and the demands for all Australians to receive a universal basic income (Khadem 2020).The core difference will be an increased global focus on issues of income inequality and poverty in the future, beyond the realm of national governments, with the ongoing integration of national economics into the global economy. For example, the global civil society organisation, Oxfam, now produces reports

PERSONAL VOICE
Nihal's social movement journey

❝ My name is Nihal Iscel and in this section I discuss the role of activism and advocacy in rights-based social movements towards meaningful inclusion of people with disability in the community. I migrated to Australia as a 15-year-old. Being totally blind and a female from a culturally and linguistically diverse (CaLD) background, I found a lot of inequalities that people from minority groups face when trying to access services in education, health, welfare, employment, housing and so on. With this in mind, I had to choose my career path carefully to influence positive systemic change.

Positive structural changes in the provision of public services for people with disability usually arise through the strong activism and effective advocacy by people who have lived experience of disability, their families and carers collectively. Rights have always been fought for and taken; they've never been given without a fight.

Disability is everybody's business. Nobody knows what will happen to them or a member of their families tomorrow. Some people are born with a disability and others acquire it later in life due to an inherited genetic condition or an accident. Disability is a part of life like being born with your specific sex, to your specific parents, religion, ethnic origin, race, etc., which you were not able to determine. Therefore, it is in the best interests of the government and the society to make disability their business and start strengthening disability discrimination legislation and policies. We must reduce discrimination on the basis of disability to provide equitable opportunities; also to prevent governments of different persuasions from using disability issues for their political advantage.

Historically, the care of people with disability mainly depended on the mercy and goodwill of their families and charitable organisations like the church. Disability in some cultures is perceived as a test—a gift of God—and in other cultures as a punishment from God for the family's past sins. In some cultures, having a family member with a disability would mean that the family was excluded from any inheritance and siblings with no disabilities could not find marriage partners. These beliefs mainly determined how the person with disability was treated in the family and the society. Putting the care of a person with disability in the hands of someone who perceives the disability as a punishment from God is very dangerous. People may not feel merciful and may wish the person to be dead. Perceiving the person as a gift is just as equally dangerous as it potentially isolates the person.

Accessing the community equally and being meaningfully included is a human right and should never depend on others' mercy, goodwill or charity.

Since the rights of people with disability were recognised by the United Nations in the 1980s (United Nations n.d.), through strong activism and effective advocacy by people with disability, people with disability in Australia have experienced many changes. Today, most children with disability are being educated in inclusive mainstream schools; while adults have the right to get a job and work, get married, and live in their choice of dwellings with supports either independently or with their family or in shared accommodations. People with disability also have improved access to public transport, health and to other services they need.

Despite this, there is a long way to go to achieve real meaningful inclusion of people with disability in economic, political, social and cultural life in the wider Australian community. Most people with disability still experience inequalities and discrimination when looking for employment, housing, legal justice, education, and disability supports to meet their own individual needs.

The difference between being an activist and an advocate

Advocacy, according to the Australian Department of Social Services (DSS), is a government program to protect the rights of people with disability and reduce discrimination. An advocate should stand on the side of the person with disability, not in front, and provide them with relevant information. An advocate should provide as much advocacy as the person wants; not more, not less. The advocate must not influence the person's decision making as the person with disability is the one to make their own decisions with the relevant information.

While I was working as an Advocacy Manager at the Ethnic Disability Advocacy Centre (EDAC) Inc. between 2010 and 2017, it came to our attention that many people with dual or multiple diagnosis of complex disability, health and mental health conditions from CaLD backgrounds did not receive adequate supports to meet their individual care needs. If the person with disability had other health and mental health issues, Disability Services Commission (DSC) expected the Health Department and the Mental Health Commission to provide the person with supports and the Health Department and the Mental Health Commission expected it from the DSC, where the individual would get very little or no supports.

To make a positive systemic change, EDAC advocated for those government departments to start talking to each other and coordinate people's disability, health and mental health supports. As a result of our three years of advocacy, eventually, we were able to initiate meetings with heads and management staff of those departments and other disability and mental health advocacy agencies on a regular basis. This enabled us to provide professional development training in cultural competency—which was linked to the National Standards for Disability Services (NSDS)—to staff working in the disability, mental health and health care services.

In Western Australia, it was also very difficult to get a disability diagnosis for people over the age of 18 years. As some people with a suspected disability migrate to Australia as adults, it would mean that if they were not diagnosed, they would not be able to get any support. Through our strong advocacy, the DSC agreed to provide opportunities for adults from CaLD backgrounds to be assessed.

Being an activist however is somewhat different. To be a good disability activist, you need to understand the cause, and recognise inequalities and the discrimination against people with disability when accessing their basic human rights and the community. You need to recognise that the person with disability is the expert in their own life and would know what works and does not work for them.

You need to always involve people with disability in making decisions about how they can be in charge of managing their own care and support system, and hear what they are saying. As an activist you can help to empower them to have a voice; give them opportunities to stand up for their rights in a safe environment; include them in the research for possible solutions for change. Be angry. Have hope and belief that positive structural change to improve the lives of people with disability is possible and may only happen by involving and including them.

Positive structural change may come about only if we work collaboratively and have one voice to say the same things. You need to identify the issues that interest you, look for likeminded people and organisations and join them. As will be discussed in the final chapter of this book, you need to do your research and be well informed. Your strategies could be to help mobilise others, write letters to your members of parliament or newspapers, use social media or rally in front of the parliament.

You may also choose to go inside and listen to the debates and hear and understand how their arguments and decisions may impact on your cause. My position is you need to have a fire in your heart to continue to fight tirelessly until the change comes through because this is our and everybody's business. If you are a person with disability, you should always look for opportunities to take charge of how you want to live your life and coordinate your supports.

(While in the concluding chapter of this book we discuss how you can help change the world, you can also see *A Beginners Guide to Activism* (Lindsey 2017) for some other ideas.)

Intersection of activism and advocacy

To make a positive systemic change, there is a need for strong activism to be mobilised as well as effective advocacy. With a great deal of activism by people with disability, their families, carers and supporters, combined with the work and advocacy from peak disability advocacy agencies, the federal government legislated the National Disability Insurance Scheme (NDIS) in 2013 and started implementing it in trial areas in 2014.

The Western Australian government, however, created its own scheme—the WA NDIS—and refused to accept the federal government's NDIS. In 2015, the WA government decided to trial the national scheme in the Perth Hills and the WA scheme in one municipality in metropolitan Perth and in one regional municipality. WA had three disability schemes going on: these were the federal government's NDIS, WA NDIS and the old Western Australian disability system. Confused? So was the community!

The disability system in WA had many problems. For example, most people with sensory, physical and psychosocial disabilities were not supported in the WA NDIS or the old disability scheme. If someone could prove that their disability was worse than all their peers with a similar disability, they could get some help, but the length of support was uncertain.

Both the WA NDIS and the old disability scheme relied heavily on the informal supports of the family and charitable organisations.

What we needed to do was empower consumer groups to have a collective voice and create safe environments for them to speak up and be heard. As such, we used the slogan 'Nothing about us, without us'. Community meetings were organised by activists and advocates with disability for people with disability and their carers to come and discuss the NDIS and WA disability scheme across Perth. It was apparent right from the beginning that people in the WA disability scheme were not getting the necessary and reasonable support they needed.

It was important for all of us to know about the various trials, what was working and what had failed. This transparency was fundamental to ensure the right system was implemented.

How social movements make systemic change

It took a long time and hard work to mobilise and empower people with disability, families and carers to have their say and ensure the government heard us: our message was clear: we wanted to join the federal government's NDIS. To do this, we formed the '#NoDisadvantage' <https://nodisadvantage.weebly.com/media.html> campaign on Facebook with the leadership of Samantha Connor. As part of the campaign we met with government ministers as well as opposition party representatives, issued media statements on a regular basis, wrote letters to the newspapers and contacted other media outlets. Whenever the WA NDIS was being debated at the WA Parliament, we went to listen and ask questions.

In 2016, the WA government engaged Stanton International Auditors to independently evaluate both the national scheme in the Perth trial areas and the WA NDIS. Although Stanton International provided their report of the evaluation to the WA government in December 2016, it was not released publicly until March 2017—just one week prior to the WA election.

As part of their evaluation process, Stanton International interviewed only 21 NDIS and WA NDIS participants out of a potential 8000. They also interviewed 65 service providers. On the basis of this report, WA government and the disability service provider organisations insisted that WA NDIS was a better choice for WA. The majority of people with disability, families and carers criticized the report as being flawed and biased towards the WA government and disability service provider agencies (Probono Australia 2017).

The #NoDisadvantage team ran a survey and in only 10 days 285 people responded, as opposed to the only 21 interviewed by Stanton International. The survey results showed that of the 285 responses, 160 people (57 per cent) wanted national NDIS as opposed to 23 people (22 per cent) who wanted WA NDIS, with 25.8 per cent of respondents unsure. (See the survey outcomes here: <www.nodisadvantage.weebly.com>.)

My dilemma

Despite the overwhelming support for the national NDIS, the entire issue divided the disability community and service provider agencies as some continued to support the WA NDIS, others the national scheme. At the EDAC where I was working, we did not want to lose our state advocacy funding and on this basis decided to support the WA scheme.

When I first started working with EDAC, it only provided disability advocacy in the Perth metropolitan areas. However, by this time EDAC's advocacy had grown significantly and was extended to some remote and regional areas of WA. The EDAC's remote and regional advocacy program includes not only people with disability from CaLD backgrounds, but also Aboriginal people with disability.

EDAC's decision made it very difficult for me to advocate for a national scheme. My dilemma was that on one hand, as a staff member, I had a loyalty to EDAC. On the other hand, I was a person with disability, and the majority of people with disability in WA preferred the nationally run NDIS.

As you journey through your own professional career, you may well confront some similar dilemmas. Our hope is that the tools offered by sociology will assist you in making the right decision for you.

I thought that if I resigned, then I would not have to be answerable to any organisation and I could still continue to campaign as an independent activist for better and fair disability supports in WA. In June 2017, I tendered my resignation.

Outcomes of activism

After my resignation, I had more time to help the #NoDisadvantage campaign team and give them as much support as I could to empower people to stand up for their human rights. I was also able to mobilise the voice of people with disability from CaLD backgrounds to join the campaign. As part of our advocacy, some of our campaigners travelled to the eastern states to gather support from the disability communities, advocacy agencies, politicians and the general public. We continued to raise these issues through media and placing pressure on politicians.

After many phone calls and emails, finally, the 'Every Australian Counts' campaign also came to support us!

In December 2017, the newly elected WA Labor Government decided to abandon the WA NDIS and joined the National Disability Insurance Scheme. We, the people with disability and our supporters in WA, through our struggles, made a positive structural change and are now included in the national scheme.

While this was an important victory, the fight for our human rights is far from over. As the NDIS is still new, it has many flaws. Further, economic financial pressures meant that the federal government cut resources from the NDIS—frustrating for many was that the defence budget and other programs were protected.

In 2019, the government cut $4 billion from the NDIS to fund bushfire and drought affected areas of Australia. This left people with complex dual and multiple disabilities, and people with sensory and psychosocial disabilities who have intermittent needs, without adequate supports to meet their individual care needs.

We still have a long way to go and continue to fight for the NDIS we need. Providing people with disability, their families and carers with the realistic supports and enabling them to meaningfully participate in the economic, political and social life in the community would give people control and autonomy and reduce their dependence on the government's welfare system in the long run.

on global inequality and poverty, including inequality measures from Australia and the United States, alongside countries from the Global South such as Cambodia and Botswana (Oxfam 2020).

A critical difference we have seen since the 2000s is the increase of technology and social media platforms to expand the boundaries of social movements generally. Through social media, social movements are able to garner greater public exposure to their concerns and build their membership base much more rapidly—as we have outlined in this chapter.

The concern that follows, however, is whether such platforms and technologies can maintain the momentum of campaigns to sustain pressure on governments, or will they be dismissed as 'just another Facebook group'? Social movements and the advocacy and activism they employ are an attempt to confront power: people in power, powerful organisations and governments. Therefore, future social movements will depend on having the right circumstances, where the use of social media as a public awareness tool transforms into technology-enabled actions, tactics and strategies. Moreover, these very technologies have their own limitations in driving social movement action as often they are inaccessible and unaffordable to some population—though this is changing with smartphones becoming increasingly affordable.

In many parts of the world, poverty has fallen dramatically. We have seen a significant increase in the middle class across China and India. Despite such positive developments, income inequality and entrenched poverty persist in most of the world. As such, historical practices of social movements, such as the street protest, will likely remain part of strategic action. There is no doubt that the broad-scale public display of social movement mobilisation, such as in Hong Kong and the street protests for democratisation, are too big to ignore—something that social media technology campaigns are unable to achieve.

We know that things like climate change have become urgent social movement concerns and across the globe there continues to be broad-scale campaigns and repertoires of action to address this issue. It is a good example of what the future holds for social movement mobilisation, campaigning and actions. It combines older social movement mobilisation strategies of the street protest with more technological savvy practices on social media platforms. It also alerts us to the ways that new issues can become prominent, reignite passion for change, and the promise of a global solidarity for a better world for all.

Critical reflection

What do you think would be the limitations of technology and social media platforms for social movement campaigns?

Conclusion

Throughout this chapter we have focused on social movements: how they came about, how they engage in social, political and cultural change, and how they emerge and mobilise different groups of people to confront power. They are made up of many different people who want to see change in the world—as well as by people who want to stop some changes from happening. As Nihal's journey illustrates, people involved in social movements are critically reflecting upon their positions, and often, to achieve the change they desire, they need to shift positions, tactics and actions. This includes small-scale social movement actions such as trying to influence policy makers through small community campaigns, or large-scale street protests to make their demands and claims public to increase the pressure on those in power.

As the examples of this chapter illustrate, across time, social movements have been able to achieve many of their goals. Before we conclude this chapter, spend some time thinking about the most recent social movement you had involvement with: Was it as someone actively campaigning, or were you just a bystander on the street watching a street protest? How did you feel when you were involved? Were you able to achieve the goals you had hoped for?

Summary points

* Social movements remain an important part of our world and will continue to exist as long as there are systems of power.
* Social movements enable people to come together around shared goals to express their dissatisfaction with those in power and to either create, resist or reverse social, political and cultural change.
* Social movements are diverse; they work in different ways, depending on the issues that they are engaged with.

Sociological reflection

1 Discuss and describe how social movements have changed over time.
2 Explain why social movements have adopted new discourses of social change and identify whether this has increased their impact.
3 Explain the importance and limitations of identity (individual and/or group) to social movement activism.

Discussion questions

Choose a social movement that you have had contact with in some way.
1 Describe the issues of the campaign.
2 How did it mobilise public interest and what tools did it use to do this (social media, street protest, media, etc.)?
3 How effective do you think this social movement was in achieving its objectives and goals?

Further investigation

1 Identify what you see to be the most important social movements in contemporary society.
2 Discuss who has the power to respond to the demands of the first three of the social movements you have identified.
3 Examine the constraints of those in power to make the change that is demanded by the social movements you have chosen.

References and further reading

REFERENCES

Biyanwila, J 2009, *Trade Unions in the Global South: Trade Unions in Sri Lanka*, Routledge, London.

Brown, M, Ray, R, Summers, E & Fraistat, N 2017, '#SayHerName: a case study of intersectional social media activism', *Ethnic and Racial Studies*, 40(11), 1831–46.

Byrne, M 2016, 'Social movements', in J Arvanitakis (ed.), *Sociologic: Analysing Everyday Life and Culture*, Oxford University Press, Melbourne.

Crenshaw, K 1991, 'Mapping the margins: intersectionality, identity politics and violence against women of color', *Stanford Law Review*, 43(6), 1241–99.

Curthoys, A 2002, *Freedom Ride: A Freedom Rider Remembers*, Allen & Unwin, Sydney.

De Sousa Santos, B 2007, *Another Knowledge is Possible: Beyond Northern Epistemologies*, Verso, London.

Doherty, B 2016, 'Revealed: the systemic exploitation of migrant workers in Australia', *The Guardian*, 29 October: <www.theguardian.com/australia-news/2016/oct/29/revealed-the-systemic-exploitation-of-migrant-workers-in-australia>.

Dondoli, G 2015, 'LGBTI activism influencing foreign legislation', *Melbourne Journal of International Law*, 16, 124–59.

Foley, G, Schaap, A & Howell, S 2013, *The Aboriginal Tent Embassy: Sovereignty, Black Power, Land Rights and the State*, Routledge, London.

Fraser, N 1997, *Justice Interruptus: Social Justice in the Post-Socialist Age*, Routledge, London.

Gurung, P 2020, 'Our lives, our story: the journey of the voiceless towards advocacy in Nepal', in K Soldatic & K Johnson (eds), *Global Perspectives on Disability Activism and Advocacy: Our Way*, Routledge, London, pp. 145–60.

Griffin, P 2019, '#MeToo, white feminism and taking everyday politics seriously in the global political economy', *Australian Journal of Political Science*, 54(4), 556–72.

Harris, A 2018, 'She founded me too. Now she wants to move past the trauma', *The New York Times*, 15 October: <www.nytimes.com/2018/10/15/arts/tarana-burke-metoo-anniversary.html>.

Hodgson, M 2011, 'Lingiari's Legacy: from little things big things grow', *ABC News*, 26 August: <www.abc.net.au/news/2011-08-26/hodgson-from-little-things-big-things-grow/2855942>.

Human Rights and Equal Opportunity Commission (HREOC) 2020, 'Case studies: complaints about Australia to the Human Rights Committee', HREOC, Sydney: <www.humanrights.gov.au/our-work/education/human-rights-explained-case-studies-complaints-about-australia-human-rights>.

Ife, J 2016, *Rethinking Human Rights in the 21st Century: The Sir John Quick Lecture*, La Trobe University Lecture Series: <www.latrobe.edu.au/__data/assets/pdf_file/0007/764746/Jim-Ife-Sir-John-Quick-Bendigo-lecture.pdf>.

Keck, M & Sikkink, K 1998, *Activists Beyond Borders*, Cornell University Press, Ithaca.

Khadem, N 2020, 'How a universal basic income could help 25 million workers at threat from coronavirus', *ABC News*, 20 March: <www.abc.net.au/news/2020-03-20/universal-basic-income-reverse-taxation-workers-coronavirus/12075260>.

Lindsey, D 2017, 'A beginners guide to activism: 10 ways to get involved with issues that matter', *The Every Girl*, 7 February: <https://theeverygirl.com/a-beginners-guide-to-activism-10-ways-to-get-involved-with-issues-that-matter/>.

Martin, G 2015, *Understanding Social Movements*, Routledge, London.

Me Too 2020, 'History and vision', *Me Too Movement*: <https://metoomvmt.org/about/>.

Meakins, F 2016, 'The untold story behind the 1966 Wave Hill Walk-Off', *ABC News*, 20 August: <www.abc.net.au/news/2016-08-19/the-untold-story-being-the-1966-wave-hill-walk-off/7764524>.

Mohanty, CP 2003, *Feminism without Borders: Decolonizing Theory, Practicing Solidarity*, Duke University Press, Durham, NC.

Moreton-Robinson, A 2000, *Talkin' Up to the White Woman*, University of Queensland Press, Queensland.

Oxfam 2020, *Dignity Not Destitution,* Oxfam International, Oxford: <www.oxfam.org.au/wp-content/uploads/2020/04/Oxfam-Dignity-not-Destitution.pdf>.

Parranas, R 2015, *Servants of Globalisation: Migration and Domestic Work*, Stanford University Press, Stanford.

Power, S 2015, 'How to make sure your partner is your next-of-kin: until marriage equality happens, the story of a gay man who was denied his rights as next-of-kin for his deceased partner should come as no surprise', *Star Observer*, November 10: <www.starobserver.com.au/news/national-news/tasmania/how-to-make-sure-your-partner-is-your-next-of-kin/142684>.

Richter, Z 2020, 'Queer-crip.blog: a virtual ethnographic comparison of social media movement-building techniques used by queer and disabled activists', in K Soldatic & K Johnson (eds), *Global Perspectives on Disability Activism and Advocacy: Our Way*, Routledge, London, pp. 193–202.

Soldatic, K 2016, 'Silent tears: violence, gender and disability', *Global Disability Watch*, 16(16): <globaldisability.org/2016/03/16/silent-tears-project-violence-gender-disability>.

Soldatic, K 2018, 'Policy mobilities of exclusion: implications of Australian disability pension retraction for Indigenous Australians', *Social Policy and Society*, 17(1), 151–67.

Soldatic, K & Johnson, K (eds) 2020, *Global Perspectives on Disability Activism and Advocacy: Our Way*, Routledge, London.

Stanley, T (ed.) 2015, *Religion after Secularisation in Australia*, Palgrave Macmillan, Basingstoke, UK.

Sur, M 2019, 'The CAA will un-make India by poisoning relationships of trust, affinity across religions', *The Wire*, December 26: <https://thewire.in/communalism/citizenship-amendment-act-trust-religion-india>.

Touraine, A 2002, 'The importance of social movements', *Social Movement Studies*, 1(1), 89–95.

Twenty10 2019, Joint LGBTIQ+ Community Statement in Support of Religious Discrimination Protections: <www.twenty10.org.au/joint-statement-on-religious-discrimination-bill-and-lgbtiq-equality/>.

United Nation n.d., *Convention on the Rights of Persons with Disabilities (CRPD)*: <www.un.org/development/desa/disabilities/convention-on-the-rights-of-persons-with-disabilities.html>.

Walters, M 2010, 'Market forces and Indigenous resistance paradigms', *Social Movement Studies*, 9(2), 121–37.

FURTHER READING

Pro Bono Australia 2017, 'WA NDIS trial evaluation slammed', Pro Bono Australia: <https://probonoaustralia.com.au/news/2017/03/wa-ndis-trial-evaluation-slammed/>.

PART 3

Social issues

CHAPTER 16

Indigenous Australia

NIKKI MOODIE

CHAPTER OVERVIEW

This chapter places the contemporary challenges facing Aboriginal and Torres Strait Islander peoples (referred to collectively as Indigenous peoples) in a global and historical context. The issues facing Indigenous peoples in Australia are similar to the issues faced by First Nations peoples around the world. The history of imperialism, civil and human rights, policy and politics are drawn together, and some explanations are given for why indigenous[1] people continue to have poorer health and economic outcomes globally.

In order to address the structural causes of inequality, it is necessary to interrogate and critique many of the taken-for-granted assumptions about how we put our world together—something this book has challenged you to do from the very start.

Ideas such as race (which we discussed in Chapter 9) are deeply embedded in our everyday life. As such, improving life expectancy or educational outcomes for Indigenous peoples cannot take place without understanding how those ideas are reproduced in the systems and institutions we work with every day.

It is important to note that while many of the insights and arguments presented here apply to First Nations people globally, there is huge diversity in the ways that Aboriginal and Torres Strait Islander peoples in Australia have experienced invasion. The experiences of people along the eastern seaboard bear both similarities and differences to those people in the south, west, north and centre of Australia. This chapter cannot do justice to the diversity and complexity of those experiences, but it will introduce some strategies you can use to think sociologically about those histories, experiences and futures.

It is also important to note that this chapter is not an introduction to Aboriginal and Torres Strait Islander *cultures*. That is not sociology. This chapter is an exploration of how the society we live in understands Indigenous people and issues, and why Indigenous people's own understanding of their own issues is often ignored.

1   You might sometimes see that the word 'Indigenous' has a capital 'I' and sometimes a lower case 'i' is used. It can be confusing! When you are referring to a specific group of people—whether you use the phrases 'Indigenous Australians', 'Aboriginal and Torres Strait Islander people' or 'First Nations'—these are proper nouns and should always be capitalised. Sometimes though it is acceptable to use the word 'indigenous' as an adjective to describe very general things, like 'the global indigenous rights movement'. You should always try to check what is appropriate in your local area and try to notice how organisations like the United Nations and local Aboriginal Land Councils use these conventions.

After reading this chapter, you should be able to:
- Explain how to use the words 'Aboriginal', 'Torres Strait Islander' and 'Indigenous'
- Describe how Aboriginal and Torres Strait Islander histories are Australian histories, and identify key events relevant to Indigenous and non-Indigenous Australians
- Explain how Australia has always been part of a global, interconnected world long before 'globalisation' became a common term in the twentieth century
- Describe the political relationship between First Australians and Europeans
- Critique contemporary systems that reproduce racist ideas about Australia's Indigenous peoples.

KEY TERMS

Aboriginal and Torres Strait Islander peoples A collective name for the First Peoples of Australia and their descendants. While this phrase can't include the diversity of languages, cultural practices and spiritual beliefs of Australia's First Peoples, it is preferred over 'Indigenous'. In this chapter you will see that 'Aboriginal and Torres Strait Islander' and 'Indigenous' are used interchangeably.

Closing the Gap An Australian Government policy and dominant political narrative in Australian Indigenous affairs.

First Peoples A broad, collective term describing the indigenous peoples of an area. Depending on the country, phrases such as 'First Peoples' and 'First Nations' can have specific meanings (for example, in Canada).

Indigeneity A term historically used to distinguish the identity of people who are 'native' from people who are 'other'. It is often more useful to explore what aspects of 'indigeneity' are being portrayed as important and relevant, by whom, and in what contexts.

Indigenous Any ethnic group originating and surviving in an area subject to colonisation. A lower-case 'i' is used when writing about general issues, such as 'the global indigenous rights movement'.

Land rights The struggle for legal recognition of Indigenous ownership of land and resources. Land rights might be granted through a claim process that then awards freehold title to an Aboriginal Land Council, for example.

Native title A type of property right recognised in Australian law that attempts to recognise the rights and interests of Aboriginal and Torres Strait Islander peoples. Native title does not grant ownership or freehold title and is the weakest form of title in common law.

Reconciliation 'Coming together' and improving the relationship between Australia's First Peoples and non-Indigenous Australians, based on recognising the ongoing impact of colonisation.

Self-determination A collective right of a people to freely decide their own political status and pursue their own economic, social and cultural development.

Whiteness The theory that there is significant power and privilege associated with being White, and that much of this privilege stems from whiteness being portrayed as 'normal'.

Introduction

The story of human civilisations can often be told as a history of warfare, colonisation and genocide. From Genghis Khan to Rwanda, the Holocaust to Bosnia and the Cambodian Killing Fields, we know that groups of humans have committed extraordinary acts of violence as a result of ideology or the desire for resources.

Just like people, nations are often born in bloodshed: the French Revolution, the American Civil War, Israel and East Timor are all examples of how nations often emerge from wars, or resistance to conquest and imperial rule. But when it comes to Australia, we are often told a different story. Somehow it seems as though our country has tried to separate itself from the global story of imperialism and conflict.

This chapter introduces a different history of Australia. Just like France, Israel, East Timor and the United States, there is a history of colonisation and warfare, but there is also a story of tremendous human resilience, friendship, and a commitment to addressing the injustices of the past through the recognition of human rights.

Moving beyond many negative dimensions of our society—including racism and inequality—requires that we not only understand history from different perspectives, but also that we understand how the society we live in reproduces inequality and makes it all seem 'normal'. Dominant cultures within colonial societies possess what French theorist Pierre Bourdieu (1989) calls a *'worldmaking power'*; that is, the ability to create and define who is included within a group, and who is excluded. This enables dominant cultures to measure, exclude, restrict and control on the basis of those definitions (all dimensions of 'power' are discussed in Chapter 8).

Chapter 9 of this book explored how race is a *social construct.* The present chapter builds on that understanding and explores how ideas of race are used by colonial powers to define, measure, and control **indigenous** peoples. In the contemporary world, this leads to policies, programs and funding based on ideas about indigenous people that have little to do with how indigenous people understand themselves.

In a fundamental way, achieving change requires undoing white definitions and categories of **'indigeneity'** (that is, of what it means to be Indigenous), and creating opportunities and partnerships with Indigenous people in order to achieve a more relevant and accurate representation in our world.

Who are Aboriginal Australians?

Before 1788, there were approximately 260 different language groups and 500 dialects spoken across Australia. Instead of 'one' Aboriginal Australia, it is more accurate to think of these groups as nations, as different to each other as Germany, France and Spain.

Aboriginal and Torres Strait Islander people tend not to refer to themselves as 'Indigenous' or 'Aboriginal', but rather as Wiradjuri, Yorta Yorta or Bigambul, for example. Moreover,

Indigenous people tend not to focus on skin colour or 'blood quantum'. The history, traditions and languages of your family—where you come from—is more important than the colour of your skin. Australia's **First Peoples** did not come up with the words 'Indigenous' or 'Aboriginal': these are imposed colonial descriptions that do not respect or adequately describe the diversity of Australia's First Nations. It is like saying 'Europeans'—think how different the cultural practices and identities of the Norwegians and the Italians are.

It is a common misconception that most Indigenous people live in remote areas and not in urban centres. Table 16.1 shows that most Aboriginal and Torres Strait Islander people in Australia live in the states of New South Wales and Queensland.

TABLE 16.1 Where do Aboriginal and Torres Strait Islander people live?

State or territory	Number of Indigenous people	Proportion of national Indigenous population living in state or territory (%)	Indigenous proportion of state or territory population (%)
New South Wales	265,685	33.3	3.4
Queensland	221,276	27.7	4.6
Western Australia	100,512	12.6	3.9
Northern Territory	74,546	9.3	30.3
Victoria	57,767	7.2	0.9
South Australia	42,265	5.3	2.5
Tasmania	28,537	3.6	5.5
ACT	7,513	0.9	1.9
Australia	798,365	**100**	3.3

Source: Adapted from ABS 2018

Contact

On 18 January 1788, the First Fleet arrived in Botany Bay. Although initial interactions between the Gadigal people of the Eora nation and the Europeans were diplomatic, resistance against the British began quickly. Governor Phillip was under instruction to establish friendly relationships with the first Australians, but the British seizure of land and resources made this difficult. The new colony was facing a food shortage, crop failures and the Aboriginal population who had little choice but to resist the occupation of their lands. Fifteen months after the First Fleet arrived, a smallpox epidemic swept through the Gadigal who had no immunity to such a virus. It is estimated that somewhere between 50 and 70 per cent of the local Aboriginal population died as a result of the introduced disease.

BOX 16.1

Sociology in history

AUSTRALIA'S INDIGENOUS PEOPLES—A DOCUMENTARY INTRODUCTION

The following two documentaries give a great introduction to the history of Australia's Indigenous peoples—before contact with Europeans (*First Footprints*) and after (*First Australians*):

- *First Footprints*: <www.abc.net.au/tv/firstfootprints>
- *First Australians*: <www.sbs.com.au/firstaustralians>

It is this year, 1788, when Australian history begins for many people. The truth is, however, that Aboriginal people have been living in Australia for at least 50,000 years and the movement of ideas, people and goods was well established before the Europeans arrived. Sites such as Cuddie Springs and Lake Mungo in New South Wales, Kow Swamp in Victoria, Camooweal in Queensland, Maxwell River in Tasmania, Malarrak in the Wellington Ranges in the Northern Territory, and Djadjiling in the Pilbara in Western Australia all contain evidence of complex Aboriginal societies existing for millennia prior to European arrival.

The British need for new penal colonies following the loss of territory in the American Revolutionary War (1775–83) is only one part of our history—a history that is long, complex and should be understood in the global context.

BOX 16.2

Sociology in history

A GLOBAL CONTEXT

As people move, they bring their cultures with them: their religions and art, their diseases and weapons. This section explores the effect of global history on Aboriginal people in Australia, comparing this with other indigenous peoples from around the world.

Following the period of Spanish and Portuguese imperial expansion in the fifteenth and sixteenth centuries, great levels of wealth were extracted from Africa and the Americas and the Atlantic slave trade began. The English, French and Dutch expanded their military operations and slavery practices throughout Asia, Africa and the Americas. Waves of colonial expansion radiated out from Europe well into the twentieth century.

The English, with their superior naval power and focus on banking and finance, established colonies in every continent. At its height in the 1920s, the British Empire was the largest single empire the world had ever seen: it covered one fifth of the planet, with more than one quarter of the world's population under its control.

As the Europeans spread their empires, they brought their diseases with them. Smallpox, measles and influenza hit people who had never been affected by these viruses. The consequences were devastating for populations around the world.

It is estimated that up 90 per cent of indigenous populations in North and Central America died as a result of introduced diseases (Lovell 1992). This spread of disease cannot be underestimated in the devastation of Aboriginal populations and the effects of ill-health and poor treatment continue across generations to this day.

In each part of the world colonised by the Europeans, different strategies, technologies, diseases and motivations were at play: the enslavement of African people on the tobacco and cotton farms of the Americas; the military conquests and economic power of the British in India; the transport of convicts to America and Australia; and the role of missionaries and Christian churches in Africa and Asia.

The unique history of each part of the world— including the specific traditions and cultures of indigenous peoples, together with the different imperial tactics used by the Europeans—have combined to shape our contemporary world. More so, this history has also shaped the contemporary experiences of indigenous peoples.

Despite the massive decolonisation and withdrawal of many colonial nations after the Second World War, the effects of European empires are still in effect today, and the impact of the violence of colonialism can still be seen in contemporary societies. While there is much diversity in the experiences of indigenous peoples globally, there are also dramatic similarities. These include:

- *The spread of diseases*: These accounted for massive and rapid depopulation among indigenous peoples.
- *The seizure of land by colonial forces*: This meant fewer natural resources for indigenous people to use, resulting in less access to food and water, traditional medicines and healing practices, and the loss of ceremonial practices that supported environmental, physical and spiritual wellbeing.
- *Massacres and conflict*: Many people have heard of the Battle of Little Bighorn in the Great Sioux War of 1876 between an alliance of Lakota and Cheyenne against George Custer and the United States 7th Cavalry. However, few have heard of the Australian Frontier Wars—the Black War (Tasmania, 1823–34), massacres at Coniston Station (Northern Territory, 1928), Convincing Ground (Victoria, 1833–4) and Myall Creek (New South Wales, 1838) are only a very few of the well-documented episodes (Tatz 2011).
- *Forced relocations*: Missions, reserves and other institutions such as boarding schools were created, and indigenous peoples were forced or coerced to leave their nations, with children often removed from their families— practices that remained common in Canada, the United States and Australia well into the twentieth century.

The History Wars: 'It wasn't me'

Before Prime Minister Kevin Rudd delivered the Apology to the Stolen Generations in 2008, one of the things that **Aboriginal and Torres Strait Islander peoples** often heard was that they should 'get over it'. Even years after the Apology, that phrase is still heard in popular culture and the media (McQuire 2014).

The usual argument is simple: any injustices happened so long ago and anyway, things can't have been that bad (Windschuttle 2003). So let's move forward.

In the 1980s and 90s, the phrase *'black armband view of history'* emerged. This phrase represents a conflict between historians, politicians, activists and the general public about how Australian history is represented.

The colonial perspective asks us to celebrate Australia's European heritage and disputes the severity of colonisation and dispossession. On the other side, Indigenous people and many eminent historians question the narrative of Australia that focuses just on our achievements and obscures the scale of injustices of the past.

Nationalism and pride

Australians have a lot of pride in the Australian nation: we see that on the sporting field and in national celebrations. There is also a need, then, to understand the patriotism and pride that Aboriginal and Torres Strait Islander people have in Australia: Aboriginal people have served in every military conflict Australia has been a part of since the Boer War (1899–1902), despite being officially banned from enlisting. Indeed, it was not until 1992 that discriminatory clauses against Aboriginal servicemen and women were removed from the *Defence Act 1903* (Riseman 2013). The story of Aboriginal men and women serving in the Australian defence forces both in Australia and internationally paints a picture that is more complex than the History Wars—which create an 'us vs them' narrative—would allow us to have.

The issue is not whether people are ashamed or proud of events in our past. If we are told stories and histories that previously were not shared, and we are given the opportunity to learn, we are then given opportunity to change. Women, immigrants and refugees, people from non-White and non-European backgrounds, and even environmental history have all played a role in shaping Australia and can help us understand who we are today. Unfortunately, these perspectives are often not prominent in the history books.

In 2014, Professor Lyndall Ryan and Dr Jonathan Richards began work on a project called 'Violence on the Australian Colonial Frontier, 1788–1960'. Their research has led to the first online interactive map documenting massacres across continental Australia, Tasmania and the Torres Strait: <https://c21ch.newcastle.edu.au/colonialmassacres>. In a rare move for Australian media, *The Guardian* has developed an investigative series called 'The Killing Times' to continue reporting on and adding to the Massacre Map: <www.theguardian.com/australia-news/series/the-killing-times>. For the first time, Australian and international audiences have access to rigorous and sensitive information about the violence of our colonial frontier.

The issue is no longer verifying what happened, but rather acknowledging that the 'History Wars' and the 'black armband view of history' speak to a deeper anxiety: How do we remember trauma and injustice, and what do we do about it today? Other nations around the world have responded to these challenges by having treaties and truth-telling commissions, but Australia finds it difficult to find a way forward on these issues.

Government policy

Part of the process of **reconciliation** involves recognising the effects of past government policies on Indigenous people: understanding both the strengths and weaknesses and how we should respond.

Table 16.2 provides a brief overview of the stages of government policy and a short discussion of the assumptions that underpin these policies. Unfortunately, these policies often demonstrate a cyclical approach to Indigenous affairs. One of the problems is the underlying idea about Indigenous people needing 'protection'—something that has not changed much. This is the case even if the language used by current governments might initially look different to what was used in the past. Australian Government policy often resists the idea that Indigenous people are capable of taking care of their own affairs.

TABLE 16.2 Stages of Indigenous policy

Policy	When	Effects
Protection	1780–1937	Underpinned by the science of eugenics, the assumption of colonial authorities was that Aboriginal and Torres Strait Islander people were an inferior race and they would 'die out'.
		This is the period of the Australian Frontier Wars and the Protection Acts that enabled governments to control where Indigenous people lived, worked, who they married and if they could keep the money they worked for.
Assimilation	1937–65	When it became apparent to governments that Aboriginal people were not 'dying out', the next phase was to require Aboriginal people to adopt the same manner of living, beliefs and cultural practices as white Australians. The policy was put into practice by removing Aboriginal children from their families and preventing family contact, the use of language, and ceremonial practices. This policy created the Stolen Generations.
Integration	1965–72	This policy recognised the right to cultural autonomy.
		Here began programs that recognised Aboriginal and Torres Strait Islander people's right to maintain languages, cultural practices and communities.
		This period saw the 1967 Referendum amend sections of the Australian Constitution.
Self-determination	1972–2005	Influenced by the Civil Rights Movement in the United States, **self-determination** is about the internationally recognised rights of Indigenous peoples to determine their own futures. It is about how Indigenous people have the right to a distinct culture and the right to decide how best to tackle the issues that face them.
		This period saw the recognition of **land rights**, **Native Title** legislation and the idea of reconciliation.
		The Aboriginal and Torres Strait Islander Commission (ATSIC) was created to give Indigenous people political representatives and a voice in how funding and services were allocated.
Normalisation	2005–	This period saw the abolition of ATSIC, the introduction of the Northern Territory Emergency Response (The Intervention) and the Stronger Futures legislation. Australia (along with the United States, Canada and New Zealand) voted against the United Nations Declaration on the Rights of Indigenous Peoples (though Australia later signed the Declaration in 2009). Despite significant movements like the Uluru Statement and Recognise, political opposition to constitutional recognition and treaty processes continues at a Commonwealth level.

Source: Adapted from ALRC 1986; Sullivan 2011

Aboriginal and Torres Strait Islander activism

By the 1960s, events in Australia and around the world brought the political, economic and social position of Indigenous people to the public's attention. The civil rights movement in the United States, the role of Australia in the creation of the United Nations, and the activism of Aboriginal people combined to influence public opinion and politicians to recognise that government policies (see Table 16.2) were still enforcing discrimination against Indigenous people and contributing to poverty and exclusion.

Aboriginal activism and resistance is as old as colonisation in Australia, but throughout the twentieth century several key events influenced public understanding of the issues Indigenous people faced:

- *26 January 1938*: The first Day of Mourning was held on the 150th anniversary of the landing of the First Fleet. Some 100 Aboriginal people gathered at Australian Hall in Sydney in one of the first public civil rights events to protest invasion, dispossession and discrimination.
- *6 December 1938*: Following *Kristallnacht* (the Night of the Broken Glass in Nazi Germany), Yorta Yorta elder William Cooper delivered a petition to the German consulate in Melbourne condemning the Nazis' treatment of the Jews. Cooper's protest came years before the Australian Government condemned the atrocity.
- *1946 Pilbara Strike*: Nearly 800 Aboriginal pastoral workers went on strike across Western Australia, protesting against being paid only in rations and having their movements limited. The strike paralysed the sheep industry for three years.
- *1963 Yirrkala Bark Petitions*: The Yolngu people protested against bauxite mining on their land by sending the first petitions prepared by Aboriginal people that included both Yolngu Matha writing as well as the English text that was required in order for them to be recognised by Parliament.
- *1965 Freedom Rides*: Inspired by the Freedom Rides in the United States, Charlie Perkins, the first Aboriginal university graduate, led a bus tour through central and western New South Wales to investigate segregation and living conditions for Aboriginal people.
- *1966 Gurindji Strike and Wave Hill walk-off*: Vincent Lingiari led 200 Aboriginal workers in a strike against low wages and poor working conditions. The strike grew into a call for land rights and lasted seven years, eventually culminating in the *Aboriginal Land Rights (Northern Territory) Act 1976*.

The 1967 Referendum

By 1967, the momentum for change in the relationship between Indigenous and non-Indigenous Australians was gathering pace. The Australian Government, increasingly embarrassed on the international stage by its discrimination against Indigenous people, moved to hold a referendum to change sections of the Constitution that discriminated against Aboriginal people.

The 1967 Referendum saw the highest 'Yes' vote of any referendum in Australia's history, with nearly 91 per cent of Australians in support of constitutional change recognising Aboriginal people (see Table 16.3). It is interesting to note, however, that the 'No' vote was the largest in the three states with the largest Aboriginal populations at that time. In New South Wales, the 'No' vote was largest in rural and regional areas where racial issues were most prominent (Gardiner-Garden 1997).

There were two other notable things about the 1967 Referendum: the first is the way it seized the public imagination; and second is the power it gave to the Commonwealth Government.

TABLE 16.3 The 'Yes' vote

Jurisdiction	Yes vote
Victoria	94.68%
New South Wales	91.46%
Tasmania	90.21%
Queensland	89.21%
South Australia	86.26%
Western Australia	80.95%
National	90.77%

Source: Gardiner-Garden 1997

BOX 16.3

Sociology in history

WHAT WAS HAPPENING IN THE WORLD IN 1967?

- The United States Supreme Court declares that all laws that prohibit interracial marriage are unconstitutional.
- Thurgood Marshall is confirmed as the first African-American Justice of the United States Supreme Court.
- Edward W Brooke III is the first African American elected to the United States Senate.
- The British Parliament decriminalises homosexuality.
- Apartheid has been in effect in South Africa for 20 years.

Aboriginal voting rights

The 1967 Referendum was and is an important part of our national identity. Such events hold a powerful place in our national psyche and record our overwhelming public support for Aboriginal civil rights. The recognition of Aboriginal and Torres Strait Islander people by governments and non-Indigenous Australians is an important part of acknowledging how Aboriginal people have been excluded and discriminated against since contact. The 1967 Referendum speaks to the healing power of recognition, equality and justice. Interestingly, a 'No' campaign was never developed for the 1967 Referendum, and the 'Yes' campaign of all political parties and Aboriginal organisations focused on the idea of rights and citizenship.

Many people—Aboriginal, Torres Strait Islander and non-Indigenous—believe that the 1967 Referendum gave Indigenous people the vote. In fact, it dealt with the seemingly more mundane issues of counting Aboriginal people in the Census, and Commonwealth Government legislative responsibilities. The truth is that Aboriginal people technically had the right to vote in all elections since 1965, but this right was not widely supported or publicised, and compulsory voting was not introduced for Aboriginal people until 1984.

> **Critical reflection**
>
> As noted, many Australians think the 1967 Referendum gave Indigenous Australians the right to vote. This is just one of many common historical errors about Aboriginal history. Do you think such confusion is problematic?

Finding the 'gap'

What is the significance of the 1967 Referendum for us today? First, the Referendum ushered in a new era of 'positive discrimination'. The Commonwealth Government was able to make policies that states wouldn't or couldn't, was able to give payments to the states for Aboriginal programs in health and education, enact land rights legislation, and create the Department of Aboriginal Affairs (in 1972). Second, the Census enabled the collection of accurate data about Indigenous people for the first time. In theory, more accurate data should lead to more effective policies and programs for people who need them.

BOX 16.4

Everyday sociology

WHY IS THE CENSUS SO IMPORTANT?

In Australia, the Census is carried out every five years. Its goal is to accurately measure the number of people in the country on Census Night. The Census gives governments, businesses and other organisations (such as not-for-profit and welfare groups) a good estimate of Australia's population so that services can be provided where they are needed. The Commonwealth Government also uses Census data to distribute funding to the states and territories, and the Australian Electoral Commission uses the data to determine electoral boundaries and estimate the number of eligible voters. The Census also provides important data on employment, housing, internet access, public transport usage and volunteering, among many other topics.

When the 1967 Referendum allowed the Census to include Aboriginal people, it meant that rigorous, longitudinal data about Indigenous Australia came into being for the first time. In a sense, Indigenous people became 'visible' to the people who rely on this data to do their jobs. Consequently, the 'gap' between Indigenous and non-Indigenous Australians also became visible. The differences in life expectancy, infant mortality rates and educational outcomes between

Indigenous and non-Indigenous Australians were no longer hidden in the administrative records of schools and hospitals, or ignored because Indigenous people weren't seen as having rights.

The gap became official. (We will discuss 'closing' the gap later in this chapter.)

Blood fetish

One of the side-effects of counting people is that you need a definition of what to count. We can count 'houses', but it is much more useful to count separate houses, semi-detached houses, terraced houses, apartments, caravans, houseboats, and flats attached to shops. Similarly, it is one thing to count the number of people who are religious, but it is much more interesting to know how many people are Protestant, Buddhist, Catholic, Hindu, Jewish or Muslim. So in order to count Indigenous people in Australia, governments needed to come up with a definition of who exactly was being counted: Who, exactly, is Indigenous?

Before 1967, an 'Aboriginal' was defined by blood quantum: a genealogical technique based on determining your 'level' of indigeneity according to how many generations you are removed from supposedly 'full blood' Indigenous forebears. Language such as 'half-caste' was enshrined in legislation and each state had a Protection Act that defined who was an Aboriginal person on the basis of how much 'pure blood' they had.

In the United States, language such as 'quadroon' and 'octoroon' was used to describe the racial heritage of African Americans, and percentages are still used today to determine membership of some Native American tribal nations.

In Australia, the eighteenth-century Protection Acts created different laws for Aboriginal people on the basis of blood quantum: so-called 'half-caste' children were removed from their parents, and the science of eugenics underpinned the assimilationist agenda of people such as the Western Australian Chief Protector of Aborigines, AO Neville, whose goal was to 'breed out the colour':

> Are we going to have a population of 1,000,000 blacks in the Commonwealth, or are we going to merge them into our white community and eventually forget that there ever were any aborigines in Australia? (Commonwealth of Australia 1937, p.11)

Developed at the time of the White Australia Policy, the Protection Acts formalised a national concern with racial purity, skin colour and blood quantum. The Acts restricted the movement of Aboriginal people and imposed curfews. They defined where Indigenous people could live, to whom and when they could marry, who could raise their own children, and what language they could speak; in short, every aspect of Indigenous peoples' lives was monitored, controlled and restricted.

Moreover, the Protector in each state had the power to exempt people from the Act and issue Certificates of Exemption (Blake 2001, p. 136). Exemption Certificates meant that an Aboriginal person would no longer be restricted by the Act, but it also meant that they would no longer legally be considered Aboriginal.

A complex history of defining who is Aboriginal

In a long history of attempts to define who is and who is not Aboriginal, researchers have found no fewer than 67 separate definitions, classifications or descriptions of Aboriginality that have been used by government since 1788 (McCorquodale 1986).

From Federation in 1901 until the 1967 Referendum, Aboriginal people were identified in the Australian Census through a question on people's 'race', and people identifying as 'half-caste' or 'full-blood' were then deducted from the population estimate. The 1971 Census included a question on 'racial origin' and Aboriginal people were officially included in estimates of the Australian population for the first time. By 1981 the question had evolved to 'Is the person of Aboriginal or Torres Strait Islander origin?', and from 1996, people of Aboriginal and Torres Strait Islander origin could indicate both.

Since 1981, indigeneity in Australia has been determined by what is known colloquially as the 'three-part test' (Gardiner-Garden 2000). The Commonwealth Department of Aboriginal Affairs (1981) suggested that:

An Aboriginal or Torres Strait Islander is a person:

- … of Aboriginal or Torres Strait Islander descent
- … who identifies as an Aboriginal or Torres Strait Islander
- … and is accepted as such by the community in which he (she) lives.

This definition is now used to determine eligibility for services (such as housing assistance or scholarships), and often needs to be formalised in a Certificate of Aboriginality or letter from an incorporated Indigenous organisation and stamped with the organisation's common seal (AIATSIS, n.d.).

It is important to note that no other ethnic or cultural group in Australia is required to meet criteria such as these, or to provide any similar documentation apart from birth certificates or passports.

So what's the problem?

So if we have a definition of who is Indigenous, what's the problem? There are a number of issues with the three-part test.

The issue of descent can be difficult to prove, and still relies on ideas of 'blood' or genetic descent. There are numerous barriers to using DNA or genetics to prove indigeneity (de Plevitz & Croft 2003), quite apart from the ethical and historical considerations that arise from using scientific methods to determine 'racial purity'.

Self-identification is the least problematic part of the test as it is the primary way in which all people decide if they belong to a group or not. We believe that individuals should be free to determine for themselves whether they are members of subcultures, families, cultural or religious groups. Community acceptance allows a group of people to determine who is in the group and who is not; this is usually quite robust because individuals and families know who their members are. However, given the high rate of child removals during the Stolen Generations and the prohibitions on family contact, it is possible for an individual to be of Aboriginal descent but not self-identify or be a part of an Aboriginal community.

To add to these complexities, ideas of racial purity, or financial and social assistance for Indigenous people, are frequently debated in public discourse. The High Court determination in the 2001 case of *Eatock v Bolt* found that journalist Andrew Bolt had violated the *Racial Discrimination Act 1975* by alleging that:

- there are fair-skinned people in Australia with essentially European ancestry but with some Aboriginal descent, of which the individuals identified in the articles are examples, who are not genuinely Aboriginal persons but who, motivated by career opportunities available to Aboriginal people or by political activism, have chosen to falsely identify as Aboriginal; and
- fair skin colour indicates a person who is not sufficiently Aboriginal to be genuinely identifying as an Aboriginal person. (Federal Court of Australia, n.d.)

In his determination, Justice Blomberg stated that Bolt's articles were not written 'reasonably and in good faith' and that fair-skinned Aboriginal people were likely to have been offended or humiliated by the articles:

> because the articles were calculated to convey a message about the race, ethnicity or colour of fair-skinned Aboriginal people, including as to whether those people were sufficiently of Aboriginal race, colour or ethnicity to be identifying as Aboriginal people (Federal Court of Australia, n.d.).

Bolt's allegations demonstrated that ideas of racial purity, skin colour and blood quantum are not relegated to the distant past of Australian colonial history. Increasingly, questioning a person's indigeneity is used to undermine their work or their influence.

Critical race theory and whiteness

One way for us to understand this is through the lens of critical race theory, or **whiteness** (which we looked at in Chapter 9). Critical race theory suggests that individual people need not hold racist beliefs for the idea of race to be an influential force in society. Indeed, this theory suggests that racism is not rare or aberrant, and we should not be surprised when we see it. It is unjust, frightening and harmful, but it is not surprising. Rather, racism should be considered integral to the operation of colonial settler societies (Delgado & Stefancic 2001). Racism isn't right, but it is very normal—especially in places like Australia.

Remember, there is no genetic basis to 'race' because it is a social construction rather than a biological reality (Delgado & Stefancic 2001). Humans have always had ways of categorising themselves; for example, by means of religion, income, literacy or fluency in a particular language. We have often been categorised ourselves and then had our value determined by other dominant groups in society. However, racial categories are a relatively recent invention and emerged only in the eighteenth century, as a result of combining Darwin's ideas on evolution with the imperial and religious ideologies used to justify colonial expansion (again, see Chapter 9).

Indeed, the Human Genome Project demonstrated that there is no genetic basis for the category of 'race', and that noticeable physical variations between human beings—such as height or skin colour—are the result of environmental factors over long periods of time.

Genetic analysis can be used to establish relatedness, but no genetic marker can be identified as belonging to one 'racial group'. In fact, what we now know is that at the DNA level there is more genetic difference between any two individuals within a 'race' than there are group differences between two 'races' (de Plevitz & Croft 2003, p. 11). A DNA test cannot confirm if someone has Aboriginal ancestry.

Despite the absence of a scientific basis for race, it has become a powerful idea, shaping peoples' beliefs about themselves and others, our education and criminal justice systems, health care, media, sport and art.

Who is Indigenous?

If there is no legitimate biological basis for race, then how do we know who is Indigenous and who is not? The United Nations Permanent Forum on Indigenous Issues addressed this by referencing the important social features defining Indigenous peoples. According to the United Nations, a useful working definition states that Indigenous peoples are those who:

- Identify themselves and are recognized and accepted by their community as Indigenous.
- Demonstrate historical continuity with pre-colonial and/or pre-settler societies.
- Have strong links to territories and surrounding natural resources.
- Have distinct social, economic or political systems.
- Maintain distinct languages, cultures and beliefs.
- Form non-dominant groups of society.
- Resolve to maintain and reproduce their ancestral environments and systems as distinctive peoples and communities (Secretariat of the Permanent Forum on Indigenous Issues 2004).

There are indigenous people on every continent, and although specific histories and contemporary issues vary, there are persistent differences in health and economic outcomes between indigenous and non-indigenous people in every colonial settler society. Maternal and infant mortality, malnutrition, cardiovascular disease, suicide rates, malaria, diabetes and mental illness are all higher among indigenous people around the world than among non-indigenous and settler peoples (United Nations 2009).

Indigenous populations constitute approximately 370 million people, or 5 per cent of the world's population, yet make up 15 per cent of the world's poor.

Despite this, Indigenous people maintain strong connections with their traditional lands: not only do Indigenous peoples' territories make up about 22 per cent of the world's land area, those areas hold 80 per cent of the planet's biodiversity (Sobrevilla 2008).

Strategies such as self-determination return important rights to indigenous peoples and support better health outcomes, but also preserve the cultural and biological diversity of the planet. Indigenous rights are a guaranteed way to support ecological restoration and environmental sustainability.

Closing the Gap

This chapter has outlined a history of Australia that includes Aboriginal and Torres Strait Islander people. The effects of this history are experienced today as significantly poorer socio-economic outcomes for Aboriginal and Torres Strait Islander peoples across the country. When health outcomes are compared to non-Indigenous Australians:

- Indigenous children are twice as likely to be of low birth weight;
- Babies born to Indigenous women are twice as likely to die in their first year;
- Diabetes is four times more common, and Indigenous people are seven times more likely to die from the disease;
- Blindness is six times more common; and
- Indigenous Australians are twice as likely to have a profound disability (Australian Indigenous HealthInfoNet 2014).

Recognising this disparity, the Australian Government implemented the **Closing the Gap** policy over a decade ago. With agreement from the states and territories, this policy worked towards achieving a set of targets that would improve life expectancy, mortality rates, education and employment outcomes for Aboriginal and Torres Strait Islander people. Table 16.4 shows the original Closing the Gap targets that were agreed upon in 2009.

TABLE 16.4 2009 Closing the Gap targets

Original Targets
Closing the life expectancy gap within a generation
Halving the gap in mortality rates for Indigenous children under five within a decade
Ensuring all Indigenous four-years-olds in remote communities have access to early childhood education within five years
Halving the gap for Indigenous students in reading, writing and numeracy within a decade
Halving the gap for Indigenous people aged 20–24 in Year 12 attainment or equivalent attainment rates by 2020
Halving the gap in employment outcomes between Indigenous and non-Indigenous Australians within a decade

Source: Adapted from COAG 2009

Whilst there were some small improvements to child mortality and Year 12 completion rates over the decade between 2009 and 2019, progress was slow towards those targets and non-existent for the others. Despite its failure, it is likely that the Closing the Gap policy will be a feature of Indigenous affairs for some time to come. This policy may begin to include some issues that are important to Indigenous people, such as a focus on incarceration or land rights, but it is likely that Indigenous people will continue to be measured against non-Indigenous Australians in ways that aren't useful or culturally relevant for Indigenous people. This shows how the shadow of colonialism continues to hang over Australia's Aboriginal and Torres Strait Islander peoples.

The demography of disadvantage

Closing the Gap is a policy based on achieving statistical equality between Indigenous and non-Indigenous Australians. The focus on measuring how outcomes for Aboriginal and Torres Strait Islander people change (or do not change) over time has received extraordinary attention from governments. But the Census, and governments more broadly, tend not to measure the kinds of things that are important or culturally relevant to Indigenous people. Instead, governments tend to determine an average or a benchmark in their statistical collections, and then Indigenous people are measured according to how far away they are from that benchmark. This is how the 'gap' between Indigenous and non-Indigenous people has become normalised and visible to governments and policy makers.

This has led to what has become known as the *'demography of disadvantage'* (Taylor 2009): the measurement, research, tracking and evaluation of the distance between socio-economic indicators for Indigenous people and everyone else in Australia.

But what is it that is really being measured? The categories used to collect data may not always be relevant in Indigenous contexts. Consider some of Taylor's examples:

- *Age*: The notion of chronological age versus social age means that a person's age in years may not have much to do with their social or cultural obligations, expectations and status. Elders do not have to be older people, and quite young people may assume significant responsibilities in their families and communities.
- *Household size*: The Australian Bureau of Statistics measures household size and composition by the number of people who usually live in a house. Large household sizes, with multiple families and high rates of mobility mean that Aboriginal and Torres Strait Islander households can look very different to the households of other Australians. For example, while a household might eat together, not everyone will sleep in the same house (Smith 1991). Cultural obligations may also change throughout the year, meaning that household size may increase significantly for several months and then reduce at other times.

These two examples of age and household composition demonstrate how definitions and categories imposed by a Eurocentric worldview tend to ignore the social and cultural reality for many Indigenous Australians (or indeed for many cultural or ethnic groups). Policies that are made on the basis of the data collected are, therefore, less likely to be effective because they are not made *by* Indigenous people, *on the basis of data that is important to* Indigenous people. Moreover, the data that is collected tends to simply keep tracking how poor, sick and uneducated Aboriginal and Torres Strait Islander people are—when compared to non-Indigenous people (Pholi, Black & Richards 2009). This in turn continues to reinforce deeply held assumptions about race and indigeneity.

Consider the challenge posed in the critical reflection question below.

Does all this mean we should not collect data on age or change our expectations of educational success for Aboriginal and Torres Strait Islander people? Probably not. But these kinds of ideas allow us to see how the technologies of colonialism (such as 'race' and measurement) are reinvented over time and used on a daily basis to make the experiences and behaviours of Indigenous Australians seem deficient or non-compliant.

The diversity of Indigenous Australia and the distribution of Aboriginal and Torres Strait Islander people around the country have an important impact on the kinds of policies and programs that respect people's rights and that are more likely to improve health and wellbeing. Where communities are able to develop their own programs and strategies, and work in partnership with government, business and non-government organisations (NGOs), health and education outcomes tend to improve.

> **Critical reflection**
>
> How might a primary school take into account a student's responsibilities to her extended family? Are cultural practices acknowledged in institutions such as schools and hospitals?

Conclusion

Policies about Aboriginal and Torres Strait Islander people are superficially concerned with making sure Indigenous people achieve the same standards of health, education and wellbeing as other Australians. On the surface this is an admirable goal, but adopting a sociological approach to Indigenous issues requires that we look a little deeper at why these gaps close so slowly, if at all.

This chapter has suggested that the ways in which indigeneity is defined, and how settler colonial societies globally continue to monitor and track Indigenous people, has little to do with achieving the outcomes that Indigenous people themselves want. Policy making, and the national discourse about Indigenous peoples, tends to be preoccupied with ideas of race, measurement, skin colour and authenticity. This tends to distract from the rights that Indigenous people are entitled to, such as those internationally recognised and enshrined in the United Nations Declaration on the Rights of Indigenous Peoples.

We know that local solutions and partnerships create better relationships between communities, businesses and governments because they require an intimate understanding of the complex social factors that affect people's everyday lives without reducing our understanding to a series of (potentially) culturally irrelevant indicators. This does not mean we should stop collecting data or doing research.

But it does require us to think critically when we collect information ourselves, use data about Indigenous people, or rely on information reported by the media. For example:

- Does the information and data that's available help Indigenous people and organisations make decisions?

- Is the research and data culturally relevant?
- How are people affected by a decision involved in the decision-making process?
- What rights do Indigenous people have?
- Are we working at the direction of Indigenous people?

Asking these kinds of questions challenges the way power usually operates and begins to bring our ideas about race and indigeneity—or even sex, gender, disability or religion—into the open; and these are issues discussed in other chapters of this book (including Chapters 7, 8 and 9). Informed by this thinking, it is possible to see how contemporary societies reproduce historical patterns of control and domination even when individual people may or may not hold racist beliefs.

As Indigenous peoples around the world continue to demonstrate, when people are given the power and resources to make decisions about issues that affect them, the benefits—for health and education outcomes, and environmentally, socially and politically—are clear.

Summary points

- Indigenous Australians remember the history of contact even today. Recognising that this is a shared history, and an integral part of Australia's story, is an important part of changing the effects of colonialism and racism.
- Settler colonial societies reinvent ways of defining and measuring Indigenous people over time. Contemporary non-Indigenous perspectives on indigeneity and authenticity have their origin in eighteenth-century ideas regarding racial purity and blood quantum.
- Australia has only recognised Aboriginal and Torres Strait Islander people by changing the Constitution to define, count and measure them (not to recognise their rights as First People). This has led to an enormous amount of data, but not necessarily the kind of data that is useful or culturally relevant for Indigenous peoples' or their organisations.
- Australian policies such as Closing the Gap tend to be based on non-Indigenous ideas of health and wellbeing. The effectiveness of policies and programs focused on Indigenous wellbeing tends to improve when they are developed and implemented at a local level.
- Focus on Indigenous disadvantage across the world tends to be less effective than focusing on:
  - how dominant systems reproduce racist assumptions about Indigenous people, perspectives and cultures;
  - the strengths and capabilities of local Indigenous communities and organisations.

Sociological reflection

1. How does Australia include (or not include) Indigenous history?
2. If 'race' is a social construction, how has this idea been used to justify colonial expansion?
3. How did the Northern Territory Emergency Response (The Intervention) (2007) differ from the policies of the protection and assimilation eras?
4. How does the impact of disease and warfare at contact impact the health outcomes of Indigenous people today?
5. What is self-determination and how could it work at the local government level?

Discussion questions

1. How do you see Indigenous Australians represented in the media?
2. Will recognising Aboriginal and Torres Strait Islander people in the Australian Constitution lead to greater equality?
3. Many Australians do not know much about Indigenous issues. Whose responsibility is it to educate Australians about our shared history?

Further investigation

1 Can a DNA test reveal if you are an Indigenous Australian? Go to <http://theconversation.com/explainer-can-a-dna-test-reveal-if-youre-an-indigenous-australian-31767>.

2 Go to the Uluru Statement website: <https://ulurustatement.org/>. What kind of political reforms are Indigenous people in Australia asking for?

3 Explore this map of gender-diverse cultures, and discuss the challenges and opportunities involved in recognising different world views: <www.pbs.org/independentlens/two-spirits/map.html>.

References and further reading

REFERENCES

Australian Bureau of Statistics (ABS) 2018, 'Estimates of Aboriginal and Torres Strait Islander Australians, June 2016', *Cat. No. 3238.0.55.001*, ABS, Canberra: <www.abs.gov.au/ausstats/abs@.nsf/mf/3238.0.55.001>.

Australian Indigenous HealthInfoNet 2014, *Summary of Australian Indigenous Health, 2013*: <www.healthinfonet.ecu.edu.au/health-facts/summary>.

Australian Institute of Aboriginal and Torres Strait Islander Studies (AIATSIS) n.d., *Confirmation of Aboriginality*, Australian Institute of Aboriginal and Torres Strait Islander Studies, Canberra: <www.aiatsis.gov.au/fhu/aboriginality.html>.

Australian Law Reform Commission (ALRC) 1986, 'Changing policies towards Aboriginal people', in *Recognition of Aboriginal Customary Laws (ALRC Report 31)*, ALRC, Sydney: <www.alrc.gov.au/publications/3.%20Aboriginal%20Societies%3A%20The%20Experience%20of%20Contact/changing-policies-towards-aboriginal>.

Blake, TW 2001, *A Dumping Ground: The History of the Cherbourg Aboriginal Reserve*, University of Queensland Press, St Lucia.

Bourdieu, P 1989, 'Social space and symbolic power', *Sociological Theory*, 7(1), 14–25.

Commonwealth Department of Aboriginal Affairs 1981, *Report on a Review of the Administration of the Working Definition of Aboriginal and Torres Strait Islanders*, Commonwealth of Australia, Canberra.

Commonwealth of Australia 1937, *Aboriginal Welfare: Initial Conference of Commonwealth and State Aboriginal Authorities, 21–23 April, Canberra*. <www.aiatsis.gov.au/_files/archive/referendum/20663.pdf>.

Council of Australian Governments (COAG) 2009, *National Indigenous Reform Agreement (Closing the Gap)*, COAG, Canberra.

Delgado, R & Stefancic, J 2001, *Critical Race Theory: An Introduction*, New York University Press, New York.

De Plevitz, L & Croft, L 2003, 'Aboriginality under the microscope: the biological descent test in Australian law', *Law and Justice Journal*, 3(1), 105–21.

Federal Court of Australia n.d., *Summaries of Judgments of Interest from 2011–12: Eatock v Bolt [2011] FCA 1103*, Federal Court of Australia, Sydney: <www.fedcourt.gov.au/publications/judgments/judgment-summaries#20111103>.

Gardiner-Garden, J 1997, *The Origin of Commonwealth Involvement in Indigenous Affairs and the 1967 Referendum*, Background Paper 11, 1996–97, Department of the Parliamentary Library, Canberra: <www.aph.gov.au/About_Parliament/Parliamentary_Departments/Parliamentary_Library/Publications_Archive/Background_Papers/bp9697/97bp11>.

Gardiner-Garden, J 2000, *The Definition of Aboriginality: Research Note 18*, Commonwealth of Australia, Canberra: <www.aph.gov.au/library/pubs/rn/2000-01/01rn18.htm>.

Lovell, WG 1992, '"Heavy shadows and black night": disease and depopulation in colonial Spanish America', *Annals of the Association of American Geographers*, 82(3), 426–43.

McCorquodale, J 1986, 'The legal classification of race in Australia', *Aboriginal History*, 10(1), 7–24.

McQuire, A 2014, 'Australia Day: Indigenous people are told to 'get over it'. It's impossible.', *The Guardian*, 27 January: <www.theguardian.com/commentisfree/2014/jan/27/australia-day-indigenous-people-are-told-to-get-over-it-its-impossible>.

Pholi, K, Black, D & Richards, C 2009, 'Is 'Close the Gap' a useful approach to improving the health and wellbeing of Indigenous Australians?', *Australian Review of Public Affairs*, 9(2), 1–14.

Riseman, N 2013, 'Serving their country: a short history of Aboriginal and Torres Strait Islander Service in the Australian Army', *Australian Army Journal*, 10(3), 11–22.

Ryan, L, Pascoe, W, Debenham, J, Gilbert, S, Richards, J, Smith, R, Owen, C, Anders, RJ, Brown, M & Price, D 2019, *Colonial Frontier Massacres in Australia, 1788–1930*, Centre for 21st Century Humanities, Newcastle: <https://c21ch.newcastle.edu.au/colonialmassacres/>.

Secretariat of the Permanent Forum on Indigenous Issues 2004, *The Concept of Indigenous Peoples*, United Nations, New York.

Smith, DE 1991, *Toward an Aboriginal Household Expenditure Survey: Conceptual, Methodological and Cultural Considerations; CAEPR Discussion Paper No 10*, Centre for Aboriginal Economic Policy Research, The Australian National University, Canberra.

Sobrevilla, C 2008, *The Role of Indigenous Peoples in Biodiversity Conservation: The Natural but Often Forgotten Partners*, The International Bank for Reconstruction and Development (World Bank), Washington DC: <http://siteresources.worldbank.org/INTBIODIVERSITY/Resources/RoleofIndigenousPeoplesinBiodiversityConservation.pdf>.

Sullivan, P 2011, *Belonging Together: Dealing with the Politics of Disenchantment in Australian Indigenous Policy*, Aboriginal Studies Press, Canberra.

Tatz, C 2011, 'Genocide in Australia: by accident or design?', *Indigenous Human Rights and History*, 1(1): <www.law.monash.edu/castancentre/research/research-projects/indigenous-human-rights/tatz-essay.pdf>.

Taylor, J 2009, 'Indigenous demography and public policy in Australia: population or peoples?', *Journal of Population Research*, 26(2), 115–30.

The Guardian 2019, *The Killing Times*, Guardian Australia: Sydney: <www.theguardian.com/australia-news/series/the-killing-times>.

United Nations 2009, *State of the World's Indigenous Peoples*, United Nations, New York: <www.un.org/esa/socdev/unpfii/documents/SOWIP/en/SOWIP_web.pdf>.

Windschuttle, K 2003, 'The fabrication of Aboriginal history', *The Sydney Papers*, 15(1), 21–9.

FURTHER READING

Altman, JC & Fogarty, W 2010, 'Indigenous Australians as 'no gaps' subjects: education and development in remote Indigenous Australia', in I Snyder & J Nieuwenhuysen (eds), *Closing the Gap in Education: Improving Outcomes in Southern World Societies*, Monash University Publishing, Clayton, pp. 109–28.

Australian Bureau of Statistics (ABS) 2011, 'Aboriginal and Torres Strait Islander peoples and the Census after the 1967 referendum', *Cat. No 2071.0*, ABS, Canberra: <http://abs.gov.au/ausstats/abs@.nsf/Lookup/2071.0Feature+Article2July+2011>.

Bennett, S 2004, 'The 1967 Aborigines referendum', in *Year Book Australia 2004*, Australian Bureau of Statistics, Canberra.

Carson, B, Dunbar, T, Chenhell, RD & Bailie, R (eds) 2007, *Social Determinants of Indigenous Health*, Allen & Unwin, Crows Nest.

Clark, M & May, SK 2013, *Macassan History and Heritage: Journeys, Encounters and Influences*, ANU E Press, Canberra: <http://press.anu.edu.au/apps/bookworm/view/Macassan+History+and+Heritage/10541/cover.xhtml>.

Dudgeon, P, Milroy, H & Walker, R 2014, *Working Together: Aboriginal and Torres Strait Islander Mental Health and Wellbeing Principles and Practice*, 2nd edn, Commonwealth of Australia, Canberra: <http://aboriginal.telethonkids.org.au/kulunga-research-network/working-together-2nd-edition-%281%29>.

Fox, C 2008, 'The fourteen powers referendum of 1944 and the federalisation of Aboriginal affairs', *Aboriginal History*, 32, 27–48.

Hollinsworth, D 2006, *Race and Racism in Australia*, 3rd edn, Thomson and Social Science Press, Melbourne.

Human Rights and Equal Opportunity Commission (HREOC) 1997, *Bringing Them Home Report: National Inquiry into the Separation of Aboriginal and Torres Strait Islander Children from their Families*, Australian Government Publishing Service, Canberra.

McKenna, M 1997, *Different Perspectives on Black Armband History: Research Paper 5, 1997–1998*, Department of the Parliamentary Library, Canberra: <www.aph.gov.au/library/pubs/rp/1997-98/98rp05.htm>.

Moreton-Robinson, A 2006, 'Towards a new research agenda? Foucault, whiteness and Indigenous sovereignty', *Journal of Sociology*, 42(4), 383–95.

Nakata, M 2007, *Disciplining the Savages: Savaging the Disciplines*, Aboriginal Studies Press, Canberra.

Paradies, Y 2006, 'Beyond black and white: essentialism, hybridity and Indigeneity,' *Journal of Sociology*, 42(4), 355–67.

Pascoe, B 2012, *The Little Red Yellow Black Book: An Introduction to Indigenous Australia*, 3rd edn, Aboriginal Studies Press, Canberra.

Walter, M 2009, 'An economy of poverty? Power and the domain of Aboriginality', *International Journal of Critical Indigenous Studies*, 2(1), 2–14.

Walter, M 2010, 'The politics of the data: how the Australian statistical indigene is constructed', *International Journal of Critical Indigenous Studies*, 3(2), 45–56.

World Health Organization (WHO) 2007, *Health of Indigenous Peoples: Fact Sheet No 326*, WHO, Geneva: <www.who.int/mediacentre/factsheets/fs326/en>.

WEBSITES

ABC—*First Footprints*: <www.abc.net.au/tv/firstfootprints>

ABC—*Gurindji Strike: The Wave Hill Walk-off*: <www.abc.net.au/archives/80days/stories/2012/01/19/3411481.htm>

ABC—*The Seed for Land Rights: Yirrkala Bark Petitions* (2013): <www.abc.net.au/local/videos/2013/07/05/3797036.htm>

AIATSIS—*Day of Mourning and Protest Aborigines Conference: 75th Anniversary* (2013): <www.aiatsis.gov.au/collections/exhibitions/dayofmourning/26jan.html>

Australian Screen—*Blood Brothers: Freedom Ride* (1993): <http://aso.gov.au/titles/documentaries/freedom-ride-blood-brothers>

Australian Screen—*How the West Was Lost* (1987): <http://aso.gov.au/titles/documentaries/how-west-was-lost> (the 1946 Pilbara Strike)

The Conversation—*Can a DNA Test Reveal if You're an Indigenous Australian?*: <http://theconversation.com/explainer-can-a-dna-test-reveal-if-youre-an-indigenous-australian-31767>

The Little Red Yellow Black Website—*An Introduction to Indigenous Australia*: <http://lryb.aiatsis.gov.au>

The Uluru Statement—<https://ulurustatement.org/>

PBS—*Two Spirits: A Map of Gender-diverse Cultures*: <www.pbs.org/independentlens/two-spirits/map.html>

SBS—*First Australians*: <www.sbs.com.au/firstaustralians>

CHAPTER 17

Youth and young people

PAULA GELDENS

> A strange new breed of students has invaded our universities. Depending on who you believe, they either bring new—even unique—ways of learning and will change higher education forever or they are intent on intellectual Armageddon: refusing to attend class, determined to finish degrees without visiting the library, demanding instant attention (and getting parents to harass staff if they do not receive it), unable to communicate without a mobile phone or computer and writing assignments in foreign languages ('omg an sa so old skool lol'). Lindsay Lohan clones already stalk our campuses and the cast of *High School Musical* are enrolling next semester. They are Generation Y.
>
> Sternberg 2012, p. 571

CHAPTER OVERVIEW

As students of sociology, we often find ourselves talking about young people. This is generally because personal anecdotes are so very accessible.

Let's face it: we are or we have been a young person at some point in our own lives, and many of the people reading this chapter are 'young'. When we discuss 'youth', we can all reference our own experiences—the same is not true for all of the categories of interest to sociologists.

In any class there will be some who can draw on the experience of a more privileged upbringing, some in the room will be able to speak with authority about being male, some may be willing to share their experiences of being queer, and others will have at their disposal personal insight into what it is like to be a member of a particular ethnic group. 'Youth', however, is different. Each of us can lay claim to having had a childhood and we have *all* been a 'young person'.

The fact that we all have firsthand experience of 'youth' can enable our learning—we can think about the issues in as much as they relate to our own lived experiences. Equally though, firsthand experience can be a barrier to a fuller understanding because it is so easy to get stuck within our own frame of reference. As you read this chapter, you will be invited to stretch beyond your own experiences and to challenge some of the ideas you might have taken for granted. We will be examining lived experiences and life chances of young people as they negotiate the 'transition' between childhood and adulthood. The content in this chapter might not mirror your own experience at all: that is part of what makes sociology great!

In this chapter, we will account for some of the key debates within the sociology of young people. After reading this chapter, you should be able to:

- Understand the socio-historical context out of which 'youth' emerged
- Critically engage with youth-related discourses
- Identify the contributions of other disciplines to our understanding of youth and transitions from childhood to adulthood
- Ask and respond to the following question: 'Which young people are we talking about?'

KEY TERMS

At risk A label indicating concern about a lack of expected/desired/required achievement or potential danger.

Discourse The ways that we think and talk about a category/issue.

Life chances A Weberian term used to describe opportunities in life; the likelihood of gaining the things we desire. While we may think that opportunities are the result of talent and effort, they are enabled and/or constrained by the class and status of our families, and by other structures that constitute our social location, such as gender, ethnicity and social capital.

Life stages A linear set of categories that mark significant periods across the human life course. Labels differ across disciplines and contexts.

Lived experiences The activities, interactions and meanings that constitute everyday life.

Moral panic An overreaction to events (that are often relatively isolated and/or seemingly inconsequential), the understanding of which is informed by the media, where particular people or actions are labelled as a threat to society and to the wellbeing of the majority of the population. This leads to widespread anxiety and fear, and calls for urgent policy action.

Transition Movement through the liminal space between childhood and adulthood.

Introduction

There is never a bad time to turn our attention to 'youth'. Youth-related issues are the focus of a great deal of attention and concern. In recent times drug and alcohol use and coward punches have attracted considerable media attention. Since the COVID-19 pandemic's social distancing measures came into effect, the media has often focused on the behaviour of young people who have desired to keep their social contexts alive as much as possible.

Other topics that frequent the commercial press about young people include underemployment and unemployment, violence and bullying, road safety, mental health and wellbeing, housing affordability and homelessness, access and affordability in tertiary education, sexting and online safety … you will also be able to think of many others too. If we were to take these reports at face value, without the benefit of a sociological lens, we would rightly be forgiven for thinking that almost no one makes it to adulthood in one piece!

Just about everyone has something to say about 'youth'. On any given day, there will be someone, somewhere, uttering in their most disparaging and exasperated voice: 'The youth of today …'. What I hear when someone uses this phrase is: 'In my day, we were more respectful, obedient, better dressed, more oriented towards family and community, less aggressive, worked harder, less promiscuous, studied harder … *blah, blah, blah*'.

In my day …

Here is an example of what I mean. This blog post appeared on a site titled 'Baby Boomer Headquarters'. The contributor shares their views about the nature of contemporary Australia and about the ways that young people are taking their place within it:

> In Australia, in the 50's a child was just that, a child! Not little adults. We called our elders Mr. Mrs. or Miss. there was no Ms. then, and definitely we did not call elders by their first name. Our parents knew exactly where we were and there were no posters seeking little children gone missing! We loved our parents, and could trust them … And, all of the parents were married, no de-facto then. In fact if a girl had a baby out of wedlock it was considered very shameful … Times were lovely and simple then, we felt safe! (Baby Boomer Headquarters n.d.)

The notion that previous times were 'simpler' and 'safer' is pervasive—you might well hear this kind of talk at your next family dinner. The problem is, however, that this is a rather idealised imagining of life six decades ago. Recollections like this conveniently overlook waves of **moral panic** (a concept we detail in Chapter 18) about the nature and behaviour of youth reaching back well beyond the 1950s.

In Australia, public disdain for the 'Bodgies' and 'Widgies' in the 1950s was as apparent as it was for the 'Pushes' in Brisbane, Sydney and Melbourne in the early 1900s (see Finch 2012). These were groups, maybe even gangs, of young people who dressed differently and to some extent, by virtue of simply being in a group, were considered menacing by respectable adult society. It would seem that young people have always caused unease and concern for adults.

Writing in the United Kingdom's *The Guardian* newspaper, Tanya Byron (2009) suggested that adults are afraid of young people: ephebiphobia. In her article she offers the following from exasperated adults:

1 'We live in a decaying age. Young people no longer respect their parents. They are rude and impatient. They frequently inhabit taverns and have no self-control.'
2 'What is happening to our young people? They disrespect their elders, they disobey their parents. They ignore the law. They riot in the streets, inflamed with wild notions. Their morals are decaying. What is to become of them?'
3 'The young people of today think of nothing but themselves. They have no reverence for their parents or old age. They are impatient of all restraint … as for the girls; they are forward, immodest and unladylike in speech, behaviour and dress.'

Any idea to whom these statements are attributed? I bet you didn't guess the following:

1 An inscription on a 6000-year-old Egyptian tomb;
2 Plato, fourth century BCE; and
3 Peter the Hermit, eleventh century CE.

The suggestion that adults are youth-phobic is an extreme position; it is wise to approach such claims with a healthy level of caution. It makes sense, though, that the moral panic associated with young people today is not a phenomenon unique to our times, and it is certainly not a phenomenon unique to Australia.

Youth studies begins …

From the 1920s, studies were coming out of the Sociology and Anthropology Department at the University of Chicago in the United States (the '*Chicago School*'), many of which explored the lives of young working-class men who were living in poverty, spending time in public places and causing concern. In the 1970s and 80s, scholars based at the Centre for Contemporary Cultural Studies at Birmingham University in England (CCCS, or the '*Birmingham School*') were writing about the spectacular, style-based youth subcultures of the time (including skinheads and punks). Again, these were groups of young people whose behaviour seemed perverse. If we look, we can find evidence of adult concerns about the doings of young people at every turn.

The views expressed in the blog post above and the quote at the beginning of this chapter highlight a fundamental paradox. The paradox is that young people are considered by many to represent all that is hopeful about the future of humankind; they are enthusiastic, optimistic and willing to take risks—they are eager to facilitate change. At the same time, many also have great reservations about young people. There is a view that young people will bring about some form of intellectual or other 'Armageddon' *because* of their enthusiasm, optimism and willingness to take risks—they lack the necessary knowledge and experience to facilitate change. In youth-related **discourses**, young people simultaneously represent a risk (a danger to themselves and others) and are **at risk** (in danger as a consequence of their inexperience). These ideas seem to sit side by side in unproblematic contradiction.

These are *really* powerful ideas … but how do they stand up against the evidence? How are young people today negotiating the **transition** between childhood and adulthood? What do their **lived experiences** and **life chances** look like? Let us start at the beginning by locating 'young people' within the broader context.

Life stages and social generations

'Youth', or 'young person', is one of several stages in the human life course. The life course is made up of a linear set of related **life stages** that represent physically, culturally and/or politically significant periods across the human lifespan. There is variation in the labels used in different disciplines and in different contexts, and some models are much more complex than others.

A basic model might employ the following categories: 'child', 'young person', 'adult' and 'elderly person'. If, however, our interest was in issues related to psycho-social development we might carve the life course up according to Erikson's (1982) eight-stage model: 'infancy', 'early childhood', 'play age', 'school age', 'adolescence', 'young adulthood', 'adulthood' and 'old age'. As an example of a further set of categories, when referencing the ageing population in Australia, the Australian Bureau of Statistics uses 'children', 'the working-age' and 'older Australians'.

Each life course model has an internal logic, and each can be shown to have established categories that are defined in part in reference to those either side; that is, life stage categories are fundamentally relational.

BOX 17.1

Thinking sociologically

LIFE STAGES—LANGUAGE MATTERS

Let's play a word game. Using a table like the one below, generate a list of words that you believe most people would use to characterise each of the life stages. It is perfectly acceptable to indulge in stereotype here ... *but don't read ahead!*

TABLE 17.1 Life stages

	'Child'	'Young person'	'Adult'	'Elderly person'
1				
2				
3				
4				
5				

OK, let's take a look.

When you were writing the lists, did you look across to what you had written in a previous column? If you look across the lists, is there overlap? It is likely that you have constructed a fairly discrete set of descriptors. Does your list for 'child' include words such as 'dependent', 'playful' and 'vulnerable'? What about for 'adult'? Did you include words like 'responsible', 'boring' and 'experienced'?

It is worth pointing out that if you are aged in your 70s, your lists will likely be very different to those of your younger classmates. If you live in a relatively affluent metropolitan area in Australia, your list will differ from that written by someone living in rural Nepal. If you have children, your responses will have been shaped by your experiences of parenthood. If you had been asked to undertake this task 100 years ago ... you can see what I am getting at. These lists will reflect your lived experiences as much as they might reflect any 'objective' assessment. And yet, it is entirely likely that you can distil your lists down to something that looks a little like this: 'child' = innocent; 'young person' = unruly; 'adult' = responsible; and 'elderly Person' = frail.

Language matters.

Sociologists choose their words very carefully. Together we construct 'discourses'—and this is quite a responsibility because discourses have power (think again of the areas we covered in Chapter 8 when discussing power). At the same time, this is an opportunity because we can choose to challenge or to strengthen a discourse though our contribution. If the discourse we construct frames children as 'innocent', then this shapes the way that we interact with them. Children in Australia today must attend school, are not permitted to work and cannot be married—this is not the result of some natural order, this is the power of discourse at work. Equally, if we perceive youth to be 'unruly', it is incumbent upon us to approach them accordingly.

Critical reflection

Our standpoint, the way we see the world, is informed by our lived experiences. In what ways did your experiences influence the lists you constructed above?

Youth = 'not adult'?

Wyn and White (1997) suggest that our understanding of 'youth' is a consequence of what we understand 'adult' to mean. That is, youth = not adult. By extension, youth = not child. As is the case in any relational arrangement, value is not apportioned equally. In the case of young person vs adult, adult is the privileged category; that is, by virtue of not yet being adult, young people are deficient (or in deficit).

While we move through childhood to become youth, and through youth to become adult, more so than any other category youth is interrogated as a transitional life stage rather than a legitimate location itself. Adulthood is the desired destination and the default against which all else is measured. As we will see in a following section, all of this would make more sense if we were able to come to a consensus about what 'adult' is!

It is a matter of sociological fact that humans are the product and beneficiary of the worlds that they are born into (as discussed in Chapter 6). One of the fundamental sociological ideas is that we are shaped, through processes of socialisation, by the context to which we are exposed. Out of these ideas comes the notion of *generation*.

There are broadly two approaches to thinking about generations. The first is the chronological approach—a cohort is born at a particular time and shares transition across the life course from birth to death.

The alternative is the sociohistorical approach—a cohort shares significant experiences and memories. Karl Mannheim (1952) drew upon both approaches to develop a useful theoretical framework for understanding how and why social generations emerge.

Mannheim wrote an influential work, first published in German in 1928 and then in English in 1952, in which he argued that generations are formed through the collective experience of living through major events or trauma. This theory was developed from his observations of the impacts of the First World War. His argument was that this war was a defining moment in human history that shaped the life chances, lived experiences and collective sense of identity for those who lived through the period—that those who survived were 'similarly located' as a consequence of having been exposed to the same horrors. For Mannheim, within each cohort location, there is 'a tendency pointing towards certain definite modes of behaviour, feeling and thought' (1952, p. 291).

Notably, Mannheim made allowances for variations within generational cohorts; that is, he did not argue that everyone who lived through the First World War had the same experience or was impacted in the same way, but that there was a legacy of some kind for all who had lived at that time. In more recent times, immersive engagement with digital technologies has been identified as characteristic with which to demark generations. When coining the term 'digital native', Prensky (2001, p. 1) observed that, young people today 'have spent their entire lives surrounded by and using computers, videogames, digital music players, video cams, cell phones, and all the other toys and tools of the digital age'. This context is widely understood as a site for generational conflict—and something that was discussed in more detail in Chapter 13. We have a generation for which, for example, sustained engagement with social media has provided unprecedented opportunities for the crafting of self. For a group of long-term Facebook users in Australia, for example, this platform 'has come to represent an archive of memories that can be edited, re-organised, modified, re-configured, re-presented, and even deleted' (Robards & Lincoln 2017, p. 717). As noted by Hugh Mackay (1997, p. 1), generational differences 'are simply the result of different generations spending their formative years in different social, cultural, economic and technological environments'.

Concerns relating to generational conflict have been present in the sociological literature for decades. Kingsley Davis' (1940) work is an early example of an intellectual project aimed at explaining why tensions can be observed between generations. Interest in generational difference and conflict remains current. For more recent scholarship referencing the generational circumstances for young Australians, see Woodman and Wyn (2015). For critiques of generational theorising in recent times, see Connolly (2019) and France and Roberts (2015).

Much of the work you will read about generations does not reflect the robust theoretical foundation offered by Mannheim. The bookshelves of airport newsagents and the World Wide Web are littered with superficial assumption and assertion about generational difference. There are resources to assist parents, employers, governments, marketing and advertising companies and a great many others who are concerned about how they might 'manage' these new generations of young people. It is quite an industry. Sources make reference to a host of labels, some of which include: 'Baby Boomers', 'Generation X', 'Generation Y', 'Generation Z' and now, 'Generation Alpha' (seen to be those born between 2010 and 2024—see McCrindle 2020). It is anyone's guess what the next cohort will be called—let us hope it is a little more creative than Generation Beta!

BOX 17.2

Thinking sociologically

GENERATIONS

Table 17.2 provides an example of some of the characteristics incorporated into generational typologies.

If the descriptions seem accurate, Mannheim (1952) would have you describe these as 'actual generations'. If you have reservations about the descriptions being representative across the group you might draw attention to a 'generational unit'—this term accounts for differences within generations. For example, despite not having grown up with the information and communications technologies that we take for granted today, some Baby Boomers are avid users of Twitter, eBay and social networking sites. Equally, some Gen Y'ers have no desire to live and work overseas. There are some within each generation who do things differently.

While it is easy to find fault with generational typologies, they do remind us of fundamental sociological ideas in relation to who we are and how we live—the importance of social context.

TABLE 17.2 Characteristics of generational typologies

'Baby Boomers' (1940s – mid 1960s)	Generation X (mid 1960s – early 1980s)	Generation Y (early 1980s – late 1990s)
Dad worked and Mum baked = unbound childhood	Both parents working = latch-key childhood	Guilt-ridden helicopter parents = coddled childhood
Work is a cornerstone of who I am. Loyalty to the company—a job for life	Work is only part of who I am. Loyal to each company—no longer a job for life	I am not defined by what I do. I am not looking for a job for life
Break the rules!	We need the rules!	We are rewriting the rules!
Change needs to be managed	Change is expected	Change is to be embraced
Face-to-face communication	Mobile phone and email communication	Email and social media communication
The war in Vietnam	The first war in Iraq	September 11 and the wars in Iraq and Afghanistan

Critical reflection

Whose voice is silenced? Take a moment to critically interrogate the generational discourses on p. 355. Who is excluded or marginalised within or by these discourses? Do they capture the lived experiences and life chances of young people living with chronic illness or disability, or those living in remote areas or on low incomes? Do they apply to young people across the globe (in Morocco or in Indonesia, for example)?

The emergence of 'youth'

Youth has always been a 'thing', right? Wrong.

Like much sociological understanding, this is more complex and interesting than you might first have imagined. Many of the life stage labels that we take for granted emerged relatively recently and, as you might expect, out of particular social contexts. Labels do not evolve in a vacuum—they are social constructs (see Chapter 3).

According to Philippe Aries (1962), 'childhood' emerged during the seventeenth and eighteenth centuries. Before this period in our human history, today's 'child' was viewed and treated as a small adult. While at the age of nine you may have spent school holidays riding around the neighbourhood on your bicycle, camping with your family or staying with your grandparents, a nine-year-old of the seventeenth or eighteenth century did not. Not only is there debate about whether the bicycle had been invented at this time, you would not have school holidays. Unless you happened to have been born into a wealthy family, you would not have the luxury of study available to you. For much of human history, education has been the sole privilege of the religious and social elite. You would be put to work alongside the rest of your family as soon as you were physically able—and often before.

Writing from a European context, Aries observed that the expansion of education, beyond the privileged few, was a defining feature in the emergence of childhood. It is worth noting that even today, for a great many children 'childhood' is not defined by the construction of elaborate cubby houses or the performance of *Frozen* tunes in the back of the car on family holidays. Many children work in dangerous and precarious roles, fight in armed conflict, and are trafficked for prostitution, marriage or forced labour (see <www.unicef.org> and <www.ilo.org> for details).

The 1800s saw the Industrial Revolution and the rise of the scientific method (which fostered the development of disciplines including psychology): you will have read about the massive social upheaval of this time in Chapter 5. During this time, a new life stage category emerged. The members of this group were no longer children, but at the same time not yet adults (does this remind anyone else of a Britney Spears song?). This group was assigned the label 'adolescent'.

With the maturing of the industrial age, the term 'youth' emerged. That is, in the late nineteenth and early twentieth century, the young men who had been providing their labour to the factories of the Industrial Revolution began to attract attention for their unruly, troublesome, violent and/or criminal behaviour. In its early usage, 'youth' captured nothing of young women's lived experiences and life chances—it was the very public male experience that drew attention. Institutions aimed at controlling 'unruly' male youth emerged during this time. The Scouting movement was among these!

The 1950s saw the emergence of the 'teenager'. It is generally argued that this term is the product of marketers and advertisers—a similar argument can be made for the use of several of the generational labels currently being used, such as 'tweens'. Teenagers emerged alongside, or as a consequence of, the new consumer market. With levels of disposable income among this group at unprecedented levels post–Second World War, they were and remain a lucrative consumer market.

It could be argued that we no longer need new labels, and that the most recent, 'Gen', is a meaningful stand-in for 'youth'. Time will tell.

Early understandings

The contributions of biology and developmental psychology

The sociology of youth is informed by work from several disciplines, including biology and psychology. The following is a very brief overview of some of the work that has come to inform the way in which sociologists approach the study of youth.

Sociologists often approach the work of biology with caution. For a long period, biological determinism was a difficult ideological position to defeat: think of the 'nature vs nurture' debate, and the tension about how much of who we are and what we do is attributable to our biological self and how much is a result of our socialisation.

For sociologists interested in the life course, the interconnection between the biological and the social has always been strong. If we think about 'early childhood' we recognise this as a period of rapid growth. If we think about 'old age' we might well think about the deterioration of our bodies and our mental capacities. There is no doubt that there is a biological aspect to youth. The physical changes that occur as a result of the onset of puberty cannot be ignored. We live in and through our bodies; this is what *embodiment* is about. We cannot, however, reduce youth to puberty—there is a lot more going on than just what is happening within our bodies!

In everyday conversations, we often default to references to chronological age. For example, we make statements like 'they are too old for that' and 'when I was that age …'. Using chronological age to make sense of the world makes a lot of sense, but it is not as definitive as we might imagine. At what age do you consider you were no longer a child? Did it correspond with getting a job, making decisions about your own body or getting your driver's licence? Was it when you cast your first vote? These markers of transition are important … but are they straightforward? The following information provided by Youthlaw on their website about the laws that apply to young people in Victoria—<http://youthlaw.asn.au>—helps us unpack this idea.

> *When can I get a job?* If you are aged 15 or over you can get a job … but if you are between 13 and 15 you can get a permit to work under certain circumstances, unless you are only working occasionally in a family business or babysitting and some other things in which case you don't need a permit … but if you are keen on a paper round or delivering pamphlets you can do that from 11. If you want to work in the entertainment industry a minimum age does not apply—but you will need your guardian or parent's consent.
>
> *When can I get a piercing?* If you want an 'intimate piercing' (nipples, genitalia, etc. …) you will need to be 18. If you are 16 or over and the piercing site is non-intimate you are right to go … but if you are under 16 you will need your parent or guardian's consent (they have to deliver this in person). And if you are aged between 10 and 16 you will need to provide written consent too.
>
> *When can I get a licence?* You can apply for a learner permit when you are 16, but if you want to ride a motorbike you need to be 18. And then things get more complicated: To apply for a probationary licence you need to be 18 … but if you are under 21 you must have completed a minimum of 120 practice hours and have had your learner permit for at least 12 months. If you are aged between 21 and 25 you will need to have had your learner permit for at least 6 months … if you over 25, 3 months will suffice.

So it is never straightforward …

This information illustrates the fundamentally social nature of our use of chronological age. In different jurisdictions the ages at which we are legally able to do things differs—there is no definitive age at which we are considered 'child', 'youth' or 'adult'. Youth services, for example, tend to be targeted at those aged 12–25. These services deliver programs and support across a broad age range. This honours the fact that there is considerable variation in the lived experiences and needs of those who access their services, and that a narrower range would prove exclusive.

Developmental psychologists have made some important contributions to our understanding of this life stage. These scholars introduced the idea that youth constitutes a period of transition between childhood and adulthood; that youth is not a destination in and of itself—it is a *liminal* position. That is, it is a position that has no boundary as such—even when you are technically an adult at 18, youth sits on both sides of this line! On the whole, developmental psychologists use the term 'adolescent'. You will recall that this label emerged at the same time as we saw the rise of the scientific method—its use is informed by a medical approach.

G Stanley Hall (1904) observed adolescence to be a time of significant upheaval or, in his terms, of 'storm and stress': a time of impulsive experimentation, rebellion and risk-taking. This perspective argues that adolescents lack the ability to manage their hormone-ridden bodies.

Another commonly cited developmental psychologist is Erik Erikson (1982). As discussed earlier in this chapter, Erikson asserted that there are eight stages of development across the human life course. He argued that 'adolescence' was a life stage (years 12–18) during which the acquisition of a sense of identity is a key priority. He labelled the stage 'Identity vs Role Confusion'. In everyday discussion we see these ideas used: 'they are experimenting with who they are' and 'they will regret that tattoo when they are older', for example. This model is linear and normative, meaning that deviation generates concern.

These contributions have enhanced our understanding of the life stage we know as youth, but they address only part of the picture. Young people are not defined through the blunt instrument of chronological age; they are not reducible to puberty, nor are they defined through identity seeking.

BOX 17.3
Thinking sociologically

'YOUNG PEOPLE': LANGUAGE MATTERS

Another word game! While there are a great many labels used interchangeably with 'young person', do they have the same connotations? In a table like the one below, list the first three words that come to mind for each label. As before, *don't read ahead yet*.

TABLE 17.3 Young people

	'Youth'	'Adolescent'	'Teenager'	'Juvenile'
1				
2				
3				

OK, let's take a look.

Do you note a difference in the tone in each column? Are some sets of descriptors more positive or affirming than others? Take a look back now at the words you documented for 'young person' in Table 17.1—is there a difference?

You will likely observe here that 'young person' carries less 'baggage' than the other labels; it is a more neutral term. A friend who works in ageing research wants you to know that they do not use the term 'elderly person'—they use 'older adult' for the same reason. This is acknowledgment that these labels are socially constructed, that their use builds discourse and that discourses have power!

> **Critical reflection**
>
> What has been your default label for young people? How does this influence the way you see young people? How much do you think language matters?

Contemporary understandings

The sociology of youth and transitions into adulthood

Unsurprisingly, the focus of sociologists is the social. Sociologists of youth draw attention to this life stage being a time of emerging independence, during which adult roles are learnt and the trappings and dependence of childhood surrendered. It is clear that young people today are 'becoming an adult' differently to the way their parents and grandparents did. This is because, as noted earlier, we are the product and beneficiary of the worlds that we are born into.

In the past, the transition into adulthood was made via a clear and well-trodden path: Once you had completed school, secured full-time employment and moved out of your parental home you could reasonably make claims to adult status—cemented further through marriage and parenthood. This model reflects a set of culturally and historically situated norms—it is a middle-class, high-income country experience of the world. It is a most orderly and linear process and, for the great majority, was the norm. In the 1940s you would likely have achieved full adult status in your 20s, and to deviate from the prescribed path would have resulted in significant social sanction (think of the stigma borne by unwed mothers and of those who cohabited outside marriage, for example).

PERSONAL VOICE

Granny's transition story

❝ I asked my 97-year-old grandmother about her transition into adulthood and discovered that her story was precisely in step with the above.

'Discouraged or not allowed to read the newspaper in case … [they] read something bad', Granny and her four siblings were largely unaffected by the Great Depression. Born and raised in a country town, Granny described a 'very protected and happy childhood', which featured drives in the bush to pick wildflowers and collect mineral water, playing cricket in the middle of the street and Sunday roasts after church. Completing primary school was a key marker of the end of childhood.

Granny and her two older sisters each achieved their Grade 8 Merit Certificates … only to return to school for an extra year because their father 'didn't like the idea' of his daughters travelling on the train at 12.

She volunteered: 'I was not a rebellious kid—it just did not occur to me not to do what I was told'. At 13, Granny began business college. The only brother in the family was not held to the same arrangement—he was off each day on the train at the age of 12.

At 16 Granny started her first full-time job and was living outside the family home for the first time; she was boarding with a family. She recounted in detail fond memories of her first job. She had never worried about finding work—she had only ever applied unsuccessfully for one job in her whole life.

Granny married at 25 and was always expected to become a mother. She recalled having told someone that she didn't think it would be 'worth getting married if you could not have children'. She had three children.

The conversation out of which the above was extracted went for well over an hour. While there is considerable detail omitted, what we see here is that the transition experienced by my grandmother was uncomplicated. She followed the clear and well-trodden path. No scandal here!

The travel metaphor

Furlong and Cartmel (2007) introduced a very useful conceptual tool for making sense of how transitions have changed: the 'travel' metaphor. The transitions into adulthood of our parents and grandparents can be described with reference to train travel; that is, successful transition required them to board the train at the first station (finishing school) and to ride it all the way to the final station (becoming a parent).

While there was only one train on a single set of tracks, there were different classes of ticket. If you were from a less wealthy family, you might have to ride on roof of the carriage rather than in the first-class cabin, which would make for a much less comfortable trip. Upgrades were possible, primarily through education, and if you had a supportive family it might have been possible to disembark and take a short break in the journey … but it would be unwise to miss the next train lest you find yourself becoming the family's 'spinster' aunt or 'confirmed bachelor' uncle.

Transitions today are much more akin to travelling in a car. We know what the destination is supposed to be, but because we are no longer constrained by the tracks we really are in the 'driver's seat'—well mostly, anyway. It is up to us to make the most of our life chances. Successful transitions into adulthood are less predictable and take longer today than they did in the past. This freedom comes at a cost though, with the blame for a lack of success resting on the shoulders of the individual. Adult status is no longer attained via progression through prescribed locations beginning with school completion and ending with becoming a parent. Young people today have greater choice of routes, and about whether they aim for the signposted destinations at all. When you are driving you can adjust your speed, stop if and when you want and revisit past locations—this is an excellent metaphor for capturing the experiences of young people today.

In Australia, young people are spending more time in non-compulsory education than any generation before. Tertiary study is increasingly the mass experience and is the result/driver of 'qualification inflation' and 'credential creep'. Young people who are unable or unwilling to engage in non-compulsory education are finding themselves left behind. Young people today are overrepresented in low-paid, insecure, low-status employment; the notion of a 'job for life' seems a thing of the past.

Young people also feature heavily in the unemployment and underemployment figures. This has resulted in this cohort remaining in the family home for longer than previous generations and returning to the familial home after periods of independent living. A great many young people in Australia today are living with and within greater precarity than we have noted for previous generations. A recent publication drawn from key longitudinal cohort studies, the Life Patterns project and the Social Futures and Life Pathways project aptly concluded:

> our analysis provides strong evidence for the erosion of a sense of personal control among young Australians in this generation. Closely linked to precarious working conditions, young people's sense of control is also linked to other life domains—education, relationships and health. This means that the precarity that young people experience in the labour market has a negative effect on many lives, and has especially negative implications for the mental health of a generation. The precarity of the labour market, and the sense of ontological insecurity that challenges young adults today is not something that they will 'grow out of' through a presumed 'transition' process (Chesters et al. 2019, p. 404).

Those who research and write about youth transitions have been using the term 'churn' and 'slow-track changes' to refer to these non-linear, precarious and increasingly protracted transitional experiences. These notions can be understood as defining features for the current generation of young people.

Again, we cannot ignore the fact that the final destination, whatever that might be, will be harder to reach for some because their vehicle will be 'unroadworthy'. As sociologists, we also have a responsibility to interrogate whether the markers against which we are measuring success are fit for purpose; that is, what does adulthood mean today? Can we be 'adult' without marrying or becoming a parent? Where does a return to study to facilitate a career change fit in this model? How do we factor in the implications of fluctuations in housing affordability? There are so many questions.

There is also reason to make visible, and subsequently interrogate, the dominant discourses and key points of intersectionality—a theme that has emerged in a number of chapters. Have we, for example, taken stock of the default to metro-centricity—that is, focusing on the experiences of young people in cities? Or have we, as urged by David Farrugia (2014, p. 303), accounted for 'rural young people? As well as a spatially informed analysis of urban, suburban, and "peri-urban"' youth?

Critical reflection

What does your transition story look like at this point? How would you describe the condition of your car? Have you been aware of the experiences of those around you?

I asked a former student to reflect upon their transition into adulthood with the view to highlighting how important it is for us to ask ourselves 'which young people' we are referring to. In asking this question, we can come to understand that while we refer to 'young people' as a single category, this is a complex grouping of people with very different life experiences, desires, ambitions and life journeys.

PERSONAL VOICE
Anonymous—Transitions

❝ I grew up in a family with two older brothers and a twin brother, making me the only girl. My mum told me that she cried with happiness when she found that she was finally getting to raise a girl. Certain gendered expectations were placed upon me because I was born female—I felt like I could never meet them.

At three or four years of age Mum used to force me kicking and screaming into a dress just so she could have one photograph of me looking girly. This rejection of female gendered social norms continued fiercely as I grew older. As I entered my teenage years I couldn't get my head around why certain restrictions were placed upon me due to my anatomy. It infuriated and grossly confused me that, for example, my brothers praised my twin brother for growing underarm hair and when I started to grow my own I was shamed and banished: his hair represented manhood, mine represented dirtiness. When I began questioning why, the answer was always something along the lines of: 'It's just the way it is so get with the program.'

My transition from child to 'adult' was messy, and I carried around a lot of guilt for not fitting into my mum's fantasy. My mum got a queer feminist daughter who rejected the white-picket fence life. She has been mourning the loss of walking me down the aisle in a white dress and marrying me off to some dude; that was never in the cards. As I carried around this guilt I also began to release the shackles that society had placed upon me, and began living my life as who I felt I really was and according to what made me happy.

I started to question my gender identity in my early 20s, and have been using a gender-neutral name ever since. I now happily identify as a transboy and have finally released the guilt I carried around for not fitting into the 'girl' I was supposed to be. I identify with the 'trans identity'. This really resonates with me, because it means that there is no need for an end goal/marker. I am not going to go 'Oh yep, I've finally reached manhood!' For me, sex, gender and sexuality are all so fluid—my identity is ever evolving.

Conclusion

Concerns about the doings of young people have a long history—as far back as the ancient Egyptians! While moral panic might be a constant, the nature of the context within which young people make their lives generates particular challenges. As the introduction to this chapter posited, you would be forgiven for thinking that almost no one makes it to adulthood in one piece! In fact, most do; but they do so differently to the way that their parents and grandparents did.

Despite having emerged over 100 years ago, 'youth' is a relatively new label and carries much of the same meaning today—unruly, troublesome and so on. It is important to recognise that we associate a great many negative descriptors with the term. As a consequence of knowing that discourses inform action, each of us has a responsibility to consider our choice of words carefully. With a sociological perspective we are able to move beyond the contributions of biology and developmental psychology to a more comprehensive understanding of the lived experiences and life chances of young people. In particular, we are encouraged to ask: 'Which young people?' If we do not ask this question, we risk further excluding and marginalising young people who are made voiceless through generational and other discursive frames … and sometimes their stories are more interesting than the noisy masses!

Summary points

* It is important to move beyond our own lived experiences if we want to develop fuller sociological understandings—the fact that we have all been young can actually constrain our capacity for understanding if we are not mindful.
* Youth is a transitionary life stage. By virtue of not yet being adult, young people are considered deficient. This positioning contributes to the paradoxical framing of young people as being a risk while also being at risk, and the ease with which they become a site for moral panic.
* While life-stage and generational models help us make sense of the human life course, and sociological transitional models assist us to make sense of how we move from childhood to adulthood, we have to ask questions about who is excluded, marginalised or made voiceless. That is what sociology does!

Sociological reflection

1. Think about recent policies that have been developed to 'deal' with young people. Can you see a connection between the ways in which young people are being constructed in and through discourses, and the introduction of mechanisms to manage them?
2. What are the implications for young people who occupy the margins or are excluded from the dominant generational discourses? In particular, what does it mean in the context of education and employment?
3. With transitions into adulthood becoming less predictable and taking longer today than in the past, what does the future hold for this life stage? Will 'youth' disappear?

Discussion questions

1. Does language matter? Does it matter whether you use 'youth', 'adolescent', 'teenager' or 'juvenile'?
2. Can you recall statements about 'the youth of today' or similar being used at a family gathering? Do the sentiments shared stand up to scrutiny? Are there specific cultural norms underpinning the statements?
3. What was the defining moment when you felt that you were no longer a child?
4. If you are a young person, is 'adulthood' what you are aiming for? What will adulthood look like when your generation arrive there?
5. With a focus on generational difference in mind, what are some of the key issues facing young people today? What will the world be like for Gen Alpha?

Further investigation

1 Visit Youth Action (www.youthaction.org.au/). You will find an enormous amount of information about the lived experiences and life chances of young people in Australia on this site.
2 You should also visit the site for ReachOut Australia (https://au.reachout.com/), which is Australia's leading online mental health organisation for young people and their parents. There is a growing suite of resources being produced by this organisation—its focus is on the intersections of health and wellbeing and technologies for young people.

References and further reading

REFERENCES

Aries, P 1962, *Centuries of Childhood*, Cape, London.

Baby Boomer Headquarters n.d., 'When I was a kid …': <www.bbhq.com/wheniwas.php>.

Byron, T 2009, 'We see children as pestilent', *The Guardian*, 17 March: <www.theguardian.com/education/2009/mar/17/ephebiphobia-young-people-mosquito>.

Chesters, J, Smith, J, Cuervo, H, Laughland-Booÿ, J, Wyn, J, Skrbiš, Z & Woodman, D 2019, 'Young adulthood in uncertain times: the association between sense of personal control and employment, education, personal relationships and health', *Journal of Sociology*, 55(2), 389–408.

Connolly, J 2019, 'Generational conflict and the sociology of generations: Mannheim and Elias reconsidered', *Theory, Culture & Society*, 1–20.

Davis, K 1940, 'The sociology of parent-youth conflict', *American Sociological Review*, Vol. 5, pp. 523–34.

Erikson, EH 1982, *The Life Cycle Completed: A Review*, WW Norton & Company, New York.

Farrugia, D 2014, 'Towards a spatialised youth sociology: the rural and the urban in times of change', *Journal of Youth Studies*, 17(3), 293–307.

Finch, L 2012, 'On the streets: working-class youth culture in the nineteenth century', in R White (ed), *Youth Subcultures: Theory, History and the Australian Experience*, Australian Clearinghouse for Youth Studies, Hobart, pp. 165–72.

France, A & Roberts, S 2015, 'The problem of social generations: a critique of the new emerging orthodoxy in youth studies', *Journal of Youth Studies*, 18(2), 215–30.

Furlong, A & Cartmel, F 2007, *Young People and Social Change: Newer Perspectives*, McGraw Hill, New York.

Hall, GS 1904, *Adolescence: Its Psychology and its Relations to Physiology, Anthropology, Sociology, Sex, Crime, Religion, and Education*, Appleton, New York.

Henderson, G 2001, 'Unleashing a "sleeper" issue: ethnic suspicion', *The Age*, 18 September, p. 5.

Kingsley, D 1940, 'The sociology of parent-youth conflict', *American Sociological Review*, 5(4), 523–35.

Mackay, H 1997, *Generations: Baby Boomers, their Parents & their Children*, Macmillan, Sydney.

Mannheim, K 1952, *Essays on the Sociology of Knowledge*, Routledge & Kegan, London (original work published 1928).

Lewis, S & McManus, G 2009, 'Revealed: Warnings about next wave of illegals', *Herald Sun*, 18 April, p. 1.

McCrindle, M 2020, *Understanding Generation Alpha*, McCrindle Research Pty Ltd, Sydney.

Prensky, M 2001, 'Digital natives, digital immigrants part 1', *On the Horizon: The Strategic Planning Resource for Education Professionals*, 9(5), 1–6.

Robards, B & Lincoln, S 2017, 'Uncovering longitudinal life narratives: scrolling back on Facebook', *Qualitative Research*, 17(6), 715–30.

Slattery, K 2003, 'Drowning not waving: the "children overboard" event and Australia's fear of the other', *Media International Australia, Incorporating Culture & Policy*, 109, 93–108.

Sternberg, J 2012, '"It's the end of the university as we know it (and I feel fine)": the Generation Y student in higher education discourse', *Higher Education Research & Development*, 31(4), 571–83 © HERDSA, reprinted permission of Taylor & Francis Ltd, tandfonline on behalf of HERDSA.

Woodman, D & Wyn, J 2015, *Youth and Generation: Rethinking Change and Inequality in the Lives of Young People*, SAGE, Los Angeles, CA.

Wyn, J & White, R 1997, *Rethinking Youth*, Allen & Unwin, St Leonards.

FURTHER READING

Beadle, S, Holdsworth, R & Wyn, J (eds) 2011, 'For we are young and …? Young people in a time of uncertainty', *Youth Studies Series*, Melbourne University Press, Melbourne.

France, A 2007, *Understanding Youth in Late Modernity*, McGraw Hill, New York.

Furlong, A 2013, *Youth Studies: An Introduction*, Routledge, New York.

Furlong, A (ed.) 2009, *Handbook of Youth and Young Adulthood: Newer Perspectives and Agendas*, Routledge, New York.

Kassem, D, Murphy, L & Taylor, E 2010, *Key Issues in Childhood and Youth Studies*, Routledge, New York.

White, RD 2012, *Youth Subcultures: Theory, History and the Australian Experience*, 2nd edn, Australian Clearinghouse for Youth Studies, Hobart.

White, R & Wyn, J 2013, *Youth and Society*, 3rd edn, Oxford University Press, South Melbourne.

MOVIES

Bailey, G (dir.) 2011, *I am 11*.

Hughes, J (dir.) 1985, *The Breakfast Club*.

Linklater, R (dir.) 2014, *Boyhood*.

Duigan, J (dir.) 1987, *The Year My Voice Broke*.

Beresford, B (dir.) 1981, *Puberty Blues*.

WEBSITES

International Labour Organization: <www.ilo.org>

UNICEF: <www.unicef.org>

Youthlaw: <http://youthlaw.asn.au>

CHAPTER 18

Deviance and moral panics

JEN COUCH AND TRUDI COOPER

CHAPTER OVERVIEW

The previous chapter presented a detailed discussion of youth and young people. In that chapter, the author outlined an important contradiction: young people are both a group that the rest of society fears, and also the site of hope for the future. Further, from Plato in ancient Greece to contemporary politicians who introduce mutual obligation 'activity tests', young people are often seen as being the site of deviance and cause of moral panics.

This chapter continues many of these important sociological concepts, including deviance, moral panic and the idea of social norms. Though this is an extension of Chapter 17, it is important to know that these broad areas are also areas of study in their own right.

After reading this chapter, you should be able to:
- Explain what sociologists mean by 'deviance' and 'social norms'
- Describe how social norms are maintained and how ideas of deviance change over time
- Define a 'moral panic'
- Discuss the role of the mass media in shaping social norms and deviance through labelling to create moral panics
- Apply the sociological concepts of deviance and moral panic to everyday life.

KEY TERMS

Deviance Any conduct, actions, traits or ideas that violate the accepted social norms of a particular society. Deviant conduct is not always illegal and may vary between groups within society, as social norms vary.

Moral panic An overreaction to events (that are often relatively isolated or seemingly inconsequential), the understanding of which is informed by the media, where particular people or actions are labelled as a threat to society and to the wellbeing of the majority of the population. This leads to widespread anxiety and fear, and calls for urgent policy action.

Othering A process whereby dominant groups in society maintain their dominance by assuming that their own features, characteristics and circumstances are the yardstick by which all others should be judged (often combined with 'totalisation').

Social customs Patterns of behaviour that contribute to social norms within a particular culture or subculture.

> **Social norms** The shared beliefs, attitudes, values and behaviours of people in a society—that is, a shared understanding of what is normal.
>
> **Totalisation** The act of labelling someone, based upon a small part of who they are. As a consequence, the person and their actions may be viewed either more, or less, sympathetically.

Introduction

When you think of '**deviance**', what is the first thing that springs to mind?

For many people the idea of deviance is strongly emotionally charged; for example, we may think of someone who does something that is morally abhorrent. To the sociologist, however, the word is purely descriptive and is separated from any moral judgment. A person who is 'deviant' is someone *who does not conform to the dominant social norms in society*. Some deviant actions are morally repugnant, but many are not.

Deviant conduct is not necessarily illegal. For example, alcohol usage may be considered deviant in some social groups (for example, in most Islamic countries; by some religious groups in Australia; in some Australian Indigenous communities; and in some age cohorts). Similarly, not consuming alcohol may be considered deviant in some cultures or subcultures.

The **social norms** of a society are formed and enforced by the laws, regulations and customs that shape our behaviour towards other people and the world around us. 'Social norms' also describe the conventional idea of the 'good life'. Social norms specify things we *must do*, things we *may do*, things we *ought to do*, and things we *must not do* if we want to be considered 'normal'.

Both social norms and what is considered 'deviant' vary from place to place and change over time. For example, in the 1950s in Australia, it was a social norm for young women to marry in their late teens or early 20s. Once married, a woman was expected to have children as soon as possible, stay at home as a housewife until the children had grown up, and stay married 'till death do us part', even if their marriage was unhappy or violent.

Think about how the social norms about marriage have changed in contemporary Australia. How would people in your social group react if an 18-year-old male they knew wanted to get married? Would the reaction be different if the 18-year-old was female? What advice would you and your friends give to someone who was desperately unhappy in their marriage, or whose partner was abusive or violent?

It is legally permissible for 18-year-olds to get married; however, in contemporary Australia it is unusual in most Australian social groups for 18-year-olds to marry. Early marriage is no longer a social norm. Therefore, from a sociological perspective, an 18-year-old who married would be considered 'deviant' in the sense of not conforming to social norms, even though marriage itself is not considered morally repugnant by most people (and even though in the 1950s in Australia early marriage was a social norm, especially for young women).

How social norms are maintained

Let us look in more detail at what we mean by 'social norms'. These are simply the 'unwritten rules'—the behaviours and hints—that exist within a society or group, and include values, beliefs and attitudes. Social norms influence what we judge as appropriate (or inappropriate) behaviour in different circumstances, including:

- How we treat other people in public and in private;
- How we expect other people to treat us; and
- What behaviour we judge as inappropriate, or rude.

Social norms can be maintained through formal methods backed by sanctions—for example, laws and regulations—or informally, through **social customs**.

Traditionally, religion was an important informal enforcement mechanism for social norms; however, in secular countries such as Australia the influence of religion has reduced for many people. Informal regulation of social norms is now more likely to occur through *peer group pressure*; for example, when we conform to the expectations of our families and friends. In Australia, most social norms are maintained informally through social customs, rather than through legal mechanisms.

Let us look at this more closely.

In our society we have *laws* that prohibit us from doing certain things, or require us to do certain other things. For example, in Australia, we *must not* use violence to force people to do what we want them to; we *must* gain a licence before we can drive a car legally; we *may* smoke cigarettes at home if we are over 18 years of age (but we are not *required* to); we *must not* take things from shops that we haven't paid for. If we break laws, we can be punished by the justice system (fined and possibly imprisoned).

In some instances, the social norms may be contrary to the law. For example, in many Australian states it is illegal to drink alcohol in a public place. However, consumption of alcohol on the beach is socially acceptable for many groups of Australians—a social norm, even though it is contrary to the law.

We also have *social customs* that influence both the way we treat other people, and the way we expect other people to treat us. For example, if we are introduced to someone, it is customary in many circumstances to shake hands. It is not legally required, but if someone offers their hand when introduced, it is considered very rude if we refuse to shake their hand. It is not illegal to refuse to shake hands, but it is contrary to social customs and social norms in many contexts. These kinds of social norms are enforced through interpersonal interactions, and if we do not conform to the norms of the group, we are made to feel socially uncomfortable by our peers.

Another example of a social custom is whether or not a 'tip' is offered to the person serving you in a restaurant. In Australia, wages are set without expectation of tips and it is customary not to offer tips. People in Australia may even be offended by being offered tips because it may imply a servile relationship. In the United States, wages are set at a lower rate with the expectation that servers will make up their wages with tips, and it is customary for people to leave tips for servers. There, restaurant staff would see it as very impolite not to leave a tip when paying for a meal.

We also have *regulations*, which fall between customs and laws. For example, the dress code of a workplace may require staff to wear particular types of clothes to work (for example, a suit, or black trousers and a white shirt). If a member of staff wears different clothing, they may be requested to conform. If they refuse, they may be disciplined or dismissed, even though in other respects their work may be satisfactory, and their attire does not break any laws.

BOX 18.1

Everyday sociology

SOCIAL NORMS AND DIFFERENCE

In some instances, different groups within society hold different social norms. In Australian society, for example, within some social groups the social use of illegal drugs is an established social norm. In other social groups the use of illegal drugs is contrary to social norms and in these groups illegal drug use would be considered deviant.

Critical reflection

What are the social norms in your life? And are they normal or deviant?

1. Provide three examples of *laws* that regulate what you may or may not do. In your social group, are there any social norms that are contrary to the law?
2. Provide three examples of *social customs* that influence what you think of as normal or polite behaviour. How do you know when someone is insulting you?
3. Provide one or two examples of *regulations* that influenced what you could or could not do at work (or when you were at school). Do these regulations align with the experiences of your peer group?

Sociology and deviance

Sociologists have asked (and answered) many different questions about deviance. Some sociologists, such as Emile Durkheim and Robert K Merton, wanted to answer the questions: 'Why are people deviant?' and 'What is the function of deviance in society?' Others, such as Michel Foucault (who was discussed in Chapter 8), asked the opposite question: 'Why aren't people more deviant?' or 'Why do people conform to social norms so readily?'

Marxist sociologists—discussed in Chapter 6—have also asked (and answered) questions such as: 'Why do people conform even when it is not in their interests to do so?', 'How do oppressed groups use deviance to resist unjust laws or customs?' and 'How does deviance contribute to social change?' Along these lines, others have asked: 'Which groups benefit by the social norms in a society?' and 'Which groups are disadvantaged by the prevailing social norms?'

So how do we answer all these questions?

Durkheim's strong social ties

Let us start at the beginning. One of the first sociologists to examine deviance methodically from a sociological perspective was Emile Durkheim (1982, original work published 1895). Durkheim wanted to know why people were deviant. He considered that strong social ties between people encouraged altruism and social integration. This strong social integration reduced deviance because people put the needs of the group ahead of their personal interests and desires.

Durkheim contended that some people did not develop strong social ties and remained *egoistical*. Their personal ties were insufficient to encourage social conformity when they wanted to do something that was against social norms. In addition, Durkheim maintained that legal sanctions and punishment were sometimes necessary to support social norms. However, he argued, this would not be successful if people felt alienated (*anomie*) from the legal system and society.

So, for Durkheim, deviance was a result of weak social ties and/or alienation from society.

Merton's five social responses

Merton (1938) was also interested in why people were deviant, and he built upon Durkheim's theory. He suggested that anomie occurred when people had no legitimate means of achieving socially sanctioned goals such as getting a job or buying a house. He suggested that the ways in which people chose to respond could be divided into five categories (which became known as his 'strain theory').

The first category is the *conformist*: someone who is well placed socially to achieve socially sanctioned outcomes—including status, respect, a good job and financial stability—when they follow a socially sanctioned pathway to success. Merton argued that this pathway was unavailable to many social groups because inequality of opportunity and inequity meant that even if they followed the socially sanctioned pathways, they had no opportunity to achieve success: think back to previous chapters about how some people are excluded (including Chapter 8 on power).

The *ritualist*—Merton's second category—is an example of someone in this latter position. Like the conformist, the ritualist accepts social norms and embarks on a socially sanctioned pathway to success, such as by being a good worker. However, in many societies access to opportunities is related to social class (see Chapter 6). Thus, working-class people may find that socially sanctioned pathways do not lead to middle-class success because of inequality of opportunity, and the achievement of socially sanctioned goals remains forever beyond their reach. Historically, working-class people who were ritualists could achieve 'working-class respectability' by following socially sanctioned pathways, but with no prospect of moving beyond this. In contemporary Australia, however, fewer working-class people are satisfied with 'working class respectability' as an alternative to socially sanctioned goals and middle-class success (Manstead 2018).

Merton's third category is the *innovator*, who accepts socially sanctioned goals, but will use any means to achieve them—including those that are not socially sanctioned and even criminal. According to Merton, such behaviour is most commonly found in people who have no ready access to legitimate means to achieve success. The innovator is deviant insofar as they reject the socially accepted ways to achieve, but they do not question the social norms about goals. Examples of innovators would be successful criminals who used their ill-gotten wealth to buy 'respectability': houses in respectable neighbourhoods, prestigious schooling for their children and so on.

Categories 4 and 5, the *retreatist* and the *rebel*, are deviant because they reject both social norms and the socially sanctioned pathways to success. The rebel actively rejects both the goals and the means, while the retreatist passively rejects them. The retreatist withdraws from society and does not pursue socially sanctioned goals. The rebel actively tries to create an alternative society or counterculture.

What is the function of deviance?

Durkheim believed that deviance was useful to society because it affirmed cultural norms by highlighting actions that were not considered normal. By naming deviance, the moral boundaries between right and wrong were affirmed, and rejection of deviance brought 'normal' people together.

At the same time, some 'boundary pushing' by people who were deviant helped to gradually change social norms, and this kept societies dynamic. We will return to this later in the chapter.

For Merton, deviance was a response to anomie and frustration, and an understandable way that people resolved tensions when legitimate means to attain socially valued roles were blocked.

TABLE 18.1 Merton's strain theory

Merton's strain theory	Accepts society's goal	Accepts means	Deviant?
Conformism (no strain)	✓	✓	No. Achieves approved goals by hard work (middle class)
Ritualism (strain between goals and means—strain resolved by prioritising the means over the goals)	✓ but does not have opportunities to succeed	✓	No. Cannot achieve goals, but works hard in jobs without prospect of advancement (working class). Respectability defined by means not goals
Innovation (strain between goals and means—rejects means to resolve strain)	✓	✗	Yes. Accepts goals but achieves them in deviant ways (informal economy)
Retreatism (rejects goals and means to resolve strain)	✗	✗	Yes. Rejects goals and means and drops out
Rebellion (rejects goals and means to resolve strain)	✗	✗	Yes. Rejects goals and means, and actively reshapes alternative

Why aren't people more deviant?

Instead of asking 'why are people deviant', some sociologists ask: 'Why do people conform?'

Sociologists such as Erving Goffman (1959) and Harold Garfinkel (1964; 1967) were interested in exploring how people understood norms and social conventions in everyday life. They wanted to know how people knew about social norms, including:

- Conventions about 'queuing';
- When and where it was permissible to talk to strangers in various social situations; and
- How to make appropriate 'small talk'.

Most people could not easily explain exactly how they knew what was expected.

This led to a series of 'breaching' experiments, or acts of deliberate deviance. Here, sociologists watched what happened when people set out to contravene social norms deliberately. They found that when people intentionally 'breached' conventions, bystanders felt uncomfortable, and would try to rationalise, or make sense of what had happened. This demonstrated that, normally, people continually adjust their actions and speech to accord with unwritten social conventions.

The people doing the breaching often also felt uncomfortable, because they were required to ignore all the social cues that would normally prevent them from acting abnormally. In other words, most people have learnt how to read non-verbal cues from other people, and to respond in ways that fit in with expectations.

> **Critical reflection**
>
> 1. a Write down the social rules for a situation you are familiar with; for example, 'how to be a student attending class', 'how to be a shopper in a grocery supermarket' or 'travelling on public transport'.
>   b In the same situation, what would count as deviant; for example, 'deviant student', 'deviant shopper' or 'deviant passenger'? What would count as a 'breach'?
> 2. Have you ever been in a social situation where you did not know the 'social rules'? What did you do? What did you feel?

The making of a deviant: labelling

Another question explored by some sociologists is *how* people became deviant. We saw in the previous section that most people who deliberately 'breach' social conventions feel very uncomfortable. If this is the case, what enables people who perform 'deviant actions' to ignore the social cues of others?

As we have seen, Durkheim suggested that alienation and lack of social connection enable people to ignore social cues, while Merton suggested that blocked access to the means of conventional success was significant. Under a number of different conditions, people were able to ignore or reject the social cues of mainstream society, or to actively challenge mainstream norms, if they had the support of their peers (Cohen 1973) or friends or family (Garfinkel 1956).

Sociologists also found that if people were *labelled* as deviant by society, they were more likely to act in accordance with these expectations even if they were negative (see the discussion of labelling in Chapter 17). Labelling theory thus explained how some people came to adopt deviant identities. Some sociologists, such as Becker (1973), Goffman (1959) and Garfinkel (1956), found that if people were persistently told that they were deviant by others who were important to them, or by those who held authority positions in society, they would come to see themselves in that way.

As such, Goffman argued, some labelling *creates* deviant identities. In his research, Goffman observed people who had been diagnosed with mental illnesses and documented how they 'learnt' to become a psychiatric patient—taking their cues from the ways in which medical staff and other patients treated them.

Matza (1969) argued that labels applied to individuals influence their self-concept and identity. Someone who has adopted a deviant identity is then likely to align their actions and behaviour with their self-concept. If a person believes they are deviant, they conform to their expectations and the expectations of others, and their deviant actions reinforce their own deviant self-image. When this happens, the deviant person conforms to both their own expectations and the expectations of others.

Totalisation of identity

Let us return to Michel Foucault. Foucault (1978) examined the effects of *emphasis on difference* on concepts of self and identity. Everyone's personal characteristics and social roles are complex, and sociologists refer to the act of labelling someone on the basis of just a small part of who they are as **totalisation**.

People are totalised frequently. The media provides good examples of this when reporting newsworthy events. Imagine a woman has been arrested in a protest against refugee policy. She may have many personal characteristics, life experiences, social roles and personal interests. She may: have five children and several grandchildren; be a prominent Christian; be widowed; be a feminist; be a librarian; be female; be a member of the Liberal Party; be a part-time student of theology; and be a lesbian. If the media select one characteristic or social role to describe the person, they totalise her. Think about the difference between the following:

- 'Prominent Christian protests against policy on refugees ...';
- 'Widow protests against policy on refugees ...';
- 'Liberal party member protests against policy on refugees ...';
- 'Lesbian protests against policy on refugees ...';
- 'Feminist protests ...';
- 'Mother of five protests ....';
- 'Grandmother protests ....';
- 'Librarian protests ....';
- 'Student protests ....'

These accounts describe the same person and the same actions, but they label and totalise her in different ways. As a consequence, the person and her actions may be viewed either more, or less, sympathetically.

FIGURE 18.1 Think about how the media might totalise these protesters.

Consider attitudes to homosexuality. Foucault (1978), writing in the twentieth century, explored how attitudes to homosexuality had changed since the seventeenth century. Before the seventeenth century, sexual orientation was not considered as a defining characteristic of a person's identity ('who they were'). Same-sex sexual activities and relationships took place, and the sexual acts were labelled as 'sinful' because they were contrary to religious teachings, but there was no concept of 'being a homosexual'. The categories of 'heterosexual/homosexual' emerged in the nineteenth century. (Note that the term 'homosexual' was a label usually applied only to men who were same-sex attracted, because lesbians were mostly ignored.) A division was established between heterosexual men (who were labelled as 'normal') and homosexual men (who were labelled as 'deviant'). This label emphasised the difference in one part of their lives (their 'sexual orientation') and ignored completely all the similarities between 'the homosexual' and 'the heterosexual'.

Differences are emphasised through use of stereotypes. Have a look at the example below and see what happens when people are labelled and such labels are 'totalised'.

Critical reflection

What's in a label?

Isabella, who is 15 years old and a very good student, went into a shop one day with a couple of friends and on impulse took various items of makeup that she didn't pay for when she left. She had never stolen anything before and didn't really need the items.

1. How would you describe Isabella?
    a. A young person who has many positive attributes, and who did something out of character on impulse;
    b. A thief;
    c. Someone who can't be trusted;
    d. Someone who is probably easily led by her friends.
2. How do you think Isabella would feel if she was described as
    a. A young person with many positive attributes who did something out of character on impulse;
    b. A thief;
    c. Someone who can't be trusted;
    d. Someone who is easily led.

Now consider some alternatives.

1. If Isabella is labelled as a thief by her family, this label may actually make it easier for her to steal in future, because it changes her family's expectations of her. She will know that they already see her as a thief, and that they expect her to steal again.
2. If Isabella is described by her family as someone who has many positive qualities, but who did something out of character on impulse, then if Isabella has strong social ties with her family, she may be reluctant to steal again, so as not to disappoint her family.
3. If Isabella is aware that all of her family habitually shoplift, and it is considered normal in her family, the label of a thief will enable her to fit in with her family's norms.
4. If Isabella's friends all shoplift but her family do not shoplift, being labelled as a thief will help her fit in with her friends and strengthen her ties with her friends; but will make her feel alienated from her family and weaken her ties with her family.

If you chose the first response in the list, then you view Isabella's decision as something that is only a small part of who she is. If you chose the second, third or fourth responses, you have labelled Isabella by this one action and have emphasised this as a central part of her identity. This is an example of totalisation.

Dividing practices

This process of totalisation is also used in conjunction with '*dividing practices*'. Dividing practices minimise the importance of all the similarities between two groups, and focus only on difference. To take the examples in the previous section, dividing practices were used to divide the world into two categories: homosexual vs heterosexual; and thieves vs non-thieves.

The reality is often more complex. Many people would not label themselves as 'thieves' if they sometimes do not pay for items if they think they will not be caught, or if it is inconvenient to do so. For example, if they find they have been undercharged for an item or an item has not registered through the till, they might not return to the shop and pay. Or if the waiter forgets to add the second dessert that they ordered, they might not point out the error. Many 'thieves' only steal under particular circumstances, and not on every occasion they could steal.

Racial profiling provides another example of how a dividing practice is used to label people—see Abdi's story below.

STUDENT VOICE

Racial profiling as a dividing practice—Abdi's* story

❝ I am from Somalia and have been in Australia 15 years. I am now 25 years old. I live in the Flemington area, just out of Melbourne. Ever since I was old enough to walk around by myself I have been harassed by the police. I have been stopped and asked for my name, address and identification as much as five times a day. Some days I lost track of the number of times I had been stopped and photographed by police.

Many times the police were racist. My friends and I have been called 'black bastards' (and much worse) and told to go back to where we came from. We have been told to move on from outside our flats; we have been hit, had our mobile phones taken, been chased in cars, and taken in police vans and dumped far, far away.

If we fought back we were charged with resisting arrest, assaulting police officers and hindering the police. We were dragged into the criminal justice system merely for resisting abuse of power.

In 2006 we had had enough and wanted to take action, so a community legal centre started to make formal complaints to Victoria Police on our behalf. At one point in 2006, 12 complaints were issued in a two-week period. By the end of that year, the legal centre had lodged 17 complaints in total (one was later withdrawn). The complaints were ignored by the (then) Office of Police Integrity (OPI), which responded that our claims were either 'unfounded' or 'unsubstantiated'.

Not all of us proceeded with formal complaints. Some were scared and worried about their safety.

You need to know that this treatment makes you feel like you will never belong in society. That you're not welcome here, and that you are a second-class citizen ... For any migrant community, police are a reflection of the government and the mainstream community.

The pressure of it all had a big effect. Some of us became homeless, some of us started using drugs, some of us self-harmed, and others were depressed, felt anxious and even became suicidal.

Others of us moved away or refused to leave their house. Many dropped out of school and became withdrawn from their friends, families and community.

Most of us felt distress and began to distrust institutions and services.

A few of us waited. It took a long time, but we continued to fight for justice.**

* Name has been changed.
** Abdi's story continues later in this chapter.

Critical reflection

Think about the following:

1 In what ways is Abdi different from other Australians?
2 In what ways is Abdi the same as other Australians?
3 How was Abdi's appearance used to 'divide' him from white Australians?

Abdi's powerful story can be analysed in many ways, not just through labelling: think, for example, about the links with Chapter 9 and the discussions on race and racism.

Ceremonies of degradation

Garfinkel (1956) investigated the concept of dividing practices further and introduced the idea of '*ceremonies of degradation*': a powerful term that describes how certain types of practices and behaviours (or what he labelled 'ceremonies') are routinely used to reinforce negative labelling and create 'outsiders' (Becker 1973). These ceremonies include the public shaming of children who break rules, and the public labelling of a person as belonging to a group that is despised by others in society.

A feature of ceremonies of degradation is that one 'unvalued' feature of a person (for example, their gender, their sexuality or their race) or action (a lie, a theft), is assumed to completely determine their whole being.

The same researchers also described how '*ceremonies of elevation*' could be used to take one valued feature of a person, and to use this to make positive generalisations about their person and being. Jane Elliott, in the classic documentary *A Class Divided* (1985), illustrated how susceptible we are to both ceremonies of degradation and ceremonies of elevation. She demonstrated how ceremonies of degradation immediately created conflict and bullying between children who had previously been friends, and reduced the academic performance of children who were treated as outsiders and inferior.

Groups labelled as deviant are *stigmatised*—meaning that they are compared negatively with 'normal' people—and then ostracised, devalued by others and blamed for their 'deviance'. Those labelled as deviant are systematically discriminated against, and their supposed deviance is presented as a rationale for discrimination.

> **Critical reflection**
>
> 1 List three 'dividing practices' that are common in Australian society. Then choose one of them and provide examples of how the 'outsiders' are stigmatised.
> 2 Can you think of any time you have been given a 'negative label' as a child (for example, about your appearance, your skills, your actions, your racial identity, or your gender or sexuality). What did you feel? Did you accept the 'label' or did you reject it?

Mass media and moral panics

So far, we have discussed what happens between individuals and groups, and between people who know each other. However, we now live in a world where *mass media* influences our beliefs and opinions. 'Mass media' refers to any mass communication; for example, internet, newspapers, television, movies and social media such as Twitter, Facebook and published blogs (which are discussed in detail in Chapter 14). Mass media provides us with access to an unprecedented volume of information and opinion, and has also enabled '**moral panics**' to emerge.

According to Stanley Cohen, a 'moral panic' is where a 'condition, episode, person or group of persons emerges to become defined as a threat to societal values and interests' (1973, p. 9). It is an overreaction to events (that are often themselves relatively isolated or seemingly inconsequential) that leads to widespread anxiety and fear, and calls for urgent policy action.

Moral panics develop because the mass media presents particular groups of people in a *stylised and stereotypical way*—think, for example, of the way young people are portrayed by the mainstream media (see Chapter 17). Claims appear in the media that a particular group will undermine supposedly shared social values and the very way of life that is assumed to be valued by the majority of people.

Very often, moral panics focus on groups of people who are already marginalised in society. Historically, the targets of moral panics have been groups that appear not to conform in some way, or who have been labelled as 'deviant' or 'other'. Such groups include: people from minority cultures; young people; particular subcultures, especially youth subcultures; feminists; LGBTIQ (lesbian, gay, bisexual, transgender, intersex and queer) people; trade unions; people who are unemployed; people who have mental illness; people who use particular illicit drugs; and people with a different lifestyle, for example, surfies or motorcycle 'gangs'.

Sometimes the moral panic is about a new phenomenon; for example, cyberbullying of children. Sometimes the object of panic is not new, but is suddenly given focus; for example, longstanding intercultural tensions. Cohen (1973) cautioned that sometimes there were long-term effects of a moral panic that could change social policy and the legal framework, and even change the way that members of society see themselves.

One example that many researchers have been discussing is the moral panic around terrorism and the rise of ISIS (originally 'Islamic State of Iraq and Syria', sometimes known as 'Daesh'). While this group has committed countless atrocities, it is not considered an immediate threat to Australia. Despite this, various governments have introduced wide-ranging laws that have removed Australian citizenship from dual nationals who supported ISIS, have rendered some children stateless, and have declined assistance to children in refugee camps whose parents supported ISIS. What we have, then, is the introduction of laws with far-reaching implications based on unsubstantiated public fears.

Moral panics develop in stages …

The first stage in the development of a moral panic is foreshadowed by sensationalised reporting about some event or group and the likely corrosive effects on society. Individuals are described negatively, and negative stereotypes are recycled to present a 'folk devil' that the public will rally against. Descriptions of the folk devil reinforce and emphasise the differences between the objects of the moral panic and 'ordinary people'.

In this first stage, the scale of the supposed problem is also exaggerated, so that readers and listeners believe that it is something that will have an immediate and severe effect on their own lives unless something is done right away. During this stage, social commentators or 'moral entrepreneurs'—such as politicians, clergy, radio shock jocks and news editors—condemn the event or group, and reinforce moral positions to justify their claim that the event or group is an immediate threat to the social order and the way of life of ordinary people.

In the next stage 'accredited experts'—such as police, lawyers, educationalists, psychologists, health promotion experts, community relations experts, social workers and youth workers—provide advice about how the threat can be managed.

What happens next is that governments develop policy, which may or may not incorporate the advice provided by experts. Usually, the response to a moral panic is harsher and more repressive laws, reductions in freedom, and legal protections for the whole population that aim to disrupt and repress the target group. This is usually enforced with a type of 'zero tolerance' policing approach.

In the final stage, the phenomenon either disappears, or becomes less visible but continues 'beneath the radar'. Alternatively, the situation can worsen and become more visible. The moral panic may be quickly forgotten but may leave a legacy of repressive policy and legal changes that persist long after the triggering events have past. Repressive legal responses may amplify the problem, as more people are criminalised and become alienated, and tolerance is reduced.

... And the targets shift

The 'war on drugs' in the early 1970s is an example of a policy response to a moral panic—in this case, about illicit drug usage, especially cannabis. The policy has since been evaluated on several occasions and has been shown to be ineffective, expensive and counterproductive. Only now is legislation beginning to be modified and repealed. More recently, the 'war on terror' has been used to justify legislation that weakens privacy and expands government surveillance.

In Australia, Indigenous people have been recurrent targets of 'moral panics' resulting in various pieces of discriminatory and repressive legislation (see Chapter 16). Historically, this has included massacres of Indigenous people and later legislation that enabled the 'Stolen Generations', enforced Indigenous curfews, and restricted freedom of movement and choice of residence for Indigenous people. The Northern Territory Emergency Response ('the Intervention') that began in 2007 and continues today is the policy result of one such recent moral panic (see Chapter 16). In the early stages of the Intervention, the army was sent to several Indigenous communities in the Northern Territory in response to high profile reporting of child sexual abuse and child exploitation material. The response of the Howard-led federal government was policy that saw Indigenous people treated more repressively and differently from non-Indigenous people. To do this, the government temporarily suspended the *Racial Discrimination Act 1975* in the Northern Territory. When this was challenged, aspects of these policies were extended to include people of all ethnicities though they continue to disproportionately affect Aboriginal and Torres Strait Islander people living in remote communities and have been continually supported by both major political parties.

Other groups targeted in the media as objects of moral panics include asylum seekers and Muslims (particularly since 11 September 2001).

Box 18.2 presents an example of how misinformation and collusion between politicians and the media in 2001 contributed to a moral panic about asylum seekers, and was used to manipulate Australian public opinion away from sympathy for people fleeing political violence and persecution in their own countries.

BOX 18.2

Sociology in history

THE MAKING OF A MORAL PANIC—POLITICAL AND MEDIA REPRESENTATION OF ASYLUM SEEKERS

On 7 October 2001, Australian Prime Minister John Howard, Immigration Minister Phillip Ruddock and Defence Minister Peter Reith accused Iraqi asylum seekers intercepted north of Christmas Island of 'throwing their children overboard' into the ocean in an attempt to pressure the crew of an Australian naval ship to pick them up and take them to Australia. These claims were supposedly supported by video footage.

When the video footage was released, the film showed the asylum seekers were signalling for help because their boat was sinking and no children were thrown overboard. Images of 'children overboard' were selected from footage filmed the day after the reported incident, when the boat sank and over 200 men, women and children ended up in the ocean.

Despite being informed of this by the Australian Defence Force, the Howard Government did not attempt to rectify the incorrect information that surrounded these images until after the planned federal election. When the boat began to sink and it was necessary to mount a rescue, the asylum seekers were labelled 'callous', and the navy who rescued them were labelled 'brave' and 'tolerant' (Slattery 2003, p. 96).

The story, constructed as it was, represented the apparent 'evil' of asylum seekers, compared with the 'goodness' of Australian values and principles. A perceived Australian national identity was pitted against the menacing 'other' presented by asylum seekers who risked their children's safety. Prime Minister Howard stated that the act 'offends the natural instinct of protection' (Slattery 2003, p. 95), and 'I certainly don't want people of that type in Australia'.

On 8 October 2001, every newspaper in the country carried front-page articles about the 'children overboard' event. Many articles quoted Howard's statement that 'we are a humane nation, but we are not a nation that's going to be intimidated by this kind of behaviour' (Henderson 2001).

The media coverage suggested that refugees pose a threat to Australia's national identity and that there was a need to control this particular group. Media reports spoke of 'waves' of refugees claiming asylum in Australia, labelling them as 'illegals'. In addition, there was also a perceived risk of refugees taking employment and welfare benefits from 'everyday Australians'. An example of racially based fear-mongering can be seen from a public comment in the *Herald Sun* that stated: 'Go back to your own country and leave jobs for white Australians only', exemplifying the resentment held by some members of the community towards refugees in Australia. Furthermore, this presents the perceived risk of refugees exploiting Australians. Some headlines presented refugees as tourists; for example: 'Refugee crisis hits home: as Christmas Island overflows, boat people are enjoying shopping trips in Queensland.' Refugees were presented as taking 'all' the jobs, and emphasis was placed upon how refugees drain resources through provision of welfare services.

The historic contribution of refugees to building Australia was ignored. Refugees, especially Muslim refugees, were presented as 'fanatics' and 'terrorists'. The fact that many refugees were trying to escape persecution by extreme Islamist regimes was ignored. Refugees were constructed as a risk and a national threat, and this was used as a dividing practice to reinforce their 'difference' from 'mainstream' Australia. Asylum seekers have become the most recent 'folk devils'.

As Cohen (1973) described in his account of how moral panics develop, what normally happens next is policy change. In this instance, the Howard

Government introduced additional policies such as temporary protection visas to restrict the rights of refugees. Ultimately this led to policies such as mandatory detention and 'tow-backs' of asylum-seeker boats, both of which may be in contravention of Australia's international obligations.

Othering

The asylum-seeker example in the previous section shows how the media can be used to present a group of people as being unlike 'normal' people. As with labelling, in this process all the similarities between the group and 'normal' people are ignored. When labelling is applied to identifiable groups of people—such as asylum seekers, Muslims, Indigenous Australians or women—the process is referred to as '**othering**'.

Through 'othering', dominant groups in society maintain their dominance by assuming that their own features, characteristics and circumstances are the yardstick by which all others should be judged, and this is often combined with totalisation. Othering can be observed in many areas of life where opposing categories are applied as totalising labels for people—for example, sexism (male/female) and racism (non-Indigenous Australian/Indigenous Australian)—and there are many other examples of othering in all areas of life, in most societies. For example, Western standards of beauty for models 'normalise' being white, blonde and thin, and consider anything else as either less desirable, 'exotic' or 'specialist'. Workplaces are organised around the needs of men in traditional roles, and women may be viewed as unreasonable if they want changes to work arrangements to accommodate caring roles.

The problem with othering and totalisation is that they enable dividing practices to become commonplace, because of under-emphasis on the *similarities* between all people as human beings. *Difference* is used to define a category of people who supposedly become the inferiors of a group of 'other' people. A contemporary Australian example of this is the way that Muslim young people are stereotyped, totalised and divided from 'ordinary' (meaning non-Muslim) Australians.

The stereotypical image presented of Muslims is overtly negative and pervasive. The overriding constructions are of Muslim young men as terrorists, rapists or gang members; and of Muslim young women as the veiled female enemy who may be concealing a bomb or who is in need of rescue and liberation from Muslim male oppression. In media accounts, Muslims have been blamed for social ills from 'banning Christmas', to being un-Australian because some women choose to wear the burqa, to turning young people into terrorists.

The media accounts present the whole Muslim community as a threat to the Australian way of life. This media presentation ignores the fact that the vast majority of Muslims reject terrorism and consider that violence is contrary to the Islamic faith. The totalisation of all Muslims as terrorists by prominent politicians and media outlets means that many Muslims find their daily lives are adversely affected by such reporting.

Deviance and resistance

At the beginning of this chapter we stated that Durkheim considered deviance was beneficial because it provided a mechanism by which social norms could change. Now we will examine how social norms have been changed by people who have resisted being labelled as deviant.

Many social norms have changed in Australia over the last century, and some of the past moral panics now look trivial to contemporary eyes. Social norms about gender roles have changed considerably; for example, married women who work are no longer viewed as deviant. This change occurred despite repeated moral panics about the changing role of women during the twentieth century.

The feminist movement challenged accepted social norms by rejecting commonly held assumptions about the inferiority of women, and drew attention to the normalisation of domestic violence. As a consequence, social norms about gender have changed; women achieved greater formal equality and now have a broader role in society. One hundred years ago working women were frequently blamed for the ills of society or for male violence; but it has now become less possible for the media and politicians to create a moral panic in this way.

At the beginning of the twentieth century, (male) homosexuality was illegal in all states in Australia, and gay men were prosecuted if they were discovered, even when sexual activity was consensual and in private. The Gay Liberation Movement successfully campaigned for the repeal of these laws. Over time, the campaign changed social norms. In 2017, the Australian Marriage Law Postal Vote found that 61.6 per cent of the Australian voters supported marriage equality (Australian Bureau of Statistics 2017) and legislation was passed to enable same-sex marriage in the same year. The passing of this legislation further removed discrimination in some spheres of life, including family law.

Indigenous Australians have challenged (white) stereotypes about Indigenous people and, as these campaigns succeed, it will become more difficult to recycle outdated negative stereotypes about Indigenous people that feed moral panics.

STUDENT VOICE

Resistance and change—Abdi's* story continues

❝ We began to work with the Flemington Legal Centre (FLC). In 2008, a partnership between FLC and the law firm Arnold Bloch Leibler was formed, and the lawyers there told FLC that we had a racial discrimination case, and we decided to lodge our complaints about racial vilification with the Australian Human Rights Commission.

We were convinced that our experiences showed that African Australian males were being singled out for different treatment from the rest of the community and that the police had stopped us on the basis of our race or skin colour rather than for any legitimate legal reason. We moved to join our individual claims to take group action that would address policing practices we knew intimately to be racist. Our claim outlined over 140 incidents, which constituted a systemic pattern of racial profiling, meaning that Victoria Police had breached the federal *Racial Discrimination Act 1975*.

At the time the claim was lodged there were 16 of us who had already committed two if not three years of our lives to seeking accountability from the police.

We felt we needed to change things for the younger generation. We feel responsible to protect our younger brothers, future children and other African Australians from the damaging experiences we have had. So we persisted, even though our community felt scared. Many elders told us this is a fight we shouldn't be partaking in, due to our refugee and immigrant backgrounds. We were also told by just about everybody, actually, that we could not win.

In 2010, after many failed mediation sessions through the Human Rights Commission, we lodged our claim at the Federal Court. Our application listed individual police officers, the State of Victoria and the Chief Commissioner of the State of Victoria. This next stage of the legal process was just as slow—it wasn't listed for a hearing until 2013, by which time only six of us were left, as the others just wanted to get on with their lives. There were times when we didn't know if our case would be heard, as there were last-minute attempts by the other side to strike out the case. Fortunately, these were unsuccessful.

Those of us who were still there felt unhopeful. We were aware that the Federal Court could well find that racial discrimination had occurred, but that it did not have the power to change the practices of Victoria Police. But we held on.

Then, as we prepared to enter a two-month trial, the matter was settled out of court. The outcome was better than we had hoped.

There were several parts of the settlement, one being that Victoria Police and the individual police officers acknowledged that any policing involving discrimination on the basis of race is unacceptable.

Two further key outcomes were that Victoria Police would hold a public inquiry inviting community comment on their 'field contact' policy, and that Victoria Police would also seek public comment on cross-cultural training provided to its police members. The inquiry opened on 1 June 2013 for an eight-week period, and received 68 submissions from organisations and individuals.

The report from the inquiry was published in December 2013 and contains actions that need to be taken in response to the report.

The inquiry was the first of its kind held by Victoria Police. Its outcomes have the potential to improve the interactions of police with Aboriginal, newly arrived and culturally diverse communities not only in Victoria, but also across Australia, as other police services take note of the Victorian response.

As part of the settlement, we were able to publicly release materials relating to the litigation process; and we maintained ownership of our individual stories and the research undertaken for the trial, which contained considerable findings. There were some materials, however, that remained sealed.

* Name has been changed

Conclusion: towards inclusion as an alternative to moral panics

As we have seen, culture and customs are not static and the dominant social norms are dynamic and change over time. Moral panics are still used to exclude some groups in society and create 'outsiders'.

Over the last two decades, the 'new outsiders' are Muslims, who are being stereotyped negatively as potential terrorists, but othering also includes the poor and unemployed—who are being stereotyped as 'dole bludgers'—as well as refugees and Indigenous people. How should Australian respond? We can see that change can happen when policy makers act in positive ways. For example, as a response to COVID-19, Newstart was renamed 'Jobseeker' with payments boosted. The unemployed were recast as innocent victims of circumstance. We do not know if this will last, but we can see that such framing can quickly change perceptions.

In Australia, there will never be a single concept of deviance that everyone agrees upon. Australia is multicultural and includes many subcultural groups who have different cultural values. Cultural groups with non-Anglo-Celtic traditions, values and beliefs include, for example, Indigenous Australians, Greek Australians, Italian Australians, Chinese Australians, Lebanese Australians and Pacific Islanders.

Australia is a liberal democracy and a pluralist society. A central value of liberalism is tolerance of groups of people who have different values and customs, as long as the customs do not interfere with the rights of others. For example, people have freedom of religion, and there is considerable latitude in personal choice about clothing, sexual relationships and expression of political views. Inclusion and pluralism strengthen liberal democracy by giving people maximum freedom consistent with the freedoms of others.

Mainstream Australian culture has been dominated by Anglo-Celtic laws and customs. Different ethnic and cultural groups have different customs, and this can be seen in many areas of life, including: what is considered decent or indecent clothing; how parents interact with their children; what food should be eaten or avoided; how children should treat their parents and grandparents; beliefs about conformity and non-conformity; and religious and spiritual explanations about the moral universe.

There are also different subcultural groups, who have differing concepts of a 'good life' and the right way to live, and have social norms that differ from those of dominant Anglo-Celtic Australian culture in some respects.

The options facing Australians are either to support maximal tolerance of difference, consistent with liberal values of not restricting the liberty of others, or to expend energy on demonising and persecuting 'folk devils'. If Australians follows the path of inclusion and understanding this will strengthen liberal democracy. If Australians follow the path of creating folk devils, they risk creating the very problem they seek to avoid—an alienated minority that has no commitment to the central liberal value of toleration.

Summary points

* Ideas about deviance and normality vary between cultures and also within a culture at different times in history. For this reason, deviance is considered a 'social construct' that reflects the dominant values and worldview within a particular culture at a given time.
* Our sense of personal identity—our concept of who we are and whether we are a valuable human being—is shaped by our social interactions with other people who are important to us. If individuals (or groups) are labelled as deviant, they become more likely to align their behaviour with the expectations that others have of them, and to believe they are deviant. This is known as 'labelling theory'.
* Moral panics arise in all modern societies when the mass media presents a particular event or group of people as a threat to the core values of society. As the moral panic unfolds, experts propose solutions to 'manage' the threat, and policies are enacted that have long-term and often negative effects on the liberty of all citizens. Frequently, these responses remain in place long after the events that prompted the moral panic have dissipated.

Sociological reflection

1 To what extent do you think recent public discussion about the radicalisation of Muslim youth constitutes a moral panic? Explain the reasons for your assessment.
2 Think about groups in Australian society that have been presented recently as posing a threat to the Australian way of life, or to Australian values. Examine how discussion developed in the media and in politics, and discuss whether you think this is an example of a moral panic, explaining your reasons.
3 Can you think of historical acts of deviance that later came to be known as heroic acts? What do these now heroic acts suggest about the perception of deviance?

Discussion questions

1 Check your understanding of the concept of 'othering', and then find examples of othering in the popular media. Some possible starting points could be:
   a Articles about celebrities, either online or in magazines: look especially at how people of colour, women, and gay and lesbian celebrities are described;
   b Movies that present the world uncritically from the perspective of dominant groups in society;
   c Newspaper reports of ethnic minorities, Aboriginal and Torres Strait Islanders, women and people with disabilities.

2   In 2012, a 17-year-old African-American boy, Trayvon Martin—who was wearing a hoodie and carrying iced tea, Skittles and his mobile phone—was fatally shot in a Florida gated community by George Zimmerman, the Neighbourhood Watch captain. Zimmerman reported seeing 'a real suspicious guy', a 'black male' walking around. What does the language Zimmerman uses to describe Martin tell us about his stereotypes of young Black men? The acquittal of Zimmerman led to the establishment of the Black Lives Matter (BLM) movement. How has the BLM movement challenged such moral panics about 'black males'?

3   Have a look at news stories online or in a few newspapers. Find examples of stories where the descriptions of people have 'totalised' their identity. Discuss how the story would have been received differently if the labels had been removed, or if different labels had been used to describe the person.

References and further readings

REFERENCES

Australian Bureau of Statistics (ABS) 2017, 'Australian Marriage Law Postal Survey, 2017', *Cat No. 1800.0*, ABS, Canberra: <www.abs.gov.au/ausstats/abs@.nsf/mf/1800.0>.

Becker, HS 1973, *Outsiders' Studies in the Sociology of Deviance*, Free Press, New York.

Cohen, S 1973, *Folk Devils and Moral Panics: The Creation of the Mods and Rockers*, MacGibbon & Kee, London.

Durkheim, E 1982, *The Rules of Sociological Method*, trans. WD Halls, The Free Press, New York (original work published 1895): <http://comparsociology.com/wp-content/uploads/2013/02/Emile-Durkheim-Rules-of-Sociological-Method-1982.pdf>.

Foucault, M 1978, *The History of Sexuality, Vol. 1: An Introduction*, trans. R Hurley, Pantheon Books, New York: <https://suplaney.files.wordpress.com/2010/09/foucault-the-history-of-sexuality-volume-1.pdf>.

Garfinkel, H 1956, 'Conditions of successful degradation ceremonies', *American Journal of Sociology*, 61(5), 420–4.

Garfinkel, H 1964, 'Studies of the routine grounds of everyday activities', *Social Problems*, Winter, 11(3), 225–50: <www.jstor.org/discover/10.2307/798722?uid=23310&uid=3737536&uid=2129&uid =2&uid =70&uid=3&uid=67&uid=62&uid=23309&uid=5909656&sid=21106009182901>.

Garfinkel, H 1967, *Studies in Ethnomethodology*, Prentice Hall, Englewood Cliffs, NJ.

Goffman, E 1959, *Presentation of Self in Everyday Life*, Doubleday, New York.

Henderson, G 2001, 'Unleashing a "sleeper" issue: ethnic suspicion', *The Age*, 18 September, p. 5.

Manstead, ASR 2018, 'The psychology of social class: How socioeconomic status impacts thought, feelings, and behaviour', *British Journal of Social Psychology*, April, 57(2), 267–91.

Matza, D 1969, *Becoming Deviant*, Prentice Hall, Englewood Cliffs, NJ.

Merton, R 1938, 'Social structure and anomie', *American Sociological Review*, 3(5), 672–82: <www.d.umn.edu/cla/faculty/jhamlin/4111/Readings/MertonAnomie.pdf>.

Slattery, M 2003, *Key Ideas in Sociology*, Nelson Thornes, Cheltenham.

FURTHER READING

A Class Divided (1985) (a classic documentary featuring Jane Elliott).

CHAPTER 19
Work and society

JUSTINE HUMPHRY

CHAPTER OVERVIEW

Work is a central feature of everyday life, but what do we actually mean by 'work'? On the surface work seems to be a straightforward idea: we all have to do it to earn a living; it takes up a great deal of the week and eats into our 'leisure' time. Yet work does not mean the same thing to all people, across all cultures and throughout all times. In fact, *work*—its meaning, organisation and practice—is going through an intense period of transformation right now in all parts of the world.

Where work is carried out, who performs it, how it is conceived and organised are all changing, in part because of the increasingly central role digital technology plays in carrying out everyday life. Just imagine how hard it would be to find employment without being able to search for a job on the internet. Think about how you would keep in contact with your friends, family and colleagues without a mobile phone. Changes to work are also due to the expansion of global capitalism and the rise of new modes of production (how people organise themselves to produce goods and services), premised on the ideal of fast-moving and flexible knowledge-based economies. It would be tempting to emphasise the globalising tendency of these changes, but in actuality these are highly uneven in and across national borders and are not driven or determined solely by one all-powerful homogenising force.

In this chapter we probe changes in contemporary work and the links between work, technology and identity. What is the place of work in our everyday lives today? What is the role of digital technology in complicating traditional divisions between 'work' and 'leisure', 'production' and 'consumption', 'public' and 'private'? What are the other factors besides technology that contribute to these changes? Work is less secure and stable today than it has been in the past, and some have described these new conditions of work as 'precarious work' (Fudge & Owens 2006; Kalleberg & Vallas 2017). Who is most affected by these changes? When addressing these questions, we are concerned not only with common experiences, but also with variations within societies and cultures that lead to distinct expressions of work, organisation and identity.

After reading this chapter, you should be able to:
- Understand that work has different meanings and histories
- Provide some explanation for why and how work is changing, with particular attention to the role of digital technology
- Understand how changes to work impact on the relationship between 'work' and 'life', and 'production' and 'consumption', and on identity processes
- Understand the impacts that these changes have on a range of social groups, such as youth and the aged.

KEY TERMS

'Anywhere, anytime' work An idealised work practice involving working 'on the move', flexibly or in different locations with the support of digital technology.

Ever-presence A new time sense, corresponding closely to the 'extended present' proposed by time philosopher Nowotny (1994), based on micro increments and continuous connectivity rather than the distinct partitioning of daily life into 'work' and 'leisure'.

Gig economy Gig economy workers are those independent contractors who work flexibly and on-call for demand companies such as Uber and Airtasker.

Global capitalism A new form of capitalism underpinned by an informational mode of production that is expanding all around the world and brings with it new ways of working and living in rapidly changing conditions.

Precarious work Insecure and poor-quality work—such as temporary employment—with lack of labour control and protection, and little income for living. More generally, the concept is used to capture a shift in modernity from stability to instability.

Prosumption The way that cultural and economic activity combines technologies of production with the labour of consumers, such as self-service food outlets like McDonald's and self-serve checkouts at supermarkets.

Respatialisation The spatial reorganisation of work using digital platforms and technologies. These changes have given rise to new forms of business and labour models. It can take multiple forms such as moving work across national boundaries (e.g. 'the call centre'), shifting work to online platforms (e.g. 'Mechanical Turk') and putting workers on the move (e.g. 'Uber' and 'Deliveroo').

Spirit of capitalism A term used by Weber in 1905 to refer to an ethic of hard work and a sense that work is inherently fulfilling and rewarding, which forms the basis of the culture of modern capitalism.

Technology A bundle of practices, techniques and materials embedded in and shaped by larger societal transformations, which plays a special role in driving and supporting the prevailing mode of production.

Work ethic An orientation and attitude towards work that an individual worker is expected to adopt.

Introduction

How and where did I work today? To begin with, I travelled by car to a university that is not my usual place of work because my son was attending a school holiday workshop at another university in the city where I live. After dropping off my son and having a coffee in a campus café, I walked to the university library. There I sat at a communal table, opened my laptop and logged on to the campus-wide guest WiFi network. I used my supplied username and password to get connected to the internet. I was then able to retrieve my emails and new messages and log in to get my work files through my own university's virtual private network. I carried out my work alongside students at an oblong table offering an array of power points. A number of smartphones lay face-up on the table within close reach of their owners. My iPhone charged at one of the power points. It buzzed frequently, notifying me of a new email or notification from Facebook, LinkedIn, WhatsApp or Twitter.

Maybe the way I described working in the paragraph above sounds familiar to you. It is typical insofar as the work many people carry out today is conducted electronically and is not restricted to a particular place and, in some instances, time. Nevertheless, this does not mean that all work is conducted '**anywhere, anytime**', a label used to describe and promote a particular mode and style of working today. There are still plenty of workers who labour in ways that do not conform to this model, just as there continues to be many different occupations and types of work.

Even factoring in the changing nature of work, what I have just been talking about is only one definition of work as *paid labour*. This commonsense understanding of work, which sums up how many of us think of and experience work, fails to capture the radically different ways that work has been conceived across different places and times, as well as ongoing disputes over its meaning.

The meaning of work

Just as the concept of 'society' is complex and changing, so too is the concept of 'work'. The ancient Greeks regarded work as an unfortunate necessity. Work—especially physical work—was rarely performed by wealthy Greeks and was carried out by the lowest in the social order, such as slaves and foreigners; issues of 'modern slavery' and the exploitation of migrant workers remain even in our modern society. Plato, an eminent Greek philosopher of the time, strongly advised that commercial activities such as working at a trade or business should only be done by immigrants (Anthony 1977, p. 17).

Because it was the slaves and immigrants doing much of the work, Greeks who were wealthier and higher in social status had more leisure time and were free to participate in other activities. Being involved in art, philosophy and politics—not work—was considered to be at the heart of citizenship. This is what the Greeks thought of as the 'good life' (Anthony 1977). As expressed in one famous ancient text by Aristotle, another Greek thinker, work got in the way of citizens' real duties of running the government:

> In the best governed states ... none of them [citizens] should be permitted to exercise any mechanic employment or follow merchandise as being capable and destructive to virtue; neither should they be husbandman, that they may be at leisure to improve in virtue and perform the duty they owe to the state (Aristotle, *Politics*, p. 1328b, cited in Anthony 1977)

Although the Hebrews and the early Christians thought differently about work to the ancient Greeks, they held in common an idea that labouring was not particularly fulfilling or rewarding and did not make you a more responsible or virtuous person. Yet today work plays a central role in how we judge ourselves and others. So when did ideas about work start to change?

We have already seen in Chapter 5 how, during the Industrial Revolution, there was a major restructuring of the idea of time, from being thought of as *seasonal* to a *linear* process. This change ran in parallel with a related shift in the meaning of work. It was during the Industrial Revolution, and in its lead-up, that work became thought of as a moral and social duty. Max Weber, in his 1905 book *The Protestant Ethic and the Spirit of Capitalism*, made the link between these new ideas about work and the doctrines of the sixteenth century Protestant reformation (Weber 1958). He argued it was at this time that the ethos or '**spirit of capitalism**' was born.

> This peculiar idea, so familiar to us today, but in reality so little a matter of course, of one's duty in a calling, is what is most characteristic of the social ethic of capitalistic culture, and is in a sense the fundamental basis of it. It is an obligation which the individual is supposed to feel and does feel towards the content of his professional activity, no matter in what it consists, in particular no matter whether it appears on the surface as a utilization of his personal powers, or only of his material possessions (as capital) (1958, p. 54).

Even though manual work was looked down on and was rarely carried out by the upper classes, the new understanding of work as having intrinsic value formed the basis for a new *ethic* of work during the Industrial Revolution. With the expansion of work to the majority, work eventually came to be seen as a natural and necessary part of everyday life—it became a cultural norm, separated from home life and distinct from 'leisure'. However, this did not come about automatically or without resistance.

Factory work was very different to work in agrarian or domestic cottage industries, where workers worked in the field or from home, breaking up their work according to cycles of the seasons and the needs of their craft. In contrast, historians have charted how during the Industrial Revolution, workers initially had to be made to work in new ways, for longer hours and without interruption (Anthony 1977). British historian Edward Palmer Thompson (1967) described the industrial strategies and techniques of controlling the volume and pace of work, as well as workers' punctuality, in terms of a 'time-discipline'. Emile Durkheim, a French sociologist writing in the late nineteenth century, argued that the centralisation of work in cities and industrial organisation brought about the pursuit of more specialised tasks and occupations, resulting in a new 'division of labour' (2014).

During this time the idea that work was a virtuous activity and inherently pleasing to God was promoted, and, as Weber said, proved integral to the expansion of industrial production. Securing workers' consent for the new demands of factory work through a **work ethic** was much more effective than coercion, though these were also used together. Thus, even though the roots of these ideas were religious, they aligned with capitalistic culture and the interests of factory owners, acting as a form of social and labour control.

The rise of capitalism therefore went hand in hand with changes in the meaning of 'work' and 'time' defined by the industrial mode of production. As noted in Chapter 5, capitalism was aggressively imposed on societies across the world by its European founders, followed by upheavals, altered structures, relationships and perceptions (Petras & Veltmeyer 2013). It involved the institution of the new industrial mode of production and the global expansion of a capitalistic culture.

Summing up this section, when we look at the different meanings of work, we see that work is moulded according to the requirements of the prevailing mode of production. It was Karl

Marx (1818–83), you might recall from Chapter 6, who argued that the 'mode of production' was the basis of societies. Yet, this is not achieved without dispute, indifference or refusal. Workers have collectively resisted and tried to gain control over the labour process to improve the quality and conditions of work. Women and carers have long argued against the distinction between paid and unpaid work predicated on the gendered division of labour to extend recognition of the domestic labour they perform (see Oakley 1974). Some cultural groups, such as ultra-Orthodox Jews, continue to believe that paid work is degrading and takes away from the more important pursuit of prayer and scholarship (Sadler 2002). The meaning of work is therefore a social negotiation that takes place within specific historical periods and cultural settings, but is it a fair negotiation for all? Those who are most powerful preserve the power to define and direct the future of work.

The rise of global capitalism

For some time now (since the latter half of the twentieth century), social and cultural theorists have been observing the emergence of a new form of capitalism underpinned by an informational mode of production. This new capitalism has been variously described as: the 'knowledge economy' (Drucker 1969), the 'information society' (Machlup 1962; Porat 1977), the 'post-industrial society' (Bell 2001), 'post-Fordism' (Ash 1994), the 'network society' (Castells 1996; Van Dijk 2012), the 'new economy' (Sennett 2006), 'soft capitalism' (Thrift 2005), 'liquid modernity' (Bauman 2000), the 'mobile society' (Urry 2008), the 'digital economy' (Malecki & Moriset 2008) and 'digital capitalism' (Schiller 2000), to name a few.

Although these models emphasise different characteristics and dynamics of the new **global capitalism**, they have in common the idea that all around the world we are working and living in new ways and in rapidly changing conditions. One longstanding popular prediction, particularly of the 1950s and 60s, was that these changes, and the progressive forces of technology, would lead to less work and more leisure, and that we would soon all enter the 'leisure society' (Veal 2009). Yet, research on work has consistently shown that many of us are doing more work than ever before.

In Australia, for example, there has been a steady increase in the average hours of paid work. In the 2008 *Australian Work and Life Index* (AWALI), around 55 per cent of employees reported long working hours, work overload and an overall poor work–life interaction (Skinner & Pocock 2010, p. 8). In an updated 2014 report, the authors found that these trends persisted (Skinner & Pocock 2014) with people working four hours more per week than they would prefer.

Significantly, this figure refers only to the hours that are counted as work. This is further explained by Pocock, Skinner and Williams as follows:

> actual hours of work are amplified by the extra time it takes getting to and from work, catching up on work at home, and recovering from it; especially among those who feel that work is becoming more demanding and intensive (2012, p. 1).

What these authors are referring to is the way that work is consuming more of our time even when what we are doing is not strictly speaking 'work', or recognised as such. The expansion of activities *oriented to our work* is an increasing feature of everyday life, as work is reorganised according to the ideals of mobility and flexibility. Gregg (2011) describes these extra activities as 'anticipatory affects', citing the myriad online tasks such as checking and monitoring emails as symptomatic of the demand on professionals to display their continuous commitment to work in today's knowledge and creative industries.

Besides working hours, many of us are also working longer into our lives. Retirees work well in to their 60s, 70s and 80s, according to Pocock, Skinner and Williams (2012), often to subsidise retirement incomes that are insufficient to cover the cost of living. These trends have coincided with long-term changes in the type of work undertaken. In Australia, like many other developed countries, information-based occupations have taken over manufacturing jobs and there has been an increase in part-time and casual work.

A chorus of writers point to the fragmented, polarised and complex picture of this transition to global capitalism, highlighting the new conditions of insecure and poor-quality employment or '**precarious work**' that are fast becoming the norm. Significantly, structural differences and inequalities mean that some groups are particularly exposed to precarious work, with gender, youth, immigrant status, ethnicity and ageing being key factors that increase the likelihood of a person being in non-standard, low-wage and insecure employment (Kalleberg 2013).

> **BOX 19.1**
> ## Thinking sociologically
>
> ### DEFINING 'PRECARIOUS WORK'
>
> 'Precarious work' is a concept used to refer to the structural features of work that make it insecure and of poor quality. Vosko (2006, p. 71) defines 'precarious work' along four dimensions as:
> 1 Less continuity of employment;
> 2 Minimal control over your own labour;
> 3 Lack of regulatory protection; and
> 4 Little income for living.
>
> More generally, the concept of 'precarious work' is used to capture a shift in modernity from stability to instability. Bourdieu (1998) talks about *précarité* or 'insecurity' as a generalised condition of society linked to the de-localisation of work in processes of globalisation. Barbier (2002) adopts the term *précarité*, which was initially used to refer to generalised poverty in France, to explain contemporary work conditions under global capitalism.
>
> Vosko (2006) and Fudge and Owens (2006) have separately referred to 'precarious work' as the feminisation of work in the shift to an information-based economy. Feminisation names the growth in the kinds of jobs once undertaken largely by women, highlighting the gendered nature of work in general and 'precarious work' in particular. This is held up in figures that show that not only is there a higher representation of women doing information work, but that women account for more of those employees engaged in part-time, casual and self-employed work.

Global capitalism brings with it many changes in how we think about and carry out work—an uneven process affecting social groups in unequal ways. How is the time and place of work changing? Are we working more than before? How is work divided up and organised? How is the relationship of work to everyday life different? All of these questions relate to aspects of this transformation. Though not exclusively a result of technological change (globalisation, deregulation and weakening of protections for workers are other key factors in the rise of global capitalism), these changes in work would not be possible if it was not for digital technology.

The role of digital technology in changing work

We know that the meaning of work changes across time and with different cultures, and is shaped by prevailing modes of production. We can now turn to the role of digital technology in the transformation of work and expansion of global capitalism.

Before we go further, it is important to be clear about what we mean by **technology**. Many philosophers and social and cultural scholars have pondered this definition, and there are many views and perspectives. The understanding adopted here is that technology is a bundle of practices, techniques and materials embedded in and shaped by larger societal transformations (see Chapter 13 as well as MacKenzie & Wajcman 1999). Technology plays a special role in driving and supporting an informational mode of production, just as technologies of manufacturing were necessary for the growth of industrial capitalism.

Digital technologies contribute to the growth of global capitalism in a number of interrelated ways:

- Respatialising and restructuring work;
- Forming new kinds of work and industries; and
- Creating a new ethic of work made possible by a range of tools and platforms that orient our attitudes and sense of time towards work in certain ways.

Respatialising and restructuring work

The idea that activities of work need not be bound to any place or time, is captured in the catchphrase 'anywhere, anytime' work coined in 1996 by American computer scientist Leonard Kleinrock (1996). First taken up by corporate managers, sales staff and creative professionals, it is now commonplace to find trade workers, freelancers, students, real estate agents and a range of other occupational types acting out some aspect of this vision: working on the move, flexibly or in different locations with the support of digital technology (Townsend & Batchelor 2005; Perry & Brodie 2006; Rossitto & Eklundh 2007).

Indeed, for many years the 'anywhere, anytime' ideal functioned more as a vision or 'myth' of the future of work, inspiring experiments in work such as the 'virtual office' of Chiat Day in 1994 (Berger 1999). Yet the idea maintained its currency and **respatialisation** is now firmly embedded in contemporary approaches to work organisation. Mobile and wireless digital technologies vastly increase the scope and range of possible work locations and modes, allowing for technology-enabled mobility (such as home-based, virtual and nomadic work) combined with some form of organisational flexibility. Odih (2003) describes 'organisational flexibility' as the breaking down of boundaries within organisations along two main fronts: in the use of existing sources of labour, and the increase in the employment of temporary staff to call on only when needed, also known as 'just-in time' labour.

In Australia, research on the location of work has shown a consistent shift to forms of work outside of the traditional workplace. In 2008, the Australian Bureau of Statistics (ABS) reported that 24 per cent of employees worked at least some hours at home. By 2013, the number of Australians working away from the office using the internet was 51 per cent of the total workforce, with 28 per cent working while travelling, according to a national survey of digital work (Gregorio 2013). The changes forced on us by the COVID-19 pandemic would have seen this number climb much higher. While we do not know what a post-COVID world will look like, we do know that the 'new normal' will see working away from the office become even more commonplace. However, not all of this out-of-office work is captured as work. In 2016, the ABS reported that just under half of the 3.5 million Australians who regularly work at home are 'catching up'(ABS 2016).

An important feature of the respatialisation of work—one that is sometimes overlooked—is that jobs and even entire industries are restructured to move them across national boundaries and in some instances to make them boundaryless, enabled by digital technology. Malecki and Moriset (2008, pp. 1–2) explain this in terms of the 'splintering of economic space', in which labour is spatially reorganised to take advantage of 'optimal combinations of (high) skills and (low) wages in various places around the world'. An example they give is the transnational call centre. One of the characteristics of this form of organisation is a disparity not just in wages, but also in conditions: low-wage information workers tend to be housed in workplaces under intensified conditions of work and surveillance, compared to a class of high-wage knowledge professionals who are mobile and relatively autonomous. These very different outcomes illustrate how the respatialisation of work is a complex and highly uneven process.

Even within highly industrialised nations, the respatialisation of work supported by digital technologies has paradoxical or what philosopher of technology Michael Arnold (2003) called 'janus-faced' effects. Studies have shown new forms of intensification, time pressure and the blurring of work–life boundaries (see Bain & Taylor 2000; Bittman, Brown & Wajcman 2009; Lowry & Moskos 2005). Others have pointed out the enhanced individual control over work and time and the ability to interact with family beyond the home (see Crowe & Middleton 2012; Wajcman 2008).

Perhaps it should not be surprising that there are contradictory effects that go with the respatialisation of work: divisions between 'work' and 'life', and 'public' and 'private' have acted as the basic building blocks of Western cultures and economies for at least two centuries These divisions are not natural but, as Davidoff and Hall (1987) documented, were historically produced over the eighteenth and nineteenth centuries to support industrial capitalism. The segregation of social spheres according to gender created a workforce of domestic labourers whose unpaid labour underpinned the formal economy (Germov 2007). The workplace provided an enclosed site for the discipline and coordination of workers and tasks in a way that could not have taken place outside of the workplace (Clarke 2006).

Significantly, these separate spheres not only supported the needs of industrial production, but also acted as anchors for a range of new social and personal identities, and cultural practices. Having 'life' opposed to 'work' created an arena of 'leisure' in which workers could partake as consumers: spending their time and money on an ever-expanding market of products and services. With the shift to a new mode of production based on information and knowledge creation, these traditional divisions are in the process of being collapsed and reassembled.

Forming new kinds of work and industries

There is very little about work today that remains untouched through its mediation by digital technology: it is not just *how* work is performed and the location of work that is transformed. New *kinds* of work are also created using the paid and unpaid labour of individuals, which in turn forms the basis of new knowledge-based and creative industries.

The blurring of boundaries between work and leisure is one aspect of a larger transformation in the relationship of production and consumption. This is captured in the neologism **'prosumption'** by Ritzer and Jurgenson (2010) to mean the way that cultural and economic activity now combines technologies of production with the labour of consumers, citing self-service food outlets such as McDonald's as their ideal type.

BOX 19.2
Thinking sociologically

DEFINING 'PROSUMPTION'

Ritzer and Jurgenson (2010) introduced the term 'prosumption' to break down the traditional approach of treating production and consumption as separate processes. They argued that these two processes have always been closely intertwined, but that in the age of the internet and social media they have become even more tightly bound. They also argued that as part of this change, there is much more of a reliance on unpaid rather than paid labour; that more products are offered at no cost; and that the economy is defined by abundance rather than scarcity (2010, p. 14). These authors note that the origins of the word 'prosumer' can be traced to Alvin Toffler's 1980 work *The Third Wave*, which argued that even though the Industrial Revolution divided production and consumption into distinct processes, the basic form of any society is in actuality a combination of the two—'prosumption'—and that we have now entered into the 'third wave' where the distinction between them disappears (1980, p. 17). In the *McDonaldization of Society*, Ritzer (2008) offers the case of McDonald's as the exemplar of this use of consumers as labourers, arguing that the acceleration of prosumption occurred in parallel with the growth of the fast-food industry from the 1950s (quoted in Ritzer & Jurgenson 2010, p. 18):

> the 'diner' at a fast food restaurant, the consumer of that food, is also, at least to some degree, a producer of the meal. Among other things, diners are expected to serve as their own waiters carrying their meals to their tables or back to their cars, sandwich makers (by adding fixings such as tomatoes, lettuce, and onions in some chains), salad makers (by creating their own salads at the salad bar), and bus persons (by disposing of their own debris after the meal is finished).

Prosumption is the engine that drives the emergence of a host of new industries and types of creative and information work. The emergence of self-service in the food industry was just the beginning. The development of the internet and web-based platforms that support user-generated content (also known as Web 2.0) facilitated new opportunities for—and indeed required—active participation by consumers. Concepts such as 'produsage' (Bruns 2008) and 'participatory culture' (Jenkins 2006) are terms that point to the types of creative activity and culture that unfolds in a system of production premised on information exchange.

While prosumption provides opportunities for consumer participation in content and even technology creation—web mashups are good examples of this—the same process also gives rise to new kinds of work, oftentimes unpaid. One example given by Terranova (2000) is the coding work of programmers and amateurs who put in large amounts of 'free labour' for the open source community and whose contributions have been key to the development of the internet. According to Terranova (2000), the ability to capture this cultural and affective labour forms the basis of the 'digital economy'.

Authors such as Burston, Dyer-Witheford and Hearn (2010), Fuchs (2010) and Scholz (2012) have similarly highlighted how new forms of 'digital labour' are a defining feature of digital economic activity. Commercially operated sites and platforms—including programs and systems—such as Facebook, Instagram, Twitter and Yelp—extract value from users in the form of online user-generated content, which, in turn, is commodified for use in targeted advertising.

While many workers are paid for building the platforms that organisations such as Facebook and Twitter use, many do not! Many workers undertake unpaid 'platform work' (Humphry 2013). This is carried out by ordinary users and collaboratively keeps office, game and entertainment systems operational. These systems in turn create platforms that support the work environment and allow things to run smoothly (see also Humphry 2014). In fact, without this kind of unpaid efforts by workers, it is doubtful that the organisations mentioned above would operate as well as they do.

All of these new forms of work are becoming an increasingly normal feature of everyday life as our activities become completely intertwined with and supported by media environments.

Digital technologies are also fuelling more precarious forms of work and what Nick Srnicek (2016) argues is a new economic paradigm premised on the extraction and use of data by these platforms. He calls this 'platform capitalism'. Kalleberg and Vallas (2017) explain that mobile technologies combined with digital platforms like Uber, Airbnb and Amazon's Mechanical Turk support the growth of more casualised mobile and distributed workforces, underpinning the emerging '**gig economy**' (see Box 19.3). In these new business models—premised on on-demand, gig work and crowd-sourced labour—the cost of production is further outsourced to workers, who take on extra costs like paying for petrol and insurance but are no longer entitled to work benefits such as superannuation, sick pay or annual leave. The automation of work by AI and robotics is an emerging area in the technologisation of work that will also have significant transformative effects and implications for work. Importantly, it is young people and other vulnerable work groups that are disproportionately affected by such trends.

BOX 19.3

Everyday sociology

WORKING IN THE 'GIG ECONOMY'

Kirin checked his backpack carefully before leaving his apartment for work. Lunch box—check. Mobile phone—check. Phone charger—check. He opened his Uber Eats app to check for delivery jobs before heading out the door, then tapped 'navigate' to map the routes on his phone. Kirin is a 'gig' worker living in Melbourne, Australia. He works two jobs: delivering meals for Uber Eats in the evenings on his electric bike and doing odd jobs as an Airtasker on the weekends. He's also a student. Kirin enrolled in a Master's degree in environmental science last year with a goal to one day get a job in wilderness conservation. Today is Kirin's 24th birthday. Having moved to Australia about five years ago on a temporary working visa, he now hopes to get permanent residency.

Kirin is a fictional character, but he is representative of the largest group of workers in the gig economy. In Australia, as in many Westernised nations, younger people (aged 18–34) and males participate in the gig economy in higher proportions than other groups. Women are half as likely as men to do gig work and those residing in cities are much more likely to partake in this emerging work trend than their country counterparts. Gig work is also carried out at a higher rate by people who are vulnerable in their employment such as students, people living with disabilities, temporary residents and people who speak a language other than English at home (Oliver et al. 2019).

The gig economy, also known as the 'on demand economy', uses digital platforms as intermediaries to match people who want work done with people who can do that work. 'Gigs' are the jobs or tasks performed by workers in this technologically mediated transaction. Mobile apps play a central role in gig work because it is often through them that gigs are generated, allocated, organised and paid for. But this is not the only model of work in the gig economy. Less well known are the freelance projects and micro-business tasks carried out by consultants and creative workers at home with their own equipment.

A survey of over 14,000 people carried out by three Australian universities for the Victorian Inquiry into the On-Demand Workforce found that about 7 per cent of the Australian workforce work in the gig economy, with over 100 digital platforms providing work for casual workers carrying out a wide range of tasks (Oliver et al. 2019).

Globally, 70 million workers are estimated to have registered with digital platforms that facilitate forms of gig work (Heeks 2017). Is gig work an exclusively Western work phenomenon? Not according to Heeks, who estimates that 36 million of these workers are concentrated in India, the Philippines, Pakistan and Bangladesh and to a more limited extent in sub-Saharan Africa and Latin America. Another 25 million estimated registered gig workers are on Chinese-based platforms (2017, p. 5).

Though gig work is embraced by some workers who experience benefits of more autonomy and flexibility over when and where they work, it also has its detractors. One of the biggest concerns is the shifting of risks, equipment costs and skill development away from employers on to individual workers (Kalleberg 2011). Another major risk is the general precarity that comes from working without institutional and social support and employment rights like sick leave, work insurance and annual leave. It has also been found that gig workers have little real choice over their work, which is mostly carried out at home or during unsocial and irregular hours (Wood et al. 2019). In times of disaster and economic upheaval, such as during the COVID-19 global pandemic, the downsides of gig work are laid bare, exposing already insecure workers to greater risks, even as they fulfil the essential work of delivering food and services to those in self-isolation.

Creating a new ethic of work

One of the key themes of this book is the issue of the relationship between the self and society. Work is a crucial component of this relationship and historically has played a central role in the way that self-identities are formed. In Chapter 5 we saw that during the Industrial Revolution work was thought to make you socially responsible and that hard work was associated with virtue. Various writers have argued that the growth of a consumer society has displaced the central role of work in identity, and that employment no longer provides individuals with meaning in their lives. In his book *Freedom* Zygmunt Bauman put it this way:

> Work has been progressively 'decentred' on the individual plane: it has become relatively less important compared to other spheres of life, and confined to a relatively minor position in individual biography; it certainly cannot compete with personal autonomy, self-esteem, family felicity, leisure, the joys of consumption and material possessions as conditions of individual satisfaction and happiness (1988, p. 74).

While there is no doubt that consumption is of fundamental importance as a source and site of identity formation, work continues to play an important role in this process. This is, first, because—as Germov (2007) points out—consumption practices cannot be divorced from work since the ability to consume is dependent on access to paid employment. Second, in an informational mode of production facilitated by digital technology, far from a reduction in work, work becomes a prerequisite for many everyday activities, as we take on the role as 'prosumers'.

The continued significance of work as a source of identity is apparent in the common question upon meeting someone new: 'What do you do?' Indeed, even though the work ethic identified by Weber (1958) belongs to a different era, elements of this ethic persist today. Many of us equate hard work with virtue, and assign value or social worth to people in high demand in the labour market. In contrast, we tend to regard those who do not work as a drain on society: think of the derogatory term 'dole bludgers' to refer to people who are unemployed and on government income benefits. The 2001 film *Time Out*, by French director Laurent Cantet, captures this sentiment, revealing the extraordinary efforts some are prepared to go to in order to disguise their unemployed work status.

A work ethic today can nevertheless not be solely defined by being in work, since the transformations such as those sketched out so far mean that there are many people without work, or with work only part of the time, casually, or with not enough work. Careers are no longer forever, and an individual worker is unlikely to be employed by a single employer or even in one industry sector for their entire working life: in this way, your working life is likely to be very different from that of your parents and grandparents. Digital technology, which is both a source of job insecurity and of new types of platform-based work, can therefore be seen as one of the ways in which a work ethic is sustained in an age of rapid transformation, uncertainty and risk (Beck 1992).

Gregg (2015) has shown how online media platforms and mobile apps generate new forms of self-governance that produce and stabilise the conditions and subjectivities appropriate to the values and qualities of the mobile and flexible knowledge worker. These technologies involve learning a set of attitudes and habits that establish an orientation to work and time. The 'Freedom' app, and other similar productivity programs such as 'Self Control', 'Omnifocus' and 'Rescue Time', promise to increase the efficiency of workers by cutting down on distractions and making better use of time.

Ironically, the time pressures that these programs promise to solve are the product of a technologically mediated culture of connectivity. Gregg sums up this contradiction as follows:

> Time management techniques offer a technological solution to an ontological and empirical problem: that the network delivers more requests for attention than it is possible to satisfy, and that these requests often come from colleagues, friends and family simultaneously (2015, p. 4).

The demand for such solutions became evident in a study conducted between 2006 and 2007 with employees of a global mobile telecommunications firm who were participating in a workplace trial of a new smartphone (Humphry 2014). Participants in the study reported a new sense of time resulting from the continuous connectivity made possible by their new mobile devices. In the words of one staff member: 'Well ... It's *ever-present*, because you can't avoid it ... even if you go on holidays, people still keep calling you and [you] are expected to take the call' (emphasis added). This '**ever-presence**' corresponds closely to the 'extended present' proposed by time philosopher Nowotny (1994), who argued that in a postmodern period, micro increments become the basic unit for structuring time.

The staff were ambivalent about this change, reporting high levels of time pressure and feelings of stress and anxiety, while simultaneously extolling a sense of 'freedom', 'flexibility' and being 'in sync' (Humphry 2014, p. 198). One reason for this ambivalence was the difficulty staying on top of work as it expanded out of its former boundaries, as well as the need to reconcile the extra work needed to maintain the conditions (including the technologies) to support mobile work. Despite this ambivalence, continuous connectivity and integrating all activities into a single time 'block' were crucial to meet the expectations of colleagues, friends and family and to maintain the sense of 'professional self' expected from their work colleagues. In this sense, 'ever-presence' was a temporality and 'time-discipline' integral to the conduct of mobile and flexible work replacing, and in some cases existing alongside, the techniques and technologies of 'clock time'.

Conclusion

In Chapter 3, we covered the idea that many scholars who have studied society have looked for universality in what makes societies function across the human experience. In the same chapter we proposed the concept of the 'interrelated rhombus' as an alternative framework for understanding contemporary society, encouraging us to draw together a range of perspectives and make connections across different areas. One area crucial to the shaping of the kind of society we live in is work, and this is what we have examined in the current chapter. However, the meaning of work and its relationship to other aspects of social life is not fixed. We know that these are contingent on specific historical, cultural and technological contexts.

We also argued that technology plays a special role in structuring the meaning of work and prevailing modes of production. In the early twenty-first century, this can be identified in the rise of an information or a knowledge-based mode of production characterised by mobile and flexible forms of work, and platform-based business models. We have outlined some of the interrelated ways that technology supports and enhances this mode of production and the rise of global capitalism more generally:

1. In the restructuring and respatialisation of work;
2. In the creation of new industries and types of paid and unpaid work; and
3. In the production of a new work ethic and identities of work.

Nevertheless, even though technology is key to these transformations, technology itself is not a predetermined force, nor is it the only factor driving these changes. Significantly, there are differences in the ability to participate and navigate this new culture and environment of work. 'Precarious work' disproportionately affects groups who are vulnerable to the structural inequalities of work in a global economy. Even within highly industrialised nations there is a great deal of variation in the quality and conditions of work, with some groups more likely to be in non-standard, low-wage and insecure employment. Moreover, consumers are now put to work in the production of products and services in a new relationship between production and consumption referred to as 'prosumption'. Despite conditions of rapid transformation and uncertainty, work still plays an important role in identity formation and takes on new meanings with the reconfiguration of 'work' and 'life', and 'work' and 'leisure'. A new work ethic and temporality of 'ever-presence' is at the heart of an informational mode of production characterised by new practices and forms of mobile and flexible work.

Summary points

- The meaning of work changes according to the historical and cultural context and the prevailing mode of production.
- The form of industrial production dominant until the mid twentieth century is now giving way to a new mode of production based on information.
- Global capitalism is a name for a form of capitalism defined by the informational mode of production and its expansion around the world.
- Although digital technology is not the only factor contributing to the rise of global capitalism, it is key to a number of interrelated processes of change. These are the respatialisation of work and everyday life, the creation of new kinds of work and industries, and the production of a new work ethic and sense of time.
- There is a cost to these changes in work, and these have a disproportionate impact on groups that are already socially and economically disadvantaged and who have traditionally been excluded from work.

Sociological reflection

1. Describe some of the ways in which your work shapes your relationships, social interactions and sense of self.
2. Reflect on some of the ways that digital technology is used for different kinds of work. Are there some kinds of activities that feel like work, but for which you do not get paid?
3. What is your dream job? How do you think you would go about getting this job? What sorts of skills and knowledge of digital technology would you need to obtain and carry out this job? Is there a job that doesn't involve technology skills?

Discussion questions

1. What is the meaning of work?
2. What influences the way we think about and carry out work?
3. What is a work ethic and how does it relate to the mode of production?
4. What are some ways that digital technology contributes to changes in work?
5. Is production still the most central form of societies, or are other processes such as consumption more important? What is 'prosumption'?
6. Who is most exposed to transformations and insecurities in contemporary work?
7. What are some of the attitudes and orientations that make up the current work ethic?
8. What are some of the technologies and tools that promote and support these attitudes and orientations?

Further investigation

1 What are your expectations of a working life today and how do they differ from those of your parents? Write down a list of what you think work will be like for you in your lifetime, and then interview your parents or a close family member about what work meant for them. Try to be attentive to what is different between your account and theirs, and also how their ideas may have changed over the course of their working lives.

2 What social theory do you think best represents the transformations in work and employment around the world? Explain your choice. Are there any aspects of these changes that this theory does not address, or does not address well?

References and further reading

REFERENCES

Anthony, PD 1977, *The Ideology of Work*, Tavistock Publications, London.

Arnold, M 2003, 'On the phenomenology of technology: the "Janus-faces" of mobile phones', *Information and Organization*, 13(4), 231–56.

Ash, A 1994, *Post-Fordism: A Reader*, Blackwell Publishers, Malden, MA.

Australian Bureau of Statistics (ABS) 2008, 'Locations of Work, Australia, November', *Cat. No. 6275.0*, ABS, Canberra.

Australian Bureau of Statistics (ABS) 2016, 'Catching up: why people work from home', *Cat. No. 6333.0*, ABS, Canberra.

Bain, P & Taylor, P 2000, 'Entrapped by the "electronic panopticon"? Worker resistance in the call centre', *New Technology, Work and Employment*, 15(1), 2–18.

Barbier, JC 2002, *A Survey of the Use of the Term Précarité in French Economics and Sociology*, Centre d'Etudes de l'Emploi, France.

Bauman, Z 1988, *Freedom*, University of Minnesota Press, MN.

Bauman, Z 2000, *Liquid Modernity*, Blackwell Publishers, Malden, MA.

Beck, U 1992, *Risk Society: Towards a New Modernity*, Vol. 17, SAGE, Thousand Oaks, CA.

Bell, D 2001, *The Coming of Post-Industrial Society: A Venture in Social Forecasting*, reissue edition, Basic Books, New York.

Berger, W 1999, 'Lost in Space', *Wired,* February, 7.02.

Bittman, M, Brown JE & Wajcman, J 2009, 'The mobile phone, perpetual contact and time pressure', *Work, Employment & Society*, 23(4), 673–91.

Bourdieu, P 1998, 'La précarité est aujord'hui partout', in P Bourdieu, *Contre-feux*, Raisons d'Agir, Paris, pp. 96–102.

Bruns, A 2008, *Blogs, Wikipedia, Second Life, and Beyond: From Production to Produsage, Vol. 45*, Peter Lang, New York.

Burston, J, Dyer-Witheford, N & Hearn, A 2010, 'Digital labour: workers, authors, citizens', *Theory and Politics in Organization*, Special Issue—Ephemera, 10(3–4), 214–21.

Castells, M 1996, *The Rise of the Network Society*, Blackwell Publishers, Malden, MA.

Clarke, J 2006, 'Style', in S Hall & T Jefferson (eds), *Resistance through Rituals: Youth Subcultures in Post-war Britain*, 2nd edn, Routledge, London and New York.

Crowe, R & Middleton, C 2012, 'Women, smartphones and the workplace: pragmatic realities and performative identities', *Feminist Media Studies*, 12(4), 560–9.

Davidoff, L & Hall, C 1987, *Family Fortunes: Men and Women of the English Middle Class, 1780–1850*, University of Chicago Press, Chicago, IL.

Drucker, P 1969, *The Age of Discontinuity: Guidelines to Our Changing Society*, Harper & Row, New York.

Durkheim, E 2014, *The Division of Labor in Society*, trans. WD Halls, The Free Press, New York.

Fudge, J & Owens, R (eds) 2006, *Precarious Work, Women and the New Economy: The Challenge to Legal Norms*, Hart Publishing, Oxford.

Fuchs, C 2010, 'Labor in informational capitalism and on the internet', *The Information Society*, 26, 179–96.

Germov, J 2007, 'The new work ethic', in J Germov & M Poole (eds), *Public Sociology: An Introduction to Australian Society*, Allen & Unwin, Crows Nest.

Gregg, M 2011, *Work's Intimacy*, Polity Press, Cambridge, UK, and Malden, MA.

Gregg, M 2015, '"Getting things done": productivity, self-management, and the order of things', in K Hillis, S Paasonen & M Petit (eds), *Networked Affect*, MIT Press, MA.

Gregorio, J 2013, 'Home is where the work is', *Australian Communications Media Authority (ACMA) Snapshot Series*, 16 October.

Heeks, R 2017, 'Decent work and the digital gig economy: a developing country perspective on employment standards in online outsourcing, crowdwork, etc.', Development Informatics Working Paper no. 7, Global Development Institute SEED, University of Manchester, Manchester: <http://hummedia.manchester.ac.uk/institutes/gdi/publications/workingpapers/di/di_wp71.pdf>.

Humphry, J 2013, 'Demanding media: platform work and the shaping of work and play', *Scan (Sydney): Journal of Media Arts Culture*, 10(2), 1–13.

Humphry, J 2014, 'Officing: mediating time and the professional self in the support of nomadic work, *Computer Supported Cooperative Work*, 23(2), 185–204.

Jenkins, H 2006, *Fans, Bloggers, and Gamers: Exploring Participatory Culture*, NYU Press, New York.

Kalleberg, AL 2011, *Good Jobs, Bad Jobs: The Rise of Polarized and Precarious Employment Systems in the United States, 1970s–2000s*, Russell Sage, New York.

Kalleberg, AL 2013, 'Globalization and Precarious Work', *Contemporary Sociology: A Journal of Reviews*, September 2013, 42 (5), 700–6.

Kalleberg, AL & Vallas, SP (eds) 2017, *Precarious Work (Research in the Sociology of Work, Vol. 31)*, Emerald Publishing Limited, Bingley, UK.

Kleinrock, L 1996, 'Nomadicity: anytime, anywhere in a disconnected world', *Mobile Networks and Applications: Special Issue on Mobile Computing and System Services*, 1(4), 351–7.

Lowry, D & Moskos, M 2005, *Hanging on the Mobile Phone: Experiencing Work and Spatial Flexibility*, National Institute of Labour Studies, Flinders University.

Machlup, F 1962, *The Production and Distribution of Knowledge in the United States*, Princeton University Press, Princeton, NJ.

MacKenzie, D & Wajcman, J (eds) 1999, *The Social Shaping of Technology*, 2nd edn, Open University Press, Buckingham.

Malecki, EJ & Moriset, B 2008, *The Digital Economy: Business Organization, Production Processes and Regional Developments*, Routledge, Abingdon and New York.

Nowotny, H 1994, *Time: The Modern and Postmodern Experience*, Polity Press, Cambridge.

Oakley, A 1974, *Housewife*, A Lane, London.

Odih, P 2003, 'Gender, work and organization in the time/space economy of "just-in-time" labour', *Time & Society*, 12(2–3), 293–314.

Oliver, D, McDonald, P, Stewart, A, Williams, P & Mayes, R 2019, 'Digital platform work in Australia: preliminary findings from a national survey', June 2019, Victorian Department of Premier and Cabinet, Victoria.

Perry, M & Brodie, J 2006, *Virtually Connected, Practically Mobile*, Springer, Berlin and Heidelberg.

Petras, J & Veltmeyer, H 2013, 'Introduction', in *Imperialism and Capitalism in the Twenty-first Century: A System in Crisis*, Ashgate, London, pp. 1–17.

Pocock, B, Skinner, N & Williams, P 2012, *Time Bomb: Work, Rest and Play in Australia Today*, NewSouth Publishing, Sydney.

Porat, MU 1977, *The Information Economy: Definition and Measurement, Vols 1–8*, Office of Telecommunications Special Publication, Department of Commerce.

Ritzer, G 2008, *The McDonaldization of Society*, Pine Forge Press, Thousand Oaks, CA (original work published 1993).

Ritzer, G & Jurgenson, N 2010, 'Production, consumption, presumption: the nature of capitalism in the age of the digital "prosumer"', *Journal of Consumer Culture*, 10(1), 13–36.

Rossitto, C & Eklundh, KS 2007, 'Managing work at several places: a case of project work in a nomadic group of students', in *Proceedings of the 14th European Conference on Cognitive Ergonomics: Invent! Explore!*, ACM, pp. 45–51.

Sadler, N 2002, 'Is profane work an obstacle to salvation? The case of Ultra Orthodox (Haredi) Jews in contemporary Israel', *Sociology of Religion*, 63(4), 455–74.

Scholz, T (ed.) 2012, *Digital Labor: The Internet as Playground and Factory*, Routledge, New York.

Sennett, R 2006, *The Culture of the New Capitalism*, Yale University Press, New Haven and London.

Schiller, D 2000, *Digital Capitalism: Networking the Global Market System*, MIT Press, Boston, MA.

Skinner, N & Pocock, B 2010, 'Work, life, flexibility and workplace culture in Australia: results of the 2008 Australian Work and Life Index (AWALI) survey', *Australian Bulletin of Labour*, 36(2), 133.

Skinner, N & Pocock, B 2014, *Work, Life, Flexibility and Workplace Culture in Australia: Results of the 2014 Australian Work and Life Index (AWALI) survey*, Centre for Work + Life, Adelaide.

Srnicek, N 2016, *Platform Capitalism*, Polity Press, Cambridge.

Terranova, T 2000, 'Free labor: producing culture for the digital economy', *Social Text*, 18(2), 33–58.

Thompson, EP 1967, 'Time, work-discipline, and industrial capitalism', *Past and Present*, 38(1), 56–97.

Thrift, N 2005, *Knowing Capitalism*, SAGE, Thousand Oaks, CA.

Toffler, A 1980, *The Third Wave*, Collins, London.

Townsend, K & Batchelor, L 2005, 'Managing mobile phones: a work/nonwork collision in small business', *New Technology, Work and Employment*, 20(3), 259–67.

Urry, J 2008, *Mobilities*, Polity Press, Malden.

Van Dijk, J 2012, *The Network Society*, SAGE, Thousand Oaks, CA.

Veal, AJ 2009, 'The elusive leisure society', in *School of Leisure, Sport and Tourism Working Paper 9*, 3rd edn, University of Technology, Sydney.

Vosko, LF (ed.) 2006, *Precarious Employment: Understanding Labour Market Insecurity in Canada*, McGill-Queen's University Press, Montréal.

Weber, M 1958, *The Protestant Ethic and the Spirit of Capitalism*, translated by Talcott Parsons with a new introduction by Anthony Giddens, Charles Scribner's Sons, New York.

Wood, AJ, Graham, M, Lehdonvirta, V & Hjorth, I 2019, 'Good gig, bad gig: autonomy and algorithmic control in the global gig economy', *Work, Employment and Society*, 33(1), 56–75.

MOVIES

Cantet, L (dir.) 1999, *Human Resources*.

Cantet, L (dir.) 2001, *Time Out*.

Judge, M (dir.) 1999, *Office Space*.

Lang, F (dir.) 1927, *Metropolis*.

Loach, K (dir.) 2007, *It's A Free World …*

Loach, K (dir.) 2016, *I, Daniel Blake*.

Niccol, A (dir.) 2011, *In Time*.

TELEVISION

Gervais, R & Merchant, S (dirs) 2001, *The Office*.

CHAPTER 20

Society and the world of sports

MAIR UNDERWOOD WITH JAMES ARVANITAKIS

CHAPTER OVERVIEW

Never been to a football match? Think sport is boring? Don't despair. The study of sport can tell us a great deal about our society, so even if you hate sport, read on—you may be surprised how interesting a sociological perspective on sport can be.

Love sport? Never miss a game? Know all the stats of your favourite athlete? Like most people, you probably have never considered the role of sport in society beyond its entertainment value. This chapter offers you the opportunity to delve into sport in a way that you never have before.

You may be wondering: What is sport doing in this textbook anyway? Sport is about physical bodies and individual motivation, isn't it? What could sociology add to understandings of something so natural and individual?

This chapter explains why a sociological perspective on sport is so important and demonstrates how the study of sport contributes to our understanding of society in general. The complex role of sport in society has been highlighted by the cancellations and postponement of all sporting events worldwide during the COVID-19 pandemic. It confirms that even if we do not think about it, sport is an integral part of our society and everyday experiences: from the weekend amateur leagues that many of us play on the weekends (netball, cricket, football) to global sporting events (like the Olympics), to local competitions such as rugby league and the Australian Football League that we follow week to week.

In this chapter you will consider sports as social constructs (something we introduced in Chapter 3), and the ways in which sport can be used to reflect society, reproduce society and provide sites for resistance. We will do this through a discussion of sport in relation to deviance, gender and sexuality—all topics we have touched on in previous chapters, but which we will now apply to the topic of sport.

After reading this chapter, you should be able to:
- Explain why a sociological approach to sport is important
- Explain why sports can be considered social constructs
- Define the terms 'overconformity' and 'underconformity', and give examples of how they relate to sport
- Explain why sport could be considered masculine territory

- List some of the consequences women in sport face because of the gendered nature of sport
- Explain the term 'hegemonic masculinity' and how it relates to sport
- Explain how success in sport may affect perceptions of an athlete's sexuality.

> **KEY TERMS**
>
> **Deviance** Any conduct, actions, traits or ideas that violate the accepted social norms of a particular society. Deviant conduct is not always illegal and may vary between groups within society, as social norms vary.
>
> **Homophobia** A dislike of, or prejudice towards, homosexuals. While homophobia may occur as a result of witnessing homosexual behaviour, it more commonly occurs as a result of perceptions of how an individual performs non-sexual behaviours, such as walking, talking or playing sport.
>
> **Overconformity** Actions, traits or ideas that are based on the uncritical acceptance of norms and extreme adherence to them.
>
> **Sexuality** Sexual behaviours and orientations.
>
> **Social construction** A social phenomenon or category created by society, such as gender.
>
> **Sport** A human activity requiring physical exertion and/or physical skill, which is competitive and is generally accepted as being a sport.
>
> **Underconformity** Actions, traits or ideas that are based on the rejection of norms.

Introduction

There are many reasons why we need to examine **sport** as a social phenomenon, not least of which is that sport engages more people in a shared experience than any other institution or cultural activity. For example, according to the International Olympic Committee, the Rio de Janeiro Olympics (2016) reached approximately five billion people worldwide—more than half the world's population! Before COVID-19 delayed the 2020 Tokyo Games, they were projected to attract even more viewers and would have had more than 11,000 athletes from 206 nations competing for 339 gold medals.

Sport holds a valued place in society. We give more prizes and awards for sport than we do in any other dimension of the social world (Leonard 1998). We idolise sports stars. This is especially the case in Australia.

Sport has such a special place in Australian culture that sporting 'heroes' have been named Australian of the Year more times than any other profession, including scientists, surgeons, diplomats and entertainers. An international survey on the sources of national pride found that Australians are excessively proud of their sporting achievements, and that they have greater pride in their sporting achievements than any other measure of success, including in science and technology, art and literature, and economic development (Kell 2000).

But what is sport?

Not only do a lot of people engage with sport and consider it important, but sports are, by definition, social phenomena. For instance, let us consider how the Australian Government (2015) defines sport:

> A human activity capable of achieving a result requiring physical exertion and/or physical skill which, by its nature and organisation, is competitive and is *generally accepted as being a sport* [emphasis added].

This definition highlights the fact that it is the social acceptance of an activity that makes it a sport—sports are socially defined. Because sports are socially defined they are contested activities. For example, there is debate over whether the kind of choreographed wrestling we see today (such as that promoted by World Wrestling Entertainment) should be considered a sport. Some people would consider bodybuilding a sport, whereas others would not.

Sports are what sociologists call '**social constructions**' (see the discussion in Chapter 3); that is, people—through their interactions with each other—*construct* sports. It is through social interaction that we construct the goals, methods and rules of each particular sport. It is also through our interactions with each other that we decide which activities are sports and which are not.

If sports are social constructs, this means that sports are not neutral activities. People create sports, and people are influenced by social structures. Those who create a certain sport, or those who decide whether an activity is a sport or not, do not stand outside of social structures. They are impacted by social structures as we all are. Sports are constructed under certain social, political and economic conditions, and therefore they are shaped by these conditions.

Sports reflect and reinforce meanings and values

The fact that sports are social constructs means that sports are not neutral activities. They reflect and reinforce meanings and values, and these meanings and values differ from culture to culture (Leonard 1998). For example, Japanese baseball is very different to American baseball. American culture emphasises individualism and competition, and thus American baseballers employ agents to look after their own individual interests and attempt to negotiate higher salaries. American baseball games never end in a draw as there is always a tiebreaker. In contrast, in Japan the emphasis is on the collective goal of winning, and individualism and egotistical behaviour are highly stigmatised. Japanese baseball games can end in a draw and players never hire agents and negotiate for higher salaries as that would imply that they have placed themselves above the team.

Because sports reflect the meanings and values of the society, we can use a sociological approach to sport to uncover these meanings and values. But what does taking a sociological approach to sport mean?

> **BOX 20.1**
> ## Everyday sociology
>
> **COVID-19, GLOBALISATION AND SPORT**
>
> When the effects of the COVID-19 pandemic impacted the global sports community, one of Australia's leading sporting sociologists, David Rowe, wrote an article outlining how global sport in contemporary society has become commercially vulnerable and is likely to change forever.
>
> In a few short months, live sport went from being widely available across a range of media to essentially non-existent.
>
> Not only did the spectacle of sports disappear, so did the ability to attend sporting events. Rowe stated that: 'Live sports events in front of boisterous crowds watched by legions of armchair viewers have suddenly become memories rather than familiar cultural furniture.'
>
> The impact has been felt by local amateur teams as much as professional teams, from the local NSW Northern Districts Cricket Club—The Butchers—to the European Champions League and Olympic Games.
>
> Sport and globalisation are now synonymous. In fact, Rowe (2020) argues that their relationship has 'supplied one of the most striking cases of the Global Village in action'. What we have seen emerge is a 'media sports cultural complex' that involves increasing 'spectacle and expanded content' that move across the world and has every step 'tracked by the media for viewing in distant places'.
>
> This creates a flow-on effect for local clubs to in a number of ways. Firstly, as more people are exposed to sport, they want to emulate their sporting heroes and seek to live this out by joining local and amateur clubs, which are often affiliated with professional organisations. Some talented players may be identified as having potential to rise through the ranks and are 'signed' by professional organisations when they are as young as 14. Some of these amateur or semi-professional local clubs also attract former star players, which assists with their broader community engagement and continues the cycle of bringing in more people to participate. This also flows into merchandise and sales of tickets. In this way, the Northern District Butchers may seem a long way from the Australian Cricket Team, but they are related in many ways.
>
> The survival of sports is not only reliant on crowds and fans coming to games, but their viewing habits that cross the globe and bring media and massive levels of sponsorship.
>
> COVID-19 has brought all this to a crashing halt. Players, for example, have taken pay cuts and are keeping up their fitness in the safety of their homes. Some are even working in other jobs such as labourers, to compensate for their lost income. Some club members are asking for their dues to be returned while other fans are watching reruns of their favourite games online. Gambling companies have lost events worldwide for punters to bet on.
>
> Globalisation turned sport into a cultural-commercial giant. This global pandemic has shown that many sports are vulnerable and we can speculate how many things about our favourite sports may never be the same.

What is a sociological approach to sport?

We usually understand sport according to a natural science approach. This approach emphasises the individual and sees success as determined by individual biology, psychology and training. In contrast, the sociological approach to sport focuses on the wider social structures and their ability to both enable and constrain. For example, why are men's competitions prioritised by both media and sponsors? The ABC (2016) reported that in 2016, an entire women's AFL team costs less than an average male player. The gap has closed somewhat, but women still earn only a fraction of the men's salary.

A sociological approach to sport is a lot less attractive than a natural science perspective for at least two reasons:

1. It suggests that success in sport is only partly determined by individual factors (such as biology, psychology and training); and
2. It highlights the fact that individuals are powerless in certain contexts.

As such, our success in sport (or lack of) is never ours alone. This is difficult for some people to handle, especially if they have been successful in sport. Understandably they want to take the credit for their success. But we all need to consider the role that social structures have played in successes and failures.

Sociologists approach sport in three ways:

1. *Sport reflects (or mirrors) society*: This approach posits that sports created in capitalist societies such as ours, in which women have less social power than men, are hardly likely to reflect socialist economic principles or gender equity. An example of how sport reflects societal issues is the 2020 National Rugby League 'simply the best' advertisement that tried to appeal to a broader cross-section of society (including women and the LGBTIQA+ community) but was criticised for trying to be too inclusive and 'politically correct' (see Kent 2020).
2. *Sport reproduces society*: This approach looks at how sport reproduces dominant social structures and values, maintaining a particular set of power relations in society.
3. *Sport provides a site for resistance*: This approach recognises that individuals have agency and are not passive victims of social structures. It is about sport as contested terrain and a site of struggles. This was highlighted by former Sydney Roosters National Rugby League player Latrell Mitchell and former Sydney Swans AFL player, and Australian of the Year, Adam Goodes, who used their profiles to confront racism and racists taunts that Aboriginal players often face. Adam Goodes' story was the subject of two documentaries, *The Final Quarter* and *The Australian Dream*.

Let us examine these three approaches in the context of some of the topics that sociologists of sport have turned their attention to: deviance, gender and sexuality.

Deviance and sport

As we have discussed throughout this book, there is nothing inevitable or natural about social norms. They are social constructs and, as such, they differ from society to society (think of the differences between Japanese and American baseball highlighted earlier in this chapter).

Deviance, as we discussed in Chapter 18, consists of actions and thoughts that fall outside the norms. The social world of sport has a unique and interesting relationship with deviance for several reasons.

The first is that sport is constructed as being beneficial in reducing deviance. Sport is thought of not only as improving your physical health, but also your morality, as is evident in government programs that redirect delinquents into sport. Whether or not sport does deter delinquency is a matter of debate (see Box 20.2).

Second, sport is unique regarding deviance because of the sense of entitlement that exists among some athletes. We value sport a great deal in our culture and therefore reward elite athletes very highly. Athletes are told that they are special and valuable in many ways: they are idolised, there is cheering and fanfare associated with their achievements, and they are given prizes, awards and huge salaries. This can lead to a sense of entitlement or *hubris* (Coakley 2009). 'Hubris' means a pride-driven arrogance or sense of self-importance and is accompanied by a sense of being above other people. This often bonds athletes together and separates them from the wider community—something that is more common today than in the past. This sense of separation can lead to deviance as athletes may not feel that the same rules apply to them.

This leads us to the third reason (because in some circumstances the same rules do not in fact apply to athletes): norms in sport are sometimes different from the norms in wider society. What is accepted in sport may be deviant in other spheres of society, such as violence and men showing emotion. But the reverse is also true: actions accepted in society may be deviant in sport, such as the asthma inhalants and nutritional supplements used by millions of non-athletes.

BOX 20.2
Everyday sociology

DOES SPORT BUILD CHARACTER AND DETER DELINQUENCY?

The fact that sport helps build character is generally accepted without question. As a result, sport has been used in numerous programs designed to reduce youth delinquency, such as the midnight basketball programs that have spread from the United States to Australia (starting in Redfern, New South Wales, in 2006). As a diversion, these programs may work; that is, the youths involved cannot be delinquent during the hours they are actually playing basketball. The question is whether sport has a longer-term effect. Does the ideology that sport builds character and deters delinquency ring true?

Most of the research in this area was conducted between the 1950s and 80s; since then it has dropped off. Why? There was a long record of inconsistent findings, and most studies found that sport had little or no significant effects (Horne et al. 2013). Despite the inconclusive findings, the ideology of sport as character building persists, due—in part—to the fact that sport is such an important part of our culture.

So does sport build character? Numerous studies have found that rather than build character, sport may actually do the opposite. Several studies conducted in the 1990s found that many athletes scored lower on moral development than their non-athlete peers (Sage 1998, p. 17). For example, a study with young male hockey players in Canada (Miracle & Rees 1994) found that the longer boys are involved in hockey:

- The more they accept the importance of cheating;
- The more they feel that violent behaviour is legitimate and expected by the coach; and
- The more they are likely to use illegal tactics learned through watching professional hockey players on television.

Another study was conducted with boys at an American summer camp (Sherif et al. 1961). The researchers created two groups and looked at how they interacted. They found that competitive sports led to greater intergroup conflict and hostility that transferred from the sport field into other situations. There were food fights, night raids on the other group's cabin, and burning of the other group's flag.

There is also evidence that sport may lead to situation-specific morality or 'game reasoning'. For example, one study found that both athletes and non-athletes tend to apply lower-level moral reasoning when thinking about sport-related dilemmas than when thinking about other dilemmas (Miracle & Rees 1994).

Despite this, research *has* found that the social context of sport can make a difference. Perhaps the most widely cited study in this area was conducted by Trulson (1986). Trulson's study was of 34 male high school students aged 13–17 who met the criteria of juvenile delinquency. Participants were divided into three groups and were each trained by the same instructor for one hour, three times per week, for six months. The three different training groups were:

1   Traditional tae kwon do training: including meditation, stretching, a brief lecture on tae kwon do philosophy (emphasising respect for others, patience, perseverance, responsibility, humility, confidence and honour), basic techniques (blocks, kicks and punches), forms (sequences of movements), free sparring and self-defence;
2   Non-traditional, modern martial arts training: including stretching, free sparring and self-defence;
3   Control group—increased physical activity: for example, basketball, jogging and football.

The results of the study were clear-cut.

Group 1, those who practised traditional tae kwon do, had decreased levels of aggressiveness, lowered anxiety, increased self-esteem, and no longer met the criteria for delinquency. Group 2, those who practised modern martial arts, had a greater tendency towards delinquency and a very large increase in aggressiveness. Group 3, the control group, had no notable differences.

So it seems that the goals or values emphasised by the coach, parent or program seem to affect the moral development of the individual. Studies have found that athletes who focus on personal improvement reported that the purpose of sport was to teach values such as working hard, cooperating with others and becoming good citizens. These athletes did not endorse cheating, but expressed approval of sporting behaviours. In contrast, individuals who focused on demonstrating greater ability than others more often viewed the intentional injuring of opponents as legitimate and were more tempted to violate sporting attitudes and behaviours (Ewing et al. 2002, p. 37).

The results of these studies are important: it is not sport per se that builds character, but the way that you teach and coach sport that makes the difference.

Critical reflection

1   What was your experience of sport at school? Did you find it 'built character', or did it promote a sense of delinquency?
2   When playing (or watching) competitive sport, do you agree with 'it's not whether you win or lose, it's how you play the game'; or would you be willing to do almost anything to win?

Underconformity

Sport is interesting in terms of deviance because a lot of the deviance in sport is about the unquestioning acceptance of norms. Coakley (2009) explains this in terms of **underconformity** and **overconformity**:

- Deviant underconformity consists of actions based on ignoring or rejecting norms.
- Deviant overconformity consists of actions based on uncritically accepting norms and being willing to follow them to extreme degrees.

All social life contains tensions between overconformity and underconformity, and sport is no exception.

Some examples of underconformity in sport are:

- *Alcohol and drug use*: Do certain sports breed a culture of excessive drinking and illicit drug use? Some research suggests that this may be the case. Indeed we have had several high-profile cases of drug use in Australian sport (such as Wendell Sailor and Ben Cousins), and many Australians considered the cricketer David Boon a 'dead-set legend' for drinking 52 beers on a flight between Sydney and London.
- *Unsanctioned violence*: Violence is part of some sports, and cannot in itself be considered an example of underconformity. But violence that is against the rules (or unsanctioned violence) is about rejecting the norms and *is* an example of underconformity. The boundary between sanctioned and unsanctioned violence is dynamic.

    For example, Australian Rugby League in the 1970s and early 80s was extremely violent and some people (especially women and children) were turned off the game. Administrators were forced to 'de-brutalise' the game in order to meet changing public demands, which shifted the boundary between sanctioned and unsanctioned violence.
- *Sexual assaults and abuse*: Are there different sexual norms in certain sports that encourage sexual abuse? There is some research suggesting that athletes are more sexually aggressive and are more likely to hold rape-supportive attitudes (Murnen & Kohlman 2007; Boeringer 1999). It seems that there may be different sexual norms in some Australian sports settings; for example, former coach Roy Masters (2006) stated that there is a tradition of 'gangbangs' (sex between one woman and a group of men) in Australian Rugby League.

Overconformity

Most of the time we think about deviance as the rejection of norms. But deviance also occurs when individuals uncritically accept norms and take them too far. This type of deviance is often ignored and even encouraged; athletes may not see overconformity as deviance, but as evidence of commitment and dedication. Much of the deviance among athletes (and coaches) involves unquestioned acceptance of and conformity to the value system embodied in the sport ethic.

Coakley (2009, pp. 171–2) describes the *sport ethic* this way:

- A player is dedicated to the game above all things.
- Sport must be a priority over other interests. An athlete must meet the expectations of fellow athletes, meet the demands of competition, and make sacrifices, all without question.

- An athlete strives for distinction.
- Being an athlete means constantly seeking to improve and achieve perfection.
- An athlete accepts risks and plays through pain.
- An athlete accepts no obstacles in the pursuit of possibilities.

Some examples of overconformity are overtraining, playing with pain and injury, and taking performance-enhancing substances. For example, you may recall the story of a man in Chapter 7 (Personal voice) who, as a child, played on in a Rugby League match with a broken arm to ensure that he did not disappoint his father.

Gender and sport

In Chapter 7, we looked at issues of gender in our society. If we look at gender and sport, we can see how sport *reflects* society, including the frequent inequalities confronted by women in our society. Sport also *reproduces* society, such as by naturalising social differences. And we can see how sport can provide sites for *resistance against norms* (see Box 20.3 and Personal voice).

Let us delve into this in a bit more detail.

Sport and masculinity

Sport as we know it today has a very masculine history. If we go back to ancient Greece, athletics were used as rehearsals for military action (Burstyn 1999). Foot and chariot races, javelin throws, wrestling and running were all events that ritualised the skills needed to play a commanding role in the armies whose campaigns were a central part of life.

The Ancient Olympic Games conducted at four-year intervals from 776 BCE to AD 394 were the premier site for the display of military prowess and were held during truces agreed upon by all city-states. Women were excluded from participation and even spectatorship for most of Olympic history, and this exclusion was enforced on pain of death.

The nineteenth century saw the creation of today's major sports. This was when they were first organised, ordered and institutionally consolidated. As discussed in Chapter 5, the nineteenth century was also a time when changes in labour were occurring, resulting in men leaving the family household to work at a distance. As a result, boys had strong attachments to their mothers and poorer attachments to their largely absent fathers. During this time sports stepped in:

> Sport emerged as an institution of social fatherhood to provide training in manly pursuits war, commerce, government—and a stepping stone out of the family of women and into the world of men (Burstyn 1999, p. 45).

Jumping to more recent times, several academics have pointed to the fact that rugby and more violent forms of football have emerged during a time of increasing women's rights (Nelson 1996). These sports have been interpreted as a response to feminism and the increasing power of women. The masculine history of sport has resulted in sociologists stating that sport is the most masculine of social institutions (Messner & Sabo 1990) reproducing masculine social values (Whitson 1990).

Sport emphasises a particular form of masculinity, which has been described as 'hegemonic masculinity' (Connell 1997)—something we discussed in detail in Chapter 7. In fact, male professional sports stars are the exemplars of hegemonic masculinity (Connell & Messerschmidt 2005). While sports stars make up a minority of men, they are the models of hegemonic masculinity to be imitated by others.

So, if athletes are the exemplars of hegemonic masculinity, then it is hardly surprising that sport is associated with heterosexism, and the subordination of women and homosexuals. In the next sections we discuss these connections.

Sport and femininity

Sport does not construct femininity in the same way that it constructs masculinity. While sport is often seen as turning 'boys into men' or creating 'real men', you never hear it said that sport turns 'girls into women' or creates 'real women'. Sport is generally a masculine terrain, so women who participate in sport cannot be made more feminine through their participation; precisely the opposite.

In the early part of the twentieth century it was feared that women who played sports would become less inhibited around men, leading to promiscuity. By the 1930s, the fear became that women participating in sports would become lesbians (Cashmore 2000). Around this time, 'virilism' was also a fear; that is, that sporting women would develop secondary male sexual characteristics such as facial hair, a deep voice and broad shoulders (Cashmore 2000). Not only were women's bodies not considered up to the task of sport, but also, they were thought to be not psychologically prepared. For instance, less than 80 years ago the respectable academic journal *Scientific American* stated that women were not competitive, assertive and aggressive enough to succeed in sport (Laird 1936).

These sorts of ideas led to women being actively excluded from participating in sports. Pierre de Coubertin, founder of the modern Olympics, publicly opposed women's participation in sport well into the 1930s. He argued that women's participation was 'un-aesthetic' and 'against the laws of nature'. He saw women's place in sport as applauding the men: 'At the Olympic Games their primary role should be, as in the ancient tournaments, to crown the victor with laurels' (cited in Kay 2003, p. 91).

The private Augusta National Golf Club in Georgia, the United States, hosts one of the most prestigious events in sport, the Masters, and some of its 300 or so members come from the echelons of American political and corporate life. It was not until 2012 that Augusta finally relented to criticism and admitted its first two female members. In Australia, one New South Wales golf club restricted female members to associate status until 1996 (Lenskyj 1998).

Even when women could compete, they faced restrictions. Women were able to compete in the Olympic 800 metres until 1928, when the organisers found the sight of women fighting for breath so repugnant that they removed the event from women's schedules (Cashmore 2000). Women were excluded from this event until 1960. Women were also excluded from the 1500 metres until 1972, and from the marathon until 1984. It was not until 1996 that women could run the 5000 metres, and 2008 that they were allowed to compete in the 3000 metres steeplechase!

Consider the following restrictions that still apply:
- There are fewer sets in women's tennis—making it 'less strenuous';
- Lacrosse women's rules limit stick and body contact—making it less violent; and
- The vertical drop is lower for women than men in alpine skiing—making it less dangerous.

Feminine sports are those that allow women to remain true to stereotyped expectations of femininity; they tend to emphasise beauty and aesthetic pleasure. Thus gymnastics and synchronised swimming are considered to be feminine sports. Feminine sports do not usually include sports that involve face-to-face competition where body contact might happen, or those that involve attempts to physically overpower opponents. And in some cases, less physically demanding female versions of male sports were created: netball from basketball; softball from baseball.

This gendered nature of sport has had numerous consequences for women. Some progress has been made in recent years with the emergence of women's professional competitions in cricket and all football codes in Australia, and the equal pay deal secured by the Australian women's soccer team, the Matildas. However, the following patterns still tend to apply:

- *Girls and women are less encouraged to play sport*: As noted above, throughout history women have not only received less encouragement to participate, but they have been actively discouraged and even excluded from sport. As a result girls do not dream of a professional sports career as much as boys (Hardin, Lynn & Walsdorf 2005).
- *Women often face a lack of options in sport*: Liz Ellis, former captain of the Australian netball team, stated that:

  > for young women there is no full-time professional career path as an athlete in a team sport. Little girls write to me and say that when they grow up they want to be a professional netballer. I am tempted to write back, 'Me too.' … On a rough count, there are over 3000 full-time jobs for men as athletes in team sport in Australia. There is not one single job for women in that role (Senate Inquiry 2006, p. 59).

  While this story is 15 years old, Alana Schetzer (2018) reminds us that not much changed when discussing the 38 per cent increase in wages for women AFL players:

  > So, yes, this is a 'huge pay increase', as the AFL has declared it, but 'huge' still doesn't mean fair, especially when you acknowledge the fact that this past season tier four players earned just $8,500. The fact that an average player increase of 38% actually represents such a bleak set of numbers illustrates what a tough battle is being fought for fair wages by women players.
  >
  > Compare that to June last year when men's AFL players signed off on a 20% increase that is collectively worth $1.84bn. That took the average salary from $309,000 to $371,000. So let's compare that again to the women players, whose top players—not average, but top—will earn $24,600 in 2019.

- *Women receive less recognition and respect*: In 1999, Prime Minister John Howard met with the Australian netball team, which had won its third consecutive world championship. The Prime Minister congratulated the 'hockey team' on their efforts! While this may seem a minor gaffe, it is inconceivable that a Prime Minister would confuse the Australian men's cricket and Rugby Union teams.

- *Women receive inferior media coverage*: Women athletes are underrepresented in the sports media. In 2006 Senate Inquiry, it was found that women's sports are represented in only 4–10 per cent of print media; 1.3–2 per cent of television (and almost exclusively by non-commercial networks); and 1.4 per cent of radio. Since then, there has been considerable change with high profile competitions across the sporting codes (Maurice 2019) including record numbers of viewers tuning into the 2020 ICC Women's T20 World Cup (AAP and Cricket Network 2020)
- *Women have a lack of role models in sport*: For example, in the 2006 Senate Inquiry into women and sport, a girl was quoted as saying, in a manner typical of many girls: 'If Don Bradman had been a woman, he would have been my role model, but because he is a man I can't take him as my role model' (Senate Inquiry 2006, p. 70).
- *Women athletes must emphasise their femininity*: Because sport masculinises, and does not feminise, women have to emphasise or even exaggerate their femininity to prevent themselves from appearing too masculine in sport. American figure-skating champion Tara Lipinski, when she was 15 and training for the Olympics, said that her most difficult challenge was maintaining the strength and power needed to do seven triple jumps in a routine while still looking cute, soft and feminine (Coakley 2009).

As mentioned, attitudes have changed considerably in recent decades, but challenges still confronting women athletes remain. This was highlighted by a photo of AFLW player Tayla Harris kicking for a goal. The photo started a national conversation about attitudes to women and changed perceptions of the AFLW after it was posted on the Seven Network's social media accounts, where it was swamped by misogynistic comments. In shock, the network deleted the image but reposted it soon after with an apology after many protested (Kelsey-Sugg & Trompf 2019).

Given all the challenges that women face in sport, we have to ask ourselves the question: Are men naturally superior at sport than women (as frequently assumed), or are the different rates of success due to social or cultural factors?

Sport was created and defined by men. Therefore, it places emphasis on aspects of the body that are more common in males than females. Sport therefore delivers 'incontrovertible evidence' of the superiority of men. In this way, sport naturalises our gender ideology. It is not that physical differences between male and female bodies do not exist; it is that these differences are socially meaningless until social practices transform them into social facts.

BOX 20.3

Everyday sociology

WOMEN BODYBUILDERS

Bodybuilding is defined as working out with weights to reshape the body, not just tone it. The strength or speed of the muscles is never tested; it is purely a sport of appearances.

Women did not enter into bodybuilding until the late 1970s and early 80s, and their participation in the sport was not encouraged (Boyle 2005). Muscles are considered masculine, so the muscular development of women was considered unfeminine.

In 1985, a documentary following a women's bodybuilding competition was made called *Pumping Iron II: The Women*. It was a follow-up to *Pumping Iron*, which was about Arnold Schwarzenegger and Lou Ferrigno competing for the title of Mr Olympia. While *Pumping Iron* focused on training and the competition, *Pumping Iron II* had an additional message to do with the gendered nature of muscle.

Pumping Iron II starred a woman bodybuilder who had achieved bigger muscles than any woman who had come before: former Australian power lifter Bev Francis. You would expect that Francis, having achieved the biggest muscles, would have won the competition. After all, the point of bodybuilding is to build muscle. However, Francis came eighth! The woman who won, while an impressive athlete, did not have Francis' level of muscularity and therefore was considered more feminine than Francis.

The message the judges were clearly sending was that a woman with Francis' level of musculature was not acceptable. In the film they are heard saying: 'women are women and men are men, there's a difference and thank god for that difference.' Women bodybuilders threaten the erasure of visible difference between men and women, and the judges saw it as their role to maintain that difference by discouraging women from achieving Francis' level of musculature.

But surely things have changed since the 1980s? Bodybuilding must be less blatantly sexist than it was back then? Well, the current International Federation of Bodybuilding (IFBB) competition rules state:

> First and foremost, the judge must bear in mind that this is a woman's body building competition and that the goal is to find an ideal female physique. Therefore, the most important aspect is shape, a muscular yet feminine shape. The other aspects are similar to those described for the male physique, but muscular development must not be carried to such an excess that it resembles the massive musculature of the male physique.

Thus, women bodybuilders still have different rules applied to them. They are actively discouraged from developing too much muscle.

Critical reflection

1 Are you comfortable with such rules as the one quoted above—from the IFBB—being implemented? Why or why not?

2 While much has changed for female athletes, does the Tayla Harris incident highlight that there are many issues left to confront?

Sexuality and sport

Understandings of **sexuality** and sport are deeply connected to the gendered meanings of sport described in the previous section. The masculinising effect of sport has very different effects on how men and women who play sport are perceived. Because sport makes men more masculine, it makes them 'real men'; it also proves heterosexuality. There is a perception by some that gay men do not enjoy sport (Bass, Hardin & Elizabeth 2015). The logic is, if you can play sport, you mustn't be gay. In fact, Plummer (2006) suggests that most **homophobia** is not triggered by sexual behaviour, but by non-sexual factors such as sports ability or the way an individual walks. A boy or man who does not play sport, or cannot play sport well, is often feminised through terms such as 'girl' and 'sissy'. Their heterosexuality is also often called into question through derogatory terms such as 'poof' and 'fag'. This explains why these terms are often used as insults during games (Ferez 2018).

Sport does not have a history of constructing femininity; quite the opposite. Therefore for women, sporting ability leads to suspicions of homosexuality. Because sporting ability often requires one to excel at being masculine, females who excel at sport may not be considered 'real women'. They are not considered feminine, and this is confused with their sexuality. As a result, sport is not a cover, but may instead be seen as 'outing' lesbians.

But are things changing?

Sport is generally described by sociologists as heterosexist and homophobic. But there is some research that suggests things are changing in sport. For example, Anderson (2009) found that sport has come a long way towards reducing homophobia since the studies of the sport scholars of the 1980s and 90s. He found that athletes were privately not homophobic, but *they assumed their teammates were*. In the absence of overt homophobic violence and marginalisation, homophobic discourse was not about personal homophobia but designed to say 'I am not gay' and 'I am not weak' as a form of heterosexual masculine social currency. In Anderson's words:

> If the softening of masculinity continues, the older conservative form of masculinity may be less alluring, and the masculinizing context of sport may have to adjust to the new version of masculinity or risk losing its effect on socialising boys and men in the culture as a whole. In other words, if everything changes around sport, sport will either have to change or it will lose its social significance and be viewed as a vestige of an archaic model of masculinity (2009, p. 4).

Another recent incident that highlights changing attitudes in sport was the sacking of high profile rugby player Israel Folau when a series of homophobic statements he made became public (Robinson 2019).

PERSONAL VOICE

Jade Alexander

❝ Sport is often regarded as a masculine (and male-dominated) social world. This is particularly true for full-contact, team-based, competitive sports. This gendering of sport sees women placed in subordinate positions; rarely are women accepted, seen as equal to, or better than, men. Until now.

Enter roller derby: a full-contact, team-based, competitive, pass-for-points sport played (predominantly) by women on quad skates.

A crash course: roller derby in Australia is played on a flat oval track, where two teams vie for points. Each team has five skaters operating at once: three blockers, one pivot and one jammer.

The blockers work together, using their hips, butts and strategy to block the opposing team's jammer, while helping their own. The pivot (recognisable by the stripe on their helmet) guides the blockers and also works to regulate the speed of the players. Collectively, the blockers and pivots form 'the pack'. The jammer (recognisable by the star on their helmet) scores the points. Each team's jammer must skate through the pack, and for each member of the opposing team they pass (after their first lap) they accumulate one point. This includes skaters sitting in the penalty area (ghost points).

Roller derby is a high-intensity and fast-paced sport that requires four to eight referees operating at once, as well as countless non-skating officials assisting behind the scene.

Roller derby, however, is best known for its unique alternative culture, including skimpy skirts and ripped fishnets. It differs from many mainstream sports due to its emphasis on women and its DIY approach; there is no commercial investment.

It provides women with a space to experiment with desire, sexuality, gender performance and physicality. As a sport and culture it emphasises fitness and an acceptance of diverse bodies and lifestyles. Women are seen here to own their sexual identities, wearing hot pants, ripped shirts (or ripped anything and everything), and rocking alternative hairstyles and tattoos.

But, roller derby is fake, isn't it? It most certainly is not. All bouts (or 'derbies') are the real deal. However, roller derby has been (and often still is) considered fake, overly theatrical, and kitsch (Coppage 1999; Joulwan 2007; Barbee & Cohen 2010). This association stems from a long history of roller derby incarnations from the 1930s until the 1990s (Coppage 1999).

Roller derby first emerged in the early 1930s as a relatively tame endurance-based, mixed-gender sport. It was created by Leo Seltzer, who, after realising that the crowd reacted strongly to falls and collisions, modified it into a full-contact team sport in 1937 (Coppage 1999; Storms 2008; Krausch 2009).

The period from 1937 until 1953 was regarded as the 'Golden Age' of roller derby (Barbee & Cohen 2010). However, offshoots emerged between the 1960s and the 1990s, beginning with Roller Games and ending with RollerJam (which was played on roller blades instead of the traditional quad skate) (Coppage 1999; Barbee & Cohen 2010). These versions are commonly compared to World Wrestling Entertainment, due to inclusions such as spandex outfits, a figure-eight track with raised turns, a 'Wall of Death' and, at one time, even a live alligator pit (Peluso 2011) RollerJam is frequently seen as the lowest point of roller derby history as it included 'fake personality conflicts, beauty over brawn, and the phoniest fights ever witnessed in the sport' (Barbee & Cohen 2010). These later versions were generally unpopular and unsuccessful, with RollerJam being cancelled before the completion of its first season.

The current incarnation of roller derby, founded in 2001, distinguishes itself from its historical cousins due to its foundation as an amateur, DIY sport organised around a principle of 'by the skaters, for the skaters', or 'by derby, for derby' (Mabe 2007; Krausch 2009; Beaver 2012). It returned to the traditional quad skate and focused on athleticism. However, contemporary flat-track roller derby does still provide a unique blend of sport and spectacle, as most leagues theme their bouts (such as Western Sydney Rollers' 'The Good, The Bad, and the Derby') and often incorporate small skater performances when they emerge onto the track (skate-outs), as well as half-time entertainment such as burlesque dancers, pole dancers, bands or BMX stunts.

Contemporary roller derby skaters position themselves in contrast to notions of femininity and women as weak, powerless, less physically able or aggressive (Mabe 2007; Finley 2010). Training from two to five days a week, roller derby skaters push their bodies. They work on skates practising drills (can you imagine doing burpees on skates?) and strategy, while also working off skates for muscle development and overall fitness. Further, as part of this gendering of roller derby and the emphasis on physicality and toughness, skaters often celebrate injuries, particularly bruises, as trophies or badges of honour (Peluso 2011; Pavlidis 2014).

For instance, according to two current members of the derby community:

> [Injuries are] badges of honour because we are women and we are not meant to have those badges of honour and we are not meant to be athletic in the sense that roller derby is because it is full contact. You know, we're meant to play the soft sports, not these ones (Skater, South Side Derby Dolls).
>
> Women aren't supposed to do things that are dangerous. Women aren't supposed to be proud of bruises. Women aren't supposed to use our bodies in this way. But we do, and we encourage it, and we support it (Referee, South Side Derby Dolls).

It is a sport of tough women doing tough femininity, but is it a feminist sport?

Roller derby offers something new—a sport developed by women, for women (initially), which was built from the ground up. It is community focused; it raises money for local charities, and leagues do blood drives and support local business through sponsorship and advertising. It provides a (much-needed) space for women, not only to commune, but also to grow, get fit, engage in a sport that is welcoming, and to be part of something where their participation isn't the subordinate version.

Here, it is 'derby' and 'men's derby', in contrast to many mainstream sports and sporting associations—such as the NBL (National Basketball League) and the WNBL (Women's National Basketball League)—where women are marked as other (and inferior). In roller derby, women in particular can experiment with their bodies, their gender presentation, their sexuality and their physicality, and can test their limits. But men can also 'play' with gender in derby.

However, roller derby has been questioned from outside, and from within, regarding the apparent emphasis on sexiness, revealing clothing and theatricality. This can be read as conformity to gender norms that work to objectify women and has been queried as potentially anti-feminist (Cohen 2008). Is roller derby just another example of women conforming to norms that subordinate and exploit women?

In the current climate of women's sport, where media coverage is minimal, roller derby could offer a new way of 'doing' women's sport. Given its incredible rise in popularity, with roller derby leagues in Australia growing from three in 2007 to over 90 in 2014, perhaps their approach offers a new framework for women's sport. The combination of theatricality and athleticism is growing, and not just in roller derby, but in men's and women's sport globally (think of the Superbowl). It has long been recognised that women's sport is judged not just on the ability of the athletes, but also on their appearance and the entertainment value of the sporting event. Is roller derby the logical extension of this? Are roller derbyists acknowledging that entertainment and sexual titillation are some reasons why people watch women's sport, and have they thus created a sport where these things are emphasised?

FIGURE 20.1 With its apparent emphasis on sexiness, revealing clothing and theatricality, is roller derby just another example of women conforming to norms that subordinate and exploit women?

Conclusion

In this chapter, we have discussed the relationship between society and sports: sport reflects society, and sport reproduces society. In our contemporary society, sports reflect the gendered, individualised and economic values that dominate. Furthermore, sport can be used to reinforce these values.

One key feature we discussed was the gendered history of sports. The impact of this history is still being felt today. It impacts on the level of encouragement, opportunity and reward that athletes receive, and it impacts on their perceived sexuality.

Research shows that attitudes are changing. In a match of rugby between the New South Wales Waratahs and the Australian Capital Territory Brumbies, the Brumbies' Captain, David Pocock, pointed out to the referee that one of the Waratahs players was using homophobic slurs (Dutton 2015). After the game, the Waratahs player identified himself and quickly apologised. Even 10 years ago, the decision to raise this issue would have been unheard of. Sport is reflecting the changing attitudes in our society, and providing a site for resistance to dominant norms and values. Throughout this chapter, we highlighted examples of how many attitudes have changed—while some remain resistant to change.

Summary points

- Sports are social constructs. They are created by people through their interactions with each other.
- Sports are not neutral activities but are shaped by social structures and therefore reflect these.
- Sport has a masculine history.
- Sports stars are exemplars of hegemonic masculinity.
- Women have been discouraged (and even excluded) from participating in sport.
- The gendered nature of sport has many consequences for women.
- Sports participation affects how people perceive an individual's sexuality.

Sociological reflection

1. Consider the gendered nature of sport. One way you could do this is as follows. Make a list of words to describe a 'real man'. Then make a list of words to describe a 'real woman'. Now consider: Which one of these lists is a better fit with how you understand sport?
2. Given what you have learnt in this chapter, take a reflexive approach to your own sporting history; that is, reflect on your choices, experiences and successes. Can you see the impact of gender? Have you been deviant by overconforming or underconforming?
3. Consider norms and values. What can a consideration of sport tell us about the norms and values in our society?
4. Consider a gay or lesbian athlete. How do you think the particular sport they play has impacted on how their coming out was received? For example, reactions to diver Matthew Mitcham's coming out were very different from the reactions to Rugby League player Ian Roberts' coming out. How much does the gendered nature of particular sports affect the ease of coming out?

Discussion questions

1. What is sport?
2. How are sports created?
3. Are sports neutral activities?
4. Why do sociologists describe sport as 'masculine'?
5. How are women treated differently in sport?
6. Why does sport have a unique relationship with deviance?
7. What is underconformity and how does it relate to sport?
8. What is overconformity and how does it relate to sport?
9. How do masculine and feminine sports differ?
10. How does the gendered nature of sport affect how an athlete's sexuality is perceived?

References and further reading

REFERENCES

AAP & Cricket Network 2020, 'Record numbers tune in to Cup final on TV', *Cricket.com.au*, 9 March: <www.cricket.com.au/news/tv-broadcast-figures-australia-india-2020-womens-t20-world-cup-final-record-figures/2020-03-09>.

Australian Broadcasting Corporation (ABC) 2016, 'An entire women's AFL team costs less than an average male player', *Triple J Hack,* 5 September: <www.abc.net.au/triplej/programs/hack/should-female-afl-players-get-paid-the-same-as-men/7817118>.

Anderson, E 2009, *Inclusive Masculinity: The Changing Nature of Masculinities*, Routledge, New York.

Australian Government 2015, *Australian Sports Commission (ASC) Recognition*: <www.ausport.gov.au/supporting/nso/asc_recognition Accessed 4.5.15>.

Barbee, J & Cohen A 2010, *Down and Derby: The Insider's Guide to Roller Derby*, Soft Skull Press, New York.

Bass, J, Hardin, R & Elizabeth, AT 2015 'The glass closet: perceptions of homosexuality in intercollegiate sport', *Journal of Applied Sport Management*, 7(4), 1–31.

Beaver, T 2012, '"By the skaters, for the skaters": the DIY ethos of the roller derby revival', *Journal of Sport and Social Issues*, 36(1), 25–49.

Boeringer, SB 1999, 'Associations of rape-supportive attitudes with fraternal and athletic participation', *Violence Against Women*, 5(1), 81–90.

Boyle, L 2005, 'Flexing the tensions of female muscularity: how female bodybuilders negotiate normative femininity in competitive bodybuilding', *Women's Studies Quarterly*, 33(1–2), 134–49.

Burstyn, V 1999, *The Rites of Men: Manhood, Politics, and the Culture of Sport*, University of Toronto Press, Toronto.

Cashmore, E 2000, *Making Sense of Sports*, Routledge, London.

Coakley, J 2009, *Sports in Society: Issues and Controversies in Australia and New Zealand*, McGraw Hill, Sydney.

Cohen, JH 2008, 'Sporting-self or selling sex: all-girl roller derby in the 21st century', *Women in Sport & Physical Activity Journal*, 17(2), 24–33.

Connell, RW 1997, 'Men, masculinities and feminism', *Social Alternatives*, 16(3), 7–10.

Connell, RW & Messerschmidt, JW 2005, 'Hegemonic masculinity: rethinking the concept', *Gender and Society*, 19(6), 829–59.

Coppage, K 1999, *Roller Derby to RollerJam: The Authorized Story of an Unauthorized Sport*, Squarebooks, Oxford.

Dutton, C 2015, 'David Pocock says no room for homophobic slurs in sport or society after incident in Brumbies clash against Waratahs', *Sydney Morning Herald*, 23 March.

Ewing, M, Gano-Overway, L, Branta, C & Seefeld, V 2002, 'The role of sports in youth development', in M Gatz, M Messner, & S Ball-Rokeach (eds), *Paradoxes of Youth and Sport*, State University of New York Press, Albany, pp. 31–47.

Ferez, S 2018, 'Everyday homophobia and imposed heterosexuality in football', *The Conversation*, 6 July: < https://theconversation.com/everyday-homophobia-and-imposed-heterosexuality-in-football-99052>.

Finley, NJ 2010, 'Skating femininity: gender maneuvering in women's roller derby', *Journal Of Contemporary Ethnography*, 39(4), 359–87.

Hardin, M, Lynn, S & Walsdorf, K 2005, 'Challenge and conformity on "contested terrain": images of women in four women's sport/fitness magazines', *Sex Roles*, 53, 105–17.

Horne, J, Tomlinson, A, Whannel, G & Woodward, K 2013, *Understanding Sport: A Socio-Cultural Analysis*, 2nd edn, Routledge, New York.

International Federation of Bodybuilding (IFBB) 2009, *IFBB Rules*: <www.ifbb.com/pdf/IFBBrulebook.pdf>.

Joulwan, M 2007, *Rollergirl: Totally True Tales from the Track*, Touchstone, New York.

Kay, T 2003, 'Gender and sport', in B Houlihan (ed.), *Sport and Society: A Student Introduction*, SAGE, London, pp. 89–104.

Kell, PM 2000, *Good Sports: Australian Sport and the Myth of the Fair Go*, Pluto Press, Sydney.

Kelsey-Sugg, A & Trompf, T 2019, 'Tayla Harris, trolls and the long-held fear of powerful women', *ABC Radio National*, 25 March.

Kent, P 2020, 'NRL devastated as majority of fans slam new TV ad as political statement', *The Daily Telegraph*, 3 March.

Krausch, M 2009, 'Feminism(s) in practice: the sport, business, and politics of roller derby', *American Sociological Association Annual Meeting*, Hilton San Francisco, San Francisco, CA.

Laird, DA 1936, 'Why aren't more women athletes?', *Scientific American*, 154, 142–3.

Lenskyj, HJ 1998, '"Inside sport" or "on the margins"? Australian women and the sport media', *International Review for the Sociology of Sport*, 33(1), 19–32.

Leonard, WM 1998, *A Sociological Perspective on Sport*, 5th edn, Allyn and Bacon, Boston, MA.

Mabe, C 2007, *Roller Derby: The History and All-Girl Revival of the Greatest Sport on Wheels*, Speck Press, New York.

Masters, R 2006, *Bad Boys: AFL, Rugby League, Rugby Union and Soccer*, Random House Australia, Milsons Point.

Maurice, M 2019, '2019: the year the Australian public bought into women's sport', *The Guardian*, 30 December.

Messner, M & Sabo, D 1990, *Sport, Men, and the Gender Order: Critical Feminist Perspectives*, Human Kinetics, Champaign, IL.

Miracle A & Rees C 1994, *Lessons of the Locker Room: The Myth of School Sports*, Prometheus Books, Amherst, NY.

Murnen, SK & Kohlman, MH 2007, 'Athletic participation, fraternity membership, and sexual aggression among college men: a meta-analytic review', *Sex Roles*, 57(1–2), 145–57.

Nelson, MB 1996, *The Stronger Women Get, the More Men Love Football: Sexism and the Culture of Sport*, The Women's Press, London.

Pavlidis, A 2014, 'The pain and pleasure of roller derby: thinking through affect and subjectification', *International Journal of Cultural Studies*, 1–17.

Peluso, NM 2011, '"Crusin' for a brusin'": women's flat track roller derby', in C Bobel & S Kwan, *Embodied Resistance: Challenging the Norms, Breaking the Rules*, Vanderbilt University Press, Nashville, pp. 37–47.

Plummer, D 2006, 'Sportophobia: why do some men avoid sport?', *Journal of Sport and Social Issues*, 30(2), 122–37.

Robinson, G 2019, 'Folau "saddened" by sacking, considering his options', *Sydney Morning Herald*, 17 May.

Rowe, D 2020, 'All sport is global: a hard lesson from the pandemic', *Open Forum Australia*, 28 March.

Sage, G 1998, 'Does sport affect character development in athletes?', *Journal of Physical Education, Recreation & Dance*, 69(1), 15–18.

Schetzer, A 2018, 'AFLW player wage rise illustrates tough battle women face', *The Guardian*, 16 November: <www.theguardian.com/sport/2018/nov/16/aflw-player-wage-rise-illustrates-tough-battle-women-face>.

Senate Inquiry 2006, *About Time! Women in Sport and Recreation in Australia*, Senate Standing Committee on Environment, Communications, Information Technology and the Arts, Parliament of Australia: <http://apo.org.au/node/3800>.

Sherif, M, Harvey, OJ, White, BJ, Hood, WR & Sherif, CW 1961, *Intergroup Conflict and Cooperation: The Robbers Cave Experiment*, University Book Exchange, Norman, OK.

Storms, CE 2008, '"There's no sorry in roller derby": a feminist examination of identity of women in the full contact sport of roller derby', *The New York Sociologist*, 3, 68–87.

Trulson, ME 1986, 'Martial arts training: a novel "cure" for juvenile delinquency', *Human Relations*, 39(12), 1131–40.

Whitson, D 1990, 'Sport in the social construction of masculinity', in M Messner & D Sabo (eds), *Sport, Men, and the Gender Order: Critical Feminist Perspectives*, Human Kinetics, Champaign, IL.

FURTHER READING

Connell, RW 1987, *Gender and Power*, Allen & Unwin, Sydney.

Connell, RW 1995, *Masculinities*, Allen & Unwin, Sydney.

Donnelly, P 2011, 'From war without weapons to sport for development and peace: the Janus-face of sport', *Sport and International Affairs Review*, 31(1), 65–76.

Fredrickson, BL & Harrison, K 2005, 'Throwing like a girl: self-objectification predicts adolescent girl's motor performance', *Journal of Sport and Social Issues*, 29(1), 79–101.

George, M 2005, 'Making sense of muscle: the body experiences of collegiate women athletes', *Sociological Inquiry*, 75(3), 317–45.

Hickey, C 2008, 'Physical education, sport and hyper-masculinity in schools', *Sport, Education, Society*, 13(2), 147–61.

Krane, V, Baird, SM, Aimar, CM & Kauer, KJ 2004, 'Living the paradox: female athletes negotiate femininity and muscularity', *Sex Roles*, 50(5–6), 315–29.

Kreager, DA 2007, 'Unnecessary roughness? School sports, peer networks, and male adolescent violence', *American Sociological Review*, 72(5), 705–24.

Sefiha, O 2012, 'Bad sports: explaining sport related deviance', *Sociology Compass*, 6, 949–61.

MOVIES

Butler, G (dir.) 1985, *Pumping Iron II: The Women*, White Mountain Films.

Darling, I (dir.) 2019, *The Final Quarter*, Shark Island Productions.

Gordon, D (dir.) 2019, *The Australian Dream*, Good Thing Productions.

Zagarella, P & Morgison, J (dirs) 2008, *Walk Like a Man: Blood, Sweat and Queers*, SBS.

CHAPTER 21

Religion and contemporary society

JOHN A REES

CHAPTER OVERVIEW

What do we mean by 'religion' and how does a better understanding of the language, communities, institutions and interests associated with this term benefit our analysis of our society, everyday life and culture? Like many important concepts, the definition of 'religion' is highly contested and linked to debates about other terms such as 'secularism', 'spirituality', and even 'colonialism'. While these complications are important for establishing the connections between religion and other spheres of society—and for resisting the temptation to isolate religion from social dynamics created by law, politics, gender, race, citizenship, ethnicity and class—it is equally useful to establish a starting definition of 'religion' in a way that allows us to develop and refine our understanding further. This is what we will attempt to do in this chapter by asking three overlapping questions:

- *What is religion?* We will take a deep dive into the way scholars from many different disciplines approach religion as a concept.
- *Where is religion?* We will identify different sites where religion can be found and think about the broader lessons to be drawn from these examples.
- *When is religion?* We will tell several stories of everyday life and together consider when and how religion matters to our understanding of these events.

After reading this chapter, you should be able to:

- Define religion in the study of contemporary society
- Understand comparative interpretations of religion as a concept
- Differentiate religion from other concepts employed to study society
- Apply concepts of religion to interpret social phenomena
- Value the importance of religion as a category in the study of society.

KEY TERMS

Adaptive response The way an entity responds and adapts to environmental and social changes.

Agency The ability (or power) of an individual or group ('agent') to act independently of the external constraints of social structures—making decisions, undertaking actions and confronting authorities.

Belief Presented by sociologist Grace Davie when discussing religion as a special mode of believing that has two collective elements: i) the chain that makes the individual believer a member of a community, and ii) the tradition (or collective memory) that becomes the basis of that community's existence (Davie 2000).

Religion A contested term variously defined as i) personal, communal and institutional practices based on believed encounters with transcendent realities beyond (or within) the material world; ii) the social dynamics created by the separation of sacred and mundane space; and iii) an idea rooted in Christian terminology employed to codify (and control) a wide variety of social and cultural practices.

Religio-secular world A concept that challenges the idea that societies can simply be split along religious or secular lines. We live in a world that can be both more religious and more secular simultaneously.

Secularism A contested term variously defined as i) the social and political subordination of religion to other, more dominant elements of social and political life; ii) a philosophy promoting the political equality of all religions in a society; and iii) a mode of dominant power that orders and controls society through the constructed definitions of 'religion'.

Secular settlement A mode of classifying and managing religion so that it serves the declared and undeclared norms of the Western secular state.

Social cohesion The concept that members of a society are willing to cooperate with each other in order to survive and prosper.

Spirituality A contested term variously understood as i) beliefs and encounters with the transcendent reality that regularly occur outside of traditional religious settings, and ii) religious practices utilising an eclectic array of everyday resources and perspectives that occur inside and outside traditional religious settings.

Tradition Individual and communal practices of religion developed over time, often adapted to answer challenges posed to belief and association in social context, that can both reinforce and challenge social norms; intended for the purpose of strengthening religious community through memory reinforcement and ethical purpose.

What is 'religion'?

Exploring **religion** as a concept is important at the outset of our chapter because not everyone agrees on its meaning, including those who doubt whether 'religion' is a useful term for studying contemporary society at all. Interrogating the definition of religion at the start of our investigation also provides a way of analysing our own biases and assumptions in the context of alternative readings that can both challenge and affirm our understanding.

As you read on, make note of the ideas that appeal, those that unsettle, and those that need further clarification and discussion. From the very beginning, this book has challenged you to reflect on different ways of seeing the world, confronting our own biases and employing our sociological imagination—this approach is fundamental as you make your way through this chapter.

While the ways to investigate the meanings of religion are almost as numerous as the definitions themselves, in this first section we aim to establish clear descriptions of three different understandings of religion, and conclude with perspectives that incorporate the multiple dimensions of religion.

Religion as a modern encounter with the gods

Do you consider yourself to be 'religious'? Does the way we answer this question influence our approach to the study of religion in contemporary society?

Although the religious landscape is incredibly diverse, one common denominator to what we might call the 'religious worldview' is that it is shaped by some sort of human encounter with divine beings and/or transcendent forces that are believed to exist independently from human experience. Whether this involves God or gods who are believed to be present in the here and now, mythic/symbolic figures from our ancient past, or guiding spiritual forces that exist beyond (or within) the physical realm, the religious encounter seems to be a significant part of individual and social identity in contemporary society.

According to one global survey, 'worldwide, more than eight in ten people identify with a religious group' (Pew Research Centre 2012). This statistic supports the statement by sociologist Peter Berger that, 'the world today … is as furiously religious as it ever was, and in some places more so than ever' (Berger 1999). (Though he wrote this in 1999, Berger echoed this position in a 2017 update of his work.)

DOES THIS SURPRISE YOU?

This might stand in tension with numerous views that we increasingly live in a religion-free society. For instance, in the Netherlands religion is described as being in 'freefall' (Pollack & Rosta 2017); and in Australia—once characterised by the scholar William Connolly as 'the most secular country I have yet to visit and the least haunted by religious wars' (Connolly 1999)—those who self-identify as having 'no religion' are now a statistically dominant group according to Census data (ABS 2018).

Religion, therefore, has long been studied in the context of **secularism**. Secularism is described by philosopher Charles Taylor as a change in social environment from where:

> belief in God is unchallenged and indeed, unproblematic, to one in which it is understood to be one option among others, and frequently not the easiest to embrace (Taylor 2007, p. 7).

Yet secularism did not mean the removal of god(s) from the public sphere altogether. In Western nations such as the United States, for example, religion is instead relocated to what sociologist Robert Bellah (2005) called the formation of 'civil religion'. That is, we see a type of political religion that serves the modern state (Bellah 2005).

Beyond the West, there are also many alternative conceptions of secularism. Anthropologist Talal Asad argues that, like religion, secularism is complex, stating: 'the secular is neither singular in origin nor stable in its historical identity' (Asad 2003). According to this position, secularism is not about life without religion but, rather, equality of religions. Here, the concern is the political status of minority religious groups rather than the diminishing of religion. In India, for example, secularism in the tradition of Gandhi can be interpreted as an attempt to treat religious communities in such a way that they may enjoy equality (Tambiah 1998).

The complexity of what we are seeing is summarised by political scientist Jonathan Fox, as follows:

> A fuller picture of the world's religious economy would show secularisation—the reduction of religion's influence in society—occurring in some parts of the religious economy, and sacralisation—the increase of religion's influence in society—occurring in other parts (Fox 2008, p. 7).

Bringing these threads together, Martin Marty (2003) suggests that we live in a **religio-secular world**. This perspective challenges the simple idea that societies can be simply seen along a secular/religious divide. Marty makes the following point when discussing religion and its place in everyday life:

> The old debates revolved around binary categories: societies were either secular or religious; worldly or otherworldly; materialist or spiritual; favouring immanence or transcendence, etc. The use of such polarising concepts is valid in some contexts, but it does not adequately express the ways that individuals, groups, and societies actually behave; most people blur, mesh, meld, and muddle together elements of both the secular and the religious, the worldly and the other worldly, etc. In adjusting to the complex world around them, people confound the categories of the social scientists, theologians, and philosophers: they simply 'make do' with a syncretic and characteristically modern blend of attitudes—call it *religio-secular* (Marty 2003, p. 42).

An important consequence of this broad and dynamic understanding of religion in society is that there is still room to include gods, spirits and super/supranatural forces—manifested in a wider variety of ways—as part of any study of the human experience. Robert Orsi, a leading religious scholar and historian, encourages us to take the encounter with religion seriously in our social analysis:

> The gods were not turned back at the borders of the modern. The unseeing of the gods [by modern social science] was an achievement; the challenge is to see them again (Orsi 2016, p. 330).

Religion as a phenomenon of social cohesion and change

The academic discipline known as the 'sociology of religion' was founded on the insights of thinkers such as Emile Durkheim (1858–1917) and Max Weber (1864–1920). These two key influential sociologists had contrasting understandings of religion's place in society and everyday life.

In contrast to the gods being 'really present', as discussed in the previous section, Durkheim challenged us to understand religion and the sacred as a social construct: 'sacredness is conferred not by God but by society' (Aldridge 2013). Durkheim defined religion as 'a unified system of beliefs and practices relative to sacred things ... beliefs and practices which unite into a single moral community' (Durkheim 1915). The strong connotation that we can draw from Durkheim's views is that religion is fundamental to the creation of community and **social cohesion**.

By contrast, Weber did not define religion as an essential and general phenomenon in society. Rather, Weber considered the role of religion in effecting social change and establishing the 'conditions and effects of a particular type of social behaviour' (Weber 1965).

The most famous example of this was Weber's idea of the 'Protestant work ethic'. Weber argued that Christians from Protestant backgrounds—such as Presbyterians, Anglicans and Baptists—are better conditioned to the demands of modern capitalism than Catholics. This was because these religious **traditions** emphasised the values of hard work, discipline and frugality. Moreover, Weber saw Protestantism as playing a role in the creation of capitalist society itself, hence a strong connection to the nexus between religion and social change.

Whilst the discussion has grown and developed significantly since the time of Durkheim and Weber, the foundational notions of religion as it relates to both social cohesion and social change remain significant for interpreting the phenomena of religion in contemporary society. The connection between religion, identity and the politics of social change serves to illustrate this.

One example is Rosa Parks, an African-American woman who famously refused to obey American racial segregation laws whilst sitting on a bus in Alabama on 1 December 1955. Her refusal to move away from the 'whites only' section of the bus and stand in the 'blacks only' section sparked a nation-wide civil rights movement. While there is no doubt that she was a heroic individual, the role of religion in the life of Rosa Parks also encourages us to think about her actions through the notions of social cohesion and social change. Scholar of religion Scott Thomas powerfully emphasises these elements as follows:

> The real Rosa Parks did not decide one fine day that she had had enough, and would no longer go to the back of the bus, and so set in motion the year-long bus boycott in Montgomery, Alabama, which turned a young Martin Luther King, Jr. into a national leader of the civil rights movement. This is to understand her social action as a matter of heroic individualism and as a quandary ethics problem. The real Rosa Parks, as a part of her faith community—the African Methodist Episcopal Church—had spent 12 years helping to lead her local NAACP [National Association for the Advancement of Coloured People] chapter and attended summer training sessions at a labour and civil rights organizing school; therefore, she was a part of an existing faith community and a social movement (Thomas 2005, p. 437).

A sociologist of religion, Grace Davie, adds an important element to our understanding of religion and community through the concept of **belief**. For Davie, religion can be defined as a special mode of believing linked to two collective elements:

1 the *chain* which makes the individual believer a member of a community—a community which gathers past, present, and future members—and

2 the *tradition* (or collective memory) which becomes the basis of that community's existence (Davie 2000).

This encourages us to think about religious belief as needing both a community location and practices and traditions. If these links are broken and the tradition becomes lost, religion becomes cut off from the social elements that give it life and vitality.

The complex links between social cohesion, social change and belief, invite one final consideration in this current section. The distinction between religion and **spirituality** can sometimes emphasise the former as linked to established religious institutions and the latter as more to do with individual choices independent of such institutions. For example, according to Census data worldwide including in Australia (see Bouma & Halafoff 2017), a growing proportion of the community self-identify as 'spiritual but not religious' ('SBNR'). This phrase is interpreted as indicating beliefs and encounters with the gods that occur outside of traditional institutional settings.

Any assumption about a disconnection between religion and spirituality needs clarifying in two ways. The first clarification comes from several important studies that show practices linked to spirituality occur both outside and inside religious institutions, with religion found in everyday life in a wide variety of spaces (Ammerman 2013; 2014). Secondly, those identifying as SBNR remain socially located in their spiritual practices (Bouma & Halafoff 2017). These clarifications point us again toward the importance of social and community contexts for religious and spiritual practice, and hence also for our own understanding of religion.

Religion as dominant power and adaptive response

A third understanding of religion combines Weber's position with the view of philosopher Karl Marx (1818–83) that religion was one of the main drivers of social inequality. In fact, Marx famously described religion as the 'opiate of the people': that is, religion leads to oppression and distracts people from the inequalities that define their lives.

According to this perspective, religion is first and foremost an agent power (something discussed in Chapter 8). This view gained significant momentum in the second half of the twentieth century as thinkers and movements fighting for independence from colonial rule associated religion with colonial power. For example, the leading postcolonial philosopher Frantz Fanon wrote of 'the pacification of the colonised by the inescapable powers of religion' (Fanon 1967, p. 28).

The negative postcolonial depiction of religion was particularly aimed at Christianity. This was both because of the colonial practices of Christian majority empires (including England, France and Spain) as well as the associated 'religion-based' strategies employed to maintain colonial control. For instance, Hinduism is considered to be a category negotiated (or perhaps even invented) by British/Christian colonial powers in India as a means of unifying (and controlling) a wide variety of spiritual and cultural practices into a unified religion (Pennington 2005).

While the implications of seeing religion as a mode and agent of dominating power are potentially far reaching, as sociologists we should delve deeper into this idea. We can do this by considering two alternative responses and their implication for an understanding of religion in contemporary society.

1 Spinning Outward: that is, to reject 'religion' as a stable category and redefine it as a tool of control in *secular societies*.

This response is held by scholars from many disciplines belonging to some traditions of critical social theory or conflict theory discussed in Chapter 3. Elizabeth Shakman Hurd, for example, argues that a focus on religion in this colonial context should be understood as establishing '**secular settlements**' around the world. What she means here is that these colonial settlements are a 'mode of containing, managing, remaking and reforming religion in a manner consistent with secularist agendas' (Hurd 2017).

Hurd's focus is on the way religion as a category is understood in different contexts and according to secular agendas. Erin K Wilson (2019) agrees with this perspective and argued that colonialism creates a set of binaries not only between the 'secular' and 'religious', but also 'modern/primitive', 'reason/emotion' and 'Western/non-Western'. These simple binaries continue to affect power relations and inequalities in global politics today (Wilson 2019).

This framework is relevant because it allows us to *spin outward*—away from a focus on the internal essence of 'religion'—and raise questions about how 'religion' is constructed as a mode of control. This is very important work, yet it is equally worth asking what might happen if we also *spin inward* toward religion and consider, for example, how religions themselves complicate our understanding of dominant and colonial forms of power. This includes Christianity and forms of political and liberation theology that exist within it (Hovey & Phillips 2015; Bretherton 2019; Wielenga 2007; Casaldaliga & Vigil 1994).

2 Spinning Inward: that is, to re-engage the question of religion and power through the responses of religious communities themselves.

While a strong and incisive focus on religion as a tool of dominant power is of clear value, it may also lead to assumptions about religion and the colonial encounter being static. This perspective can be challenged by a more dynamic reading of **adaptive responses** by religious communities.

We will consider the complex case of Korea as a way to illustrate this point. Modern colonialism brought with it a tide of religious change in Korea. Most notably was the rise of Christianity in the twentieth century—but in a way that complicates the narrative of religion as a tool of domination. Here are four dynamics of religion that enhance our understanding:[1]

a *Religion under occupation*: Japan exercised colonial rule in Korea (1910–45) which also reinforced the power of Shintoism and Buddhism. The rise of Christianity—now Korea's most prominent religion—is partly attributed to Christian involvement in the resistance movement as 'the self-assertion of Korea against colonial influence' (Pollack & Rosta 2017).

b *Religion and the influence of new urban community*: Christian networks formed new communities in growing cities created by rapid modernisation. The potential for social, commercial and political influence in such circumstances was realised, notably through megachurches like Yoido Full Gospel that preached a message of material prosperity.

---

1   Adapted from John A. Rees, 'Megachurches and the living dead: intersections of religion & politics in Korea', *The Religion Gap*, June 18 2018: <www.e-ir.info/2018/06/18/megachurches-and-the-living-dead-intersections-of-religion-politics-in-korea/>. Used with permission.

c *Religious advocacy for the poor*: Alternative expressions to megachurch powerplay also grew via Christian movements for the empowerment of women, Christian urban missions in support of labour rights, and Christian interfaith networks with Buddhist leaders focused on issues of social justice. These are all expressions of *Minjung* theology that places advocacy for the poor and oppressed at the centre of religious practice.

d *Theology in cultural context*: According to the theologian David Kwang-sun Suh, 'Korean Christianity, although so Western in its liturgy and appearances, is obviously quite Shamanistic in its belief and behaviour' (Suh 2000). In this context, even Yoido Full Gospel, with its emphasis on healing and the claimed authority of its leader to have a hotline to God, can be comprehended through a shamanistic lens: that is, the practice of reaching different states of consciousness in order to reach out to and perceive and interact with the spirit world.

The interweaving of these contextual threads creates a complex tapestry where religion, popular practice and cultural politics intersect. Yes, colonial influence is an important part of the story—but it is more complex than the simple binaries described above.

While this example offers insights that are specific to the Korean context, it points to dynamics that are more generally applicable. Perhaps the most important one is that religious traditions and practices often display **agency**: that is, power to adapt to the conditions of the time, whether they be ones of domination and control or liberation and justice. Atalia Omer calls this the 'interpretive processes and fluid conceptions of traditions' that allow us to study religion beyond merely the perspective of power alone (Omer 2018).

Overview: religion as a multidimensional concept

In this first part of the chapter, I have offered three introductory responses to the question, 'What is religion in the study of contemporary society?': a modern encounter with the gods; a phenomenon of social cohesion and change; and dominant power and adaptive response.

Hopefully there are elements of these three perspectives that you will find both relevant and challenging. We conclude this first section by summarising two frameworks that help us to further appreciate religion as a multidimensional concept.

The first framework is by the sociologist of religion Linda Woodhead. We stated at the start of this chapter that interrogating the definition of religion provides a way of analysing our own biases and assumptions in the context of alternative readings that can both challenge and affirm our understanding. Woodhead's highly regarded approach offers a set of conceptual lenses that can help us to view religion from a variety of perspectives and to reflect on our assumptions in a productive way. Woodhead's approach describes 'five concepts' and encourages us to value the concept of religion, despite its contested nature. Woodhead suggests that:

> Rather than responding to criticisms of the concept of religion by abandoning the term … it is more fruitful for scholars of religion to become critically aware of the scope, variety and contingency of the term and its uses and so better able to justify and critique their own conceptual choices (Woodhead 2011, p. 126).

Woodhead's five concepts of religion appear in a modified summary in Table 21.1.

TABLE 21.1 Five concepts of religion

Concept	Meaning
Culture	Religious beliefs creating meaning, values, social order and behavioural norms
Identity	Religion creating community, defining the 'other', and ways of belonging
Relationship	Religion connecting the local and global, the immanent and transcendent, and the past-present-future
Practice	Religion generating forms of ritual and embodiment
Power	Religion linked to economic and political influence, status and recognition

Source: Woodhead 2011

Critical reflection

- Can you situate each concept above in our larger discussion of religion thus far? Which concept sounds most interesting to you?
- Does your current social context reflect the reality of some concepts more than others?
- Might this change over time or do you think that some concepts will always be more dominant than others?
- Are you familiar with the beliefs and practices of a religious tradition, and if so, how do the five concepts of religion manifest themselves?
- How does your understanding of 'religion' change, if at all, by considering Woodhead's framework?

The second example of religion as a multidimensional concept is particularly relevant to the study of contemporary society at the global level. Adapting categories originally devised by the anthropologist Clifford Geertz, scholar of international relations Ron E. Hassner offers an approach to the study of religion in global affairs via three dimensions:

- Deep religion: which displays 'an intimate familiarity with a particular religious movement or a particular geographical region'. Importantly, however, while we gain a deep understanding of this religion or region, deep religion argues against offering generalisations.
- Broad religion: an approach that tends to 'essentialise religion and reduce it to its social, economic, or political implications' (Hassner 2011, p. 43). Each of these dimensions are important but Hassner warns against both keeping them apart or prioritising one over other.
- Thick religion: an approach that traces international phenomena to their religious origins. While acknowledging specific contexts, Hassner also argues that we can identify 'generalisable patterns across states and regions' (Hassner 2011, p. 51). Hassner employs the acronym T-H-I-C-K to illustrate further: see Table 21.2.

TABLE 21.2 Five elements of THICK religion

Element	Meaning
Theology	What are the tenets of this religious movement? What do its most important texts and scholars propose?
Hierarchy	How is the religious movement organised, socially and politically? Who rules and makes decisions? How are these individuals chosen and ranked?
Iconography	How does this religious movement use symbols, myths, images, words or sounds to convey its ideas? How do believers treat these icons?
Ceremony	How do believers act out the theology, hierarchy and iconography of this religious movement? What are their rituals, practices, feasts and commemorations?
Knowledge	What do members of this religious community believe in? What are the foundations of their faith?

Source: Hassner 2011

Hassner's framework is appealing because it highlights the complex, multifaceted nature of different religious traditions. It is also a recognition that different fields of knowledge are needed to maximise our appreciation of religion at the global level:

> Thick religion rests on the assumption that the study of religion and international politics is necessarily an interdisciplinary exercise. Viewing religion merely through a political lens will not do. In addition to politics, we ought to also study religion directly, be it through the sociology of religion, comparative religious analysis, or theology (Hassner 2011, p. 178).

This multi-disciplinary emphasis is a good place to conclude our first section. Even though we have covered much ground, we have only taken a small number of possible pathways in our quest to answer the question 'What is religion?' Recommended readings at the conclusion of the chapter will assist you to further extend your understanding of the concept of religion, to explore new terrain and discover new points of interest and challenge.

Where is religion?

Having considered the definition of religion, we now turn to some examples of sites where religion can be analysed. They are:

- *Organisations*: For example, how an international organisation like the World Bank became interested in religion as a resource for its own mission;
- *Nationalism*: For example, on the complex connection between the Christian celebration of Easter and ANZAC Day in Australia;
- *Human rights*: For example, on how Tibetan Buddhism counters the dominating power of China;
- *The internet*: For example, on the way religious practice occurs in and through the use of online technologies;
- *Environment*: With a focus on religious tradition, networks and communities.

There are of course many other sites that we could choose. For instance, take a look at the chapters in this book and think about sites related to each chapter theme that have a religious dimension that could be analysed. As this kind of exercise would show, the possibilities are endless! What follows is not extensive treatment of each topic but is instead designed to give you a taste of many different contexts where the dynamics of religion can be studied.

Religion and organisations: how the World Bank got religion

The World Bank is arguably the most influential international financial institution worldwide. It sets the agenda for the way countries conduct financial borrowing in response to fundamental social and economic development needs around the world. It might surprise you that the World Bank has a substantial track record in thinking about ways to harness the capabilities of religion as a way of furthering its mission. Although there is a larger story to tell, what follows is a brief analysis of how this global corporation came to be interested in religion in the mid 1990s (see Rees 2011).

First, we need to acknowledge that other international organisations such as the International Labour Organization and United Nations Development Program have been working in partnership with religious communities for some time. The World Bank's faith and development thinking emerged from this broader process of engagement with religion.

Second, the World Bank was confronted directly and indirectly by religious civil society groups advocating for change to its environmental and debt-reduction policies. These groups were representing both formal religious organisations and informal social movements (discussed in Chapter 15). The concerns raised by these groups was that the Bank's policies were negatively impacting vulnerable communities that should not be ignored. The Bank came to realise that these religious networks could mobilise large populations and lead influential campaigns for change.

Third, since the 1980s a network of the Bank's own employees had been meeting in a forum called the Friday Morning Group to discuss issues of religion and ethics. These regular meetings resulted in convincing the Bank's stakeholders that religion and religious communities were key themes relevant to the work and mission of the organisation.

Fourth, these factors were emerging at a time when the understanding of 'development' for poorer nations was broadening beyond the delivery of economic assistance. Rather, development was seen to have a broader definition that included community empowerment. The World Bank asked itself: 'How would this be done most effectively?' It was obvious that gender empowerment and a focus on environmental sustainability were of central importance. In addition, when the Bank surveyed over 60,000 of the poorest people on Earth in an attempt to hear their concerns, religion emerged as a significant factor. It was identified that 'churches and mosques, as well as sacred trees, rivers, and mountains, were mentioned time and again as important and valued by poor men and women' (Narayan 2001, p. 45).

As a result of such factors, in 1998 the World Bank sponsored a program called the World Faiths Development Dialogue that would prioritise the role of faith communities and resources in the delivery of international development assistance. While the program had mixed results, what is key for us is that religion became recognised as a fundamental part of understanding and working with communities around the world.

This account is one example of a larger story—both in public and private sector organisations—of religion being included in the corporate emphasis on human capability.

> **Critical reflection**
>
> Do you think religion can be a productive force in corporate culture and performance, or is this understanding of religion in contemporary society misplaced?

Religion and nationalism: is there an ANZAC–Easter connection? [2]

The service of soldiers of the Australian and New Zealand Army Corps (ANZAC) is commemorated annually on ANZAC Day, April 25. The fabled and catastrophic landing of ANZAC forces at Gallipoli, Turkey, during the Great War holds central place in the ANZAC tradition. For many Australian citizens, to recognise ANZAC is to recognise the very birth of the nation itself in the crucible of war. Indeed, the ANZAC story is memorialised in ways that highly resemble religious practice. These can take standard forms of 'civic religiosity': that is, where the nation itself becomes the object of ritualised devotion.

Further, the memorialisation of the ANZAC story is intrinsically linked to traditional faith practices and beliefs. For instance, the central Easter theme of the sanctity of life upheld in the shadow of death 'belongs naturally' with the commemoration of ANZAC. In a homily delivered at the Vigil Mass of Remembrance for the ANZAC Centenary, a ceremony attended by the highest political and military representatives of the nation, the Catholic Archbishop of Sydney summarised it thus:

> Anzac Day always falls in the season of Easter. For all the seeming pointlessness of these young deaths, the white crosses that once marked the Gallipoli hills and the more permanent walled cross now at the beach cemetery are portents of Easter.

Another theme intrinsic to both Easter and ANZAC is reconciliation between enemies. At Gallipoli there is a Turkish memorial quoting Mustafa Kemal Ataturk on the fallen Allied foes. The memorial includes the following words:

> Those heroes that shed their blood, and lost their lives ... You are now lying in the soil of a friendly country. Therefore, rest in peace ... After having lost their lives on this land, they have become our sons as well.

A third intrinsic connection is the theme of sacrifice. Monumentalised separately at cenotaphs and in churches, at times each are represented as belonging together. The Archbishop of Sydney, once more:

> At one end of this cathedral is a very fine statue of a young man, an unknown ANZAC, who died for his country. At the opposite end, on the front of our main altar, is an image

---

2   Adapted from John A. Rees, 'Lest we forget: religion and the remembrance of war in a secular state', *The Religion Gap*, 7 May 2015: <www.e-ir.info/2015/05/07/lest-we-forget-religion-and-the-remembrance-of-war-in-a-secular-state/>. Used with permission.

similar in some ways, of another young man who died for His people, for all people. The echo is not accidental.

As we analyse this site of religion in Australia, it is important to distinguish the connection between ANZAC and Easter and not conflate these two quite separate events. ANZAC Day is not Easter, the memorialisation of war by an Enlightenment settler state cannot be confused with a transnational religious tradition of ancient origins. Yet at the conceptual level, sanctity, reconciliation and sacrifice are three binding concepts that seem intrinsic to both ANZAC and Easter.

Critical reflection

The ANZAC–Easter connection may be a premium example of a 'secular settlement' between the state and Christianity. Alternatively, others may suggest that there is a clear distinction between the two events, and that the Easter religious observance plays a broader role in society well beyond—and in competition with—the civil religion at the heart of ANZAC.

What do you think?

Religion and rights: how reincarnation informs resistance in Tibet [3]

One important dimension in studying religion in contemporary society is the way religious communities can be subject to discrimination and ill-treatment. As such, they can fall victim to human rights abuses at the hands of communities and countries alike. It is important to be cautious in assuming that maltreatment of a religious group is always because of their religion, when issues of ethnicity, race, or historic grievance may be more primary factors. On other occasions, religious practice seems to be at the heart of events.

Consider, for example, the conflict in 2015 between China's Communist authorities and the 14th Dalai Lama over the question of reincarnation. The incident centres on the suggestion by the present Dalai Lama about the possible cessation of his own reincarnation as a protest against Chinese oppression in Tibet. In a remarkable response, the Communist authorities accused him of blasphemy against Tibetan Buddhism. How can we interpret these events?

We might initially be surprised that an officially atheist regime would bother to have a view on the matter of spiritual rebirth. However, when an ageing 14th Dalai Lama passes away, Beijing hopes for someone more politically compliant to their rule of Tibet to be reborn as the 15th Dalai Lama. Someone, perhaps, like Bainqen Erdini Qoigyijabu, a member of the Chinese People's Political Consultative Conference and the 11th Panchen Lama, the second highest authority in Tibetan Buddhism. Bainqen Erdini Qoigyijabu was handpicked by the Chinese

---

3   Adapted from John A. Rees, 'To be, or not to be [reincarnated]—that is the [political] question', *The Religion Gap*, 1 April 2015: < www.e-ir.info/2015/04/01/to-be-or-not-to-be-reincarnated-that-is-the-political-question>. Used with permission.

leadership in 1995 after rejecting the exiled Dalai Lama's identification of another child as the next Holiness.

We might be equally surprised that the Dalai Lama can choose not to reincarnate. Yet, through the exercise of his religious authority, the Dalai Lama has shown time and time again that religious traditions have the capacity to innovate, adopt and even co-opt modern influences for their own growth and success.

Could we offer an authoritative theological comment on the Dalai Lama's suggestion that Buddhist rebirth can cease? Likely not. Can we observe that such a statement represents a nimble wielding of spiritual tradition in answer to a present and grave political danger? Indeed, we can.

In the above example we learn how religion can provide a unique protective resource in the face of human rights challenges.

Religion and the internet: which influences which?

Technology has always played an important role in the transmission of faith. In turn, faith has at times encouraged the growth in technology. One of the best historic examples of this two-way exchange is the astrolabe. Described as 'the original smartphone' (Poppick 2017), the astrolabe was an ancient navigation device that became popularised throughout the Islamic world as a way to help the faithful establish the direction of prayer toward Mecca—known as the Qibla.

In this way, technology aided the believer to practise their regular devotion 'in synchrony with the heavens' (King 2005). Fast forward to today and any basic app search on a smartphone will produce options such as 'qibla compass', 'qibla connect' and 'qibla finder', illustrating an unbroken thread between technology and faith from the premodern to the postmodern world.

As the example of the astrolabe shows, internet technology impacts the everyday experience of faith. For instance, consider the passage below from a recent text on 'religion online'. As you read, locate elements of religious encounter and/or social binding/cohesion, and the role played by internet technologies to support them:

> Yashir is working at his home desk Saturday afternoon when his smartphone issues a special chime. He quickly closes his laptop and opens his mat on the floor so that he is facing Ka'ba. He does not need the phone's reminder of what direction to face—that direction is an established habit by now. At the same time, Mary is using her laptop to connect to the video stream from her best friend's wedding. Her broken leg has kept her from flying the 1,500 miles to attend it, but her video connection lets her celebrate along with everyone who is there in person. Halfway around the world, Sangjae is trying to make reference to a scriptural passage but can't remember the exact words. He is saved by a student who starts reading the passage from his e-reader (Grant and Stout 2019, p. 1).

A fascinating line of investigation is whether internet technology not only supports religion but also creates it. That is, through new dimensions within existing traditions, can it generate new forms of religion itself?

Previous study in this area answers with an emphatic 'yes' to both options. On the creation of religion, one prominent tech entrepreneur offers the stimulating thought that 'technology-oriented religions are coming' (Stalnaker 2019). By linking this view to our broader consideration of religion in everyday life, we might understand the connections between religion and internet technologies to be yet another expression of religion as social connection and change, adaptive response, and even spiritual encounter. Do you agree?

Religion and climate change: where is religion?[4]

Conceptualising religion as multidimensional is important to understanding why global attention has recently focused on how faith-based organisations (FBOs) are responding to climate change. As the conversation on the climate crisis develops, international organisations like the United Nations are increasingly acknowledging the agency of religious communities (Haynes 2014). Where can religion be found in response to the climate change challenge?

There are three places where we can look at this relationship: the teachings of religious traditions; the power of religious networks; and the connections of religious community. Let's discuss each of these in turn.

First, religions can influence their followers through teachings developed from rituals and scripture, which can cultivate responses to world events (Haluza-DeLay 2014). This is because religion can help conceptualise the human experience including how we define the relationship humans have with the physical world.

Responding to climate change arguably requires individual engagement, and through ritual, scripture and practice, religion can influence how people address the climate challenge on a personal level.

Judaism, specifically, is a faith praised for its environmental stewardship. The commandment of *bal tashchit* is a teaching central to the faith's ethics, making environmental protection a fundamental tenet of Jewish tradition. *Bal tashchit* teaches believers not to waste or destroy and demonstrates how scripture and practice can instil in individuals a moral obligation to protect God's creation (Gunter-Goldstein 2010).

Second, religions provide a powerful mechanism through which the global community can cohesively respond to climate change. In 2015, Islamic leaders including clerics, academics and policymakers, urged the global Muslim community to be proactive in combating climate change. Further, these leaders advocated to international government leaders to conclude an effective universal climate change agreement (United Nations 2015). The Islamic Declaration on Climate Change was instrumental to global discussions that occurred at the 2015 UN Climate Change Conference, demonstrating the influence religious communities can have on promoting political change.

Finally, religion provides a sense of connectivity across communities in a time of crisis. This is often cultivated by religious leaders and interfaith cohesion within a community. This cooperation can lead to tangible change when addressing issues experienced by all of humankind, with climate change being a pertinent example.

---

4   The author acknowledges the research assistance of Ms Jasmine Robertson in making a core contribution to the content and writing of this section: Religion and climate change.

Indonesia, which recognises Islam, Buddhism, Christianity, Hinduism and Indigenous faiths as official religions, is an example here. Religion has an important social function in Indonesian society. Due to its location, Indonesia is particularly vulnerable to the effects of climate change. In 2007 at the UN Climate Summit in Bali, an interfaith statement on the obligation of religious communities to address climate change was presented (Smith 2019). Since 2007, interfaith cooperation in Indonesia has been used proactively to address domestic environmental issues.

This has played out in many ways. One is the joint effort of Christian and Indigenous leaders in the 'Save Aru Islands' movement, which kept 5000 square kilometres of land from being developed by a multinational corporation (The Gecko Project & Mongabay 2019).

When answering the question, 'Where is religion?', the global climate crisis demonstrates the individual, community and international roles religion has to play in humanity's response to collective hardship. For many people, religion is a necessary part of the human experience, and this has contributed to its multidimensional nature. Religion has agency, and this needs to be acknowledged and considered when analysing how to collectively address social and political issues.

When is religion?

We have explored answers to the questions 'What?' and 'Where?' is religion. Our final section offers you a chance to consider 'When?' religion might be important to apply in analysing distinct social phenomena. This will be done through three brief accounts of different types of religious events and contexts. The first story focuses on a moment in the life of an individual, the second on the public action of a prominent faith community, the third on how a religious tradition is adapting to the challenge of COVID-19.

BOX 21.1

Everyday sociology

RAY ENCOUNTERS HOPE

A man sits in the chapel of a hostel for homeless men. He is somewhat aware of those around him, residents and workers who have also gathered for the daily church service, but his alcohol-induced dementia has made communication very difficult. Like many residents of the hostel in Sydney's inner city, Ray has lived a troubled life that has taken a toll on his wellbeing. Sitting quietly in a psychosocial haze, he seems lost in his own world for much of the service—though he is the first to arrive at the chapel every day, Ray seems almost always 'hidden' from view. Yet as the final hymn is played on a small organ that is slightly out of tune, something quite remarkable occurs. The hymn is titled 'The Old Rugged Cross', and for those gathered at the hostel it is a song of hope about the god worshipped by Christians who has saved humanity and who offers liberation from affliction.

Suddenly, Ray stands to his feet, and with a clarity in his voice and a sharp, lucid look in his eye, begins to sing the hymn loudly and with full conviction. It is as if another man is standing there—a new man, or maybe a younger man—somehow retrieved from the past by the power of the song, now (re)introducing himself to the world, no longer crouched in a defeated funk but standing tall in confidence. Yet, inevitably perhaps, as the final verse of the hymn is sung, Ray begins to retreat into his former self. By the time it is over, Ray is slumped down in his seat, quietly lost in his own thoughts once more. Every day, during every service, Ray's transformation would occur and be witnessed by others.

As you re-read Ray's story, critically consider the following:
1 Which of the characteristics of religion—encounter, social cohesion/change, and power—are represented?
2 Can any of the elements of Woodhead's concept of religion be used to interpret the story?
3 Could any connections be established between Ray's story and the sites of analysis discussed in this chapter?

Discuss your insights with others.

BOX 21.2

Everyday sociology

AUSTRALIAN MUSLIMS PRAY FOR RAIN DURING EID AL-ADHA

In 2018, Muslims across Australia prayed for rain to help drought-affected Australian farmers.

During the holy celebration of Eid al-Adha, one of the two main religious holidays for the Muslim community and one of Islam's holiest festivals, mosques dedicated their celebrations to praying for rain for the farmers.

The Grand Mufti of Australia encouraged the Australian Muslim community to work together in partnership with farmers: 'For they are our fellow human being and our brothers, they are our partners in this country. What pains them pains us and what harms them harms us.'

Adapted from Erwin Renaldi's article for the ABC, 22 August 2018, 'Muslims pray for rain for Australian farmers during religious holiday Eid al-Adha': <www.abc.net.au/news/2018-08-22/muslim-rain-prayer-call-to-end-the-drought-for-farmers/10152076>.

As you re-read the 2018 media report of the Australian Muslim community praying for rain to break the drought in Australia, critically consider the following:
1 Are any of the characteristics of religion—encounter, social cohesion/change, and power—represented?
2 Can any of the elements of Hassner's concept of religion be used to interpret the event?
3 Can any connections be established between this story and the sites of analysis discussed in this chapter?

Discuss your insights with others.

> **BOX 21.3**
> ## Everyday sociology
>
> **WORSHIP IN AN AGE OF COVID-19**
>
> In March 2020, the ABC ran a story about Hemangini Patel, a devout Hindu who looks forward to going to the temple for the weekly 'sabha' or congregation.
>
> Responding to the government's restrictions on public gatherings to curb the spread of COVID-19, her local temple replaced the in-person assembly with a live stream. She found it comforting to have 'some form of normality and routine', and the message of 'hope, unity and fraternity'. 'To have those messages as a reminder of what our priorities are in these times, it really helps to keep everyone calm,' she said.
>
> Kunal Patel, BAPS's (Bochasanwasi Akshar Purushottam Sanstha) national community relations volunteer, agrees that 'the most important feedback we received was that for practising Hindus this is an important milestone, to attend a congregation on a weekly basis, and the fact it's still accessible puts people at ease.'
>
> Adapted from the ABC article, 24 March 2020, 'How the internet is bringing comfort to faith communities during coronavirus social isolation' by Siobhan Hegarty with extra reporting from Alison Xiao: <www.abc.net.au/news/2020-03-24/hindu-christian-worship-in-the-time-of-covid-19-coronavirus/12081284>.

As you re-read the story of the BAPS community, critically consider the following:
1. Are any of the characteristics of religion—encounter, social cohesion/change, and adaptive change—represented?
2. Can any of the elements of Woodhead's concept of religion be used to interpret the story (e.g. religion as relationship and practice)?
3. Can any connections be established between Hemangini's story and the sites of analysis? Discuss your insights with others.

Summary of main points

* *What is religion?* Religion is a contested term that can be defined according to the contrasting modes of personal and communal encounter, social cohesion and change, dominant power and adaptive response.
* Religion as encounter recognises the lived experience of individuals and communities who uphold a belief in the present and formative interaction with gods, myths and divine forces in contemporary society.
* Religion as social cohesion and change prioritises the immanent and temporal effects of religion in society, both in terms of how society defines itself and the way religion influences social development.
* Religion as dominant power and adaptive response situates the creation of 'religion' as a category of modern secular control, leading to either a rejection of religion as a term that only masks other more important social dynamics (the dominant power position) or a study of the way religious practices inform actions that counter dominant power (the adaptive response position).
* Frameworks such as those by Woodhead (2011) and Hassner (2011) are salient examples of approaches that offer insight into the multiple dimensions of religion.
* *Where is religion?* Studies of religion and organisations, nationalism and human rights offer contexts through which to understand the conceptual richness of religion as a category.
* *When is religion?* Stories of religion in society provide an opportunity to apply 'religion' to an analysis of everyday life.

Sociological reflection

1. Would you describe your life as informed by religious belief? Have you had personal or communal experiences that are best explained in religious terms?
2. To paraphrase John Lennon, 'imagine there is no religion'. In your view, would this be a good, bad or neutral thing for society?
3. Do religious authorities have too much, too little or irrelevant levels of power in the contemporary society that you live in?
4. Is it better to consider religious conversion negatively or as a normal and healthy part of civil society? When, and under what conditions, might each option apply?

Essay topics

1. What is 'religion'? Answer this question from two different theoretical perspectives, applying each perspective to an example of religion in contemporary society.
2. Is Australia a 'secular settlement'? In your answer, define 'secular settlement' and provide examples of possible linkages between religion and the modern state that could support this view.

3   Is religion an agent of social cohesion or social disruption? Answer giving examples from Australian or international contexts.

4   How important is religion to the peace and stability of society? Answer citing the role religious belief and practices play in everyday community life.

5   Is the difference between the classification of 'religion' and being 'spiritual but not religious' important for understanding the makeup of Australian society?

Further investigation

* Next time you visit a new city, take a walk around the downtown area and count the number of religious institutions that are visible, noting the different kinds of religions and religious denominations there are. Although this is an informal exercise, consider what this observation exercise might tell you (or not) about the religious subculture that resides in the city you are visiting.

* Reach out to a friend who belongs to a different religious tradition than you (doing the same if you do not belong to a religious tradition). Ask them if it is possible to visit their community religious gathering and/or observe a religious ceremony with them. Following this experience, discuss the relevance (or not) of our definitions of religion as encounter, social cohesion/change, dominant power and adaptive response.

References and further reading

REFERENCES

Aldridge, A 2013, *Religion in the Contemporary World: A Sociological Introduction*, 3rd edn, Polity Press, Cambridge, UK.

Ammerman, NT 2013, 'Spiritual but not religious? Beyond binary choices in the study of religion', *Journal for the Scientific Study of Religion*, 52(2), 258–78.

Ammerman, NT 2014, 'Finding religion in everyday life', *Sociology of Religion* 75(2), 189–207.

Asad, T 2003, *Formations of the Secular: Christianity, Islam, Modernity*, Stanford University Press, Stanford, CA.

Australian Broadcasting Corporation (ABC) 2018, 'Muslims pray for rain for Australian farmers during religious holiday Eid al-Adha', *ABC News*, 22 August: <www.abc.net.au/news/2018-08-22/muslim-rain-prayer-call-to-end-the-drought-for-farmers/10152076>.

Australian Broadcasting Corporation (ABC) 2020, 'How the internet is bringing comfort to faith communities during coronavirus social isolation', *ABC News*, 24 March: <www.abc.net.au/news/2020-03-24/hindu-christian-worship-in-the-time-of-covid-19-coronavirus/12081284>.

Australian Bureau of Statistics (ABS) 2018, 'Census reveals Australia's religious diversity on World Religion Day', ABS, Canberra: <www.abs.gov.au/AUSSTATS/abs@.nsf/mediareleasesbyReleaseDate/8497F7A8E7DB5BEFCA25821800203DA4?OpenDocument>.

Bellah, RN 2005, 'Civil religion in America', *Daedalus*, 134(4), 40–55.

Berger, PL 1999, 'The desularisation of the world: a global overview', in *The Desularisation of the World: Resurgent Religion and World Politics*, Eerdmans, Grand Rapids, Michigan, pp. 1–18.

Bouma, G & Halafoff, A 2017, 'Australia's changing religious profile—rising nones and pentecostals, declining British protestants in superdiversity: views from the 2016 Census', *Journal for the Academic Study of Religion*, 32(2), 129–43.

Bretherton, L 2019, *Christ and the Common Life: Political Theology and the Case for Democracy*, Eerdmans, Grand Rapids, Michigan.

Casaldaliga, P & Vigil JA 1994, *The Spirituality of Liberation*, Burns & Oats, Kent, UK.

Connolly, W 1999, *Why I Am Not a Secularist*, University of Minnesota Press, Minneapolis, Minnesota.

Davie, G 2000, *Religion in Modern Europe: A Memory Mutates*, Oxford University Press, Oxford.

Durkheim, E 1915, *The Elementary Forms of Religious Life*, trans. J Ward Swain, Allen & Unwin, London.

Fanon, F 1967, *The Wretched of the Earth*, Penguin, London.

Fox, J 2008, *A World Survey of Religion and the State*, Cambridge University Press, New York.

Grant, AE & Stout, DA 2019, 'Introduction: religion in cyberspace', in *Religion Online: How Digital Technology Is Changing the Way We Worship and Pray*, ABC-CLIO, Santa Barbara, CA, pp. 1–10.

Gunter-Goldstein, S 2010, 'Sowing the seeds for a greener Jewish future', *The Canadian Jewish News*, no. January 28: <www.cjnews.com/news/canada/sowing-seeds-greener-jewish-future>.

Haluza-DeLay, R 2014, 'Religion and climate change: varieties in viewpoints and practices', *Wires Climate Change*, 5(2), 261–79.

Hassner, RE 2011, 'Religion and international affairs: state of the art', in P James (ed.), *Religion, Identity, and Global Governance: Ideas, Evidence, and Practice*, University of Toronto Press, pp. 37–56: <www.jstor.org/stable/10.3138/j.ctt2ttp51.7>.

Haynes, J 2014, *Faith-Based Organizations at the United Nations*, Palgrave MacMillan, New York.

Hovey, C & Phillips, E 2015, 'Preface', in *Christian Political Theology*, Cambridge University Press, Cambridge, UK.

Hurd, E 2017, 'Religion and secularism', in R Devetak, J George & P Percy (eds), *An Introduction to International Relations*, 3rd edn, Cambridge University Press, UK, pp. 356–70

King, DA 2005, *In Synchrony with the Heavens, Volume 2: Instruments of Mass Calculation: Studies X–XVIII*, Brill, Leiden, Netherlands.

Marty, ME 2003, 'Our religio-secular world', *Daedalus*, 132(3), 42–0.

Narayan, D 2001, 'Voices of the poor,' in D Belshaw, R Calderisi & C Sugden (eds), *Faith in Development. Partnership Between the World Bank and the Churches of Africa*, Regnum Books, Oxford & Washington, DC, pp. 39–48.

Omer, A 2018, 'When "good religion" is good', *Journal of Religious & Political Practice*, 4(1), 122–36.

Orsi, R 2016, *History and Presence*, Harvard University Press, Cambridge, MA.

Pennington, BK 2005, *Was Hinduism Invented?: Britons, Indians, and the Colonial Construction of Religion*, Oxford University Press, New York: <https://doi.org/10.1093/0195166558.001.0001>.

Pew Research Centre 2012, 'The global religious landscape: a report on the size and distribution of the world's major religious groups as of 2010', Washington, DC.

Pollack, D & Rosta, G 2017, *Religion and Modernity: An International Comparison*, Oxford University Press, Oxford, UK.

Poppick, L 2017, 'The story of the astrolabe, the original smartphone', *The Smithsonian Magazine*, no. January 31: <www.smithsonianmag.com/innovation/astrolabe-original-smartphone-180961981/>.

Rees, JA 2011, *Religion in International Politics and Development: The World Bank and Faith Institutions*, Edward Elagar, Cheltenham, UK.

Rees, JA 2015a, 'To be, or not to be [reincarnated]—that is the [political] question', *The Religion Gap*, 1 April: <www.e-ir.info/2015/04/01/to-be-or-not-to-be-reincarnated-that-is-the-political-question>.

Rees, JA 2015b, 'Lest we forget: religion and the remembrance of war in a secular state', *The Religion Gap*, 7 May: <www.e-ir.info/2015/05/07/lest-we-forget-religion-and-the-remembrance-of-war-in-a-secular-state/>.

Rees, JA 2018, 'Megachurches and the living dead: intersections of religion & politics in Korea', *The Religion Gap*, June 18: <www.e-ir.info/2018/06/18/megachurches-and-the-living-dead-intersections-of-religion-politics-in-korea/>.

Smith, J 2019, 'Turning to faiths to save the planet; how religions shape environmental movement in Indonesia', *The Conversation*, November 11: <https://theconversation.com/turning-to-faiths-to-save-the-planet-how-religions-shape-environmental-movement-in-indonesia-126506>.

Stalnaker, S 2019, 'Technology-oriented religions are coming', *Quartz*, October 10: <https://qz.com/1723739/technology-oriented-religions-are-coming/>.

Suh, DK 2000, *The Korean Minjung in Christ*, Wipf & Stock, Eugene, Oregon.

Tambiah, SJ 1998, 'The crisis of secularism in India', in R Bhargava (ed.), *Secularism and Its Critics*, Oxford University Press, New Delhi.

Taylor, C 2007, *The Secular Age*, Harvard University Press, Cambridge, MA.

The Gecko Project & Mongabay 2019, 'Saving Aru: the epic battle to save the islands that inspired the theory of evolution', *Mongabay*, October 10: <https://thegeckoproject.org/saving-aru-the-epic-battle-to-save-the-islands-that-inspired-the-theory-of-evolution-b96a5c2b9c32>.

Thomas, SM 2005, *The Global Resurgence of Religion and the Transformation of International Relations: The Struggle for the Soul of the Twenty-First Century*, Palgrave Macmillan, New York.

United Nations 2015, 'Islamic declaration on climate change (external statement)', *United Nations Climate Change*, August 18: <https://unfccc.int/news/islamic-declaration-on-climate-change>.

Weber, M 1965, *The Sociology of Religion*, trans. E Fischoff, MacMillan, London.

Wielenga, B 2007, 'Liberation theology in Asia', in C Rowland (ed.), *Liberation Theology*, 2nd edn, Cambridge Companion Series, Cambridge University Press, Cambridge, UK, pp. 55–78.

Wilson, EK 2019, 'Being "critical" of/about/on "religion" in international relations', in J Edkins (ed.), *Routledge Handbook of Critical International Relations*, Routledge, Florence, USA, pp. 143–60.

Woodhead, L 2011, 'Five concepts of religion', *International Review of Sociology*, 21(1), 121–43.

FURTHER READING

Becci, I, Burchardt, M & Casanova, J 2013, *Topographies of The Faith: Religion in Urban Spaces*, Brill, Leiden, Netherlands.

Bouma, G & Halafoff, A 2017, 'Australia's changing religious profile—rising nones and Pentecostals, declining British Protestants in superdiversity: views from the 2016 Census', *Journal for the Academic Study of Religion*, 32(2), 129–43.

Daniel, P 2014, *Nine Theories of Religion*, 3rd edn, Oxford University Press, Oxford.

Grace, D 2004, *The Sociology of Religion*, SAGE, London.

Hecht, RD & Biondo, VF (eds) 2010, *Religion and Everyday Life and Culture*, Praeger, CA.

Marshall, K 2013, *Global Institutions of Religion: Ancient Movers Modern Shakers*, Routledge, New York.

Orsi, R 2016, *History and Presence*, Harvard University Press, Cambridge, MA.

CHAPTER 22
Conclusion and how to change the world

JAMES ARVANITAKIS AND MITRA GUSHEH

CHAPTER OVERVIEW

From risotto to a coffee …

When I wrote this conclusion to the first edition of this book, it was 7.30am and I was sitting in a café at one of the busiest intersections in Sydney, smiling at the very nice barista who had just made my coffee: three-quarter full flat white in case you are wondering. Just as we are finishing this second edition, COVID-19 has resulted in a massive lockdown—the once busy streets are empty and cities like Sydney, Melbourne and Brisbane are starting to feel like some of the ghost towns I visited while in the United States.

At both these times, I have paused to contemplate the many goings on around me, reflecting on what we can observe as 'active sociologists'. Right now, during this difficult and often heartbreaking time, we can begin to reflect on the many things we used to think were 'normal' and take for granted: our ability to see live bands, go out for dinner, meet friends at the beach or park, catch public transport or even give a loved one or friend a hug. Where we once sat with friends and family, we now talk to them over Skype or other such tools and it 'kind of feels normal'.

What irreversible societal changes will come from this pandemic? Only time will tell but making sense of it all will certainly raise new and important questions for sociologists for many years to come. Many of you will be reading this book when the COVID-19 lockdowns have (hopefully) become a thing of the past. If so, then consider what things have returned to how they were before, what things have changed, and what has even been created as a 'new normal'.

In this chapter, we will begin by contemplating how we can apply the many sociological concepts we have learnt in this book to everyday experiences like ordering a cup of coffee and move to discuss how we can use the insights we have learnt to—and we are not joking—'change the world'.

Returning to the café then.

Let me return to life before COVID-19 to reflect on my experiences—and hopefully when you are reading this the 'lockdown' will be nothing more than a memory!

As a researcher, I spend a lot of time sitting in cafés reading, writing and interviewing people—it is also where I prefer to do my marking. Many of the scenes I describe are common and everyday events.

Looking up and down the busy street, there is so much going on it is difficult to know where to begin. The most distracting thing is the traffic and the number of people beeping their horns. Watching this scene, I imagine the exhaust fumes making their way into the atmosphere. I wonder whether so many thousands of people would use their cars (and hence contribute to the destruction of our environment) if there were a genuine alternative to driving to work, such as an integrated public transport system and better bike lanes.

The problem, however, is that cars are not simply a way of getting around; they are an integral part of our contemporary society and culture. The car you drive helps define your identity: it tells the world about you including your tastes, your income and whether you care enough to keep it clean. When we are old enough to get our driver's licence, buying a car is part of the transition to adulthood and a taste (and symbol) of freedom.

The other thing about our cars is that there are hundreds of thousands of people whose livelihood is dependent on these vehicles. There are the car makers, designers and mechanics. There are also the people who import tyres, clean cars and install stereos. Also, in each Australian state, entire government departments and specific ministers of parliament are responsible for looking after our roads.

Each year, organisations spend billions of dollars on research and development of new features: from new safety equipment, making cars more efficient, designing driverless cars and making them more aesthetically appealing. The emergence of driverless cars has opened up many debates about the future of work (will taxi or delivery drivers be needed), safety (should a driver pay attention when the car is driving or can we read a book) and ethics (should a car be programmed to save the life of a passenger, driver or pedestrian in a collision).

Serious traffic snarls are reported on the news and are discussed in parliament. Helicopters fly over and monitor the traffic, and report to radio and television stations all over the country. The 'trip to work' and the 'trip home' are focal points on every news bulletin in the morning and late afternoon.

Traffic is not only discussed during special events—grand finals, New Year's Eve celebrations and some important national commemorations such as ANZAC Day—discussions about traffic happen every single day!

For the sociologist, this scene tells us a lot about our society. It explains to us how we have socially constructed our society around a piece of technology: the car. Furthermore, many dimensions of our contemporary society are integrated around this technology. As we discussed in Chapter 13, society and technology have always been interrelated—so in some ways, while the technologies we are witnessing today are new, the relationships that emerge and the power structures around them have long existed.

Now for the interrelated rhombus

If you return to the interrelated rhombus (see Chapter 3), you will see how cars, a part of life that seems almost mundane, have important social, economic, political and environmental consequences. Nothing stands alone—things are always connected. Not only do our identities, cultures and economies revolve around cars, but our entire neighbourhoods and cities are designed to make sure that there is enough parking and space for these vehicles. (For those of you that drive to university, handling staff and student parking is one of the most challenging things for university management!)

I mentioned earlier that cars have also become part of our identity and culture. Think about the way people express themselves with the car they drive: what image is portrayed by a four-wheel drive, a hybrid Prius or Tesla, a brand-new BMW with L-plates, a Hummer, or an old beaten-up Corolla with P-plates? Think of the billions of dollars spent on advertising cars and the amount of time and energy we put into learning to drive.

Just across from me there is a bunch of school students—boys and girls—dressed in their very well-designed school uniforms. They are talking about someone's TikTok video that has had thousands and thousands of views.

They stop talking as two motorists start yelling at each other. Road rage, which is seen as a crime, can also be analysed from a sociological and cultural studies perspective as we attempt to understand why we drive, why time is such an important element in our society and why people do not use public transport.

Back to the students. They are talking about a new video released by an American band about to tour Australia and are all sharing it with one another via WhatsApp. At 16 years of age these students are part of the global economy and society: they are shaped by it and are shaping it. They have, like the rest of us, helped to socially construct globalisation in the way it now exists.

Maybe on the weekend, if they were dressed in hoodies, the six or so boys standing on the corner would be a cause for concern to someone walking past: Aren't all young people dangerous and/or waiting to commit a crime? As we saw in Chapter 17, young people are often the source of many moral panics.

Contrasts and contradictions

Near us, there is a homeless man with a sign asking for spare change. His head is lowered to avoid eye contact while he holds out the sign. Comparing this man to the many people in business suits walking past him and to the private school students in the café near me shows that class structures are alive in Australia. The schools that these students go to cost tens of thousands of dollars per year—something that many people cannot afford.

The interesting thing about the homeless man is that he seems to be ignored—not purposely, but almost incidentally. In cities like Sydney, Melbourne and Brisbane and across the world, homelessness is a growing concern, and the homeless seem to blend into the streetscape, like some unsightly building or bus shelter. A sociologist would ask: 'What is it about our culture that allows us to ignore homelessness so easily?' A sociologist would also question why we spend more money on pet food in Australia than we do on the overseas aid that assists the poorest around the world.

I sip my coffee and return to my online news feed—I am reading about Donald Trump's latest speech in the United States and I click a link to see extracts from that speech. In the speech, the President is criticising Barack Obama—the 44th president of the United States and the first African-American president. It is hard to imagine that only three generations ago, slavery still existed in the United States, and now they have had an African-American president. This prompts me to wonder when Australia will elect our first Indigenous prime minister. When this happens, will this be part of a broader conversation about the ways Indigenous Australians were treated not so long ago, as well as the disadvantage many continue to face (see Chapter 16)?

My friend Victoria appears; she smiles at me as she orders her coffee and asks me about my weekend. I tell her I went shopping with one of my friends to help her find an outfit for a wedding. She laughs and tells me: 'You are such a chick.' We both laugh in response.

This phrase, while harmless between two friends, also tells the sociologist a great deal about gender relations in our society: how boys and girls are expected to behave and what is considered 'masculine' and 'feminine'. As a 'bloke', my pastime of helping my female friends choose clothes is something that many of my friends find amusing.

With such a phrase, we also gain insights into how power operates: while Victoria used the word 'chick' as a 'term of endearment', such a word can also be used as an insult. Many young men and women who do not achieve the expectations around their gender may be forced to conform or will otherwise be identified as 'deviant' (see Chapters 7 and 18). When I was at school, I saw many young men bullied and even physically attacked and violently assaulted because they were 'sissies'. It is something that we should always be mindful of, as we do not want to perpetuate the mistreatment of people that leads to exclusion and, in the worst of circumstances, young people dying by suicide.

All the things I have observed are not unique events but things that happen every day and all the time. It is by analysing these everyday events that we can gain great insights into our contemporary society—insights that tell us about power relations, social expectations and the priorities of our society. They also provide us with insights into our own role in perpetuating or challenging these social structures.

Before talking about 'what next', we would now like to present six themes that appeared throughout this book.

1 Society is (mostly) socially constructed

As the many authors have repeatedly said throughout the chapters in this book, there is very little in our society that is 'natural' or 'innate': from gender roles to the category of youth, and from the uses of technology to our relationship to the environment. Rather, the way our society is organised is a result of the social relations between people just like us.

One example we discussed in detail concerned the ways in which gender relations are socially constructed (see Chapter 7). What we see as acceptable norms of masculinity and femininity revolve around the issue of social expectations and informal rules, not what is innate (or natural) to us. From the moment a child is born, the colour of their clothes, the toys they are given and often the dreams they are encouraged to have revolve around their biology—it is a function of the social relations around them.

As noted, our understanding of poverty, class relations, race and ethnicity, technology and globalisation should also be seen as being socially constructed. Importantly, if these social relations were constructed by society, then we as members of that society can change them.

2   Power is everywhere

The issue of power is everywhere in our society (see Chapter 8). As we have seen, power can be understood both in traditional ways and through relationships. We need to understand how power is used to shape our perceptions, thoughts, bodies and the way we are in the world.

Understanding how power operates through social relations opens up many new ways of seeing the world. While not all power relations are negative, power relations can be harmful. Power can be used to exclude; to ensure people do not even have a voice, to remove a sense of agency and to repress or exploit.

Sometimes the use of power is obvious and sometimes it is more subtle. For example, one way for us to understand power is to see the priorities the government sets—how our tax dollars are spent, which technological advancements are given priority and what programs are supported. In this way, we can see how the coal industry has much greater power than the solar industry. Or, even more bleakly, we can see how the health priorities of wealthy countries are the focus of research and development. Bill Gates, one of the founders of Microsoft, for example, stated that the world spends more money on researching minor ailments such as baldness than on diseases such as malaria that kill millions of people in poor countries around the world (Chu 2013).

3   Everything is interrelated

Let me remind you again of the interrelated rhombus in Chapter 3. This was my way of explaining that everything we see around us is related to everything else. Like my car example at the beginning of this chapter, we should always look at the broader links and consequences of our actions and the way we live our lives.

Understanding such interconnectedness means we can understand how, for example, our relationships with the environment and environmental challenges are linked with our attitudes towards the economy and the structure of our political system. For example, many environmental challenges such as global warming will take decades if not centuries to confront—but our political cycles take place every three or four years. One of the reasons that we cannot deal with environmental challenges is that political cycles and environmental challenges—two things that should be intricately linked—are disconnected in our political system.

This is also part of developing your 'sociological imagination' (see Chapter 2). By employing your sociological imagination, it is possible to see what is happening beyond our own everyday experiences.

A number of authors throughout this book have used the term 'intersectionality'. For example, in Chapter 9 we saw how, if we are to study the concept of 'race' and 'racism', it should be understood in relation to other influencing issues such as class, gender, ethnicity, the state and sexuality. This gives us important insights, but also highlights the incredible difficulties confronted by policymakers when they try to find solutions to challenges such as youth homelessness, discrimination and exclusion.

4 We reflect our culture in our everyday actions

When you go into a café and order a coffee, you are taking part in a cultural event that confirms you are part of a capitalist system (as you pay money for it), integrated within a global economy (as the chances are that the coffee was imported, since coffee beans are the second-most traded commodity in the world) and that drinking coffee has become an incredibly important social event for Australians.

It is within such daily rituals of everyday life that we can understand our culture and how it shapes and is shaped by our contemporary society. Within these daily actions we find the rules and values that shape our lives, the way we see the world and how power operates.

Now, when I say 'rituals', I am not referring to those things that happen rarely, but those that occur regularly: the daily, weekly, monthly and annual rituals. Often, we do not even realise that we are following rituals. So, when we look at a society like Australia, we can see what binds us and what is our culture: language, beliefs, institutions, stories and myths, but also our everyday practices or rituals.

5 There is never only one way to see the world

Another point that has emerged repeatedly throughout this book is that there are many ways to see and analyse the world around us. When analysing our contemporary society, you should never rely on one argument or theory—not even your lecturer's.

In this book you have been exposed to many different concepts and theorists; but never once has someone insisted that 'this is the answer'. Part of the aim of developing your skills as a sociologist is to encourage you to reflect on various theories, picking and choosing what you feel best explains the phenomenon you are analysing. I often draw on various perspectives to gain an understanding of something I am investigating and, based on my research, will weave these various concepts together. This is how we learn and develop new knowledge. It is one of the reasons that sociology and cultural studies are such fascinating fields of study.

As I said in Chapter 1, never feel that you have to agree with any one argument or theory: as long as you can justify your analysis, then you should be prepared to make your own case and argue your point.

6 If humans made it this way, then we can change it

As I noted above, one thing that is difficult for us to comprehend when we analyse the world around us is that most things are socially constructed. If this is the case, it means that humans made it this way. If humans made it this way, then each of us has the ability to change it—this is what we turn to next.

HOW TO CHANGE THE WORLD

Over the years, many students have approached us after sitting through our classes or reading a book like this and said: 'What should I do next?'

Our answer is simple: 'You can change the world.'

There are two ingredients you need to change the world. The first is education and knowledge—which is what this book is all about. The second is a belief that 'a better world is possible'—something that we describe as 'hope'. These are the two ingredients that have been evident in the work of many who have brought positive change in the world: from the abolitionist movement (which ended slavery) to antiracism movements (discussed in Chapter 15).

Education and knowledge are still the most powerful tools in the world; and the knowledge that is contained in this text gives you insights into the world around us—insights that can be used to promote a society that has justice at its core. As such, the final part of this book is a guide in how you can help change the world.

What, you may ask, is a textbook doing telling me to change the world? Well, we hope that by reading the first 21 chapters, the conversations we've had have made you look more critically at the world around you, and you may now recognise injustices: bullying in your neighbourhood, homelessness, racism, issues around access to food, or the health and wellbeing of your community.

We would like you to use your knowledge to reflect on the world and consider if you are happy with the way things are. The reality is that there will be something, if not many things, that you will recognise as needing change.

Now that you have this knowledge of injustice and have insights into how the world works, the question is: What are you going to do about it? You may think, 'What do these things have to do with me', or 'What can I do about it? I'm just one person.'

The answer is that you can do a great deal.

You may recall that in our discussion about globalisation (Chapter 11), we looked at how we are increasingly an interlinked community. Globalisation is about more than goods travelling across borders. It is also about the speed at which things happen, how frequently they happen, the social consequence of this process and the range of people involved. It is this last factor that we want to draw your attention to—the 'range of people' encompasses all of humanity. *We are all part of the process; it influences us and we influence it.* Whether we are conscious of it or not, we *are* changing the world every day just by living in it and our actions, intended or unintended, impact others. Being mindful of this can help you to shift the question from 'Can I impact the world?' to 'How can I make my impact more positive?'

It can still be overwhelming, thinking about how you can bring about change in respect to some of the complex problems we face today. Remember one of the key points above, that most of this world is socially constructed (constructed by our society). As such, if the social issues we see surrounding us are in part made by us, then we can change them.

The question that we are often asked is: How can one person change the world? Well, it is never one person—it is one person working with a group of other people, who then connect with even more people, and all of a sudden massive change is possible.

You will remember the Wave Hill Walk-Off discussed in Chapter 15 or the Freedom Rides discussed in Chapter 16. We now look back at the ways in which Indigenous Australians were discriminated against and wonder how this could have been possible. Today it seems absurd. It took some people making small—or perhaps significant—changes in their lives and working with others to achieve this major change. In the future people will look back on many of the things happening now, such as the disproportionate rates of incarceration and deaths in custody of Indigenous Australians and feel the same way.

For the rest of this chapter we will outline some strategies that can be implemented to assist you in confronting challenges that you believe are important. These strategies do not necessarily require you to dramatically change your life. On the contrary, they are about using your strengths, resources and networks to change the things you care about for the better. It is all about incremental steps towards a more peaceful, just and sustainable world.

This is the path we are hoping to take you on. What you do on this path, how fast and far you go and where you end up is ultimately up to you.

The recipe for change

To make a good pizza, you need to get the right mix of ingredients. You then put your skills to the test and knead the flour, yeast, salt, water and olive oil to get the right foundation—the pizza dough. You set aside the dough and concentrate on the toppings. You need to consider the people you are sharing the pizza with—what is their taste in food? Are they vegetarian? You might even get them to come and give you a hand to put the toppings on. The pizza is then put in the oven and, when ready, you can sit, eat and enjoy what you have created together.

Change also has a recipe. It is not a 'one size fits all'. Just as different regions have different cooking styles, bringing about change has many variations. A basic recipe can get you cooking and once you get the fundamentals under your belt, you can mix and match to make your own creation—something that is suitable for your context.

In this section we start the conversation about the basics. Once you have a better idea about your needs, you will be able to search for the appropriate ways to go forward.

Let us begin the journey and start planning for change!

Step 1: Start with the right mindset—change is possible

Have you ever been sitting on the couch watching television, seen something and said to yourself: 'That's not fair!' and 'I want to do something about that!'

Have you felt that there are so many important issues in the world—poverty, climate change, war, homelessness—that seem so large they cannot be solved? At the same time, you may think that you have no time to do something about any of these things and that you are insignificant in the face of so many global (or even local) issues. That is, you feel you lack the resources, knowledge or power to make a difference.

It seems like a huge leap from watching television to having a positive impact on global challenges. Sometimes, bringing about change seems impossible—there are injustices in our lives that are so common that we begin to accept that they are almost 'natural'. Injustices such as poverty, however, are not natural but are socially constructed; that is, they exist because of decisions made by humans at some point in history. If people have created poverty, then it is logical that people—just like us—can undo it! We can all have a positive effect on these very important and serious issues. We hope this is something that you have learnt reading this book.

If you still do not think change is possible, let us look at one of the most successful campaigns for change in human history—the campaign to end slavery. Slavery existed for thousands of years, but it became a lucrative trade in the late fifteenth century in England. People were usually captured in tribal wars or seized especially for the slave trade, and then sent by ship to England and its colonies to be sold as slaves.

The conditions on the slave ships were horrible: people were packed so tightly they could hardly move, and they were often chained down. It is estimated that by the mid eighteenth century, British ships were transporting about 50,000 enslaved people a year. The people who managed to survive the journey were taken ashore and sold like any other commodity.

In response to this, an antislavery movement started that was formed by both white abolitionists and Black resistance movements. The ultimate aim of the movement was the abolition of the slave trade—something that seemed almost impossible at the time. Reflecting on what we learnt about social movements, this was a combination of Black resistance leaders such as David Walker, Frederick Douglass and Sojourner Truth, as well as allies and advocates.

Initially, the movement consisted of small pockets of resistance, which grew to form a network that spanned the British Isles. The movement was built up slowly, and it began by distributing information about slavery. One of the members of the movement was Granville Sharp, who worked with others to publish pamphlets to stir public opinion against the trade. In her *New York Times* article, Marilynne Robinson (2005) describes Sharp as:

> [a] minor government clerk who educated himself in the law in the course of defending the rights of Africans brought into England as slaves. He devoted himself and his slender resources to this work over decades with the object of finally putting an end to slavery itself.

This was not some high-profile politician or celebrity; this was an ordinary person who saw slavery for what it was and wanted to do something about it. And he had limited resources and time—just like the rest of us!

Such efforts where simultaneously happening across the world. In the midst of this, the Haitian Revolution, which began in 1791 and ended in 1804, freed the slaves of the French colony to create the now sovereign state of Haiti. This successful revolt was led by liberated slaves and gave momentum to other resistance groups both in the United States and across the world.

Forming alliances with religious groups, such as the Quakers, and with parliamentarians including William Wilberforce, Sharp achieved a great number of changes. By 1807 the slave trade in the British colonies was abolished and it became illegal to carry enslaved people in British ships; and in 1833 the British Parliament passed the *Abolition of Slavery Act*.

We need to acknowledge that even after the Act was passed and the slave trade ended, many people of colour continued to confront prejudice and exclusion. Ultimately this led to the civil rights movement and the fight for equality continues today.

This is an amazing story. People from all parts of society worked together to achieve a change that was thought to be almost impossible; this process began by people imagining a change in a part of life that seemed 'natural' or 'normal'. Believing in change was an important step in the journey for ending slavery.

If the story of the slave trade seems too distant from where you are today, then all you have to do is look around you. Every day people bring about change—even you! In one of the workshops that we run we ask participants to share their story of a time when they consciously changed the way they did something. In a matter of minutes we start hearing about the amazing things people are doing every day: a boy shared a story about renting chickens to keep in his backyard so that he could be sure that his eggs came from animals that were treated fairly; two girls told their story of successfully campaigning for their university to only sell fair trade coffee; someone else told us that they started composting at home and had managed to get their whole family in on the act. If you look around your world, you will find many similarly inspiring stories.

Most, if not all, of the stories of successful change start by people *learning* about something. They find out about the treatment of chickens or the positive impact of fair trade on coffee farmers and their communities. It is said that knowledge is power—and this is really true. It can carry with it great emotion and can motivate you to break down the perceived barriers and come to understand that change is possible. Gaining knowledge can help you to develop the mindset you need to go forward.

This is of course only a foundation. You also need to *think* about how this knowledge fits in with your personal context and what an appropriate *action* might look like for you.

BOX 22.1
Method to action

THE INSTIGATORS OF CHANGE

In this first in a series of activities, we want you to reflect on successful social changes that you have contributed to in the past and use this as a learning process to help you plan the pathway forward.

- Make a list of five things you have consciously changed in your life. Maybe you started recycling or composting at home; or growing your own vegies; or buying organic eggs; or donating to a particular charity.
- In each case, write down what helped you change your mindset and what supported you to change your behaviour. What motivated you and what helped you to start taking action?

Step 2: Broaden your understanding and become active

When we say 'become active', we are referring to many things including 'active citizenship'. But what does this actually mean? There are many formal definitions that you can look up, but we are more interested in the practicalities of being active.

Being active has two important dimensions: empowerment and engagement:

- *Empowerment* is about ensuring that you have the skills and knowledge to influence decision makers and the community.
- *Engagement* is about feeling that your efforts to make change are valued and have impact on the world.

As we discussed in Step 1, learning about the issues you care about and seeing others achieve success can support you to realise that change is possible. Learning can also help you to become more empowered and engaged.

In the context of being active, learning should not be viewed as something that is limited to a personal, local or national level. In a globalised and interconnected world, our decisions and actions have a real impact on people's lives all over the globe (see the discussion in Chapter 11). We need to be aware of this and to respond appropriately by being engaged and empowered on local, national and international levels. We need to understand the issues that are important to us from our own perspective and also from a broader global perspective. Therefore, we should all be aware of the many issues facing the world and we should understand how the world works economically, politically, socially, culturally, technologically and environmentally. It is important to recognise how the issues that concern us fit into a broader context.

This is exactly what this book has tried to achieve! So even by reading this book and becoming more aware of the world around you, you can say that you have taken a step towards being a more active citizen.

BOX 22.2

Method to action

WHAT'S IMPORTANT TO YOU?

Reading this book is the start of a journey. We have shared information about many complex issues that affect us all. Using this as a starting point, write down three areas that interest you. It could be something you have come across in this book—maybe you see something from a different perspective now and realise that you are not happy with it. Write a strategy for how you can find out more information about what concerns you … and start *learning*. Consider each issue from a personal, local, national and global perspective.

There are many pathways to starting your learning journey. One approach is to turn to organisations that focus on your interest area. These organisations are experts in their field and are able to provide you with information about the issues confronting the world today. Examples of organisations focusing on young people include:

- *ReachOut.com*: a leading youth mental health service that provides information and support through its online platform: <https://au.reachout.com>

- *Oxfam Australia*: an international aid and development organisation that collaborates with communities to act against poverty and injustice: <www.oxfam.org.au>

- *Per Capita*: an independent progressive think tank dedicated to building a new vision for Australia: <www.percapita.org.au>.

What organisations can you approach about the issues that concern you?

Step 3: Fit the change you want to bring about into your life

The third step is to consider how the change you want to bring about fits into your life.

This is an important consideration and will help you to do things in a sustainable way. We see a lot of passionate people who have learnt about something they care about and want to dive in deep and give it all they have. Volunteering three to four days a week is a great thing to do, unless you have full-time study commitments; or you have to work to pay rent; or you have a family that you need to spend time with … the list goes on. Unless you acknowledge the context within which you operate, you risk not being able to sustain your engagement.

There is also another reason why understanding your world is important. Your context impacts what you are trying to do—both in positive and negative ways. You can use what is around you to help you achieve your goals. At the same time, there are things within your life that limit you. It is important to recognise that the issues that you are concerned about, and the changes that you want to achieve, are integrated into your world.

BOX 22.3

Method to action

VISUALISE YOUR CONTEXT

Take a blank piece of paper and draw a large circle on it. Spend about five minutes mapping out your world within this circle. Try to create a picture of your context and get a sense of what your life looks like. You can use symbols, words, stick figures—anything that gets the message across. You can include things that occupy your time, your affiliations and networks, things and people that you care about and are important to you, and so on.

In Box 22.2, you started your learning process about the things you care about. These concerns cannot be disconnected from your world.

Select one of the issues you have been looking into. We are going to use this as an example of how we can use our world and our circle of influence to bring about change.

Now think about the issue you have selected. Based on everything you have learnt about this issue, add to the image of your world three specific actions that you think can be done to bring about positive change. Focus the actions as follows—write down:

- One thing that you can do personally;
- One thing that can be done in your community (local or national); and
- One thing that can be done on a global scale.

So for example, if you are concerned about fair trade, then:

- Personally, you can start purchasing fair trade;

- On a community level, you might work with your university or place of employment to stock fair trade coffee or chocolates; and
- Globally, you might consider working with an organisation to lobby governments for improved policies.

Change can happen on many levels. You need to consider where you are best placed to have the most impact.

Next, place a star next to the level of change that you think best reflects where you are now in terms of what you can achieve. It is important to note that this is not a static position. As we move on, you may change your mind and think you can have better impact elsewhere. That is fine—it is more about being mindful of where you can have the most impact.

Now we need to think of all the things that can help us achieve change and all the things that will stop us from achieving change. On the left side of the paper, next to your circle, write a list of all the things that can help you to act on the issue that you have identified; that is: What things make you feel bringing about change is possible? This could be specific people, your university, your knowledge or education, your mindset, your experience or any resources you have access to, and so on. Be very specific and avoid broad generalisations. Try to write at least 15 things!

Now, on the right side of the paper, write down the factors that stop you and the things that make change less likely. Again, list at least 15 things. These may include lack of confidence, not having enough information and lacking time.

Analysing what you have created is an important step towards understanding how you can begin to have an impact on the issues that concern you. From your plan, you can see the complexities that you will have to navigate on your journey towards change. Documenting the landscape that you will have to navigate in this way also allows you to break up a complex issue into manageable parts and start the planning process.

Reflecting on the content of the image you have drawn, start writing notes as follows:

1. Why is this issue important to you?
2. What encourages and inspires you?
3. What do you need to bring about the change you have identified with a star?
4. What are the things and people you can begin to influence, starting today?
5. What is stopping you, and how can you use your enabling factors and resources to overcome those things that prevent you from taking action?
6. List some milestones that will indicate you are on your way to achieving your goal.
7. What can you do to change things by tomorrow?
8. What can you do to change things within a month?
9. What can you do to change things in six months?
10. What else do you need that you currently do not have?

Step 4: Realise that you are not alone

When we face a large problem or injustice, our first thought is: 'What can I do about it? I'm just one person.'

Even when we feel empowered, we often try to tackle the problem on our own and end up struggling. The reality is that we rarely do anything alone. We are part of multiple networks that support us to bring about change.

This focus on groups working together to make change is a shift from thinking about an individual 'hero'. Over the last decade, we have seen the emergence of alternative leadership models including *distributed leadership* (see Bolden 2011), *shared leadership* (Pearce, Conger & Locke 2007) and *collective leadership* just to name a few. What binds these theories is the understanding that leadership cannot be the responsibility of a single individual. We can be more effective through strategic collaboration where we each work to our strengths.

As we covered in the Step 3, it is important to recognise where you are best placed to bring about change. It is also important to consider the *stakeholders* and the power players that relate to the change you want to bring about (a stakeholder is someone who has an interest in or is impacted by what you want to do). If you begin the process of involving others by having conversations about the issues that concern you, you will be amazed at the level of generosity you will be offered. No doubt there will be some people who will think differently to you, and this is not a bad thing. But you will find others who will give you the knowledge, time, connections or resources that you need to make change happen.

BOX 22.4

Method to action

PLAN YOUR CHANGE AND MEET PEOPLE

Look over your answers to the questions in Box 22.3.

Hopefully you have identified many enablers that can help you to bring about change, and you have started planning what you want to achieve. You will also notice that there are gaps. In this activity we want you to address these gaps by thinking about how you can make use of your networks and people of influence around you.

Make a list of people that you can meet and talk to about what you have planned. This will give you an opportunity to tap into other people's knowledge, resources and networks. If people cannot help you, they may be able to point to others who can.

Put at least two names against each of the categories below. If you do not know any specific people for any of the points, leave it blank for now, but make a point of asking the people you are approaching if they can introduce you to others who may be relevant. (Some of the points may not be appropriate to your issue—in which case leave them blank.)

- People who have the things you listed in question 10 of Box 22.3;
- People who can be considered 'stakeholders' and who are relevant to what you plan to do;
- Others who work in this space;
- Experts on the topic; and
- People or organisations who have the potential to influence you or who can help you.

Now that you have a list, start calling people and arrange to meet them for coffee. Talk to people about what concerns you. Ask their opinion of your plan. Tell them what you have and what you need and ask them to support you. Importantly, also consider how you can reciprocate and support others.

Step 5: Test your ideas and be prepared to fail

The final step is to move beyond ideas and take action. Sometimes the biggest barrier we face is the fear of failure. This can be so overwhelming that we do not even take the first step. It is no wonder either. Failure is not something that is celebrated in our society. We associate it with weakness, lack of intelligence, an inability to perform and so on.

There are two points to be made here.

The first is in relation to where success comes from. When inspiring others to take action we often share case studies or success stories. Hearing about the success of others can help improve understanding by demonstrating what theories look like in practice. Seeing the accomplishments of others can provide useful frameworks that we can then use to achieve similar results. These can be great motivators and points of inspiration. The downside of success stories is that, often, they do not tell the whole story.

The simple truth is that behind every success, there are many failures that work to expand our understanding and improve our experience. Did you know, for example, that Walt Disney's concept of Mickey Mouse was rejected 302 times! Entrepreneur Richard Branson (2013) has said that the secret to success is failure.

Much of what we have achieved in life, from walking and talking to what we do professionally, is based on learning from experience and making mistakes along the way. If we approach failures with a mindset that they are part of our growth, and look at them as an opportunity for improvement, then failures should be celebrated. They are in fact an inevitable part of everyday life and so we should learn to use them effectively.

That brings us to the second point: if we are going to embrace failing, then we need to develop a strategic approach that results in the best outcome. One feature of *design thinking* or a *start-up mentality* offers a useful framework here; that is, rapid prototyping to test and improve what you are doing in an ongoing way.

Traditional ways of working involve making a grand plan and then putting it into practice. Say, for example, you decide that you are passionate about refugee rights. Through the research you do, you come up with a great idea about creating a magazine that shares the stories of refugees in your local community and distributing it to the schools around your area. Producing a magazine is costly and time consuming, and therefore failing in this context may be incredibly expensive and exhausting.

Prototyping your ideas and making them tangible early on would allow you to get immediate feedback from your various stakeholders. In the case of the magazine project, you could collect a small sample of the kind of stories you are thinking. You could then print a mock-up of the magazine on your home printer and take this sample to your local school for feedback. Having a conversation over a tangible object can help bring to the surface any assumptions or misunderstandings. You can learn from the people you are ultimately trying to reach, to ensure that what you are creating has the most impact. This is a low-cost way of obtaining this information—creating 10 mock-ups of a magazine on your home printer and realising they are not going to get picked up is much cheaper than doing a print run of 5000!

There is an important thing to keep in mind about prototypes. They are meant to convey your idea rather than be a finished product. Rapid prototyping will give you the opportunity to learn about what you are doing quickly and cheaply. They reduce the cost of failing, allow you to take more risks and support you to build towards a more effective solution.

> **BOX 22.5**
> ## Method to action
>
> **TEST YOUR CONCEPT AND TAKE ACTION**
>
> Think about the change that you want to bring about. We want you to start planning how you can prototype your concept and test your idea.
>
> Prototyping is not necessarily about building a product; it is more about making your idea tangible so that you can seek feedback and improve on what you plan to do.

Getting active in other ways

So far, we have focused on supporting you to initiate and work through the changes that you believe to be important. Another strategy you may employ is volunteering for organisations you care about.

Healthy volunteering, however, is a two-way process. As you make your contribution, think about whether the organisation can support you to find the appropriate resources and capacity-building opportunities that will enable you to take personal and collective action.

When volunteering, it is important to find a like-minded organisation that you can connect with. You could connect with them on an issue, your ideology or faith, or simply the fact that you like the way they carry out their practice. Finding the right organisation for you will ensure that your volunteering experience lines up with your interests and values.

You should do your own research to find the most appropriate organisation for you. Many organisations—including many universities—promote volunteering opportunities through their websites, so look around and decide what suits you best.

If you are travel-inclined, you could also look for organisations—including your university—that offer the opportunity to volunteer overseas.

Things to remember

There are some things that you need to keep in mind when working towards making change:
- *Maintain balance*: When we get involved in things that we are passionate about, we often forget other things in our lives, such as studying for exams. It is important that you keep a balance in your life. This ensures that your actions remain sustainable.
- *Embed actions into your life*: Think about the way you live; do not think about change as something that you do on a part-time basis. In this way, change becomes a way of life and not a phase. So if climate change is important to you, think about all the things that you can do every day to help, such as walking to the shops rather than driving.
- *Learn more about your interests and consider the resources that you need*: Information will empower you to bring about change. Also learn about yourself. Consider what you have to offer and what else you may need to make your change happen.

- *Work with others*: To fill the gaps you may have and to have the most impact, you need to work with others. Bringing about social change is complex and not something you can do on your own.
- *Fail*: Fail often, fail fast and test your ideas as you go. But make sure you are learning from your mistakes.

Conclusion

How do you conclude a book that started with pirates and ended with changing the world?

Simply, by telling you that we have been lucky enough to work with people like you all over the world who have witnessed injustices and have decided to do something about them. They have done this with the help of their friends, connecting with allies and advocates, by obtaining more knowledge, and by using some of the strategies we discussed here.

Over the 22 chapters, many authors have presented you with different slices of our society. While doing this, they have also attempted to explain how these slices are interlinked.

As you have read these pages, you have been challenged in many ways: from the introduction of new ideas to being encouraged to ask your lecturer if a siesta would be acceptable! You have also been challenged to use the various tools of analysis presented to you in an attempt to change the world.

As I write these final lines, there are things happening all around us that may make some of the things we have discussed seem a little 'old'. Think of it this way, if this book was written:

- Twelve months earlier, no one would have heard of coronavirus;
- Five years ago, TikTok and the Apple Watch did not exist;
- Ten years ago, Facebook would have just become the world's most popular social media, and many authors in this book would have been referring to 'MySpace', a social networking website that few people can even remember.

That is what makes studying our society both challenging and exciting. So, fellow sociologists and cultural theorists: go forth and analyse the world—and if you see something you do not like, I encourage you to challenge it. Such an attitude will make a better world possible—and that should be our aim—for it is the only world we have.

Good luck and best.

James and the rest of the team.

References and further reading

REFERENCES

Bolden, R 2011, 'Distributed leadership in organizations: a review of theory and research', *International Journal of Management Reviews, Special Issue: Distributed Leadership*, September, 13(3), 251–69.

Branson, R 2013, 'Richard Branson on the secret to success: failure', *Entrepreneur*: <www.entrepreneur.com/article/226811>.

Chu, B 2013, 'Bill Gates: why do we care more about baldness than malaria?', *The Independent*, 16 March: <www.independent.co.uk/news/world/americas/bill-gates-why-do-we-care-more-about-baldness-than-malaria-8536988.html>.

Pearce, CL, Conger, JA & Locke, EA 2007, 'Shared leadership theory', *Management Department Faculty Publications. Paper 74*: <http://digitalcommons.unl.edu/managementfacpub/74>.

Robinson, M 2005, '"Though the heavens may fall" and "Bury the chains": freed', *New York Times*, 9 January.

FURTHER READING

Gladwell, M 2011, *Outliers*, Back Bay Books, New York.

Hochschild, A 2004, *Bury the Chains: Prophets and Rebels in the Fight to Free an Empire's Slaves*, Houghton Mifflin, Boston, MA.

Wise, SM 2004, *Though the Heavens May Fall: The Landmark Trial That Led to the End of Human Slavery*, Da Capo Press, New York.

WEBSITES

Bloy, M, 'The anti-slavery campaign in Britain': <www.victorianweb.org/history/antislavery.html>.

Glossary

Aboriginal and Torres Strait Islander peoples
A collective name for the First People of Australia and their descendants. While this phrase does not emphasise the diversity of languages, cultural practices and spiritual beliefs of Australia's First People, it is preferred over 'Indigenous'.

Academic literacy
A capacity to write in different styles at university level, to apply academic referencing, to understand academic vocabulary and terminology, to interpret and produce information and academic texts, to research and to evaluate evidence.

Actor–Network Theory (ANT)
An approach to social theory that treats technologies as networks of human and non-human actors. ANT calls for symmetry, with human and non-human actors being treated and discussed in the same terms.

Adaptive response
The way an entity responds and adapts to environmental and social changes

Agency
Refers to the ability (or power) of an individual or group ('agent') to act independently of the external constraints of social structures—making decisions, undertaking actions and confronting authorities.

Alienation
A process present in pre-socialist economies, whereby a person is separated from their true nature and highest purpose in life via the labour process, and in particular, by selling their labour power. A worker could be alienated from themselves, from other workers, from their working life and from the product of their labour.

'Anywhere, anytime' work
An idealised work practice involving working 'on the move', flexibly or in different locations with the support of digital technology.

Assimilation
The process of becoming similar to something; the absorption of minorities into the mainstream culture.

At risk
A label indicating concern about a lack of expected/desired/required achievement or potential danger.

Backroads
The geographies of globalisation that are often unseen but are vibrant.

Belief
Presented by sociologist Grace Davie when discussing religion as a special mode of believing that has two collective elements: i) the chain that makes the individual believer a member of a community, and ii) the tradition (or collective memory) that becomes the basis of that community's existence (Davie 2000).

Biological determinism
The belief that human traits and behaviours are created by genes and biology, rather than social factors.

Bureaucracy
A type of organisation based on rational principles, hierarchy of authority and written rules, and staffed by full-time officials.

Campaign
A sustained, organised public effort making collective claims on specific authorities and institutions such as governments, corporations and the global governance institutions.

Capitalism
An economic system based on the private ownership of wealth, which is invested to produce profit. Its driving principle is the accumulation of profit, which demands ever-increasing levels of consumption.

Carbon pricing
The application of a price on carbon, internalising the environmental cost of carbon emissions, within the context of climate change.

Child development domains
Five domains in which children mature and grow: language development, cognition, learning, physical development and social development.

Childhood
The age span ranging from birth to adolescence.

Circular economy
In recognition of the limit in availability of resources, they are instead recovered and reused in this economic system, rather than being disposed of.

Citizenship
Legal membership of a political community, normally a state (that is, a 'country') that provides individuals with both rights (or protections and provisions) and obligations (or loyalty and duties).

Class
A process of ordering people in society by a set of divisions based on both real and perceived differences in social and economic status.

Climate justice
Justice that aims to ensure that those more likely to experience environmental risk and harm as a consequence of climate change are heard, can participate in decision

making affecting them, and are supported so that they can be resilient.

Closing the Gap
An Australian Government policy and dominant political narrative in Australian Indigenous affairs.

Collective action
A variety of actions (such as campaigns) taken by a group of people with a specific set of objectives and goals to achieve a shared purpose.

Colonialism
The political rule, and often cultural domination, of one nation over another.

Conflict theory
A social theory linked with Marxism that argues different individuals and groups have different levels of resources and power. These groups come into 'conflict' as the more powerful aim to exploit the less powerful, who in turn resist and fight back.

Covert power
Power that is exerted when issues are excluded from discussion in decision making. In this way, issues not on the agenda are neither discussed nor decided. It is evident when, for example, 'a person or group—consciously or unconsciously—creates or reinforces barriers to the public airing of policy conflicts' (Bachrach & Baratz 1970, p. 8).

Cultural capital
The social exchange of accumulated cultural knowledge that provides an individual with power and status in society. It is a form of capital based in modes of thinking, dispositions or cultural goods (such as books, art, music, furniture, food and wine).

Cultural studies
An academic discipline that investigates the symbolic meanings and cultural practices of our everyday experiences.

Culture
Encompasses the rules and processes of everyday life and includes the symbolic and learned aspects of human society, such as language, custom and convention.

Cyberspace
Electronically mediated and simulated space in which individuals play, debate, create and form relationships. Cyberspace is used to refer to the virtual spaces created by the digital computing technologies of the internet.

Data
Information collected and/or analysed to answer research questions. Data comes in all manner of forms—surveys, contents analysis, secondary data and so on.

Democracy
In a general sense, the 'rule of the people'. There are different interpretations of democracy, encompassing the principles of the participation of citizens in political decision making, the presence of civil liberties and equality.

Democratic revolution
The idea, sparked by the American Revolution (1775–83) and the French Revolution (1789–99), that people should have a say in how they are governed.

Deviance
Any conduct, actions, traits or ideas that violate the accepted social norms of a particular society. Deviant conduct is not always illegal and may vary between groups within society, as social norms vary.

Digital technology
Computerised devices such as a laptop, tablet and/or a mobile phone and related systems, methods and processes.

Disciplinary power
Power that reflects a move away from overt power through physical punishment to the expansion of a kind of disciplinary net over the moral character of individual (Foucault 1977). Rather than being purely restrictive of behaviour, disciplinary power is productive, influencing and controlling the ways that people think about and see the world.

Discourse
The ways that we think and talk about a category/issue.

Ecological economics
An economic model that internalises environmental costs and operates at a sustainable level in response to the knowledge that resources are finite.

Ecological footprint
An ecological measure of the impact of a person's lifestyle.

Economic capital
For Bourdieu, this is simply cash, or capital that an individual can convert to cash, such as property, businesses and shares.

Empirical
Data that is collectable and related to observable social phenomena.

Environmental inequality
The unequal distributions of environmental risk and harm, and unequal access to environmental amenities.

Environmental justice
Justice that aims to bring about accountability and seeks to prevent environmental inequality for both current and future generations.

Environmental racism
The unequal distribution of environmental risk and harm, and

OXFORD UNIVERSITY PRESS

unequal access to environmental amenities on the basis of 'race'.

Epistemology
The theory of knowledge and how we learn what we know.

Ethics
A set of values that guide how we interact with others in the practice of research.

Ethnicity
The categorisation of groups of people on the basis of cultural characteristics and shared heritage; belonging to a group bonded by the common historical linkages of language, tradition, religion or cultural practice.

Ethno-symbolism
A theory that nations originate in both the historical development of ethnicity and the creation of a modern political community.

Ever-presence
A new time sense, corresponding closely to the 'extended present' proposed by time philosopher Nowotny (1994), based on micro increments and continuous connectivity rather than the distinct partitioning of daily life into 'work' and 'leisure'.

Expert knowledge
Specialised knowledge acquired through professional experience and advanced education. It is also the knowledge that arises from conducting systematic, scholarly research.

Exploitation
For Marx, this is the nexus of class relations. Capitalists, who own the means of production, exploit workers by paying them less than the full value of their labour. The gap between the full value of the worker's labour and their wage determines the extent to which the worker is exploited.

Feminism
A diverse set of theories and actions that have the following elements as their starting point: that gender is a significant element of social organisation, that gender relations are patriarchal, and that this inequality needs to be transformed.

First Nations
A term used initially to describe the Indigenous peoples of Canada. It is now widely used in the United States, Australia and other places. Unless otherwise specified, it refers to Indigenous peoples globally.

First Peoples
A broad, collective term describing the indigenous peoples of an area. Depending on the country, phrases such as 'First Peoples' and 'First Nations' can have specific meanings (for example, in Canada).

Fourth estate
The conceptualisation of the news media as guardians of democracy and the public interest. Fourth estate journalism is that which scrutinises the activities of social elites (including politicians) to expose abuses of power and ensure accountability.

Framing
The process of selecting and highlighting some aspects of a story or situation in order to influence how the audience interprets an event or issues.

Gender
Social and cultural traits associated with males and females that shape roles, behaviours and expectations around what it means to be a man (masculine) or a woman (feminine).

Gender performativity
The ways in which gender is constructed by the repetitive performing or acting out of gender conventions.

Gig economy
Gig economy workers are those independent contractors who work flexibly and on-call for demand companies such as Uber and Airtasker.

Global capitalism
A new form of capitalism underpinned by an informational mode of production that is expanding all around the world and brings with it new ways of working and living in rapidly changing conditions.

Globalisation
A contested term—often described as the processes that bring the world closer together, for others it is something to be opposed.

Grand narrative
A theory that attempts to explain social history through a single 'master' idea, such as 'class conflict' or 'conflict theory'.

Habitus
Acquired modes of thought and unthinking dispositions learnt in early childhood. People who move between habitus (for example, when a working-class person enters an elite university) may suffer cleft-habitus, an uncomfortable form of social dislocation.

Hegemony
The dominance of one state, social group or ideology over others.

Holism
A conceptualisation recognising the reciprocal links between nature and culture.

Homophobia

A dislike of, or prejudice towards, homosexuals. While homophobia may occur as a result of witnessing homosexual behaviour, it more commonly occurs as a result of perceptions of how an individual performs non-sexual behaviours, such as walking, talking or playing sport.

Human Exemptionalist Paradigm

A way of viewing humans as superior to and exempt from the natural world.

Human rights activism

Campaigns that utilise the language, processes and institutions of human rights to position their collective action and organising.

Imagined community

A theory that in the modern world, members of nations are bound together by a constructed image of how fellow members live the same way and share the same values.

Indigeneity

A term historically used to distinguish the identity of people who are 'native' from people who are 'other'. It is often more useful to explore what aspects of 'indigeneity' are being portrayed as important and relevant, by whom, and in what contexts.

Indigenous

Any ethnic group originating and surviving in an area subject to colonisation. A lower-case 'i' is used when writing about general issues, such as 'the global indigenous rights movement'.

Individualisation

The expansion of the scope of individual preference and choice in defining our identities, our life paths and our relationships.

Industrial revolution

The economic and related social transformations produced by industrialisation.

Industrialisation

The harnessing of advanced forms of energy to power mechanised production. It involves the application of science and technology to industrial processes.

Integration

The process of mixing, blending into a unified whole, with adaptation from both sides.

Intersectionality

The interconnected nature of social categories such as gender, race, class, (dis)ability and sexuality that create overlapping systems of inequality.

Instrumentarian power

Power that shapes human behaviour toward the ends of others (namely corporations) through automated networked devices, things and spaces (Zuboff 2019).

Land rights

The struggle for legal recognition of Indigenous ownership of land and resources. Land rights might be granted through a claim process that then awards freehold title to an Aboriginal Land Council, for example.

Lay knowledge

The everyday, common knowledge based on lived experiences.

Left–Right political spectrum

A system of classifying political ideologies, positions and parties.

Life chances

A Weberian term used to describe opportunities in life; the likelihood of gaining the things we desire. While we may think that opportunities are the result of talent and effort, they are enabled and/or constrained by the class and status of our families, and by other structures that constitute our social location, such as gender, ethnicity and social capital.

Life stages

A linear set of categories that mark significant periods across the human life course. Labels differ across disciplines and contexts.

Liquid surveillance

A sociological concept that emphasises the diffused, mobile and flexible methods of surveillance, from CCTV cameras on the streets to software that tracks our digital footprints. Liquid surveillance can come from government agencies, corporations, social networks, partners and parents, and even employers.

Lived experiences

The activities, interactions and meanings that constitute everyday life.

Lukes' third face of power

Power that is characterised by the capacity to change, shape or regulate the wants of someone without their knowledge.

Mass communication

The transmission of information to large audiences. Mass communication is made possible in advanced industrial societies because of mass media technologies.

Mass media

Diversified communication technologies that reach a large audience and include print (books, newspapers, magazines, etc.), recordings (CDs, DVDs, digital data files, etc.), cinema, radio, television and the internet.

McDonaldisation

George Ritzer's term for the intensification of rationalisation in contemporary societies. It refers to the extension of the principles of fast-food restaurants—such as efficiency, calculation and predictability—to more and more spheres of social life.

Media power
The concentration of power in the media. This has three primary aspects: discursive power (the ability to influence how we think and act regarding particular phenomena); access power (the ability to control which voices and perspectives are present within the public sphere); and resource power (the ability to use media assets to leverage certain policy outcomes).

Method
The technique used to collect and analyse research data.

Methodology
How to approach the research that is to be undertaken. It is more than just the method used—it also represents how the researcher sees the world around them.

Mixed methods
A research process that combines both qualitative and quantitative research.

Modernisation
The social processes that brought about the transition from traditional to modern societies. These include industrialisation, urbanisation, rationalisation, and a shift in consciousness that fostered the idea that human beings have agency.

Modernism
A theory that nations were created in the Industrial Revolution by the need to develop a large-scale sense of community, identity and order.

Modernity
The social structures and ways of thinking that have been shaped by the industrial, scientific and democratic revolutions.

Moral panic
An overreaction to events (that are often relatively isolated or seemingly inconsequential), the understanding of which is informed by the media, where particular people or actions are labelled as a threat to society and to the wellbeing of the majority of the population. This leads to widespread anxiety and fear, and calls for urgent policy action.

Multiculturalism
Policies that support the maintenance of different cultural groups within one society. The term is also used to mean cultural diversity, whether that is supported by policy or not.

Multiple modernities
The many different forms that modernity takes around the globe. Patterns vary across nations, regions and civilisations.

Nation
A group of people with a common identity and a public culture rooted in ethnicity or created by industrial society.

Nation state
A political community in a recognised territorial space in which a centralised government exercises authority to rule on behalf of a national community or communities; among its citizens, there is a strong sense of belonging to a shared community.

Nationalism
A set of symbols and beliefs that provide the sense of being part of a single political community; also refers to loyalty to and promotion of the nation.

Native title
A type of property right recognised in Australian law that attempts to recognise the rights and interests of Aboriginal and Torres Strait Islander peoples. Native title does not grant ownership or freehold title and is the weakest form of title in common law.

Nature/culture dualism
A conceptualisation of nature and culture as two opposing and disconnected elements.

Neoliberalism
The political ideology and economic policies that promote a 'pure' form of capitalism, as free as possible from government regulation.

New Ecological Paradigm
A way of viewing humans as interdependent with the natural world.

New Sociology of Childhood
Social construction of childhood in which childhood identities are interpreted as multidimensional and children are active constructors of their own identities.

Occupy Movement
International progressive socio-political movement that, using many global technologies, opposed social and economic inequality brought on by the global financial crisis.

Ontology
The way we see the world: how we classify things, people and other entities around us.

Othering
A process whereby dominant groups in society maintain their dominance by assuming that their own features, characteristics and circumstances are the yardstick by which all others should be judged (often combined with 'totalisation').

Overconformity
Actions, traits or ideas that are based on the uncritical acceptance of norms and extreme adherence to them.

Overshoot
The point after which the share of resources available to ensure sustainability are expended.

Overt power
Power that exists in a direct gain of preference in a visible conflict. It takes place when actor A has the power over actor B to the extent that A can get B to do something that B would not otherwise do (Lukes 1974, p. 12).

Patriarchy
A social system in which men and masculinity are privileged, and women and femininity made subordinate.

Postmodernism
A movement of thought in the late twentieth century that that was sceptical of any grand narrative.

Precarious work
Insecure and poor-quality work—such as temporary employment—with lack of labour control and protection, and little income for living. More generally, the concept is used to capture a shift in modernity from stability to instability.

Primordialism
A theory that nations are timeless because they are rooted in the language and culture of pre-modern societies.

Prosumption
The way that cultural and economic activity combines technologies of production with the labour of consumers, such as self-service food outlets like McDonald's and self-serve checkouts at supermarkets.

Public sphere
A concept used to discuss the networked areas of public life in which ideas, information and knowledge are exchanged and debated. The media help to constitute society's public sphere by providing news and information, which is the raw material people use to discuss matters of public concern.

Qualitative research
Research that focuses on the investigation and understanding of opinions, motivations and feelings.

Quantitative research
Research that aims to explain phenomena by collecting numerical data that are analysed by using mathematically based methods, including statistics.

Race
The hierarchical categorisation of groups of people on the basis of physical characteristics such as skin colour or eye shape.

Racism
Ideology and practices that discriminate against people based on assumptions about their biological or cultural inferiority.

Rationalisation
The spread of precise calculation and efficiency as the primary principles for social organisation.

Reconciliation
'Coming together' and improving the relationship between Australia's First Peoples and non-Indigenous Australians, based on recognising the ongoing impact of colonisation.

Religion
A contested term variously defined as i) personal, communal and institutional practices based on believed encounters with transcendent realities beyond (or within) the material world; ii) the social dynamics created by the separation of sacred and mundane space; and iii) an idea rooted in Christian terminology employed to codify (and control) a wide variety of social and cultural practices.

Religio-secular world
A concept that challenges the idea that societies can simply be split along religious or secular lines. We live in a world that can be both more religious and more secular simultaneously.

Respatialisation
The spatial reorganisation of work using digital platforms and technologies. These changes have given rise to new forms of business and labour models. It can take multiple forms such as moving work across national boundaries (e.g. 'the call centre'), shifting work to online platforms (e.g. 'Mechanical Turk') and putting workers on the move (e.g. 'Uber' and 'Deliveroo').

Scholarly information
Encyclopedias, textbooks, journal articles, conference proceedings, or any other information that is written by people with expertise and authority in a subject area.

Scientific revolution
The origins of modern Western science in the sixteenth century, based on detached observation, evidence and reason.

Secularism
A contested term variously defined as i) the social and political subordination of religion to other, more dominant elements of social and political life; ii) a philosophy promoting the political equality of all religions in a society; and iii) a mode of dominant power that orders

and controls society through the constructed definitions of 'religion'.

Secular settlement
A mode of classifying and managing religion so that it serves the declared and undeclared norms of the Western secular state.

Self-determination
A collective right of a people to freely decide their own political status and pursue their own economic, social and cultural development.

Sex
The biological categories: male and female.

Sexuality
Sexual behaviours and orientations.

Snapchat
A social media platform that young people use to post statuses, updates, photos, and videos to friends to comment on. Posts automatically disappear after 24 hours.

Social capital
For Bourdieu, the resources and benefits that derive from our social networks.

Social cohesion
The concept that members of a society are willing to cooperate with each other in order to survive and prosper.

Social construction
A social phenomenon or category created by society, such as gender.

Social contract
Society's tacit acceptance of how we will be governed and the laws we will follow.

Social customs
Patterns of behaviour that contribute to social norms within a particular culture or subculture.

Social facts
A concept identified with the French sociologist, Emile Durkheim (1858–1917), that refers to the way that social forces—external to an individual—influence the feeling, thinking and behaviours of an individual.

Social interaction
The interactions within the society of people (both as part of groups and as individuals) and both informal and formal institutions.

Social media
Websites and apps that enable users to create and share content or to participate in social networking.

Social movement
A large grouping of people and organisations that focus on specific social, political or cultural issues with the aim of achieving, resisting or reversing social change.

Social norms
The shared beliefs, attitudes, values and behaviours of people in a society—that is, a shared understanding of what is normal.

Social research
A systematic investigation of society.

Social settings
The range of environments that children engage in socially including home, school and other institutions.

Social stratification
The ranking of individuals or groups based on factors such as income, wealth, occupational status and education.

Social structures
The social systems and institutions that underpin a society and the relationships within it. Social systems include work, education and religion, for example, while social institutions include family, schools, hospitals, government and other institutions that exist within our legal, economic and political systems.

Social theory
The frameworks used to explain how society works.

Socialisation
The process of transmission of culture from one generation to the next; the ongoing social processes by which we learn the norms, customs and values of our society.

Socially constructed
The concept that society is built by individuals and groups through various social processes. In turn, the processes established shape expectations for those individuals and groups.

Society
A social system made up of many smaller parts that share a culture: these smaller parts include both formal institutions (such as schools, hospitals and government) and informal social groups (such as families).

Sociological imagination
The capacity to see how social factors influence the life of an individual in society.

Sociological research
Research that seeks to advance our understanding of social phenomena and the social world.

Sociology
The study of society. In order to study society, we must look at the interactions within the society of people (both as part of groups and as individuals) and both informal and formal institutions (such as schools, hospitals and government).

Sovereignty
The autonomous power to exercise supreme legal and political authority over a given domain, commonly measured in territorial terms.

Spirit of capitalism
A term used by Weber in 1905 to refer to an ethic of hard work and a sense that work is inherently fulfilling and rewarding, which forms the basis of the culture of modern capitalism.

Spirituality
A contested term variously understood as i) beliefs of and encounters with the transcendent reality that regularly occur outside of traditional religious settings, and ii) religious practices utilising an eclectic array of everyday resources and perspectives that occur inside and outside traditional religious settings.

Sport
A human activity requiring physical exertion and/or physical skill, which is competitive and is generally accepted as being a sport.

State
A form of modern political organisation where a government exercises sovereign power over a population of citizens. Often synonymous with 'country'.

Status
A Weberian term to describe the degree of power possessed by an individual on the basis of honour or prestige.

Supraterritorial
The ability of a state to engage with its citizens or corporations beyond its borders.

Surplus value
The portion of the value of a product or service that exceeds the cost of producing it; that is, the labour of producing it.

Symbolic capital
When cultural capital is legitimated or not legitimated by others, it becomes symbolic capital. What is deemed valuable or not valuable by others is always objectively determined by the dominant middle classes.

Technology
A bundle of practices, techniques and materials embedded in and shaped by larger societal transformations, which plays a special role in driving and supporting the prevailing mode of production.

Techno-social life
Seamless integration of technology into our social lives.

Theory
An explanation for patterns of meaning or trends and the relationship between the key concepts that we find in our data.

Totalisation
The act of labelling someone, based upon a small part of who they are. As a consequence, the person and their actions may be viewed either more, or less, sympathetically.

Tradition
Individual and communal practices of religion developed over time, often adapted to answer challenges posed to belief and association in social context, that can both reinforce and challenge social norms; intended for the purpose of strengthening religious community through memory reinforcement and ethical purpose.

Traditional societies
The range of pre-modern societies. These varied widely, but all were non-industrial, primarily rural, and characterised by meaning-based rather than reason-based world views.

Transition
Movement through the liminal space between childhood and adulthood.

Transnational actor
A community or political movement that defines its identity or activity beyond the sovereign boundary of the state.

Underconformity
Actions, traits or ideas that are based on the rejection of norms.

White Australia Policy
A legislated practice that started at Federation and continued for almost 70 years, which essentially ensured that 'people of colour' could not migrate to Australia and made it difficult for those already living in Australia to remain.

Whiteness
The theory that there is significant power and privilege associated with being White, and that much of this privilege stems from whiteness being portrayed as 'normal'.

Work ethic
An orientation and attitude towards work that an individual worker is expected to adopt.

Index

Abbott Government 290
Abolition of Slavery Act 1833 463
Aboriginal and Torres Strait Islander Commission (ATSIC) 332
Aboriginal and Torres Strait Islander people 180, 302, 325
   activism 333, 334–5, 461
   Closing the Gap 326, 340–1
   cultural land management 14
   demography of disadvantage 341–2
   documentaries about 329
   early childhood education experience 79
   ethics process for research 82–3
   first contact with settlers 328–30
   Frontier Wars 330
   government reconciliation policies 331–2
   the Intervention 381
   levels of indigeneity (blood quantum) 336–9
   long-term social movement 304–5
   massacres 331
   Redfern Address 199
   self-identification 327–8, 337
   service in military 331
   states and territories of residence 328
   underclass stereotypes 118–19
   voting rights 334–5
   Wave Hill walk-off 306–7, 333, 461
   See also Stolen Generations
Aboriginal Land Rights (Northern Territory) Act 1976 333
Aboriginal Tent Embassy 307
academic literacy 20, 30–1
access power 280, 281
active citizenship 464
activism
   Aboriginal and Torres Strait Islander 333, 334–5, 461
   black rights movement 204–5
   difference from advocacy 314–15
   disability 313–17
   intersection of advocacy and 315
   power through 152, 159
   youth strikes on climate change 158
   WA disability scheme 317
   See also human rights activism
Actor-Network Theory (ANT) 255, 258–9
adaptive response 432, 436–8
Adelaide News 281
Admission Impossible (documentary) 181
adolescent 357, 358
Adorno, Theodor 278
Adu-Gyamfi, J. 157

Advertiser Code of Ethics 288
advertising 399
   gender analysis 140–1
   social media 165, 289
   sport 413
advocacy
   difference from activism 314–15
   disability 313–17
affordance 272
Age of Enlightenment 160, 176
ageing population
   sociological research 66–7
   work trends 395
ageism 166–7
agency 20, 22, 46, 49, 89, 91, 258–9, 432
   Agentic Child construction 267, 268
   in homeless 70
   modern ideas 98–9
   religious adaptive response 438
Airbnb 399
Alexander, Jade 422–4
Al-Hudaydah *See* Yemen
alienation 108, 111–12
Alone Together (Turkle) 286
Althusser, Louis 278–9
Amazon 264, 399
American Psychological Association Style (APA) 33
American Revolution 89, 91
Amnesty International 8
analysis
   class 107, 125–6
   discourse 79–80
   gender 132, 140–1
   merit-based 114
   secondary information sources 77, 79
   social and cultural personal reflection 16–17
   social research 69
   social research data 74
   for sociology assignments 34–5
   statistical 77
Anderson, Benedict 96, 196, 200
   See also imagined communities
Anderson, E. 422
anomie 26, 372, 373, 374
anti-globalisation 207
anti-globalisation movement 220
anti-racism 188–9
antislavery movement 462
'anywhere, anytime' work 391, 392, 396
ANZAC-Easter connection 442–3
Apology to the Stolen Generations 2008 330
apps 272, 287, 401–2, 444
   role in gig economy 400
   surveillance 268
Aristotle 392

Arnold Bloch Leibler 384
Arvanitakis, James 119–20
asset-based class 123, 125
assimilation 174, 182
asylum seekers 184
   media portrayal 33, 280
   targets of moral panic 381, 382–3
   street art mural 260
The Australian 281
Australian Association of National Advertisers (AANA) 288
Australian Bureau of Statistics 67, 341, 352
   groups showing environmental concern 246
   homelessness 68
   Social Economic Indicators for Areas (SEIFA) 71
   work locations 397
Australian Critical Race and Whiteness Studies Association 186
The Australian Dream (documentary) 189, 413
Australian Government
   Closing the Gap targets 340
   definition of sport 411
   Gonski Review 155–6
   Indigenous reconciliation policies 331–2
   multiculturalism policy 182–90, 197
   types of social contract 55, 56
   White Australia Policy 180–1, 197
Australian Housing and Urban Research Institute (AHURI) 125
Australian Human Rights Commission 384, 385
Australian Institute of Aboriginal and Torres Strait Islander Studies (AIATSIS) 238
Australian Marriage Act 1961 280
Australian Marriage Law Postal Vote 384
Australian National University Energy Change Institute 240
Australian Productivity Commission 2018, Rising Inequality 2018 report 124
Australian Sociological Association 24
Australian Women Against Violence Alliance 8
Australian Work and Life Index (AWALI) 394
Austudy 55
autonomy 99

Baby Boomers 355, 356
background information 35, 37
backroads 216, 219–20, 221, 225
Bainqen Erdini Qoigyijabu 443–4
Banton, Michael 175

Barth, Frederik   178
Bateson, Gregory   234
Bauman, Zygmunt   278, 287, 291, 401
Beattie, Alix   260
Beck, Ulrich   100, 218
Beck-Gernsheim, Elisabeth   100
belief   432, 435–6
Bellah, Robert   433
Bentham, Jeremy   160, 164
   See also Panopticon concept
Berger, Peter   433
bias
   media   274
   mobilisation of   155, 168
   political   282
biological determinism   10, 133, 135, 357–8
the Birmingham School   352
Black Lives Matter   189
Black Skin, White Masks (Fanon)   176
Blomberg, Justice   338
Boas, Franz   177
Bolt, Andrew   338
boomerang social movement   312
bottom-up technology transmissions   262
Bourdieu, Pierre   30–1, 278, 327
   on culture   115–17
   on work   395
bourgeoisie   110, 115
breaching experiments   374
Breuilly, John   204
Brexit   207, 290
British Sociological Association   22
broad religion   439
Bullard, Robert   237
The Bulletin   181
Bulmer, M. & Solomos, J.   180
bureaucracy   89, 96–7
bushfires 2019–20   241
   interrelated rhombus   60–1
   use of social media to discuss   260
Butler, Judith   53, 138
bystander anti-racism   188

CAARP evaluation technique   39
Calwell, Arthur   181
campaign   302
Canavan, Matt   159, 166
Capital in the Twenty-First Century (Piketty)   123
capitalism   89, 95, 99, 391, 393, 399
   See also global capitalism; surveillance capitalism
carbon pricing   232, 246
Cartesian Philosophy   233–4
Castells, Manuel   284

categorical data   78
Catholic Education   156
Census
   data on Indigenous people   335–6, 337
   data on religiousness   433, 436
   1971   337
   Population and Housing 2016   68
Centre for Contemporary Cultural Studies (CCCS)   352
ceremonies of degradation   379
ceremonies of elevation   379
Certificate of Aboriginality   337
Certificates of Exemption   336
Chauncy, Merrin   31
the Chicago School   352
child development domains   255, 261–2
childhood   255
   language used to frame   353
   social construction   255, 266–8
   technological impacts on   254, 263–5
   techno-social life   261
children
   changed relationships with adults   262
   connection to digital technology   256–7
   connection to environment   247–8
   moral panic over technology use   254–5, 266
   reasons for excelling at technology   261–2
'Children are Vulnerable' construct   267–8
China   238
   forms of modernity   92–3, 97
   restrictions on e-waste   238
   Tibetan resistance via religion   443–4
circular economy   232, 245
citizenship   197, 464
civic nationalism   178, 197, 205
class   108
   asset-based   123–4
   and place   121–2
   personal reflection   119–20
   ruling   278
   structures   112–13
   as taboo subject   109
   Weber on   113–15
   and women   120–1
   See also Marxism
class analysis   107, 120–1
class conflict   58
class culture   115
A Class Divided (documentary)   379
class mobility   124–5
Climate Action Summit 2019 report   240
climate change   206, 239–40

religious-based responses   440, 445–6, 447
   role of education   158, 159
   youth protests   159
climate justice   232, 240–4
Closing the Gap   326, 340–1
CNN   51, 290–1
Coleman, Alexandra   16–17
collective action   302, 303, 305
collective identity   96, 201–2, 247
colonialism   89, 92
   knowledge systems   14
   secular settlements   437–8
   technologies of power   175–6, 342
   See also History Wars
colonisation   59, 92, 174, 329–30
Commonwealth Games 1994   198
communication   6–7
   technological impact on   259
communism   109
The Communist Manifesto (Marx)   109
competition   56, 57–8
Comte, Auguste   26, 53, 56, 58, 75
   See also social evolution
conflict theory   46, 54, 57–8, 275, 278, 437
   media influence   280
conformism   372
Connell, R.W.   148
Connolly, William   433
Connor, Samantha   316
consensus   56–7
   See also organic analogy
consumer society   101–2
consumption   225–6, 241–4, 277, 401
   See also prosumption
contact hypothesis   188
content words   35
cooperation   56–7
Copernican paradigm   258
Copernicus   258
Copper, William   333
counterculture   97–8
covert power   153, 167
   corporate vested interests   158
   impact on youth   166, 168
   school funding models   155–6
COVID-19
   use of apps during   287, 448
   impact on society   7, 454
   impact on sport   409, 410, 412
creativity   100
Crenshaw, Kimberle   310
critical discourse analysis   80
critical race theory   338–9
critical thinking   20, 24
Cronulla Riots 2003   7
cultural awareness training   188

cultural capital   21, 30–1, 108, 115
    rural/regional reflection   116–17
cultural groups   22–3
cultural norms   22–3
cultural racism   178
cultural studies   3, 5, 6–7, 50, 51–3
    difference from sociology   51–2
cultural theorists   50, 52
culture   3, 8, 11–12, 51–3, 97–8, 115–17
    changes in   48–9
    consumption of non-Western   226
    consumption of Western   225–6
    daily rituals   459
    of excess   244
    Goffman and Butler on   52–3
    hybrid   226
    and identity   12
    narcissistic   286
cyberbullying   285
cyber-safety   268
cyberspace   273, 284–5

Damiens, Robert-Francois   159–60
Darwin, Charles   53–4, 174, 176
data   68
    breach scandal   290
    categorical   78
    empirical   66, 73–4
    government online surveillance   290
    HILDA   124–5
    on Indigenous people   335–6, 341, 342–3
    social research process   72–3
database   37, 38, 40
Davie, Grace   435–6
Day of Mourning 1938   333
d'Azeglio, Massimo   200
de Beauvoir, Simone   134
de Coubertin, Pierre   418
The Death of Class (Pakulski & Waters)   109
Defence Act 1903   331
Deliveroo   164
'on demand' economy   400
democracy   89, 97, 99
    compulsory voting   276–7
    modern forms   157
    monitory   275
    surveillance expansion powers   290–1
democratic revolution   89, 91
Department of Aboriginal Affairs   335, 337
Department of Social Services (DSS)   314
Descartes, René   233
The Descent of Man (Darwin)   176
design thinking   468
determinism   10
deviance   368, 369, 410
    breaching experiments   374
    ceremonies of degradation   379

dividing practices   377–9
Durkheim on   372, 373, 374, 384
functions of   373
Goffman on   374, 375
labelling   374–5
Merton on   372–3
othering   383
overconformity   416–17
resistance   384–5
and sport   413–17
totalisation of identity   375–7
underconformity   416
Dictation Test   181
digital economy   399
digital labour   399
digital literacy   32
digital media   284
Digital Natives   261, 354
digital pictograms   286
digital technology   255, 262
    convergence   274
    role in changing work   396–402
Disability Services Commission (DSC)   314
discimination, positive   335
disciplinary power   153, 159–65
    models of public health and prevention   162
Discipline and Punish (Foucault)   159
discourse   80, 350, 353
    youth-related   352
discourse analysis   79–80
discursive power   280
dividing practices   377–9, 383
doctors and influence of social factors   9–10, 29
'Dominant Western Worldview'   234
dramaturgical theory   52–3, 138
drugs, moral panic   381
Du Bois, W.E.B.   177
dualism
    nature/culture   232–4, 248
    sex   136, 232
Durkheim, Emile   11, 21, 26, 371
    on deviance   372, 373, 374, 384
    on religion   434, 435
    on work   393
Dutton, Peter   282

Eatock v Bolt 2001   338
echo chambers   276, 279, 291
ecological economics   232, 245–6
ecological footprint   232, 243
Ecological Footprint Calculators   243
economic capital   108, 115
economic growth and impact on environment   245–6
Edmund Rice Centre   8

education   460
    role in combating climate change   158, 159
education funding models   155–6
eight-stage model   352–6, 357
E.L.K. (street artist)   260
Elliott, Jane   379
Ellis, Liz   419
emojis   286
empirical data   66, 73–4
Engels, Friedrich   109
environmental accountability   233
environmental inequality   232, 236–9
environmental justice   232, 238–9
environmental racism   232, 237
environmental sociology   234–6, 246
epistemology   3, 14
Erikson, Erik   352, 357
    See also eight-stage model
Ethical Conduct in Research with Aboriginal and Torres Strait Islander Peoples and Communities: Guidelines for Researchers and Stakeholder (2018b)   82
ethics   66
    social media   288
    social research   69, 72
    sociological research   81–3
Ethnic Disability Advocacy Centre (EDAC) Inc.   314, 316
ethnic nationalism   197, 205
ethnicity   174, 195, 197
    race and nation   177–8
    race and nationalism   183–6
ethnie   201
ethno-symbolism   196–7, 201
European Enlightenment   93, 98
European Union (EU)   206
    Emissions Trading Scheme (ETS)   246
    impact of importing fish   221, 223–4
    nationalist movements   309
ever-presence   391, 402, 403
'Every Australian Counts' campaign   317
evidence, using and citing   39–40
e-waste   238–9
expert knowledge   21, 29
exploitation   108, 110–11, 112

fa'afafine   135
Facebook   165, 276, 279, 286, 470
    social movements   305, 316
    targeted advertising   289, 399
Facebook-Cambridge Analytica scandal   290
Fanon, Frantz   176, 436
Fausto-Sterling, Anne   136
Femen   159
The Feminine Mystique (Friedan)   147

femininity   457–8
feminism   132, 133, 144–6, 384
    views on power   159
feminist movements   308
feudal systems   95
filter bubbles   276, 279
The Final Quarter (documentary)   189, 413
First Australians (documentary)   329
First Contact (documentary)   118
First Footprints (documentary)   329
First Nations National Constitutional Convention 2017   202
First Nations peoples   198, 200, 202, 203, 306–7, 325
First Peoples   302, 326, 328
Flemington Legal Centre (FLC)   384
The Flip-FLop Trail: A Journey Through Globalisation's Backroad (Knowles)   219
Folau, Isreal   422
food
    as symbol capital   115–16
    Yemen fish export   217, 221–4
Food and Agriculture Organization   217
Foucault, Michel   153, 291, 371
    on normalisation   15
    on power   159–61, 163, 164
    on totalisation   375, 376
fourth estate   273, 277
Fox, Jonathan   434
Fox News   51, 280, 282
framing   273
    childhood   267, 353
    heteronormative   308
    holistic   233
    media power and influence   280
Francis, Bev   421
Frankfurt School scholars   278
Freedom (Bauman)   401
Freedom Rides 1965   307, 333, 461
Freeman, Cathy   198–9, 202
French Revolution   89, 91
Friedan, Betty   147
Frontier Wars   330, 332
functionalist theory   275, 277–8

Galileo   258
game reasoning   415
Garfinkel, Howard   374, 375, 379
Gay Liberation Movement   384
Geertz, Clifford   196, 439
Gellner, Ernest   196, 200, 201, 204
gender   13–14, 131–2
    difference from sex   135–6
    'doing gender' concept   139–43
    identity   53

framing heteronormative   308
    intersectionality   146–8
    personal reflection on masculinity   141–3
    social construction   133–4, 135, 136, 137, 457
    and sport   417–21, 425
    symbolic interactionism   138
    and work   143–4
    See also femininity; masculinity
gender analysis   132
gender discrimination   144
gender inequality   146
gender lens   132, 140, 148
Gender Pay Gap (GPG)   143
gender performativity   133, 139, 141
gender socialisation   137–8, 144
Generation Alpha   355
generation gap   351, 354–5
Generations X and Y   355, 356
Generation Z   355
generational typologies   355–6
GetUp!   284
ghettos   122
Giddens, Anthony   29, 52, 157
gig economy   164, 391, 399–400
    See also 'on demand' economy
Gillard Government   155–6, 282
global capitalism   391, 394–6, 403
Global Financial Crisis   95
globalisation   215, 460
    difficulties defining   218–20
    forms of inequality   225
    impact on nationhood   206
    impact on societal inequality   223
    mobility of workers   224–5
    sport and impact of COVID-19   412
    Yemen case study   216–18, 221–4
glocalisation   278
Goffman, Erving   51, 52, 138, 140, 285
    on deviance   374, 375
Gonski 2.0   156
Gonski Review   155–6
Goodes, Adam   189, 413
Google   38–9, 152, 165
Google data   290
government
    communicative links   276–7
    corporate covert power over   158
    media influence over   281–4
    online surveillance   290–1
    shifting response to moral panics   381
Government Communications Headquarters (GCHQ)   290
governmentality   161, 163
Gramsci, Antonio   158
grand narrative   46, 59, 60
Great Chain of Being concept   175–6

Great Depression   95
Groopman, Jerome   9–10
Gross Domestic Product (GDP)   244
The Guardian   331, 351
Gurindji Strike 1966   333

Habermas, Jürgen   275–6, 278, 281
habitus   108, 115
Hage, Ghassan   187
Haitian Revolution   462
Hanson, Pauline   187, 197
Harris, Tayla   420
Hassner, Ron E.   439–40
Health Department   314
hegemonic masculinity   148, 418
Henderson, Debra   118
Herald   113
Herald & Weekly Times   282
Hing, Michael   195
History Wars   59, 330–2
Hobbes, Thomas   54, 55
Hobsbawm, Eric   201
holism   232, 233, 235–6
homelessness   446–7, 456–7
homophobia   410, 421–2, 425
hooks, bell   109, 121, 147
Horkheimer, Max   278
'The House of Young Prisoners in Paris' (Foucault)   160
Household Income and Labour Dynamics Australia (HILDA)   124–5
Howard, John   282, 419
Howard Government
    moral panic over asylum seekers   382–3
    new citizenship tests   183
human ecology   234
Human Exemptionalist Paradigm   232, 234–5
Human Genome Project   175, 338–9
Human Research Ethics Committee (HREC)   72, 82
human rights activism   302, 311–12, 334
    Tibetan use of religion as resistance   440
ideal speech situations   276
identity   52–3
    collective   96, 201–2, 247
    and culture   12
    gendered   53, 363
    modern ideas of agency   98–9
    national and personal   204–5
    online   285
    politics   310
    totalisation   375–7
imagined communities   96, 198, 200

Imagined Communities (Anderson)   196
Immigration Restriction Act 1901   180–1
imperialism   51
India
   Hinduism as dominant power   436
   reactionary movements   309
   secularism   434
indigeneity   326, 327, 336–9
Indigenous people   302, 304, 325, 326, 327
   challenges to stereotypes   384
   civil and constitutional rights movement   308
   data collection on   335–6, 337, 341, 342–3
   environmental inequality and racism   237–8
   evolution approaches towards   54
   philosophical ecology   235–6
   as targets of moral panic   381
   working definitions   339
   See also Aboriginal and Torres Strait Islander people; First Peoples: First Nations
individualisation   89, 100–1
Indonesia's interfaith response to climate issues   446
Industrial Revolution   6, 50–1, 89, 307, 357
   meaning of work   392–3
industrialisation   89, 92, 94–5
information literacy   32–9
   evaluation of information   39
   reliable internet information   38–9
   where to find   36–7
innovation   373
Instagram   265, 272–3, 286, 399
   social movements   305
instrumental rationality   98
instrumentarian power   153, 165
integration   174, 183
interactionist theory   275
Intergovernmental Panel on Climate Change   206
International Covenant on Civil and Political Rights   312
International Federation of Bodybuilding (IFBB)   421
International Labour Organization   441
International Olympic Committee   410
internet
   anti-social behaviours   285
   reliable information techniques   38–9
   role in transmission of faith   440, 444–5
   user-generated content   398, 399
interpretation   69–70, 73
interrelated rhombus   60–1, 402, 456, 458–9

intersectionality   133, 146–8, 174, 187, 302, 310–11, 458–9
the Intervention   381
interviews, qualitative   80–1
Iscel, Nihal   303–4, 313–17
Islamic Declaration on Climate Change   445

Journal of Sociology   24, 25
journal subscriptions and access   33–4
journalism *See* fourth estate
Judaism   445
'just-in time' labour   396

Kaepernick, Colin   204–5
Kanakas   180
Kant, Immanuel   93
Keating, Paul   199
Keeping Research on Track II (2018c)   82
keywords   36
Kimmel, Michael   147–8
knowledge   14, 459, 463
   expert   21, 29
   lay   21, 29–30
   scientific   98, 257–8
   sociological   24, 28–30
   See also epistemology
Knowles, Christine   219
Kohn, Hans   205
Korean adaptive response to religion   437–8
Kuhn, Thomas   257–8

labelling theory   374–9
labour power   110
land rights   326, 332
language
   discourse analysis   79–80
   labels associated with youth   359
   life stages   353
   used to frame emotive issues   188, 280
Latour, Bruno   258–9
   See also Actor-Network Theory (ANT)
lay knowledge   21, 29–30
LBGTIQA people
   movies reflecting individualisation   101
   sexuality and health interviews   81
   social movements   308, 311, 312
   totalisation of identity   376
   transitions personal reflection   363
leadership models   467
Lebow, Victor   241
Left-Right political spectrum   216, 220
leisure class   124
leisure society   394
Lévi-Strauss, Claude   234

liberalism   102, 386
life chances   108, 114–15, 350, 352
Life Patterns project   362
life stages   350, 352–6, 357, 360–1
   See also eight-stage model
limiting words   35
Lindt Cafe siege 2014   7
Lingiari, Vincent   306–7, 333
LinkedIn   286
Linnaeus, Carl   176
liquid love theory   287
liquid surveillance   273, 291
literacy cultural capital   30–1, 32
lived experience   350, 352
The Longitudinal Study of Indigenous Children (LSIC)   79
Lukes, Steven   153, 156–7, 168
Luke's third face of power   153, 156–9, 167–8
Lydon, Jane   177
Lyon, David   291

macro level analysis   25, 27, 40, 112
Mannheim, Karl   354
Maori identity and racism   179–80
Maralinga nuclear tests   237–8
Marcuse, Herbert   278
Martin, Trayvon   189
Marty, Martin   434
Marx, Karl   58, 95, 109, 393–4
   on deviance   371–2
   on exploitation   110, 112
   on religion   436
   on ruling class   278
   See also structuralism
Marxism
   analytical   112–15
   classical   110–11, 112
masculinity   15, 457–8
   hegemonic   148
   male subjectivity   13–14
   personal reflection   141–3
   and sport   417–18
mass communication   273, 276
mass media   273, 277
   targets of moral panic   379–83
McDonaldisation   89, 102
McDonaldization of Society (Ritzer)   398
Mechanical Turk   399
media
   concerns about new platforms   284–91
   coverage of women's sport   420, 424
   critical thinking about content   278–80
   digital   284
   gender analysis of advertising   140–1

power of influence 274, 281
role and function 275–8
as sources of information 32–3
totalisation tactics 376
youth-related topics 350
See also mass media
media power 273, 274, 280–4
Melbourne Response compensation scheme 80
Mental Health Commission 314
Merton, Robert K. 371, 372–3, 374
See also strain theory
Messenger 286
method 66, 68
methodological individualism 113
methodology 66, 70, 75–6
micro level analysis 25, 27, 40, 112, 161, 275
Microsoft 165
Middle East Broadcasting Center (MBC) 217
migrant workers 224–5
Mills, Charles Wright 26
See also sociological imagination
Mitchell, Latrell 413
mixed methods 66, 77
mobile devices 261–2, 264–5, 274–5
modernisation 89, 92–4
modernism 196, 198, 200, 201
modernity 88, 89, 90–1
core components 94–9
disciplinary power 161–3
dynamics underpinning 99–100
moral panic 273, 292, 350, 368
children's technology use 266, 268
mass media 379–83
stages in development 380–1
targeted groups 351, 364, 379–83, 385–6
Morrison, Scott 282, 284, 304
multiculturalism 174, 182–90, 197
personal reflection on racism 184–6
phases in 183
multiple modernities 89, 93–4
Murdoch, Rupert 113, 281–4
Murray, Charles 118
Muslims 184
climate change activism 445, 447
racialisation 178, 188, 381, 382–3
stereotypes 383, 385–6

NASA 239
nation 198, 199
Australian context 201–2
debates and approaches 200–3
emergence of 327
nation states 89, 198, 199, 200

as component of modernity 95–7
purpose of nationalism 204
National Disability Insurance Scheme (NDIS) 315, 317
National Health and Medical Research Council 81–2
National Security Agency (NSA) 290
National Standards for Disability Services (NSDS) 314
National Statement on Ethical Conduct in Research Involving Humans 81–2
national surveys 77
nationalism 89, 96, 198, 200, 201
civic 178, 197, 205
debates and approaches 200–3, 208
ethnic 197, 205
ethnicity, race and 183–6
flags as symbols of 183–4, 206
and religion 440, 442–3
symbols of 203–6
theoretical approaches 196–7
types of 207
nationality 195
Native Title 326, 332
natural environment 231
children's connection to 247–8
groups showing environmental concern 246–7
holistic thinking 235–6
nature/culture dualism 232–4, 248
neoliberalism 89, 102–3
neo-racism 178
neo-Weberians 114
Netflix 264
New Ecological Paradigm 232, 234–5
new racism 178
New Sociology of Childhood 255, 267
New York Times 462
News Corp 281, 282
News Ltd 113
no-fault divorce laws 68, 117
normalisation 15
Northern Territory Emergency Response (the Intervention) 381
Nowotny, H. 391, 402

observation in social research 69
Occupy movement 97, 216, 220
Olympic Games 198, 202 410, 417, 418
Online Hate Prevention Institute 189
ontology 3, 13
organic analogy 56–7
organisations, faith and development programs 440, 441–2
On the Origin of Species (Darwin) 53
Orsi, Robert 434
othering 368, 383

Out Watch 8
overconformity 410, 416
overshoot 232, 241–4
overt power 153, 154, 166
Oxfam Australia 8, 312, 317, 465

paid labour 392, 394, 398
Pakulski, Jan 109
Palm Island Riots 2004 7
Panopticon concept 160, 164, 291
Parks, Rosa 435
Parsons, Talcott 56–7, 137–8
participatory culture 398
patriarchy 133, 145–6, 148, 159
peer group pressure 370–1
peer-reviewed information 32, 33, 37, 73
people with disabilities
#NoDisadvantage campaign 316, 317
participation via social media 286
personal reflection on social movement 313–17
Per Capita 465
Perkins, Charles 307, 333
petit bourgeoisie 110, 115
Pew Research Center 265, 279
Piketty, Thomas 123, 124
Pilbara Strike 1946 333
place (location), and class 121–2
platform capitalism 399
Plato 14, 392
political economy 280
politics
as form of entertainment 278
power relations 152
voting rights for women 162–3
postmodernism 46, 59–60, 275
See also History Wars
postmodernity 100
post-nations 197, 206–8
power 51, 113–14, 458
access 280, 281
citizenship, control and modern state 157
colonial 175–6, 342
cultural 158
disciplinary 153, 159–65
discursive 280
Foucault on 159–61, 163, 164
in gig economy 164
instrumentarian 153, 165
Luke's third face 153, 156–9, 167–8
media 274, 280, 281–4
overt 153, 154, 166
politics 152
prisons 160–1
relational 154, 159–65, 168
religious 436–8

power (*continued*)
  resource   280, 281
  social media   287–9
  surveillance and monitoring   164–5, 289–91
  worldmaking   327
  youth's experience of   152, 159, 166–8
  See also covert power
Power: A Radical View (Lukes)   153
precarious work   390, 391, 395, 399, 403
primary information sources   40
primordialism   196, 198, 201
prisons and power   160–1
probability sampling   77
produsage   398
progress   59, 60
proletariat   110, 111, 115
prosumers   401
prosumption   391, 398–9, 403
Protection Acts   336
The Protestant Ethic and the Spirit of Capitalism (Weber)   393
Protestant work ethic   435
prototyping ideas   468–9
Ptolemaic paradigm   258
public health and disciplinary power   162
public sphere   274, 275–7, 278, 286
Pumping Iron II: The Women (documentary)   421

qualitative interviews   80–1
qualitative research   66, 77, 80–1
quantitative research   66, 77, 78
queer studies   132

r > g model   123, 124
race   458–9
  ethnicity and nation   177–8
  ethnicity and nationalism   183–6
  social construction   175, 327, 338
  system of categorisation   174–6
Racial Discrimination Act 1975   189, 338, 381, 385
racial profiling   378, 384–5
Racial Theories (Banton)   175
racialisation process   178
racism   174, 175, 178–80, 458–9
  dividing practices   378
  flags as symbols of   173
  internet   285
  mixed identity personal reflection   179–80
  new   178
  personal reflection   184–6
  in sport   413
  stereotypes   118, 383, 384, 385–6
  See also environmental racism; nationalism

Racism (Bulmer & Solomos)   180
racism awareness   188
rationalisation   89, 102
Reach Out   8, 464
rebellion   373
Reclaim Australia   197
reconciliation   326, 331–2
Redfern Address   199
referencing   33, 39–40
Referendum 1967   308, 332, 333–5
relational power   154, 159–65, 168
religion   431, 432
  as adaptive response   437–8
  catholic church sexual abuse of children   80
  as dominant power   436–8
  event and contexts   446–8
  Great Chain of Being concept   175–6
  and human rights   443–4
  and internet   444–5
  as modern encounter with gods   433–4
  as multidimensional concept   438–40
  and nationalism   442–3
  and organisations   441–2
  response to climate change   440, 445–6
  sites of analysis   440–6
  as social cohesion and change   434–6
  as social construction   435
religio-secular world   432, 434
reproductive work   144
research *See* social research; sociological research
Resende, Michael   28
resource power   280, 281
respatialisation   391, 396–7
retreatism   373
revenge porn   285
Rheingold, Howard   285, 286
Richards, Jonathan   331
Richter, Zahari   311
at risk   350, 352
ritualism   372
Ritzer, George 89, 102, 398 *See also* McDonaldisation
Robinson, Marilynne   462
roller derby   422–5
Romantic movement   98
Rose, Deborah Bird   235, 236
Rose, Nikolas   163
Rudd, Kevin   282, 283
Rudd Government Apology to the Stolen Generations 2008   330
rural/regional communities   116–17, 122
Rushton, Philippe   177
Ryan, Lyndall   331

same-sex marriage   280, 308, 309, 384
Samoan variants of gender identity   135
Saunders, Peter   122
SBS   118
Schetzer, Alana   419
scholarly information   21, 32
Scholte, Jan Aarte   219, 222
Scientific American   418
scientific knowledge   98, 257–8
scientific method   357, 358
scientific revolution   89, 91, 98, 257–8
secondary information sources   40, 77, 79
secular settlement   432, 437, 443
secularism   432, 433–4
self-determination   326, 332, 339, 343
self-discipline, technologies   163–4
self-identification   337
selfies   286
Senate Inquiry into Women and Sport 2006   420
separatism   207
sex   133, 134
  difference from gender   135–6
  dualism   135
sexting   78, 272
sexual harassment   285
sexual norms   15
sexuality   410
  and sport   421–5
Sharp, Granville   462–3.
Shils, Edward   196
Sieyes, Emmanuel-Joseph   26
Siri   256–7
Sky News   282
Small, Albion   29
Smith, Anthony   196–7, 200, 201, 202, 204
Snapchat   255, 264, 265
Snowden, Edward   290
social and cultural analysis personal reflection   16–17
social capital   108, 115, 116–17
social change   47–8, 459–60
  mode of communication   6–7
  recognition of issues to focus   465–7
  ways to enact   461–70
social class   114–15
social cohesion   432, 435
social construction   14–15
  childhood   255, 256, 266–8
  gender   133–4, 135, 136, 137, 457
  race   175, 327, 338
  religion   435
  society   457–8
  sport   410, 411
  youth   364
social contract   46, 54–6
social currency   288
social customs   368, 370–1

social darwinism   176
social enterprises   167
social evolution   53, 58
social factors   22
   influence on decision making   9–10
   influence on scientific knowledge   258
social facts   21
Social Futures and Life Pathways project   362
social generations   355–6
social geography   219, 222
social interaction   21, 22
social justice approaches   188
social media   256, 259
   anti-racism campaigns   189
   disability activism and advocacy   316, 317
   expansion of boundaries of social movements   317–18
   facilitation of street art and environmental issues   260
   impact on traditional media   279
   influence   275–6
   influence on news agendas   279–80
   influencers   287–9
   negative aspects   265, 272
   power and surveillance   164–5, 289–91
   recent platforms   48
   short-term social campaign   304, 305
   social benefits   286–7
social movements   97, 301, 302–4
   anti-racism   188
   antislavery   462
   boomerang   312
   disability   316
   environmental   238, 308
   feminist   147, 308
   future predictions   312, 317–18
   human rights as key principle   311–12
   intersectional power within   311
   long-term campaign   304–5
   marriage equality   308
   #MeToo movement   164–5, 311
   reactionary   309–10
   short-term campaign   304, 305
   transgender   138
   use of social media to expand   317
social norms   21, 22–3, 26
   attitudes to marriage   369
   maintenance   370–1
   ways to change   384–5
social positions   76
social research   21, 24, 25, 65
   ethics   69
   objectivity and methodology   75–6
   research process   70–3

scientific inquiry process   68–70
   See also sociological research
social scientific inquiry   24
social settings   256, 259
social stratification   108, 114–15
social structures   21, 22, 24, 46, 49
social theory   21, 24, 137–8
socialisation   3, 4–5, 12, 133, 277–8
socially constructed   46, 49
society   3, 4–9, 11, 45, 49–51
   awareness of determinism   10
   consumer   101–2
   diversity of views   46–7
   impact of cars on   455, 456
   pace of changes in   47–9
   role of sport   409
   social and cultural norms   22–3
   social construction   46, 49, 457–8
   universal rules   58–9
SOCIndex   38
socio-economic status   108, 114
sociohistorical approach   354
sociological imagination   20, 21, 26–8, 40, 67–8, 458–9
   media influences   273
   personal reflection   28
sociological knowledge   24, 28–30
sociological research   66, 67–8
   discourse analysis   79–80
   ethics   81–3
   surveys and statistical analysis   78–9
sociologists   5, 21–2, 50, 91, 454
sociology   4, 5, 21, 22, 26
   difference from cultural studies   51–2
   sport   412–13
   youth and young people   360–1
sociology assignments, approaches to research   34–7
Solomos, J. & Bulmer, M.   180
South Sea Islander people 180 *See also* Kanakas
sovereignty   198, 202
Spencer, Herbert   53–4, 56
spirit of capitalism   391, 393
spirituality   432, 436
sport
   AFL player salaries   111
   anti-racism campaigns   189
   cheating in cricket   12
   deviance   413–17
   femininity and   418–21
   and gender   417–21, 425
   impact of COVID-19   409, 410, 412
   programs for delinquency   414–15
   reflector of cultural value   410, 411
   role in society   409
   and sexuality   421–5
   as social and cultural process   277–8

   social construction   410, 411
   sociological approach   412–13
   types of conformity   416–17
   women's exclusion from   418
   women's pay inequality   412–13, 419
sport ethic   416–17
Stanton International Auditors   316
start-up mentality   468
state   198, 199
status   108, 114
status anxiety   273
stereotypes   376
   challenges to   384
   Muslims   383, 385–6
   nationality   195
   racist   118, 383, 384, 385–6
   welfare   118–19
Stokes, Kerry   282
Stolen Generations   330, 332, 337, 381
strain theory   372–3
streaming services   264
Street, John   280
street art and use of social media   260
street protests   318
structural functionalism   57, 74
structuralism   113
subjectivity   13–14
The Sun   282
supraterritorial   216, 222
surplus value   108, 110
surveillance capitalism   164–5
surveys   77, 78
Swing Riots   307
symbolic capital   108, 115–16
symbols, societal and cultural   11–12
systematic and public processes   70

Tamir, Yael   205, 207
Tanner, Lindsay   163
task words   35
Taylor, Charles   98, 99, 433
technological determinism   258
technology   48
   colonial power   175–6, 342
   convergent   274–5
   expansion of social movements   317–18
   impact on adult–children relationships   262
   impact on childhood   254–5
   impact on society   455
   impact on work   391, 396
   reasons for children excelling in   261–2
   role in transmission of faith   444–5
   self-discipline   161, 163–4
   See also digital technology

techno-social life   256, 259, 261
teenager   357
terra nullius   176
terrorism and moral panic   380, 381
Tettey, Kwasi   184–6
theory   66, 73, 74–5
thick religion   439–40
The Third Wave (Toffler)   398
Thomas, Scott   435
Thunberg, Greta   22, 152, 264
Tickamyer, Ann   118
TikTok   265, 470
Toffler, Alvin   398
Toonen, Nicholas   312
Toonen v Australia (1994)   312
totalisation   369, 383
Trade Union movement   307, 308
tradition   432, 435
traditional society   89, 90, 97–8
transgender people   135, 139
transition   350, 352
transnational actor   198, 200
Trans-Pacific Partnership (TPP)   207
travel metaphor for adulthood transition   361–2
Treaty of Westphalia   199
triangulation   77
trolling   272, 285
Trump, Donald   32, 207, 280, 290–1, 309
Tunstall, Arthur   198, 199
Turkle, Sherry   286
Turnbull, Malcolm   282, 283
tweens   357
Twitter   32, 189, 276, 286, 399
  short-term social campaign   304, 305

Uber   399
Uber Eats   399–400
Uluru Statement from the Heart   202–3, 302
underclass   117–20
underconformity   410, 416
unequal pay   144
United Kingdom
  antislavery movement   462–3
  Brexit movement   302, 309
  Murdoch's media power   282
  online surveillance   290
United Nations   177, 313
  Climate Action Summit 2019 report   240
  Food and Agriculture Organization   217
  Paris Agreement   239–40
United Nations Climate Change Conference 2015   445

United Nations Climate Summit 2007   446
United Nations Declaration of Human Rights   94
United Nations Declaration on the Rights of Indigenous Peoples   305, 342
United Nations Development Program   441
United Nations Intergovernmental Panel of Climate Change   239–40
United Nations International Year of the World's Indigenous People 1993   199
United Nations Permanent Forum on Indigenous Issues   339
United Nations Treaty system   312
United States
  Black Lives Matter   189
  civil rights movements   308
  determining levels of indigeneity   336
  Federal Trade Commission   288
  ghettos   122
  human rights activism   334
  Murdoch's media power   282
  overt power structures   154
  underclass stereotypes   118
  use of Twitter to predict election outcomes   32
unpaid work 143–4, 394, 398, 399 *See also* reproductive work
Uranium Mining, Processing and Nuclear Energy Review Taskforce   238
urban migration process   6, 7
user-generated content   265, 399

vaccine hesitancy   279
Victoria Police   378, 385
Victorian Inquiry into the On-Demand Workforce   400
virtual communities   285, 286
The Virtual Community (Rheingold)   285
volunteering   465, 469
Vosko, L.F.   395

Wacquant, Loïc   122
Waters, Malcolm   109
Wave Hill walk-off   306–7, 333, 461
wealth inequality   123, 125
Web 2.0   398
Weber, Max   96, 97, 98
  on class structures   113–15
  on ethnicity   177–8
  on life chances   114–15
  on power   154
  on religion   434, 435
  on work   393
  See also methodological individualism

welfare culture stereotypes   118–19
welfare states   95
West, C.   139
West, Rebecca   144–5
Western Australia disability scheme activism and advocacy   314–17
WhatsApp   286
White Australia Policy   174, 180–1, 182–90, 197, 336
whiteness   186–7, 326, 338–9
Whiteness Studies   186–7
Whitlam, Gough   282, 307
Whitlam Government   182
Winipilin, Riley Young   236
Winton, Tim   109
women
  and class   120–1
  concern about environment   246
  exclusion from sports   418
  femininity and sport   418–21
  movies reflecting individualisation   101
  pay inequality in sport   412–13, 419
  precarious work   395
  roller derby personal reflection   422–4
  social theory   138
  transnational movement   310
  unpaid work   144, 394
  voting rights   162–3
Wong, Melissa   122
Woodhead, Linda   438–9
work
  ancient Greek views   392
  blurred work-life boundaries   397, 398
  changing conditions   390
  feminisation   395
  and gender   143–4, 395
  Industrial Revolution   392–3
  precarious   390, 391, 395, 399, 403
  respatialisation and restructure   396–7
  See also paid labour; unpaid work
work ethic   391, 393, 400–2
World Bank faith and development programs   441–2
World Faiths Development Dialogue   441
World Food Programme   217
World Health Organization (WHO)   279
World Trade Organization (WTO)   222
World Wide Fund for Nature (WWF)   241–3
World Wide Web   284
Wright, Erik Olin   112–13

Yelp 399
Yemen
    consumption of Western culture 225–6
    fish exports 215–16, 221–4
    migrant workers 224–5
Yinger, J Milton 178
Yirrkala Bark Petitions 333
Yoido Full Gospel 437
Youth Allowance 55
youth and young people 349, 354–7
    biological and developmental psychology 357–9
    discourse 352
    experiences of power 166–8
    gig economy 164
    labels associated with 359
    older person reflection on youth 360–1
    power through activism 152, 159
    research into sexting behaviours 78
    social construction 364
    sports programs for delinquency 414–15
    technological impact on 263–5
    time spent on social media 164–5
    transitions into adulthood 360–2
    youth-produced content 265
youth services 358
Youthlaw 358
YouTube 264, 265, 276, 279, 286

Zimmerman, D.H. 139
Zizek, Slovaj 58
Zuboff, Shoshana 153, 165